UNCERTAIN COMPUTATION-BASED
DECISION THEORY

T0350116

UNCERTAIN COMPUTATION-BASED DECISION THEORY

Rafik Aliev
Azerbaijan State Oil and Industry University, Azerbaijan

World Scientific

NEW JERSEY · LONDON · SINGAPORE · BEIJING · SHANGHAI · HONG KONG · TAIPEI · CHENNAI · TOKYO

Published by

World Scientific Publishing Co. Pte. Ltd.
5 Toh Tuck Link, Singapore 596224
USA office: 27 Warren Street, Suite 401-402, Hackensack, NJ 07601
UK office: 57 Shelton Street, Covent Garden, London WC2H 9HE

Library of Congress Cataloging-in-Publication Data
Names: Aliev, R. A. (Rafik Aziz ogly), author.
Title: Uncertain computation-based decision theory / by Rafik Aliev
    (Azerbaijan State Oil and Industry University, Azerbaijan).
Other titles: Uncertain computation based decision theory
Description: New Jersey : World Scientific, 2017.
Identifiers: LCCN 2017026645 | ISBN 9789813228931 (hc : alk. paper)
Subjects: LCSH: Uncertainty--Mathematical models.
Classification: LCC QA273 .A3435 2017 | DDC 519.2--dc23
LC record available at https://lccn.loc.gov/2017026645

British Library Cataloguing-in-Publication Data
A catalogue record for this book is available from the British Library.

Copyright © 2018 by World Scientific Publishing Co. Pte. Ltd.

All rights reserved. This book, or parts thereof, may not be reproduced in any form or by any means, electronic or mechanical, including photocopying, recording or any information storage and retrieval system now known or to be invented, without written permission from the publisher.

For photocopying of material in this volume, please pay a copying fee through the Copyright Clearance Center, Inc., 222 Rosewood Drive, Danvers, MA 01923, USA. In this case permission to photocopy is not required from the publisher.

For any available supplementary material, please visit
http://www.worldscientific.com/worldscibooks/10.1142/10679#t=suppl

Desk Editor: Herbert Moses

Typeset by Stallion Press
Email: enquiries@stallionpress.com

Printed in Singapore

To the memory of my wife Aida Alieva

To my mentor, the father of fuzzy logic, Prof. Lotfi
Zadeh
To universally recognized metaphysical poet, fuzzy
thinker Ramiz Rovshan

— Rafik Aliev

Preface

The evolution of decision theories passed a long way since the development of the expected utility theory. However, the existing decision theories still suffer from the series of disadvantages. First, existing theories rely on the use of precise (numerical) techniques for decision analysis. However, real-world decision-relevant information on objective conditions and behavioral determinants is naturally characterized by a combination of probabilistic and fuzzy uncertainties. Second, existing theories follow a bivalent logic-based description of preferences. In contrast, real-world preferences may be vague due to uncertainty and complexity of decision problems. Third, a small attention is paid to reliability of decision relevant information. Indeed, decision relevant information is often partially reliable. This is naturally conditioned by uncertainty, incomplete data, incomplete knowledge and restricted experience of a decision maker and other reasons.

One of the main insights stemming from these points is that a decision analysis should have an ability of computation with uncertain information. Computation with uncertain information, uncertain computation for short, is a system of computation and reasoning in which the objects of computation are not values of variables but restrictions on values of variables. Principal levels of generality of restrictions are real numbers (ground level), intervals (level 1), fuzzy numbers and random numbers (level 2), Z-numbers (level 3) and visual representation of restrictions (level 4). Decision making and modeling in social and other spheres as economics, business, production, etc., falls within the province of uncertain computation and reasoning.

In this book, we intend to overcome the gap between real-world decision problems and formal decision analysis. We consider decision problems under all the levels of generality of uncertain information. In the most general scope, we suggest the fundamentals of a new general theory of decisions based on the principles of a combined state and fuzzy logic, mainly, Z-restrictions. The formalism of Z-restrictions suggested by Prof. Zadeh provides the most adequate framework for description of imprecise and partially reliable information and is more general than formalisms of interval, fuzzy and second-order hierarchical imprecise models.

The book is organized into 12 chapters. The first chapter is devoted to a review of the main existing decision theories developed for the classical framework of decision-relevant information. The certain, risk and uncertain decision environments are considered.

In Chapter 2, we analyze the existing theories and outline the main disadvantages of them, which consist in incapability to deal with imperfect relevant information.

Chapter 3 covers the basics of interval arithmetic for computation information at level 1 of generalization. Mainly, the classical interval arithmetic and relative distance measure-based interval arithmetic are described.

Chapters 4 and 5 cover the basics of computation under level 2 of information generalization. In Chapter 4, the basics of operations over random variables and other related problems are described. Chapter 5 discusses foundations of fuzzy sets theory, fuzzy logic and fuzzy arithmetic.

Chapter 6 is devoted to important directions of computation with Z-numbers. The chapter includes the principles of arithmetic of continuous and discrete Z-numbers, the basic properties of Z-number valued functions, the basics of reasoning with Z-information, aggregation of Z-information and other related problems.

Computation with information in the scope of the usuality concept is considered in Chapter 7. The proposed approach is based on the computation with Z-information outlined in Chapter 6.

Chapter 8 is devoted to computation with uncertain information expressed in the form of visual images. The proposed study relies on fuzzy logic-based reasoning with geometric objects. An approach to decision making under visual information by using the proposed formalism is described.

The basics of decision making under interval-valued information are described in Chapter 9. Decision making under interval probabilities and multi-attribute decision making under interval-valued information is considered.

Chapter 10 covers various approaches to decision making under fuzzy information and related techniques. A theory of decision making under linguistic information on states of nature, probabilities and alternatives is described. The foundations of behavioral decision making under imperfect information are given. An alternative approach to decision making under imperfect information based on fuzzy optimality principle is described. Fuzzy decision making perspectives in the field of economics are expressed. The important techniques to be used for decision analysis under imperfect information, including type-2 fuzzy clustering and fuzzy regression analysis, are described.

Chapter 11 is devoted to decision analysis under Z-information. In the first section, we describe the basics of Z-restriction centered general decision theory. This theory is developed for behavioral decision analysis when the relevant information on objective and subjective conditions of decision making is expressed by Z-numbers. In the second section, we consider an approach to linear programming when decision variables, coefficients of objective function and right-hand sides of constraints are described by Z-numbers. In the third section, we outline an approach to solving a regression problem with Z-number valued variables and parameters.

Chapter 12 presents applications of the uncertain computation-based decision theory to real-world decision problems with imperfect information in economics, business, production, IT and other areas.

This book is intended for researchers and practitioners and will be useful for anyone who is interested in solving real-world decision problems with imperfect information. The reason is that the book is self-containing and includes detailed advice on the application of the suggested theory. The book will be helpful for teachers and students of universities and colleges, for managers and specialists from various fields of business and economics, production and social sphere.

I would like to express my thanks to Professor Lotfi Zadeh, the founder of the fuzzy set and Soft Computing theories, for his permanent support, invaluable ideas and advice for my research.

R.A. Aliev

Contents

Chapter 1

Decision Environment

1.1 Certain environment

Decision making involves making a choice among available alternatives. Some decisions can be made simply on the base of intuitive judgments. However, in general, making sound decisions requires complex analysis of decision environment which includes such factors as objective and subjective conditions, consequences and relevant information. Such analysis is out of a highly constrained computational ability of a human brain. Thus, decision making mandates the use of mathematical methods as a strong language of reasoning. This requires imposing a formal structure of a decision making problem. Despite that various routine decision making problems were formulated subject to specific decision environment, all the formulations include the common main elements outlined below.

The first element is a set $\mathcal{A}$ of alternatives (alternative actions, strategies etc) to choose from:

$$\mathcal{A} = \{f_1, ..., f_n\}, n \geq 2,$$

where $n \geq 2$ implies that decision making may take place when at least two alternatives exist. For instance, in the problem of business development, alternatives like f_1– "to extend business", f_2– "to improve quality of products", f_3– "to open a new direction" can be considered.

The second element is used to model objective conditions which influence the results of any chosen alternative. This element is called *a set of states of nature*: $\mathcal{S} = \{S_1, ..., S_m\}$. A state of nature S_i is a possible objective condition. s is considered as a "*a space of **mutually exclusive***

1

and **exhaustive states**", according to a formulation suggested by L. Savage [664]. This implies that possible objective conditions are known in advance, and only one S_i, $i = 1,...,m$ will take place. For example, in the problem of business development, the set of states of nature may include four conditions $S = \{S_1, S_2, S_3, S_4\}$, where S_1 denotes "high demand and low competition", S_2 –"high demand and medium competition", S_3 – "medium demand and low competition", S_4 – "medium demand and high competition".

The third element is consequences (results) of actions in various states of nature, termed as outcomes. An alternative results in an outcome in any state of nature. For example, extending business under high demand results in high profit. If a low demand occurs, then extension may result in a loss. The outcomes may be quantitative or qualitative, monetary or non-monetary. A set of outcomes is commonly denoted $\mathcal{X}$. As an outcome $X \in \mathcal{X}$ is a result of an action f taken at a state of nature S, it is written $X = f(S)$. So, an action f is considered as a function whose domain is a set of states of nature S and the range is the set of outcomes $\mathcal{X}$: $f: S \rightarrow \mathcal{X}$. In order to compare alternatives $f \in \mathcal{A}$, it is needed to measure all their outcomes $X \in \mathcal{X}$, especially when the latter are qualitative. For this purpose, a numeric function $u: \mathcal{X} \rightarrow R$ is used to measure an outcome $X \in \mathcal{X}$ in terms of its *utility* for a decision maker (DM). In general, utility $u: \mathcal{X} \rightarrow R$ should take into account various factors like reputation, health, mentality, psychology [484] etc.

The fourth element is preferences of a DM. The fact that a DM prefers an alternative $f \in \mathcal{A}$ to an alternative $g \in \mathcal{A}$ is denoted $f \succ g$. Indifference among f and g is denoted $f \sim g$. The fact that f is at least as good as g is denoted $f \succsim g$. Preferences are described as a binary relation $\succsim \in \mathcal{A} \times \mathcal{A}$.

Thus, a decision making problem is formulated as follows:

Given

the set of alternatives $\mathcal{A}$,

the set of states of nature S,

the set of outcomes $\mathcal{X}$

Determine an action $f^* \in \mathcal{A}$ such that $f^* \succsim f$ for all $f \in \mathcal{A}$.

Certain decision environment implies that a state of nature S that will take place is known. In the considered example of business development, assume a simple situation when uncertainty in decision environment related to demand and competition can be reduced by using a DM's long-time experience and knowledge, customer surveys, interviewing of experts and various market analysis techniques. As a result, a DM can for sure predict the future state of nature. In such cases, determining of $f^* \in \mathcal{A}$ is formally reduced to comparison of numeric utilities $u(X_i) = u(f(S_i))$ of outcomes that alternatives $f \in \mathcal{A}$ produce under a known state of nature S. In other words, given S that will take place for sure, it is needed to find an alternative whose outcome in this state of nature has the highest utility for a DM.

Without doubt, certain environment is an idealized case as it is rarely possible to know an actual state of nature in real-world problems. Our knowledge, experience and other information sources we can use may not uncover real-world uncertainty of various economic, social, political and other factors that form actual objective conditions of our choices.

1.2 Risk environments

1.2.1 *Expected utility theory of von Neumann and Morgenstern*

When objective (actual) probability $p(S_i)$ of occurrence of each state of nature S_i, $i = 1,...,m$ is known, we deal with *decision making under risk*. In this case, it becomes more difficult to determine the best alternative. The issue is that we need to compare alternatives as vectors of the outcomes they generate $(f(S_1),...,f(S_m))$ by taking into account the corresponding probabilities $p(S_1),...,p(S_m)$. For this purpose, a quantification of preferences is used. One approach to quantify preferences is to use a *utility function* [664, 749]. Utility function is a function $U : \mathcal{A} \to R$ that satisfies

$$U(f) \geq U(g) \text{ iff } f \succsim g, \ \forall f, g \in \mathcal{A}.$$

The first axiomatic foundation of the utility function for risk environment was the expected utility (EU) theory of von Neumann and Morgenstern [749]. In this theory, an alternative is described as a collection $f = (X_1, P_1; \ldots; X_n, P_n)$ of its outcomes with the associated probabilities and is termed as a lottery. In the EU theory of von Neumann and Morgenstern, preferences over alternatives as finite-outcome lotteries are encoded by utility function when numeric utilities and numeric objective probabilities of outcomes are given. Let $\mathcal{X}$ be a set of outcomes without any additional structure imposed on it. Formally, the set of lotteries in the EU theory is the set of distributions P of objective probabilities over $\mathcal{X}$ with finite supports [316]:

$$\mathcal{L} = \left\{ P : \mathcal{X} \to [0,1] \Big| \sum_{X \in \mathcal{X}} P(X) = 1 \right\}.$$

The EU model was not initially based on a general decision problem framework which includes the concept of a set of states of nature. However, it can be applied in this framework also, once we consider an action f as a lottery $f = \left\{ P : f(\mathcal{S}) \to [0,1] \Big| \sum_{S \in \mathcal{S}} P(f(S)) = 1 \right\}$, $f(\mathcal{S}) \subset \mathcal{X}$.

More complicated cases may be considered, if various lotteries $\mathcal{L}$ can be faced with various probabilities. Such case is referred to as a compound, or a two-stage lottery. In other words, outcomes of a lottery are lotteries. To model this within $\mathcal{L}$, a compound lottery is defined as a convex combination in $\mathcal{L}$: for any $P, Q \in \mathcal{L}$ and any $\alpha \in [0,1]$ $\alpha P + (1-\alpha)Q = R \in \mathcal{L}$, where $R(X) = \alpha P(X) + (1-\alpha)Q(X)$. The axioms describing the assumptions on preference which underlie EU model are the following:

(i)   **Weak-order:**
   (a) Completeness. Any two alternatives are comparable with respect to $\succsim$: for all f and g in $\mathcal{A}$ one has $f \succsim g$ or $g \succsim f$.
   (b) Transitivity. For all f, g and h in $\mathcal{A}$ If $f \succsim g$ and $g \succsim h$ then $f \succsim h$.

(ii) **Continuity:** For all f, g and h in $\mathcal{A}$, if $f \succ g$ and $g \succ h$ then there are α and β in $\alpha, \beta \in (0,1)$ such that $\alpha f + (1 - \alpha)h \succ g \succ \beta f + (1 - \beta)h$.

(iii) **Independence:** For all acts f, g and h in $\mathcal{A}$, if $f \succsim g$ then $\alpha f + (1 - \alpha)h \succsim \alpha g + (1 - \alpha)h$ for all $\alpha \in (0,1)$.

The completeness property implies that despite the fact that each alternative f or g may have better or worse outcomes with respect to the other one, a DM supposed to be always able to compare two alternatives: either f is preferred to g or g is preferred to f, or f and g are considered equivalent. Transitivity is an obvious condition stating that it is possible to order alternatives from the better to the worst one. The independence assumption implies that preference over two lotteries does not depend on introducing some third lottery to produce compound lotteries. In other words, a compound lottery in which f takes places with probability α and h with probability $1 - \alpha$ is better than the analogous compound lottery of g and h as soon as f is better than g. The continuity assumption is a technical requirement needed to construct continuous utility function.

Example 1. (Completeness). Bob feels that he have got a cold, but in two days he will have a trip abroad. He considers two alternatives: f – to have a hot tea with raspberry jam and g – to take medicine. Bob cannot exactly know state of his organism. In general f is not so strong tool to get better as g, but as opposed to g, f is harmless for his stomach. Moreover, why to use medicine if the organism is able to recover in two days without it? From the other side, the trip is a too important for him to risk by not taking medicine. So, at first he is not sure what to do and decides to take his temperature. If his temperature is below 37°C then he will have tea with raspberry jam, otherwise he definitely will take the medicine to be surer that he will recover in two days.

So, even having non-comparable alternatives, Bob finds a way to define his preference among them by obtaining the additional information as his temperature value.

Example 2. (Independence). Suppose that you are planning to go to a small shop just near your house where they sell fruits and prefer buying apples to buying pears. If we denote buying apples by f and buying pears by g, then your preferences are $f \succ g$. Suppose now that there is also another shop located at the other side of the street you live in, where the same apples and pears are sold at the lower prices. So, you can save your expenses going to the shop at the other side of the street, but then buying fruits for you will be connected with a danger to become a victim of a road accident. Let us denote the danger by h. This means that after deciding to go to the shop located at the other side of the street you will no more have 'pure' alternatives f and g, but instead of them you will have $\alpha f + (1-\alpha)h$ and $\alpha g + (1-\alpha)h$ respectively, where $1-\alpha$ is the probability of h. However, it would be strange to suppose that after crossing the street, you will prefer to buy pears instead of apples. It is reasonable to suppose that you will buy apples and not pears after crossing the street. The reason is that crossing the street is just related to saving expenses and in no way is connected with your preferences with respect to apples and pears. So, your preferences should be $\alpha f + (1-\alpha)h \succ \alpha g + (1-\alpha)h$.

Below we present the result on the existence of the EU function:

Theorem 1.1 [749]. $\succsim \subset \mathcal{L} \times \mathcal{L}$ *satisfies (i)-(iii) if and only if there exists* $u : \mathcal{X} \to \mathcal{R}$ *such that for every* P *and* Q *in* $\mathcal{L}$:

$$P \succsim Q \ \text{ iff } \ \sum_{X \in \mathcal{X}} P(X)u(X) \geq \sum_{X \in \mathcal{X}} Q(X)u(X).$$

Moreover, in this case, u is unique up to a positive linear transformation.

Thus, a value $U(P)$ of utility function for a finite-outcome lottery $P = (X_1, P(X_1); ...; X_n, P(X_n))$ is defined as $U(P) = \sum_{i=1}^{n} u(X_i)P(X_i)$.

The problem of decision making is to find such P^* that $U(P^*) = \max_{P \in A} U(P)$.

The utility function in EU theory is simple from computational point of view. However, the main criticism related to this theory concerns objective probabilities. In real problems, there is no perfect information (sufficient amount of data etc) to determine exact objective probabilities. At the same time, when the latter are unknown, independence assumption becomes not realistic [263].

1.2.2 *Prospect theory*

In EU theory they assume that individuals maximize utility in a rational way. This means that individuals update beliefs following Bayes' rule [109]. However, even thought experiments show violation of the EU axioms. Indeed, in this model people are considered as making decisions according to predefined mathematical algorithms, like 'computational machines' function. From the other side, these models are developed for a perfect decision relevant information.

Humans' decision making is subject to psychological issues, mental, social and other aspects. These insights motivated studying how people actually make decisions. A related field called *behavioral economics* emerged in the Prospect Theory (PT) of Kahneman and Tversky [404]. PT is based on psychological insights uncovered during experiments [404, 732, 733, 734]. The first is that deviations from initial wealth, i.e. gains or losses, rather than final wealth matter. A lottery includes outcomes as changes from current wealth called *reference point*. Such a lottery is termed a prospect.

Moreover, a gain-loss asymmetry takes place: losses influence choices stronger than gains do. A loss aversion plays an important role in decision making. Attitudes to risk differ in gains and losses domains. People wish to risk to escape loss, i.e. they are risk seeking dealing with losses.

In order to representing the mentioned features, Kahneman and Tversky introduced a value function $v(\ )$ with the following properties: 1) it is steeper in losses domain than in gains domain; 2) it is concave in gains domain and is convex in losses domain; 3) it is steepest in the reference point. A value function is schematically given in Fig. 1.1.

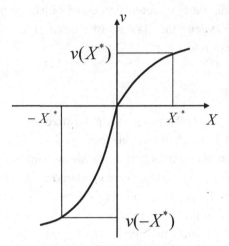

Fig. 1.1. Value function

The second main insight is distortion of probabilities. For example, the change of probability from 0 to 0.1 or from 0.9 to 1 is more important than the change from 0.3 to 0.4. Indeed, appearance of a chance or a guaranteed outcome is more sufficient than just a change of a probability. As a result, people overestimate low and underestimate high probabilities. Kahneman and Tversky introduced a so-called weighting function $w:[0,1]\rightarrow[0,1]$ to replace probabilities P with weights $w(P)$. A weighting function is schematically shown in Fig. 1.2:

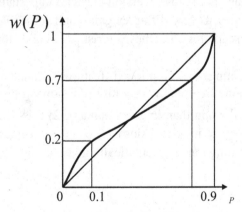

Fig. 1.2. Weighting function

Thus, a value function $v(\ )$ is used instead of utility function $u(X)$ and a weighting function $w(\ )$ is used instead of probability measure in PT. The model has the following form (compare with the expected utility):

$$U((X_1, P(X_1); ...; X_n, P(X_n)) = \sum_{i=1}^{n} v(X_i)w(P(X_i)).$$

However, PT model was formulated for at most two non-zero outcomes [404]. There are various forms of a value function $v(\ )$ and a weighting function $w(\ )$ suggested by various authors [578]. However, any weighting function is non-decreasing with $w(0) = 0$, $w(1) = 1$ and is nonadditive, $w(P + Q) \neq w(P) + w(Q), P + Q \leq 1$.

PT is a successful theory and explains such choice phenomena as Allais paradox [70], certainty effect and framing effects [404].

1.3 Uncertain environment

1.3.1 *The Laplace criterion, the Hurwitz criterion and the minimax regret criterion*

In the situations when there is no information on probabilities of states of nature we deal with *decision making under uncertainty* (in the existing theories this is also referred to as *decision making under complete ignorance*). For this situation the following typical decision making approaches are used: Laplace criterion, Wald Maximin criterion, Hurwitz criterion, Savage Minimax Regret criterion.

In Laplace criterion, as no information on chances of objective conditions is available, they consider states of nature as equiprobable. Thus, given m states of nature, probability of each $S_i, i = 1, ..., m$ is $p(S_i) = \dfrac{1}{m}$. Then the utility of alternative f is computed by using the EU approach:

$$U(f) = \sum_{i=1}^{m} u(f(S_i))p(S_i) = \frac{1}{m}\sum_{i=1}^{m} u(f(S_i))$$

The disadvantage of this approach is that it is quite 'inanimate'. In real-world problems, due to psychology, welfare and other factors, a DM rarely consider states of nature as equiprobable, especially when some of them are related to gains and some of them — to losses.

Wald criterion (Maximin criterion) models pessimistic behavior of a DM under uncertainty. For each alternative, its overall utility $U(f)$ is defined as a utility of its worst possible outcome:

$$U(f) = \min_{i=1,\ldots,m} u(f(S_i)).$$

Next, an action whose worst outcome is better than those of the others is chosen as an optimal one. In other words, an incentive of a DM is to chose an action which is less harmful than the others. This is more realistic approach from psychological point of view than the Laplace criterion. However, a utility in this approach is evaluated only on the base of one outcome and the rest information is disregarded.

Due to the fact that in general, a DM is not fully pessimistic, the Hurwitz criterion is a more adequate approach where a degree of pessimism is used. A degree of pessimism, $\alpha \in [0, 1]$ describes a level of pessimistic behavior of a DM. An overall utility $U(f)$ is defined then as a convex combination of utilities of the worst and the best possible outcomes:

$$U(f) = \alpha \min_{i=1,\ldots,m} u(f(S_i)) + (1-\alpha) \max_{i=1,\ldots,m} u(f(S_i))$$

where $(1-\alpha)$ is referred to as a degree of optimism. Thus, the higher α is, the stronger the influence of the worst possible outcome on a choice of a DM.

The Minimax Regret criterion models a DM's tendency of minimizing a regret. Regret is measured as a relative loss resulting from selecting an alternative which is not the best for a particular state of nature. Regret is the opportunity loss (OL) faced when an action (alternative) f_k is chosen and a state of nature s_j occurs. Formally speaking, OL a DM face at a state s_j after f_k is chosen is equal to the difference between the highest utility that can be obtained when state of nature s_j occurs and $u(f_k(s_j))$:

$$\Delta u(f_k(s_j)) = \max_{i=1,\ldots,n} u(f_i(s_j)) - u(f_k(s_j)).$$

So, $\Delta u(f_k(s_j))$ is the difference between the maximal utility value among all the alternatives in state s_j and a utility value $u(f_k(s_j))$ of alternative f_k at s_j. According to Minimax Regret criterion, an action f_k is optimal if its maximum regret is minimal:

$$\max_{j=1,\ldots,m} \Delta u(f_k(s_j)) = \min_{i=1,\ldots,n} \left(\max_{j=1,\ldots,m} \Delta u(f_i(s_j)) \right).$$

1.3.2 *Subjective expected utility theory of Savage*

The assumptions of von Neumann and Morgenstern expected utility model stating that objective probabilities of events are known makes this model unsuitable for majority of real-world applications. For example, what is an actual probability of an oil prize increase in few months? What is an actual probability of high competition in car industry in a region? What is an actual probability that I will not get the flu upcoming winter? What is an actual probability of whether it will rain in the mid of Autumn?

In such examples we deal either with the completely new phenomena, or phenomena which notably differs from the previous events, or phenomena that depends on uncertain or unforeseen factors. This means we have no representative experimental data or complete knowledge to determine objective probabilities. For such cases, Savage suggested a subjective expected utility (SEU) theory able to compare alternative actions on the base of a DM's experience or vision [664]. Savage's theory is based on a concept of subjective probability suggested by Ramsey [128] and de Finetti [219]. Subjective probability is DM's probabilistic belief concerning occurrence of an event and is assumed to be used by humans when no information on objective (actual) probabilities of outcomes is known. SEU became a base of almost all the utility models for decision making under uncertainty.

The Savage's utility representation is as follows: provided that $\succsim$ satisfies all the axioms [664], there exists a unique probability measure μ on $\mathcal{S}$ and a function $u : \mathcal{X} \rightarrow \mathcal{R}$ such that

$$f \succsim g \text{ iff } \int_S u(f(S))d\mu \geq \int_S u(g(S))d\mu.$$

The problem of decision making consist in determination of an action $f^* \in \mathcal{A}$ such that

$$U(f^*) = \max_{f \in \mathcal{A}} \int_S u(f(S))d\mu.$$

In quantitative sense, SEU model coincides with the EU theory of von Neumann and Morgenstern — we again have expectation with respect to a probability measure. However, qualitatively, these theories differ. The main implications of SEU model are the following: 1) beliefs of a DM are probabilistic; 2) the beliefs are to be used linearly in utility representation of an alternative.

1.3.3 *Choquet expected utility*

SEU is based on modeling of belief by an additive probability measure. Choquet Expected Utility (CEU) was suggested by Schmeidler [669] to model intrinsic non-additivity of belief under uncertainty. Schmeidler considered a simple example. Suppose you have a coin for which frequencies of falls of heads and tails are equal. Therefore, your belief would be the frequencies-based probabilities of falls of heads equal to 0.5. Consider now a coin you did not tossed and don't know if it is ideal. You may assume that the probabilities of heads and tails for this coin are 0.5. This is the same beliefs as those for your own coin. However, they are not based on real evidence, but are assumption-based. Certainly, the first beliefs are more reliable. For the second coin, heads and tails are symmetric — for example, there is no reason to believe in occurrence of falls more than in that of tails or vice-versa. However, it is reasonable to think that one of the results of tossing is more likely than the other. Then belief may be, for instance, $v(heads) = v(tails) = 0.3$. But, naturally $v(heads \, or \, tails) = 1$. So, one has non-additivity: $v(heads \, or \, tails) \neq v(heads) + v(tails)$.

In CEU a non-additive belief is described by a capacity η [196, 669]:

1. $\eta(\varnothing) = 0$

2. $\forall A, B \subset \mathcal{S}$, $A \subset B$ implies $\eta(A) \leq \eta(B)$

3. $\eta(\mathcal{S}) = 1$

Capacity is also termed non-additive probability.

CEU is based on Choquet integral. This integral is a generalization of Lebesgue integral if a capacity is used instead of an additive measure. The use of a capacity in Riemann integration (Riemann integration is used in SEU) is not correct. Particularly, Riemann integration depends on how an act is written. The other problems are violation of continuity and monotonicity [316].

The main feature of preferences in CEU is that independence property is assumed only for comonotonic acts. Two acts f and g are comonotonic if for no S and S' in $\mathcal{S}$, $f(S) \succ f(S')$ and $g(S') \succ g(S)$ hold. Motivation of a departure from the independence axiom may be shown in the following example. Consider a box containing balls of the same color. The only information is that the color is either white or black. Assume the two acts which can be chosen prior to open the box: the first gives $10 if the color is white and 0 if it is black, the second gives $0 if the color is white and $10 if is black. These acts can be written as functions f and g: $f(white)=10$, $f(black)=0$, $g(white)=0$, $g(black)=10$. As information on white and black is symmetric, we sup-pose $\tilde{f} \sim \tilde{g}$. Consider now the following mixes of these acts with act $h=g$:

$f_h = \frac{1}{2}f + \frac{1}{2}h$ and $g_h = \frac{1}{2}g + \frac{1}{2}h$. This will produce $f_h(white) = 5$, $f_h(black) = 5$ and $g_h(white) = g(white) = 0$, $g_h(black) = g(black) = 10$. Whereas f and g are qualitatively similar, f_h and g_h – not. In the first pair we have uncertain acts. In the second we have a certain act and an uncertain act: f_h gives a certain outcome $5 whether g is uncertain to give $10 or $0. These acts differ qualitatively and one may prefer certain $5 (reliable result) to $10 about which it is not known whether it will occur (not reliable result): $f_h = \frac{1}{2}f + \frac{1}{2}h \succ g_h = \frac{1}{2}g + \frac{1}{2}h$. Hence, the independence is violated: $\tilde{f} \sim \tilde{g}$ and $f_h = \frac{1}{2}f + \frac{1}{2}h \succ g_h = \frac{1}{2}g + \frac{1}{2}h$. In this example, uncertainty of the results disappears when mixing f with $h = g$. The effect of uncertainty decrease is called hedging effect [318]. This may lead to violation of independence, but for comonotonic acts hedging is impossible [316]. The co-monotonic independence axiom is the following:

Co-monotonic Independence. *For all pairwise co-monotonic acts* f, g *and* h *in* A *if* $f \succsim g$, *then* $\alpha f + (1 - \alpha)h \succsim \alpha g + (1 - \alpha)h$ *for all* $\alpha \in (0, 1)$.

For finite S, CEU representation is as follows:

$$U(f) = \sum_{i=1}^{n} (u(f(S_{(i)})) - u(f(S_{(i+1)})))\eta(\{S_{(1)},...,S_{(i)}\}),$$

where (i) implies index permutation $u(f(S_{(i)})) \geq u(f(S_{(i+1)}))$, and $u(f(S_{(n+1)})) = 0$ by convention. Sometimes an equivalent expression is used:

$$U(f) = \sum_{i=1}^{n} u(f(S_{(i)}))(\eta(\{S_{(1)},...,S_{(i)}\}) - \eta(\{S_{(1)},...,S_{(i-1)}\}))$$

with $\{S_{(1)},...,S_{(i-1)}\} = \varnothing$ for $i = 1$.

The disadvantages of CEU relates to interpretation difficulties of η. One of the typical cases is to consider η as a lower envelope of a set of possible probability distributions for a considered problem (when a single true distribution is unknown). Lower envelope assigns minimal probability to an event among all the possible probabilities. This requires solving optimization problems which increases complexity of computations. In general, non-additive measure construction may be difficult from intuitive and computational points of view.

1.3.4 *Multiple priors models*

In CEU, non-additivity of beliefs is modeled by a non-additive probability. Another way is to model non-probabilistic beliefs by a set of probability distributions (priors). This class of models is termed as multiple priors models. They are used when a DM can not have a precise (single) probabilistic belief, but has to allow for a range of values of probabilities. Indeed, various priors assign various probabilities to an event. At the same time, imprecise beliefs imply existence of multiple priors.

The well-known examples showing incompatibility of a single probability measure with human choices under uncertainty were suggested by Daniel Ellsberg in 1961 [263]. One example is called Ellsberg two-urn paradox. In this experiment they present a DM two urns each containing 100 balls. A DM is allowed to see that urn I contains 50 white and 50 black balls, whereas no information is provided on a ratio of white and black balls in urn II. A DM is suggested to choose from bets on a color of a ball drawn at random: on a white color and on a black color. Each bet produces a prize of $100. After bet is chosen, a DM needs to choose the urn to play. Majority of people were indifferent whether to bet on white or on black. However, whatever bet was chosen, most of people strictly preferred choose urn I to play — they prefer betting on an outcome with known probability 0.5 to betting on an outcome with probability that may take any value from [0,1]. This choice is inconsistent with any probabilistic belief on a color of a ball taken at random from urn II. Indeed, betting on white and then choosing urn I means that a DM believes on the number of white balls in urn II being smaller than in urn I, whereas betting on black and then choosing urn I means that a DM believes on the number of black balls in urn II being smaller than in urn I. No single probabilistic belief on colors for urn II may simultaneously explain these two choices — the probabilities of a white and a black balls drawn at random from urn II cannot be simultaneously smaller than 0.5.

The second example is called Ellsberg single-urn paradox. In this example a DM is offered to choose among bets on colors of balls in one urn. An urn contains 90 balls — 30 are white and the other 60 are black and yellow in an unknown proportion. The following bets on a color of a ball taken at random are suggested (Table 1.1).

Table 1.1. Ellsberg single-urn decision problem

	White	Black	Yellow
f	$100	0	0
g	0	$100	0
f	$100	0	$100
g	0	$100	$100

For example, f yields $100 if a ball drawn is white and 0 otherwise whereas f' yields $100 whether a ball drawn is white or yellow and 0 otherwise. Majority of subjects prefer f to g (i.e. they prefer an outcome with known probability 1/3 to an outcome with unknown probability being somewhere between 0 and 2/3). At the same time, majority prefer g' to f' (i.e. they prefer an outcome with known probability 2/3 to an outcome with unknown probability being somewhere between 1/3 and 1). These two choices cannot be explained by beliefs described by a single probability distribution. Indeed, if to suppose that the beliefs are probabilistic, then the first choice implies that subjects think that a white ball is more probable to be drawn than a black ball: $P(w) > P(b)$. The second choice implies subjects thinking that a black or yellow ball drawn is more probable than a white or yellow ball drawn — $P(b) + P(y) > P(b) + P(y)$ which means that $P(b) > P(w)$. This contradicts the beliefs underlying the first choice.

Indeed, information on occurrence of complementary events *black* and *yellow* represented only by probability of their union cannot be uniquely separated into probabilities of *black* and *yellow*.

The interpretation of these choices is that probabilistic outcomes are preferred to uncertain ones. This phenomenon is termed as uncertainty aversion, or ambiguity aversion. Term ambiguity was introduced by Daniel Ellsberg as follows: "a quality depending on the amount, type, reliability and 'unanimity' of information, and giving rise to one's 'degree of confidence' in an estimate of relative likelihoods" [263]. In its essence, ambiguity is considered as uncertainty of probabilities [146].

The axiomatization of uncertainty aversion was proposed by Gilboa and Schmeidler [318]. To understand its formal description, let us recall the Ellsberg two-urn example. Suppose an act f yielding $100 for a white ball drawn from an unknown urn and an act g yielding $100 for a black ball drawn from an unknown urn. It is reasonable to consider these acts equivalent: $f \sim g$. Now mix these acts as $\frac{1}{2}f + \frac{1}{2}g$, obtaining an act which yields a lottery of getting \$100 with probability ½ and 0 with probability ½ no matter what ball is drawn. That is, by combining two uncertain bets, one gets a risky bet (hedging effect). This act is equivalent to a bet on any color for a known urn that yields the same lottery. But as this act is preferred to f and g, we write $\frac{1}{2}f + \frac{1}{2}g \succsim f$. The uncertainty aversion axiom states that for equivalent f and g, their combination is weakly preferred to each of them: $\alpha f + (1-\alpha)g \succsim f$. This is the main axiom of a famous Maximin Expected Utility (MMEU) model [318]. According to this model, a unique closed and convex set C of priors p exist such that

$$f \succsim g \Leftrightarrow \min_{P \in C} \int_S u(f(S))dP \geq \min_{P \in C} \int_S u(g(S))dP,$$

where u is unique up to a positive linear transformation. In simple words, an overall utility of an act is a minimal expected utility over priors $P \in C$. The consideration of C as convex does not affect generality. MMEU allows to model the observed preferences in Ellsberg paradoxes.

A generalization of MMEU was suggested in [312]. This model is termed α-MMEU and states that $f \succsim g$ iff

$$\alpha \min_{P \in C} \int_S u(f(S))dP + (1-\alpha)\max_{P \in C} \int_S u(f(S))dP \geq$$
$$\alpha \min_{P \in C} \int_S u(g(S))dP + (1-\alpha)\max_{P \in C} \int_S u(g(S))dP$$

$\alpha \in [0,1]$ is a degree of ambiguity aversion, or an ambiguity attitude. The higher α reflects stronger ambiguity aversion a DM is; when $\alpha = 1$ we get MMEU. When $\alpha = 0$, the model describes *ambiguity seeking*, — a DM may seek for ambiguity to possibly get the best realization of priors. The values $\alpha \in (0,1)$ describe the fact that a person may not exhibit extreme ambiguity attitudes.

It is important to consider relation between CEU and MMEU. The Ellsberg single-urn paradox may be explained by CEU if the capacity η

is defined as

$$\eta(\{S_w\}) = \eta(\{S_w, S_b\}) = \eta(\{S_w, S_y\}) = \frac{1}{3},$$

$$\eta(\{S_b\}) = \eta(\{S_y\}) = 0,$$

$$\eta(\{S_b, S_y\}) = \frac{2}{3},$$

where S_w, S_b, S_y denote states of nature as extractions of a white, a black and a yellow balls respectively. Schmeidler showed that an ambiguity aversion is modeled by a capacity that satisfies $\eta(H \cup G) + \eta(H \cap G) \geq \eta(H) + \eta(G)$. Such η is termed a convex capacity. Schmeidler showed that for the case of ambiguity aversion, CEU is a special case of MMEU:

$$(Ch)\int_S u(f(S))d\eta = \min_{P \in C} \int_S u(f(S))dP,$$

$(Ch)\int_S$ denotes Choquet integral, η is a convex capacity, and C is a set of probability measures defined as $C = \{P | P(H) \geq \eta(H), \forall H \subset S\}$. Such C is called a core of a convex η. The capacity given above that expresses Ellsberg paradox, is a capacity whose value for each event is equal to a minimum among all the possible probabilities for this event, and therefore, satisfies $\eta(H) \leq P(H), \forall H \subset S$. Given a set of priors C, a convex capacity η satisfying $\eta(H) = \min_{P \in C} P(H)$ is called a lower envelope of C.

However, MMEU is not always a generalization of CEU as CEU does not presuppose an ambiguity aversion. If η is not convex, there is no C for which CEU and MMEU coincide. For concave η, CEU models ambiguity seeking [316]. Also, a capacity may not have a core.

If to compare CEU and MMEU, the latter has important advantages. Choquet integral and a non-additive measure are not widely known concepts and use of them requires specific mathematical knowledge. From the other side, there exist difficulties of interpretation and construction of a capacity. In contrast, a set of priors is straightforward and clear as a possible 'range' for unknown probability distribution. The idea to compute minimal EU is very intuitive and accepted easily. At the same time, it often requires to solve well-known optimization problems like those of linear programming. However, determination of a set of priors as the problem of strict constraining a range of possible probabilities is influenced by insufficient knowledge. In contrast, the use of a non-additive belief obtained from experience-based knowledge may be a good alternative.

As to the MMEU main disadvantage, in this model all the priors are assumed to be equally relevant to a decision problem. However, it is not the case for real decision problems. From the other side, in MMEU each act is evaluated on the base of only one prior. They propose to resolve this issue by introducing of a subjective second-order probability measure defined over multiple priors [194, 195, 436]. A smooth ambiguity model of Klibanoff *et al.* [436] is based on the following utility function:

$$U(f) = \int_C \phi\left(\int_S u(f(S))dP\right)dv,$$

v is a probabilistic belief over a set of priors C and ϕ is a nonlinear function reflecting extent of ambiguity aversion. ϕ rules out reduction of a second-order probability model to a first-order model.

In [176] they suggested to use confidence function to measure relevance of priors:

$$U(f) = \min_{\rho \in \mathcal{L}_\beta} \frac{1}{\varphi(\rho)} \int_S u(f(S))d\rho$$

Here $_\varphi$ is a confidence function, $\varphi(\rho) \in [0,1]$ is a relevance of prior ρ, $\mathcal{L}_\beta = \{\rho : \varphi(\rho) \geq \beta\}, \beta \in (0,1]$ is a set of priors.

A wide class of multiple priors models is termed as variational preferences models [489, 770], robust control idea-based model [350], ε contamination model [259]. The generalized representation for these models is the following:

$$U(f) = \min_{\rho \in \Delta(S)} \left[\int_S u(f(S))d\rho + c(\rho) \right]$$

where c is a "cost function". A value $c(\rho)$ is higher for less relevant distribution ρ, and $\Delta(S)$ is the set of priors over s.

1.3.5 *Cumulative prospect theory*

Cumulative Prospect Theory (CPT) [732] was proposed by Kahnemann and Tversky as a further development of PT for decision making under uncertainty. A CPT for risk environment was proposed in [175].

In CPT, gains and losses are aggregated separately by Choquet integrals with different capacities:

$$U(f) = \int_S v(f^+(S))d\eta^+ + \int_S v(f^-(S))d\eta^-,$$

where $f^+(S) = \max(f(S),0)$ and $f^-(S) = \min(f(S),0)$, $\int_S$ is Choquet integral, v is a value function, η^+, η^- are capacities.

Such a utility function is used to describe dependence of beliefs on the sign of outcomes, referred to as *sign-dependence*. Sign-dependence for the case of decisions under uncertainty is modeled by using two different capacities η^+, η^-. When $\eta^+(A) = 1 - \eta^-(S \setminus A), A \subset S$, the sign-dependence disappears and CPT is reduced to CEU.

CPT is one of the most successful theories — it encompasses advantages of PT and CEU: it describes loss aversion and models non-additivity of beliefs under uncertainty.

However, CPT suffers from a series of disadvantages. Gains and losses are aggregated separately that often contradicts experimental evidence [118, 119, 790].

The main disadvantage is that CPT for risk problems is due to the fact that CPT is highly conditioned by parameters of value and weighting functions [551]. Roughly speaking, the same combination works well in one choice problem but badly in another. For example, CPT fails to model choices under moderate and equal probabilities [83].

1.4 General theory of decisions

It should be mentioned that evolution of decision analysis goes along particular directions. Despite that existing theories account for important issues as risk, gain-loss and ambiguity attitudes, altruism, trust etc, these behavioral determinants are considered independently of each other. In view of this, several studies were devoted to the idea of a general decision theory [314, 364, 753]. The progress achieved in these works includes consideration of a multi-decision problem, the use of cross-disciplinary decision model, account for mental and psychological factors. However, these works are based on the probability theory and precise computations, whereas real-world decision-relevant information is imperfect and involves a combination of probabilistic and possibilistic information.

The evolution of modeling decision-relevant information has led to formation of the following hierarchy with increase of adequacy: numerical information (ground level), interval-valued information (first level), probabilistic or fuzzy information (second level), information with second-order uncertainty (third level), Z-information and visual information (fourth level) [821, 856]. In existing studies, the ground, first, second, and, sometimes, the third levels of information is considered. Unfortunately, reliability of information is rarely considered whereas real-world information is often partially reliable. This implies that results of decision analysis is also partially reliable.

As it was proposed in [60], the behavioral aspects which form subjective conditions of decision making, and states of nature which form objective conditions, should be considered jointly as two main dimensions of the fundamental basis of decision analysis. The joint consideration of objective and subjective conditions reflects the fact that a human behavior to some extent depends on objective conditions. Unfortunately, in existing studies states of nature are the main basis of decision analysis and behavioral determinants are introduced parametrically.

In order to cope with the above mentioned problems, in [54] they proposed the basics of a general theory of decisions to outline these fundamental aspects of decision making in one model. This general theory of decisions rely on the following principles:

1) General theory of decisions is based on fuzzy logic, not on binary logic. This allows for construction of better models of reality where uncertainty and imprecision play a critical role, as it is mentioned by Prof. L.A. Zadeh. Fuzzy logic-based modeling languages help to better describe human reasoning in economic, social and political spheres.

2) The general theory is developed to resolve the existing paradoxes of decision by using a general approach to modeling subjective and objective conditions of choice. The existing theories fail to do so as they are developed to model some specific decision phenomena by using parametric approaches and disregarding imperfect decision relevant information.

3) Systemic view on a unified multidisciplinary model to account for psychological, mental, cultural, intellectual, social, material and other decision factors.

4) Account for vague preferences. Vagueness of preferences reflects the fact that a DM often cannot surely give preference to one alternative, but the preference is 'distributed' among alternatives. This is due to limited knowledge of a human being, imperfect information, psychological biases.

5) Joint consideration of objective conditions and subjective conditions. A human behavior is modeled by a set of states of a DM to represent his/her principal mental conditions inspired by important behavioral determinants. For instance, a state of a DM may be considered as a vector of such determinants as attitudes to risk, altruism, responsibility. States of a DM and states of nature form a whole space of combined states as a basis of decision analysis. A joint probability distribution in this space measures whether a considered subjective condition can take place at a considered objective condition.

6) Taking into account non-additivity of preferences. Modeling of non-additivity of DM's preferences should be based on the use of a bi-capacity. The bi-capacity [451] is used to describe interaction between positive and negative values (outcomes, criteria values) as gains and losses.

7) The use of Z-information [821] to describe partial reliability of information stemming from partial reliability of the source of

information, misperceptions, psychological biases, incompetence etc. Z-information represents an NL-described value of a variable of interest and the related NL-described reliability. This is important as information on states of nature, future outcomes and behavioral determinants is partially known.

These principles allow to better understand the phenomena of motivation, bounded rationality and imperfect information as leading factors of economic agents behavior. Following these principles, in [54] they propose a unified decision model. This model is based on a space of combined states and utilizes computation with Z-numbers as mathematical language to handle imperfect information. It is shown that existing decision theories such as CEU, CPT and others are special cases of the suggested general theory of decisions.

Chapter 2

Analyses of the Existing Decision Theories

2.1 A brief review of the main existing decision theories

Analyzing the above mentioned decision theories we arrived at conclusion that these theories are developed for a decision environment characterized by well-described information on alternatives, states of nature, probabilities and outcomes. Let us shortly overview the existing decision theories.

The main shortcoming of decision making methods developed for situations of uncertainty is that most of them are not developed to deal with any information on probabilities of states of nature, whereas in real-life, a DM almost always have some amount of such information.

The main methods of decision making under risk are von Neumann and Morgenstern EU, Hodges-Lehmann criterion [360] and Prospect theory. Despite strong scientific foundations and simplicity of the utility models, they are based on idealized decision environment. A DM is considered fully rational and relying on coarsely computational, inanimate reasoning. It is considered that future may be perfectly described by means of states of nature like extraction of a white or a black ball. However, as David Schmeidler states, *"Real life is not about balls and urns"*. Often, available information is not sufficient to describe likelihood of states of nature by objective probabilities. The use of subjective probabilities is slightly more realistic, but is often not suitable to describe choices under uncertainty even in thought experiments.

Reconsideration of preferences framework of EU resulted in development of two types generalizations: rank-dependence generalization and sign-dependence generalization [175]. These generalizations include various reconsiderations and weakening of independence axiom [97, 270, 311, 318, 669], measuring human attitudes to risk and uncertainty (rank-dependent generalization), gains and losses [404, 732] etc.

A large number of studies is devoted to decision making under ambiguity when probabilities are not exactly known [6, 146, 192, 258, 260, 287, 309, 310, 312, 337, 370, 411, 412, 718]. This is related to non-probabilistic uncertainty. In this regard, decision making under uncertainty often is considered as an extreme case — ambiguity represented by simultaneous consideration of all the probability distributions. The studies on decision making under ambiguity are conducted in two directions — a development of models based on multi-ple probability distributions, called multiple priors models [318, 319], and a formation of approaches based on non-additive measures [755, 768] such as CEU.

CEU is a nice model as describing non-additivity of beliefs conditioned by scarce relevant information on likelihood of events. CEU is a one of the most successful utility models of decision making under ambiguity and risk.

CPT follows both rank-dependent and sign-dependent generalization of EU that allows to take into account both asymmetry of gains and losses and ambiguity attitudes. From the other side, the psychological biases are precisely described, that may be done hardly under qualitative nature of relevant information.

Multiple priors models were suggested for situations when a DM has imprecise beliefs in form of ranges of probabilities. Moreover, sometimes a DM has different degrees of belief to different relevant probability distributions. For addressing this issue, models with second-order probabilities were suggested [97, 194, 195]. In the smooth ambiguity model [436] a subjective probability measure is used to reflect a DM's belief on whether a considered subset of multiple priors contains a 'true' prior. However, for a human being an assessment of a precise subjective probability to each prior does not correspond to extremely limited computational capability of humans. The other disadvantage of the belief representation suggested in [436] is that the problem of investigation of consistency of subjective probability-relevant information is not discussed. An extensive investigation of consistency issue is covered in [756].

The model based on confidence function and the variational preferences models [489] also use complicated techniques to account for a relevance of a prior to a considered problem. From the other side, each decision is evaluated only on one prior and the pessimistic evaluation (min operator) is used.

Let us note that existing utility models are based on rather complicated techniques and may be too subtle to be applied under imperfect decision-relevant information. As Prof. L. Zadeh states, imperfect information is information which is in one or more respects is imprecise, uncertain, incomplete, unreliable, vague or partially true [855]. Even the advanced utility models are developed for decision environment where real-world imperfect information is degenerated to some typical cases. This presents some difficulties in application of the existing models and decreases trust to the obtained results.

In [315, 320] they propose a new theory referred to as case-based decision theory. The motivation behind this theory is that in real-world problems, it may be impossible to determine all the states of nature, possible outcomes and probabilities. In such cases human rely on their experience, that is, consider decision problems they dealt with in the past. Given a current decision problem, they tend to recall similar problems in the related decisions. In the proposed theory, a decision situation is termed a case, and is formally considered as a triple (q,f,r), where q is a decision problem, f is an act, r is a result. A set of cases, M, is referred to as a memory. A decision maker choices is based on a utility function u, which measures utility of r, and a similarity function s, which measures a similarity $s(p,q)$ between a current problem p and any problem q stored in M. A similarity $s(p,q)$ is a non-negative value, and naturally satisfies $s(p,q') > s(p,q'')$ if q' is more similar to p than q'', $q',q'' \in M$. A problem of decision making is to find f that maximizes the following utility function:

$$U(f) = U_{p,M}(f) = \sum_{(q,f,r) \in M} s(p,q)\, u\,(r).$$

As based on a paradigm which people actually apply, this theory allows to find solutions for many decision problems where EU theories fail. However, despite that information stored in our memory is likely to be uncertain, imprecise and partially reliable, numerical utility function and numerical similarity measure are used in this theory.

2.2 Comparison of existing decision theories

The evolution of decision theories starting from EU theory achieved a sufficient progress that is represented by formation of three main directions: normative theories, descriptive theories and prescriptive theories [102, 427, 428, 485].

The normative theories are used to model fully rational decisions without consideration of psychological, mental or other factors, and requires perfect decision-relevant information.

The descriptive theories [671, 698] are used to account for important behavioral factors, including psychology, perception, attitudes of a DM toward people, tolerance to imprecision and uncertainty, understanding of imperfect nature of decision environment.

However, the majority of decision theories are not purely normative or descriptive. For example, the Prospect theory [732] can be considered as synthesis of normative EU paradigm and formalization of psychological biases. In this regard, a concept of a prescriptive theory was proposed to as a interdisciplinary fusion of economics, psychology and other fields. The related research is conducted in the field of neuro-economics [144, 145, 402] where they study neurobiological activity of human brain underlying decision making and economic behavior.

The important direction of decision analysis in the stream of prescriptive models is referred to as discrete choice models [107, 429, 494, 503, 504, 505, 693]. These models are based on the evidence that in real-world problems one usually has a discrete and finite set of mutually exclusive alternatives. The main important achievement of this research is that real decisions depend on relation between attributes of alternatives and behavioral determinants of a DM. However, the main disadvantage is that in such a complex consideration, real-world imperfect information is modeled by using a precise joint probability distribution.

A series of works is devoted to development of a general decision theory which could unite previous findings within a single framework as soon as these findings describe various important features of decisions.

In [753] Wald suggested basics of a general theory for statistical decisions. However, it is not possible to create general theory within probabilistic uncertainty because real-world decision-relevant information is a combination of probabilistic and possibilistic information.

The research suggested in [364] represents construction of a general decision theory as a synthesis of psychological economic theory principles and a general model of decisions under uncertainty. The cross-disciplinary decision model based on the achievements in economics, psychology, computer science, mathematics and neurobiology is used. One advantage of the suggested model is consideration of a real-world outcome as a pair of a benefit and a cost. Values of outcomes may be determined based not only on financial impact, but also on time impact, personal principles of a decision maker and other issues. Despite of notable progress achieved, this theory is based on the probability theory and precise numerical techniques whereas real decision-relevant information includes both probabilistic and possibilistic information.

In [314] Gilboa discusses important questions in the present decision theories, which complicate a formulation of a general theory and offer a unified decision model to better capture real-world decision behavior.

It may be considered that development of decision theories, while achieving good results, still requires sufficient improvement. A decision theory should be able to account for imperfect information on states of nature, probabilities, outcomes and behavioral determinants. A fundamental basis instead of parametrical modeling is needed to account for behavioral determinants and their interaction. It is needed to take into account vagueness of preferences stemming from imperfect decision relevant information and behavioral aspects such as psychological, mental features (attitudes to risk and uncertainty), social norms etc.

A series of works is proposed to cope with these shortcomings [18, 19, 20, 24, 40, 44, 58, 60, 61].

In [18, 20, 24, 44] they proposed a theory of decision making under linguistically described decision relevant information on states of nature, probabilities and outcomes. Decision model in this theory is expressed as a fuzzy-valued Choquet integral-based utility function used to describe natural vagueness of preferences in a framework of linguistic information.

In [60] a further research is proposed which extends the study in [20] to behavioral decision making framework. In this theory, behavior of a DM is modeled by a set of his/her states each representing one principal behavioral condition a DM may exhibit. States of a DM and states of nature constitute in this theory a general basis for decision analysis. Such framework is more general than behavioral basics of the existing theories. From the other side, the theory allows for a transparent analysis. It is shown that existing theories including EU, CEU and CPT are special cases of the suggested theory of behavioral decision making under imperfect information.

The theories based on the use of a utility function have at least one disadvantage. This is related to evaluation of a vector-valued alternative by a scalar-valued utility. Indeed, it may not suit well human intuition and leads to information loss. Utility function is constructed on the basis of restrictive assumptions on preferences, e.g. independence, completeness, transitivity etc. Relaxations of these assumptions allow to obtain more adequate but more complex models. In contrast, humans directly compare alternatives as vectors of attributes' values and don't adopt some scalar values. From the other side, utility function construction may not be practical or even may not possible. In order to cope with these problems, an approach to decision making with imperfect information based on the Fuzzy Pareto optimality (FPO) principle is suggested in [61]. In contrast to the classical Pareto optimality principle according to which all Pareto alternatives are considered equally optimal, FPO concept allows to determine degrees of optimality. This is also important when decision-relevant information is imperfect.

In real-life decision problems perception-based decision-relevant information may be too vague to use some reliable analytical precisiation. In contrast, information is described by using uncertain visual constraints. In [58] they propose an approach to decision making based on a new fuzzy geometry and the extended fuzzy logic of Prof. Lotfi Zadeh. In this approach unprecisiated information is described by means of fuzzy geometric objects. The decision model is expressed as fuzzy if-then rules with fuzzy geometric primitives.

In [54] they propose foundations of a general decision theory in order to cope with all the above-mentioned main shortcomings of existing theories. The proposed theory relies on two main aspects. The one is the use of combined states as an adequate basis of behavioral decision analysis. The other one is the use of Z-valued information to model imperfect information of real decision problems. The theory utilizes a utility function described as a Z-valued Choquet like with the Z-valued bi-capacity. This theory is of a more general and a more transparent decision model than existing decision theories.

The theories proposed in [18, 19, 20, 24, 40, 44, 60, 61] are able to handle uncertain information. The main difficulty of handling uncertain information is related to analytical and computational complexities. However, this difficulty is not so restrictive taking into account two main achievements. The first is related to a sufficient progress in the field of fuzzy arithmetic related to achievement of a good tradeoff between reducing a range of uncertainty and loss of informativeness of results. The second is related to an increased computational power of information processing systems for effective computations with imprecise, partially true and partially reliable information.

Chapter 3

Interval Computation

3.1 Classical interval arithmetic

In real-life decision making uncertainty almost always arises due to use of information which come from expert estimations and measurements. Instead of crisp number as approximation for the value of a real variable interval arithmetic presents a set of reals as possible values. These sets are restricted to intervals.

First we consider the classical interval arithmetic. Classical interval theory began with [540]. The closed interval

$$[\underline{x}, \overline{x}] = \{x \in R \mid \underline{x} \le x \le \overline{x}\},$$

is defined as the interval of certainty about the value of x. We are certain that the true value of x is in the interval $[\underline{x}, \overline{x}]$.

Interval number [217]. Let's $\underline{x}, \overline{x} \in R$ such that $\underline{x} \le \overline{x}$. An interval number $[\underline{x}, \overline{x}]$ is a closed and bounded nonempty real interval, that is

$$[\underline{x}, \overline{x}] = \{x \in R \mid \underline{x} \le x \le \overline{x}\}.$$

Here $\underline{x} = \min([\underline{x}, \overline{x}])$ and $\overline{x} = \max([\underline{x}, \overline{x}])$ are the lower and upper endpoints of $[\underline{x}, \overline{x}]$.

The equality of interval numbers is defned as

$$[\underline{x}, \overline{x}] = [\underline{y}, \overline{y}] \Leftrightarrow \underline{x} = \underline{y} \wedge \overline{x} = \overline{y}.$$

A strict partial order on the set of interval numbers R is denied as

$$[\underline{x},\overline{x}] < [\underline{y},\overline{y}] \Leftrightarrow \overline{x} = \underline{y}.$$

Here $<$ is transitive, asymmetric, and irreflexive on R.

We now define the basic arithmetic and algebraic operations for interval numbers. As interval numbers are sets, the algebraic operations for them can be characterized by set-theoretic definitions. Taking this into account, below we give these operations.

Addition: Assume that two interval $[\underline{x},\overline{x}]$ and $[\underline{y},\overline{y}]$ are given. Interval addition is formulated as

$$[\underline{x},\overline{x}] + [\underline{y},\overline{y}] = [\underline{x}+\underline{y},\overline{x}+\overline{y}].$$

Example

$$[2, 5] + [1, 3] = [2+1, 5+3] = [3, 8].$$

Multiplication: Two interval numbers $[\underline{x},\overline{x}]$ and $[\underline{y},\overline{y}]$ are given. Interval multiplication is defined as

$$[\underline{x},\overline{x}] \times [\underline{y},\overline{y}] = [\min\{\underline{xy},\underline{x}\overline{y},\overline{x}\underline{y},\overline{xy}\}, \max\{\underline{xy},\underline{x}\overline{y},\overline{x}\underline{y},\overline{xy}\}].$$

Example

$$[-1,1]\cdot[-2,0.5]$$
$$= [\min(-1\cdot(-2),-1\cdot0.5, \ 1\cdot(-2), \ 1\cdot0.5), \ \max(-1\cdot(-2),-1\cdot0.5, \ 1\cdot(-2),1\cdot0.5))]$$
$$= [\min(2,-0.5,-2, \ 0.5), \ \max(2,-0.5,-2, \ 0.5)] = [-2, \ 2].$$

Multiplication to scalar number $k \in R$. If $k > 0$, then $k \cdot A = k[a_1,a_2] = [ka_1,ka_2]$, if $k<0$, then $k \cdot A = k[a_1,a_2] = [ka_2,ka_1]$.

Negation: For $[\underline{x},\overline{x}]$ interval negation is defined as

$$-[\underline{x},\overline{x}] = [-\overline{x},-\underline{x}].$$

Example

$$-[1,3] = [-3,-1].$$

Reciprocal: For $\left[\underline{x},\overline{x}\right]$ ($0 \notin [\underline{x},\overline{x}]$), interval reciprocal is defined as

$$[\underline{x},\overline{x}]^{-1} = [\overline{x}^{-1}, \underline{x}^{-1}].$$

Example

$$[1,2]^{-1} = \left[2^{-1}, 1^{-1}\right] = [0.5, 1].$$

Subtraction: Assume that interval numbers X and Y are given. Interval subtraction is defined by

$$X - Y = X + (-Y).$$

Example

$$[2,5] - [1,3] = [2 - 3,\ 5 - 1] = [-1, 4],$$

$$[0,1] - [-6,5] = [0 - 5,\ 1 + 6] = [-5,\ 7].$$

Division: For any two interval numbers X and any Y division is defined as

$$X/Y = X \times (Y^{-1}), 0 \notin Y.$$

Example

$$[-1,1]/[-2,-0.5] = [-1,1] \cdot [1/(-0.5), 1/(-2)]$$
$$= [\min(-1/(-2), -1/(-0.5), 1/(-2), 1/(-0.5)),$$
$$\max(-1/(-2), -1/(-0.5), 1/(-2), 1/(-0.5))]$$
$$= [\min(0.5, 2, -0.5, -2), \max(0.5, 2, -0.5, -2)] = [-2, 2].$$

Exponentiation: For X and integer n, the exponents of X are formulated as

$$X^0 = [1,1],$$
$$0 < n \Rightarrow X^n = X^{n-1} \times X,$$
$$0 \notin X \wedge 0 \leq n \Rightarrow X^{-n} = (X^{-1})^n.$$

The square of $[\underline{x},\overline{x}]$ is defined as

$$[\underline{x},\overline{x}]^2 = [\underline{x},\overline{x}] \times [\underline{x},\overline{x}]$$
$$= [\min\{\underline{x}^2, \underline{x}\overline{x}, \overline{x}^2\}, \max\{\underline{x}^2, \underline{x}\overline{x}, \overline{x}^2\}]$$
$$= [\underline{x}\overline{x}, \max\{\underline{x}^2, \overline{x}^2\}].$$

Example

$$[2,5]^2 = \left[\min\left\{2^2, 2*5, 5^2\right\}, \max\left\{2^2, 2*5, 5^2\right\}\right] = \left[2^2, \max\left\{2^2, 5^2\right\}\right] = [4,25].$$

Infimum: The infimum of $[\underline{x}, \overline{x}]$ is defined as

$$\inf([\underline{x}, \overline{x}]) = \min([\underline{x}, \overline{x}]) = \underline{x}.$$

Supremum: The supremum of $[\underline{x}, \overline{x}]$ is defined as

$$\sup([\underline{x}, \overline{x}]) = \max([\underline{x}, \overline{x}]) = \overline{x}.$$

Interval Width: The width of $[\underline{x}, \overline{x}]$ is defined as

$$w([\underline{x}, \overline{x}]) = \overline{x} - \underline{x}.$$

Example

$$w[5,7] = 7 - 5 = 2.$$

Absolute Value: The absolute value of $[\underline{x}, \overline{x}]$ is defined as

$$\|[\underline{x}, \overline{x}]\| = \max(\{|\underline{x}|, |\overline{x}|\}).$$

Example

$$\|[-6,4]\| = \max(\{|-6|, |4|\}) = 6.$$

Distance: The distance (metric) between $[\underline{x}, \overline{x}]$ and $[\underline{y}, \overline{y}]$ is defined as

$$d\left([\underline{x}, \overline{x}], [\underline{y}, \overline{y}]\right) = \max(\{|\underline{x} - \underline{y}|, |\overline{x} - \overline{y}|\}).$$

Example

$$d([2,3], [4,6]) = \max(\{|2 - 4|, |3 - 6|\}) = 3.$$

In classical interval arithmetic the interval result tends to be wider than one could reasonably expect, the result contains all possible values.

3.2 Preference relations of interval values

To create preference relations under interval values we here use a satisfaction function approach [2]. Assume that the interval numbers $A = [\underline{a}, \overline{a}]$ and $B = [\underline{b}, \overline{b}]$ are given. The satisfaction functions $(S(A < B), S(A > B),$ and $S(A = B))$ are:

$$S(A < B) = \frac{w(\{x \in A \mid x < y \ \forall y \in B\}) + w(\{x \in B \mid x > y \ \forall y \in A\})}{w(A) + w(B)}, \quad (3.1)$$

$$S(A > B) = \frac{w(\{x \in A \mid x > y \ \forall y \in B\}) + w(\{x \in B \mid x < y \ \forall y \in A\})}{w(A) + w(B)}, \quad (3.2)$$

$$S(A = B) = \frac{w(\{x \in A \mid x = y \ \forall y \in B\}) + w(\{x \in B \mid x = y \ \forall y \in A\})}{w(A) + w(B)}, \quad (3.3)$$

S will be applied for solving interval linear programming problem in Chapter 9. Now let us to introduce upper and lower satisfaction functions. Upper satisfaction functions, i.e., $S_U(A > B)$, $S_U(A < B)$, $S_U(A \geq B)$ and $S_U(A \leq B)$ are defined as the following [2]:

$$S_U(A > B) = \frac{w(\{x \in A \mid x > y \ \forall y \in B\})}{w(A) + w(B)},$$

$$S_U(A \geq B) = \frac{w(\{x \in A \mid x > y \ \forall y \in B\}) + w(\{x \in A \mid x = y \ \forall y \in B\})}{w(A) + w(B)},$$

$$S_U(A < B) = \frac{w(\{x \in B \,|\, x > y \;\; \forall y \in A\})}{w(A) + w(B)},$$

$$S_U(A \geq B) = \frac{w(\{x \in B \,|\, x > y \;\; \forall y \in A\}) + w(\{x \in B \,|\, x = y \;\; \forall y \in A\})}{w(A) + w(B)},$$

Similarly the lower satisfaction functions (i.e., $S_L(A > B)$, $S_L(A < B)$, $S_L(A \geq B)$ and $S_L(A \leq B)$ are expressed as

$$S_L(A > B) = \frac{w(\{x \in B \,|\, x < y \;\; \forall y \in A\})}{w(A) + w(B)},$$

$$S_L(A \geq B) = \frac{w(\{x \in B \,|\, x < y \;\; \forall y \in A\}) + w(\{x \in B \,|\, x = y \;\; \forall y \in A\})}{w(A) + w(B)},$$

$$S_L(A < B) = \frac{w(\{x \in A \,|\, x < y \;\; \forall y \in B\})}{w(A) + w(B)},$$

$$S_L(A \geq B) = \frac{w(\{x \in A \,|\, x < y \;\; \forall y \in B\}) + w(\{x \in A \,|\, x = y \;\; \forall y \in B\})}{w(A) + w(B)}.$$

3.3. Relative distance measure based interval arithmetic

Most frequently used interval arithmetic is Moore arithmetic [539, 540, 597]. However there are some limitations and the drawbacks of the Moore interval arithmetic [252, 456, 616, 683]. They are mainly the larger excess width effect problem, dependency problem, solving interval equation problem, etc. The alternative for interval arithmetic is relative distance measure (RDM) interval arithmetic [610, 612-615]. In [612-615] value x from $X = [\underline{x}, \overline{x}]$ is described by using RDM variable $\alpha_x, \alpha_x \in [0,1]$

$$x = \underline{x} + \alpha_x (\overline{x} - \underline{x}). \tag{3.4}$$

Interval $X = [\underline{x}, \overline{x}]$ is described as

$$X = \{x : x = \underline{x} + \alpha_x (\overline{x} - \underline{x}), \alpha_x \in [0,1]\}. \tag{3.5}$$

By α_x one can obtain any value in $[\underline{x}, \overline{x}]$.

In this arithmetic for interval numbers A, B, C following properties are satisfied [236]:

1. $A + B = B + A$, $AB = BA$ (commutativity laws).

2. $A + (B + C) = (A + B) + C$, $A(BC) = (AB)C$ (associativity laws).

3. $A + (-A) = (-A) + A = 0$, $-A$ is the additive inverse of a A.

4. $A(B + C) = (AB) + (AC)$ (left distributivity law)
   $(B + C)A = (BA) + (CA)$ (right distributivity law).

5. $A^{-1} = 1/A$ $AA^{-1} = A(1/A) = 1$, A^{-1} multiplicative inverse of A.

6. $A + C = B + C \Rightarrow A = B$ (cancellation law).

7. $CA = CB \Rightarrow A = B$ (cancellation law).

In classical interval arithmetic, Laws 3, 4, 5, 7 do not hold. For example, in the equation $A + X = C$, $X = C - A$ is not allowed due to the fact that law 3 does not hold.

Arithmetic operations on interval numbers in PDM arithmetic are performed as follows. Assume that two intervals X and Y are given: $X = [\underline{x}, \overline{x}] = \{x : x = \underline{x} + \alpha_x (\overline{x} - \underline{x}), \alpha_x \in [0,1]\}$ and $Y = [\underline{y}, \overline{y}] = \{y : y = \underline{y} + \alpha_y (\overline{y} - \underline{y}), \alpha_y \in [0,1]\}$.

Addition of X and Y is defined as following

$$X + Y = \{x + y : x + y = \underline{x} + \alpha_x (\overline{x} - \underline{x}) + \underline{y} + \alpha_y (\overline{y} - \underline{y}), \alpha_x, \alpha_y \in [0,1]\}. \tag{3.6}$$

Subtraction is defined as

$$X - Y = \{x - y : x - y = \underline{x} + \alpha_x(\overline{x} - \underline{x}) - \underline{y} - \alpha_y(\overline{y} - \underline{y}), \alpha_x, \alpha_y \in [0,1]\}. \quad (3.7)$$

Multiplication is defined as

$$X \cdot Y = \{xy : xy = [\underline{x} + \alpha_x(\overline{x} - \underline{x})] \cdot [\underline{y} + \alpha_y(\overline{y} - \underline{y})], \alpha_x, \alpha_y \in [0,1]\}. \quad (3.8)$$

Division is defined as

$$X / Y = \{x / y : x / y = [\underline{x} + \alpha_x(\overline{x} - \underline{x})] / [\underline{y} + \alpha_y(\overline{y} - \underline{y})], \alpha_x, \alpha_y \in [0,1]\}, \\ \text{if } 0 \notin Y \quad (3.9)$$

For operations $* \in \{+, -, \cdot, /\}$ span is defined as

$$s(X * Y) = [\min\{X * Y\}, \max\{X * Y\}] \quad (3.10)$$

Example

Assume that two intervals A = [1, 2] and B = [3, 4] are given. Operations $X \in \{+, -, \cdot, /\}$ are performed as follows. First, we have to write A and B using variable α_a and α_b

To find solutions by RDM arithmetic we should write intervals in RDM notation using RDM variable α_a and α_b, where $\alpha_a \in [0, 1]$ and $\alpha_b \in [0, 1]$.

$$A = [1,2] = \{a : a = 1 + \alpha_a, \ \alpha_a \in [0,1]\} \quad (3.11)$$
$$B = [3,4] = \{b : b = 3 + \alpha_b, \ \alpha_b \in [0,1]\}$$

Then solutions may be defined as

$$A + B = \{a + b : a + b = 4 + \alpha_a \alpha_b, \ \alpha_a, \alpha_b \in [0,1]\}$$

$$A - B = \{a - b : a - b = -2 + \alpha_a - \alpha_b, \ \alpha_a, \alpha_b \in [0,1]\}$$

$$A \cdot B = \{ab : ab = 3 + 3\alpha_a + \alpha_b + \alpha_a\alpha_b, \ \alpha_a, \alpha_b \in [0,1]\}$$

$$A / B = \{a / b : a / b = (1 + \alpha_a) / (3 + \alpha_b), \ \alpha_a, \alpha_b \in [0,1]\}.$$

Inverse of interval is defined as

$$X - X = \{x - x : x - x = \underline{x} + \alpha_x(\overline{x} - \underline{x}) - \underline{x} - \alpha_x(\overline{x} - \underline{x}), \ \alpha_x \in [0,1]\} = 0$$
$$X / X = \{x / x : x / x = [\underline{x} + \alpha_x(\overline{x} - \underline{x})] / [\underline{x} - \alpha_x(\overline{x} - \underline{x}], \ \alpha_x \in [0,1]\} = 1.$$

3.4 Solving interval equations

Let consider the interval equation

$$[\underline{a}, \overline{a}] + [\underline{x}, \overline{x}] = [\underline{c}, \overline{c}],$$

$$[1,3] + [\underline{x}, \overline{x}] = [3,4].$$
$$(3.12)$$

By using conventional interval arithmetic we have

$$1 + \underline{x} = 3, \qquad\qquad \underline{x} = 2;$$

$$3 + \overline{x} = 4, \qquad\qquad \overline{x} = 1.$$

Let's solve (3.12) by using RDM arithmetic. In this case the interval $[\underline{a}, \overline{a}] = [1,3]$ takes the form $a = 1 + 2\alpha_a \ \alpha_a \in [0,1]$, and the interval $[\underline{c}, \overline{c}] = [3,4]$ takes the form $c = 3 + \alpha_c, \ \alpha_c \in [0,1]$. So, (3.12) can be rewritten as

$$(1 + 2\alpha_a) + x = 3 + \alpha_c,$$

$$x = 2 - 2\alpha_a + \alpha_c, \ \alpha_a \in [0,1], \ \alpha_c \in [0,1]. \qquad (3.13)$$

The correct solution has the form

$$[\underline{a},\overline{a}]+[\underline{x}(a),\overline{x}(a)]=[\underline{c},\overline{c}],$$

$$[1,3]=[\underline{x}=3-a,\overline{x}=4-a]=[3,4].\qquad(3.14)$$

Example

$$[\underline{a},\overline{a}]+[\underline{x},\overline{x}]=[\underline{c},\overline{c}],$$

$$[0,2]+[\underline{x},\overline{x}]=[1,6].\qquad(3.15)$$

Use of Moore-arithmetic for solution (3.15) gives $[\underline{x},\overline{x}]=[1,4]$.

By using RDM arithmetic equation (3.15) is described as

$$\underline{a}+\alpha_a(\overline{a}-\underline{a})+x=\underline{c}+\alpha_c(\overline{c}-\underline{c}),$$

$$0+2\alpha_a+x=1+\alpha_c,\qquad(3.16)$$

$$\alpha_a\in[0,1],\ \alpha_c\in[0,1].$$

The solution will be

$$x=\underline{c}-\underline{a}+\alpha_c(\overline{c}-\underline{c})-\alpha_a(\overline{a}-\underline{a}),$$

$$x=1+5\alpha_c-2\alpha_a,\qquad(3.17)$$

$$\alpha_a\in[0,1],\ \alpha_c\in[0,1].$$

Solution ($[\underline{x},\overline{x}]=[1,4]$) does not contain (0.5, 5) though it satisfies the equation $[0,2]+[\underline{x},\overline{x}]=[1,6]$.

One of drawback of conventional interval-arithmetic is so-called the principle of increasing entropy [252].

Now we consider the system of linear interval equations which can be presented as follows:

$$[A][x] = [b] \tag{3.18}$$

where [A], [b], [x] are interval matrix, interval vector and interval solution vector. Generally such a system has no exact solutions. There are, however, methods for approximate solution of (3.18). The dominant approaches to the solution of interval linear system are based on the treating (3.18) as a set of real valued equations whose parameters belong to the corresponding intervals [423]. These approaches are NP hard problems, and finding a solution of even a small system is a very difficult task. Main drawback of exsisting approaches to the solution of (3.18) is the increasing width effect.

Equation (3.18) can be extended to

$$[\underline{a}, \overline{a}] \cdot [\underline{x}, \overline{x}] - [\underline{b}, \overline{b}] = [-y, y] \tag{3.19}$$

where [-y,y] is interval extension of 0. If interval values are positive (3.19) can be transformed to

$$\begin{cases} \underline{a} \cdot \underline{x} - \overline{b} = -y \\ \overline{a} \cdot \overline{x} - \underline{b} = y \end{cases} \tag{3.20}$$

Consequently,

$$\underline{a}\underline{x} - \overline{b} + \overline{a}\,\overline{x} - \underline{b} = 0. \tag{3.21}$$

With given constraints on the values of $\underline{x}$ and $\overline{x}$, (3.21) is Constraint Satisfaction Problem (CSP) [198] and its solution may be obtained:

$$[\underline{x}] = \left[\underline{x}_{\max}, \frac{\overline{b} + \overline{b}}{\underline{a} + \overline{a}} \right], [\overline{x}] = \left[\frac{\overline{b} + \overline{b}}{\underline{a} + \overline{a}}, \overline{x}_{\min} \right] \tag{3.22}$$

where $x_{\max} = \max\left(\dfrac{\underline{b}}{\underline{a}}, \dfrac{\underline{b} + \overline{b}}{\underline{a}} - \dfrac{\overline{a}\,\overline{b}}{\underline{a}^2} \right), \overline{x}_{\min} = \min\left(\dfrac{\overline{b}}{\overline{a}}, \dfrac{\underline{b} + \overline{b}}{\overline{a}} - \dfrac{\underline{a}\,\underline{b}}{\overline{a}^2} \right)$

$$y_{\max} = \frac{\overline{a}\,\overline{b}}{\underline{a}} - \underline{b}, \ y_{\min} = \frac{\overline{a}\,\overline{b} - \underline{a}\,\underline{b}}{\underline{a} + \overline{a}}.$$

In [617] it is introduced

$$\alpha = 1 - \frac{y - y_{\min}}{y_{\max} - y_{\min}} \tag{3.23}$$

as measure of certainty of interval solution of (3.19).

In [250, 251] it is shown that this method leads to considerable reducing of resulting interval's length.

Chapter 4

Probabilistic Arithmetic

4.1 Operations on random variables

The problem of operations on random variables arises in a wide range of applications where calculation of functions of random variables are required. In some cases analytical solutions exist, but in other cases numerical methods are used. In this section we will consider both analytical and numerical methods for arithmetic operations on random variables.

Usually determination of distributions of functions of random variables was based on search for analytical solutions. For some restricted classes of problems a formula for the required distributions can be tabulated, but in general it is not practicable to give such results. Exact analytical techniques for determining distributions arising in statistics is described in [500]. An alternative approach is to use numerical methods for calculating the required distributions.

General solution to the distribution of functions of random variables in terms of the Jacobian of transformation is given in [783]. In this chapter we will consider calculation for a function of only one and two random variables. It is very easy to extend the results to functions of n random variables.

A random variable, X, is a variable whose possible values x are numerical outcomes of a random phenomenon. Random variables are of two types: continuous and discrete.

A continuous random variable X is a variable which can take an infinite number of possible values x. A discrete random variable is a variable which can take only a countable number of distinct values.

To determine a probability that a continuous random variable X takes any value in a closed interval $[a, b]$, denoted $P(a \le X \le b)$, a concept of probability distribution is used. A probability distribution or a probability density function is a function $p(x)$ such that for any two numbers a and b with $a \le b$:

$$P(a \le X \le b) = \int_a^b p(x)dx,$$

where $p(x) \ge 0, \int_{-\infty}^{\infty} p(x)dx = 1$.

Consider a discrete random variable X with outcomes space $\{x_1,...,x_n\}$. A probability of an outcome $X = x_i$, denoted $P(X = x_i)$ is defined in terms of a probability distribution. A function p is called a discrete probability distribution or a probability mass function if

$$P(X = x_i) = p(x_i),$$

where $p(x_i) \in [0,1]$ and $\sum_{i=1}^{n} p(x_i) = 1$.

Let us consider operations on Random Variables [696].

Adding Constant to Random Variable

Let X be a random variable and $Y = X + c, \ c \in R$. Then the probability density function (pdf) of Y, p_Y, will be

$$p_Y(y) = p_X(y - c).$$

It is obvious that the density function is simply shifted c units to the right $(c > 0)$ or left $(c < 0)$.

Scalar Product of Random Variable

X is a random variable and $Y = aX, \ a \in R$. Density function $p_Y(y)$ is determined as

$$p_Y(y) = \frac{1}{a} p_X(y/a) \quad if \quad a > 0,$$

$$p_Y(y) = -\frac{1}{a} p_X(y/a) \quad if \quad a < 0.$$

Linear Transformation of Random Variable

Let Y be a continuous random variable, which is linear function of a continuous random variable X. For

$$Y = aX + b \tag{4.1}$$

a density function $p_Y(y)$ is determined as

$$p_Y(y) = \frac{1}{a} p_X\left(\frac{y-b}{a}\right). \tag{4.2}$$

If X is a normal random variable with

$$p_X(x) = \frac{1}{\sqrt{2\pi}} e^{-(x-\mu)^2/2}, \tag{4.3}$$

then

$$p_Y(y) = \frac{1}{a\sqrt{2\pi}} e^{-(\frac{y-b}{a}-\mu)^2/2}. \tag{4.4}$$

A linear function of a normal random variable is

$$X \sim \mathcal{N}(\mu, \sigma^2) \quad \Rightarrow \quad Y \sim \mathcal{N}(a\mu + b, a^2\sigma^2).$$

Square of a Random Variable

X is a random variable and $Y = X^2$. The density function is determined as

$$p_Y(y) = \frac{1}{2\sqrt{y}}\left[p_X(\sqrt{y}) + p_X(-\sqrt{y})\right], \ y \geq 0. \quad (4.5)$$

Example. Square of a Gaussian random variable is a Chi-square random variable

$$X \sim \mathcal{N}(0,1) \ \Rightarrow \ Y \sim X_2^2, \ p_Y(y) = \frac{e^{-y/2}}{\sqrt{2\pi y}}, \ y \geq 0$$

Square Root of a Random Variable

Assume that X is a continuous random variable with density function p_X. It is required to find the pdf p_Y for

$$Y = \sqrt{X} . \quad (4.6)$$

If $y \geq 0$ then

$$p_Y(y) = 2yp_X(y^2) . \quad (4.7)$$

Square root of a random variable with exponential distribution is determined as follows. Suppose that X is random variable with density function

$$p_X(x) = \lambda e^{-\lambda x} (x \geq 0)$$

and consider the distribution of $Y = \sqrt{X}$. The transformation

$$y = g(x) = \sqrt{x}, \ x \geq 0$$

gives

$$p_Y(y) = p_X(y^2)2y = 2\lambda y e^{-\lambda y^2}, \ y \geq 0$$

Consider two independent random variables X and Y with probability distributions p_X and p_Y respectively [174, 782]. Let $Z = X * Y$, $* \in \{+, -, \cdot, /\}$. Suppose we would like to determine a probability distribution p_z of Z .

If the considered function f of the two random variables X and Y is one of the four arithmetic operations, we have the four convolution equations [580, 696, 783]

$$Z = X + Y: \quad p_Z(z) = \int_{-\infty}^{\infty} p_{XY}(z - x, x)\,dx, \qquad (4.8)$$

$$Z = X - Y: \quad p_Z(z) = \int_{-\infty}^{\infty} p_{XY}(z + x, x)\,dx, \qquad (4.9)$$

$$Z = X \times Y: \quad p_Z(z) = \int_{-\infty}^{\infty} \frac{1}{|x|} p_{XY}(z / x, x)\,dx, \qquad (4.10)$$

$$Z = X / Y: \quad p_Z(z) = \int_{-\infty}^{\infty} |x| p_{XY}(zx, x)\,dx. \qquad (4.11)$$

In case when X and Y are independent we can obtain

$$Z = X + Y: \quad p_Z(z) = \int_{-\infty}^{\infty} p_X(z - x, x) p_Y(x)\,dx, \qquad (4.12)$$

$$Z = X - Y: \quad p_Z(z) = \int_{-\infty}^{\infty} p_X(z + x, x) p_Y(x)\,dx, \qquad (4.13)$$

$$Z = X \times Y: \quad p_Z(z) = \int_{-\infty}^{\infty} \frac{1}{|x|} p_X(z / x, x) p_Y(x)\,dx, \qquad (4.14)$$

$$Z = X / Y: \quad p_Z(z) = \int_{-\infty}^{\infty} |x| p_X(zx, x) p_Y(x)\,dx. \qquad (4.15)$$

Equations (4.12)–(4.15) are basic for calculation probability distributions of sum, subtraction, product and quotient of two independent random variables.

For calculation of distributions of sums and subtractions of two normal random variables exact formulae do exist. If $Z = f(X_1, X_2) = X_1 \pm X_2$ [783]

$$\mu_Z = \mu_{X_1} \pm \mu_{X_2}, \qquad (4.16)$$

$$\sigma_Z^2 = \sigma_{X_1}^2 + \sigma_{X_2}^2. \tag{4.17}$$

If X_i, $i = \overline{1,n}$ are normal independent random variables such that $X_i \sim N(\mu_i, \sigma_i^2)$, then $Y = \sum_{i=1}^{n} X_i$ is normally distributed with [366]

$$\mu = \sum_{i=1}^{n} \mu_i \text{ and } \sigma^2 = \sum_{i=1}^{n} \sigma_i^2,$$

$$Y \sim N(\mu, \sigma^2).$$

If a_i, $i = \overline{1,n}$ are real constants, then $Y = \sum_{i=1}^{n} a_i X_i$ is normal distributed with

$$\mu = \sum_{i=1}^{n} a_i \mu_i \text{ and } \sigma^2 = \sum_{i=1}^{n} a_i^2 \sigma_i^2,$$

$$Y \sim N(\mu, \sigma^2).$$

Unfortunately, exact formulae for moments of products and quotients do not exist. In this case approximations are useful for application in applied probability theory. For an arbitrary function of n independent random variables $Z = f(X_1, \ldots, X_n)$ approximate formulae is [343]

$$\mu_Z \approx f(\mu_{X_1}, \ldots, \mu_{X_n}) + \frac{1}{2} \sum_{i=1}^{n} \frac{\partial^2 f}{\partial X_i^2} \sigma_{X_i}^2 \tag{4.18}$$

$$\sigma_Z^2 \approx \sum_{i=1}^{n} \left(\frac{\partial f}{\partial X_i} \right)^2 \sigma_{X_i}^2 + \left(\frac{\partial f}{\partial X_i} \right) \left(\frac{\partial^2 f}{\partial X_i^2} \right) \mu_{X_i}^3 \tag{4.19}$$

Let us consider product and quotient of two independent normal random variables X_1 and X_2. If $Z = h(X_1, X_2) = X_1 X_2$,

$$\mu_Z \approx \mu_{X_1} \mu_{X_2}, \tag{4.20}$$

$$\sigma_Z^2 \approx \mu_{X_1}^2 \sigma_{X_2}^2 + \mu_{X_2}^2 \sigma_{X_1}^2 + \sigma_{X_1}^2 \sigma_{X_2}^2. \tag{4.21}$$

If $Z = f(X_1, X_2) = X_1 / X_2$,

$$\mu_Z \approx \frac{\mu_{X_1}}{\mu_{X_2}} + \frac{\mu_{X_1} \sigma_{X_2}^2}{4\mu_{X_2}^3}, \tag{4.22}$$

$$\sigma_Z^2 \approx \frac{\sigma_{X_1}^2}{\mu_{X_2}^2} + \frac{\mu_{X_1}^2 \sigma_{X_2}^2}{\mu_{X_2}^4} - \frac{\mu_{X_1}^2 \mu_{X_2}^3}{2\mu_{X_2}^5} \tag{4.23}$$

A different approach to calculation of distribution of product of random variables is given in [322].

In [385] it is considered different numerical solution methods of the problem of calculation of distributions of product and subtraction of random variables. It is considered families which contain practically all distributions used in practice and which are closed under the four arithmetic operations [385]. The families include distributions with infinite supports and a finite number of singularities [385]. Wide class of distributions is embraced by software PaCAL [385].

Convolution $p_{12} = p_1 \circ p_2$ of probability distributions p_1 and p_2 is defined as follows:

$$p_{12}(z) = \frac{b(z) \cdot c(z)}{a^3(z)} \frac{1}{\sqrt{2\pi}\sigma_x \sigma_y} \left[2\Phi\left(\frac{b(z)}{a(z)}\right) - 1 \right] +$$
$$+ \frac{1}{a^2(z) \cdot \pi \sigma_x \sigma_y} e^{-\frac{1}{2}\left(\frac{\mu_x^2}{\sigma_x^2} + \frac{\mu_y^2}{\sigma_y^2}\right)} . \tag{4.24}$$

where

$$a(z) = \sqrt{\frac{1}{\sigma_x^2} z^2 + \frac{1}{\sigma_y^2}}, \quad b(z) = \frac{\mu_x}{\sigma_x^2} z + \frac{\mu_y}{\sigma_y^2},$$

$$c(z) = \exp\left(\frac{1}{2}\frac{b^2(z)}{a^2(z)} - \frac{1}{2}\left(\frac{\mu_x^2}{\sigma_x^2} + \frac{\mu_y^2}{\sigma_y^2}\right)\right) \tag{4.25}$$

$$\Phi(z) = \int_{-\infty}^{z} \frac{1}{\sqrt{2\pi}} e^{-\frac{1}{2}u^2 du}.$$

For the case $\mu_X = \mu_Y = 0$ and $\sigma_X = \sigma_Y = 1$, (4.24) is reduced to

$$p_{12}(z) = \frac{1}{\pi} \frac{1}{1+z^2}.$$

Let X_1 and X_2 be two independent discrete random variables with the corresponding outcome spaces $X_1 = \{x_{11},...,x_{1i},...,x_{1n_1}\}$ and $X_2 = \{x_{21},...,x_{2i},...,x_{2n_2}\}$, and the corresponding discrete probability distributions p_1 and p_2. The probability distribution of $X_1 * X_2$, where $*$ is some binary operation, is the convolution $p_{12} = p_1 \circ p_2$ of p_1 and p_2 which is determined as follows [33]:

$$p_{12}(x) = \sum_{x=x_{1i}*x_{2j}} p_1(x_{1i}) p_2(x_{2j}),$$

for any $x \in \{x_1 * x_2 \mid x_1 \in X_1, x_2 \in X_2\}$.

Below we provide formulas for convolution $p_{12} = p_1 \circ p_2$ as a probability distribution of $X = X_1 * X_2$ for several typical binary operations.

Addition $X = X_1 + X_2$:

$$p_{12}(x) = \sum_{x=x_{1i}+x_{2j}} p_1(x_{1i}) p_2(x_{2j}). \tag{4.26}$$

Subtraction $X = X_1 - X_2$:

$$p_{12}(x) = \sum_{x=x_{1i}-x_{2j}} p_1(x_{1i}) p_2(x_{2j}). \tag{4.27}$$

Multiplication $X = X_1 X_2$:

$$p_{12}(x) = \sum_{x = x_{1i} \cdot x_{2j}} p_1(x_{1i}) p_2(x_{2j}).$$

(4.28)

Division $X = X_1 / X_2$:

$$p_{12}(x) = \sum_{x = x_{1i} / x_{2j}} p_1(x_{1i}) p_2(x_{2j}).$$

(4.29)

Minimum $X = \min(X_1, X_2)$:

$$p_{12}(x) = \sum_{x = \min(x_{1i}, x_{2j})} p_1(x_{1i}) p_2(x_{2j}).$$

(4.30)

Maximum $X = \max(X_1, X_2)$:

$$p_{12}(x) = \sum_{x = \max(x_{1i}, x_{2j})} p_1(x_{1i}) p_2(x_{2j}).$$

(4.31)

4.2 Estimation of statistical characteristic of interval uncertainty[45]

In many practical situations, it is important to estimate the mean E and the variance V from the sample values $x_1, \ldots, x_n$. Usually, in statistics, we consider the case when the parameters like E and V do not change with time and when the sample values x_i are known exactly. In practice, the values x_i come from measurements, and measurements are never 100% accurate. In many cases, we only know the upper bound Δ_i on the measurement error. In this case, once we know the measured value $\tilde{x}_i$, we can conclude that the actual (unknown) value x_i belongs to the interval $[\tilde{x}_i - \Delta_i, \tilde{x}_i + \Delta_i]$. Different values x_i from these intervals lead, in general, to different values of E and V. It is therefore desirable to find the ranges E and V of all possible values of E and V. While this problem is, in general, NP-hard, in many practical situations, there exist efficient algorithms for computing such ranges. In practice, processes are dynamic. As a result, reasonable estimates for E and V assign more weight to more recent measurements and less weight to the past ones. In this session, we extend known algorithms for computing the ranges **E** and **V** to such dynamic estimates.

4.2.1 *Statistical estimates*

Lets consider Normal distribution and the standard estimates for E and V. Standard methods for estimating E and V are based on the assumption that the corresponding random quantity is normally distributed, with a probability density

$$\rho(x) = \frac{1}{\sqrt{2\pi \cdot V}} \cdot \exp\left(-\frac{(x-E)^2}{2V} \right).$$

This assumption is often empirically valid. The explanation for a frequent occurrence of normal distribution comes from the Central Limit Theorem, according to which if the random variable consists of several small independent components, then its distribution is close to normal- and it is often the case that the desired value x_i is influenced by a large number of different independent factors [211].

It is usually assumed that different sample values are independent. In this case, for each pair of values E and V, the probability L that the observed sample $x_1, \ldots, x_n$ occurs for these particular values of E and V can be found as simply the product of the corresponding probabilities:

$$L = \prod_{i=1}^{n} \rho(x_i) = \prod_{i=1}^{n} \frac{1}{\sqrt{2\pi \cdot V}} \cdot \exp\left(-\frac{(x_i - E)^2}{2V} \right).$$

It is reasonable to select the *most probable* values E and V, i.e., the values for which the above probability is the largest. This idea is known as the *Maximum Likelihood (ML) approach*.

We can find the corresponding maximum if we differentiate the expression L with respect to E and V and equate derivatives to 0. As a result, we get the following estimates:

$$E = \frac{1}{n} \cdot \sum_{i=1}^{n} x_i; \quad V = \frac{1}{n} \cdot \sum_{i=1}^{n} (x_i - E)^2.$$

These are the estimates that are most frequently used to estimate the mean and variance.

Sometimes, statisticians use instead an un-biased estimate for the variance, i.e., an estimate for which the expected value is exactly the desired variance. This un-biased estimate $\frac{1}{n-1} \sum_{i=1}^{n} (x_i - E)^2$ differs from the ML estimate by a constant factor in front of the sum. Thus, from the computational viewpoint, we can easily reduce the computation of the un-biased estimate to the computation of the ML estimate. Namely, to compute the un-biased estimate, we can simply compute the ML estimate and multiply the result by $\frac{n}{n-1}$. Because of this reduction, in the following text, we will mainly talk about computing the ML estimate.

4.2.2 *In general case when the distributions are not necessarily Gaussian*

While these estimates are justified as optimal only for the normal distributions, they are used for other distributions as well. Their application to arbitrary distributions is justified by the fact that the mean can be equivalently defined as the limit of the arithmetic averages when the sample size n grows to infinity — similarly to how the probability can be defined as limit of the frequency when the sample size increases $n \to \infty$.

The variance is, by definition, the expected value of the square of the difference $(x - E)^2$: $V = E[(x - E)^2]$. It can be equivalently described as the difference $E[x^2] - (E[x])^2$. Similarly, the above formula can be described as $M - E^2$, where $M \overset{\text{def}}{=} \dfrac{1}{n} \cdot \displaystyle\sum_{i=1}^{n} x_i^2$. The arithmetic average of x_i^2 tends to $E[x^2]$, the arithmetic average E tends to $E[x]$, so our estimate $M - E^2$ tends to the difference $E[x^2] - (E[x])^2$, i.e., to the actual variance.

The limits mean, in effect, that the estimates based on large n can serve as *good* estimates for the actual mean and variance; the larger the sample size n, the better these estimates.

The values $\tilde{x}_i$ resulting from the measurement are, in general, different from the actual (unknown) values x_i of the corresponding quantities, and the corresponding measurement errors $\Delta x_i \overset{\text{def}}{=} \tilde{x}_i - x_i$ are non-zero.

Sometimes, we know the probabilities of different values of measurement errors. However, in many cases, we only know the upper bound Δ_i on the (absolute value of the) measurement error: $|\Delta x_i| \leq \Delta_i$. In this case, once we know the measured value $\tilde{x}_i$, we can conclude that the actual (unknown) value x_i belongs to the interval

$$\mathbf{x}_i = [\underline{x}_i, \overline{x}_i] \overset{\text{def}}{=} [\tilde{x}_i - \Delta_i, \tilde{x}_i + \Delta_i].$$

Different values x_i from these intervals lead, in general, to different estimates of $E(x_1, \ldots, x_n)$ and $V(x_1, \ldots, x_n)$. It is therefore desirable to find the ranges

$$\mathbf{E} = [\underline{E}, \overline{E}] = \{E(x_1, \ldots, x_n) \mid x_1 \in \mathbf{x}_1, \ldots, x_n \in \mathbf{x}_n\} \text{ and}$$

$$\mathbf{V} = [\underline{V}, \overline{V}] = \{V(x_1, \ldots, x_n) \mid x_1 \in \mathbf{x}_1, \ldots, x_n \in \mathbf{x}_n\}$$

of all possible values of E and V.

The general problem of estimating the range of a function under interval uncertainty is known as the *main problem of interval computations* [539].

The situation is the simplest with the mean $E(x_1,\ldots,x_n) = \frac{1}{n} \cdot \sum_{i=1}^{n} x_i$: since the mean is an increasing function of each of its variables $x_1,\ldots,x_n$, its smallest possible value $\underline{E}$ is attained when we take the smallest possible values $x_i = \underline{x}_i$ of all the inputs, and its largest possible value $\overline{E}$ is attained when we take the largest possible values $x_i = \overline{x}_i$ of all the inputs. Thus, the desired range has the form $[\underline{E}, \overline{E}] = \left[\frac{1}{n} \cdot \sum_{i=1}^{n} \underline{x}_i, \frac{1}{n} \cdot \sum_{i=1}^{n} \overline{x}_i \right]$.

In contrast, the variance $V(x_1,\ldots,x_n)$ is not always monotonic, so for the variance, estimating the range is a more complex task. It is known that in general, the problem of computing this range is NP-hard [650, 651]. Specifically, the lower endpoint $\underline{V}$ can be computed in feasible time [650, 651], but computing $\overline{V}$ is NP-hard. For some practically useful situations, there exist efficient algorithms for computing $\overline{V}$ [652, 742, 743].

Usually, in statistics, we consider the case when the parameters like E and V do not change with time. In practice, processes are dynamic.

As a result, reasonable estimates for E and V should assign more weight to more recent measurements and less weight to the past ones. Specifically, if we sort the values x_i from the most recent one x_1 to the least recent one x_n, then, for each function $y(x)$, to estimate the mean value of y, instead of the arithmetic mean, we take the weighted mean

$$E[y] \approx \sum_{i=1}^{n} w_i \cdot y(x_i),$$

where $w_1 \geq w_2 \geq \cdots \geq w_n > 0$, and $\sum_{i=1}^{n} w_i = 1$. In particular, for the mean E, we have the estimate

$$E = \sum_{i=1}^{n} w_i \cdot x_i.$$

Similarly, as an estimate for the actual variance $E[x^2] - (E[x])^2$, we take

$$V = \sum_{i=1}^{n} w_i \cdot x_i^2 - \left(\sum_{i=1}^{n} w_i \cdot x_i \right)^2.$$

One can show that this expression is equivalent to

$$V = \sum_{i=1}^{n} w_i \cdot (x_i - E)^2.$$

If $w_i = 0$, this simply means that we do not take into account the corresponding value x_i. Thus, if we restrict ourselves only to the inputs on which the characteristics actually depend, we conclude that $w_i > 0$.

In this session, we extend known algorithms for computing the ranges **E** and **V** to such dynamic estimates.

Let us first consider the simplest case: estimates for the mean. Since all the weights are non-negative, the function $E = \sum_{i=1}^{n} w_i \cdot x_i$ is an increasing function of all its variables. Thus:

• the smallest possible value $\underline{E}$ is attained when we take the smallest possible values $x_i = \underline{x}_i$ of all the inputs, and

• the largest possible value $\overline{E}$ is attained when we take the largest possible values $x_i = \overline{x}_i$ of all the inputs.

Thus, the desired range of E has the form

$$[\underline{E}, \overline{E}] = \left[\sum_{i=1}^{n} w_i \cdot \underline{x}_i, \sum_{i=1}^{n} w_i \cdot \overline{x}_i \right].$$

A function $f(x)$ defined on an interval $[\underline{x}, \overline{x}]$ attains its minimum on this interval either at one of its endpoints, or in some internal point of the interval. If it attains is minimum at a point $x \in (a,b)$, then its derivative at this point is 0: $\frac{df}{dx} = 0$.

If it attains its minimum at the point $x = \underline{x}$, then we cannot have $\frac{df}{dx} < 0$, because then, for some point $x + \Delta x \in [\underline{x}, \overline{x}]$, we would have a smaller value of $f(x)$. Thus, in this case, we must have $\frac{df}{dx} \geq 0$.

Similarly, if a function $f(x)$ attains its minimum at the point $x = \overline{x}$, then we must have $\frac{df}{dx} \leq 0$.

For the maximum, a similar thing happens. If $f(x)$ attains is maximum at a point $x \in (a,b)$, then its derivative at this point is 0: $\frac{df}{dx} = 0$.

If it attains its maximum at the point $x = \underline{x}$, then we must have $\frac{df}{dx} \leq 0$.

Finally, if a function $f(x)$ attains its maximum at the point $x = \overline{x}$, then we must have $\frac{df}{dx} \geq 0$.

We are interested in range of the expression $V = \sum_{i=1}^{n} w_i \cdot x_i^2 - E^2$, where $E \overset{\text{def}}{=} \sum_{i=1}^{n} w_i \cdot x_i$. For this estimate, $\frac{\partial E}{\partial x_i} = w_i$, hence

$$\frac{\partial V}{\partial x_i} = 2w_i \cdot x_i - 2E \cdot \frac{\partial E}{\partial x_i} = 2w_i \cdot (x_i - E).$$

To find this range, we must find the point where this expression attains its minimum, and the point where it attains its maximum.

By considering the variance V as a function of x_i, for the point $(x_1, \ldots, x_n)$ at which V attains its minimum, we can make the following conclusions:

- if $x_i = \underline{x}_i$, then $x_i \geq E$;
- if $x_i = \overline{x}_i$, then $x_i \leq E$;
- if $\underline{x}_i < x_i < \overline{x}_i$, then $x_i = E$.

So, if $\overline{x}_i < E$, this means that for the value $x_i \leq \overline{x}_i$ also satisfies the inequality $x_i < E$. Thus, in this case:

- we cannot have $x_i = \underline{x}_i$ — because then we would have $x_i \geq E$; and
- we cannot have $\underline{x}_i < x_i < \overline{x}_i$ — because then, we would have $x_i = E$.

So, if $\overline{x}_i < E$, the only remaining option for x_i is $x_i = \overline{x}_i$.

Similarly, if $E < \underline{x}_i$, this means that the value $x_i \geq \underline{x}_i$ also satisfies the inequality $x_i > E$.

Thus, in this case:

- we cannot have $x_i = \overline{x}_i$ — because then we would have $x_i \leq E$; and
- we cannot have $\underline{x}_i < x_i < \overline{x}_i$ — because then, we would have $x_i = E$.

So, if $E < \underline{x}_i$, the only remaining option for x_i is $x_i = \underline{x}_i$.

What if $\underline{x}_i < E < \overline{x}_i$? In this case:

- the minimum cannot be attained for $x_i = \underline{x}_i$, because then we should have $x_i \geq E$, while we have $x_i < E$;
- the minimum cannot be attained for $x_i = \overline{x}_i$, because then we should have $x_i \leq E$, while we have $x_i > E$.

Thus, the minimum has to be attained when $x_i \in (\underline{x}_i, \overline{x}_i)$. In this case, we have $x_i = E$. So:

If $\overline{x}_i \leq E$, i.e., if the interval $\mathbf{x}_i$ is fully to the left of the mean E, the minimum is attained for $x_i = \overline{x}_i$.

If $E \leq \underline{x}_i$, i.e., if the interval $\mathbf{x}_i$ is fully to the right of the mean E, the minimum is attained for $x_i = \underline{x}_i$.

If $\underline{x}_i < E < \overline{x}_i$, i.e., if the interval $\mathbf{x}_i$ contain the mean E, the minimum is attained for $x_i = E$.

In all three cases, once we know where E is attained in relation to the endpoints $\underline{x}_i$ and $\overline{x}_i$, we can find out, for each i, where the minimum is attained — actually at the point which is the closest to E.

This conclusion is in good accordance with common sense: the variance is the smallest when all the values are the closest to the mean.

The value E must be found from the condition that it is the weighted mean of all corresponding minimal values, i.e., that

$$\sum_{i:\overline{x}_i \leq E} w_i \cdot \overline{x}_i + \sum_{j:E \leq \underline{x}_j} w_j \cdot \underline{x}_j + \sum_{k:\underline{x}_i < E < \overline{x}_i} w_k \cdot E = E.$$

By moving all the terms proportional to E to the right-hand side and dividing by the coefficient at E, we conclude that

$$E = \frac{\displaystyle\sum_{i:\overline{x}_i \leq E} w_i \cdot \overline{x}_i + \sum_{j:E \leq \underline{x}_j} w_j \cdot \underline{x}_j}{\displaystyle\sum_{i:\overline{x}_i \leq E} w_i + \sum_{j:E \leq \underline{x}_j} w_j}.$$

This conclusion will be used to design an efficient algorithm for computing V.

The function $V(x_1, \ldots, x_n)$ is convex. Thus, its maximum is always attained at one of the endpoints of each intervals $[\underline{x}_i, \overline{x}_i]$.

From our calculus-based analysis, we can now come up with the following conclusions:

- if the maximum is attained for $x_i = \underline{x}_i$, then we should have $x_i \leq E$, i.e., $\underline{x}_i \leq E$;

- if the maximum is attained for $x_i = \overline{x}_i$, then we should have $x_i \geq E$, i.e., $E \leq \overline{x}_i$.

Thus, if $\overline{x}_i < E$, we cannot have $x_i = \overline{x}_i$, so the maximum is attained for $x_i = \underline{x}_i$.

Similarly, if $E < \underline{x}_i$, then we cannot have $x_i = \underline{x}_i$, so the maximum is attained for $x_i = \overline{x}_i$.

If $\underline{x}_i \leq E \leq \overline{x}_i$, then we can have both options $x_i = \underline{x}_i$ and $x_i = \overline{x}_i$.

So:

• If $\overline{x}_i \leq E$, i.e., if the interval $\mathbf{x}_i$ is fully to the left of the mean E, the maximum is attained for $x_i = \underline{x}_i$.

• If $E \leq \underline{x}_i$, i.e., if the interval $\mathbf{x}_i$ is fully to the right of the mean E, the maximum is attained for $x_i = \overline{x}_i$.

• If $\underline{x}_i < E < \overline{x}_i$, i.e., if the interval $\mathbf{x}_i$ contain the mean E, the maximum can be attained at both values $\underline{x}$ and $\overline{x}$.

In all three cases, once we know where the maximum is attained in relation to the endpoints $\underline{x}$ and $\overline{x}_i$, we can find out, for each i, where the minimum is attained — actually at the point which is the farthest away from E.

This conclusion is also in good accordance with common sense: the variance is the largest when all the values are the farthest way from the mean.

Now, we are ready to describe the corresponding algorithms.

First, we sort all $2n$ endpoints $\underline{x}_i$ and $\overline{x}_i$ of the given intervals into a non-decreasing sequence $r_1 \leq r_2 \leq \ldots \leq r_{2n-1} \leq r_{2n}$.

To cover the whole straight line, we add the points $r_0 = -\infty$ and $r_{2n+1} = +\infty$. As a result, the whole real line is divided into $2n+1$ zones $[r_k, r_{k+1}]$, with $k = 0, 1, \ldots, 2n$.

For each zone, we find the values x_i which minimize V under the condition that their weighted average E is contained in this zone. Namely, we compute $E_k = \dfrac{N_k}{D_k}$, where

$$N_k \stackrel{\text{def}}{=} \sum_{i:\overline{x}_i \leq r_k} w_i \cdot \overline{x}_i + \sum_{j:r_{k+1} \leq \underline{x}_j} w_j \cdot \underline{x}_j; \quad D_k = \sum_{i:\overline{x}_i \leq r_k} w_i + \sum_{j:r_{k+1} \leq \underline{x}_j} w_j.$$

If E_k is not within the zone $[r_k, r_{k+1}]$, we dismiss it and move to the next zone. If it is within the zone, we compute the corresponding value of the variance

$$V_k = \sum_{i:\overline{x}_i \leq r_k} w_i \cdot (\overline{x}_i - E_k)^2 + \sum_{j:r_{k+1} \leq \underline{x}_j} w_j \cdot (\underline{x}_j - E_k)^2.$$

This expression can be equivalently reformulated a $V_k = M_k - W_k \cdot E_k^2$, where we denoted

$$M_k = \sum_{i:\overline{x}_i \leq r_k} w_i \cdot (\overline{x}_i)^2 + \sum_{j:r_{k+1} \leq \underline{x}_j} w_j \cdot (\underline{x}_j)^2; \quad W_k = \sum_{i:\overline{x}_i \leq r_k} w_i + \sum_{j:r_{k+1} \leq \underline{x}_j} w_j.$$

Once the computations are performed for all $2n+1$ zones, we find the smallest of the corresponding values V_k as the desired smallest value $\underline{V}$.

4.2.3 *Complexity of the estimation calculation*

Sorting takes time $O(n \log \log(n))$ [707].

Computing the sums D_0, N_0, M_0, and W_0 corresponding to the first zone take linear time $O(n)$.

Each new sum is obtained from the previous one by changing a few terms which go from $\underline{x}$ to $\overline{x}$; each value x_i changes only once, so we only need totally linear time to compute all these sums — and we also need linear time to perform all the auxiliary computations. Thus, the total computation time is $O(n \cdot \log(n)) + O(n) + O(n) = O(n \cdot \log(n))$.

This computation time can be reduced to $O(n)$ if we use the ideas from [294], where instead of sorting, we used the known linear time algorithm for computing the median.

Now we consider the efficient Algorithm for Computing $\overline{V}$ under a Reasonable Condition.

We assume that for some integer C, each set of more than C intervals has an empty intersection. For example, for $C = 1$, no two intervals have a common point. For $C = 2$, two intervals may have a common point, but no three intervals share a common point, etc.

As with computing $\underline{V}$, we start by sorting all $2n$ endpoints $\underline{x_i}$ and $\bar{x_i}$ of the given intervals into a non-decreasing sequence $r_1 \leq r_2 \leq \ldots \leq r_{2n-1} \leq r_{2n}$.

To cover the whole straight line, we then add the points $r_0 = -\infty$ and $r_{2n+1} = +\infty$. As a result, the whole real line is divided into $2n+1$ zones $[r_k, r_{k+1}]$, with $k = 0, 1, \ldots, 2n$.

For each zone, we find the values x_i which maximize V under the condition that their weighted average E is contained in this zone:

- for those i for which $\bar{x_i} \leq r_k$, we take $x_i = \underline{x_i}$;
- for those i for which $r_{k+1} \leq \underline{x_i}$, we take $x_i = \bar{x_i}$;
- for all other indices i, for which $[r_k, r_{k+1}] \subseteq \mathbf{x}_i$, we consider both possibilities $x_i = \underline{x_i}$ and $x_i = \bar{x_i}$.

Because of our condition, for each zone, there are no more than C indices i in the third category. Thus, for each zone, we have to consider $\leq 2^C$ possible combinations of values $\underline{x_i}$ and $\bar{x_i}$.

For each of these combinations, we compute the weighted average E and, if this weighter average is within the zone $[r_k, r_{k+1}]$, we compute the weighted variance V e.g., $V = M - E^2$, where $M = \sum_{i=1}^{n} w_i \cdot x_i^2$ is the weighted average of the squared values x_i^2.

The largest of all such computed values V is then returned as $\bar{V}$.

Sorting takes time $O(n \cdot \log(n))$. Computing the original values of E and M requires linear time. Similarly to the case of computing $\underline{V}$, each new sum is obtained from the previous one by changing a few terms which go from $\underline{x_i}$ to $\bar{x_i}$; each value x_i changes only once, so we only need totally linear time to compute all these sums and we also need linear time to perform all the auxiliary computations. Thus, the total computation time is also $O(n \cdot \log(n)) + O(n) + O(n) = O(n \cdot \log(n))$.

A similar modification of an algorithm presented in [382] can lead to a polynomial-time algorithm for computing the range of the weighted covariance

$$C = \sum_{i=1}^{n} w_i \cdot (x_i - E_x) \cdot (y_i - E_y) = \sum_{i=1}^{n} w_i \cdot x_i \cdot y_i,$$

where

$$E_x \overset{\text{def}}{=} \sum_{i=1}^{n} w_i \cdot x_i \text{ and } E_y \overset{\text{def}}{=} \sum_{i=1}^{n} w_i \cdot y_i,$$

under the condition that all x-intervals $\mathbf{x}_i$ are of the form $[t_0^{(x)}, t_1^{(x)}]$, $[t_1^{(x)}, t_2^{(x)}], \ldots, [t_{N_x-1}^{(x)}, t_{N_x}^{(x)}]$ for some x-threshold values $t_0^{(x)} < t_1^{(x)} < \ldots < t_{N_x}^{(x)}$, and all y-intervals $\mathbf{y}_i$ are of the form $[t_0^{(y)}, t_1^{(y)}], [t_1^{(y)}, t_2^{(y)}], \ldots$, $[t_{N_y-1}^{(y)}, t_{N_y}^{(y)}]$ for some y-threshold values $t_0^{(y)} < t_1^{(y)} < \ldots < t_{N_y}^{(y)}$.

This situation occurs in statistical data processing, when we use, as input, answers to threshold-related questions: e.g., whether the age is from 0 to 20, from 20 to 30, etc.

Chapter 5

Fuzzy Type-1 and Fuzzy Type-2 Computations

5.1 Type-1 fuzzy sets and numbers

Let X be a classical set of objects, called the universe, whose generic elements are denoted x. Membership in a classical subset A of X is often viewed as a characteristic function μ_A from $[0,1]$ to $\{0,1\}$ such that

$$\mu_A(x) = \begin{cases} 1 \ \textit{iff} \ x \in A \\ 0 \ \textit{iff} \ x \notin A \end{cases}$$

where $\{0,1\}$ is called a valuation set; 1 indicates membership while 0 - non-membership. If the valuation set is allowed to be in the real interval $[0,1]$, then A is called a Type-1 fuzzy set A [15, 27, 34, 59, 437, 438, 822, 828, 881]. $\mu_A(x)$ is the grade of membership of x in A

$$\mu_A : X \to [0,1].$$

As closer the value of $\mu_A(x)$ is to 1, so much x belongs to A. $\mu : X \to [0,1]$ is reffered to as a membership function (MF).

A is completely characterized by the set of pairs:

$$A = \{(x, \mu_A(x)), \ x \in X\}$$

Fuzzy sets with crisply defined membership functions are called ordinary fuzzy sets or Type-1 fuzzy sets.

Equality of fuzzy sets. Two fuzzy sets A and B are said to be equal denoted $A = B$ if and only if

$$\forall x \in X, \quad \mu_A(x) = \mu_B(x).$$

The support of a fuzzy set A is the ordinary subset of X that has nonzero membership in A:

$$\text{supp}(A) = A^{+0} = \{x \in X, \mu_A(x) > 0\}.$$

The elements of x such as $\mu_A(x) = 1/2$ are the crossover points of A.

A fuzzy set that has only one point in X with $\mu_A = 1$ as its support is called a singleton.

The height of a fuzzy set. Normal and subnormal sets. The height of A is

$$hgt(A) = \sup_{x \in X} \mu_A(X)$$

i.e., the least upper bound of $\mu_A(x)$.

A is said to be normalized iff $\exists x \in X, \mu_A(x) = 1$. This implies $hgt(A) = 1$. Otherwise A is called subnormal fuzzy set.

The empty set $\varnothing$ is defined as

$$x \in X, \mu_\varnothing(x) = 0.$$

The universe of discourse X is defined as

$$\forall x \in X, \mu_X(x) = 1.$$

α-level fuzzy sets. One of important ways of representation of fuzzy sets is α-cut method. Such type of representation allows us to use properties of crisp sets and operations on crisp sets in fuzzy set theory.

The (crisp) set of elements that belongs to the fuzzy set A at least to the degree α is called the α-level set:

$$A^\alpha = \left\{ x \in X, \mu_A(x) \geq \alpha \right\}$$

$A^\alpha = \left\{ x \in X, \mu_A(x) \geq \alpha \right\}$ is called "strong α-level set" or "strong α-cut".

The cardinality of a fuzzy set. When X is a finite set, the scalar cardinality $|A|$ of a fuzzy set A on X is defined as

$$|A| = \sum_{x \in A} \mu_A(x).$$

Sometimes $|A|$ is called the power of A. $\|A\| = |A|/|X|$ is the relative cardinality. When X is infinite, $|A|$ is defined as

$$|A| = \int_X \mu_A(x)\, dx.$$

In modeling of systems the internal structure of a system must be described first. An internal structure is characterized by connections (associations) among the elements of system. As a rule these connections or associations are represented by means of relation. We will consider here fuzzy relations which gives us the representation about degree or strength of this connection.

There are several definitions of fuzzy relation [419, 858]. Each of them depends on various factors and expresses different aspects of modeling systems.

Fuzzy relation. Let $X_1, X_2, ..., X_n$ be nonempty crisp sets. Then, a $R(X_1, X_2, ..., X_n)$ is called a fuzzy relation of sets $X_1, X_2, ..., X_n$, if $R(X_1, X_2, ..., X_n)$ is the fuzzy subset given on Cartesian product $X_1 \times X_2 \times ... \times X_n$.

If $n = 2$, then fuzzy relation is called binary fuzzy relation, and is denoted as $R(X_1, X_2)$. For three, four, or n sets the fuzzy relation is called ternary, quaternary, or n-ary, respectively.

To relate the fuzzy subsets A and B of disparate universes of discourse X and Y, the concept of a fuzzy conditional statement (linguistic implication) is introduced, that is

$$A => B \text{ or } \text{“if } A \text{ then } B\text{”}.$$

Then implied relation R is expressed in terms of the Cartesian product of the subsets A and B denoted by $R = A \times B$ and its membership function is defined by

$$\mu_R(x,y) = \mu_{AxB}(x,y) = \min\left[\mu_A(x), \mu_B(y)\right], \quad x \in X, \quad y \in Y.$$

Linguistic variable [825, 851]. A linguistic variable is characterized by the set (u, T, X, G, M), where u is the name of variable; T denotes the term-set of u that refer to as base variable whose values range over a universe X; G is a syntactic rule (usually in form of a grammar) generating linguistic terms; M is a semantic rule that assigns to each linguistic term its meaning, which is a fuzzy set on X.

Linguistic IF-THEN rules. Fuzzy sets and lingusitic variables are widely used for modeling nonlinear uncertain objects and for approximating functions [34, 59, 249, 592]. The idea of fuzzy modeling consists in substituting the precise mathematical relation between object parameters by some qualitative relations expressed via linguistic IF-THEN rules.

The structure of linguistic IF-THEN rules for objects or systems with multiple inputs (n) and outputs (m) (MIMO models) is expressed as follows:

$$IF \ x_1 \ is \ A_{11} \ AND \ x_2 \ is \ A_{12} \ AND \ \dots \ x_n \ is \ A_{1n} \quad THEN$$
$$IF \ y_1 \ is \ B_{11} \ AND \ y_2 \ is \ B_{12} \ AND \ \dots \ y_m \ is \ B_{1m}$$

$$ALSO$$

$$IF \ x_1 \ is \ A_{21} \ AND \ x_2 \ is \ A_{22} \ AND \ \dots \ x_n \ is \ A_{2n} \quad THEN$$
$$IF \ y_1 \ is \ B_{21} \ AND \ y_2 \ is \ B_{22} \ AND \ \dots \ y_m \ is \ B_{2m}$$

$$ALSO$$

$$IF \ x_1 \ is \ A_{r1} \ AND \ x_2 \ is \ A_{r2} \ AND... \ x_n \ is \ A_{r\,n} \qquad THEN$$

$$IF \ y_1 \ is \ B_{r1} \ AND \ y_2 \ is \ B_{r2} \ AND... \ y_m \ is \ B_{r\,m}.$$

Here $x_i(i=\overline{1,n})$, $y_j(j=\overline{1,m})$ are input and output linguistic variables of the fuzzy system, A_{ij}, B_{ij} are fuzzy sets. Each rule can be represented by IF-THEN fuzzy relation (linguistic implication). The calculus of IF-THEN rules is based on composition of fuzzy relations. It is explained in more details in Section 5.8.

Type-1 Continuous fuzzy number. A fuzzy number is a fuzzy set A on $\mathcal{R}$ which possesses the following properties: a) A is a normal fuzzy set; b) A is a convex fuzzy set; c) α-cut of A, A^α is a closed interval for every $\alpha \in (0,1]$; d) the support of A, supp(A) is bounded.

There is an equivalent parametric definition of fuzzy number [95, 324]. A fuzzy number A is a pair $(\underline{\mu_A}, \overline{\mu_A})$ of functions $\underline{\mu}_A(\alpha), \overline{\mu}_A(\alpha)$; $0 \le \alpha \le 1$ with following requirements:

1) $\underline{\mu}_A(\alpha)$ is a bounded monotonic increasing left continuous function;

2) $\overline{\mu}_A(\alpha)$ is a bounded monotonic decreasing left continuous function;

3) $\underline{\mu}_A(\alpha) \le \overline{\mu}_A(\alpha), 0 \le \alpha \le 1$.

Discrete Type-1 fuzzy number [16, 44, 152, 153]. A fuzzy subset A of the real line $\mathcal{R}$ with membership function $\mu_A : \mathcal{R} \to [0,1]$ is a discrete fuzzy number if its support is finite, i.e. there exist $x_1,...,x_n \in \mathcal{R}$ with $x_1 < x_2 < ... < x_n$, such that $supp(A) = \{x_1,...,x_n\}$ and there exist natural numbers s,t with $1 \le s \le t \le n$ satisfying the following conditions:

1) $\mu_A(x_i) = 1$ for any natural number i with $s \le i \le t$;

2) $\mu_A(x_i) \le \mu_A(x_j)$ for each natural numbers i,j with $1 \le i \le j \le s$;

3) $\mu_A(x_i) \geq \mu_A(x_j)$ for each natural numbers i,j with $t \leq i \leq j \leq n$.

5.2 Type-2 fuzzy sets and numbers

Fuzzy Type-2 sets possess more expressive power to create models adequately describing uncertainty. The three-dimensional membership functions of Type-2 fuzzy sets provide additional degrees of freedom that make it possible to directly and more effectively model uncertainties.

Type-2 fuzzy set [159, 416, 417, 517, 519-522, 657, 865]. Type-2 fuzzy set (T2 FS) in the universe of discourse X can be represented as follows:

$$\tilde{A} = \{((x,u), \mu_{\tilde{A}}(x,u)) | \forall x \in X, \forall u \in J_x \subseteq [0,1]\} \tag{5.1}$$

where $0 \leq \mu_{\tilde{A}}(x,u) \leq 1$. The Type-2 fuzzy set $\tilde{A}$ also can be represented as follows:

$$\tilde{A} = \int_{x \in X} \int_{u \in J_x} \mu_{\tilde{A}}(x,u) / (x,u) \tag{5.2}$$
$$= \int_{x \in X} [\int_{u \in J_x} \mu_{\tilde{A}}(x,u) / u] / x$$

where x is the primary variable, $J_x \subseteq [0,1]$ is the primary membership of x, u is the secondary variable. $f(x) = \int_{u \in J_x} \mu_{\tilde{A}}(x,u) / u$ is the secondary membership function at x. $\iint$ denotes the union over all admissible x and u.

If X is a discrete set with elements $x_1, ..., x_n$ then Type-2 fuzzy set $\tilde{A}$ can be as follows:

$$\tilde{A} = \sum_{x \in X}\left[\sum_{u \in J_x} f_x(u)/u\right]\bigg/x = \sum_{i=1}\sum_{u \in J_x}[f_x(u)/u]\bigg/x_i. \qquad (5.3)$$

Interval Type-2 fuzzy set. As special case of a general T2 FS, Interval Type-2 fuzzy sets uses a subinterval of [0,1] as its membership value. Interval Type-2 fuzzy sets (IT2 FSs) in comparison with general T2 FSs are more effective from computational point of view. This fact made IT2 FSs a widely used framework for design of fuzzy systems.

When all $\mu_{\tilde{A}}(x,u) = 1$ in (5.2) then $\tilde{A}$ is an interval Type-2 fuzzy set (IT2 FS).

Consequently IT2 FS can be expressed as

$$\tilde{A} = \int_{x \in X}\int_{u \in J_X} 1/(x,u), \; J_x \subseteq [0,1]. \qquad (5.4)$$

First we consider some properties of Type-2 fuzzy sets. To indicate second order uncertainty one can use the concept of the footprint of uncertainty.

The footprint of uncertainty (FOU) of a Type-2 fuzzy set $\tilde{A}$ is a region with boundaries covering all the primary membership points of elements x, and is defined as follows [158, 159, 161, 510, 512-514, 517-521]:

$$FOU(\tilde{A}) = \bigcup_{x \in X} J_x. \qquad (5.5)$$

Embedded fuzzy sets. The embedded Type-2 fuzzy set of Type-2 fuzzy set $\tilde{A}$ is defined as follows [521]:

$$\tilde{A}_0 = \int_{x \in X} [f_x(\theta)/\theta]/x, \qquad (5.6)$$

where θ is the element, which can be chosen from each interval J_x. For discrete case, $\tilde{A}_0$ is defined as follows:

$$\tilde{A}_0 = \sum_{i=1}^{R} [f_{x_i}(\theta_i) / \theta_i] / x_i.$$

Let us consider theoretic operations on Type-2 fuzzy sets. Two Type-2 fuzzy sets $\tilde{A}$ and $\tilde{B}$ in a universe X with membership functions $\mu_{\tilde{A}}(x)$ and $\mu_{\tilde{B}}(x)$ are given: $\mu_{\tilde{A}}(x) = \int_u f_x(u)/u$ and $\mu_{\tilde{B}}(x) = \int_w g_x(w)/w$, where $u, w \subseteq J_x$ indicate the primary memberships of x and $f_x(u), g_x(w) \in [0,1]$ indicate the secondary memberships (grades) of x. Using Zadeh's Extension Principle, the membership grades for union, intersection and complement of Type-2 fuzzy sets $\tilde{A}$ and $\tilde{B}$ can be defined as follows [416]:

Union:

$$\tilde{A} \cup \tilde{B} \Leftrightarrow \mu_{\tilde{A} \cup \tilde{B}}(x) = \mu_{\tilde{A}}(x) \quad \mu_{\tilde{B}}(x)$$
$$= \int_u \int_w (f_x(u) * g_x(w)) / (u \vee w), \tag{5.7}$$

Intersection:

$$\tilde{A} \cap \tilde{B} \Leftrightarrow \mu_{\tilde{A} \cap \tilde{B}}(x) = \mu_{\tilde{A}}(x) \sqcap \mu_{\tilde{B}}(x) = \int_u \int_w (f_x(u) * g_x(w)) / (u * w), \tag{5.8}$$

Complement:

$$\tilde{A} \Leftrightarrow \mu_{\tilde{A}}(x) = \neg \mu_{\tilde{A}}(x) = \int_u f_x(u) / (1 - u). \tag{5.9}$$

Here $\sqcap$ and $\sqcup$ are intersection/meet and union/join operations on two membership function Type-2 fuzzy sets, * indicates the chosen T-norm.

T-norm and T-conorm

A T-norm can be extended to be a conjunction in Type-2 logic and an intersection in Type-2 fuzzy set theory, such as a Minimum T-norm and a Product T-norm [597].

A T-conorm of operation can be used to stand for a disjunction in Type-2 fuzzy logic and a union in Type-2 fuzzy set theory, such as maximum T-conorm.

Type reduction

To defuzzify Type-2 fuzzy sets one can use type reduction procedure. By this procedure, we can transform a Type-2 fuzzy set into a Type-1 fuzzy set. The centroid of a Type-2 set, whose domain is discretized into points, can be defined as follows [417]:

$$
C_{\tilde{A}} = \int_{\theta_1} \cdots \int_{\theta_N} \left[\mu_{D_1}(\theta_1) * \cdots * \mu_{D_N}(\theta_N) \right] \Bigg/ \frac{\sum_{i=1}^{N} x_i \theta_i}{\sum_{i=1}^{N} \theta_i}.
$$

where $D_i = \mu_{\tilde{A}}(x_i), \theta_i \in D_i$.

Type-2 fuzzy number. Let $\tilde{A}$ be a Type-2 fuzzy set defined in the universe of discourse R. If $\tilde{A}$ is normal, $\tilde{A}$ is a convex set, and the support of $\tilde{A}$ is closed and bounded, then $\tilde{A}$ is a Type-2 fuzzy number.

5.3 Arithmetic with continuous type-1 fuzzy numbers

5.3.1 *Method based on the extension principle*

Extension Principle extends crisp domains of functions to fuzzy domains, and generalizes a mapping of a function $f(\cdot)$ to a mapping between fuzzy sets.

Assume that f is a function from X to Y. A is a fuzzy set on X

$$
A = \mu_A(x_1)/(x_1) + \mu_A(x_2)/(x_2) + \cdots + \mu_A(x_n)/(x_n).
$$

In accordance with the extension principle the image of A under the mapping $f(\cdot)$ is defined as

$$B = f(A) = \mu_A(y_1)/(y_1) + \mu_A(y_2)/(y_2) + \cdots + \mu_A(y_n)/(y_n).$$

Here $y_i = f(x_i), i = 1,...,n$. If $f(\cdot)$ is a many-to-one mapping then

$$\mu_B(y) = \max_{x=f^{-1}(y)} \mu_A(x).$$

Assume that function $y = f(x) = 0.6x + 4$ is given

If $x = around5 = \left\{ \dfrac{0.3}{3} + \dfrac{1.0}{5} + \dfrac{0.3}{7} \right\}$, then

$$f(around\,5) = \left\{ \dfrac{0.3}{f(3)} + \dfrac{1.0}{f(5)} + \dfrac{0.3}{f(7)} \right\}$$

$$= \left\{ \dfrac{0.3}{0.6 \cdot 3 + 4} + \dfrac{1.0}{0.6 \cdot 5 + 4} + \dfrac{0.3}{0.6 \cdot 7 + 4} \right\} == \left\{ \dfrac{0.3}{5.8} + \dfrac{1}{7} + \dfrac{0.3}{8.2} \right\}.$$

Let us consider arithmetic operations on fuzzy numbers using Extension Principle.

Addition.

$$\mu_{A+B}(z) = \bigvee_{z=x+y} (\mu_A(x) \wedge \mu_B(y))$$

Subtraction.

$$\mu_{A-B}(z) = \bigvee_{z=x-y} (\mu_A(x) \wedge \mu_B(y))$$

Multiplication.

$$\mu_{A\cdot B}(z) = \bigvee_{z=x\cdot y} (\mu_A(x) \wedge \mu_B(y))$$

Division.

$$\mu_{A/B}(z) = \bigvee_{z=x/y} (\mu_A(x) \wedge \mu_B(y))$$

5.3.2 *Method based on interval arithmetic and α-cuts*

This method is based on representation of arbitrary fuzzy numbers by their α-cuts and use interval arithmetic to the α-cuts. Let $A, B \subset \mathcal{R}$ be fuzzy numbers and $*$ denote any of four operations. For each $\alpha \in (0,1]$, the α-cut of $A * B$ is expressed as

$$(A * B)^\alpha = A^\alpha * B^\alpha. \tag{5.10}$$

For division we assume $0 \notin \text{supp}(B)$.

The resulting fuzzy number $A * B$ can be defined as

$$A * B = \bigcup_{\alpha \in [0,1]} \alpha (A * B)^\alpha. \tag{5.11}$$

Next using (5.10), (5.11) we illustrate four arithmetic operations on fuzzy numbers.

Addition. Let A and B be two fuzzy numbers and A^α and B^α be their α cuts

$$A^\alpha = [a_1^\alpha, a_2^\alpha]; B^\alpha = [b_1^\alpha, b_2^\alpha] \tag{5.12}$$

Then we can write

$$A^\alpha + B^\alpha = [a_1^\alpha, a_2^\alpha] + [b_1^\alpha, b_2^\alpha] = [a_1^\alpha + b_1^\alpha, a_2^\alpha + b_2^\alpha], \forall \alpha \in [0,1] \tag{5.13}$$

here

$$A^\alpha = \{x / \mu_A(x) \geq \alpha\}; B^\alpha = \{x / \mu_B(x) \geq \alpha\} \tag{5.14}$$

Subtraction. Subtraction of given fuzzy numbers A and B can be defined as

$$(A - B)^\alpha = A^\alpha - B^\alpha = [a_1^\alpha - b_2^\alpha, a_2^\alpha - b_1^\alpha], \forall \alpha \in [0,1]. \tag{5.15}$$

We can determine (5.15) by addition of the image B to A

$$\forall \alpha \in [0,1], B^\alpha = [-b_2^\alpha, -b_1^\alpha]. \tag{5.16}$$

Multiplication. Let two fuzzy numbers A and B be given. Multiplication $A \cdot B$ is defined as

$$(A \cdot B)^\alpha = A^\alpha \cdot B^\alpha = [a_1^\alpha, a_2^\alpha] \cdot [b_1^\alpha, b_2^\alpha] \quad \forall \alpha \in [0,1]. \tag{5.17}$$

Multiplication of fuzzy number A in $\mathcal{R}$ by ordinary numbers $k \in \mathcal{R}_+$ is performed as follows

$$\forall A \subset \mathcal{R} \ kA^\alpha = [ka_1^\alpha, ka_2^\alpha], \forall \alpha \in [0,1]. \tag{5.18}$$

Division. Division of two fuzzy numbers A and B is defined by

$$A^\alpha : B^\alpha = [a_1^\alpha, a_2^\alpha] : [b_1^\alpha, b_2^\alpha] \quad \forall \alpha \in [0,1] \tag{5.19}$$

Absolute Value of a Fuzzy Number

Absolute value of fuzzy number is defined as:

$$abs(A) = \begin{cases} \max(\mu_A(x), \mu_{-A}(x)), & \text{for } \mathcal{R}_+ \\ 0, & \text{for } \mathcal{R}_- \end{cases} \tag{5.20}$$

Square of a Continuous Fuzzy Number

The square of fuzzy number A denoted by μ_{A^2}, is a continuous fuzzy number defined by [95]

$$\mu_{A^2}(y) = \max(\mu_A(\sqrt{y}), \mu_A(-\sqrt{y})). \tag{5.21}$$

Denote $\mathcal{R}_{\mathcal{F}}$ the set of fuzzy numbers defined on $\mathcal{R}$, and $\mathcal{R}_{U\mathcal{F}}$ the set of fuzzy numbers defined on $U = [0, \infty)$.

Square Root of a Continuous Fuzzy Number

The square root of a fuzzy number X is a function $F : \mathcal{R}_{\mathcal{F}} \to \mathcal{R}_{U\mathcal{F}}$ denoted by $F(X) = \sqrt{X}$ with α-cut $[\sqrt{X}]^{\alpha} = \left\{ \sqrt{x} \mid x \in X^{\alpha} \right\}$.

Since $f(x) = \sqrt{x}$ is a continuous function on $U = [0, \infty)$, we get $F(X) = \sqrt{X}$ is a continuous function on $\mathcal{R}_{U\mathcal{F}}$. Because f is increasing on U, we have

$$\left[\sqrt{X} \right]^{\alpha} = \left[\sqrt{X_1^{\alpha}}, \sqrt{X_2^{\alpha}} \right]. \tag{5.22}$$

The Exponential of a Fuzzy Number

The exponential of a fuzzy number $X \in \mathcal{R}_{\mathcal{F}}$ is a function $F : \mathcal{R}_{\mathcal{F}} \to \mathcal{R}_{U\mathcal{F}}$ denoted by $F(X) = e^X$ with α-cut $(e^X)^{\alpha} = \left\{ e^x \mid x \in X^{\alpha} \right\}$.

Since $f(x) = e^x$ is a continuous function on $\mathcal{R}$, we get $F(X) = e^X$ is a continuous function on $\mathcal{R}_{\mathcal{F}}$. Because f is increasing on R, we get $(e^X)^{\alpha} = [e^{X_1^{\alpha}}, e^{X_2^{\alpha}}]$.

The Logarithm of a Fuzzy Number

The natural logarithm of a fuzzy number $X \in \mathcal{R}_{\mathcal{F}}$ is a function F: $\mathcal{R}_{U\mathcal{F}} \to \mathcal{R}_{\mathcal{F}}$ denoted by $F(X) = \ln X$ with α-cut $(\ln X)^{\alpha} = \{\ln x \mid x \in X^{\alpha}\}$.

Since $f(x) = \ln x$ is a continuous function on $[\varepsilon, \infty)$, $\varepsilon > 0$, we get $F(X) = \ln X$ is a continuous function on $\mathcal{R}_{U\mathcal{F}}$. Because f is increasing on $[\varepsilon, \infty)$, $\varepsilon > 0$, we have $(\ln X)^{\alpha} = \left[\ln X_1^{\alpha}, \ln X_2^{\alpha} \right]$.

For positive fuzzy numbers $A, B \in \mathcal{R}_{U\mathcal{F}}$, we have

$\ln 1 = 0$; $\ln AB = \ln A + \ln B$; $\ln A / B = \ln A - \ln B$; $\ln A^{\alpha} = \alpha \ln A$ [15].

Let $A \in \mathcal{R}_{\mathcal{F}}$ and $B \in \mathcal{R}_{U\mathcal{F}}$, then we have $\ln(\exp A) = A$; $\exp(\ln B) = B$.

5.4 Arithmetic with discrete type-1 fuzzy numbers

In general, the extension of arithmetical or lattice operations, $\mathcal{O}$, to fuzzy numbers A, B [531] can be approached either by the direct use of their membership function $\mu_A(x)$, $\mu_B(x)$ as fuzzy subsets of $\mathcal{R}$ with Zadeh's extension principle:

$$\mu_{\mathcal{O}(A,B)}(z) = \sup\{\mu_A(x) \wedge \mu_B(y) \mid \mathcal{O}(x,y) = z\},$$

or by the equivalent use of the α-cuts representation [531, 676]:

$$\mathcal{O}(A,B)^{\alpha} = O(A^{\alpha}, B^{\alpha}) = \{O(x,y) \mid x \in A^{\alpha}, y \in B^{\alpha}\}$$

and

$$\mu_{\mathcal{O}(A,B)}(z) = \sup\{\alpha \in [0,1] \mid z \in \mathcal{O}(A,B)^{\alpha}\}.$$

Nevertheless, in the discrete case, this process can yield a fuzzy subset that does not satisfy the conditions to be a discrete fuzzy number [153, 761].

In order to overcome this drawback, several authors [152, 153, 761] have proposed other methods:

Addition of discrete fuzzy numbers [152, 153, 750, 761]. For discrete fuzzy numbers A_1, A_2 their addition $A_{12} = A_1 + A_2$ is the discrete fuzzy number whose α-cut is defined as

$$A_{12}^{\alpha} = \{x \in \{\mathrm{supp}\,(A_1) + \mathrm{supp}\,(A_2)\} \mid \min\{A_1^{\alpha} + A_2^{\alpha}\} \leq x \leq \max\{A_1^{\alpha} + A_2^{\alpha}\}\},$$

where

$$\mathrm{supp}\,(A_1) + \mathrm{supp}\,(A_2) = \{x_1 + x_2 \mid x_j \in \mathrm{supp}\,(A_j), j = 1,2\}, \min\{A_1^{\alpha} + A_2^{\alpha}\} =$$
$$= \min\{x_1 + x_2 \mid x_j \in A_j^{\alpha}), j = 1,2\},$$

$\max\{A_1^{\alpha} + A_2^{\alpha}\} = \max\{x_1 + x_2 \mid x_j \in A_j^{\alpha}, j = 1,2\}$ and the membership function is defined as

$$\mu_{A_1 + A_2}(x) = \sup\{\alpha \in [0,1] \mid x \in \{A_1^{\alpha} + A_2^{\alpha}\}\}. \tag{5.23}$$

Below we provide several definitions of the other operation of arithmetic of discrete fuzzy numbers. In these definitions, non-interactive fuzzy numbers are considered.

Standard subtraction of discrete fuzzy numbers [16, 44]. For discrete fuzzy numbers A_1, A_2 their standard subtraction $A_{12} = A_1 - A_2$ is the discrete fuzzy number whose α-cut is defined as

$$A_j^\alpha = \{x \in \{\text{supp}(A_1) - \text{supp}(A_2)\} \mid \min\{A_1^\alpha - A_2^\alpha\} \leq x \leq \max\{A_1^\alpha - A_2^\alpha\}\},$$

where

$$\text{supp}(A_1) - \text{supp}(A_2) = \{x_1 - x_2^- \mid x_j \in \text{supp}(A_j), j = 1, 2\},$$

$$\min\{A_1^\alpha - A_2^\alpha\} = \min\{x_1 - x_2 \mid x_j \in A_j^\alpha, j = 1, 2\},$$

$$\max\{A_1^\alpha - A_2^\alpha\} = \max\{x_1 - x_2 \mid x_j \in A_j^\alpha, j = 1, 2\}$$

and the membership function is defined as

$$\mu_{A_1 - A_2}(x) = \sup\{\alpha \in [0,1] \mid x \in \{A_1^\alpha - A_2^\alpha\}\} . \tag{5.24}$$

For the standard subtraction one has:

$$A_2 + (A_1 - A_2) \neq A_1 .$$

Hukuhara difference of discrete fuzzy numbers [16, 44]. For discrete fuzzy numbers A_1, A_2 their Hukuhara difference denoted $A_1 -_h A_2$ is the discrete fuzzy number A_{12} such that

$$A_1 = A_2 + A_{12} . \tag{5.25}$$

Hukuhara difference exists only if $n \geq m$.

Multiplication of discrete fuzzy numbers [16, 44]. For discrete fuzzy numbers A_1, A_2 their multiplication $A_{12} = A_1 \cdot A_2$ is the discrete fuzzy number whose α-cut is defined as

$$A_j^\alpha = \{x \in \{\text{supp}(A_1) \cdot \text{supp}(A_2)\} \mid \min\{A_1^\alpha \cdot A_2^\alpha\} \leq x \leq \max\{A_1^\alpha \cdot A_2^\alpha\}\},$$

where

$$\text{supp}(A_1) \cdot \text{supp}(A_2) = \{x_1 \cdot x_2 \mid x_j \in \text{supp}(A_j), j = 1,2\},$$

$$\min\{A_1^\alpha \cdot A_2^\alpha\} = \min\{x_1 \cdot x_2 \mid x_j \in A_j^\alpha, j = 1,2\},$$

$$\max\{A_1^\alpha \cdot A_2^\alpha\} = \max\{x_1 \cdot x_2 \mid x_j \in A_j^\alpha, j = 1,2\}$$

and the membership function is defined as

$$\mu_{A_1 \cdot A_2}(x) = \sup\{\alpha \in [0,1] \mid x \in \{A_1^\alpha \cdot A_2^\alpha\}\}. \tag{5.26}$$

Standard division of discrete fuzzy numbers [16, 44]. For discrete fuzzy numbers A_1, A_2 given that $0 \notin \text{supp}(A_2)$ their standard division $A_{12} = {A_1}\big/{A_2}$ is the discrete fuzzy number whose α-cut is defined as

$$A_{12}^\alpha = \{x \in \{\text{supp}(A_1)/\text{supp}(A_2)\} \mid \min\{A_1^\alpha/A_2^\alpha\} \le x \le \max\{A_1^\alpha/A_2^\alpha\}\},$$

where

$$\text{supp}(A_1)\big/\text{supp}(A_2) = \{x_1/x_2 \mid x_j \in \text{supp}(A_j), j = 1,2\},$$

$$\min\{A_1^\alpha/A_2^\alpha\} = \min\{x_1/x_2 \mid x_j \in A_j^\alpha, j = 1,2\},$$

$$\max\{A_1^\alpha/A_2^\alpha\} = \max\{x_1/x_2 \mid x_j \in \text{supp}(A_j), j = 1,2\}.$$

and the membership function is defined as

$$\mu_{A_1/A_2}(x) = \sup\{\alpha \in [0,1] \mid x \in \{A_1^\alpha/A_2^\alpha\}\}. \tag{5.27}$$

For the standard division one has:

$$A_2 \cdot (A_1/A_2) \ne A_1.$$

A square of a discrete fuzzy number [16, 44]. For a discrete fuzzy number A its square A^2 is the discrete fuzzy number whose α-cut is defined as

$$\left[A^2 \right]^\alpha = \{ y \in \mathrm{supp}(A^2) \mid \min((A^\alpha)^2) \le y \le \max((A^\alpha)^2) \}$$

where

$$\mathrm{supp}(A^2) = \{ y \mid y = x^2, x \in \mathrm{supp}(A) \},$$

$$\min(A^\alpha)^2 = \min\{ y \mid y = x^2, x \in A^\alpha \},$$

$$\max(A^\alpha)^2 = \max\{ y \mid y = x^2, x \in A^\alpha \}.$$

Thus, $\left[A^2 \right]^\alpha = \left(A^\alpha \right)^2$. The membership function of A^2 is defined as

$$\mu_{A^2}(y) = \sup\{ \alpha \in [0,1] \mid y \in [A^2]^\alpha \}. \qquad (5.28)$$

A square root of a discrete fuzzy number [16, 44]. For a discrete fuzzy number A, where $\mathrm{supp}(A) \subset [0, \infty)$, its square root $\sqrt{A}$ is the discrete fuzzy number whose α-cut is defined as

$$\left[\sqrt{A} \right]^\alpha = \{ y \in \mathrm{supp}(\sqrt{A}) \mid \min\sqrt{A^\alpha} \le y \le \max\sqrt{A^\alpha} \}$$

where

$$\mathrm{supp}(\sqrt{A}) = \{ y \mid y = \sqrt{x}, x \in \mathrm{supp}(A) \},$$

$$\min\sqrt{A^\alpha} = \min\{ y \mid y = \sqrt{x}, x \in A^\alpha \},$$

$$\max\sqrt{A^\alpha} = \max\{ y \mid y = \sqrt{x}, x \in A^\alpha \}.$$

Thus, $\left[\sqrt{A} \right]^\alpha = \sqrt{A^\alpha}$. The membership function of $\sqrt{A}$ is defined as

$$\mu_{\sqrt{A}}(y) = \sup\left\{\alpha \in [0,1] \mid y \in \left[\sqrt{A}\right]^{\alpha}\right\}. \tag{5.29}$$

Minimum and maximum of discrete fuzzy numbers [155]. For discrete fuzzy numbers (DFNs) A_1, A_2, $A_1 = \{x_1^{\alpha}, ..., x_p^{\alpha}\}$ $A_2 = \{y_1^{\alpha}, ..., y_k^{\alpha}\}$, their minimum $A_{12} = MIN(A_1, A_2)$ is the DFN whose α-cut is defined as

$$A_{12}^{\alpha} = \{z \in \{\text{supp}(A_1) \wedge \text{supp}(A_2)\} \mid \min\{x_1^{\alpha}, y_1^{\alpha}\} \leq z \leq \min\{x_p^{\alpha}, y_k^{\alpha}\}\}$$

where
$$\text{supp}(A_1) \wedge \text{supp}(A_2) = \{z = \min(x, y) \mid x \in \text{supp}(A_1), y \in \text{supp}(A_2)\}.$$

Then
$$MIN(A_1, A_2)(z) = \sup\{\alpha \in [0,1] \mid z \in A_{12}^{\alpha}\}. \tag{5.30}$$

For DFNs A_1, A_2, $A_1 = \{x_1^{\alpha}, ..., x_p^{\alpha}\}$, $A_2 = \{y_1^{\alpha}, ..., y_k^{\alpha}\}$ their maximum $A_{12} = MAX(A_1, A_2)$ is the DFN whose α-cut is defined as

$$A_{12}^{\alpha} = \{z \in \{\text{supp}(A_1) \vee \text{supp}(A_2)\} \mid \max\{x_1^{\alpha}, y_1^{\alpha}\} \leq z \leq \max\{x_p^{\alpha}, y_k^{\alpha}\}\},$$

where
$$\text{supp}(A_1) \vee \text{supp}(A_2) = \{z = \max(x, y) \mid x \in \text{supp}(A_1), y \in \text{supp}(A_2)\}.$$

Then
$$MAX(A_1, A_2)(z) = \sup\{\alpha \in [0,1] \mid z \in A_{12}^{\alpha}\}. \tag{5.31}$$

Denote $\mathcal{D}$ the set of DFNs defined on $\mathcal{R}$. As it shown in [155], the triple $(\mathcal{D}, MIN, MAX)$ is a distributive lattice.

An absolute value of a discrete fuzzy number. For a discrete fuzzy number A its absolute value $abs(A)$ is the discrete fuzzy number whose α -cut is defined as

$$\left[abs(A)\right]^{\alpha} = \{y \in \text{supp}(abs(A)) \,|\, \min(abs(A^{\alpha})) \leq y \leq \max(abs(A^{\alpha}))\}$$

where

$$\text{supp}(abs(A^{\alpha})) = \{y \,|\, y = abs(x), x \in \text{supp}(A)\},$$

$$\min abs(A^{\alpha}) = \min\{y \,|\, y = abs(x), x \in A^{\alpha}\},$$

$$\max abs(A^{\alpha}) = \max\{y \,|\, y = abs(x), x \in A^{\alpha}\}.$$

Thus, $\left[abs(A)\right]^{\alpha} = abs\left(A^{\alpha}\right)$. The membership function of $abs(A)$ is defined as

$$\mu_{abs(A)}(y) = \sup\{\alpha \in [0,1] \,|\, y \in \left[abs(A)\right]^{\alpha}\}. \tag{5.32}$$

A discrete fuzzy exponential function. The discrete fuzzy exponential function is a function $f : \mathcal{D} \rightarrow \mathcal{D}$ denoted $f(A_X) = e^{A_X}$ whose α -cut is defined as

$$\left[e^{A_X}\right]^{\alpha} = \{y \in \text{supp}(e^{A_X}) \,|\, \min(e^{A_X^{\alpha}}) \leq y \leq \max(e^{A_X^{\alpha}})\}$$

where

$$\text{supp}(e^{A_X}) = \{y \,|\, y = e^x, x \in \text{supp}(e^{A_X})\},$$

$$\min(e^{A_X^{\alpha}}) = \min\{y \,|\, y = e^x, x \in A_X^{\alpha}\},$$

$$\max(e^{A_X^{\alpha}}) = \max\{y \,|\, y = e^x, x \in A_X^{\alpha}\}.$$

Thus, $\left[e^{A_X}\right]^{\alpha} = e^{A_X^{\alpha}}$. The membership function of e^{A_X} is defined as

$$\mu_{e^{A_X}}(y)=\sup\{\alpha\in[0,1]\,|\,y\in[e^{A_X}]^\alpha\}. \tag{5.33}$$

A discrete fuzzy natural logarithm. A discrete fuzzy exponential function is a function $f:\mathcal{D}\to\mathcal{D}$ denoted $f(A_X)=\ln(A_X)$ whose α-cut is defined as

$$\left[\ln(A_X)\right]^\alpha=\{y\in\mathrm{supp}(\ln(A_X))\,|\,\min(\ln(A_X^{\;\alpha}))\le y\le\max(\ln(A_X^{\;\alpha}))\}$$

where

$$\mathrm{supp}(\ln(A_X))=\{y\,|\,y=\ln(x),x\in\mathrm{supp}(\ln(A_X))\},$$

$$\min(\ln(A_X^{\;\alpha}))=\min\{y\,|\,y=e^x,x\in\ln(A_X^{\;\alpha})\},$$

$$\max(\ln(A_X^{\;\alpha}))=\max\{y\,|\,y=\ln(x),x\in\ln(A_X^{\;\alpha})\}.$$

Thus, $\left[\ln(A_X)\right]^\alpha=\ln(A_X^{\;\alpha})$. The membership function of $\ln(A_X)$ is defined as

$$\mu_{\ln(A_X)}(y)=\sup\{\alpha\in[0,1]\,|\,y\in[\ln(A_X)]^\alpha\}. \tag{5.34}$$

5.5 Arithmetic of type-2 fuzzy numbers

As it was shown above a type-2 fuzzy set $\tilde{A}$ is defined as

$$\tilde{A}=\left\{\left((x,u),\mu_{\tilde{A}}(x,u)\right)\,|\,\forall x\in X,\forall u\in J_x\subseteq[0,1]\right\},\ 0\le\mu_{\tilde{A}}(x,u)\le1.$$

Type-2 fuzzy set alternatively can be described as

$$\tilde{A}=\int_{x\in X}\int_{u\in J_x}\mu_{\tilde{A}}(x,u)/(x,u).$$

Type-2 fuzzy sets also can be expressed by vertical slice representation.

$$\tilde{A} = \left\{ \left(x, \mu_{\tilde{A}}(x) \right) | \ \forall x \in X \right\}$$

$$\tilde{A} = \int_{x \in X} \mu_{\tilde{A}}(x) / x$$

$$\mu_{\tilde{A}}(x) = \int_{u \in J_x} f_x(u) / u \ , \quad J_x \subseteq [0,1].$$

As it is shown abowe a bounded region obtained as union of all primary membership of $\tilde{A}$ is footprint of uncertainty (FOU)

$$FOU(\tilde{A}) = \bigcup_{x \in X} J_x.$$

Upper and lower membership functions of $\tilde{A}$ defined as the upper and lower bounds of the FOU are expressed as

$$\bar{\mu}_{\tilde{A}}(x) = \overline{FOU\left(\tilde{A}\right)} = \overline{\bigcup_{x \in X} J_x} \ , \quad \forall x \in X$$

$$\underline{\mu}_{\tilde{A}}(x) = \underline{FOU(\tilde{A})} = \underline{\bigcup_{x \in X} J_x} \ , \quad \forall x \in X.$$

For discret case of X and J_x $\tilde{A}$ can be expressed as

$$\tilde{A} = \sum_{x \in X} \left[\sum_{u \in J_x} f_x(u) / u \right] \Bigg/ x = \sum_{i=1}^{N} \left[\sum_{u \in J_{x_i}} f_{x_i}(u) / u \right] \Bigg/ x_i$$

$$= \left[\sum_{k=1}^{M_1} f_{x_1}(u_{1k}) / u_{1k} \right] \Bigg/ x_1 + \cdots + \left[\sum_{k=1}^{M_N} f_{x_N}(u_{Nk}) / u_{Nk} \right] \Bigg/ x_N$$

For discrete X and U an embedded type-2 fuzzy set $\tilde{A}_e$ with N elements is defined as

$$\tilde{A}_e = \sum_{i=1}^{N} \left[f_{x_i}(u_i) / u_i \right] / x_i \ , \quad u_i \in J_{x_i} \subseteq U = [0,1]$$

An embedded type-1 fuzzy set A_e is union of all membership of $\tilde{A}_e$ and is defined as

$$A_e = \sum_{i=1}^{N} u_i / x_i , \ u_i \in J_{x_i} \subseteq U = [0,1].$$

Wavy slice representation (WSR) of $\tilde{A}$ is expessed as [7].

$$\tilde{A}_e^j \equiv \left\{ (u_i^j, f_{x_i}(u_i^j)), i = 1,...,N \right\}, \ u_i^j \in \{ u_{ik}, k = 1,...,M_i \}$$

$$\tilde{A} = \sum_{j=1}^{n} \tilde{A}_e^j , \ n \equiv \prod_{i=1}^{N} M_i.$$

Here M_i is the cardinality of type-1 fuzzy sets.

In case $f_x(u) = 1, \forall u \in J_x \subseteq [0,1], \forall x \in X,$ $\mu_{\tilde{A}}(x)$ are interval sets and $\tilde{A}$ is called an interval type-2 fuzzy set.

$$\tilde{A} = \int_{x \in X} \left[\int_{u \in J_x} 1 / u \right] / x = \int_{x \in X} \left[\int_{u \in [\underline{\mu}_{\tilde{A}}(x), \overline{\mu}_{\tilde{A}}(x)]} 1 / u \right] / x.$$

WSR can be applied to operations on type-2 fuzzy sets. For example the union of two type-2 fuzzy sets $\tilde{A}$ and $\tilde{B}$ is defined as

$$\tilde{A} \cup \tilde{B} = \sum_{j=1}^{n_A} \tilde{A}_e^j \cup \sum_{i=1}^{n_B} \tilde{B}_e^i = \sum_{j=1}^{n_A} \sum_{i=1}^{n_B} \tilde{A}_e^j \cup \tilde{B}_e^i. \tag{5.35}$$

Now by using (5.35) we can find the arithmetic operations of type-2 fuzzy numbers. By replacing the union operator in (5.35) with a arithmetical operator $* \in (-,+,\times,\div)$ one can represent any binary function

$$\tilde{A} * \tilde{B} = \sum_{j=1}^{n_A} \tilde{A}_e^j * \sum_{i=1}^{n_B} \tilde{B}_e^i = \sum_{j=1}^{n_A} \sum_{i=1}^{n_B} \tilde{A}_e^j * \tilde{B}_e^i.$$

To date computational complexity of using a general Type-2 fuzzy sets is with some extent high. To simplify computation with Type-2 fuzzy sets we usually use interval Type-2 fuzzy sets.

As it was mentioned above a general Type-2 fuzzy set is expressed as

$$\tilde{A} = \int_{x \in X} \int_{u \in J_X} \mu_{\tilde{A}}(x,u) / (x,u) \ J_X \subseteq [0,1]. \tag{5.36}$$

where $\iint$ denotes union over all admissible x and u. For discrete universes of discourse, $\int$ is replaced by $\sum$.

As it is mentioned above when all $\mu_{\tilde{A}}(x,u) = 1$ then $\tilde{A}$ is an interval Type-2 fuzzy set (IT2FS).

Consequently İT2 FS can be expressed as

$$\tilde{A} = \int_{x \in X} \int_{u \in J_X} 1/(x,u), \quad J_X \subseteq [0,1].$$ (5.37)

At each value of x, say $x = x'$, in (5.36) the 2-D plane whose axes are u and $\mu_{\tilde{A}}(x',u)$ is called a vertical slice of $\mu_{\tilde{A}}(x,u)$.

Based on the concept of secondary sets, we can reinterpret an IT2 FS as the union of all secondary sets, and we can reexpress $\tilde{A}$ in a vertical-slice manner as [522]

$$\tilde{A} = \{(x, \mu_{\tilde{A}}(x)) \mid \forall x \in X\}$$

or, alternatively, as

$$\tilde{A} = \int_{x \in X} \mu_{\tilde{A}}(x)/x = \int_{x \in X} \left[\int_{u \in J_x} 1/u \right]/x, \quad J_x \subseteq [0,1].$$

IT2 FS footprint of uncertainty can be described as

$$FOU(\tilde{A}) = \bigcup_{x \in X} J_x.$$ (5.38)

In accordance with Mendel-John representation theorem for an IT2 FS $\tilde{A}$ is the union of all of its embedded IT2 FSs.

Assume that $X = \{x_1, x_2, \ldots, x_n\}$ is discrete or discretized primary variable, $U_i^j \in \{\underline{\mu}_{\tilde{A}}(x_i), \ldots, \overline{\mu}_{\tilde{A}}(x_i)\}$ is sampled secondary variables. In accordance with Mendel-John representation Interval Type-2 fuzzy sets (IT2FS) can be expressed as follows:

$$\tilde{A} = 1/FOU(\tilde{A}) = 1/U_{j=1}^{n_A} A_e^j \text{ where } A_e^j = \sum_{i-1}^{n} U_i^j / x_i \qquad (5.39)$$

$$\tilde{A} = \sum_{j=1}^{n_A} \tilde{A}_e^j$$

where $j = 1, \ldots, n_A$

$$\tilde{A}_e^j = \sum_{i=1}^{N} [1/u_i^j] / x_i, \quad u_i^j \in J_{x_i} \subseteq U = [0,1]$$

and

$$n_A = \prod_{i=1}^{N} M_i$$

in which M_i denotes the discretization levels of secondary variable u_i^j at each of the N x_i.

Arithmetic operations on IT2 fuzzy numbers

Type-2 fuzzy number (T2FN) is very frequently used in type-2 fuzzy decision making and control. We concentrate on triangular type-2 fuzzy number (TIT2FN).

The TIT2FN can be determined as follows:

$$\tilde{a}_i = \left(a_i^l, a_i^u \right) = \left([a_{i1}^l, a_{i2}^l], [a_{i1}^u, a_{i2}^u]; \tilde{s}_i^l, \tilde{s}_i^u \right),$$

where a_i^l and a_i^u are Type-1 fuzzy sets, $a_{i1}^l, a_{i2}^l, a_{i1}^u, a_{i2}^u$ are the reference points of the interval Type-2 fuzzy set $\tilde{a}_i, s_i^l$ is the upper membership function and s_i^u is the lower membership function, $s_i^l \in [0,1]$ and $s_i^u \in [0,1]$ and $1 \le i \le n$.

Let us consider arithmetic operations on TIT2FN [861].

Addition

Two TIT2FN are given

$$\tilde{a}_1 = \left(a_1^l, a_1^u \right) = \left([a_{11}^l, a_{12}^l], [a_{11}^u, a_{12}^u]; s_1^l, s_1^u \right)$$

$$\tilde{b}_2 = \left(b_2^l, b_2^u \right) = \left([b_{21}^l, b_{22}^l], [b_{21}^u, b_{22}^u]; s_2^l, s_2^u \right).$$

The addition of $\tilde{a}_1$ and $\tilde{b}_2$ is defined as:

$$\tilde{a}_1 + \tilde{b}_2 = \left(a_1^l, a_1^u \right) + \left(b_2^l, b_2^u \right) = \begin{bmatrix} \left(a_{11}^l + b_{21}^l, a_{12}^l + b_{22}^l; \min\left(s_1^l, s_2^l \right) \right), \\ \left(a_{11}^u + b_{21}^u, a_{12}^u + b_{22}^u; \min\left(s_1^u, s_2^u \right) \right) \end{bmatrix}.$$

Subtraction

The subtraction of $\tilde{a}_1$ and $\tilde{b}_2$ is defined as:

$$\tilde{a}_1 - \tilde{b}_2 = \left(a_1^l, a_1^u \right) - \left(b_2^l, b_2^u \right) = \begin{bmatrix} \left(a_{11}^l - b_{21}^l, a_{12}^l - b_{22}^l; \min\left(s_1^l, s_2^l \right) \right), \\ \left(a_{11}^u - b_{21}^u, a_{12}^u - b_{22}^u; \min\left(s_1^u, s_2^u \right) \right) \end{bmatrix}.$$

Multiplication

The multiplication of $\tilde{a}_1$ and $\tilde{b}_2$ is defined as:

$$\tilde{a}_1 \times \tilde{b}_2 = \left(a_1^l, a_1^u \right) \times \left(b_2^l, b_2^u \right) = \begin{bmatrix} \left(a_{11}^l \times b_{21}^l, a_{12}^l \times b_{22}^l; \min\left(s_1^l, s_2^l \right) \right), \\ \left(a_{11}^u \times b_{21}^u, a_{12}^u \times b_{22}^u; \min\left(s_1^u, s_2^u \right) \right) \end{bmatrix}.$$

Division

The division of $\tilde{a}_1$ and $\tilde{b}_2$ is defined as:

$$\tilde{a}_1 \div \tilde{b}_2 = \left(a_1^l, a_1^u\right) : \left(b_2^l, b_2^u\right) = \begin{bmatrix} \left(a_{11}^l : b_{21}^l, a_{12}^l : b_{22}^l; \min\left(s_1^l, s_2^l\right)\right), \\ \left(a_{11}^u : b_{21}^u, a_{12}^u : b_{22}^u; \min\left(s_1^u, s_2^u\right)\right) \end{bmatrix}.$$

5.6 Horizontal membership function based fuzzy arithmetic

Fuzzy arithmetic based on classical interval arithmetic and α-cuts approach is not ideal, though it can solve certain problems. Below we give a version of fuzzy arithmetic that is based on horizontal membership functions and on α-cuts [456, 457, 608-615].

Classical arithmetic uses vertical membership functions.

Let consider trapezoidal membership function (Fig. 5.1) [606, 607]. As it is shown from Fig. 5.1 membership function assigns two values of x for one value of μ. Use $\alpha_x \in [0,1]$ allows to determine any point between borders $x_L(\mu)$ and $x_R(\mu)$.

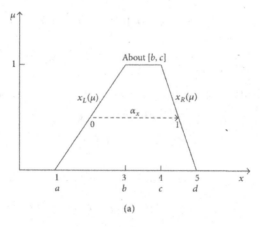

Fig. 5.1. Visualization of the horizontal approach to fuzzy membership functions

The interval $x(\mu)$ is defined as

$$x = x_L + (x_R - x_L)\alpha_x, \quad \alpha_x \in [0,1],$$
$$x = [a + (b-a)\mu] + [(d-a) - \mu(b-a) + (d-c))]\alpha_x.$$

In this arithmetic the element $X(\mu, \alpha_x)$ is expressed as

$$X(\mu, \alpha_x) = \left\{ x(\mu, \alpha_x) : x(\mu, \alpha_x) = x_L(\mu) + \alpha_x(x_R(\mu) - x_L(\mu)), \ \alpha_x \in [0,1], \right\}.$$

Its negative element $-X(\mu, \alpha_x)$ is determined as

$$-X(\mu, \alpha_x) = \left\{ x(\mu, \alpha_x) : x(\mu, \alpha_x) = -x_L(\mu) - \alpha_x(x_R(\mu) - x_L(\mu)), \ \alpha_x \in [0,1] \right\}.$$

Subtraction result $X - X$ is

$$X(\mu, \alpha_x) - X(\mu, \alpha_x) = 0.$$

In conventional fuzzy arithmetic

$$X(\mu) - X(\mu) = \left[-(x_R(\mu) - x_L(\mu)), x_R(\mu) - x_L(\mu) \right] \neq [0,0].$$

Let us consider addition of two fuzzy numbers X_1 and X_2 by using horizontal membership function.

Horizontal MF of X_1 and X_2 are given below

$$x_1 = \left[a_1 + \mu(b_1 - a_1) \right] + \alpha_{x_1}(d_1 - a_1)(1 - \mu),$$

$$x_2 = \left[a_2 + \mu(b_2 - a_2) \right] + \alpha_{x_2}(d_2 - a_2)(1 - \mu).$$

For simplisity here we consider triangular fuzzy numbers.

The sum $y = x_1 + x_2$ is determined as

$$x_1 \in [a_1, d_1], \ x_2 \in [a_2, d_2],$$

$$y = x_1 + x_2 = \left[(a_1 + a_2) + \mu(b_1 + b_2 - a_1 - a_2) \right]$$
$$+ \left[\alpha_{x_1}(d_1 - a_1) + \alpha_{x_2}(d_2 - a_2) \right](1 - \mu).$$

Example. If X_1 is $(0.9, 1.0, 1.1)$ and X_2 is $(1.0, 1.1, 1.2)$ then we can write

$$x_1 = \left[0.9 + 0.1\mu \right] + 0.2\alpha_{x_1}(1 - \mu), \ \alpha_{x_1} \in [0,1]$$

$$x_2 = \left[1.0 + 0.1\mu \right] + 0.2\alpha_{x_2}(1 - \mu), \ \alpha_{x_2} \in [0,1].$$

The sum $y = x_1 + x_2$ will be

$$y = [1.9 + 0.2\mu] + 0.2(\alpha_{x_1} + \alpha_{x_2})(1-\mu), \quad \alpha_{x_1}, \alpha_{x_2}, \mu \in [0,1].$$

Main problem in interval, fuzzy and Z-arithmetic is informativeness problem. Operations on large number of interval, fuzzy numbers lead to significant increase of resulting number's support. By appropriate choosing of cardinality level of resulting values we can handle informativeness of operations on interval and fuzzy numbers. Cardinality distribution of the sum $y = x_1 + x_2$ is given in Fig. 5.2.

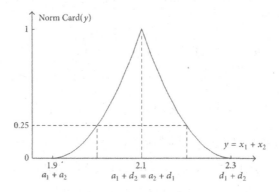

Fig. 5.2. Normalised cardinality distribution

5.7 Adequacy of fuzzy models [25]

Let $R_i = \bigcup_{i=1}^{n} = X_i \times Y_i$. If for each X_i,

$$Y_i = X_i \circ R, \tag{5.40}$$

then the compositional rule of inference is executed strictly; otherwise it is done approximately.

Below, theorems about the strict execution of the compositional rule of inference are formulated, defining the conditions of minimizing the adequacy criterion.

Theorem 5.1. Let R be a regular fuzzy relation matrix:

$$R = X \times Y \quad (n = 1).$$

If fuzzy sets X and Y are normal, then the expression (5.40) is executed strictly.

Proof of Theorem 5.1. We assume that

$$X = \left\{ (\mu_X(x), x) \right\}, \ Y = \left\{ (\mu_Y(y), y) \right\}, R = \left\{ (\mu_R(x, y), (x, y)) \right\}.$$

In view of a theorem of Tong [723], when fuzzy sets X and Y are normal and R is a regular relation matrix, then R has column x^* and row y^*, such that

$$\mu_X(x) = \mu_R(x^*, y), \ \mu_Y(y) = \mu_R(x, y^*) \tag{5.41}$$

or

$$\mu_X(x) = \max_y \mu_R(x, y), \ \mu_Y(y) = \max_x \mu_R(x, y). \tag{5.42}$$

Since for elements (x, y) of relation matrix R the expressions

$$\mu_R(x^*, y) \geq \mu_R(x, y), \ \mu_R(x, y^*) \geq \mu_R(x, y),$$

hold, it follows that
$$\min\left\{ \mu_R(x^*, y), \mu_R(x, y) \right\} = \mu_R(x, y),$$
$$\min\left\{ \mu_R(x, y^*), \mu_R(x, y) \right\} = \mu_R(x, y). \tag{5.43}$$

As

$$\mu_Y(y) = \max_x \min\left\{ \mu_X(x), \mu_R(x, y) \right\}, \tag{5.44}$$

then inserting (5.41) in (5.44), taking (5.42) and (5.43) into account, we get

$$\mu_Y(y) = \max_x \min\left\{ \mu_X(x), \mu_R(x, y) \right\}$$

$$= \max_x \min\left\{ \mu_R(x^*, y), \mu_R(x, y) \right\} = \max_x \mu_R(x, y) = \mu_Y(y)$$

Then theorem is proved.

Theorem 5.2. Let non-regular fuzzy relation matrix $R = \bigcup_{i=1}^{n} R_i$ be given. Here $\tilde{R}_i = X_i \times Y_i$ are regular relation matrices. If fuzzy sets X_i and Y_i $(i=1,..., n)$ are normal and satisfy the conditions

$$\bigcap_{i=1}^{n} X_i = \varnothing, \quad \bigcap_{i=1}^{n} Y_i = \varnothing$$

then the expression (5.40) is executed strictly.

Here for simplicity only the binary relation was considered when the object is one-dimensional. The obtained results are true for multidimensional processes when the rules have a nested structure.

Proof of theorem 5.2. We assume that

$$X_i = \left\{ (\mu_{X_i}(x), x) \right\}, \ Y_i = \left\{ (\mu_{Y_i}(y), y) \right\},$$
$$\mu_{Y_i}(y) = \max_{x} \min \left\{ \mu_{X_i}(x) \mu_R(x, y) \right\}. \tag{5.45}$$

The relation matrix R is non-regular, so

$$R = \bigcup_{i=1}^{n} R_i \tag{5.46}$$

where $R_i = X_i \times Y_i$. According to the conditions of Theorem 5.2, the fuzzy sets X_i and Y_i satisfy

$$\bigcap_{i=1}^{n} X_i = \varnothing, \quad \bigcap_{i=1}^{n} Y_i = \varnothing. \tag{5.47}$$

Then from expression (5.46) taking (5.47) into account it follows that

$$\mu_{R_i} = \begin{cases} \mu_{R_i}, & \text{if } (x, y) \in \operatorname{supp} X_i \times Y_i, \\ 0, & \text{if } (x, y) \in \operatorname{supp} X_i \times Y_i. \end{cases}$$

Therefore

$$\mu_R = \begin{cases} \mu_{R_1}, & \text{if}(x,y) \in \text{supp}\,X_1 \times Y_1, \\ \mu_{R_2}, & \text{if}(x,y) \in \text{supp}\,X_2 \times Y_2, \\ \vdots & \vdots \qquad\qquad \vdots \\ \mu_{R_n}, & \text{if}(x,y) \in \text{supp}\,X_n \times Y_n. \end{cases}$$

Consequently $\min(\mu_{X_i}, \mu_{R_j}) = 0$ for all $\mu_R = \mu_{R_j} (j = 1, ..., n)$ with the exception of $\mu_R = \mu_{R_i} (i = j)$. Taking this into account in (5.45), we obtain

$$\mu_{Y_i}(y) = \max_x \min(\mu_{X_i}(x), \mu_R(x,y)) = \max_x \min(\mu_{X_i}(x), \mu_{R_i}(x,y)).$$

As X_i is normal fuzzy set and R is a regular relation matrix, according to the conditions of Theorem 1, the expression (5.40) holds strictly.

The theorem is proved [25].

5.8 Fuzzy logic formalization for approximate reasoning

In our daily life we often make inferences where *antecedents* and *consequents* are represented by fuzzy sets. Such inferences cannot be realized adequately by the methods, which are based either on two-valued logic or many-valued logic. In order to facilitate such an inference, Zadeh [822-826, 842] suggested an inference rule called a "compositional rule of inference". Using this inference rule, Zadeh, Mamdani [492], Mizumoto *et al.* [290, 529, 530], R.Aliev and A.Tserkovny [32, 36, 43] suggested several methods for fuzzy reasoning in which the antecedent contain a conditional proposition involving fuzzy concepts:

Ant 1: If x is P then y is Q
Ant2: x is P'

---------------------------------   (5.48)

Cons: y is Q'.

Those methods are based on implication operators present in various fuzzy logics. This matter has been under a thorough discussion for the last couple decades. Some comparative analysis of such methods was presented in [86-91, 290, 306, 367, 384, 405-407, 498, 499, 529, 530, 679, 799, 800]. A number of authors proposed to use a certain suite of fuzzy implications to form fuzzy conditional inference rules [36, 43, 87, 91, 442, 443, 492, 529, 530]. The implication operators present in the theory of fuzzy sets were investigated in [36, 43, 81, 101, 106, 121, 123, 141, 167, 216, 230, 235, 254, 272, 286, 328, 333, 367, 386, 426, 444, 452, 466, 478, 488, 499, 506, 507, 516, 535, 543, 546, 559, 599, 630, 649, 674, 687, 791, 792, 796, 871, 872, 874]. On the other hand, statistical features of fuzzy implication operators were studied in [560, 773]. In turn, the properties of stability and continuity of fuzzy conditional inference rules were investigated in [276, 290, 387, 433].

We investigate a systemic approach toward fuzzy logic formalization for an approximate reasoning. We will begin with a *formation* of a fuzzy logic regarded as an *algebraic system closed under all its operations*. In the sequel an investigation of statistical characteristics of the proposed fuzzy logic will be presented. Special attention will be paid to building a set of fuzzy conditional inference rules on the basis of the fuzzy logic proposed in this study. Next, continuity and stability features of the formalized rules will be investigated.

In what follows, we introduce some required notation. x and y are the names of objects, while P, P', Q and Q' are fuzzy concepts represented by fuzzy sets defined in the universes of discourse U, U, V and V, respectively. This form of inference may be viewed as a generalized *modus ponens,* which reduces to modus ponens when $P'=P$ and $Q'=Q$. Let P and Q be fuzzy sets in U and V, respectively, while the corresponding fuzzy sets are represented as

$$P \subset U \big| \mu_P : U \to [0,1], Q \subset V \big| \mu_Q : V \to [0,1],$$

where

$$P = \int_U \mu_P(u)/u \quad Q = \int_V \mu_Q(v)/v. \tag{5.49}$$

Let $\times, \cup, \cap, \neg$ and $\oplus$ denoted a Cartesian product, union, intersection, complement and bounded-sum for fuzzy sets, respectively. Then the following fuzzy relations in $U \times V$ can be derived from the fuzzy conditional proposition "If x is P then y is Q" in Ant 1 of (5.48). The fuzzy relations R_m and R_a were proposed by Zadeh [461, 478], R_c by Mamdani [492], R_s, R_g are by Mizumoto [276, 288, 290], while R_{ALI2} and R_{ALI3} are by Aliev and Tserkovny [32, 36, 43].

$$R_m = (P \times Q) \cup (\neg P \times V) = \int_{U \times V} (\mu_P(u) \wedge \mu_Q(v)) \vee (1 - \mu_P(u)) / (u, v) \quad (5.50)$$

$$R_a = (\neg P \times V) \oplus (U \times Q) = \int_{U \times V} 1 \wedge (1 - \mu_P(u) + \mu_Q(v)) / (u, v). \quad (5.51)$$

$$R_c = (P \times Q) = \int_{U \times V} (\mu_P(u) \wedge \mu_Q(v)) / (u, v). \quad (5.52)$$

$$R_s = (P \times V \underset{s}{\Rightarrow} U \times Q) = \int_{U \times V} (\mu_P(u) \underset{s}{\rightarrow} \mu_Q(v)) / (u, v), \quad (5.53)$$

where

$$\mu_P(u) \underset{s}{\rightarrow} \mu_Q(v) = \begin{cases} 1, & \mu_P(u) \le \mu_Q(v), \\ 0, & \mu_P(u) > \mu_Q(v). \end{cases}$$

$$R_g = (P \times V \underset{g}{\Rightarrow} U \times Q) = \int_{U \times V} (\mu_P(u) \underset{g}{\rightarrow} \mu_Q(v)) / (u, v), \quad (5.54)$$

and

$$\mu_P(u) \underset{g}{\rightarrow} \mu_Q(v) = \begin{cases} 1, & \mu_P(u) \le \mu_Q(v), \\ \mu_Q(v), & \mu_P(u) > \mu_Q(v). \end{cases}$$

$$R_b = (\neg P \times V \bigcup U \times Q) = \int_{U \times V} (1 - \mu_P(u)) \vee \mu_Q(v) / (u,v), \qquad (5.55)$$

$$R_\Delta = (P \times V \underset{\Delta}{\Rightarrow} U \times Q) = \int_{U \times V} [\mu_P(u) \underset{\Delta}{\rightarrow} \mu_Q(v)] / (u,v), \qquad (5.56)$$

where

$$\mu_P(u) \underset{\Delta}{\rightarrow} \mu_Q(v) = \begin{cases} 1, & \mu_P(u) \leq \mu_Q(v), \\ \dfrac{\mu_Q(v)}{\mu_P(u)}, & \mu_P(u) > \mu_Q(v). \end{cases}$$

$$R_* = (P \times V \underset{*}{\Rightarrow} U \times Q) = \int_{U \times V} [\mu_P(u) \underset{*}{\rightarrow} \mu_Q(v)] / (u,v), \qquad (5.57)$$

where

$$\mu_P(u) \underset{*}{\rightarrow} \mu_Q(v)$$
$$= (\mu_P(u) \wedge \mu_Q(v)) \vee (1 - \mu_P(u) \wedge 1 - \mu_Q(v)) \vee (\mu_Q(v) \wedge 1 - \mu_P(u))$$

$$R_\Diamond = (P \times V \underset{\Diamond}{\Rightarrow} U \times Q) = \int_{U \times V} [\mu_P(u) \underset{\Diamond}{\rightarrow} \mu_Q(v)] / (u,v), \qquad (5.58)$$

where

$$\mu_P(u) \underset{\Diamond}{\rightarrow} \mu_Q(v) = \begin{cases} 1, & \mu_P(u) < 1, \quad or \quad \mu_Q(v) = 1, \\ 0, & \mu_P(u) = 1 \quad or \quad \mu_Q(v) < 1. \end{cases}$$

$$R_{ALI_1} = (P \times V \underset{ALI_1}{\Rightarrow} U \times Q) = \int_{U \times V} [\mu_P(u) \underset{ALI_1}{\rightarrow} \mu_Q(v)] / (u,v), \qquad (5.59)$$

where

$$\mu_P(u) \underset{ALI_1}{\to} \mu_Q(v) = \begin{cases} 1 - \mu_P(u), & \mu_P(u) < \mu_Q(v), \\ 1, & \mu_P(u) = \mu_Q(v), \\ \mu_Q(v), & \mu_P(u) > \mu_Q(v). \end{cases}$$

$$R_{ALI_2} = (P \times V \underset{ALI_2}{\Rightarrow} U \times Q) = \int\limits_{U \times V} [\mu_P(u) \underset{ALI_2}{\to} \mu_Q(v)] / (u, v), \qquad (5.60)$$

where

$$\mu_P(u) \underset{ALI_2}{\to} \mu_Q(v) = \begin{cases} 1, & \mu_P(u) \le \mu_Q(v), \\ (1 - \mu_P(u)) \wedge \mu_Q(v), & \mu_P(u) > \mu_Q(v). \end{cases}$$

$$R_{ALI_3} = (P \times V \underset{ALI_3}{\Rightarrow} U \times Q) = \int\limits_{U \times V} [\mu_P(u) \underset{ALI_3}{\to} \mu_Q(v)] / (u, v), \qquad (5.61)$$

where

$$\mu_P(u) \underset{ALI_3}{\to} \mu_Q(v) = \begin{cases} 1, & \mu_P(u) \le \mu_Q(v), \\ \dfrac{\mu_Q(v)}{\mu_P(u) + (1 - \mu_Q(v))}, & \mu_P(u) > \mu_Q(v). \end{cases}$$

A necessary observation to be made in the context of this discussion is that with the only few exceptions for *S-logic* (5.53) and *G-logic* (5.54), and ALI$_1$-ALI$_3$(5.59)-(5.61), all other known fuzzy logics (5.50)-(5.52), (5.55)-(5.58) do not satisfy either the classical "modus-ponens" principle, or other criteria which appeal to the human perception of mechanisms of a decision making process being formulated in [530]. The proposed fuzzy logic comes with an implication operator, which satisfies the classical principle of "modus-ponens" and meets some additional criteria being in line with human intuition.

Consider a continuous function $F(p,q) = p - q$ which defines a distance between p and q where p, q assume values in the unit interval. Notice that $F(p,q) \in [-1,1]$, where $F(p,q)^{min} = -1$ and $F(p,q)^{max} = 1$. The normalized version of $F(p,q)$ is defined as follows

$$F(p,q)^{norm} = \frac{F(p,q)-F(p,q)^{min}}{F(p,q)^{max}-F(p,q)^{min}} = \frac{F(p,q)+1}{2} = \frac{p-q+1}{2}. \quad (5.62)$$

It is clear that $F(p,q)^{norm} \in [0,1]$. This function quantifies a concept of "closeness" between two values (potentially the ones for the truth values of antecedent and *consequent*), defined within unit interval, which therefore could play significant role in the formulation of the implication operator in a fuzzy logic.

Definition 5.1. An *implication* is a continuous function I from $[0, 1] \times [0, 1]$ into $[0, 1]$ such that for $\forall p, p', q, q', r \in [0,1]$ the following properties are satisfied

(I1) If $p \leq p'$ then $I(p,q) \geq I(p',q)$; (Antitone in first argument),

(I2) If $q \leq q'$ then $I(p,q) \leq I(p,q')$; (Monotone in second argument),

(I3) $I(0,q) = 1$, (Falsity),

(I4) $I(1,q) \leq q$, (Neutrality),

(I5) $I(p, I(q,r)) = I(q, I(p,r))$, (Exchange),

(I6) $I(p,q) = I(n(q), n(p))$. (Contra positive symmetry), where $n(.)$ — is a negation, which could be defined as $n(q) = T(\neg Q) = 1 - T(Q)$.

Definition 5.2. [91] Given a fuzzy implication operator $\rightarrow$ and a fuzzy subset Q of universe U, the *fuzzy power set* PQ of Q is given by the membership function μ_{PQ}, where

$$\mu_{PQ}P = \bigcap_{x \in U}(\mu_P x \rightarrow \mu_Q x). \quad (5.63)$$

The degree to which F is subset of Q is defined as

$$\pi(P \subseteq Q) = \mu_{PQ}P.$$

Definition 5.3. [91] The degree to which the fuzzy sets F and C are the same, or their *degree* of *similarity*, is

$$\pi(P \equiv Q) = \pi(P \subseteq Q) \wedge \pi(P \supseteq Q). \tag{5.64}$$

The following proposition is immediate.
Proposition 5.1. [91]

$$\pi(P \equiv Q) = \bigcap_{x \in U}(\mu_P x \leftrightarrow \mu_Q x). \tag{5.65}$$

Definition 5.4. [91] The degree of disjointness of F and C, or degree to which F and C are disjointed, in the first and second sense, is defined as follows

$$(1)\, \pi(Pdisj_1 Q) = \pi(P \subseteq Q^C) \wedge \pi(Q \supseteq B^C) \tag{5.66}$$

$$(2)\, \pi(Pdisj_2 Q) = \pi(P \cap Q \equiv \varnothing). \tag{5.67}$$

Definition 5.5. [91] A degree to which a set is a subset of its complement is defined in the form $\pi(P \subseteq P^C)$.

Definition 5.6. [91] A degree to which a set is disjointed from its complement, in terms of the two interpretations provided above is defined as $\pi(Pdisj_1 P^C)$ and $\pi(Pdisj_2 P^C))$.

Let us define the implication operation

$$I(p,q) = \begin{cases} 1 - F(p,q)^{norm}, & p > q; \\ 1, & p \le q, \end{cases} \tag{5.68}$$

where $F(p,q)^{norm}$ is expressed by (5.62). Before showing that operation $I(p,q)$ satisfies axioms (I1)-(I6), let us show some basic operations encountered in proposed fuzzy logic.

Let us designate the truth values of the *antecedent* P and *consequent* Q as $T(P) = p$ and $T(Q) = q$, respectively. The relevant set of proposed fuzzy logic operators is shown in Table 5.1.

Table 5.1. Fuzzy logic operators

Name	Designation	Value
Tautology	$\overset{\bullet}{P}$	1
Controversy	$\overset{\circ}{P}$	0
Negation	$\neg P$	$1 - P$
Disjunction	$P \vee Q$	$\begin{cases} \dfrac{p+q}{2}, p+q \neq 1, \\ 1, p+q = 1 \end{cases}$
Conjunction	$P \wedge Q$	$\begin{cases} \dfrac{p+q}{2}, p+q \neq 1, \\ 0, p+q = 1 \end{cases}$
Implication	$P \rightarrow Q$	$\begin{cases} \dfrac{1-p+q}{2}, p \neq q, \\ 1, p = q \end{cases}$
Equivalence	$P \leftrightarrow Q$	$\begin{cases} \min((p-q),(q-p)), p \neq q, \\ 1, p = q \end{cases}$
Pierce Arrow	$P \downarrow Q$	$\begin{cases} 1 - \dfrac{p+q}{2}, p+q \neq 1, \\ 0, p+q = 1 \end{cases}$
Shaffer Stroke	$P \uparrow Q$	$\begin{cases} 1 - \dfrac{p+q}{2}, p+q \neq 1, \\ 1, p+q = 1 \end{cases}$

To obtain the truth values of these expressions, we use well known logical properties such as

$$p \rightarrow q = \neg p \vee q; \ p \wedge q = \neg(\neg p \vee \neg q) \text{ and alike.}$$

In other words, we propose a new many-valued system, characterized by the set of *union* ($\cup$) and *intersection* ($\cap$) operations with relevant *complement*, defined as $T(\neg P) = 1 - T(P)$. In addition, the operators $\downarrow$ and $\uparrow$ are expressed as negations of the $\cup$ and $\cap$, respectively. It is well known that the *implication* operation in fuzzy logic supports the foundations of decision-making exploited in numerous schemes of approximate reasoning. Therefore let us prove that the proposed *implication* operation in (5.68) satisfies axioms (5.58)-(5.63). For this matter, let us emphasize that we are working with a many-valued system, which values for our purposes are the elements of the real interval $\Re = [0, 1]$. For our discussion the set of of truth values $V_{11} = \{0, 0.1, 0.2\ldots 0.9, 1\}$ is sufficient. In further investigations, we use this particular set V_{11}.

Theorem 5.3. Let a continuous function $I(p,q)$ be defined by (5.68), i.e.,

$$I(p,q) = \begin{cases} 1 - F(p,q)^{norm}, p > q, \\ 1, p \le q, \end{cases} = \begin{cases} \dfrac{1-p+q}{2}, p > q, \\ 1, p \le q. \end{cases} \tag{5.69}$$

where $F(p,q)^{norm}$ is a defined by (5.48).

Then axioms (5.58)-(5.63) are satisfied and, therefore (5.69) is an *implication* operation. Proof of the Theorem 5.3 is given in [28] .

In addition, the proposed fuzzy logic is characterized by the following properties:

Commutativity of both conjunction ($\cap$) and disjunction ($\cup$) operations, i.e.: $p \wedge q = q \wedge p$ and

$$p \vee q = q \vee p;$$

Assotiativity of these operations:

$$p \wedge (q \wedge r) = (p \wedge q) \wedge r$$

and

$$p \vee (q \vee r) = (p \vee q) \vee r;$$

Partial idempotency:

$$p \wedge p = \begin{cases} p, p > 0.5, \\ 0, p \le 0.5 \end{cases}$$

$$p \vee p = \begin{cases} p, p < 0.5, \\ 1, p \ge 0.5 \end{cases}$$

Partial Distributivity:

$$(p \vee q) \wedge r = (p \wedge r) \vee (q \wedge r), \quad if \ p + q + 2r \le 1, \tag{5.70}$$

$$(p \vee q) \wedge r \ne (p \wedge r) \vee (q \wedge r), if \ p + q + 2r > 1,$$

$$p \vee (q \wedge r) = (p \vee q) \wedge (p \vee r), if \ 2p + q + r \le 1, \tag{5.71}$$

$$p \vee (q \wedge r) \ne (p \vee q) \wedge (p \vee r), if \ 2p + q + r > 1.$$

To prove (5.70), we note that

$$p + q + 2r \le 1 \mid (p \vee q) \wedge r = (\frac{p+q}{2}) \wedge r = \frac{\frac{p+q}{2} + r}{2} = \frac{p+q+2r}{4} \tag{5.72}$$

On the other hand, we have

$$(p \wedge r) \vee (q \wedge r) = (\frac{p+r}{2}) \vee (\frac{q+r}{2})$$
$$= (\frac{p+r}{2} + \frac{q+r}{2})/2 = \frac{p+q+2r}{4}, \tag{5.73}$$

Therefore expression (5.72) is the same as (5.73) Q.E.D.
To prove (5.71), we carry out the following calculations,

$$2p+q+r \leq 1 \mid p \vee (q \wedge r) = p \vee \left(\frac{q+r}{2} \right)$$

$$= \left(p + \frac{q+r}{2} \right) \Big/ 2 = \frac{(2p+q+r)}{4}.$$

(5.74)

$$(p \vee q) \wedge (p \vee r) = \left(\frac{p+q}{2} \right) \wedge \left(\frac{p+r}{2} \right) = \frac{(2p+q+r)}{4}.$$ (5.75)

Therefore expression (5.74) is the same as (5.75) Q.E.D.
DeMorgan theorems,

$$\neg(p \wedge q) = \neg p \vee \neg q,$$

$$\neg(p \vee q) = \neg p \wedge \neg q;$$

hold as well. To prove them, let us notice that

$$\neg(p \wedge q) = \begin{cases} \neg \left(\dfrac{p+q}{2} \right) \\ 1 \end{cases} = \begin{cases} 1 - \left(\dfrac{p+q}{2} \right) \\ 1 \end{cases} = \begin{cases} \dfrac{2-p-q}{2} \\ 1 \end{cases}.$$ (5.76)

On the other hand

$$\neg p \vee \neg q = \begin{cases} \dfrac{\neg p + \neg q}{2} \\ 1 \end{cases} = \begin{cases} \dfrac{2-p-q}{2} \\ 1 \end{cases}.$$ (5.77)

Therefore expression (5.76) is the same as (5.77) Q.E.D.
By analogy

$$\neg(p \vee q) = \begin{cases} \neg(\dfrac{p+q}{2}) \\ 0 \end{cases} = \begin{cases} 1-(\dfrac{p+q}{2}) \\ 0 \end{cases} = \begin{cases} \dfrac{2-p-q}{2} \\ 0 \end{cases} \quad (5.78)$$

On the other hand

$$\neg p \wedge \neg q = \begin{cases} \dfrac{\neg p + \neg q}{2} \\ 0 \end{cases} = \begin{cases} \dfrac{2-p-q}{2} \\ 0 \end{cases} . \quad (5.79)$$

Therefore expression (5.78) is the same as (5.79) Q.E.D.

It should be mentioned that the proposed fuzzy logic could be characterized by yet some other three features: $p \wedge 0 \equiv 0, p \le 0$, whereas $p \vee 0 \equiv 0, p \ge 0$ and $\neg \neg p = p$. As a conclusion, we should admit that all above features confirm that *resulting system* can be applied to V_{11} for every finite and infinite n up to that $(V_{11}, \neg, \wedge, \vee, \rightarrow)$ is then *closed* under all its operations.

Considering (5.63)-(5.65) and taking into account (5.69), we can formulate the following propositions.

Proposition 5.2. (Degree of possibility of *set-inclusion*)

$$\pi(P \subseteq Q) = \begin{cases} \dfrac{1-\mu_P x + \mu_Q x}{2}, \mu_P x > \mu_Q x, \\ 1, \mu_P\, x \le \mu_Q x, \end{cases} \quad (5.80)$$

Proposition 5.3. (Degree of possibility of *set-equality*)

$$\pi(P \equiv Q) = \begin{cases} \dfrac{1-\mu_P x + \mu_Q x}{2}, \mu_P x > \mu_Q x, \\ 1, \mu_P x = \mu_Q x, \\ \dfrac{1-\mu_Q x + \mu_P x}{2}, \mu_P x < \mu_Q x, \end{cases} \quad (5.81)$$

From (5.81) it is clear that $\pi(P \equiv Q) = 1$ in case when $\mu_P x = \mu_Q$ x and $\pi(P \equiv Q) \leq 0.5$ otherwise. As it was mentioned in [86], there seem to be two plausible ways to define the degree to which sets P and Q may be said to be *disjointed*. One is the degree to which each is a subset of the other's complement. The second is the degree to which their intersection is empty.

Proposition 5.4. (Degree of disjointness of P and Q, or degree to which P and Q are disjointed)

For the case (5.48) from (5.66)

$$\pi(P \subseteq Q^C) = p \to (1-q) = \begin{cases} \dfrac{1-p+1-q}{2}, p > 1-q, \\ 1, p \leq 1-q, \end{cases} = \begin{cases} \dfrac{2-(p+q)}{2}, p+q > 1, \\ 1, p+q \leq 1. \end{cases} \quad (5.82)$$

$$\pi(Q \supseteq B^C) = q \to (1-p) =$$

$$= \begin{cases} \dfrac{1-q+1-p}{2}, q > 1-p, \\ 1, q \leq 1-p, \end{cases} = \quad (5.83)$$

$$= \begin{cases} \dfrac{2-(p+q)}{2}, p+q > 1, \\ 1, p+q \leq 1. \end{cases}$$

Therefore from (5.82) and (5.83), the definition (5.48) can arise in the form

$$\pi(P disj_1 Q) = \begin{cases} \dfrac{2-(p+q)}{2}, p+q > 1, \\ 1, p+q \leq 1. \end{cases} \quad (5.84)$$

For case (5.49) from (5.67) and given that

$$p \wedge q = \begin{cases} \dfrac{p+q}{2}, p+q > 1, \\ 0, p+q \leq 1. \end{cases}$$

We have

$$\pi(Pdisj_2 Q) = \pi(p \wedge q \equiv 0) = \begin{cases} 1, p+q \leq 1, \\ 0, p+q > 1. \end{cases} \tag{5.85}$$

Proposition 5.5.

Based on Definition 5.5 the degree to which a set is a subset of its complement is formulated as follows.

$$\pi(P \subseteq P^C) = p \rightarrow (1-p) = \begin{cases} \dfrac{1-p+1-p}{2}, p > 1-p, \\ 1, p \leq 1-p, \end{cases} = \begin{cases} 1-p, p > 0.5, \\ 1, p \leq 0.5. \end{cases}$$

Proposition 5.6.

The degree to which a set is disjointed from its complement is based on the Definition 5.6. From expressions (5.84), (5,85) we make an observation: $\pi(Pdisj_1 P^C) \equiv 1$ whereas $\pi(Pdisj_2 P^C) \equiv 0$.

In this section, we discuss some properties of the proposed fuzzy implication operator (5.68), assuming that the two propositions (*antecedent/consequent*) in a given compound proposition are independent of each other and the truth values of the propositions are uniformly distributed in the unit interval. In other words, we assume that the propositions P and Q are independent from each other and the truth values $v(P)$ and $v(Q)$ are uniformly distributed across the interval [0, 1]. Let $p = v(P)$ and $q = v(Q)$. Then the value of the implication $I = v(p \rightarrow q)$ could be represented as the function $I = I(p,q)$.

Because p and q are assumed to be uniformly and independently distributed across [0, 1], the expected value of the implication is

$$E(I) = \iint_{\Re} I(p,q) dp dq. \tag{5.86}$$

Its variance is equal to

$$Var(I) = E[(I - E(I))^2] =$$
$$= \iint_{\Re} (I(p,q) - E(I))^2 \, dpdq = E[I^2] - E[I]^2, \tag{5.87}$$

where $\Re = \{(p,q) : 0 \leq p \leq 1, 0 \leq q \leq 1\}$. From (5.86) and given (5.68) as well as the fact that

$$I(p,q) = \begin{cases} I_1(p,q), p > q, \\ I_2(p,q), p \leq q \end{cases} \quad \text{we have the following}$$

$$E(I_1) = \iint_{\Re} I_1(p,q) dpdq = \int_0^1 \int_0^1 \frac{1-p+q}{2} dpdq = \frac{1}{2} \int_0^1 (\int_0^1 (1-p+q) dp) dq =.$$

$$= \frac{1}{2} \int_0^1 ((p - \frac{p^2}{2} + q) \big|_{p=0}^{p=1}) dq] = \frac{1}{2} [\frac{1}{2} + \frac{q^2}{2} \big|_{q=0}^{q=1}] = \frac{1}{2}. \tag{5.88}$$

As $E(I_2) = 1$, therefore $E(I) = (E(I_1) + E(I_2))/2 = 0.75$.

From (5.87) we have

$$I_1^2 (p,q) = \frac{1}{4}(1-p+q)^2 = \frac{1}{4}(1 - 2p + 2q + p^2 - 2pq + q^2).$$

$$E (I_1^2) = \iint_{\Re} I_1^2(p,q) dpdq = \frac{1}{4} \int_0^1 (\int_0^1 (1 - 2p + 2q + p^2 - 2pq + q^2) dp) dq$$

$$dq = \frac{1}{4} \int_0^1 [p - 2\frac{p^2}{2} + \frac{p^3}{3} - 2\frac{p^2}{2} q + 2q + q^2] \big|_{p=0}^{p=1} dq =$$

$$= \frac{1}{4} \int_0^1 (\frac{1}{3} + q + q^2) dq = \frac{1}{4} [\frac{q}{3} + \frac{q^2}{2} + \frac{q^3}{3}] \big|_{q=0}^{q=1} = \frac{7}{24}.$$

Here $E(I_2^2) = 1$. Therefore $E(I^2) = (E(I_1^2) + E(I_2^2))/2 = \dfrac{31}{48}$. From

(5.87) and (5.88) we have $Var(I) = \dfrac{1}{12} = 0.0833$.

Both values of $E(I)$ and $Var(I)$ demonstrate that the proposed fuzzy implication operator could be considered as one of the fuzziest from the list of the exiting implications [15]. In addition, it satisfies the set of important Criteria I-IV, which is not the case for the most implication operators mentioned above. These criteria are given below.

Criterion I

       Ant 1: If x is P then y is Q

       Ant2: x is P

       Cons: y is Q.

Criterion II-1

       Ant 1: If x is P then y is Q

       Ant2: x is *very P*

       Cons: y is *very Q*.

Criterion II-2

       Ant 1: If x is P then y is Q

       Ant2: x is *very P*

       Cons: y is Q.

Criterion III

       Ant 1: If x is P then y is Q

       Ant2: x is *more or less P*

       Cons: y is *more or less Q*.

Criterion IV-1

Ant 1: If x is P then y is Q

Ant2: x is *not P*

Cons: y is *unknown.*

Criterion IV-2

Ant 1: If x is P then y is Q

Ant2: x is *not P*

Cons: y is *not Q.*

As it was mentioned in [290] "…in the semantics of natural language there exist a vast array of concepts and humans very often make inferences antecedents and consequences of which contain fuzzy concepts …". A formalization of methods for such inferences is one of the most important issues in fuzzy sets theory, in particular Artificial Intelligence, in general. For this purpose, let U and V (from now on) be two *universes of discourses* and corresponding fuzzy sets P and Q are the same as in (5.49).

Given (5.49), a *binary relationship* for the fuzzy conditional proposition of the type: "*If x is P then y is Q*" for proposed fuzzy logic is defined as

$$R(A_1(x), A_2(y)) = P \times V \to U \times Q =$$
$$= \int_{U \times V} \mu_P(u) / (u,v) \to \int_{U \times V} \mu_Q(v) / (u,v) =$$
$$= \int_{U \times V} (\mu_P(u) \to \mu_Q(v)) / (u,v). \qquad (5.90)$$

Given (5.68), expression (5.90) reads as

$$\mu_P(u) \to \mu_Q(v) = \begin{cases} \dfrac{1 - \mu_P(u) + \mu_Q(v)}{2}, \mu_P(u) > \mu_Q(v), \\ 1, \mu_P(u) \le \mu_Q(v). \end{cases} \qquad (5.91)$$

It is well known that given a *unary relationship* $R(A_1(x)) = P$ one can obtain the consequence $R(A_2(y))$ by applying a compositional rule of inference (CRI) to $R(A_1(x))$ and $R(A_1(x), A_2(y))$ of type (5.90):

$$R(A_2(y)) = P \circ R(A_1(x), A_2(y))$$
$$= \int_U \mu_P(u)/u \circ \int_{U \times V} \mu_P(u) \to \mu_Q(v)/(u,v)$$

$$= \int_V \bigcup_{u \in U} [\mu_P(u) \wedge (\mu_P(u) \to \mu_Q(v))]/v. \qquad (5.92)$$

In order to have Criterion I satisfied, that is $R(A_2(y)) = Q$ from (5.92), the equality

$$\bigcup_{u \in U} [\mu_P(u) \wedge (\mu_P(u) \to \mu_Q(v))] = \mu_Q(v) \qquad (5.93)$$

has to be satisfied for any arbitrary v in V To satisfy (5.93), it becomes necessary that the inequality

$$\mu_P(u) \wedge (\mu_P(u) \to \mu_Q(v)) \leq \mu_Q(v) \qquad (5.94)$$

holds for arbitrary $u \in U$ and $v \in V$. Let us define a new method of fuzzy conditional inference of the following type:

Ant 1: If x is P then y is Q
Ant2: x is P' (5.95)

Cons: y is Q',

where $P, P \subseteq U$ and $Q, Q \subseteq V$. Fuzzy conditional inference in the form given by (5.95) should satisfy Criteria I-IV.
It is clear that the inference (5.95) is defined by the expression (5.92), when $R(A_2(y)) = Q'$.

Theorem 5.4.

If fuzzy sets $P \subseteq U$ and $Q \subseteq V$ are defined by (5.90) and (5.91), respectively and $R(A_1(x), A_2(y))$ is expressed as

$$R(A_1(x), A_2(y)) = P \times V \xrightarrow{L4} U \times Q$$

$$= \int_{U \times V} \mu_P(u)/(u,v) \xrightarrow{L4} \int_{U \times V} \mu_Q(v)/(u,v)$$

$$= \int_{U \times V} (\mu_P(u) \xrightarrow{L4} \mu_Q(v))/(u,v) \text{, where}$$

$$\mu_P(u) \xrightarrow{L4} \mu_Q(v) = \begin{cases} \dfrac{1 - \mu_P(u) + \mu_Q(v)}{2}, \mu_P(u) > \mu_Q(v), \\ 1, \mu_P(u) \le \mu_Q(v). \end{cases} \qquad (5.96)$$

then Criteria I, II, III and IV-1 [290] are satisfied.

Proof:

For Criteria I-III let $R(A_1(x)) = P^\alpha (\alpha > 0)$ then

$$R(A_2(y)) = P^\alpha \circ R(A_1(x), A_2(y))$$

$$= \int_U \mu_P^\alpha(u)/u \circ \int_{U \times V} \mu_p(u) \xrightarrow{L4} \mu_Q(v)/(u,v)$$

$$= \int_V \bigcup_{u \in U} [\mu_P^\alpha(u) \wedge (\mu_P(u) \xrightarrow{L4} \mu_Q(v))]/v. \qquad (5.97)$$

$$\exists U_1, U_2 \subset U | U_1 \cup U_2 = U; | U_1 \cap U_2 = \varnothing \Rightarrow$$

$$\forall u \in U_1 | \mu_P(u) > \mu_Q(v) ; \forall u \in U_2 | \mu_P(u) \le \mu_Q(v). \qquad (5.98)$$

From (5.97) and given subsets from (5.98), we have

$$R(A_2(y)) = \left[\int_V \bigcup_{u \in U_1} [\mu_P^\alpha(u) \wedge (\frac{1 - \mu_P(u) + \mu_Q(v)}{2})] / v \right] \vee$$

$$\vee \left[\int_V \bigcup_{u \in U_2} [\mu_P^\alpha(u) \wedge 1] / v \right] \tag{5.99}$$

Let us introduce the following function

$$f(u,v) = \frac{1 - \mu_P(u) + \mu_Q(v)}{2}. \tag{5.100}$$

Then the following relationship is satisfied:

$$\forall u \in U_1 \left| \mu_P^\alpha(u) \wedge f(u,v) = \begin{cases} \mu_P^\alpha(u), \mu_P^\alpha(u) \le f(u,v), \\ f(u,v), \mu_P^\alpha(u) > f(u,v), \end{cases} \right. \tag{5.101}$$

$$\forall u \in U_2 \left| \mu_P^\alpha(u) \wedge 1 = \mu_P^\alpha(u), \right. \tag{5.102}$$

From (5.101) and (5.102) we have

$$(5.99) = \left[\int_V \bigcup_{u \in U_2} \mu_P^\alpha(u) / v \right] = \int_V \mu_Q^\alpha(v) / v = Q^\alpha . \text{ (Q.E.D.)}.$$

For Criteria IV-2 [290] let $R(A_1(x)) = \neg P = 1 - P$ then

$$R(A_2(y)) = \neg P \circ R(A_1(x), A_2(y))$$

$$= \int_U (1 - \mu_P(u)) / u \circ \int_{U \times V} \mu_P(u) \xrightarrow[L4]{} \mu_Q(v) / (u,v)$$

$$= \int_V \bigcup_{u \in U} [(1 - \mu_P(u)) \wedge (\mu_P(u) \xrightarrow[L4]{} \mu_Q(v))] / v. \tag{5.103}$$

From (5.103) and given subsets (5.98) we have

$R(A_2(y)) =$

$$\left[\int_V \bigcup_{u \in U_1} [(1 - \mu_P(u)) \wedge (\frac{1 - \mu_P(u) + \mu_Q(v)}{2})] / v \right] \vee \left[\int_V \bigcup_{u \in U_2} [(1 - \mu_P(u)) \wedge 1] / v \right]$$

$$= \left[\int_V \bigcup_{u \in U_1} [(1 - \mu_P(u)) \wedge f(u,v)] / v \right] \vee \left[\int_V \bigcup_{u \in U_2} [(1 - \mu_P(u)) \wedge 1] / v \right] \quad (5.104)$$

Apparently the following holds

$$\left[(1 - \mu_P(u)) \wedge f(u,v) \right] \leq \left[(1 - \mu_P(u)) \wedge 1] \right], \text{ therefore}$$

$$(5.104) = \left[\int_V \bigcup_{u \in U_2} [(1 - \mu_P(u)) \wedge 1] / v \right] = \left[\int_V 1 / v \right] = unknown . \text{ (Q.E.D.)}$$

Theorem 5.5.
If fuzzy sets $P \subseteq U$ and $Q \subseteq V$ are defined by (5.90) and (5.91), respectively, and $R(A_1(x), A_2(y))$ is defined as

$$R(A_1(x), A_2(y)) = (P \times V \underset{L4}{\to} U \times Q) \cap (\neg P \times V \underset{L4}{\to} U \times \neg Q)$$

$$= \int_{U \times V} (\mu_P(u) \underset{L4}{\to} \mu_Q(v)) \wedge ((1 - \mu_P(u)) \underset{L4}{\to} (1 - \mu_Q(v))) / (u,v) . \quad (5.105)$$

where

$$(\mu_P(u) \underset{L4}{\to} \mu_Q(v)) \wedge ((1 - \mu_P(u)) \underset{L4}{\to} (1 - \mu_Q(v)))$$

$$= \begin{cases} \dfrac{1 - \mu_P(u) + \mu_Q(v)}{2}, \mu_P(u) > \mu_Q(v), \\ 1, \mu_P(u) = \mu_Q(v), \\ \dfrac{1 - \mu_Q(v) + \mu_P(u)}{2}, \mu_P(u) < \mu_Q(v). \end{cases}$$

Then Criteria I, II, III and IV-2 [290] are satisfied.

Proof:

$$\exists U_1, U_2, U_3 \subset U \,|\, U_1 \cup U_2 \cup U_3 = U; |U_1 \cap U_2 \cap U_3 = \varnothing \Rightarrow$$

$$\forall u \in U_1 |\mu_P(u) > \mu_Q(v) \,;\, \forall u \in U_2 |\mu_P(u) = \mu_Q(v), \forall u \in U_3 |\mu_P(u) < \mu_Q(v) \,. \quad (5.106)$$

Let us introduce the following functions

$$h_1(u,v) = \frac{1 - \mu_P(u) + \mu_Q(v)}{2}, h_2(u,v) = \frac{1 - \mu_Q(v) + \mu_P(u)}{2}. \quad (5.107)$$

Therefore from (5.105)–(5.107) for Criteria I-III let
$R(A_1(x)) = P^{\alpha} \,(\alpha > 0)$ then

$$R(A_2(y)) = P^{\alpha} \circ R(A_1(x), A_2(y))$$

$$= \int_U \mu_P^{\alpha}(u) / u \circ \int_{U \times V} (\mu_P(u) \underset{L4}{\to} \mu_Q(v)) \wedge ((1 - \mu_P(u)) \underset{L4}{\to} (1 - \mu_Q(v))) / (u,v)$$

$$= \int_V \bigcup_{u \in U} [\mu_P^{\alpha}(u) \wedge (\mu_P(u) \underset{L4}{\to} \mu_Q(v)) \wedge ((1 - \mu_P(u)) \underset{L4}{\to} (1 - \mu_Q(v)))] / v. \quad (5.108)$$

From (5.107), (5.108) and given subsets by (5.106) we have

$$R(A_2(y)) = \left[\int_V \bigcup_{u \in U_1} [\mu_P^{\alpha}(u) \wedge h_1(u,v)] / v \right] \vee \left[\int_V \bigcup_{u \in U_2} [\mu_P^u(u) \wedge 1] / v \right]$$

$$\vee \left[\int_V \bigcup_{u \in U_3} [\mu_P^{\alpha}(u) \wedge h_2(u,v)] / v \right] \quad (5.109)$$

Then the following is satisfied

$$\forall u \in U_1 \left| \mu^\alpha{}_P(u) \wedge h_1(u,v) = \begin{cases} \mu^\alpha{}_P(u), \mu^\alpha{}_P(u) \leq h_1(u,v), \\ h_1(u,v), \mu^\alpha{}_P(u) > h_1(u,v), \end{cases} \right. \tag{5.110}$$

$$\forall u \in U_2 \left| \mu^\alpha{}_P(u) \wedge 1 = \mu^\alpha{}_P(u), \right. \tag{5.111}$$

$$\forall u \in U_3 \left| \mu^\alpha{}_P(u) \wedge h_2(u,v) = \begin{cases} \mu^\alpha{}_P(u), \mu^\alpha{}_P(u) \leq h_2(u,v), \\ h_2(u,v), \mu^\alpha{}_P(u) > h_2(u,v), \end{cases} \right. \tag{5.112}$$

From (5.110) - (5.112) we have

$$(5.108) = \left[\int_V \bigcup_{u \in U_2} \mu_P^\alpha(u)/v \right] = \int_V \mu_Q^\alpha(v)/v = Q^\alpha . \quad \text{(Q.E.D.)}.$$

For Criteria IV-2 let $R(A_1(x)) = \neg P = 1 - P$ then

$$R(A_2(y)) = \neg P \circ R(A_1(x), A_2(y))$$

$$= \int_U (1 - \mu_P(u))/u \circ \int_{U \times V} (\mu_P(u) \underset{L4}{\rightarrow} \mu_Q(v)) \wedge ((1 - \mu_P(u)) \underset{L4}{\rightarrow} (1 - \mu_Q(v)))/(u,v)$$

$$= \int_V \bigcup_{u \in U} [(\mu_P(u) \underset{L4}{\rightarrow} \mu_Q(v)) \wedge ((1 - \mu_P(u)) \underset{L4}{\rightarrow} (1 - \mu_Q(v)))]/v. \tag{5.113}$$

From (5.109), (5.113) and given subsets from (5.106) we have

$$R(A_2(y)) =$$

$$\left[\int_V \bigcup_{u \in U_1} [(1 - \mu_P(u)) \wedge h_1(u,v))]/v \right] \vee \left[\int_V \bigcup_{u \in U_2} [(1 - \mu_P(u)) \wedge 1]/v \right] \vee .$$

$$\vee\left[\int_V \bigcup_{u\in U_3}[(1-\mu_P(u))\wedge h_2(u,v))]/v\right] \tag{5.114}$$

As a conclusion we have

$$\left[(1-\mu_P(u))\wedge h_1(u,v)\right]\leq\left[(1-\mu_P(u))\wedge 1]\right] \text{ and}$$

$$\left[(1-\mu_P(u))\wedge h_2(u,v)\right]\leq\left[(1-\mu_P(u))\wedge 1]\right], \text{ therefore}$$

$$(5.114)=\left[\int_V \bigcup_{u\in U_2}[(1-\mu_P(u))\wedge 1]/v\right]=\left[\int_V (1-\mu_Q(u))/v\right]=\neg Q. \text{ (Q.E.D.)}$$

Theorems 5.4 and 5.5 show that fuzzy conditional inference rules, defined in (5.105) could adhere with human intuition to the higher extent as the one defined by (5.96). The major difference between mentioned methods of inference might be explained by the difference between *Criteria IV-1* and *IV-2*. In particular, a satisfaction the *Criterion IV-1* means that in case of logical negation of an original antecedent we achieve an ambiguous result of an inference, whereas for the case of the *Criterion IV-2* there is a certainty in a logical inference.

Now we revisit the fuzzy conditional inference rule (5.95). It will be shown that when the membership function of the observation P is continuous, then the conclusion Q depends continuously on the observation; and when the membership function of the relation R is continuous then the observation Q has a continuous membership function.

Let A be a fuzzy number, then for any $\theta \geq 0$ we define $\omega_A(\theta)$, the modulus of continuity of A by

$$\omega_A(\theta) = \max_{|x_1-x_2|\leq\theta} |\mu_A(x_1)-\mu_A(x_2)|. \tag{5.115}$$

An α-level set of a fuzzy interval A is a non-fuzzy set denoted by $[A]^\alpha$ and is defined by $[A]^\alpha = \{t\in\Re\,|\,\mu_A(t)\geq\alpha\}$ for $\alpha\in(0,1]$ and

$[A]^\alpha = cl(\text{supp}\,\mu_A)$ for $\alpha = 0$. Here we use a metric of the following type

$$D(A,B) = \sup_{\alpha\in[0,1]} d([A]^\alpha,[B]^\alpha), \qquad (5.116)$$

where d denotes the classical Hausdorff metric expressed in the family of compact subsets of $\Re^2$, i.e.

$$d([A]^\alpha,[B]^\alpha) = \max\{|a_1(\alpha)-b_1(\alpha)|,|a_2(\alpha)-b_2(\alpha)|\},$$

where as $[A]^\alpha = [a_1(\alpha),a_2(\alpha)],[B]^\alpha = [b_1(\alpha),b_2(\alpha)|]$. when the fuzzy sets A and B have finite support $\{x_1,...,x_n\}$, then their Hamming distance is defined as

$$H(A,B) = \sum_{i=1}^{n} |\mu_A(x_i)-\mu_B(x_i)|.$$

In the sequel we will use the following lemma.

Lemma 5.1 [123] Let $\delta \geq 0$ be a real number and let A, B be fuzzy intervals. If
$D(A,B) \leq \delta$, Then

$$\sup_{t\in\Re}|\mu_A(t)-\mu_B(t)| \leq \max\{\omega_A(\delta),\omega_B(\delta)\}.$$

Consider the fuzzy conditional inference rule with different observations P and P':

Ant 1: If x is P then y is Q	Ant 1: If x is P then y is Q
Ant2: x is P	Ant2: x is P'
Cons: y is Q	Cons: y is Q'

According to the fuzzy conditional inference rule, the membership functions of the conclusions are computed as

$$\mu_Q(v) = \bigcup_{u \in \Re} [\mu_P(u) \wedge (\mu_P(u) \to \mu_Q(v))],$$

$$\mu_{Q'}(v) = \bigcup_{u \in \Re} [\mu_{P'}(u) \wedge (\mu_P(u) \to \mu_Q(v))]$$

or

$$\mu_Q(v) = \sup_{u \in \Re} [\mu_P(u) \wedge (\mu_P(u) \to \mu_Q(v))],$$

$$\mu_{Q'}(v) = \sup_{u \in \Re} [\mu_{P'}(u) \wedge (\mu_P(u) \to \mu_Q(v))] \qquad (5.117)$$

of the conclusions.

Theorem 5.6. (*Stability* theorem) Let $\delta \geq 0$ and let P, P' be fuzzy intervals and an implication operation in the fuzzy The following theorem shows the fact that when the observations are closed to each other in the metric $D(.)$ of (5.116) type, then there can be only a small deviation in the membership functions conditional inference rule (5.117) is of type (5.91). If $D(P, P') \leq \delta$, then

$$\sup_{v \in \Re} |\mu_Q(v) - \mu_{Q'}(v)| \leq \max\{\omega_P(\delta), \omega_{P'}(\delta)\}$$

Proof: Given an implication operation in the fuzzy conditional inference rule (5.117) is of type (5.91), for the observation P we have

$$Q = P \circ R(A_1(x), A_2(y))$$
$$= \int_U \mu_P(u)/u \circ \int_{U \times V} \mu_P(u) \underset{L4}{\to} \mu_Q(v)/(u,v)$$

$$= \int_V \bigcup_{u \in U} [\mu_P(u) \wedge (\mu_P(u) \underset{L4}{\to} \mu_Q(v))]/v. \qquad (5.118)$$

It was shown above that for

$$U, V \subset \Re; \exists U_1, U_2 \subset U | U_1 \cup U_2 = U; | U_1 \cap U_2 = \varnothing \Rightarrow$$

$$\forall u \in U_1 \Big| \mu_P(u) > \mu_Q(v) \,;\, \forall u \in U_2 \Big| \mu_P(u) \le \mu_Q(v),$$

$$\forall u \in U_1 \Bigg| \mu_{p}(u) \wedge f(u,v) = \begin{cases} \mu_{p}(u), \mu_{p}(u) \le f(u,v), \\ f(u,v), \mu_{p}(u) > f(u,v), \end{cases}$$

$$\forall u \in U_2 \Big| \mu_{p}(u) \wedge 1 = \mu_{p}(u),$$

where $f(u,v)$ is from (5.100). Applying the observation P' to (5.118) we obtain the following

$$Q' = P' \circ R(A_1(x), A_2(y)) = \int_U \mu_{P'}(u)/u \circ \int_{U \times V} \mu_P(u) \underset{L4}{\rightarrow} \mu_Q(v)/(u,v)$$

$$= \int_V \bigcup_{u \in U} [\mu_{P'}(u) \wedge (\mu_P(u) \underset{L4}{\rightarrow} \mu_Q(v))]/v. \qquad (5.119)$$

We also have

$$\forall u \in U_1 \Bigg| \mu_{p'}(u) \wedge f(u,v) = \begin{cases} \mu_{p'}(u), \mu_{p'}(u) \le f(u,v), \\ f(u,v), \mu_{p'}(u) > f(u,v), \end{cases}$$

$$\forall u \in U_2 \Big| \mu_{p'}(u) \wedge 1 = \mu_{p'}(u).$$

From (5.118) and (5.119), we see that the difference of the values of conclusions for both P and P' observations for arbitrary fixed $v \in \Re$ $|\mu_Q(v) - \mu_{Q'}(v)|$ is defined as follows

$$\forall u \in U_1 \Bigg| \mu_Q(v) - \mu_{Q'}(v)| = \begin{cases} |\mu_p(u) - \mu_{p'}(u)|, \\ 0, \end{cases}$$

$$\forall u \in U_2 \left\| \mu_{.Q}(v) - \mu_{Q'}(v) \right| = |\mu_P(u) - \mu_{P'}(u)|,$$

and therefore from Lemma 5.1 we have

$$\sup_{v \in \Re} |\mu_Q(v) - \mu_{Q'}(v)| = \sup_{u \in \Re} |\mu_P(u) - \mu_{P'}(u)| \le \max\{\omega_P(\delta), \omega_{P'}(\delta)\}$$

(Q.E.D.)

Theorem 5.7. (*Continuity* theorem) Let *binary relationship* $R(u,v) = \mu_P(u) \underset{L4}{\to} \mu_Q(v)$ be continuous. Then Q is continuous and $\omega_Q(\delta) \le \omega_R(\delta)$ for each $\delta \ge 0$.

Proof: Let $\delta \ge 0$ be a real number and let $v_1, v_2 \in \Re$ such that $|v_1 - v_2| \le \delta$. From (5.115) we have

$$\omega_Q(\delta) = \max_{|v_1 - v_2| \le \delta} |\mu_Q(v_1) - \mu_Q(v_2)|.$$

Then

$$\left| \mu_Q(v_1) - \mu_Q(v_2) \right|$$

$$= \left| \sup_{u \in \Re}[\mu_P(u) \wedge (\mu_P(u) \underset{L4}{\to} \mu_Q(v_1))] - \sup_{u \in \Re}[\mu_P(u) \wedge (\mu_P(u) \underset{L4}{\to} \mu_Q(v_2))] \right|$$

$$\le \sup_{u \in \Re}[\mu_P(u) \wedge \left| (\mu_P(u) \underset{L4}{\to} \mu_Q(v_1)) - (\mu_P(u) \underset{L4}{\to} \mu_Q(v_2)) \right|]$$

$$\le \sup_{u \in \Re}[\mu_P(u) \wedge \omega_R(|v_1 - v_2|)]$$

$$\le \sup_{u \in \Re}[\mu_P(u) \wedge \omega_R(\delta)] = \omega_R(\delta)$$

In this section, we proposed the fuzzy logic as an *algebraic system closed under all its operations* in which truth values of an implication operator need to be based on truth values of both the antecedent and the consequent. This implication operator has to be considered to be one of the fuzziest implication from a list of implication operators known so far.

It was shown that the fuzzy logic presented here forms a basis for fuzzy conditional inference rules, which satisfy the set of known important criteria and seem to be suitable for capturing human intuition. The important features of stability and continuity of the proposed fuzzy conditional inference rules were also investigated.

Chapter 6

Computation with Z-Numbers

6.1 Z-number, Z-information

Decisions are based on information. To be useful, information must be reliable. Basically, the concept of a Z-number relates to the issue of reliability of information. A Z-number, Z, has two components, $Z = (A, B)$ [821]. The first component, A, is a restriction (constraint) on the values which a real-valued uncertain variable, X, is allowed to take. The second component, B, is a measure of reliability (certainty) of the first component. Typically, A and B are described in a natural language. The concept of a Z-number has a potential for many applications, especially in the realms of economics, decision analysis, risk assessment, prediction, anticipation and rule-based characterization of imprecise functions and relations.

The concept of a restriction has greater generality than the concept of a constraint. A probability distribution is a restriction but is not a constraint [820]. A restriction may be viewed as a generalized constraint [829].

The concept of a Z-number is based on the concept of a fuzzy granule [829, 853, 857]. It should be noted that the concept of a Z-number is much more general than the concept of confidence interval in probability theory. There are some links between the concept of a Z-number, the concept of a fuzzy random number and the concept of a fuzzy random variable [137, 420, 421, 550]. An alternative interpretation of the concept of a Z-number may be based on the concept of a fuzzy-set-valued random variable — a concept which is discussed in [853].

6.2 The arithmetic with continuous Z-numbers

Unfortunately, up to day works devoted to arithmetic of continuous Z-numbers in existence are very scarce. An original formulation of operations over continuous Z-numbers proposed by Zadeh includes complex non-linear variational problems. In this section we consider on approach which has a better computational complexity and accuracy tradeoff. The proposed approach is based on linear programming and other simple optimization problems. We develop basic arithmetic operations such as addition, subtraction, multiplication and division, and some algebraic operations as maximum, minimum, square and square root of continuous Z-numbers.

6.2.1 *State-of-the-art*

In [821] the author suggests a general approach for computations over Z-numbers on the base of the Zadeh's extension principle. The approach is used to solve a problem of computation of a Z-number-valued function of Z-number-valued arguments.

Let us note that the Z-number concept is not the first attempt to model real-world uncertainty which is too complex to be captured by interval or fuzzy number-based representations. In fuzzy numbers, uncertainty is described by a numerical membership function. This means that they do not take into account inferred uncertainty interval. The first attempt to deal with such uncertainty intervals was made in the theory of type-2 fuzzy sets [159-161, 509]. However, in contrast to a type-2 fuzzy set, a Z-number explicitly represents reliability described in NL, and is a more structured formal construct. Hence, processing of Z-information requires to develop a new theory, new approaches and methodologies of computation with Z-numbers.

A general framework to computation with Z-numbers is suggested in [821]. In particular, implementation of arithmetic operations over two Z-numbers is expressed. However, practical realization of the suggested framework is computationally very complex, it includes several variational problems. As Zadeh claims, "Problems involving computation with Z-numbers is easy to state but far from easy to solve", and there is no detailed and effective methods in existence to develop arithmetic, algebraic and other operations of Z-numbers. The author also raises important issues of computations with Z-numbers including ranking of Z-numbers and calculus of IF-THEN rules with Z-number valued components. In general, paper [821] opens a door for a lot of potential investigations of computation with Z-numbers.

Let us overview the existing works devoted handling of Z-numbers and its practical applications.

In [410] they suggest an approach to dealing with Z-numbers which naturally arise in the areas of control, decision making, modeling and others. The approach is based on converting a Z-number to a fuzzy number on the base of an expectation of a fuzzy set. However, converting Z-numbers to fuzzy numbers [421, 438] leads to loss of original information reducing the benefit of using original Z-number-based information.

In [408] they considered an approach to multi-criteria decision making with Z-numbers on the base of the approach given in [410]. In the suggested framework, criteria weights and criteria values of alternatives are given as Z-numbers. However, the resulting overall performance evaluations of alternatives are computed as real numbers. This significant loss of information contained in Z-numbers is likely to lead to an inadequate multicriteria choice.

Papers [802, 803] are devoted to new approaches of processing Z-numbers in various important fields. It is suggested to deal with Z-number $Z = (A, B)$ in terms of a possibility distribution $G(p)$ of probability distributions p which underlie $Z = (A, B)$. Based on such representation, the author suggests manipulations over Z-numbers and their applications to reasoning, decision making and answering questions. Several detailed examples on computation with Z-information are provided to illustrate usefulness of the suggested approach. Another important potential impact of the suggested research is application to formalization of linguistic summaries. The author also suggests an alternative formulation of Z-information in terms of a Dempster-Shafer belief structure [682] which involves type-2 fuzzy sets [514, 645, 865]. In the paper, it is also suggested to rank Z-numbers by proceeding to the corresponding fuzzy numbers. The resulting fuzzy numbers are then compared on the base of their defuzzified values. However, this comparison is based on reducing a Z-number to a numeric value which is naturally characterized by a sufficient loss of information.

The work [837] is devoted to computation over continuous Z-numbers and several important practical problems in control, decision making and other areas. The suggested investigation is based on the use of normal probability density functions for modeling random variables. A special emphasis in some of the examples is made on calculus of Z-numbers based IF-THEN rules. A series of illustrative examples is provided on problems with Z-information in economics, social sphere, engineering, everyday activity and other fields.

Paper [29] is the first work devoted to decision making under uncertainty when probabilities of states of nature and outcomes of alternatives are described by Z-numbers. The suggested decision analysis is based on two main stages. At the first stage, Z-numbers are reduced to fuzzy numbers on the base of the approach suggested in [410]. At the second stage, values of fuzzy utility function for alternatives are computed to choose the best one. The main disadvantage is related to the loss of information resulting from converting Z-numbers to fuzzy numbers.

Paper [92] is devoted to potential contributions of application of the Z-number concept to development of computing with words (CWW) methodology. The authors suggest an approach to CWW using Z-numbers and provide a real-life illustrating example.

In [575] they suggest an outline of the general principles, challenges and perspectives of CWW in light of the Z-number concept and consider issues of integration of CWW and Natural Language Processing technology.

The work [574] is also devoted to Z-numbers based approach to CWW. The authors suggest basis for a system of processing sentences in NL by using Bayes' approach and Shannon's entropy theorem.

In [431] they suggest an enhanced inference engine toolkit for implementation of CWW technologies in a general scope including combinations of fuzzy IF-THEN rules, fuzzy arithmetic and fuzzy probabilities. The authors mention that the suggested toolkit can be further developed to apply for computation with Z-numbers, without involvement into problems with high computational complexity.

In [79] they consider an application of the AHP approach under Z-information. The suggested procedure is based on the approach proposed in [410]. Despite that in the suggested procedure alternatives are described in the realm of Z-information, they are compared on the basis of numeric overall utilities. Unfortunately, this significantly reduces benefits of using Z-information.

In [479] decision making under interval, set-valued, fuzzy, and Z-number uncertainty are considered. The decision analysis technique suggested by the authors is based on the fair price approach.

In [708] they suggest several approaches of approximate evaluation of a Z-number in order to reduce computational complexity. One of the suggested approaches is based on approximation of a fuzzy set of probability densities by means of fuzzy IF-THEN rules.

In [16, 17, 44] a general and computationally effective approach to computation with discrete Z-numbers is suggested. The authors provide strong motivation of the use of discrete Z-numbers as an alternative to the continuous counterparts. In particular, the motivation is based on the fact that NL-based information has a discrete framework. From the other side, in a discrete framework it is not required to decide upon a reasonable assumption to use some type of probability distributions. The suggested arithmetic of discrete Z-numbers includes basic arithmetic operations and important algebraic operations. The proposed approach allows dealing with Z-numbers directly without conversion to fuzzy numbers.

Let us mention, that despite of wide applicability of computation of discrete Z-numbers, in a lot of real-world problems relevant information comes in a continuous framework which may require computing with continuous Z-numbers. We can conclude that today there is no general and computationally effective approach to computations with continuous Z-numbers. In the existing papers, information described by continuous Z-numbers is reduced to fuzzy numbers or crisp numbers that always leads to loss and distortion of information. However, processing of original Z-numbers-based information is very important for solving a large variety of real-world problems.

A new approach should be developed to introduce basic arithmetic, algebraic and other important operations for Z-numbers, which are worth to consider from theoretical and practical perspectives. This approach needs to be relatively easily applied for problems in realms control, decision analysis, optimization, forecasting and other areas. Computation with Z-numbers is characterized by propagation of combinations of possibilistic-probabilistic restrictions, that is, involves restriction-based computation.

Nowadays, existing literature devoted to computation and reasoning with restrictions includes well-developed approaches and theories to deal with pure probabilistic or pure possibilistic restrictions.

For computation with probabilistic restrictions as probability distributions the well-known probabilistic arithmetic is used [572, 580, 782, 783]. Fuzzy arithmetic [421, 438] deals with possibilistic constraints, which describe objects as classes with "unsharp" boundaries.

6.2.2 *General procedure of computation with Z-numbers*

6.2.2.1. *A general approach suggested by L. Zadeh*

Let us shortly express the general framework of computation with Z-numbers suggested by Zadeh [821].

Let $Z_1 = (A_1, B_1)$ and $Z_2 = (A_2, B_2)$ be continuous Z-numbers describing values of random variables X_1 and X_2. Assume that it is needed to compute $Z_{12} = Z_1 * Z_2$, $* \in \{+, -, \cdot, /\}$. This computation starts with a computation over the corresponding continuous Z^+-numbers

$$Z_1^+ = (A_1, R_1) \text{ and } Z_2^+ = (A_2, R_2):$$

$$Z_{12}^+ = Z_1^+ * Z_2^+ = (A_1 * A_2, R_1 * R_2).$$

where R_1 and R_2 are pdfs p_{R_1} and p_{R_2}. For simplicity, consider the case when $*$ is a sum and suppose that X_1 and X_2 are independent. As the operands in $A_1 * A_2$ and in $R_1 * R_2$ are represented by different types of restrictions, the meanings of $*$ are also different [821]. Therefore, $A_1 + A_2$ and $R_1 + R_2$ are defined as

$$\mu_{A_1 + A_2}(x) = \sup_{x_1}(\min\{\mu_{A_1}(x_1), \mu_{A_2}(x - x_1)\})$$

$$p_{12}(x) = \int_{\mathcal{R}} p_1(x_1) p_2(x - x_1) dx_1.$$

Thus, $Z_{12}^+ = (A_{12}, p_{12})$ is obtained. Next we realize that 'true' pdfs p_1 and p_2 are not known but the following fuzzy restrictions are given [821]:

$$\int_{\mathcal{R}} \mu_{A_j}(x_j) p_j(x_j) dx_j \text{ is } B_j, j = 1, 2,$$

which are represented in terms of membership functions as [821]

$$\mu_{p_{R_1}}(p_{R_1}) = \mu_{B_j}\left(\int_{\mathcal{R}} \mu_{A_j}(x_j) p_j(x_j) dx_j\right), j = 1, 2.$$

Thus, an available information about p_{12} will also be represented by a fuzzy restriction construction of which is formulated as

$$\mu_{p_{12}}(p_{12}) = \sup_{p_{R_1}, p_{R_2}} \left(\min\{\mu_{p_{R_1}}(p_{R_1}), \mu_{p_{R_2}}(p_{R_2})\}\right), \tag{6.1}$$

subject to

$$p_{R_1 + R_2}(x) = \int_{\mathcal{R}} p_{R_1}(x_1) p_{R_2}(x - x_1) dx, \tag{6.2}$$

$$\mu_{p_j}(p_{Rj}) = \mu_{B_j}\left(\int_{\mathcal{R}} \mu_{A_j}(x_j) p_j(x_j) dx_j\right), j = 1, 2, \tag{6.3}$$

$$\int_{\mathcal{R}} p_{R_j}(x_j) dx_j = 1, j = 1, 2 \tag{6.4}$$

(compatibility conditions):

$$\int_{\mathcal{R}} x_j p_j(x_j) dx_j = \frac{\int_{\mathcal{R}} x_j \mu_{A_j}(x_j) dx_j}{\int_{\mathcal{R}} \mu_{A_j}(x_j) dx_j}, \quad j = 1, 2. \tag{6.5}$$

Once $\mu_{p_{R_1 + R_2}}$ is constructed, we proceed to determination of B_{12}. This problem is formulated as follows:

$$\mu_{B_{12}}(b_{12}) = \sup(\mu_{p_{R_1 + R_2}}(p_{R_1 + R_2})) \tag{6.6}$$

subject to

$$b_{12} = \int_R p_{R_1 + R_2}(x) \mu_{A_{12}}(x) dx \tag{6.7}$$

Thus, $Z_{12} = (A_{12}, B_{12})$ is computed.

6.2.2.2 *The suggested approach*

We suggest an approach to computation with continuous Z-numbers according to basic two-place arithmetic and algebraic operations $+, -, \cdot, /, \min, \max$ and one-place algebraic operations as a square and a square root of continuous Z-numbers.

Let $Z_1 = (A_1, B_1)$ and $Z_2 = (A_2, B_2)$ be continuous Z-numbers describing values of two random variables X_1 and X_2. Assume that it is needed to compute the result of a two-place operation $* \in \{+, -, \cdot, /, \min, \max\} : Z_{12} = Z_1 * Z_2$. The cases of computation of one place operations $Z = Z_1^2$ and $Z = \sqrt{Z_1}$ are treated analogously.

The computation with continuous Z-numbers starts with computation of continuous Z^+-number $Z_{12}^+ = (A_{12}, R_{12})$ as a result of operation $Z_1^+ * Z_2^+$ over continuous Z^+-numbers $Z_1^+ = (A_1, R_1)$ and $Z_2^+ = (A_2, R_2)$:

$$Z_1^+ * Z_2^+ = (A_1 * A_2, R_1 * R_2).$$

Therefore, at the *first step* it is needed to compute $A_{12} = A_1 * A_2$ by using methods given in Chapter 5 (depending on the considered operation). For example, when * is sum, A_{12} is a sum of continuous fuzzy numbers [421, 438].

At the *second step*, $R_{12} = R_1 * R_2$ is computed (or approximated) as a convolution $p_{12} = p_1 \circ p_2$ of continuous pdfs defined in accordance with definitions and equations in Chapter 4. For example, when * is the sum, p_{12} is defined based on Equation (4.12).

At the *third step* it is needed to compute discretized μ_{p_j}. Construction of continuous μ_{p_j} requires solving a complex variational problem. Discretization of μ_{p_j} leads to reducing of computational complexity. It allows to achieve a required tradeoff between accuracy and computational efficiency. We recall that 'true' pdfs p_1 and p_2 are unknown, and we have to consider all the pdfs p_1 and p_2 satisfying the available restrictions:

$$\sum_{i=1}^{n_j} \mu_{A_j}(x_{ji}) p_j(x_{ji}) \text{ is } B_j,$$

described by a membership function as

$$\mu_{p_j}(p_j) = \mu_{B_j}\left(\sum_{i=1}^{n_j} \mu_{A_j}(x_{ji}) p_j(x_{ji})\right), j = 1, 2. \tag{6.8}$$

Thus, a fuzzy number $B_j, j = 1, 2$ plays the role of a soft constraint on a value of a probability measure of A_j. In other words, an element $b_j \in B_j, j = 1, 2$ is induced by some probability distribution p_j. We will use discretized version of $B_j, j = 1, 2$, i.e. the latter will be described as discrete fuzzy sets. This is more practical as we will deal with finite number of probability distributions underlying $B_j, j = 1, 2$. In general, two approaches exist for discretization of fuzzy numbers [351]. The first approach is to divide support of a considered fuzzy number into subintervals, particularly into subintervals of the same length. The second approach is to divide membership axis μ_{B_j} into subintervals. More detailed discussion of these two approaches is given in [351]. Both two approaches can be used to discretize $B_j, j = 1, 2$. We will use the first approach. We will split up $\text{supp}(B_j)$ into discrete elements $b_{jl}, l = 1, ..., m$ such that the spacing is the constant interval $\Delta b_j = b_{jl+1} - b_{jl}$, $l = 1, ..., m - 1$. For example, consider $B_j = (0.6, 0.7, 0.8)$. Let us discretize the support of this fuzzy number into $m = 9$ points as follows: $b_{j1} = 0.6, b_{j2} = 0.625, ..., b_{j9} = 0.8$. Therefore, the following discretized fuzzy number will be obtained:

$$B = 0/0.6 + 0.25/0.625 + 0.5/0.65 + 0.75/0.675 + 1/0.7$$
$$+ 0.75/0.725 + 0.5/0.75 + 0.25/0.775 + 0/0.8.$$

Any $b_l, l = 1, ..., 9$ is induced by some probability distribution p_{jl} as

$$b_{jl} = \sum_{i=1}^{n_j} \mu_{A_j}(x_{ji}) p_{jl}(x_{ji}).$$

In this case basic values $b_{jl} \in \text{supp}(B_j); j = 1, 2; l = 1, ..., m$ of a fuzzy number $B_j, j = 1, 2$ are values of a probability measure of $A_j, b_{jl} = P(A_j)$ Thus, given b_{jl}, we have to find such pdf p_{jl} which satisfies:

$b_{jl} = (\mu_{A_j}(x_{j1}) p_{jl}(x_{j1}) + \mu_{A_j}(x_{j2}) p_{jl}(x_{j2}) + ... + \mu_{A_j}(x_{jn_j}) p_{jl}(x_{jn_j}))$. At the same time we know that p_{jl} has to satisfy:

$$\sum_{i=1}^{n_j} p_{jl}(x_{ji}) = 1, p_{jl}(x_{ji}) \geq 0,$$

$$\sum_{i=1}^{n_j} p_{jl}(x_{ji})x_{ji} = \frac{\sum_{i=1}^{n_j} \mu_{A_j}(x_{ji})x_{ji}}{\sum_{i=1}^{n_j} \mu_{A_j}(x_{ji})} \text{ (compatibility conditions).}$$

Therefore, the following goal programming problem should be solved to find p_j:

$$\mu_{A_j}(x_{j,1})p_{jl}(x_{j,1}) + \mu_{A_j}(x_{j,2})p_{jl}(x_{j,2}) + ... + \\ + \mu_{A_j}(x_{j,n_j})p_{jl}(x_{j,n_j}) \to b_{jl} \tag{6.9}$$

subject to

$$\left.\begin{array}{l} p_{jl}(x_{j,1}) + p_{jl}(x_{j,2}) + ... + p_{jl}(x_{j,n_j}) = 1 \\ p_{jl}(x_{j,1}), p_{jl}(x_{j,2}), ..., p_{jl}(x_{j,n_j}) \ge 0 \end{array}\right\}. \tag{6.10}$$

$$\sum_{i=1}^{n_j} p_{jl}(x_{j,i})x_{j,i} = \frac{\sum_{i=1}^{n_j} \mu_{A_j}(x_{j,i})x_{j,i}}{\sum_{i=1}^{n_j} \mu_{A_j}(x_{j,i})} \tag{6.11}$$

(compatibility conditions).

Let us now use new notations. At first, we fix $j \in \{1,2\}$, choose points $x_{j,i}$ and denote $c_{j,i} = \mu_{A_j}(x_{j,i})$ for $i=1,..,n_j$. Second, we choose m and

fix an index $l \in \{1,...,m\}$. Third, we compute $\gamma_j = \sum_{i=1}^{n_j} c_{j,i}$,

$\beta_j = \dfrac{1}{\gamma_j}\sum_{i=1}^{n_j} c_{j,i}x_{j,i}$ and solve the linear goal programming problem with n_j

variables $v_1, v_2, ..., v_{n_j}$:

$$c_{j,1}v_1 + c_{j,2}v_2 + ... + c_{j,n_j}v_{n_j} \to b_{j,l} \tag{6.12}$$

subject to

$$\left.\begin{array}{l} v_1 + v_2 + ... + v_{n_j} = 1 \\ v_1, v_2, ..., v_n \geq 0 \end{array}\right\} \tag{6.13}$$

$$x_{j,1}v_1 + x_{j,2}v_2 + ... + x_{j,n_j}v_{n_j} = \beta_j. \tag{6.14}$$

Having obtained the solution vector $v_i, i=1,2,...,n_j$ the values of the probabilities $p_{j,l}(x_{j,l})$, for the fixed indices j and l, are given by the found values v_i. Thus, each pdf $p_{j,l}(x_{j,l})$ is approximated at the same points $x_{j,l}, i=1,2,...,n_j$ for all l. Next, as $p_{j,l}$ is obtained given $b_{j,l}$, the membership degree of $p_{j,l}$ in the fuzzy set of distributions is

$$\mu_{P_j}(p_{j,l}) = \mu_{B_j}(b_{j,l}), \quad j=1,2, \text{ that is } \mu_{P_j}(p_j) = \mu_{B_j}\left(\sum_{i=1}^{n_j} \mu_{A_j}(x_{j,i})p_{j,l}(x_{j,i})\right). \ .$$

Thus, to construct a fuzzy set of pdfs p_j, it is needed to solve m simple goal linear programming problems (6.12)-(6.14), which is easier to be solved than the original formulation (6.3)-(6.5). Let us mention that discretized $p_{j,l}$ can be further approximated by continuous pdfs of the type assumed for the considered real-world problem (e.g. normal pdf).

At the *fourth step* we compute discretized $\mu_{P_{12}}$. The fuzzy sets of pdfs $p_{1l_1}, l_1 = 1,...,m$ and $p_{2l_2}, l_2 = 1,...,m$ induce the fuzzy set of convolutions p_{12s} with the membership function defined as

$$\mu_{P_{12}}(p_{12s}) = \max_{p_{1l_1}, p_{2l_2}} [\mu_{P_1}(p_{1l_1}) \wedge \mu_{P_2}(p_{2l_2})] \tag{6.15}$$

$$\text{subject to } p_{12s} = p_{1l_1} \circ p_{2l_2}, \tag{6.16}$$

where $\wedge$ is *min* operation. Depending on operation convolution (6.16) is determined by using (4.12-4.16). Let us mention that the number of pdfs p_j is equal to the number of points of discretized B_j, m. Thus, to construct all the convolutions p_{12s}, one will consider m^2 possible combinations of p_1 and p_2. Therefore, the number of convolutions p_{12s} is in general equal to $m^2 : p_{12s}$, $s = 1, ..., m^2$. It is natural that the value of m is chosen on the basis of computational efficiency and accuracy tradeoff. For example, if $m=10$ then one will have to solve 20 problems (6.12)-(6.13) (10 problems for each B_j) to find distributions p_j and then construct $10^2=100$ convolutions. If $m = 20$ then one will have to solve 40 problems (6.12)-(6.13) and construct $20^2=400$ convolutions, i.e. if m increases λ times, m^2 increases λ^2 times.

At the *fifth step* we need to compute approximated $\mu_{B_{12}}$. At first we should compute probability measure of $A_{12} = A_1 * A_2$ given p_{12}, that is, compute probability measure $P(A_{12})$ of the fuzzy event X_{12} *is* A_{12} as

$$P(A_{12}) = \sum_{i=1}^{n} \mu_{A_{12}}(x_{12,i}) p_{12s}(x_{12,i}).$$

Thus, when p_{12} is known, $P(A_{12})$ is a number $P(A_{12}) = b_{12}$. However, what is only known is a fuzzy restriction on pdfs p_{12s} described by the membership function $\mu_{p_{12}}$. Therefore, $P(A_{12})$ will be a fuzzy set B_{12} with the membership function $\mu_{B_{12}}$ defined as follows:

$$\mu_{B_{12}}(b_{12s}) = \max \mu_{p_{12s}}(p_{12s}) \tag{6.17}$$

subject to

$$b_{12s} = \sum_{i=1}^{n} \mu_{A_{12}}(x_i) p_{12s}(x_i). \qquad (6.18)$$

The sense of equations (6.17)-(6.18) is as follows. In general, several convolutions p_{12s} may induce the same numeric value of probability measure $b_{12s} = P(A_{12})$ as a basic value of the fuzzy set B_{12}. Then, the membership degree $\mu_{B_{12}}(b_{12s})$ is equal to the maximum of the membership degrees $\mu_{p_{12s}}(p_{12s})$ of all the convolutions p_{12s} which induce the value

of $b_{12s} = P(A_{12}) = \sum_{i=1}^{n} \mu_{A_{12}}(x_i) p_{12s}(x_i)$.

As a result, $Z_{12} = Z_1 * Z_2$ is obtained as $Z_{12} = (A_{12}, B_{12})$.

Let us now discuss advantages of this approach with respect to the approach suggested in [821]. In [821] Zadeh suggested a conceptual basis for computation with continuous Z-numbers. However, he mentioned that it is characterized by high complexity and may not be practical. In this regard, he suggested two simplifications. The first is related to use normal pdfs $p_j = N(m_j, \sigma_j)$. Moreover, taking into account compatibility conditions (6.5), for the case of addition one may fix mean m_j and conduct optimization with respect to σ_j only. The second simplification concerns approximation of a continuous fuzzy number A_j of $Z_j = (A_j, B_j)$ by its bandwidth $A_j^{\ b}$ which is a closed interval (a crisp set). Then computation of $Z_{12} = Z_1 * Z_2$ is quite simple: $Z_{12} = (A_1, B_1) * (A_2, B_2) = (A_1 * A_2, B_1 \cdot B_2)$, i.e. $B_1 \cdot B_2$ is just a multiplication of continuous fuzzy numbers B_1 and B_2. Let us mention that these two simplifications may be too restrictive for some practical problems. Below we provide comparison of advantages of the suggested approach.

As one can see, the considered computational framework includes two non-linear variational problems (6.1)-(6.5) and (6.6)-(6.7) which sufficiently complicate computation with continuous Z-numbers. (6.1)-(6.5) is a problem of construction of a membership function over a set of convolutions $p_{R_1+R_2}(x)$ and the operands of the problem are pdfs p_{R_1} and p_{R_2} which are considered in a general sense. Such a problem with non-linear constraints and objective function is very complex to be solved as a single whole both from analytical and computational points of view. In the suggested approach instead of (6.1)-(6.5), we consider to consecutively solve two problems. First, we suggest solving LP problems (6.12)-(6.14) to extract pdfs $p_j, j = 1, 2$. Second, given the extracted pdfs $p_j, j = 1, 2$, we compute membership degrees $\mu_{p_{12}}(p_{12})$ of convolutions $p_{12} = p_1 \circ p_2$ by solving a problem (6.15)-(6.16). One can see that (6.15)-(6.16) is just a problem of determination of maximum for a membership degree over a finite set of pdfs, as compared to a quite complex variational problem (6.1)-(6.5). Therefore, discretization of continuous fuzzy numbers and continuous pdfs and consecutive solving of simple optimization problems (6.12)-(6.14) and (6.15)-(6.16) is sufficiently easier and clearer than solving the whole nonlinear variational problem (6.1)-(6.5) in continuous framework. Also, discretization allows considering a general case of random variables when an actual form of pdf is unknown.

The problem (6.6)-(6.7) is a variational problem. In the suggested approach we consider (6.17)-(6.18) instead where a membership degree in B_{12} is found as a maximum within a finite countable set.

6.2.3 Operations on continuous Z-numbers

6.2.3.1 Addition of continuous Z-numbers

In this section we describe basic arithmetic and some algebraic operations of continuous Z-numbers following the approach provided in Section 6.2.2.2.

Let $Z_1 = (A_1, B_1)$ and $Z_2 = (A_2, B_2)$ be continuous Z-numbers describing imperfect information about values of random variables X_1 and X_2. The procedures of computation of addition $Z_{12} = Z_1 + Z_2$ are as follows.

Step 1. Compute addition $A_{12} = A_1 + A_2$ of fuzzy numbers (Section 5.3).

Step 2. Compute discretized $R_{12} = R_1 + R_2$ as convolution $p_{12} = p_1 \circ p_2$ of pdfs p_1 and p_2 (Section 4.1). A broad family of pdfs p_1 and p_2 can be considered.

Step 3. Compute discretized $\mu_{p_j}, j = 1,2$. For this purpose, at first we should discretize fuzzy numbers A_j and B_j and formulate m goal linear programming problems (6.12)-(6.14). Next, we should solve problems (6.12)-(6.14) to obtain m discretized distributions p_{jl}. Finally, we compute μ_{p_j} as $\mu_{p_j}(p_{jl}) = \mu_{B_j}\left(\sum_{i=1}^{n_j} p_{jl}(x_{ji}) \mu_{A_j}(x_{ji}) \right)$.

Step 4. Given $\mu_{p_j}, j = 1,2$, compute discretized $\mu_{p_{12}}$ by using (6.15)-(6.16).

Step 5. Given discretized $\mu_{p_{12}}$ and discretized $\mu_{A_{12}}$, compute discretized $\mu_{B_{12}}$ by using (6.17)-(6.18). The obtained discretized $\mu_{B_{12}}$ can then be approximated by an appropriate typical continuous membership function. Thus, the addition $Z_{12} = Z_1 + Z_2$ is obtained as $Z_{12} = (A_{12}, B_{12})$.

6.2.3.2 *Standard subtraction of continuous Z-numbers*

There are two main types of subtraction operations in existence: standard subtraction and Hukuhara difference. Let us note that for standard subtraction $Z_{12} = Z_1 - Z_2$ one has $Z_1 \neq Z_2 + Z_{12}$. However, standard subtraction always exists. In contrast, Hukuhara difference Z_{12} is that which satisfies $Z_1 = Z_2 + Z_{12}$, but it does not always exist. The conditions on existence of Hukuhara difference of fuzzy numbers is widely investigated in [99, 699] (and the references therein). Existence of Hukuhara difference Z_{12} requires existence of A_{12} and analysis of some additional conditions for B_1 and B_2. In this section we don't consider Hukuhara difference but consider standard subtraction $Z_{12} = Z_1 - Z_2$. Let us mention that whatever subtraction operation is used, the suggested main ideas of operations over continuous Z-numbers remain the same.

Step 1. Compute standard subtraction $A_{12} = A_1 - A_2$ of fuzzy numbers (Section 5.3.2).

Step 2. Compute discretized $R_{12} = R_1 - R_2$ as convolution $p_{12} = p_1 \circ p_2$ of pdfs p_1 and p_2 (Section 4.1). A broad family of pdfs p_1 and p_2 can be considered.

Step 3. Compute discretized $\mu_{p_j}, j = 1,2$. This step is analogous to that of the addition. Indeed, the extraction of discretized distributions p_j and computation of $\mu_{p_j}(p_j)$ does not depend on a type of operation over Z-numbers.

Step 4. Given $\mu_{p_j}, j = 1,2$, compute discretized $\mu_{p_{12}}$ by using (6.15)-(6.16). This computation also does not depend on a type of operation ove Z-numbers

Step 5. Given discretized $\mu_{p_{12}}$ and discretized $\mu_{A_{12}}$, compute discretized $\mu_{B_{12}}$ by using (6.17)-(6.18). The obtained discretized $\mu_{B_{12}}$ can be approximated by a typical continuous membership function.

As a result, standard subtraction $Z_{12} = Z_1 - Z_2$ is obtained as $Z_{12} = (A_{12}, B_{12})$.

6.2.3.3 *Multiplication of continuous Z-numbers*

Consider multiplication $Z_{12} = Z_1 \cdot Z_2$ of $Z_1 = (A_1, B_1)$ and $Z_2 = (A_2, B_2)$. Let us mention that multiplication is not a linear operation. This leads to some differences in the results as compared to those of addition and subtraction which are shown below.

Step 1. Compute multiplication $A_{12} = A_1 \cdot A_2$ of fuzzy numbers (Section 5.3.2). Let us mention that $\mu_{A_{12}}$ does not preserve the form of μ_{A_1} or μ_{A_2} due to nonlinearity of multiplication.

Step 2. Compute discretized $R_{12} = R_1 \cdot R_2$ as convolution $p_{12} = p_1 \circ p_2$ of pdfs p_1 and p_2 (Section 4.1). A broad family of pdfs p_1 and p_2 can be considered. Moreover, the use of discretization is very important as for multiplication p_{12} can not in general be found analytically even when p_1 and p_2 have analytical descriptions.

Step 3. Compute discretized $\mu_{p_j}, j = 1,2$. This computation does not depend on a type of operation over Z-numbers and is processed as shown above.

Step 4. Given $\mu_{p_j}, j = 1,2$, compute discretized $\mu_{p_{12}}$ by using (6.15)-(6.16).

Step 5. Given discretized $\mu_{p_{12}}$ and discretized $\mu_{A_{12}}$, compute discretized $\mu_{B_{12}}$ by using (6.17)-(6.18).

As a result, multiplication $Z_{12} = Z_1 \cdot Z_2$ is obtained as $Z_{12} = (A_{12}, B_{12})$.

6.2.3.4 *Standard division of continuous Z-numbers*

Consider standard division $Z_{12} = \dfrac{Z_1}{Z_2}$ of $Z_1 = (A_1, B_1)$ and $Z_2 = (A_2, B_2)$, where $0 \notin \mathrm{supp}(A_2)$. Let us mention that computation of standard division has some specific issues as compared to addition or standard subtraction.

Step 1. Compute multiplication $A_{12} = \dfrac{A_1}{A_2}$ of fuzzy numbers by using (Section 5.23). Let us mention that $\mu_{A_{12}}$ does not preserve the form of μ_{A_1} or μ_{A_2}.

Step 2. Compute discretized $R_{12} = R_1 * R_2$ as convolution $p_{12} = p_1 \circ p_2$ of pdfs p_1 and p_2 (Section 4.1). A broad family of pdfs p_1 and p_2 can be considered. The use of discretization is very important as for standard division, p_{12} can not in general be found analytically even when p_1 and p_2 have analytical descriptions.

Steps 3, 4, 5 are the same as those for addition, standard subtraction and multiplication.

As a result, division $Z_{12} = \dfrac{Z_1}{Z_2}$ is obtained as $Z_{12} = (A_{12}, B_{12})$.

6.2.3.5 *Square of a continuous Z-number*

Let us now consider computation of a square of a continuous Z-number: $Z_Y = Z_X^2$. Let us mention that the square operation is one-place operation. However, the computation of one-place operations can be conducted based on the approach suggested in Section 6.2.2 analogously to that of two-place operations. Below we will explain this computation.

Step 1. Compute square root $A_Y = A_X^2$ of a fuzzy numbers (Section 5.3.2).

Step 2. Compute $R_Y = R_X{}^2$ as a pdf p_Y obtained form p_X (Section 4.1). A broad family of pdfs p_X can be considered.

Step 3. Compute discretized μ_{p_X}. This step is the same as that of addition. At first, pdfs p_X are extracted by solving (6.12)-(6.14) and then $\mu_{p_X}(p_X)$ are computed.

Step 4. Given μ_{p_X}, compute discretized μ_{p_Y} analogously to (6.15)-(6.16):

$$\mu_{p_Y}(p_Y) = \mu_{p_X}(p_X),$$

where p_Y is induce by p_X in accordance to (4.5).

Step 5. Given discretized μ_{p_Y} and discretized μ_{A_Y}, compute discretized μ_{B_Y} analogously to (6.17)-(6.18):

$$\mu_{B_Y}(b_Y) = \max \mu_{p_Y}(p_Y)$$

subject to

$$b_Y = \sum_{i=1}^{n} \mu_{A_Y}(x_i) p_Y(x_i).$$

As a result, the square Z^2 is obtained as $Z^2 = (A_Y, B_Y)$.

Let us mention that computation of $Z_Y = Z_X^n$, where n is any natural number, is carried out analogously.

6.2.3.6 *Square root of a continuous Z-number*

In [821] Zadeh poses a question: "What is a square root of a Z-number?". In this section we will try to answer this question. Let us consider computation of $Z_Y = \sqrt{Z_X}$.

Step 1. Compute square root of $A_Y = \sqrt{A_X}$ of a fuzzy numbers (Section 5.3.2).

Step 2. Compute $R_Y = \sqrt{R_X}$ as a pdf p_Y obtained form p_X (Section 4.1). A broad family of pdfs p_X can be considered.

Step 3. Compute discretized μ_{p_X}. This step is the same as that of addition. At first, pdfs p_X are extracted by solving (6.12)-(6.14) and then $\mu_{p_X}(p_X)$ are computed.

Step 4. Given μ_{p_X}, compute discretized μ_{p_Y} analogously to (6.15)-(6.16):

$$\mu_{p_Y}(p_{Y,l}) = \mu_{p_X}(p_{X,l}),$$

where $p_{Y,l}$ is defined on the base of $p_{X,l}$ according to (4.7).

Step 5. Given discretized μ_{p_Y} and discretized μ_{A_Y}, compute discretized μ_{B_Y} analogously to (6.17)-(6.18).

As a result, the square $\sqrt{Z}$ is obtained as $Z^2 = (A_Y, B_Y)$.

6.2.3.7 *Minimum and maximum of continuous Z-numbers*

Let us consider computation of $Z_{12} = Z_1 * Z_2$, $* \in \{MIN, MAX\}$ of Z-numbers $Z_1 = (A_1, B_1)$ and $Z_2 = (A_2, B_2)$.

Step 1. Compute minimum $A_{12} = A_1 * A_2$ of fuzzy numbers (Section 5.3.2).

Step 2. Compute $R_{12} = R_1 * R_2$ as convolution $p_{12} = p_1 \circ p_2$ of pdfs p_1 and p_2 (Section 4.1). A broad family of pdfs p_1 and p_2 can be considered.

Steps 3, 4, 5 are the same as those for addition, standard subtraction and multiplication.

Thus, the minimum (maximum) $Z_{12} = Z_1 * Z_2$ is obtained as

$$Z_{12} = (A_{12}, B_{12}) .$$

In the examples given in the sequel, we show how the ideas underlying the suggested approach can be applied.

6.3 The arithmetic of discrete Z-numbers

6.3.1 *Discrete Z-numbers*

In [16] they considered discrete Z-numbers, that is, Z-numbers whose components are discrete fuzzy numbers. The motivation behind the use of discrete Z-numbers is three-fold. The first is that due to the highly constrained computational ability of the human brain as a human being uses linguistic description of real-world information. In turn, linguistic information, as a rule, is represented on the basis of a discrete set of linguistic terms. The second aspect is that computation with discrete fuzzy numbers [153, 761] and discrete probability distributions are characterized by a significantly lower computational complexity than that involving continuous fuzzy numbers and probability density functions. The third aspect is the universality of uncertainty modeling. In discrete case one does not need to assume a type of probability distribution that will constrain modeling abilities, but can consider a general case.

For example, consider the following Z-number-based evaluation [821]:

(the price of oil in the near future is *medium, very likely*)

As one can see, linguistic terms are used in this evaluation. This means that Z-numbers are based on the use of a sets of linguistic terms. Such sets can be represented by ordinal linguistic scales. In the considered case, one may consider the ordinal linguistic scales with, for example, eleven linguistic terms $\mathcal{M} = \{VL, L, ..., M, ..., H, VH\}$, where the letters denote linguistic terms *very low, low,...,medium,..., high, very high* and $\mathcal{N} = \{U, NVL,...,L,...,VL,EL\}$, where the letters denote linguistic terms *unlikely, not very likely,..., likely,..., very likely, extremely likely.* The terms of the considered scales are ordered in an increasing order: $VL \prec L \prec ... \prec M \prec ... \prec H \prec VH$ and $U \prec NVL \prec ... \prec L \prec ... \prec VL \prec EL.$ Therefore, one can consecutively number the linguistic terms in the considered scales and arrive at an ordered set $\mathbf{L} = \{0,1,...,n\}$.

Consideration of discrete Z-numbers instead of their continuous counterparts also allows us to significantly improve tradeoff between adequacy and universality from the one side and computational complexity from the other side. Concerning loss of accuracy as a result of proceeding from continuous forms of membership functions and probability distributions to discrete forms, in many problems it may not be significant from qualitative point of view. As it will be shown, operations over discrete Z-numbers involve only linear programming problems but not non-linear variational problems.

6.3.1.1 *Addition of discrete Z-numbers*

Let $Z_1 = (A_1, B_1)$ and $Z_2 = (A_2, B_2)$ be discrete Z-numbers describing imperfect information about values of real-valued random variables X_1 and X_2. Consider the problem of computation of addition $Z_{12} = Z_1 + Z_2$. Computation with discrete Z-numbers, as that with continuous Z-numbers, starts with the computation over the corresponding discrete Z^+-numbers. The discrete Z^+-number $Z_{12}^+ = Z_1^+ + Z_2^+$ is determined as follows:

$$Z_1^+ + Z_2^+ = (A_1 + A_2, R_1 + R_2)$$

where R_1 and R_2 are represented by discrete probability distributions:

$p_1 = p_1(x_{11}) \backslash x_{11} + p_1(x_{12}) \backslash x_{12} + ... + p_1(x_{1n}) \backslash x_{1n}$,

$p_2 = p_2(x_{21}) \backslash x_{21} + p_2(x_{22}) \backslash x_{22} + ... + p_2(x_{2n}) \backslash x_{2n}$,

for which one necessarily has

$$\sum_{k=1}^{n} p_1(x_{1k}) = 1,$$

$$\sum_{k=1}^{n} p_2(x_{2k}) = 1.$$

As the operands in $A_1 + A_2$ and in $R_1 + R_2$ are represented by different types of restrictions, then the meanings of $*$ are also different [821].The addition $A_1 + A_2$ of discrete fuzzy numbers is defined in accordance with (5.23) and $R_1 + R_2$ is a convolution $p_{12} = p_1 \circ p_2$ of discrete probability distributions defined as:

$$p_{12}(x) = \sum_{x = x_{1i} + x_{2j}} p_1(x_{1i}) p_2(x_{2j}).$$

So, we will have Z_{12}^+ as $Z_{12}^+ = (A_1 + A_2, p_{12})$, which is the result of computation with discrete Z^+-numbers being the first step of computation with Z-numbers. The further computations are condacted by using (6.8-6.18).

6.3.1.2 *Standard subtraction of discrete Z-numbers*

Let us consider standard subtraction $Z_{12} = Z_1 - Z_2$ of discrete Z-numbers $Z_1 = (A_1, B_1)$ and $Z_2 = (A_2, B_2)$. First, a discrete Z^+-number $Z_{12}^+ = Z_1^+ - Z_2^+$ should be determined:

$$Z_1^+ - Z_2^+ = (A_1 - A_2, R_1 - R_2)$$

where R_1 and R_2 are represented by discrete probability distributions:

$$p_1 = p_1(x_{11}) \backslash x_{11} + p_1(x_{12}) \backslash x_{12} + \ldots + p_1(x_{1n}) \backslash x_{1n},$$

$$p_2 = p_2(x_{21}) \backslash x_{21} + p_2(x_{22}) \backslash x_{22} + \ldots + p_2(x_{2n}) \backslash x_{2n},$$

for which (6.25)-(6.26) are satisfied.

The difference $A_1 - A_2$ of discrete fuzzy numbers is defined in accordance with (5.24) and $R_1 - R_2$ is a convolution $p_{12} = p_1 \circ p_2$ of discrete probability distributions defined as:

$$p_{12}(x) = \sum_{x=x_1-x_2} p_1(x_1)p_2(x_2).$$

So, we will have Z_{12}^+ as $Z_{12}^+ = (A_1 - A_2, p_{12})$, which is the result of standard subtraction of discrete Z^+-numbers being the first step of standard subtraction of Z-numbers.

Third, we construct the fuzzy sets $\mu_{p_{jl}}(p_{jl}) = \mu_{B_j}\left(\sum_{k=1}^{n_j} \mu_{A_j}(x_{jk})p_{jl}(x_{jk})\right)$, $j = 1,2$, $l = 1,...,m$ by solving (6.12)-(6.14). *Fourth,* the fuzzy set of convolutions p_{12s}, $s = 1,...,m^2$, with the membership function constructed by solving (6.15)-(6.16), where convolution is computed according to (4.27).

At the *fifth step*, we proceed to construction of B_{12}. First we should compute probability measure of $A_{12} = A_1 - A_2$ given p_{12}, i.e. to compute probability of the fuzzy event X *is* A_{12}. Finally, we compute a fuzzy set B_{12} according to (6.17)-(6.18). As a result, $Z_{12} = Z_1 - Z_2$ is obtained as $Z_{12} = (A_{12}, B_{12})$.

6.3.1.3 *Multiplication of discrete Z-numbers*

Let us consider multiplication $Z_{12} = Z_1 \cdot Z_2$ of $Z_1 = (A_1, B_1)$ and $Z_2 = (A_2, B_2)$. First, $Z_{12}^+ = Z_1^+ \cdot Z_2^+$ should be determined:

$$Z_1^+ \cdot Z_2^+ = (A_1 \cdot A_2, R_1 \cdot R_2),$$

where R_1 and R_2 are represented by discrete probability distributions:

$$p_1 = p_1(x_{11}) \setminus x_{11} + p_1(x_{12}) \setminus x_{12} + ... + p_1(x_{1n}) \setminus x_{1n},$$

$$p_2 = p_2(x_{21}) \setminus x_{21} + p_2(x_{22}) \setminus x_{22} + ... + p_2(x_{2n}) \setminus x_{2n}.$$

The product $A_1 \cdot A_2$ of discrete fuzzy numbers is defined and $R_1 \cdot R_2$ is a convolution $p_{12} = p_1 \circ p_2$ of discrete probability distributions defined as

$$p_{12}(x) = \sum_{x=x_1 \cdot x_2} p_1(x_1)p_2(x_{2j}).$$

Thus, we will have $Z_{12}^+ = (A_1 \cdot A_2, p_{12})$. Next, we construct the fuzzy sets $\mu_{p_{jl}}(p_{jl})$, $l = 1, ..., m$, and the fuzzy set of convolutions p_{12s}, $s = 1, ..., m^2$, with the membership function defined by solving (6.15)–(6.16).

At the next step probability measure of $A_{12} = A_1 \cdot A_2$ is computed Finally, a fuzzy set B_{12} is constructed according to (6.17)-(6.18). As a result, $Z_{12} = Z_1 \cdot Z_2$ is obtained as $Z_{12} = (A_{12}, B_{12})$.

6.3.1.4 *Standard division of discrete Z-numbers*

Let us consider standard division $Z_{12} = Z_1 / Z_2$ of $Z_1 = (A_1, B_1)$ and $Z_2 = (A_2, B_2)$, where $0 \notin \operatorname{supp}(A_2)$. First, $Z_{12}^+ = (A_{12}, p_{12})$ is determined:

$$Z_{12}^+ = (A_{12}, p_{12}),$$

where the standard division $A_{12} = A_1 / A_2$ of discrete fuzzy numbers is defined in accordance with (5.27) and a convolution $p_{12} = p_1 \circ p_2$ of discrete probability distributions is defined as

$$p_{12}(x) = \sum_{\substack{x=x_1/x_2, \\ x_2 \neq 0}} p_1(x_1)p_2(x_2).$$

Next, we construct the fuzzy sets $\mu_{p_{jl}}(p_{jl})$, $j = 1, 2$, $l = 1, ..., m$ and the fuzzy set of convolutions p_{12s}, $s = 1, ..., m^2$, with the membership function defined by solving (6.15)-(6.16).

At the next step probability measure of A_{12} is computed. Finally, a fuzzy set B_{12} is constructed according to (6.17)-(6.18) . As a result, $Z_{12} = Z_1 \big/ Z_2$ is obtained as $Z_{12} = (A_{12}, B_{12})$.

6.3.2 *Power of a discrete Z-number*

6.3.2.1 *Square of a discrete Z-number*

Let us now consider computation of $Z_Y = Z_X^2$. Let $Z_X^+ = (A_X, R_X)$ where R_X is represented as

$$p_X = p_X(x_1) \backslash x_1 + p_X(x_2) \backslash x_2 + ... + p_X(x_n) \backslash x_n .$$

Then the discrete Z^+-number Z_Y^+ is determined as follows:

$$Z_Y^+ = (A_Y, R_Y),$$

where $A_Y = A_X^2$, A_X^2 is determined on the base of (5.27) and R_Y is represented by a discrete probability distribution

$$p_Y = p_Y(y_1) \backslash y_1 + p_Y(y_2) \backslash y_2 + ... + p_Y(y_m) \backslash y_m , \tag{6.19}$$

such that

$$y_r = x_k^2 \text{ and } p_Y(y_r) = \sum_{y_r = x^2} p_X(x), r = 1, ..., m . \tag{6.20}$$

Next we compute $\mu_{p_X}(p_{X,l}) = \mu_{B_X}\left(\sum_{k=1}^{n} \mu_{A_X}(x_k) p_{X,l}(x_k)\right)$ by solving linear programming problem (6.12)-(6.14).

Now, recalling (6.19)-(6.20), we realize that the fuzzy set of probability distributions p_X with membership function $\mu_{p_X}(p_{X,l})$ naturally induces the fuzzy set of probability distributions $p_{Y,l}$ with the membership function defined as

$$\mu_{p_Y}(p_{Y,l}) = \mu_{p_X}(p_{X,l}),$$

subject to (6.19)-(6.20).

Next, we should compute probability measure of A_Y given p_Y. Finally, given a fuzzy restriction on p_Y described by the membership function μ_{p_Y}, we construct a fuzzy set B_Y with the membership function μ_{B_Y} defined as follows:

$$\mu_{B_Y}(b_{Y,l}) = \sup(\mu_{p_Y}(p_{Y,l}))$$

subject to

$$b_{Y,l} = \sum_k p_{Y,l}(x_k)\mu_{A_Y}(x_k).$$

As a result, Z^2 is obtained as $Z^2 = (A_Y, B_Y)$. Let us mention that for $x_i \geq 0, i = 1,...,n$, one has $p_{Y,l}(y_k) = p_{X,l}(x_k)$, $\mu_{p_Y}(p_{Y,l}) = \mu_{p_X}(p_{X,l})$, and $\mu_{A_Y}(y_k) = \mu_{A_X}(x_k)$ with $y_k = x_k^2$. Thus, one has

$$b_{Y,l} = b_{X,l} \text{ and } \mu_{B_Y}(b_{Y,l}) = \mu_{B_X}(b_{X,l}),$$

which means $B_Y = B_X$. Therefore, for the case $x_i \geq 0, i = 1,...,n$, it is not needed to carry out computation of B_Y because it is the same as B_X.

Let us mention that computation of $Z_Y = Z_X^n$, where n is any natural number, is carried out analogously.

6.3.2.2 *Square root of a discrete Z-number*

Let us consider computation of $Z_Y = \sqrt{Z_X}$. Then the discrete Z^+-number Z_Y^+ is determined as follows:

$$Z_Y^+ = (A_Y, R_Y),$$

where $A_Y = \sqrt{A_X}$ is determined on the base of (5.29) and R_Y is represented by a discrete probability distribution.

$$p_{R_Y} = p_{R_Y}(y_1)\backslash y_1 + p_{R_Y}(y_2)\backslash y_2 + \ldots + p_{R_Y}(y_n)\backslash y_n, \quad (6.21)$$

such that

$$y_k = \sqrt{x_k} \text{ and } p_{R_Y}(y_k) = p_{R_X}(x_k). \quad (6.22)$$

Next we construct $\mu_{p_X}(p_{X,l}) = \mu_{B_X}\left(\sum_{k=1}^{n}\mu_{A_X}(x_k)p_{X,l}(x_k)\right)$ and recall that

$$\mu_{p_Y}(p_{Y,l}) = \mu_{p_X}(p_{X,l}),$$

subject to (6.21)-(6.22).

Next we compute probability measure of A_Y and, given the membership function μ_{p_Y}, we construct a fuzzy set B_Y analogously to that we did in Section 6.3.3.1. As a result, $\sqrt{Z}$ is obtained as $\sqrt{Z} = (A_Y, B_Y)$. Let us mention that analogously to the case of the square of a discrete Z-number, it is not needed to carry out computation of B_Y. One can easily verify that for the case of the square root of a discrete Z-number, $B_Y = B_X$ holds.

6.4 Z-numbers valued functions

A wide class of problems in science and engineering requires mathematical formalization. One of the important aspects in this regard is that we should account for various types of uncertainties, which are simultaneously present in real-world problems and result from imprecise and partially reliable information. This mandates a need for a theoretical basis of uncertain functional dependencies. The theories of interval-valued functions, functions of random variables, and fuzzy functions are well-developed. The main disadvantage of these theories is that each of them can deal with only a single type of uncertainty. In this section, we consider a general methodology for a construction of Z-valued functions on the basis of the extension principle applied to Z-numbers. Some properties of functions of Z-numbers are considered.

In general, a function is defined as a mapping between two spaces. In mathematics, it is presumed that information related to elements of domain and a range of a function is precise. For example, in calculus this means that a value of an argument should be a precise number, and then the corresponding value of a function will be determined as a precise number. Mathematical analysis, calculus and functional analysis in mathematics are well developed. However, an important problem arises when applying these theories to real-world problems: values of arguments to compute with are not precisely known but are impacted by various facets uncertainties. This naturally implies uncertainties related to the values of a function. In real-world problems, we do not have the exact and reliable information on values of variables of interest, but have to deal with some restrictions over these values. Therefore, the exact values of functions cannot be found, but only some restrictions over these values can be described. Therefore, new mathematical problems appear related to how to handle uncertainties, which naturally propagate from values of arguments to values of functions. The theory of probabilistic arithmetic was developed to construct a function when its arguments are not precise number-valued variables but random variables [174, 579, 696, 782, 783]. This helps us formalize randomness of a value of a function, which naturally results from the randomness of its arguments. In order to process imprecise measurements, when restrictions on accuracy are described by intervals defined over the space of reals, a theory of interval calculus was developed [13, 424, 538]. A more general and adequate formalism to deal with imprecise and vague information, especially linguistic information, the theory of fuzzy calculus was developed [421, 449, 757, 819]. This theory serves the purposes of computations when the restrictions over values are linguistically specified. This means that feasibility of a value within restriction is a matter of a degree. The book of Kaufmann and Gupta [420] is devoted to the development of the extension principle-based fuzzy arithmetic and other important directions of research on fuzzy functions including factorials, sequences, series of fuzzy numbers, and a derivative of functions of fuzzy numbers. The suggested fuzzy arithmetic includes basic arithmetic operations such as addition and multiplication, algebraic operations and comparison operations over fuzzy numbers. The commonly encountered functions as fuzzy trigonometric functions and fuzzy hyperbolic functions based on the extension principle are considered. The book includes many examples offering an in-depth explanation of the considered fuzzy arithmetic operations.

The development of the fuzzy calculus uncovered important issues, which required developing theoretical basis for fuzzy functions. In general, at least two different concepts of fuzzy functions exist. The first concept is based on the extension principle suggested by L. A. Zadeh [825] according to which a fuzzy function is considered as a generalization of a classical function to the case when values of its arguments are fuzzy sets. This was a starting point of research on fuzzy functions. Further significant developments of a fundamental basis of fuzzy functions were suggested in [233] where a wide theoretical research framework was suggested. Fuzzy functions were considered as mappings from the real line to the space of normal and convex fuzzy sets with upper semicontinuous membership functions and compact support. Various metric in the considered space are provided. Formulated were definitions of a limit, continuity, boundedness, integrability, differentiability and other concepts for a fuzzy function. Applications of a suggested analysis to fuzzy differential equations and to other important fields are considered. The studies in [454] were devoted to research on fuzzy functions, mainly related to fuzzy differential equations.

Nowadays a diversified series of studies on the extension principle based research on fuzzy functions exists [226, 227, 434, 602-605]. These works include research on fuzzy equations [69, 602, 603, 605], fuzzy differential equations [21, 98, 453], fuzzy valued measures and fuzzy valued integrals [335, 593, 701, 869] etc. A series of the related applications to decision making, control and other fields were considered in [20-22, 24].

As it has been mentioned in [604], another important view on a concept of a fuzzy function is to consider the latter as a fuzzy relation between a domain and a range of a function [226, 227, 344, 434]. In [604] the authors suggest to combine the extension principle-based and fuzzy relations-based concepts of fuzzy function. It has been shown that a fuzzy relation based fuzzy function determines the extension principle based fuzzy function. The relationship between these two concepts has been investigated.

The theories outlined above, viz. the one of probabilistic calculus and fuzzy calculus, deal with the unique types of uncertainty. However, real-world information is characterized by both probabilistic and fuzzy uncertainties. This calls for the development of a sound formalism being able to simultaneously deal with randomness and fuzziness.

In [16, 44] a general and computationally effective approach to computation with discrete Z-numbers has been introduced. The authors provide a strong motivation behind the use of discrete Z-numbers regarded as an alternative to the continuous counterparts. In particular, the motivation is based on the fact that linguistic information can be cast in a discrete framework. On the other hand, in a discrete framework it is not required to make a reasonable assumption about a type of probability distribution. The suggested arithmetic of discrete Z-numbers includes basic arithmetic operations and important algebraic operations. The proposed approach supports coping with Z-numbers directly without their conversion to fuzzy numbers.

The book [33] is devoted to computations over continuous and discrete Z-numbers. The authors considered some arithmetic operations. They also focused on solving of equations with Z-numbers. On the basis of the suggested methods, several important problems and their solution were developed. One of them concerns linear programming with Z-number valued decision variables and Z-number valued parameters. The other problem considers a Z-number valued regression analysis. The foundations of decision making with Z-number valued information were also suggested. The book covers several applications of the suggested approach to decision making, marketing, and optimal planning.

In the mentioned studies, a sound systematic theory of functions of Z-numbers has not been developed. The existing important theoretical and practical problems in system analysis, decision, control, economics, ecology and other fields are more or less well-developed for solely precise information framework. Some of them were developed solely in the probabilistic information framework or fuzzy information framework. However, there is no theoretical basis to develop formal statement of real world problems and the solution methods for Z-number valued information framework. Formally, correct processing of such information becomes important for formulating adequate solutions to real-world problems.

This section is devoted to theoretical investigations of functions of Z-numbers and establishing their properties under assumption that Z-numbers describe imperfect information on independent random variables. The general methodology of construction of functions of Z-numbers based on the extension principle is suggested.

6.4.1 *Methodology for construction of functions of Z-numbers*

Let us elaborate on the general methodology of the construction of a Z-number valued function. Consider a function $f : \mathcal{R} \times \mathcal{R} \to \mathcal{R}$ of two independent random variables X_1 and X_2. Suppose now that values of X_1 and X_2 are not exactly known, but restrictions over their values described as Z-numbers are only available. These restrictions will naturally induce not the exact value $X_{12} = f(X_1, X_2)$ but a restriction over X_{12} described as a Z-number. Therefore, we need to consider a two place Z-number valued function $f : \mathcal{Z} \times \mathcal{Z} \to \mathcal{Z}$ defined over the sets of Z-numbers. Precisely speaking, the arguments of f are not the values of X_1 and X_2 but are restrictions on values of X_1 and X_2. For simplicity, below we will use the term 'value' instead of 'restriction over a value'. Consider computation of a value $Z_{12} = f(Z_1, Z_2)$ of this function. These restrictions induce a Z-number valued restriction $Z_{12} = f(Z_1, Z_2)$ on a value of f.

Thus, in general, the extension principle for computation with Z-numbers can be described in the form:

The value of the mapping: $Z = f(X_1, X_2)$
The restriction on $X_1 : X_1$ is $Z_1 = (A_1, B_1)$
The restriction on $X_2 : X_2$ is $Z_2 = (A_2, B_2)$
The induced restriction Z is $Z_{12} = (A_{12}, B_{12})$ is constructed as:
$A_{12} = f(A_1, A_2)$ is a fuzzy number (Section 5.3).

B_{12} is a fuzzy number computed as a inner product of $\mu_{A_{12}}$ and pdfs
$p_{12} = f(p_1, p_2)$, where p_1, p_2 are obtained by solving (6.12)-(6.14).

6.4.2 Basic properties of functions of Z-numbers

In this section we formulate basic properties of functions of discrete Z-numbers. In other words, we will deal with properties of discrete functions. Formulation of properties of discrete functions is important as the approach we propose is based on discretization of continuous Z-numbers, and this, in turn, requires to consider the issue of accuracy. A new fundamental theory of discrete functions was suggested in [138, 139]. This theory presented offers a systematic approach to dealing with discrete structures. We will adopt a general framework of the theory proposed in [138, 139] to formulate properties of functions of discrete Z-numbers.

Let us denote by $\mathcal{Z}^n$ the space of elements which are *n*-vectors of discrete Z-numbers
$$\mathbf{Z} = (Z_1, Z_2, ..., Z_n) = ((A_1, B_1), (A_2, B_2), ..., (A_n, B_n)) .$$
Denote $\mathcal{Z}_{[c,d]} = \left\{ (A, B) \middle| A \in \mathcal{D}_{[c,d]}, B \in \mathcal{D}_{[0,1]} \right\}$, $[c, d] \subset \mathcal{R}$, and
$$\mathcal{Z}_+ = \left\{ (A, B) \in \mathcal{Z} \middle| A \in \mathcal{D}_{[0,\infty)} \right\}, \quad \mathcal{Z}_- = \mathcal{Z} \backslash \mathcal{Z}_+ .$$

Let us consider a subset $\mathcal{A} \subset \mathcal{Z}$. Let $Z_1 = (A_1, B_1)$ and $Z_2 = (A_2, B_2)$ be two Z-numbers. Denote by $A_i^{\alpha_k}$ and $B_i^{\beta_k}$ *k*-th α-cuts of A_i and B_i respectively, $\alpha_k \in \{\alpha_1, \alpha_2, ..., \alpha_n\} \subset [0,1]$, $\beta_k \in \{\beta_1, \beta_2, ..., \beta_n\} \subset [0,1]$. Denote $a_{i\alpha_k}^L = \min A_i^\alpha$, $a_{i\alpha_k}^R = \max A_i^\alpha$ and $b_{i\beta_k}^L = \min B_i^{\beta_k}$,

$b_{i\beta_k}^R = \max B_i^{\beta_k}$, $i = 1,2$. Below we propose a definition for a distance between Z-numbers.

Definition 6.1. The Hamming distance based metrics on $\mathcal{Z}$. The Hamming distance based Z-metrics on $\mathcal{Z}$ is defined as

$$D(Z_1, Z_2) =$$

$$\left(\frac{1}{n+1} \sum_{k=1}^{n} \left\{ \left| a_{1\alpha_k}^L - a_{2\alpha_k}^L \right| + \left| a_{1\alpha_k}^R - a_{2\alpha_k}^R \right| \right\} + \frac{1}{m+1} \sum_{k=1}^{m} \left\{ \left| b_{1\beta_k}^L - b_{2\beta_k}^L \right| + \left| b_{1\beta_k}^R - b_{2\beta_k}^R \right| \right\} \right)$$

Proposition. The Hamming distance-based metric satisfies the metric properties:

    i. $D(Z_1, Z_2) \geq 0$ for any $Z_1, Z_2 \in \mathcal{Z}$.

    ii. $D(Z_1, Z_2) = 0$ iff $Z_1 = Z_2$.

    iii. $D(Z_1, Z_2) = D(Z_2, Z_1)$ for any $Z_1, Z_2 \in \mathcal{Z}$.

    iv. $D(Z_1, Z_2) \leq D(Z_1, Z) + D(Z, Z_2)$ for any $Z, Z_1, Z_2 \in \mathcal{Z}$.

Proof.

i.   As $\left| a_{1\alpha_k}^L - a_{2\alpha_k}^L \right|, \left| a_{1\alpha_k}^R - a_{2\alpha_k}^R \right|, \left| b_{1\beta_k}^L - b_{2\beta_k}^L \right|, \left| b_{1\beta_k}^R - b_{2\beta_k}^R \right| \geq 0$ then

$D(Z_1, Z_2) \geq 0$.

ii.   Let $Z_1 = Z_2$, that is $A_1 = A_2$ and $B_1 = B_2$. This means that the corresponding α-cuts are equal, that is $a_{1\alpha_k}^L = a_{2\alpha_k}^L, a_{1\alpha_k}^R = a_{2\alpha_k}^R$, $b_{1\beta_k}^L = b_{2\beta_k}^L, b_{1\beta_k}^R = b_{2\beta_k}^R \geq 0$.

Thus $\left| a_{1\alpha_k}^L - a_{2\alpha_k}^L \right|, \left| a_{1\alpha_k}^R - a_{2\alpha_k}^R \right|, \left| b_{1\beta_k}^L - b_{2\beta_k}^L \right|, \left| b_{1\beta_k}^R - b_{2\beta_k}^R \right| = 0 \Rightarrow D(Z_1, Z_2) = 0$.

At the same time, $D(Z_1, Z_2) = 0$ only if $\left| a_{1\alpha_k}^L - a_{2\alpha_k}^L \right|, \left| a_{1\alpha_k}^R - a_{2\alpha_k}^R \right|$,

$\left| b_{1\beta_k}^L - b_{2\beta_k}^L \right|, \left| b_{1\beta_k}^R - b_{2\beta_k}^R \right| = 0$. This means that $A_1^{\alpha_k} = A_2^{\alpha_k}$, $B_1^{\beta_k} = B_2^{\beta_k}$.

Therefore $A_1 = A_2$ and $B_1 = B_2$.

iii.   As $\left| a_{1\alpha_j}^L - a_{2\alpha_j}^L \right| = \left| a_{2\alpha_j}^L - a_{1\alpha_j}^L \right|, \left| b_{1\beta_k}^R - b_{2\beta_k}^R \right| = \left| b_{2\beta_k}^R - b_{1\beta_k}^R \right|$ then $D(Z_1, Z_2) = D(Z_2, Z_1)$.

iv.   Denote $a_{\alpha_k}^L = \min A^{\alpha_k}, a_{\alpha_k}^R = \max A^{\alpha_k}$ and $b_{\beta_k}^L = \min B^{\beta_k}$, $b_{\beta_k}^R = \max B^{\beta_k}$, $i = 1, 2$. It is obvious that

$$\left| a_{1\alpha_k}^L - a_{\alpha_k}^L \right| + \left| a_{\alpha_k}^L - a_{2\alpha_k}^L \right| \geq \left| a_{1\alpha_k}^L - a_{2\alpha_k}^L \right|,$$

$$\left| a_{1\alpha_k}^R - a_{\alpha_k}^R \right| + \left| a_{\alpha_k}^R - a_{2\alpha_k}^R \right| \geq \left| a_{1\alpha_k}^R - a_{2\alpha_k}^R \right|,$$

$$\left| b_{1\beta_k}^L - b_{\beta_k}^L \right| + \left| b_{\beta_k}^L - b_{2\beta_k}^L \right| \geq \left| b_{1\beta_k}^L - b_{2\beta_k}^L \right|,$$

$$\left| b_{1\beta_k}^R - b_{\beta_k}^R \right| + \left| b_{\beta_k}^R - b_{2\beta_k}^R \right| \geq \left| b_{1\beta_k}^R - b_{2\beta_k}^R \right|.$$

Thus, $D(Z_1, Z_2) \leq D(Z_1, Z) + D(Z, Z_2)$.

An ordered set of discrete Z-numbers. A discrete ordered set $\mathcal{A} = \{Z_1, Z_2, ..., Z_n\} \subseteq \mathcal{Z}$ is called:

1) *uniform* if $D(Z_i, Z_{i+1}) = const$ for any $Z_i, Z_{i+1} \in \mathcal{A}$, that is, all distances between any two consecutive points in $\mathcal{A}$ are equal;

2) *bounded down* if for some $t > 0$ one has $D(Z_i, Z_{i+1}) > t$ for any $Z_i, Z_{i+1} \in \mathcal{A}$, that is, all distances between any two consecutive points in $\mathcal{A}$ are larger than some $t > 0$;

3) *bounded up* if for some $t > 0$ one has $D(Z_i, Z_{i+1}) < t$ for any $Z_i, Z_{i+1} \in \mathcal{A}$, that is, all distances between any two consecutive points in $\mathcal{A}$ are less than some $t > 0$;

Definition 6.2. Spacing of a uniform set of discrete Z-numbers.

1) In a uniform discrete set $\mathcal{A}$, the distances between any two consecutive points is called the *spacing* of $\mathcal{A}$.

2) In a bounded down discrete set $\mathcal{A}$, the lower bound of distances between consecutive points in $\mathcal{A}$ is called the *lower inner bound* of $\mathcal{A}$; it is denoted by *libA*.

3) In a bounded up discrete set $\mathcal{A}$, the lower bound of distances between consecutive points in $\mathcal{A}$ is called the *upper inner bound* of $\mathcal{A}$; it is denoted by *uibA*.

The concept of the lower and upper inner bounds are mainly used for a choice of a discretization in concrete practical problems of construction of functions of Z-numbers. Particularly, when we use a set of discrete Z-numbers as values of argument of a function, the lower and upper inner bounds of this set should be chosen by taking into account the fact that the values of lower and upper inner bounds of the set of the resulted Z-values of a function will naturally increase. In other words, in a practice, a choice of these bounds is based on a trade-off of accuracy and computational complexity.

Lemma 6.1. *If $\mathcal{A}$ and $\mathcal{A}'$ are discrete sets and $\mathcal{A} \subseteq \mathcal{A}'$, then $lib\mathcal{A}' \le lib\mathcal{A}$ and $uib\mathcal{A}' \le uib\mathcal{A}$.*

The proof is obvious.

Definition 6.3. A discrete Z-number valued infinity. Let $Z = (A, B)$ be a discrete Z-number. If for every positive real number M, there exists $\alpha_0 \in (0,1]$ such that $M < A_2^{\alpha_0}$ or $A_1^{\alpha_0} < -M$, then $Z = (A, B)$ is called discrete Z-number valued infinity, denoted by Z_∞.

Denote by $\mathcal{F}$ a σ-algebra of $\mathcal{A}$. Let us define for two Z-numbers $Z_1 = (A_1, B_1)$ and $Z_2 = (A_2', B_2)$ and state that $Z_1 = Z_2$ iff $A_1 = A_2$ and $B_1 = B_2$. The equality of fuzzy numbers is defined as

$$A_1 = A_2 \text{ iff } \forall x \in X, \quad \mu_{A_1}(x) = \mu_{A_2}(x).$$

Let $\mathcal{A} \subseteq \mathcal{Z}$ be a metric space with a metric D, and r be a non-negative real number, and $Z = \{Z_i | Z_i \in \mathcal{A}, i = 1, 2, ..., n, ...\}$ be a sequence in $\mathcal{A}$.

Definition 6.4. An r-limit. An element $Z \in \mathcal{A}$ is called an r-limit of Z (denoted $Z = r\text{-lim}Z$) if for any $t \in R^+ \setminus \{0\}$ the inequality $D(Z, Z_i) \le r + t$ is valid for almost all Z_i.

For the case of a sequence of continuous Z-numbers, one would have a definition of a limit where $r = 0$.

Definition 6.5. A discrete Z-number valued function of discrete Z-numbers. A discrete Z-number valued function of discrete Z-numbers is a mapping $f : \mathcal{A} \to \mathcal{A}$.

Analogously, in a continuous setting, the Z-function is defined as a mapping between spaces of continuous Z-numbers.

Consider a general case $f : \Omega \to \mathcal{A}$, where Ω is a universe of discourse. Given a Z-number valued function $f : \Omega \to \mathcal{Z}$, a fuzzy number valued function $\varphi : \Omega \to \mathcal{D}$ is called its $\mathcal{A}$-valued function whenever for any $\omega \in \Omega$ one has $\varphi(\omega) = A \in \mathcal{D}$ iff $f(\omega) = (A, B) \in \mathcal{Z}$. A fuzzy number valued function $\gamma : \Omega \to \mathcal{D}_{[0,1]}$ is called $\mathcal{B}$-valued function for $f : \Omega \to \mathcal{Z}$ whenever for any $\omega \in \Omega$ one has $\gamma(\omega) = B \in \mathcal{D}_{[0,1]}$ iff $f(\omega) = (A, B) \in \mathcal{Z}$.

Definition 6.6. An $_r$-limit of discrete Z-number valued function of discrete Z-numbers. An element $Z_d \in f(Z)$ is called an $_r$-limit of f at a point $Z_{a,i} \in Z$ and denoted $Z_d = r\text{-}\lim_{Z_x \to Z_a} f(Z_x)$ if for any sequence $\bar{Z}$ satisfying the condition $Z_a = \lim Z$, the equality $Z_d = r\text{-}\lim f(Z)$ is valid.

Theorem 6.1. If $Z_d = r\text{-}\lim_{Z_x \to Z_a} f(Z)$ and $q \in R^+$, then qZ_d is $rq\text{-}\lim_{Z_x \to Z_a} qf(Z)$.

Proof. Denote $f(Z_x) = Z_y = (A_y, B_y)$ and $Z_d = (A_d, B_d)$. As for a Z-number $Z = (A, B)$, $qZ = q(A, B) = (qA, B)$ holds, one has:

$$D(qZ_d, qf(Z_x)) = D(qZ_d, qZ_y)$$

$$= \left(\frac{1}{n+1} \sum_{k=1}^{n} \left\{ \left| qa_{d1\alpha_k}^L - qa_{y2\alpha_k}^L \right| + \left| qa_{d1\alpha_k}^R - qa_{y2\alpha_k}^R \right| \right\} + \frac{1}{m+1} \sum_{k=1}^{m} \left\{ \left| b_{d1\beta_k}^L - b_{y2\beta_k}^L \right| + \left| b_{d1\beta_k}^R - b_{y2\beta_k}^R \right| \right\} \right)$$

$$= \left(q \frac{1}{n+1} \sum_{k=1}^{n} \left\{ \left| a_{d1\alpha_k}^L - a_{y2\alpha_k}^L \right| + \left| a_{d1\alpha_k}^R - a_{y2\alpha_k}^R \right| \right\} + \frac{1}{m+1} \sum_{k=1}^{m} \left\{ \left| b_{d1\beta_k}^L - b_{y2\beta_k}^L \right| + \left| b_{d1\beta_k}^R - b_{y2\beta_k}^R \right| \right\} \right)$$

$$\leq q \left(\frac{1}{n+1} \sum_{k=1}^{n} \left\{ \left| a_{d1\alpha_k}^L - a_{y2\alpha_k}^L \right| + \left| a_{d1\alpha_k}^R - a_{y2\alpha_k}^R \right| \right\} + \frac{1}{m+1} \sum_{k=1}^{m} \left\{ \left| b_{d1\beta_k}^L - b_{y2\beta_k}^L \right| + \left| b_{d1\beta_k}^R - b_{y2\beta_k}^R \right| \right\} \right)$$

$$= qD(Z_d, f(Z_x)).$$

Thus, $D(qZ_d, qf(Z_x)) \leq qD(Z_d, f(Z_x))$. As $Z_d = r\text{-}\lim_{Z_x \to Z_a} f(Z)$ then $D(Z_d, f(Z_x)) \leq r + t$ for any $t > 0$. Thus, $D(qZ_d, qf(Z_x)) \leq q(r + t)$, and, therefore, qZ_d is an $rq\text{-}\lim_{Z_x \to Z_a} qf(Z)$.

Definition 6.7. (q, r)-continuous Z-function. A function $f : \mathcal{A} \to \mathcal{A}$ is called (q, r)-*continuous* at a point $Z_a \in \mathcal{A}$ if for any $\varepsilon > 0$ there is $\delta > 0$ such that the inequality $D(Z_a, Z_x) < q + \delta$ implies the inequality

$D(f(Z_a), f(Z_x)) < r + \varepsilon$,   or   in   other   words,   for   any Z_x with $D(Z_a, Z_x) < q + \delta$, we have $D(f(Z_a), f(Z_x)) < r + \varepsilon$.

For the spaces of continous Z-numbers the continuity of Z-valued function is defined in a traditional sense, that is, when $q = 0$ and $r=0$.

In [814] they provide a definition of a measurability of a fuzzy number valued function. By using this concept, below we formulate a definition of measurability of a Z-number valued function:

.**Definition 6.8.** Measurability of a discrete Z-number valued function. A Z-valued function $f : \Omega \to \mathcal{Z}$ is called a measurable Z-valued function if its A-valued function $\varphi : \Omega \to \mathcal{D}$ and L-valued function $\gamma : \Omega \to \mathcal{D}_{[0,1]}$ are measurable fuzzy mappings.

Examples.

Let us provide examples illustrating the concept of r-limit.

Example 1. Consider the following function:

$$f(Z_x) = \begin{cases} Z_c^2 + 1/i \, when \, Z_x = Z_c - 1/i \, for \, i = 1,2,3,...; \\ Z_c^2 + 1 - 1/i \, when \, Z_x = Z_c + 1/2i \, for \, i = 1,2,3,...; \\ Z_c^2 + (-1)^i \, when \, Z_x = Z_c + 1/(2i+1) \, for \, i = 1,2,3,...; \\ Z_x^2 \, otherwise \end{cases},$$

where Z_c is a Z-number $Z_c = ((3,4,5),(0.7,0.8,0.9))$.

f has no conventional limit at the point $Z_x = Z_c$, but has various r-limits at this point. Consider the Z-number $Z = (A, B)$, where A is described by the following membership function:

$$\mu_A(x) = \begin{cases} 0, & if \, x < 9 \, \, x > 25 \\ -3 + \sqrt{x}, & if \, 9 \leq x < 16 \\ 5 - \sqrt{x}, & if \, 16 \leq x < 25 \end{cases},$$

and B is a triangular fuzzy number $B = (0.7, 0.8, 0.9)$.

For simplicity, consider parameters $n = m = 2$ in the formula of distance D (Definition 6.1). First, consider the sequence $Z_x = Z_c - 1/i$ *for* $i = 1, 2, 3, \ldots$. Then $f(Z_x) = (A_y, B)$ (as the square operation does not change B part), where $A_y^\alpha = [(3 + \alpha)^2 + 1/i, (5 - \alpha)^2 + 1/i]$. In this case we have:

$D(f(Z_x), (A, B))$

$$\frac{1}{2+1} \sum_{k=1}^{2} \left\{ \left| a_{1\alpha_k}^L - a_{2\alpha_k}^L \right| + \left| a_{1\alpha_k}^R - a_{2\alpha_k}^R \right| \right\} + \frac{1}{2+1} \sum_{k=1}^{m} \left\{ \left| b_{1\beta_k}^L - b_{2\beta_k}^L \right| + \left| b_{1\beta_k}^R - b_{2\beta_k}^R \right| \right\}$$

$$= \frac{1}{3} \left(\left| a_{1\alpha_1}^L - a_{2\alpha_1}^L \right| + \left| a_{1\alpha_1}^R - a_{2\alpha_1}^R \right| + \left| a_{1\alpha_2}^L - a_{2\alpha_2}^L \right| + \left| a_{1\alpha_2}^R - a_{2\alpha_2}^R \right| \right)$$

$$= \frac{1}{3} \left(\left| (3 + \alpha_1)^2 + 1/i - (3 + \alpha_1)^2 \right| + \left| (5 - \alpha_1)^2 + 1/i - (5 - \alpha_1)^2 \right| \right)$$

$$+ \frac{1}{3} \left(\left| (3 + \alpha_2)^2 + 1/i - (3 + \alpha_2)^2 \right| + \left| (5 - \alpha_2)^2 + 1/i - (5 - \alpha_2)^2 \right| \right) = \frac{1}{3} \cdot 4/i.$$

Thus, when $Z_x = Z_c - 1/i \to Z$, i.e. when $i \to \infty$, one has $D(f(Z_x), (A, B)) \to 0$.

For the sequence $Z = Z_x = Z_c + 1/2i$, $i = 1, 2, 3, \ldots$, one has $f(Z_x) = (A_y, B)$, where $A_y^\alpha = [(3 + \alpha)^2 + 1 - 1/i, (5 - \alpha)^2 + 1 - 1/i]$. In this case we have:

$D(f(Z_x), (A, B))$

$$\frac{1}{3} \left(\left| (3 + \alpha_1)^2 + 1 - 1/i - (3 + \alpha_1)^2 \right| + \left| (5 - \alpha_1)^2 + 1 - 1/i - (5 - \alpha_1)^2 \right| \right)$$

$$+ \frac{1}{3} \left(\left| (3 + \alpha_2)^2 + 1 - 1/i - (3 + \alpha_2)^2 \right| + \left| (5 - \alpha_2)^2 + 1 - 1/i - (5 - \alpha_2)^2 \right| \right)$$

$$= \frac{1}{3} \cdot 4(1 - 1/i).$$

Therefore, $\lim D(f(Z_x), Z) = 4/3$ when $Z_x = Z_c + 1/2i \to Z_c, i = 1, 2, 3, \ldots,$.

Third, it can be shown that for sequence $Z_x = Z_c + 1/(2i+1)$ *for* $i = 1,2,3,...$ the limit is also $\lim D(f(Z_x), Z) = 4/3$.

Fourth, it can be shown that for any other sequence one has $D(f(Z_x),(A,B)) \to 0$ (as for any other sequence except those considered above, the considered function is defined as $f(Z_x) = Z_x^2$. Thus, we can say that the considered Z-number $Z = (A,B)$ is a 4/3-limit of f.

From a practical point of view, this result can be interpreted as follows. Assume that in a whole, the considered function is defined as $f(Z_x) = Z_x^2$. However, for a practical problem this can be an approximated form. Due to measurement errors, missed factors and other issues, a real value of some variable described by this function can deviate from $f(Z_x) = Z_x^2$. In accordance with the example, it can be $Z_c^2 + 1/5$, $Z_c^2 + 1 - 1/2$ or $Z_c^2 - 1$ when $Z_x \approx Z_c$. Thus, we can say that the function can be in general described as $f(Z_x) = Z_x^2$, but with accuracy level of 4/3.

6.5 Reasoning with Z-information

6.5.1 *State-of-the-art*

In essence, approximate reasoning refers to a process of inferring imprecise conclusions from imprecise premises [244, 536, 577, 677, 804]. As one can witness, this process often takes place in various fields of human activity including economics, decision analysis, system analysis, control, everyday activity etc. The reason for this is that information relevant to real-world problems is, as a rule, imperfect. We can state that in a wide sense, approximate reasoning is reasoning with imperfect information.

The research on approximate reasoning was initiated by Zadeh in [827, 843]. As Zadeh mentioned, fuzzy logic is logic of approximate reasoning. Nowadays, existing approaches to approximate reasoning form a large family of methods for reasoning under fuzzy uncertainty. In [573] the authors overviewed the state-of-the-art of the paradigm and widely discuss the fields of its practical applications. A real-world example of an approximate reasoning based linguistic recognition system is suggested. In [492] an application of approximate reasoning to construction of fuzzy controllers for industrial plants is considered.

The recent results on approximate reasoning and its applications in business, economics, healthcare and other fields can be found in [247, 468, 747, 766]. A series of works are devoted to lattice-valued logic, fuzzy implication algebra and fuzzy lattice reasoning methods including applications in classification and pattern recognition [149, 383, 398, 576, 598].

In [798] they introduce various settings of the theory of approximate reasoning. Particularly, approximate reasoning equipped with capability of probability theory is considered. As an alternative to the compositional rule of inference method which is characterized by computational complexity, the interpolation-based approaches to approximate reasoning were suggested [397, 830]. The approach suggested in [397] is based on the well-known and effective linear interpolation technique. The coefficients of linearity are determined based on the distances between a current input and the antecedents. Nowadays a wide class of interpolative reasoning methods and its applications exists [171, 183, 184, 193, 391, 392, 601].

A comparative analysis of fuzzy reasoning methods based on implication operators is offered in [28]. A new fuzzy reasoning approach is suggested.

As it can be seen, a paradigm of approximate reasoning is tightly connected with the essence of imperfect information. Real-world imperfect information is mainly characterized by two features. On the one hand, real-world information is often described based on perception, experience and knowledge of a human being. In turn, these operate with linguistic description carrying imprecision and vagueness, for which fuzzy sets based formalization can be used. In general, an idea of modeling combination of fuzzy and probabilistic uncertainties is considered in a series of works, including works on fuzzy belief rule based systems, fuzzy belief networks, imprecise probabilities, fuzzy and probabilistic information fusion and other works [202, 203, 245, 246, 248, 390, 726, 877]. However, the idea of Z-number concept is a more general and intuitive basis for dealing with combination of fuzzy and probabilistic uncertainties.

Unfortunately, as of now, there is no fundamental research on approximate reasoning based on Z-rules in existence. We need a new formalism able to derive Z-number valued conclusions from Z-number valued information that can serve as a basis of real-world approximate reasoning with imprecision and partial reliability. A problem of calculus of If-Then rules with Z-number based antecedents and consequents, termed as Z-rules, was first addresses by Zadeh as a very important problem with potential practical application [821]. Indeed, for real-world approximate reasoning, presence of incomplete beliefs is unavoidable. The Z-rule base is complete when for all the possible observations at least one rule exists whose Z-antecedent part overlaps the current Z-number-valued antecedent, at least partially. Otherwise, the Z-rule base is incomplete. This is a more realistic view, as there is often no sufficient knowledge in existence to construct a base taking into account all the possible cases with fuzzy and probabilistic uncertainties, or construction of such base may be too costly. In case if there is incomplete (sparse) Z-rule base, the classical reasoning methods based on compositional rule of inference [28, 823-826, 828], including Mamdani [492], Takagi-Sugeno [704] or Aliev [15] reasoning approaches are not so effective to adapt generating an output for the observation covered by none of the rules. In such cases, for reasoning with Z-rules it would be adequate to utilize the idea underlying interpolation based approaches [830].

The objective of this section is to propose an approach for reasoning with Z-rules. On the one hand, a new approach should be able to deal with combination of fuzzy and probabilistic uncertainties. A reduction to pure fuzzy case or pure probabilistic case would not preserve important features of information. On the other hand, a new approach should be computationally effective in order to cope with complexity of processing combination of fuzzy and probabilistic information. The use of an approach based on the composition rule of inference would be quite complex from theoretical and computational points of view. In view of this, we propose an approach based on an interpolation idea, namely a Z-interpolation method. The computational and theoretical complexities of such approach are sufficiently low to effectively process both fuzziness and probabilistic uncertainty. This forms a perspective of potential application of the approach for a wide class of real-world problems.

6.5.2 *Fuzzy and Z-number-valued If-Then rules*

There are two main approaches to reasoning with fuzzy If-Then rules in existence. The first is the classical fuzzy reasoning which is based on the composition rule of inference [244, 804]. In this approach, a fuzzy relation between fuzzy inputs and fuzzy outputs of rules is constructed on the basis of implication operators [28, 244, 804]. The reasoning is implemented by using a composition of a current fuzzy input with a fuzzy relation matrix to produce a corresponding fuzzy output. The main problem here is that it can be used only when a complete rule base is available, i.e. any possible fuzzy input in a considered problem will necessarily overlap with at least one rule in a rule base. Otherwise, the method will not produce a fuzzy output.

The second approach is the so-called interpolation fuzzy reasoning [397, 830]. It facilitates reasoning when a current fuzzy input does not intersect with inputs of existing rules. For a new fuzzy input, a corresponding fuzzy output is computed as an interpolation of fuzzy outputs. The coefficients of interpolation are computed subject to distance of a new input to the antecedents of rules. This approach is more practical as it allows constructing only most important rules to be used. On the other hand, the approach is of a lower computational complexity than the classical fuzzy reasoning.

Let us discuss abilities of fuzzy If-Then rules to operate under combination of fuzzy and probabilistic uncertainties. Assume that we need to model relationships between independent random variables X_1, X_2 and dependent random variable Y. Assume also one constructed the following two fuzzy If-Then rules to model these relationships:

If X_1 is low and X_2 is high Then Y is low

If X_1 is high and X_2 is low Then Y is high.

However, as X_1 and X_2 are random variables, an adequate description of a new input to the rules would be, for example, X_1 *is low is with medium probability* and X_2 *is high with high probability*. This implies that formalization of uncertainty in the evaluations requires the use of both membership function and probability density functions (pdfs). Moreover, the used probability evaluations are imprecise, e.g. *probability is medium*. This implies that the 'true' pdf is unknown and one has to consider a set of pdfs behind the evaluation. However, the calculus of fuzzy If-Then rules is not able to process pdfs. Thus, the considered evaluations cannot be processed 'as is'. In contrast, combination of probabilistic and fuzzy uncertainty should be reduced to fuzzy uncertainty in some way to apply fuzzy reasoning. This will lead not only to loss of information but also to disregarding the property of X_1 and X_2 to be the random variables.

In [825] suggested was a way to construct probabilistic fuzzy logic systems to be applied for problems characterized by both fuzzy and probabilistic (stochastic) uncertainties. This approach is based on construction of fuzzy sets with membership functions whose values are randomized based on a predefined pdf (often a normal random variable is used). However, the main problem is that in real world settings, a 'true' pdf is not exactly known. For an expert, it is likely to express a conclusive imprecise degree of belief for an adequacy of a considered fuzzy value, but not to search for an adequate randomization of its membership function. This imprecision of belief naturally implies necessity to deal with a set of pdfs. Therefore, for some problems, the use of probabilistic fuzzy If-Then rules may not be adequate. Incorporating probabilistic uncertainty directly into membership function is complex and counterintuitive.

Let us consider ability of probabilistic fuzzy rules to process combination of fuzzy and probabilistic information. The following two rules are given:

$$\textit{If } X_1 \textit{ is } A_{11,prob} \textit{ and } X_2 \textit{ is } A_{12,prob} \textit{ Then } _Y \textit{ is } C_{1,prob}$$

$$\textit{If } X_1 \textit{ is } A_{21,prob} \textit{ and } X_2 \textit{ is } A_{22,prob} \textit{ Then } _Y \textit{ is } C_{2,prob}$$

where $A_{ij,prob}$, C_i, $i, j = 1, 2$ are probabilistic fuzzy sets.

The problem is to realize reasoning on the basis of these rules given the inputs X_1 is (A_1, B_1) and X_2 is (A_2, B_2). The formal description of combination of fuzzy and probabilistic uncertainties for the considered inputs (Z-valued formalization) differs from that of the considered rules. Therefore, it is needed to use some transformation of (A_i, B_i), $i = 1, 2$ into $A_{i,prob}$, where the latter is a probabilistic fuzzy set. However, as (A_i, B_i), $i = 1, 2$ handles a fuzzy set of pdfs, and $A_{i,prob}$ is based on randomization of membership function by only one pdf, the loss of useful information related to probabilistic uncertainty is inevitable.

In [390, 766] fuzzy belief-rule based systems are considered which are designed as an improvement of fuzzy systems for modeling complex uncertain processes. In these systems, probabilistic information is introduced in the consequent parts in terms of an exact probability distribution over possible fuzzy outputs. In other words, a consequent part is composed of pairs with each pair containing the fuzzy value of a possible output and an associated precise probability. Such a pair can be considered as a special case of a Z-number. However, in real-world applications, assigning a precise accurate probability to a fuzzy value is counterintuitive and difficult due to absence of relevant information. Z-number valued If-Then rules are of a more adequate and intuitive formalization in which imprecise values of probability measure is used in both antecedent and consequent parts.

Let us now consider Z-number valued If-Then rules:

If X_1 is (A_{11}, B_{11}) and X_2 is (A_{12}, B_{12}) Then $_Y$ is (A_1, B_1)

If X_1 is (A_{21}, B_{21}) and X_2 is (A_{22}, B_{22}) Then $_Y$ is (A_2, B_2).

These rules provide a more adequate description of relation between random variables X_1, X_2 and $_Y$ under combination of fuzzy and probabilistic uncertainties. Of course, computation with such rules is of a higher computational complexity as compared to that of pure fuzzy rules. In order to reduce computational complexity of dealing with Z-numbers, in [408] they suggest converting a Z-number to a fuzzy number. However, the loss of information related to such conversion may lead to the following situation. Consider the following Z-number valued If-Then rules:

$$If\ _x is\ ((26,28,30),(0.6,0.64,0.7))$$

$$Then\ _Y is\ ((40,50,60),(0.7,0.8,0.9))$$

$$If\ _x is\ ((34.7,37.3,40),(0.3,0.36,0.42))$$

$$Then\ _Y is\ ((20,30,40),(0.5,0.6,0.7)).$$

We have converted the Z-numbers in the considered If-Then rules into fuzzy numbers on the basis of the approach in [408]. As a result, the following fuzzy If-Then rules are obtained:

$$If\ _x is\ (20.8,22.4,24)\ Then\ _Y is\ (35.8,44.7,53.7)$$

$$If\ _x is\ (20.8,22.4,24)\ Then\ _Y is\ (15.5,23.23,31).$$

One can see that these rules are contradictory. Despite the fact that the inputs coincide, the outputs differ substantially. Thus, loss of information related to conversion of Z-number valued information into fuzzy-valued one may lead to serious mistakes.

Let us now consider conversion of Z-numbers into generalized fuzzy numbers.

$$If\ _x is\ ((26,28,30),(0.6,0.64,0.7))$$

$$Then\ _Y is\ ((40,50,60),(0.7,0.8,0.9))$$

$$If\ _x is\ ((34.7,37.3,40),(0.3,0.36,0.42))$$

$$Then\ _Y is\ ((20,30,40),(0.5,0.6,0.7)).$$

The obtained generalized fuzzy If-Then rules are as follows.

$$If\ _x is\ (26,28,30;0.64)\ Then\ _Y is\ (40,50,60;0.8)$$

$$If\ _x is\ (34.7,37.3,40;0.36)\ Then\ _Y is\ (20,30,40;0.6).$$

As one can see, in these rules information on probabilistic uncertainty is lost. This implies that the important fact that $_x$ and $_y$ are indeed random variables is disregarded.

6.5.3 *Approximate reasoning with Z-rules*

6.5.3.1 *Linear interpolation-based reasoning with Z-rules*

A problem of interpolation of Z-rules is the generalization of interpolation of fuzzy rules [439]. The problem of Z-interpolation is given below.
Given the following Z-rules:

$$\text{If } X_1 \text{ is } Z_{X_1,1} = (A_{X_1,1}, B_{X_1,1}) \text{ and, ..., and } X_m \text{ is } Z_{X_m,1} = (A_{X_m,1}, B_{X_m,1}) \text{ then } _Y$$
$$\text{is } Z_Y = (A_{Y,1}, B_{Y,1})$$

$$\text{If } X_1 \text{ is } Z_{X_1,2} = (A_{X_1,2}, B_{X_1,2}) \text{ and, ..., and } X_m \text{ is } Z_{X_m,2} = (A_{X_m,2}, B_{X_m,2}) \text{ then } _Y$$
$$\text{is } Z_Y = (A_{Y,2}, B_{Y,2})$$

.

.

.

$$\text{If } X_1 \text{ is } Z_{X_1,n} = (A_{X_1,n}, B_{X_1,n}) \text{ and, ..., and } X_m \text{ is } Z_{X_m,n} = (A_{X_m,n}, B_{X_m,n}) \text{ then } _Y$$
$$\text{is } Z_Y = (A_{Y,n}, B_{Y,n})$$

and a current observation

$$X_1 \text{ is } Z'_{X_1} = (A'_{X_1}, B'_{X_1}) \text{ and, ..., and } X_m \text{ is } Z'_{X_m} = (A'_{X_m}, B'_{X_m}),$$

find the Z-value of $_Y$.

The idea underlying the suggested interpolation approach is that the resulting output should be computed as a convex combination of consequent parts. The coefficients of linear interpolation are determined on the basis of the similarity between a current input and the antecedent parts [439]. This implies for Z-rules that the resulting output Z'_Y is computed as

$$Z'_Y = \sum_{j=1}^{n} w_j Z_{Y,j} = \sum_{j=1}^{n} w_j (A_{Y,j}, B_{Y,j}) \qquad (6.23)$$

where $Z_{Y,j}$ is the Z-valued consequent of the j-th rule, $w_j = \dfrac{\rho_j}{\sum_{k=1}^{n} \rho_k}$,

$j = 1,...,n$; $k = 1,...,n$ are coefficients of linear interpolation, $_n$ is the number of Z-rules. ρ_j is defined as follows.

$$\rho_j = \min_{i=1,...,m} S(Z'_{X_i}, Z_{X_i,j}) \qquad (6.24)$$

where s is the similarity between current i-th Z-number-valued input and the i-th Z-number-valued antecedent of the j-th rule. Thus, ρ_j computes the similarity between a current input vector and the vector of the antecedents of j-th rule [868].

Formula (6.24) requires using a similarity measure of Z-numbers, and formulating operations of addition and scalar multiplication of discrete Z-numbers. As similarity measure Jacard index may be used.

Definition 6.9. Jaccard index based similarity of discrete Z-numbers. A Jaccard index similarity $J(Z_1, Z_2)$ of discrete Z-numbers Z_1, Z_2 is defined as follows.

$$J(Z_1, Z_2)$$

$$= \frac{1}{2} \frac{\sum_{k=1}^{K} \mu_{A_1}(x_k) \cdot \mu_{A_2}(x_k)}{\sum_{k=1}^{K} \left(\mu_{A_1}(x_k)\right)^2 + \sum_{k=1}^{K} \left(\mu_{A_2}(x_k)\right)^2 - \sum_{k=1}^{K} \mu_{A_1}(x_k) \cdot \mu_{A_2}(x_k)}$$

$$+ \frac{1}{2} \frac{\sum_{k=1}^{K} \mu_{B_1}(x_k) \cdot \mu_{B_2}(x_k)}{\sum_{k=1}^{K} \left(\mu_{B_1}(x_k)\right)^2 + \sum_{k=1}^{K} \left(\mu_{B_2}(x_k)\right)^2 - \sum_{k=1}^{K} \mu_{B_1}(x_k) \cdot \mu_{B_2}(x_k)}.$$

6.6 Ranking of Z-numbers

6.6.1 *State-of-the-art*

Real-world problems are characterized by information which can be adequately described by Z-numbers. Therefore, as decision making involves choice among available alternatives, one of the most important problems arising is ranking of Z-numbers. Indeed, as soon as the basic components of decision problems including possible results of alternative course of actions, objective conditions of decision environment, criteria evaluation of alternatives are described by using Z-numbers, ranking of Z-numbers is a desired operation for a valid decision analysis.

A huge number of studies is devoted to ranking of intervals and fuzzy numbers and their application to decision making [60, 75, 130, 182, 418, 557, 628, 682, 737, 765, 818]. From the other side, there are a lot of approaches in existence devoted to comparison of random variables [221, 222, 533, 537, 745, 875]. However, ranking of Z-numbers which involves dealing with both fuzzy and probabilistic information is in its initial stage of development. The problem of ranking of Z-numbers is first addressed by Zadeh in [821].

As Zadeh mentions, the problems of computation and ranking of Z-numbers fall within an uncharted territory of processing information characterized by both fuzziness and partial reliability. Nowadays there are a few approaches to this problem in existence, which are shortly overviewed below.

In [410, 802, 803] it is suggested to rank Z-numbers by proceeding to the corresponding fuzzy numbers. The comparison of Z-numbers by reducing them to fuzzy numbers and its application to management, decision making, risk analysis, and forecasting is studied in [79, 80, 532, 659].

Ranking Z-numbers on the basis of transformation into generalized fuzzy numbers is proposed in [82]. Let us mention that all these methods are characterized by loss of information (due to conversion of Z-numbers to fuzzy numbers or generalized fuzzy numbers) and may lead to counterintuitive results.

In [16] they propose a new basis for ranking of discrete Z-numbers. As compared to the works [29, 409, 410, 802, 803], this approach does not lead to conversion of Z-numbers to fuzzy numbers. In contrast, two Z-numbers are formally considered as multiattribute alternatives evaluated with respect to two criteria: the first one measures the value of interest, and the other one estimates reliability of the value. This is a more adequate view on formal and informational structures of Z-numbers.

6.6.2 *Ranking of Z-numbers*

For adequate ranking of Z-numbers in real-world decision problems, it is important to consider at least two main aspects. The first is that in contrast to real numbers, Z-numbers are ordered pairs. This implies that no universal approach may exist for ranking of Z-numbers. For purpose of comparison, we suggest to consider a Z-number as a pair of values of two attributes – one attribute measures value of a variable, the other one measures the associated reliability. Then it will be adequate to compare Z-numbers as multiattribute alternatives. The basic concept of comparison of multiattribute alternatives is the Pareto optimality concept based on a counterintuitive assumption to consider non-dominated alternatives without any information on a degree of dominance. The fuzzy Pareto optimality (FPO) concept [61, 273] fits very well multiattribute problems. This concept is an implementation of the ideas of CW-based redefinitions of the existing scientific concepts [829]. In this approach, by directly comparing alternatives, one arrives at total degrees to which one alternative is better than, is equivalent to and is worse than another one. These degrees are determined as graded sums of differences between attribute values for considered alternatives [61, 273]. This approach is closer to the way humans compare alternatives by confronting their attribute values.

The second aspect is that a Z-number contains fuzzy uncertainty and probabilistic uncertainty. In such settings, the well known behavioral phenomenon of real decision making under uncertainty arises. This phenomenon is the uncertainty aversion [312, 316, 318], i.e. humans prefer less uncertain situations to more uncertain ones, even when the latter may provide higher benefit. In this regard, the well known techniques based on a degree of uncertainty aversion, referred to as uncertainty attitude, should be used in comparison of Z-numbers.

Taking into account the mentioned aspects we suggest to consider comparison of Z-numbers on the basis of the FPO principle [61, 273] and uncertainty attitude as follows. Let Z-numbers $Z_1 = (A_1, B_1)$ and $Z_2 = (A_2, B_2)$ be given. The comparison consists of two main stages. At the first stage it is needed to compare the corresponding components of these Z-numbers to measure how much one of the Z-numbers is better, equivalent and worse than the other one. For this purpose, the functions n_b, n_e, n_w are computed. The function n_b measures the number of components with respect to which $Z_1 = (A_1, B_1)$ dominates $Z_2 = (A_2, B_2)$ (minimum is 0, maximum is 2). The function n_w measures the number of components with respect to which $Z_1 = (A_1, B_1)$ is dominated by $Z_2 = (A_2, B_2)$ (minimum is 0, maximum is 2). The function n_e measures the number of components with respect to which $Z_1 = (A_1, B_1)$ is equivalent to $Z_2 = (A_2, B_2)$ (minimum is 0, maximum is 2).The functions n_b, n_e, n_w are defined as follows:

$$n_b(Z_i, Z_j) = P_b(\delta_A^{i,j}) + P_b(\delta_B^{i,j}), \tag{6.25}$$

$$n_e(Z_i, Z_j) = P_e(\delta_A^{i,j}) + P_e(\delta_B^{i,j}), \tag{6.26}$$

$$n_w(Z_i, Z_j) = P_w(\delta_A^{i,j}) + P_w(\delta_B^{i,j}), \tag{6.27}$$

where $\delta_A^{i,j} = A_i - A_j, \delta_B^{i,j} = B_i - B_j$,$i, j = 1, 2, i \neq j$. The meaning of these functions is as follows. As superiority, equivalence and inferiority are indeed a matter of a degree for human intuition, $P_l()$ may be used as follows:

$$P_l(\delta_A^{i,j}) = \frac{Poss\left(\delta_A^{i,j} | n_l\right)}{\sum_{t \in \{b,e,w\}} Poss\left(\delta_A^{i,j} | n_t\right)},$$

$$P_l(\delta_B^{i,j}) = \frac{Poss\left(\delta_B^{i,j} | n_l\right)}{\sum_{t \in \{b,e,w\}} Poss\left(\delta_B^{i,j} | n_t\right)},$$

where *Poss* is a possibility measure [18] to fuzzy terms of n_b, n_e, n_w. Following [61, 273], we will use the terms shown in Fig. 6.1, $t \in \{b, e, w\}$, $i, j = 1, 2, i \neq j$.

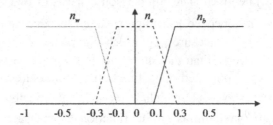

Fig. 6.1. The membership functions for n_b, n_e, n_w

The function $P_l()$ is therefore used as a weighted possibility measure. It is clear that the functions n_b, n_e, n_w may take non-integer values within $[0,2]$. As $\sum_{t \in \{b,e,w\}} P_l(\delta_k^{i,j}) = 1$ will always hold, one will always have

$$n_b(Z_i, Z_j) + n_e(Z_i, Z_j) + n_w(Z_i, Z_j) = N,$$ where N is the number of components of a Z-number, i.e. $N = 2$.

Next, on the basis of n_b, n_e, n_w, the $(1-k)$-dominance is determined which is a degree of dominance. This suggests that $Z_1[A1][A2](1-k)$-dominates Z_2 iff [273]

$$n_e(Z_i, Z_j) < 2, \ n_b(Z_i, Z_j) \geq \frac{2 - n_e(Z_i, Z_j)}{k+1}, \tag{6.28}$$

with $k \in [0,1]$.

Next, one needs to find the highest degree $(1-k)$ to which Z_i Pareto dominates Z_j. For this aim, a function d is used [273]:

$$d(Z_i, Z_j) = \begin{cases} 0, \text{ if } n_b(Z_i, Z_j) \leq \dfrac{2 - n_e(Z_i, Z_j)}{2} \\ \dfrac{2 \cdot n_b(Z_i, Z_j) + n_e(Z_i, Z_j) - 2}{n_b(Z_i, Z_j)}, \text{ otherwise.} \end{cases} \tag{6.29}$$

Then the desired smallest k is determined as $k = 1 - d(Z_i, Z_j)$, i.e. $(1-k) = d(Z_i, Z_j)$. Indeed, $d(Z_i, Z_j) = 1$ implies Pareto dominance of Z_i

over Z_j, whereas $d(Z_i, Z_j) = 0$ implies no Pareto dominance of Z_i over Z_j.

Finally, the degree of optimality $do(Z_i)$ is determined as follows:

$$do(Z_i) = 1 - d(Z_j, Z_i). \tag{6.30}$$

Thus, we can consider $do(Z_i)$ as the overall degree of optimality of a Z-number. Then, one may consider

$$Z_i > Z_j \underset{\text{iff}}{} do(Z_i) > do(Z_j),$$

$$Z_i < Z_j \underset{\text{iff}}{} do(Z_i) < do(Z_j),$$

and $Z_i = Z_j$ otherwise.

This FPO-based procedure may be considered as a first stage for a human-oriented ranking of Z-numbers. One of the main issues inspiring human decision making is that of optimism and pessimism. These are fundamental psychological factors that drive human choices related to consideration of good and bad outcomes and attitudes to ambiguity [666, 667]. Optimistic choices rely on good possible outcomes, brave attitude to uncertainty, assured relation to difficulties and active behavior, but sometimes on naïve and unrealistic expectations. Pessimistic choices are inspired by escaping bad outcomes, cautious attitude to uncertainty, mental numbness under difficulties and passive behavior. In the realm of decision analysis under uncertainty, they were systematically investigated for a long time. One can recall the studies of Hurwitz, Gilboa and Schmeidler and others [312, 318, 371]. Multicriteria decision making, which is characterized by complexities as relation among criteria, imprecise criteria evaluation etc, should also be considered in view of optimism and pessimism profiles. The investigations of the matter in decisions under fuzzy environment are proposed in [186-189, 662, 795].

Thus, the issue of comparison of Z-numbers characterized by dependence of criteria and the presence of probabilistic and fuzzy uncertainty mandates taking into account optimism and pessimism. In view of this, at the second stage of the proposed approach, given the results of the FPO-based procedure we suggest to account for a degree of pessimism $\beta \in [0,1]$ as a mental factor which influences the choice of a preferred Z-number. The degree of pessimism is submitted by a human observer who wishes to compare the considered Z-numbers but does not completely rely on the results obtained by the above mentioned FPO approach. This attitude may result from the different importance of $\measuredangle$ and $\measuredangle$ components for a human being and other issues.

In this viewpoint, given $do(Z_j) \leq do(Z_i)$, we define for two Z-numbers Z_1 and Z_2:

$$r(Z_i, Z_j) = \beta do(Z_j) + (1-\beta)do(Z_i),\tag{6.31}$$

where $(1-\beta)$ is a degree of optimism. Then

$$\left. \begin{array}{l} Z_i > Z_j \text{ iff } r(Z_i, Z_j) > \dfrac{1}{2}(do(Z_i)+do(Z_j)) \\[2mm] Z_i < Z_j \text{ iff } r(Z_i, Z_j) < \dfrac{1}{2}(do(Z_i)+do(Z_j)) \\[2mm] \text{and} \\[1mm] Z_i = Z_j \text{ otherwise} \end{array} \right\}\tag{6.32}$$

Thus, $r(Z_i, Z_j)$ is a convex combination of the degrees of optimality $do(Z_i), i = 1,2$. The use of degree of pessimism $\beta \in [0,1]$ adjusts ranking of Z-numbers to reflect human attitude to the do-based comparison. By assigning β, a human being 'weakens' superiority of a Z-number of the highest do, or completely changes preferences. Without loss of generality suppose that $do(Z_1) < do(Z_2)$. Then, given interval $[do(Z_1), do(Z_2)]$, an assigned β 'shifts' a 'strength' of preference from off $do(Z_2)$. Then, $r(Z_i, Z_j)$ can be considered as a value of a function F which assigns to each interval $[do(Z_1), do(Z_2)]$ a number $F([do(Z_1), do(Z_2)])$:

$$F([do(Z_1), do(Z_2)]) = \beta do(Z_j) + (1-\beta)do(Z_i).$$

F can be considered as a fair price under interval uncertainty, a concept suggested in [479] by one of the co-authors of the present section and his colleagues. In view of this, we formulate the following

Proposition. F has the following properties:

1) Conservativeness: $do(Z_1) \leq F([do(Z_1), do(Z_2)]) \leq do(Z_2)$

2) Monotonicity: If $do(Z_1) = do(Z_1')$ and $do(Z_2) < do(Z_2')$ then
$$F([do(Z_1), do(Z_2)]) \leq F([do(Z_1'), do(Z_2')])$$

3) Additivity:
$$F([do(Z_1) + do(Z_1'), do(Z_2) + do(Z_2')])$$
$$= F([do(Z_1), do(Z_2)]) + F([do(Z_1'), do(Z_2')]).$$

Proof. Here we shortly show that F exhibits the above mentioned properties.

1. The existence of the conservativeness property is obvious.

2. Concerning the monotonicity property, as $do(Z_1) = do(Z_1')$, $do(Z_2) < do(Z_2')$ and $\beta \in [0,1]$, then

$$F([do(Z_1), do(Z_2)]) - F([do(Z_1'), do(Z_2')])$$

$$= \beta do(Z_1) + (1 - \beta) do(Z_2) - (\beta do(Z_1') + (1 - \beta) do(Z_2'))$$

$$= (1 - \beta)(do(Z_2) - do(Z_2')) \leq 0.$$

3. F satisfies the additivity property:

$$F([do(Z_1) + do(Z_1'), do(Z_2) + do(Z_2')])$$

$$= \beta do(Z_1) + (1 - \beta) do(Z_2) + \beta do(Z_1') + (1 - \beta) do(Z_2')$$

$$= F([do(Z_1), do(Z_2)]) + F([do(Z_1'), do(Z_2')]).$$

This completes the proof.

The case of interval, fuzzy and Z-number valued do can also be treated analogously.

Below we consider an example of application of the proposed approach to ranking of Z-numbers.

The suggested approach to ranking of discrete Z-numbers is analogous to that for the continuous framework. At the first stage, the degree of

Pareto optimality is computed for Z-numbers on the basis of (6.25)-(6.27). The main difference is that standard subtraction used in (6.25)-(6.27) is computed based on (5.24) The stage results in computation of degrees of Pareto optimality $do(Z_i), i = 1, 2$ for considered discrete Z-numbers. At the second stage, the obtained degrees of optimality are adjusted by using (6.31)-(6.32) to implement a human like ranking of discrete Z-numbers.

6.7 Aggregation of Z-information

Aggregation of information is important in various fields, especially for decision analysis related to analyzing information obtained from various sources. Aggregation becomes complicated by the fact that information itself is imperfect. On the one hand, this means that information comes in the form of some linguistic description carrying imprecision and vagueness. On the other hand, perception, experience, and knowledge of a human being are not completely, but are partially reliable. A lot of effective approaches exist for aggregation of numerical, interval, probabilistic and fuzzy information. Unfortunately, up to day in the existing literature there is no comprehensive approach to aggregation of Z-number based information. In this section we consider aggregation methods for Z-number based information. We consider averaging, conjunctive and disjunctive operators and Choquet integral based operator for Z-number based information.

6.7.1 *State-of-the-art*

Aggregation of information from various sources in real-world applications is exacerbated by the fact that information itself is imperfect. On the one hand, this means that information is often inherently associated with imprecision [446]. In such cases, linguistic estimates described by fuzzy numbers or intervals are used to deal with imprecise information [27, 28]. On the other hand, sometimes the use of fuzzy numbers may not be sufficient to adequately describe information. The reason is that sources of information such as a human being's perception, experience or knowledge are not completely but partially reliable. As a result, the assigned fuzzy number can be trusted only to some degree of belief, i.e., the provided information is partially reliable. This degree of belief is also naturally described in a linguistic form.

Nowadays a large number of studies exist on aggregation operators for different information frameworks including interval-valued information, probabilistic information and fuzzy information, and their applications in various fields. Such operators as arithmetic and geometric means, maximum and minimum operators and their extensions for aggregation of fuzzy information are well known. The ordered weighted averaging (OWA) operator suggested by [812] as the generalization of these operators found a lot of applications under both precise and fuzzy information in decision analysis and other fields [103, 330, 525, 769, 793, 794, 878]. The Choquet integral based on the use of a capacity (non-additive measure) is able to account for dependence between aggregated values. One of the most commonly considered is the Choquet Expected Utility developed in [669]. Let us mention that the famous Cumulative prospect theory is based on the Choquet integral [734]. For fuzzy framework, this integral was developed in [20, 24, 814, 869]. In [20] proposed was the theory of decision making under fuzzy information based on the use of fuzzy valued Choquet integral. [705] suggested concepts of fuzzy integral and fuzzy measure [329]. The Sugeno integral generalizes maximum and minimum operators.

The nature of information is one of the important issues to account for aggregation purposes. In the case of complex quantities such as linguistic quantities, aggregation can be provided in the framework of fuzzy sets [851]. In the probability theory aggregation problem is supported by the calculus of functions of random variables [782]. Aggregation in real-world settings often requires combining Z-number valued information obtained from a set of sources. Let us consider a typical example. Suppose that each member of a group of experts provides his own evaluation of a value of a variable of interest. The experts naturally have various degrees of competence which play the role of the partial reliability of the provided evaluations. Thus, what will be the resulting aggregated value and what will be its associated partial reliability? In other words, we need to determine the final opinion of the group and the associated partial reliability. Answering this question requires combining both imprecise evaluations and partial reliability in a single processing framework. Another example can be found in the area of an employee evaluation. Suppose that a manager of a firm need to express his opinion on one of his employees. The manager considers the following criteria: initiative, problem solving, job knowledge, human relation skills. On the one side, values of these criteria are assigned based on perception, knowledge and intuition of the manager. As a result, these are imprecise and linguistically described. On the other side, the manager is not completely sure in his evaluation as it is impossible to predict human behavior for sure always. Moreover, degrees of beliefs vary with respect to criteria evaluation. In evaluating job knowledge, the manager can be surer than in evaluating problem solving or human relations skills as these criteria are more complex and depend on psychological condition of the employee. Suppose that the manager provides his opinion: (high, likely), (medium, medium), (high, likely), (medium, not very likely). The degrees of belief are based on the manager's experience of working with his employee and the general life experience, and therefore, is of probabilistic character. The problem is to determine the overall performance of the employee and the associated degree of belief. For solving this problem, some combination of fuzzy and probabilistic computations is needed.

Nowadays a series of works devoted to Z-numbers and their application in decision making, control and other fields [17, 29, 79, 92, 409, 431, 479, 575, 708, 802, 803, 837] exists. However, in all these studies, they reduced the original Z-number valued information to fuzzy information and then apply various operators to aggregate the latter. The drawback of this approach is that this evidently leads to substantial loss of information, especially information concerning partial reliability. As a result, the idea underlying the concept of the Z-number is disregarded. Unfortunately, nowadays there is no research on aggregation operators for Z-number valued information.

Z-number valued information is characterized by fuzziness (fuzzy uncertainty) and probabilistic uncertainty and as such is referred to as bimodal information. Processing of bimodal information requires some synergy of fuzzy arithmetic and probabilistic arithmetic. Only recently, in [16] for the first time the arithmetic of Z-numbers has been introduced, which opens a door to shift the use of aggregation operators to the environment of Z-number valued information.

The novelty of the approach suggested in this section is that this study extends information processing ability of aggregation operators to the environment of Z-number valued information in this way offering solutions to essential problems while contributing to the fundamentals of the discipline of Z numbers. In this study, we studied aggregation operators such as averaging operators, conjunctive and disjunctive operators, and Choquet integral for Z-number valued information. The suggested operations are based on basic arithmetic operations and important algebraic operations [33]. The suggested approach is characterized by a relatively low computational complexity. This offers a perspective of potential application for a wide class of real-world problems.

6.7.2 Aggregation operators for Z-numbers based information

6.7.2.1 Z-arithmetic mean

In general, arithmetic mean is an aggregation operator of the simplest structure. Let us consider Z-arithmetic mean, the arithmetic mean for Z-numbers. Let a Z-valued vector $Z = (Z_1, Z_2, ..., Z_n)$ be given. The arithmetic mean operator $M\,()$ assigns to any vector Z a unique Z-number $Z_M = M(Z_1, Z_2, ..., Z_n) = (A_M, B_M)$:

$$M(Z_1, Z_2, ..., Z_n) = \frac{1}{n}\sum_{i=1}^{n} Z_i \,. \qquad (6.33)$$

The operation of addition and scalar multiplication of discretized Z-numbers used in (6.33) is performed as it is shown in Section 6.3.

6.7.2.2 Z-geometric mean

Let us consider a Z-valued vector $Z = (Z_1, Z_2, ..., Z_n)$. The geometric mean operator G assigns to any vector Z a unique Z-number $Z_G = G(Z_1, Z_2, ..., Z_n) = (A_G, B_G)$:

$$G(Z_1, Z_2, ..., Z_n) = \sqrt[r]{\prod_{i=1}^{r} Z_i} \,. \qquad (6.34)$$

The operation of multiplication of discrete Z-numbers and r-th root of discrete Z-number are performed in accordance with the approach shown in Section 6.3.

Let us mention that for even r and for $x_i \geq 0, i = 1,...,n$, one has $B_Y = B_X$ (see section 6.3.3.2)[16].

6.7.2.3 Z-weighted arithmetic mean

Let us consider real-valued weighting vector $W = (W_1, W_2,...,W_n)$ and Z-valued vector $Z = (Z_1, Z_2,...,Z_n)$. A weighted arithmetic mean operator WA assigns to any two vectors W and Z a unique Z-number $Z_W = (A_W, B_W) = WA(Z_1, Z_2,...,Z_n)$:

$$WA(Z_1, Z_2,...,Z_n) = \sum_{i=1}^{n} W_i Z_i .$$ (6.35)

The operations of addition and scalar multiplication of discrete Z-numbers used in (6.35) are described in Section 6.3.

6.7.2.4 Z-T-norm and Z-T-conorm operators

As it was mentioned above, T-norm operators and T-conorm operators are typical conjunctive operators and disjunctive operators respectively. In fuzzy settings, they are widely used in linguistic IF-THEN rules based control, modeling, forecasting and other approaches. In this section we develop T-norm operators and T-conorm operators for Z-numbers.

Z-T-norm operators. Assume that a vector of Z-numbers $Z = (Z_1, Z_2,...,Z_n)$ is given. There is a unique Z-number $Z_T = (A_T, B_T)$ built by T-norm operation in existence. For simplicity, assume that *n=2*. Then $A_T = T(A_1, A_2)$ is determined as follows [151,156].

$$T(A_1, A_2) = \bigcup_{\alpha \in (0,1]} \alpha T(A_1^\alpha, A_2^\alpha), \; T(A_1^\alpha, A_2^\alpha) = \left\{ T(x,y) \middle| x \in A_1^\alpha, y \in A_2^\alpha \right\},$$ (6.36)

The convolutions $p_{12} = p_1 \circ p_2$ of distributions p_1 and p_2 are determined as

$$p_{12}(x) = \sum_{x=T(x_1,x_2)} p_1(x_1)p_2(x_2) \cdot$$

Calculation of B_T is performed analogously to the procedure shown in Section 6.3. Let us mention that the minimum operator is the highest T-norm operator.

Z-T-conorm operators. For a vector of Z-numbers $Z = (Z_1, Z_2, ..., Z_n)$ a unique Z-number $Z_S = (A_S, B_S)$ built by T-conorm operation exists. For simplicity, assume that $n=2$. $A_S = S(A_1, A_2)$ is determined as follows [151, 156].

$$S(A_1, A_2) = \bigcup_{\alpha \in (0,1]} \alpha S(A_1^\alpha, A_2^\alpha), \ S(A_1^\alpha, A_2^\alpha) = \left\{ S(x,y) \middle| x \in A_1^\alpha, y \in A_2^\alpha \right\}, \quad (6.37)$$

The convolutions $p_{12} = p_1 \circ p_2$ of distributions p_1 and p_2 are determined as

$$p_{12}(x) = \sum_{x=S(x_1,x_2)} p_1(x_1)p_2(x_2) \cdot \quad (6.38)$$

Calculation of B_S is performed by the methodology described in Section 6.3.

6.7.2.5 *Z-ordered weighted averaging operators*

Assume that a vector of Z-numbers $Z = (Z_1, Z_2, ..., Z_n)$ is given. The Z-Ordered Weighted Averaging (Z-OWA) Operator aggregates $Z = (Z_1, Z_2, ..., Z_n)$ into a unique Z-number that will be denoted by $Z_{OWA} = OWA(Z_1, Z_2, ..., Z_n) = (A_{OWA}, B_{OWA})$ as follows.

$$OWA(Z_1, Z_2, ..., Z_n) = \sum_{j=1}^{n} W_j Z_{(j)}$$

Here $(\cdot)$ implies permutation $Z_{(1)} \geq Z_{(2)} \geq ... \geq Z_{(n)}$; $W_j \geq 0, \sum_{j=1}^{n} W_j = 1.$ The addition and scalar multiplication in (6.38) are computed based on the approaches given in Sections 6.3. The important issue is the sense of $\leq$. A new approach to ranking of Z-numbers as multicriteria alternatives on base of fuzzy Pareto optimality concept [61, 273] and a degree of pessimism is suggested in [16]. An alternative approach to ranking Z-numbers is to use the idea of the method proposed in [476] to rank the elements of a non-totally ordered lattice. According to this idea, given Z_j one can construct a chain by means of the minimum and maximum operators of Z-numbers.

As for the traditional case, the OWA operator for the case of Z-numbers describes a family of aggregation operators, including the maximum, the minimum and the arithmetic mean. These operators can be obtained as special cases by customizing values of weights in (6.38). For example, the minimum operator is obtained under $W_1 = 1, W_j = 0, j \neq 1$

$$OWA(Z_1, Z_2, ..., Z_n) = 0 \cdot Z_{(1)} + 0 \cdot Z_{(2)} + ... + 1 \cdot Z_{(n)} = Z_{(n)} \text{ and as}$$

$$Z_{(1)} \geq Z_{(2)} \geq ... \geq Z_{(n)} \text{ then one has}$$

$$Z_{(n)} = \min(Z_{(1)}, Z_{(2)}, ..., Z_{(n)}) = \min(Z_1, Z_2, ..., Z_n).$$

The other operators as Z-arithmetic mean, Z-geometric mean, maximum of Z-numbers are obtained analogously as special cases of Z-OWA.

Fuzzy integrals, also referred to as non-additive integrals, are aggregation operators based on the use of fuzzy (also referred to as non-additive) measure. Fuzzy measure [811] is not constrained by additivity property, and this allows measuring a set not just as collection of independent elements (i.e. not related one to another), but also to take into account relations between elements. The definition of a fuzzy measure is as follows.

Denote $S = \{s_1, s_2, ..., s_n\}$ be a set of sources of Z-number valued information and $P(S)$ be a set of all subsets of S, referred to as the power set of S.

A fuzzy measure on S is a set function $g : P(S) \rightarrow [0,1]$ satisfying the following conditions:

(1) $g(\emptyset) = 0$, $g(S) = 1$; normalization

(2) for $V, W \in P(S)$, if $V \subset W$ then $g(V) \leq g(W)$; monotonicity.

Let $\mathcal{Z} = \{Z_1, Z_2, ..., Z_n\}$ be a set of Z-numbers obtained from the sources of information $\mathcal{S} = \{s_1, s_2, ..., s_n\}$. The discrete Choquet integral of Z-numbers $\mathcal{Z} = \{Z_1, Z_2, ..., Z_n\}$ with respect to the fuzzy measure g is defined as

$$C_g(Z_1, ..., Z_n) = \sum_{i=1}^{n} (Z_{(i)} -_h Z_{(i+1)}) g(S_{(i)}), \tag{6.39}$$

where $(\cdot)$ implies indices are permuted such that $Z_{(1)} \geq Z_{(2)} \geq ... \geq Z_{(n)}$, $Z_{(n+1)} = (0,1)$ $S_{(i)} = \{s_{(1)}, s_{(2)}, ..., s_{(i)}\}$, $S_{(n+1)} = \varnothing$. $-_h$ denotes the Hukuhara difference. The conditions on existence of Hukuhara difference of discrete Z-numbers and the computation procedure for it are given in [33].

Choquet integral is a linear operator and computes distorted average of $Z_1, ..., Z_n$. The Z-weighted arithmetic mean, Z-maximum, Z-minimum and Z-OWA operators are special cases of the considered Choquet integral of Z-numbers.

6.8 Z-numbers and type-2 fuzzy sets: A representation result

Traditional [0,1]-based fuzzy sets were originally invented to describe expert knowledge expressed in terms of imprecise ("fuzzy") words from natural language. To make this description more adequate, several generalizations of the traditional [0,1]-based fuzzy sets have been proposed, among them type-2 fuzzy sets and Z-numbers. In this section we will investigate the relation between these two generalizations. As a result of this study, we show that if we apply data processing to Z-numbers, then we get type-2 sets of special type — that we call monotonic. We also prove that every monotonic type-2 fuzzy set can be represented as a result of applying an appropriate data processing algorithm to some Z-numbers.

6.8.1 *Z-numbers and type-2 fuzzy sets*

In this section, we formulate — and answer — a question about the relation between Z-numbers and type-2 fuzzy sets, two generalizations of the traditional fuzzy sets. To understand why this question is important, let us first recall why we need fuzzy sets — both traditional and generalized — in the first place: this need comes from the need to formalize expert knowledge.

In many application areas, we reply on human expertise: when we want to fly to a conference, we rely on a pilot; when we get sick, we go to a doctor, etc.

Some experts are better than others. In the ideal world, we should all be served by the best experts: every plane should be controlled by the most skilled pilot, every patient should be treated by the best medical doctor. In practice, however, a few best doctors cannot cure all the patients, and a few most skilled pilots cannot navigate all the planes.

It is therefore important to design computer-based systems that will incorporate the knowledge and skills of the best experts and thus, help other experts make better decisions. For that, we need to describe the expert knowledge in computer-understandable terms.

Some of the experts' knowledge is precise and thus, easy to describe in computer-understandable terms. For example, one can easily describe, in such terms, a medical doctor's recommendation that any patient with a body temperature of 38°C or higher will be given a dose of aspirin proportional to his/her body weight.

However, many expert rules are not that precise. For example, instead of specifying a 38°C threshold, a medical doctor may say that a patient with high fever be given aspirin — without explicitly specifying what "high fever" means.

Rules and statements using such imprecise ("fuzzy") words from natural language like "high" are ubiquitous in our knowledge. To describe such knowledge in precise terms, Lotfi Zadeh invented a special technique that he called *fuzzy logic* [438, 555, 822]. According to this technique, to describe the meaning of each imprecise term like "high", we ask the expert to describe, for each possible value x of the corresponding quantity (e.g., temperature) the degree $\mu(x) \in [0,1]$ to which this value can be characterized by this term, so that 0 means absolutely not high, 1 means absolutely high, and intermediate values mean somewhat high. One way to get each value $\mu(x)$ is ask an expert to indicate his/her degree by a point on a scale — e.g., on a scale from 0 to 10. If an expert marks 37.9°C as corresponding to 7 on this scale, then we describe his/her degree of 37.9°C being "high" by the ratio 7/10.

A function assigning, to each possible value x, the corresponding degree $\mu(x)$, as it is shown in section 5.1 is known as a *membership function* or, alternatively, as a *fuzzy set*.

Note that, in general, the quantity x does not need to be numbervalued: alternatively, its values can be, e.g., vectors.

Many expert rules involve several conditions. For example, since some efficient fever-lowering medicines increase blood pressure, a medical doctor may recommend the corresponding medicine is the fever is high *and* the blood pressure is not high.

Ideally, we should consider all possible pairs $(x; y)$ of temperature and blood pressure, and for each such pair, elicit, from the expert, his/her degree that the corresponding "and"-condition is satisfied. However, in practice, there is a large number of such combinations, so it may not be possible to ask the expert's opinion about all of them. This is especially true if we take into account that sometimes, expert rules include three, four (and even more) conditions — in this case, asking the expert about all such combinations is plainly impossible.

In such situations, since we cannot elicit the expert's degree of confidence about a composite statement $A\&B$, we have to estimate this degree based on the known degree of confidence a and b in the components statements A and B. In our example, A is the statement that x is a high temperature, and B is the statement that y is not a high blood pressure.

The corresponding estimate depends only on a and b, so it has the form $f_\&(a,b)$ for an appropriate algorithmic function $f_\&$. This function is known as an *"and"-operation* or a *t-norm*. Similarly, to estimate the expert's degree of confidence in a statement $A \vee B$, we need an \or*"-operation* $f_\vee(a,b)$; "or"- operations are also known as *t-conorms*.

The corresponding operations should satisfy some reasonable properties. For example, since $A\&B$ is equivalent to $B\&A$, it makes sense to require that the "and"-operation provide the same estimate for both expressions — i.e., that it be commutative: $f_\&(a,b) = f_\&(b,a)$. Similarly, since $A\&(B\ \&C)$ is equivalent to $(A\&B)\&C$, the "and"-operation must be associative, etc.

The simplest operations that satisfy all these properties are $f_\&(a,b) = \min(a,b)$ and $f_\vee(a,b) = \max(a,b)$. These operations are among the most widely used in applications of fuzzy techniques [438, 555, 822].

In case of precise rules, we use the values of the inputs $x_1,...,x_n$ to determine the values of the desired quantity y — e.g., the value of the parameter that describes the appropriate control. Let us denote the corresponding algorithmic function by $y = f(x_1,...,x_n)$. Computing the corresponding values y is an important part of *data processing*.

If instead of measured values, we use expert estimates, then instead of the values x_i of the corresponding quantities X_i, we have fuzzy sets $\mu_i(x_i)$ that describe our knowledge about these quantities. In such situations, it is desirable to come up with a similar description for the possible values y of the desired quantity Y.

A number y is a possible value of the quantity Y if there exists a tuple of values $x_1,...,x_n$ for which $y = f(x_1,...,x_n)$ and each x_i is a possible value of the corresponding quantity X_i. For each number x_i, the degree to which this number is a possible value of the quantity X_i is equal to $\mu_i(x_i)$. Thus, if we use the min "and"-operation, the degree to which x_1 is a possible value of X_1 *and* x_2 is a possible value of X_2, etc., is equal to $\min(\mu_1(x_1),....,\mu_n(x_n))$.

The condition $y = f(x_1,...,x_n)$ is either absolutely true (i.e., has degree 1) or absolutely false (degree 0). Thus, the degree to which each x_i is a possible value of X_i and $y = f(x_1,...,x_n)$ is equal to $\min(\mu_1(x_1),....,\mu_n(x_n))$ when $y = f(x_1,...,x_n)$ and to 0 otherwise.

The phrase "there exists a tuple" means that either the corresponding property holds for one tuple, or for another tuple, etc. If we use the simplest max "or"-operation, then the degree $\mu(y)$ to which y is a possible value of Y takes the following form:

$$\mu(y) = \max\{\min(\mu_1(x_1),...,(\mu_n(x_n)) : y = f(x_1,...,x_n)\}.$$

As it is shown in section 5.3 this formula — first proposed by Zadeh — extends functions from real numbers to fuzzy inputs and is thus known as *Zadeh's extension principle* [438, 555, 822].

In describing the degree of confidence $\mu(y)$, in principle, we can use a different "and"-operation, e.g., the algebraic product $f_\&(a,b) = a \cdot b$.

However, we do not have much choice with the "or"-operation. Indeed, if instead of $f_\vee(a,b) = \max(a,b)$, we use, e.g., the algebraic sum $f_\vee(a,b) = a+b-a\cdot b$, then the "or"-combination of infinitely many degrees will lead to a meaningless $\mu(y) = 1$ for all y.

The traditional $[0, 1]$-based fuzzy techniques are based on the implicit assumption that an expert can always describe his/her degree of confidence in a statement by a number. In practice, this may be difficult: an expert may be able to meaningfully distinguish between 7 and 8 on a 0-to-10 scale, but hardly anyone can differentiate between, say 7.0 and 7.1 on this scale. In other words, instead of selecting a single number, an expert may be more comfortable selecting several numbers – maybe with the degree to which each of these numbers describes his/er opinion.

So, for each value x, the expert describes, for each possible degree μ, a degree $d(x,\mu)$ to which μ is a reasonable degree of x being high. Thus, the degree $\mu(x)$ characterizing the expert's opinion about the value x is no longer a number, it is itself a fuzzy set. Membership functions that assign such a fuzzy set to each values x are known as *type-2* fuzzy set; see, e.g., [512, 513, 554].

Another generalization of the traditional fuzzy sets is related to the fact that experts are often not 100% confident in their degrees. So, in addition to eliciting a degree $\mu(x)$, it makes sense to also elicit the degree $v(x)$ to which the expert is certain in his/her evaluation. The corresponding pairs $(\mu(x), v(x))$ is known as a *Z-number* as it is shown in Section 6.1.

Note that this is one possible definition of a Z-number; different formalization of the original Zadeh's idea of a Z-number may lead to slightly different definitions. For example, in [479], we used a single degree $v(x) = const$ to describe the expert's degree of confidence for all x. In this section, we consider a more general definition, in which we allow the degrees $v(x)$ to depend on x.

For both generalizations, instead of a single value $\mu(x)$, we have degrees describing to what extend different degrees are possible. In other words, while the meanings of two extensions are different, from the purely mathematical viewpoint, these two extensions seem similar. So what is the relation between the two extensions?

In this study, we explain the relation between Z-numbers and type-2 fuzzy sets. Specifically, we prove that if we apply data processing to

Z-numbers, then we get type-2 fuzzy sets of a special type — which we will call *monotonic*, and that, vice versa, every monotonic type-2 fuzzy set can be represented as a result of applying some data processing algorithm to appropriate Z-numbers.

6.8.2 Data processing to Z-numbers and type-2 fuzzy set

In the usual Zadeh's extension principle, when we apply the data processing algorithm $y = f(x_1, ..., x_n)$, we assume that for each i and for each possible value x_i of the quantity X_i, we know the degree $\mu_i(x_i)$ to which this value x_i is possible.

In the Z-number case, in addition to each degree $\mu_i(x_i)$, we also know the degree $v_i(x_i)$ to which the expert is confident in the degree $\mu_i(x_i)$. How will this additional information affect the result of data processing?

In our derivation of Zadeh's extension principle, we used the "and" and "or"-operations — namely, min and max. To extend Zadeh's extension principle to Z-numbers, it is therefore necessary to extend the usual "and"- and "or"-operations to Znumbers.

Let us assume that the expert's degree of confidence in a statement A is a and the expert's degree of confidence in this estimate is v_a. Let us also assume that the expert's degree of confidence in a statement B is b and the expert's degree of confidence in this estimate is v_b.

Then, the expert's degree of confidence in a composite statement $A\&B$ is $f_\&(a,b)$. If we use the simplest possible "and"-operation $f_\&(a,b) = \min(a,b)$, then this degree is equal to min(a; b).

What is the expert's degree of confidence in the estimate min(a;b)? This estimate makes sense only if both estimates a and b make sense. In other words, an expert is confident in the combined estimate min(a; b) if the expert is confident in the estimate a *and* confident in estimate b. So, the expert's degree of confidence in the combined estimate min(a; b) can be obtained by applying the "and"-operation to the degrees of confidence v_a and μ_b in both estimates: $f_\&(\mu_a, \mu_b)$. In particular, if we use the min "and"-operation, we get the degree $\min(v_a, v_b)$,

The degrees v_a and v_b are usually viewed as subjective probabilities, with the "and"-operation $f_\&(a,b) = a \cdot b$. In general, this is OK, but, as we will see, the choice of the algebraic product "and"-operation lead to meaningless 0 values for the results of data processing – similar to the fact that the use of the algebraic sum leads to meaningless 1 for the usual Zadeh's extension principle. To avoid such meaningless values, in this section, we use the min "and"-operation.

What about the "or"- operation? What is the expert's degree of confidence in the corresponding estimate $f_\vee(a,b) = \max(a,b)$? At first glance, by analogy, it may seem that we get $\max(v_a,v_b)$, but a more detailed analysis shows that this is a wrong formula. Indeed, an expert is confident in the combined estimate max(*a; b*) if the expert is confident in the estimate *a and* confident in estimate *b*. So, similar to the case of the "and"-operations, the expert's degree of confidence in the combined estimate min(*a; b*) can be obtained by applying the "and"-operation to the degrees of confidence v_a and μ_b in both estimates: $f_\&(\mu_a,\mu_b)$. In particular, if we use the min "and"-operation, we get the degree $\min(v_a,v_b)$ — the same degree as for the "and"-operation.

Now, we are ready to describe a natural way to generalize Zadeh's extension principle to Z-numbers.

Let us now consider the case when all the inputs to a data processing algorithm $y = f(x_1,...,x_n)$ are Z-numbers, i.e., that for each input *i* and for each possible value x_i of the *i*-th quantity X_i, we know not only the expert's degree of confidence $\mu_i(x_i)$ that *xi* is a possible value of *Xi*, but also the expert's degree of confidence $v_i(x_i)$ in this estimate.

Based on this information, what can we say about the possible values *y* of the desired quantity *Y*?

In line with the above description of "and"- and "or"-operations for Z-numbers, for each tuple $x_1,...,x_n$ for which $y = f(x_1,...,x_n)$, the resulting value *y* is possible with degree $\min(\mu_1(x_1),...,\mu_n(x_n))$, and the expert's confidence in this estimate is equal to $\min(v_1(x_1),...,v_n(x_n))$.

In principle, we could do what we did when we derived Zadeh's extension principle, and for each y, simply combine the estimates corresponding to all the tuples $x_1,...,x_n$ for which $y = f(x_1,...,x_n)$. As a result, we would get the same degree $\mu(y)$ as in the traditional $[0; 1]$-based fuzzy case, but the problem is that the expert's confidence in this estimate would then be equal to

$$v(y) = \min\{\min(v_1(x_1),...,(v_n(x_n))): y = f(x_1,...,x_n)\}.$$

Since some of the degrees $v_i(x_i)$ may be very low, we will get the degree $v(y)$ very low — or even equal to 0. This means that the expert's confidence in the degree $\mu(y)$ is very low.

It make no sense to produce an estimate $\mu(y)$ in which the expert is not confident at all. Thus, we need to modify our approach.

The above formula shows that to compute the v-degrees, we do not have much of a choice in selecting an "and"-operation. Indeed, if instead of min, we use, e.g., the algebraic product "and"-operation $f_\&(a,b) = a \cdot b$, then by taking the product of infinitely many degrees corresponding to infinitely many tuples, we will have a meaningless value $\mu(y) = 0$ always, even if — as we propose in the following text — we do not consider tuples with small value $v_i(x_i)$.

We do not want to have an estimate with degree of confidence 0. Let us therefore select the desired degree of confidence $v > 0$, and let us try to come up with an estimate $\mu(y)$ for which the expert's degree of confidence $\mu(y)$ is at least as large as this threshold value: $v(y) \geq v$.

In other words, the minimum of the degrees of confidence corresponding to different tuples $x_1,...,x_n$ must be at least μ. This is equivalent to saying that all these degrees of confidence must be at least μ. In other words, we should only consider tuples $x_1,...,x_n$ for which $\min(v_1(x_1),...,v_n(x_n)) \geq v$. This inequality, in its turn, is equivalent to requiring that $v_i(x_i) \geq v$ for each i. Thus, we arrive at the following definition.

Let us assume that for each input i and for each possible value x_i of the ith quantity X_i we know the expert's degree of confidence $\mu_i(x_i)$ that x_i is a possible value of X_i, and the expert's degree of confidence $v_i(x_i)$ in this estimate. Then, for each value $v \in [0,1]$, we compute

$$\mu_v(y) = \max\{\min(\mu_1(x_1), ..., \mu_n(x_n)) : y = f(x_1, ..., x_n)$$

and $v_i(x_i) \geq v$ for all $i\}$.

The function that assigns, to each $v \in [0,1]$, the corresponding value $\mu_v(y)$, is the result of applying the data processing algorithm to Z-numbers — i.e., it is the desired extension of Zadeh's extension principle to Z-numbers. Let us describe this in precise terms.

Definition 6.10. By a Z-number, we mean a mapping that assigns, to every element x of a universal set, two numbers $mu(x)$ and $v(x)$ from the interval [0,1]. We will say that:

• $\mu(x)$ is the expert's degree of confidence that x is a possible value, and

• $v(x)$ is the the expert's degree of confidence in the estimate $\mu(x)$.

Definition 6.11. Let $F : U_1 \times ... \times U_n \to U$ be a function, and for each $i = 1, ..., n$ let X_i be a Z-number defined on the universal set U_i. By the result $f(X_1, ..., X_n)$ of applying the function $f(x_1, ..., x_n)$ to the Z-numbers $X_1, ..., X_n$, we mean a function that assigns, to each $v \in [0,1]$, the value

$$\mu_v(y) = \max\{\min(\mu_1(x_1), ..., \mu_n(x_n)) : y = f(x_1, ..., x_n)$$

and $v_i(x_i) \geq v$ for all $i\}$.

This is the desired extension of Zadeh's extension principle to Z numbers.

Let us recall that we get a type-2 fuzzy set if instead of a single value $\mu(x)$, we get a function that assigns, to each value $\mu \in [0,1]$, a degree $d(\mu, x) \in [0,1]$.

Here, we have exactly this situation: to each value v, we assign, a degree $\mu_v(x)$. Thus, from the purely mathematical viewpoint, the result of applying data processing to Z-numbers is a type-2 fuzzy set.

Can every type-2 fuzzy number be so represented? We have shown that the result of applying data processing to Z-numbers is a type-2 fuzzy set. A natural question is: can every type-2 fuzzy number be thus represented?

In the following text, we will prove that this is not the case: namely, that the type-2 fuzzy sets which are obtained as a result of applying data processing to Z-numbers have an additional property — that we will call monotonicity.

Monotonicity property. When the value v increases, fewer and fewer tuples $(x_1, ..., x_n)$ satisfy the inequalities $v_i(x_i) \geq nu$. Thus, the maximum in the definition of $\mu_v(y)$ is over a smaller set of values – and, is thus, in general, smaller. In other words, if $v < v'$, then $\mu_v(x) \leq \mu'_v(x)$. In this section, we will call type-2 fuzzy sets with this property monotonic.

We started with a question of whether every type-2 fuzzy number can be represented as a result of applying data processing to Z-numbers. We have shown that this is not the case, by proving that a type-2 fuzzy numbers obtained as a result of applying data processing to Z-numbers is always monotonic.

A natural next question is: Can every monotonic type-2 fuzzy set be represented as a result of applying data processing to Z-numbers? Our – positive – answer to this question is provided in the theorem given below.

Definition 6.12. We say that a type-2 fuzzy number $d(y, \mu)$ is monotonic if $\mu < \mu'$ implies $d(y, \mu) \geq d(y, \mu')$.

Representation Theorem 6.2. Every monotonic type-2 fuzzy set $d(y, \mu)$ can be represented as a result of applying an appropriate data processing algorithm $y = f(x_1, ..., x_n)$ to some Z-numbers $X_1, ..., X_n$. Proof is given in [38].

Chapter 7

Computation with U-Numbers

7.1 Usuality and U-number concept

The theory of usuality suggested by L.A. Zadeh is widely used in many areas including decision analysis, system analysis, control and others where commonsense knowledge plays an important role. As a rule, this knowledge is imprecise, incomplete, and partially reliable. The concept of usuality is characterized by a combination of fuzzy and probabilistic information. Formally, it is handled by possibilistic-probabilistic constraint "Usuality X is A", where A is a fuzzy restriction on a value of a random variable X, and "usually" is a fuzzy restriction on a value of probability measure of A. Thus, usuality is a special case of a Z-number where second component is "usually", and is referred to as U-number. Humans mainly use U-numbers in everyday reasoning.

The importance of the concept of usuality is dictated by the fact that it underlies commonsense knowledge-based human decision making and reasoning. Zadeh for the first time suggested the concept of "usuality" which plays central role in a theory of commonsense. In [834-836] Zadeh has suggested main principles of theory of usuality. In [840] the author shows that the concept of dispositionality is closely related to the notion of usuality. Theory of usuality is defined as a tool for computational framework for commonsense reasoning.

In [838] author outlines a theory of usuality based on a method of representing the meaning of usuality-qualified propositions. A system of inference for usuality-qualified propositions is developed. In [809] Yager introduces a formal mechanism for representing and manipulating of usual values. This mechanism is based upon a combination of the linguistic variables and Shafer evidential structures [685]. In [774] authors analyze the concepts usuality, regularity and dispositional reasoning from the point of view of approximate reasoning. Schwarts in [673] discusses fuzzy quantifiers, fuzzy usuality modifiers and fuzzy likelihood modifiers. He analyzes these notions with unified semantics.

The main conclusion stemming from review of the mentioned above works is that arithmetic of U-numbers and reasoning under U-information should be rather approximate than exact. Indeed, for commonsense knowledge-based everyday reasoning, approximate and sufficient results are more effective than absolutely exact and time consuming results. Thus, a computational framework of operations of U-numbers should be based on a practically suitable tradeoff between accuracy and computational complexity. In this section we develop a new approach to approximate arithmetic operations on U-numbers.

Let X be a random variable and A be a fuzzy number playing a role of fuzzy constraint on values that the random variable may take: X is A. The definition of a usual value of X may be expressed in terms of the probability distribution of X as follows [838]. If $p(x_i)$ is the probability of X taking x_i as its value, then

$$usually(X \text{ is } A) = \mu_{usually}\left(\sum_i p(x_i)\mu_A(x_i)\right) \qquad (7.1)$$

or

$$usually(X \text{ is } A) = \mu_{most}\left(\sum_i p(x_i)\mu_A(x_i)\right) \qquad (7.2)$$

A usual number describing, "usually, professor's income is medium" is shown Fig.7.1.

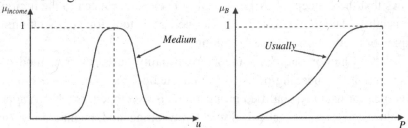

Fig. 7.1. An example of U-number

Formula (7.2) indicates that the probability that the event A occurs as the value for the variable X, is "*most*". As it was mentioned above, in [838] Zadeh provided an outline for the theory of usuality, however this topic requires further investigation. It is needed a more general approach for other usuality quantifiers. In this study "usuality" will be a composite term characterized by fuzzy quantities as *always, usually, frequently/ often, occasionally, seldom, almost never/rarely, never*. The codebook for "usuality" is shown in Fig. 7.2.

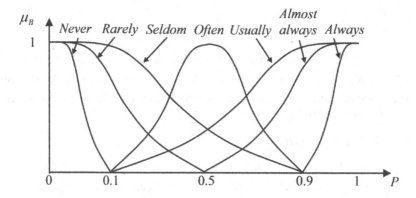

Fig. 7.2. The codebook of the fuzzy quantifiers of usuality

Operations over U-numbers are considered below.

7.2 A general approach to computation with U-numbers

We try to answer the questions raised by Zadeh [838] concerning the concept of usuality. These basic questions are:

- How can a usual value of a variable be computed?

- How can the usual values of two or more variables be combined? More concretely, if $X_{12} = X_1 + X_2$, and the usual values of X_1 and X_2 are given, what will be the usual value of X_{12}?

- How can we construct an inference system for reasoning with usuality-qualified propositions?

- How can decisions be made in usuality-qualified knowledge-based environment (i.e. when we know only usual values of probabilities, payoff's, etc)?

The most critical question is that related to combination of U-numbers. It should be taken into account whether the variables X_1 and X_2 are dependent or independent. This will influence how a usuality quantifier related to the result $X_{12} = X_1 * X_2$ should be determined on the basis of the usuality quantifiers related to X_1 and X_2:

In this study the modality of a generalized constraint is considered as usuality:

$$X\, is\, u\, A \quad or \quad Usuality(r=u),$$

where X is the constrained variable, A is a constraining relation, and r identifies the semantics of the constraint. The usuality constraint presupposes that X is a random variable and the probability that X isu A is "usually":

$$Prob\{X\, is\, A\}\ is\ usually,$$

where A is a usual value of X, for example A is "*small*".

Computation with U-numbers is related to usuality constraint propagation. Assume that X is a random variable taking values $x_1, x_2, ...$ and p is probability distribution of X. The constraint propagation is as follows:

$$\frac{X\ isu\ A}{Prob\{X\ is\ B\}\ is\ C},$$

$$X\ isu\ A \rightarrow Prob\{X\ is\ A\}\ is\ usually \rightarrow \mu_{usually}\left(\int_R \mu_A(x)p(x)dx\right),$$

$$\mu_C(y) = \sup_{p(x)}(\mu_{usually}(\int_R \mu_A(x)p(x)dx)),$$

subject to

$$y = \int_R \mu_B(x)p(x)dx.$$

We consider an approach to computation with U-numbers according to basic two-place arithmetic operations $+,-,\cdot,/$ and one-place algebraic operations as a square and a square root of U-numbers.

Let $U_1 = (A_1, B_1)$ and $U_2 = (A_2, B_2)$ be U-numbers (B_1 and B_2 are fuzzy terms of the usuality codebook) describing values of random variables X_1 and X_2. Assume that it is needed to compute the result $U_{12} = (A_{12}, B_{12})$ of a two-place operation $* \in \{+,-,\cdot,/\} : U_{12} = U_1 * U_2$. Computation of one-place operations $U = U_1^2$ and $U = \sqrt{U_1}$ is treated analogously.

Consider the case of discretized version of components of usual numbers. The first stage is the computation of two-place operations $*$ of fuzzy numbers A_1 and A_2 on the basis of fuzzy arithmetic. For example, for sum $U_{12} = U_1 + U_2$ we have to calculate $A_{12} = A_1 + A_2$.

The second stage involves step-by-step construction of B_{12} and is related to propagation of probabilistic restrictions. We realize that in U-numbers $U_1 = (A_1, B_1)$ and $U_2 = (A_2, B_2)$, the 'true' probability distributions p_1 and p_2 are not exactly known. In contrast, the information available is represented by the fuzzy restrictions:

$$\sum_{k=1}^{n_1} \mu_{A_1}(x_{1k}) p_1(x_{1k}) \ is \ B_1 \qquad \sum_{k=1}^{n_2} \mu_{A_2}(x_{2k}) p_2(x_{2k}) \ is \ B_2$$

which are represented in terms of the membership functions as

$$\mu_{p_1}(p_1) = \mu_{B_1}\left(\sum_{k=1}^{n_1} \mu_{A_1}(x_{1k}) p_1(x_{1k})\right)$$

$$\mu_{p_2}(p_2) = \mu_{B_2}\left(\sum_{k=1}^{n_2} \mu_{A_2}(x_{2k}) p_2(x_{2k})\right).$$

Given these fuzzy restrictions, extract probability distributions $p_j, j = 1, 2$ by solving the following goal linear programming problem:

$$c_1 v_1^j + c_2 v_2^j + ... + c_n v_n^j \to b_{jl} \tag{7.3}$$

subject to

$$\left. \begin{array}{c} v_1^l + v_2^l + ... + v_n^l = 1 \\ v_1^l, v_2^l, ..., v_n^l \geq 0 \end{array} \right\}, \tag{7.4}$$

where $c_k = \mu_{A_j}(x_{jk})$ and $v_k = p_j(x_{jk})$, $k = 1,..,n_j$, $k = 1,..,n_j$. As a result, $p_{jl}(x_{jk})$, $k = 1,..,n_j$ is found and, therefore, distribution p_{jl} is obtained. Thus, to construct the distributions p_{jl}, we need to solve m simple problems (7.3)-(7.4).

Distributions $p_{jl}(x_{jk})$, $k = 1,..,n_j$ naturally induce probabilistic uncertainty over the result $X_{12} = X_1 * X_2$. This is a critical point of computation of U-numbers, at which the issue of dependence between X_1 and X_2 should be considered. For simplicity, here we consider the case of independence between X_1 and X_2. This implies that given a pair p_{1l_1}, p_{2l_2}, the convolution $p_{12s} = p_{1l_1} \circ p_{2l_2}$, $s = 1,...,m^2$ is to be computed as on the basis of (4.26)-(4.31).

For the case of dependence between X_1 and X_2, p_{12s} should be computed as a joint probability distribution by taking into account dependence between random variables [783, 786].

Given p_{12s}, the value of probability measure of A_{12} can be computed: $P(A_{12}) = \sum_{k=1}^{n} \mu_{A_{12}}(x_{12k}) p_{12}(x_{12k})$. However, the 'true' p_{12s} is not exactly known as the 'true' p_{1l_1}, p_{2l_2} are described by fuzzy restrictions. These fuzzy restrictions induce the fuzzy set of convolutions $p_{12s}, s = 1,...,m^2$ with the membership function defined as

$$\mu_{p_{12}}(p_{12s}) = \max_{p_{12s} = p_{1l_1} \circ p_{2l_2}} [\mu_{p_1}(p_{1l_1}) \wedge \mu_{p_2}(p_{2l_2})] \tag{7.5}$$

subject to

$$\mu_{p_j}(p_{jl_j}) = \mu_{B_j}\left(\sum_{k=1}^{n_j} \mu_{A_j}(x_{jk}) p_{jl_j}(x_{jk})\right), \; j = 1,2 \tag{7.6}$$

where $\wedge$ is *min* operation.

As a result, fuzziness of information on p_{12s} described by $\mu_{p_{12}}$ induces fuzziness of the value of probability measure $P(A_{12})$ in a form of a fuzzy number B_{12}. The membership function of B_{12} is defined as

$$\mu_{B_{12}}(b_{12s}) = \max(\mu_{p_{12}}(p_{12s}))$$ (7.7)

subject to

$$b_{12s} = \sum_k \mu_{A_{12}}(x_k) p_{12s}(x_k)$$ (7.8)

As a result, $U_{12} = U_1 * U_2$ is obtained as $U_{12} = (A_{12}, B_{12})$.

Square of a U-number

Let us now consider construction of $U = U_1^2$. $A = A_1^2$ is determined as follows:

$$A_1^2 = \bigcup_{\alpha \in [0,1]} \alpha [A_1^2]^\alpha$$ (7.9)

$$[A_1^2]^\alpha = \{x_1^2 \mid x_1 \in A_1^\alpha\}.$$ (7.10)

The probability distribution p is determined given p_1 as

$$p(x) = \frac{1}{2\sqrt{x}} \left[p_1(\sqrt{x}) + p_1(-\sqrt{x}) \right], \quad x \geq 0.$$ (7.11)

Next by noting that a 'true' p_1 is not known, one has to consider fuzzy constraint μ_{p_1} to be constructed by solving a certain LP problem (7.3)-(7.4). The fuzzy set of probability distributions $p_{1,l}$ with membership function μ_{p_1} naturally induces the fuzzy set of probability distributions p_l with the membership function $\mu_p(p_l)$ defined as

$$\mu_p(p_l) = \mu_{p_1}(p_{1l}), l = 1, ..., m$$

where p is determined from p_1 based on (7.11).

The probability measure $P(A)$ given $\tilde{p}$ is produced. Finally, given a fuzzy restriction on $\tilde{p}$ described by μ_p, we extend $P(A)$ to a fuzzy set B by solving a problem analogous to (7.7)-(7.8). As a result, U^2 is obtained on the basis of the extension principle for computation with U - numbers as $U^2 = (A, B)$. Let us mention that for $X_1 \geq 0$, it is not needed to compute of B because it is the same as B_1 [16]. Computation of $U = U_1^n$, where n is any natural number, is carried out in an analogous fashion.

Square Root of a U-number

Let us consider computation of $U = \sqrt{U_1}$ based on the extension principle for computation with U-numbers. $A = \sqrt{A_1}$ is determined as follows:

$$\sqrt{A} = \bigcup_{\alpha \in [0,1]} \alpha [\sqrt{A_1}]^\alpha, \tag{7.12}$$

$$[\sqrt{A_1}]^\alpha = \{\sqrt{x_1} \mid x_1 \in A_1^\alpha\}. \tag{7.13}$$

The probability distribution p is determined given p_1 as

$$p(x) = 2x p_1(x^2). \tag{7.14}$$

Then we compute μ_p by solving problem (7.3)-(7.4) and recall that $\mu_p(p_l) = \mu_{p_1}(p_{1l})$,

where $\tilde{p}$ is determined from p_1 on the basis of (7.14). Next we compute probability measure $P(A)$. Finally, given the membership function μ_p, we construct a fuzzy set B by solving a problem analogous to (7.7)-(7.8). Let us mention that for the square root of a U-number, it is not needed to carry out computation of B because it is the same as B_1 [16].

As a U-number is a specific type of a Z-number, see Section 6.3 for more detailed description of the considered operations.

7.3 Approximate reasoning with usual information

The approximate reasoning can be considered as a formal model of commonsense knowledge-based reasoning with imprecise and uncertain information [24, 27]. Approximate reasoning is based on fuzzy logic [28, 31] and has found a lot of successful applications in various fields [18, 23].

The problem of approximate reasoning with usual information is started as follows:

Given the following U-rules:

If X_1 is $U_{X_{1,1}} = (A_{X_{1,1}}, B_{X_{1,1}})$ and,..., and X_m is $U_{X_{m,1}} = (A_{X_{m,1}}, B_{X_{m,1}})$ then Y is $U_Y = (A_{Y,1}, B_{Y,1})$

If X_1 is $U_{X_{1,2}} = (A_{X_{1,2}}, B_{X_{1,2}})$ and,..., and X_m is $U_{X_{m,2}} = (A_{X_{m,2}}, B_{X_{m,2}})$ then Y is $U_Y = (A_{Y,2}, B_{Y,2})$

...

If X_1 is $U_{X_{1,n}} = (A_{X_{1,n}}, B_{X_{1,n}})$ and,..., and X_m is $U_{X_{m,n}} = (A_{X_{m,n}}, B_{X_{m,n}})$ then Y is $U_Y = (A_{Y,n}, B_{Y,n})$

and a current observation

X_1 is $U_{X_1} = (A'_{X_1}, B'_{X_1})$ and,..., and X_m is $U'_{X_m} = (A'_{X_m}, B'_{X_m})$,

find the U-value of Y.

The idea underlying the suggested interpolation approach is that the resulting output should be computed as a convex combination of consequent parts. The coefficients of linear interpolation are determined on the basis of the similarity between a current input and the antecedent parts [439]. This implies for U-rules that the resulting output U'_Y is computed as

$$U'_Y = \sum_{j=1}^{n} w_j U_{Y,j} = \sum_{j=1}^{n} w_j (A_{Y,j}, B_{Y,j}),$$ (7.15)

where $U_{Y,j}$ is the U-valued consequent of the j-th rule, $w_j = \dfrac{\rho_j}{\sum\limits_{k=1}^{n} \rho_k}$,

$j = 1, ..., n;\ k = 1, ..., n$ are coefficients of linear interpolation, n is the number of U-rules. ρ_j is defined as follows:

$$\rho_j = \min_{i=1,...,m} S(U'_{X_i}, U_{X_i,j}), \tag{7.16}$$

where S is the similarity between current i-th U-valued input and the i-th U-valued antecedent of the j-th rule. Thus, ρ_j computes the similarity between a current input vector and the vector of the antecedents of j-th rule.

Example. Let us consider modeling of a fragment of a relationship between the student motivation, attention, anxiety and educational achievement [23]. The information on the considered characteristics is naturally imprecise and partially reliable. Indeed, one deals mainly with intangible, non-measurable mental indicators. For this reason, the use of Z-rules, as rules with Z-number valued inputs and outputs is an adequate way for modeling of this relationship. This rules will help to evaluate a student with a given Z-number based evaluations of the characteristics. Consider the following Z-rules which describe a fragment of this relationship:

Rule 1: *If Motivation is (M,U) and Attention is (H,U) and Anxiety is (L,U) Then Achievement is (E,U).*

Rule 2: *If Motivation is (M,U) and Attention is (M,U) and Anxiety is (M,U) Then Achievement is (G,U).*

Here the pairs (,) are Z-numbers where uppercase letters denote the following linguistic terms: H-High; L-Low; M- Medium; G-Good; E-Excellence; U-Usually. A solution of this example is given in Section 12.6.

Chapter 8

Fuzzy Geometry Based Computations

İn this chapter we present the fuzzy logic for formal geometric reasoning with extended objects. Based on the idea that extended objects may be seen as location constraints to coordinate points, the geometric primitives point, line, incidence and equality are interpreted as fuzzy predicates of a first order language. An additional predicate for the "distinctness" of point like objects is also used. Fuzzy Logic [28] is discussed as a reasoning system for geometry of extended objects. A fuzzification of the axioms of incidence geometry based on the proposed fuzzy logic is presented. In addition we discuss a special form of positional uncertainty, namely positional tolerance that arises from geometric constructions with extended primitives. We also address Euclid's first postulate, which lays the foundation for consistent geometric reasoning in all classical geometries by taken into account extended primitives and gave a fuzzification of Euclid's first postulate by using of our fuzzy logic. Fuzzy equivalence relation "Extended lines sameness" is introduced. For its approximation we use fuzzy conditional inference, which is based on proposed fuzzy "Degree of indiscernibility "and "Discernibility measure "of extended points.

In [777, 779, 780] it was mentioned that there are numerous approaches by mathematicians to restore Euclidean Geometry from a different set of axioms, based on primitives that have extension in space. These approaches aim at restoring Euclidean geometry, including the concepts of crisp points and lines, starting from different primitive objects and relations. An approach, aimed at augmenting an existent axiomatization of Euclidean geometry with grades of validity for axioms (fuzzification) is also presented in [777, 779, 780]. It should be mentioned, that in [777, 779, 780] the *Lukasiewicz* Logic was only proposed as the basis for "fuzzification" of axioms. And also for both fuzzy predicates and fuzzy axiomatization of incidence geometry no proofs were presented. The goal of this study is to fill up above mentioned "gap". In addition we use fuzzy logic, proposed in [28] for all necessary mathematical purposes.

8.1　Geometric primitives and incidence

Similarly to [18, 19, 44, 777, 779, 780] we will use the following axioms from [357]. These axioms formalize the behaviour of points and lines in incident geometry, as it was defined in [779].

($I1$) *For every two distinct point p and q, at least one **line** l exists that is incident with p and q.*

($I2$) *Such a **line** is unique.*

($I3$) *Every **line** is incident with at least two points.*

($I4$) *At least three points exist that are not incident with the same **line**.*

The uniqueness axiom $I2$ ensures that geometrical constructions are possible. Geometric constructions are sequential applications of construction operators. An example of a construction operator is

Connect: point × point → line.

This means taking two points as an input and returning the line through them. For *connect* to be a well-defined mathematical function, the resulting line needs always to exist and needs to be unique. Other examples of geometric construction operators of 2D incidence geometry are

Intersect: line × line → point,

Parallel through point: line × point → line.

The axioms of incidence geometry form a proper subset of the axioms of Euclidean geometry. Incidence geometry allows for defining the notion of parallelism of two lines as a derived concept, but does not permit to express betweenness or congruency relations, which are assumed primitives in Hilbert's system [357]. The complete axiom set of Euclidean geometry provides a greater number of construction operators than incidence geometry. Incidence geometry has very limited expressive power when compared with the full axiom system.

The combined incidence axioms *I*1 and *I*2 state that it is always possible to connect two distinct points by a unique line. In case of coordinate point *a* and *b*, Cartesian geometry provides a formula for constructing this unique line: $l = \{a + t(b - a) \mid t \in R\}$.

As it was shown in [777, 779, 780], when we want to connect two extended geographic objects in a similar way, there is no canonical way of doing so. We cannot refer to an existing model like the Cartesian algebra. Instead, a new way of interpreting geometric primitives must be found, such that the interpretation of the incidence relation respects the uniqueness property *I*2.

Similarly to [777, 779, 780] we will refer to extended objects that play the geometric role of points and lines by *extended points* and *extended lines*, respectively. The following section gives a brief introduction in proposed fuzzy logic and discusses possible interpretations of fuzzy predicates for extended geometric primitives. The Fuzzy logic from [28] is introduced as a possible formalism for approximate geometric reasoning with extended objects and based on extended geometric primitives a fuzzification of the incidence axioms *I*1-*I*4 is investigated.

8.2 Fuzzification of incidence geometry

8.2.1 *Proposed fuzzy logic*

Let $\forall p,q \in [0,1]$ a continuous function $F(p,q) = p-q$, which defines a distance between p and q be given. Notice that $F(p,q) \in [-1,1]$, where $F(p,q)^{\min} = -1$ and $F(p,q)^{\max} = 1$. The normalized value of $F(p,q)$ is defined as follows

$$F(p,q)^{norm} = \frac{F(p,q) - F(p,q)^{\min}}{F(p,q)^{\max} - F(p,q)^{\min}} = \frac{F(p,q)+1}{2} = \frac{p-q+1}{2}; \quad (8.1)$$

It is clear that $F(p,q)^{norm} \in [0,1]$. This function represents the value of "closeness" between two values (potentially *antecedent* and *consequent*), defined within single interval, which therefore could play significant role in formulation of an implication operator in a fuzzy logic. Given $I(p,q)$ defined as

$$I(p,q) = \begin{cases} 1 - F(p,q)^{norm}, p > q; \\ 1, p \leq q, \end{cases} \tag{8.2}$$

and $F(p,q)^{norm}$ is from (8.1), let us show some basic operations in proposed fuzzy logic. Let us designate the truth values of logical *antecedent* P and *consequent* Q as $T(P) = p$ and $T(Q) = q$ respectively. Then relevant set of proposed fuzzy logic operators is shown in Table 8.1. To get the truth values of these definitions we use well known logical properties such as $p \rightarrow q = \neg p \vee q$; $p \wedge q = \neg(\neg p \vee \neg q)$ and alike.

Table 8.1. Fuzzy logic operators

Name	Designation	Value
Tautology	P^1	1
Controversy	P^0	0
Negation	$\neg P$	$1 - P$
Disjunction	$P \vee Q$	$\begin{cases} \dfrac{p+q}{2}, p+q < 1, \\ 1, p+q \geq 1 \end{cases}$
Conjunction	$P \wedge Q$	$\begin{cases} \dfrac{p+q}{2}, p+q > 1, \\ 0, p+q \leq 1 \end{cases}$
Implication	$P \rightarrow Q$	$\begin{cases} \dfrac{1-p+q}{2}, p > q, \\ 1, p \leq q \end{cases}$
Equivalence	$P \leftrightarrow Q$	$\begin{cases} \dfrac{1-p+q}{2}, p > q, \\ 1, p = q, \\ \dfrac{1-q+p}{2}, p < q \end{cases}$
Pierce Arrow	$P \downarrow Q$	$\begin{cases} 1 - \dfrac{p+q}{2}, p+q < 1, \\ 0, p+q \geq 1 \end{cases}$

(Continued)

Table 8.1. (*Continued*)

Name	Designation	Value
Shaffer Stroke	$P \uparrow Q$	$\begin{cases} 1 - \dfrac{p+q}{2}, p+q > 1, \\ 1, p+q \leq 1 \end{cases}$

In [28] we proposed a new many-valued system, characterized by the set of base *union* $(\cup)$ and *intersection* $(\cap)$ operations with relevant *complement*, defined as $T(\neg P) = 1 - T(P)$. In addition, the operators $\downarrow$ and $\uparrow$ are expressed as negations of $\cup$ and $\cap$ correspondingly. For this matter let us pose the problem very explicitly.

We are working in many-valued system, which for present purposes is all or some of the real interval $\mathfrak{R} = [0, 1]$. As was mentioned in [28], the rationales there are more than ample for our purposes in very much of practice, the following set $\{0, 0.1, 0.2,...,0.9, 1\}$ of 11 values is quite sufficient, and we shall use this set V_{11} in our illustration. Table 8.2 shows the operation *implication* in proposed fuzzy logic.

Table 8.2. Operation implication

$p \rightarrow q$	0	.1	.2	.3	.4	.5	.6	.7	.8	.9	1
0	1	1	1	1	1	1	1	1	1	1	1
.1	.45	1	1	1	1	1	1	1	1	1	1
.2	.4	.45	1	1	1	1	1	1	1	1	1
.3	.35	.4	.45	1	1	1	1	1	1	1	1
.4	.3	.35	.4	.45	1	1	1	1	1	1	1
.5	.25	.3	.35	.4	.45	1	1	1	1	1	1
.6	.2	.25	.3	.35	.4	.45	1	1	1	1	1
.7	.15	.2	.25	.3	.35	.4	.45	1	1	1	1
.8	.1	.15	.2	.25	.3	.35	.4	.45	1	1	1
.9	.05	.1	.15	.2	.25	.3	.35	.4	.45	1	1
1	0	.05	.1	.15	.2	.25	.3	.35	.4	.45	1

8.2.2 *Geometric primitives as fuzzy predicates*

It is well known, that in Boolean predicate logic atomic statements are formalized by predicates. Predicates that are used in the theory of incidence geometry may be denoted by p (a) ("a is a point"), l (a) ("a is a line"), and inc (a, b) ("a and b are incident"). The predicate expressing equality can be denoted by eq (a, b) ("a and b are equal"). Traditionally predicates are interpreted by crisp relations. For example, eq: $N \times N \rightarrow \{0, 1\}$ is a function that assigns 1 to every pair of equal objects and 0 to every pair of distinct objects from the set N. Of course, predicates like p (.) or l (.), which accept only one symbol as an input are unary, whereas binary predicates, like inc (.,.) and eq (.,.), accept pairs of symbols as an input. In a fuzzy predicate logic, predicates are interpreted by fuzzy relations, instead of crisp relations. For example, a binary fuzzy relation eq is a function eq: $N \times N \rightarrow [0, 1]$, assigning a real number $\lambda \in [0, 1]$ to every pair of objects from N. In other words, every two objects of N are equal to some degree. The degree of equality of two objects a and b may be 1 or 0 as in the crisp case, but may as well be 0.9, expressing that a and b are almost equal. In [777, 779, 780] the fuzzification of p (.), l (.) inc (.) and eq (.) predicates were proposed.

Similarly to [777, 779, 780] we define a bounded subset Dom $\subseteq R^2$ as the domain for our geometric exercises. Predicates are defined for two-dimensional subsets A, B, C.., of Dom, and assume values in [0, 1]. We may assume two-dimensional subsets and ignore subsets of lower dimension, because every measurement and every digitization introduces a minimum amount of location uncertainty in the data [780]. For the point-predicate p (.) the result of Cartesian geometric involve a Cartesian point does not change when the point is rotated: Rotation-invariance seems to be a main characteristic of "point likeness" with respect to geometric operations: it should be kept when defining a fuzzy predicate expressing the "point likeness" of extended subsets of R^2. As a preliminary definition let

$$\theta_{\min} (A) = \min_{t} | ch(A) \cap \{c(A) + t \bullet R_\alpha \bullet (0,1)^T | t \in \Re\} | \qquad (8.3)$$

$$\theta_{\max} (A) = \max_{t} | ch(A) \cap \{c(A) + t \bullet R_\alpha \bullet (0,1)^T | t \in \Re\} |$$

be the minimal and maximal diameter of the convex hull ch (A) of A $\subseteq$ Dom, respectively. The convex hull regularizes the sets A and B and eliminates irregularities. c (A) denotes the centroid of ch (A), and Rα denotes the rotation matrix by angle α (Figure 8.1(a)) [777, 779, 780].

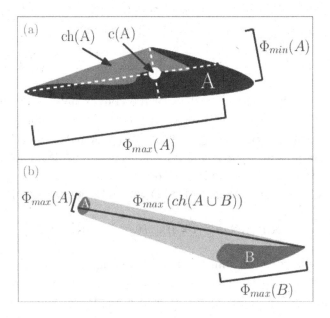

Fig. 8.1. (a) Minimal and maximal diameter of a set A of Cartesian points. (b) Grade of distinctness dc (A, B) of A and B.

Since A is bounded, ch (A) and c (A) exist. We can now define the fuzzy point-predicate p(.) by

$$p(A) = \theta_{min}(A) / \theta_{max}(A). \tag{8.4}$$

For A ⊆ Dom p (.) expresses the degree to which the convex hull of a Cartesian point set A is rotation-invariant: If p (A) =1, then ch (A) is perfectly rotation invariant; it is a disc. Here, $\theta_{max}(A) \neq 0$ always holds, because A is assumed to be two-dimensional. Converse to p(.), the fuzzy line-predicate

$$l(A) = 1 - p(A). \tag{8.5}$$

Let's express the degree to which a Cartesian point set A ⊆ Dom is sensitive to rotation. Since we only regard convex hulls, l (.) disregards the detailed shape and structure of A, but only measures the degree to which A is directed.

A fuzzy version of the incidence-predicate inc(.,.) is a binary fuzzy relation between Cartesian point sets A, B $\subseteq$ Dom :

$$inc(A, B) = \max\Big(| \, ch(A) \cap ch(B) \, | \, / \, | \, ch(A) \, |, | \, ch(A) \cap ch(B) \, | \, / \, | \, ch(B) \, |\Big) \qquad (8.6)$$

Inc measures the relative overlaps of the convex hulls of A and B and selects the greater one. Here |ch (A)| denotes the area occupied by ch (A). The greater inc (A, B), "the more incident" are A and B: If A $\subseteq$ B or B $\subseteq$ A, then inc (A, B) =1, and A and B are considered incident to degree one. Conversely to inc(.,.), a graduated equality predicate eq(.,.) between the bounded Cartesian point sets A, B $\subseteq$ Dom can be defined as follows:

$$eq(A, B) = \min\Big(| \, ch(A) \cap ch(B) \, | \, / \, | \, ch(A) \, |, | \, ch(A) \cap ch(B) \, | \, / \, | \, ch(B) \, |\Big) \qquad (8.7)$$

eq (A, B) measures the minimal relative overlap of A and B, whereas $\neg$ eq (A, B) = 1 − eq (A, B) measures the degrees to which the two point sets do not overlap: if eq (A, B) $\approx$ 0, then A and B are "almost disjoint".

The following measure of "distinctness of points", dp (.), of two extended objects tries to capture this fact (Figure 8.1(b)). We define

$$dp \, (A, B) = \max(0, \, 1- \, \max(\theta_{max} (A), \, \theta_{max} (B)) \, / \, \theta_{max} (ch(A \cup B))) \qquad (8.8)$$

dp (A, B) expresses the degree to which ch (A) and ch (B) are distinct: The greater dp (A, B), the more A and B behave like distinct Cartesian points with respect to connection. Indeed, for Cartesian points a and b, we would have dp (A, B) = 1. If the distance between the Cartesian point sets A and B is infinitely big, then dp (A, B) = 1 as well. If $\max(\theta_{max} (A), \, \theta_{max} (B)) > \theta_{max} (ch(A \cup B)))$ then dp (A, B) = 0.

8.2.3 *Formalization of fuzzy predicates*

To formalize fuzzy predicates, defined in subsection 8.2.2 both implication → and conjunction operators are defined as in Table 8.1:

$$A \wedge B = \begin{cases} \dfrac{a+b}{2}, a+b>1, \\ 0, a+b \le 1 \end{cases} \qquad (8.9)$$

$$A \rightarrow B = \begin{cases} \dfrac{1-a+b}{2}, a>b, \\ 1, a \le b. \end{cases} \qquad (8.10)$$

In our further discussions we will also use the disjunction operator from the same table.

$$A \vee B = \begin{cases} \dfrac{a+b}{2}, a+b<1, \\ 1, a+b \ge 1. \end{cases} \qquad (8.11)$$

Now let us re-define the set of fuzzy predicates (8.6)–(8.8), using proposed fuzzy logic's operators.

Proposition 8.1.
If fuzzy predicate inc(…) is defined as in (8.6) and conjunction operator is defined as in (8.9), then

$$inc(A,B) = \begin{cases} \dfrac{a+b}{2a}, a+b>1 \ \& \ a<b, \\ \dfrac{a+b}{2b}, a+b>1 \ \& \ a>b, \\ 0, a+b \le 1. \end{cases} \qquad (8.12)$$

Proof: Lets present (8.6) as follows:

$$inc(A, B) = \frac{|A \cap B|}{\min(|A|, |B|)}, \tag{8.13}$$

And given that

$$\min(|A|, |B|) = \frac{a + b - |a - b|}{2}, \tag{8.14}$$

from (8.6) and (8.9) we are getting (8.12). (Q.E.D.).

It's important to notice that for the case when a + b > 1 in (8.12), the value of inc (A, B) ≥ 1, which means that (8.12) in fact reduced into the following:

$$inc(A, B) = \begin{cases} 1, a + b > 1 \, \& \, a = b \, \& \, a > 0.5 \, \& \, b > 0.5, \\ 0, a + b \leq 1. \end{cases} \tag{8.15}$$

Proposition 8.2.
If fuzzy predicate eq(...) is defined as in (8.7) and disjunction operator is defined as in (8.11), then

$$eq(A, B) = \begin{cases} \dfrac{a + b}{2b}, a + b > 1 \, \& \, a < b, \\[2mm] \dfrac{a + b}{2a}, a + b > 1 \, \& \, a > b, \\[2mm] 0, a + b \leq 1. \end{cases} \tag{8.16}$$

Proof:
Let's re-write (8.7) in the following way:

$$eq(A, B) = \min\left(A \cap B / A, A \cap B / B\right). \tag{8.17}$$

Let's define P = $A \cap B / A$ and Q = $A \cap B / B$ and given (8.9) we have got the following:

$$P=\begin{cases}\dfrac{a+b}{2a}, a+b>1, \\ 0, a+b\le1\end{cases} \qquad Q=\begin{cases}\dfrac{a+b}{2b}, a+b>1, \\ 0, a+b\le1\end{cases} \qquad (8.18)$$

Therefore, given (8.14), we use (8.18) in the expression of min (8.14) and first find the following:

$$P+Q=\begin{cases}\dfrac{a+b}{2a}+\dfrac{a+b}{2b}, a+b>1, \\ 0, a+b\le1\end{cases}=\begin{cases}\dfrac{(a+b)^2}{2ab}, a+b>1, \\ 0, a+b\le1\end{cases} \qquad (8.19)$$

In a meantime we can show that the following is also taking place

$$P-Q=\begin{cases}\dfrac{a+b}{2a}-\dfrac{a+b}{2b}, a+b>1, \\ 0, a+b\le1\end{cases}=\begin{cases}\dfrac{b^2-a^2}{2ab}, a+b>1, \\ 0, a+b\le1\end{cases} \qquad (8.20)$$

From (8.20) we are getting

$$|P-Q|=\begin{cases}\dfrac{b^2-a^2}{2ab}, a+b>1\ \&\ b>a, \\ \dfrac{a^2-b^2}{2ab}, a+b>1\ \&\ a>b, \\ 0, a+b\le1\end{cases} \qquad (8.21)$$

But from (8.17) we have the following:

$$eq(A,B)=\min(P,Q)=\dfrac{P+Q-|P-Q|}{2}=$$

$$\begin{cases}\dfrac{(a+b)^2-b^2+a^2}{2ab}, a+b>1\ \&\ b>a, \\ \dfrac{(a+b)^2-a^2+b^2}{4ab}, a+b>1\ \&\ a>b, \\ 0, a+b\le1\end{cases}=\begin{cases}\dfrac{a+b}{2b}, a+b>1\ \&\ a<b, \\ \dfrac{a+b}{2a}, a+b>1\ \&\ a>b, \\ 0, a+b\le1\end{cases} \qquad (8.22)$$

(Q.E.D.).

Corollary 8.1.

If fuzzy predicate eq (A, B) is defined as (8.22), then the following type of transitivity is taking place

$$eq(A,C) \rightarrow eq(A,B) \wedge eq(B,C),$$ (8.23)

where A, B, C $\subseteq$ Dom, and Dom is partially ordered space, i.e. either A $\subseteq$ B$\subseteq$ C or vice versa. (Note: both conjunction and implication operations are defined in Table 8.1).

Proof:

From (8.16) we have

$$eq(A,B) = \begin{cases} \dfrac{a+b}{2b}, a+b>1 \& a<b, \\ \dfrac{a+b}{2a}, a+b>1 \& a>b, \\ 0, a+b \le 1 \end{cases}$$

and

$$eq(B,C) = \begin{cases} \dfrac{b+c}{2c}, b+c>1 \& b<c, \\ \dfrac{b+c}{2b}, b+c>1 \& b>c, \\ 0, b+c \le 1 \end{cases}$$

then

$$eq(A,B) \wedge eq(B,C) = \begin{cases} \dfrac{eq(A,B)+eq(B,C)}{2}, eq(A,B)+eq(B,C)>1, \\ 0, eq(A,B)+eq(B.C) \le 1 \end{cases}$$ (8.24)

Meanwhile, from (8.16) we have the following:

$$eq(A,C)=\begin{cases}\dfrac{a+c}{2c},a+c>1\ \&\ a<c,\\[2mm]\dfrac{a+c}{2a},a+c>1\ \&\ a>c,\\[2mm]0,a+c\le1\end{cases} \qquad (8.25)$$

Case 1: $a < b < c$
From (8.24) we have:

$$(eq(A,B)\wedge eq(B,C))/2=\frac{a+b}{2b}+\frac{b+c}{2c}=\frac{ac+2bc+b^2}{4bc}. \qquad (8.26)$$

From (8.25) and (8.26) we have to proof that

$$\frac{a+c}{2c}\rightarrow\frac{ac+2bc+b^2}{4bc}. \qquad (8.27)$$

But (8.27) is the same as

$$\frac{2ab+2bc}{4bc}\rightarrow\frac{ac+2bc+b^2}{4bc},\text{ from which we get the following }2ab\rightarrow$$

$ac+b^2$
From definition of implication in fuzzy logic (8.10) and since for $a < b < c$ condition the following is taking place

$2ab < ac+b^2$, therefore $2ab\rightarrow ac+b^2=1$. (Q.E.D.).

Case 2: $a > b > c$
From (8.24) we have:

$$(eq(A,B)\wedge eq(B,C))/2=\frac{a+b}{2a}+\frac{b+c}{2b}=\frac{ac+2ab+b^2}{4ab} \qquad (8.28)$$

. From (8.25) and (8.28) we have to proof that

$$\frac{a+c}{2a} \to \frac{ac+2ab+b^2}{4ab}.$$ (8.29)

But (8.29) is the same as

$$\frac{2ab+2bc}{4ab} \to \frac{ac+2ab+b^2}{4ab},$$ from which we get the following $2bc \to ac+b^2$.

From definition of implication in fuzzy logic (8.10) and since for $a > b > c$ condition the following is taking place

$2bc < ac+b^2$, therefore $2bc \to ac+b^2 = 1$. (Q.E.D.).

Proposition 8.3.
If fuzzy predicate dp(...) is defined as in (8.8) and disjunction operator is defined as in (8.11), then

$$dp(A,B) = \begin{cases} 1-a, a+b \geq 1\ \&\ a \geq b, \\ 1-b, a+b \geq 1\ \&\ a < b, \\ 0, a+b < 1 \end{cases}$$ (8.30)

Proof:
From (8.8) we get the following:

$$dp(A,B) = \max\left\{0, 1 - \frac{\max(A,B)}{A \cup B}\right\}.$$ (8.31)

Given that $\max(A,B) = \dfrac{a+b+|a-b|}{2}$, from (8.31) and (8.8) we are getting the following:

$$dp(A,B) = \begin{cases} \max\{0, 1 - \dfrac{a+b+|a-b|}{a+b}\}, a+b < 1, \\ \max\{0, 1 - \dfrac{a+b+|a-b|}{2}\}, a+b \geq 1. \end{cases} \quad (8.32)$$

1. From (8.32) we have:

$$\max\left\{0, 1 - \frac{a+b+|a-b|}{2}\right\} = \max\left\{0, \frac{2-a-b-|a-b|}{2}\right\} =$$
$$\begin{cases} 1-a, a+b \geq 1 \, \& \, a \geq b, \\ 1-b, a+b \geq 1 \, \& \, a < b. \end{cases} \quad (8.33)$$

2. Also from (8.32) we have:

$$\max\left\{0, 1 - \frac{a+b+|a-b|}{a+b}\right\} = \max\left\{0, -\frac{|a-b|}{a+b}\right\} = 0, a+b < 1. \quad (8.34)$$

From both (8.33) and (8.34) we have gotten that

$$dp(A,B) = \begin{cases} 1-a, a+b \geq 1 \, \& \, a \geq b, \\ 1-b, a+b \geq 1 \, \& \, a < b, \text{ (Q.E.D.).} \\ 0, a+b < 1 \end{cases} \quad (8.35)$$

8.3 Fuzzy axiomatization of incidence geometry

Using the fuzzy predicates formalized in subsection 8.2, we propose the set of axioms as fuzzy version of incidence geometry in the language of a fuzzy logic [28] as follows:

$$I1' : dp(a, b) \rightarrow \sup_{c}[l(c) \wedge inc(a,c) \wedge inc(b,c)]$$

$I2': dp(a,b) \rightarrow [l(c) \rightarrow [inc(a,c) \rightarrow [inc(b,c) \rightarrow l(c') \rightarrow$
$\rightarrow [inc(a,c') \rightarrow [inc(b,c') \rightarrow eq(c,c')]]]]]]$

$I3': l(c) \rightarrow \sup_{a,b}\{p(a) \wedge p(b) \wedge \neg eq(a,b) \wedge inc(a,c) \wedge inc(b,c)\}$

$I4': \sup_{a,b,c,d} [p(a) \wedge p(b) \wedge p(c) \wedge l(d) \rightarrow \neg(inc(a,d) \wedge inc(b,d) \wedge inc(c,d))]$

In axioms I1'-I4' we also use a set of operations (8.9)-(8.11).

Proposition 8.4.

If fuzzy predicates dp (...) and inc (...) are defined like (8.35) and (8.12) respectively, then axiom I1' is fulfilled for the set of logical operators from a fuzzy logic [28]. (For every two distinct point a and b, at least one line l exists that is incident with a and b.)

Proof:

From (8.15)

$$inc(A,C) = \begin{cases} 1, a+c>1 \& a=c \& a>0.5 \& c>0.5, \\ 0, a+c \leq 1 \end{cases}$$

$$inc(B,C) = \begin{cases} 1, b+c>1 \& b=c \& b>0.5 \& c>0.5, \\ 0, b+c \leq 1 \end{cases} \qquad (8.36)$$

$$inc(A,C) \wedge inc(B,C) = \frac{inc(A,C)+inc(B,C)}{2} \equiv 1,$$

$\sup_{c}[l(c) \wedge inc(a,c) \wedge inc(b,c)]$ and given (8.36)

$\sup_{c}[l(c) \wedge 1] = 0 \wedge 1 \equiv 0.5$. From (8.35) and (8.9) $dp(a,b) \leq 0.5$ we are getting

$dp(a,b) \leq \sup_{c}[l(c) \wedge inc(a,c) \wedge inc(b,c)]$ (Q.E.D.).

Proposition 8.5.

If fuzzy predicates dp (...), eq(...) and inc (...) are defined like (8.35), (8.16) and (8.15) respectively, then axiom I2' is fulfilled for the set of logical operators from a fuzzy logic [28]. (For every two distinct point a and b, at least one line l exists that is incident with a and b and such a line is unique)

Proof:

Let's take a look at the following implication:

$$inc(b,c') \rightarrow eq(c,c'). \tag{8.37}$$

But from (8.25) we have

$$eq(C,C') = \begin{cases} \dfrac{c+c'}{2c'}, c+c'>1 \,\&\, c<c', \\[2mm] \dfrac{c+c'}{2c}, c+c'>1 \,\&\, c>c', \\[2mm] 0, c+c' \leq 1. \end{cases} \tag{8.38}$$

And from (8.15)

$$inc(B,C) = \begin{cases} 1, b+c>1 \,\&\, b=c \,\&\, b>0.5 \,\&\, c>0.5, \\ 0, b+c \leq 1. \end{cases} \tag{8.39}$$

From (8.38) and (8.39) we see that $inc(B,C) \leq eq(C,C')$, which means that

$$inc(b,c') \rightarrow eq(c,c') \equiv 1,$$

therefore the following is also true

$$inc(a,c') \rightarrow [inc(b,c') \rightarrow eq(c,c')] \equiv 1. \tag{8.40}$$

Now let's take a look at the following implication $inc(b,c) \rightarrow l(c')$. Since $inc(b,c) \geq l(c')$, we are getting $inc(b,c) \rightarrow l(c') \equiv 0$. Taking into account (8.40) we have the following

$$inc(b,c) \rightarrow l(c') \rightarrow [inc(a,c') \rightarrow [inc(b,c') \rightarrow eq(c,c')]] \equiv 1. \tag{8.41}$$

Since from (8.15), $inc(a,c) \leq 1$, then with taking into account (8.41) we've gotten the following:

$$inc(a,c) \rightarrow [inc(b,c) \rightarrow l(c') \rightarrow [inc(a,c') \rightarrow [inc(b,c') \rightarrow eq(c,c')]]] \equiv 1. \quad (8.42)$$

Since $l(c) \leq 1$, from (8.42) we are getting:

$$l(c) \rightarrow [inc(a,c) \rightarrow [inc(b,c) \rightarrow l(c') \rightarrow [inc(a,c') \rightarrow [inc(b,c') \rightarrow eq(c,c')]]]] \equiv 1$$

Finally, because $dp(a,b) \leq 1$ we have

$$dp(a,b) \leq \{l(c) \rightarrow [inc(a,c) \rightarrow [inc(b,c) \rightarrow l(c') \rightarrow [inc(a,c') \rightarrow [inc(b,c') \rightarrow eq(c,c')]]]]\}$$
(Q.E.D.).

Proposition 8.6.
If fuzzy predicates eq(…) and inc (…) are defined like (8.16) and (8.15) respectively, then axiom I3' is fulfilled for the set of logical operators from a fuzzy logic [28]. (Every line is incident with at least two points.)

Proof:
It was already shown in (8.36) that

$$inc(a,c) \wedge inc(b,c) = \frac{inc(a,c) + inc(b,c)}{2} \equiv 1.$$

And from (8.16) we have

$$eq(A,B) = \begin{cases} \dfrac{a+b}{2b}, a+b>1 \,\&\, a<b, \\[2mm] \dfrac{a+b}{2a}, a+b>1 \,\&\, a>b, \\[2mm] 0, a+b \leq 1 \end{cases}$$

The negation $\neg eq(A,B)$ will be

$$\neg eq(A,B) = \begin{cases} \dfrac{b-a}{2b}, a+b>1 \,\&\, a<b, \\[2mm] \dfrac{a-b}{2a}, a+b>1 \,\&\, a>b, \\[2mm] 1, a+b \leq 1 \end{cases} \quad (8.43)$$

Given (8.36) and (8.43) we get

$$\neg eq(A,B) \wedge 1 = \begin{cases} [1+\dfrac{b-a}{2b}]/2, a+b>1 \,\&\, a<b, \\[2mm] [1+\dfrac{a-b}{2a}]/2, a+b>1 \,\&\, a>b, \\[2mm] 1, a+b\leq 1 \end{cases}$$

$$\begin{cases} \dfrac{3b-a}{4b}, a+b>1 \,\&\, a<b, \\[2mm] \dfrac{3a-b}{4a}, a+b>1 \,\&\, a>b, \\[2mm] 1, a+b\leq 1 \end{cases} \qquad (8.44)$$

Since $\neg eq(A,B) \wedge 1 \equiv 0.5 \mid a = .1, b = 1$, from which we are getting

$$\frac{\sup}{a,b}\{p(a) \wedge p(b) \wedge \neg eq(a,b) \wedge inc(a,c) \wedge inc(b,c)\} = 1 \wedge 0.5 = 0.75.$$

And given, that $l(c) \leq 0.75$ we are getting

$$l(c) \to \frac{\sup}{a,b}\{p(a) \wedge p(b) \wedge \neg eq(a,b) \wedge inc(a,c) \wedge inc(b,c)\} \equiv 1 \text{ (Q.E.D.).}$$

Proposition 8.7.

If fuzzy predicate inc (...) is defined like (8.15), then axiom I4' is fulfilled for the set of logical operators from a fuzzy logic [28]. (At least three points exist that are not incident with the same line.)

Proof:

From (8.15) we have

$$inc(A,D) = \begin{cases} 1, a+d>1 \,\&\, a=d \,\&\, a>0.5 \,\&\, d>0.5, \\ 0, a+d\leq 1 \end{cases}$$

$$inc(B,D) = \begin{cases} 1, b+d>1 \,\&\, b=d \,\&\, b>0.5 \,\&\, d>0.5, \\ 0, b+d\leq 1 \end{cases}$$

$$inc(C,D) = \begin{cases} 1, c+d > 1 \ \& \ c = d \ \& \ c > 0.5 \ \& \ d > 0.5, \\ 0, c+d \le 1 \end{cases}$$

But from (8.36) which we have

$$inc(A,D) \wedge inc(B,D) = \frac{inc(A,D) + inc(B,D)}{2} \equiv 1$$

$(inc(a,d) \wedge inc(b,d) \wedge inc(c,d)) = 1 \wedge inc(c,d) \equiv 1$, from where we have $\neg(inc(a,d) \wedge inc(b,d) \wedge inc(c,d)) \equiv 0$. Since $l(d) \equiv 0 \,|\, d = 1$ we are getting $l(d) == \neg(inc(a,d) \wedge inc(b,d) \wedge inc(c,d))$, which could be interpreted like $l(d) \to \neg(inc(a,d) \wedge inc(b,d) \wedge inc(c,d)) = 1$, from which we finally get the following

$$\sup_{a,b,c,d} [p(a) \wedge p(b) \wedge p(c) \wedge 1] \equiv 1 \text{ (Q.E.D.)}.$$

8.3.1 *Equality of extended lines is graduated*

In [778] it was shown that the location of the extended points creates a constraint on the location of an incident extended line. It was also mentioned, that in traditional geometry this location constraint fixes the position of the line uniquely. And therefore in case points and lines are allowed to have extension this is not the case. Consequently Euclid's First postulate does not apply: Figure 8.2 shows that if two distinct extended points P and Q are incident (i.e. overlap) with two extended lines L and M, then L and M are not necessarily equal.

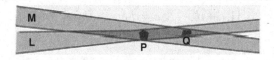

Fig. 8.2. Two extended points do not uniquely determine the location of an incident extended line

Yet, in most cases, L and M are "closer together", i.e. "more equal" than arbitrary extended lines that have only one or no extended point in common. The further P and Q move apart from each other, the more similar L and M become. One way to model this fact is to allow degrees of equality for extended lines. In other words, the equality relation is graduated. It allows not only for Boolean values, but for values in the whole interval [0, 1].

As it was demonstrated in [778], there is a reasonable assumption to classify an extended point and an extended line as incident, if their extended representations in the underlying metric space overlap. We do this by modelling incidence by the subset relation:

Definition 8.1: For an extended point P, and an extended line L we define the incidence relation by

$$R_{inc}(P, L) := (P \subseteq L) \in \{0,1\} \,, \tag{8.45}$$

where the subset relation $\subseteq$ refers to P and L as subsets of the underlying metric space.

The extended incidence relation (8.45) is a Boolean relation, assuming either the truth value 1 (true) or the truth value 0 (false). It is well known that since a Boolean relation is a special case of a graduated relation, i.e. since $\{0, 1\} \subset [0, 1]$, we will be able to use relation (8.45) as part of fuzzified Euclid's first postulate later on.

8.4 Equality of extended points and lines

As stated in previous sections, equality of extended points, and equality of extended lines is a matter of degree. Geometric reasoning with extended points and extended lines relies heavily on the metric structure of the underlying coordinate space. Consequently, it is reasonable to model graduated equality as inverse to distance.

8.4.1 *Metric distance*

In [778] was mentioned that a pseudo metric distance, or pseudo metric, is a map $d : M^2 \to \Re^+$ from domain M into the positive real numbers (including zero), which is minimal, symmetric, and satisfies the triangle inequality:

$$\forall p, q \in [0,1] \Rightarrow \begin{cases} d(p,p) = 0 \\ d(p,q) = d(q,p) \\ d(p,q) + d(q,r) \geq d(p,r). \end{cases} \qquad (8.47)$$

d is called a metric, if additionally holds:

$$d(p,q) = 0 \Leftrightarrow p = q, \qquad (8.48)$$

Well known examples of metric distances are the Euclidean distance, or the Manhattan distance. Another example is the elliptic metric for the projective plane defined in (8.46) [778]. The "upside-down-version" of a pseudo metric distance is a fuzzy equivalence relation w.r.t. a proposed t-norm. The next section introduces the logical connectives in a proposed t-norm fuzzy logic. We will use this particular fuzzy logic to formalize Euclid's first postulate for extended primitives. The reason for choosing a proposed fuzzy logic is its strong connection to metric distance.

8.4.2 *The t-norm*

Proposition 8.8. In proposed fuzzy logic the operation of conjunction (8.9) is a t-norm.

Proof:
The function f(p, q) is a t-norm if the following

1.   Commutativity: $p \wedge q = q \wedge p$
2.   Associativity: $(p \wedge q) \wedge r = p \wedge (q \wedge r)$
3.   Monotonity: $p \leq q, p \wedge r \leq q \wedge r$

4. Neutrality: $1 \wedge p = p$
5. Absorption $0 \wedge p = 0$

Commutativity:

$$f(p,q) = P \cap Q = \begin{cases} \dfrac{p+q}{2}, p+q > 1 \\ 0, p+q \leq 1 \end{cases} \qquad \text{and}$$

$$f(q,p) = Q \cap P = \begin{cases} \dfrac{q+p}{2}, q+p > 1 \\ 0, q+p \leq 1 \end{cases}, \text{ therefore}$$

$$f(p,q) = f(q,p) \text{ (Q.E.D.).}$$

Associativity:
Case: $f(p,q) \wedge r$

$$f(p,q) = \frac{p+q}{2}, p+q > 1 \Rightarrow f(p,q) \wedge r$$

$$= \begin{cases} \dfrac{f(p,q)+r}{2}, f(p,q)+r > 1 \\ 0, f(p,q)+r \leq 1 \end{cases} = \begin{cases} \dfrac{p+q+2r}{4}, \dfrac{p+q}{2}+r > 1 \\ 0, \dfrac{p+q}{2}+r \leq 1 \end{cases}$$

From where we have that

$$f_1(p,r) = \begin{cases} \dfrac{p+q+2r}{4}, p+q+2r > 2 \\ 0, p+q+2r \leq 2 \end{cases} \qquad (8.49)$$

In other words $f_1(p,r) \subseteq (0.5;1]\,|\,p+q+2r > 2$ and $f_1(p,r) = 0\,|$
$p+q+2r \leq 2$.

For the case: $p \wedge f(q,r)$ we are getting similar to (8.49) results

$$f_2(p,r) = \begin{cases} \dfrac{q+r+2p}{4}, q+r+2p > 2 \\ 0, q+r+2p \le 2 \end{cases}$$
(8.50)

i.e. $f_2(p,r) \subseteq (0.5;1] \mid q+r+2p > 2$ and $f_2(p,r) = 0 \mid q+r+2p \le 2$.

$f_1(p,r) \approx f_2(p,r)$ (Q.E.D.).

Monotonity:

If $p \le q \Rightarrow p \wedge r \le q \wedge r$ then given

$$p \wedge r = \begin{cases} \dfrac{p+r}{2}, p+r > 1 \\ 0, p+r \le 1 \end{cases} \text{ and } q \wedge r = \begin{cases} \dfrac{q+r}{2}, q+r > 1 \\ 0, q+r \le 1 \end{cases}$$ we are getting the

following

$$\frac{p+r}{2} \le \frac{q+r}{2} \Rightarrow p+r \le q+r \Rightarrow p \le q \mid p+r > 1 \text{ and } q+r > 1.$$

Whereas for the case $p+r \le 1$ and $q+r \le 1 \Rightarrow 0 \equiv 0$ (Q.E.D.).

Neutrality: $1 \wedge p = \begin{cases} \dfrac{1+p}{2}, 1+p > 1 \\ 0, 1+p \le 1 \end{cases} = \begin{cases} \dfrac{1+p}{2}, p > 0 \\ 0, p \le 0 \end{cases} = \begin{cases} \dfrac{1+p}{2}, p > 0 \\ 0, p = 0 \end{cases}$,

from which the following is apparent

$$1 \wedge p = \begin{cases} \dfrac{1+p}{2}, p \in (0,1) \\ p, p = 0, p = 1 \end{cases} \text{ (Q.E.D.).}$$

Absorption:

$$0 \wedge p = \begin{cases} \dfrac{p}{2}, p > 1 \\ 0, p \leq 1 \end{cases}, \text{ but since } p \in [0,1] \Rightarrow 0 \wedge p \equiv 0 \, (\text{Q.E.D.}).$$

8.4.3 *Fuzzy equivalence relations*

As mentioned above, the "upside-down-version" of a pseudo metric distance is a fuzzy equivalence relation w.r.t. the proposed t-norm $\wedge$. A fuzzy equivalence relation is a fuzzy relation $e : M^2 \rightarrow [0,1]$ on a domain M, which is reflexive, symmetric and $\wedge$-transitive:

$$\forall p, q \in [0,1] \Rightarrow \begin{cases} e(p,p) = 1 \\ e(p,q) = e(q,p) \\ e(p,q) \wedge e(q,r) \leq e(p,r). \end{cases} \tag{8.51}$$

Proposition 8.9.

If fuzzy equivalence relation is defined (Table 8.1) as the following

$$e(p,q) = P \leftrightarrow Q = \begin{cases} \dfrac{1-p+q}{2}, p > q, \\ 1, p = q, \\ \dfrac{1-q+p}{2}, p < q \end{cases} \tag{8.52}$$

then conditions (8.51) are satisfied.

Proof:

1. Reflexivity: $e(p,p) = 1$ comes from (8.52) because $p \equiv p$.

2. Symmetricity: $e(p,q) = e(q,p)$.

$$e(p,q) = \begin{cases} \dfrac{1-p+q}{2}, p > q, \\ 1, p = q, \\ \dfrac{1-q+p}{2}, p < q \end{cases} \text{ but } e(q,p) = \begin{cases} \dfrac{1-q+p}{2}, q > p, \\ 1, q = p, \\ \dfrac{1-p+q}{2}, q < p \end{cases} \text{ therefore}$$

$e(p,q) \equiv e(q,p) \, (\text{Q.E.D.}).$

3. Transitivity: $e(p,q) \wedge e(q,r) \leq e(p,r) \mid \forall p,q,r \in L[0,1]$ -lattice.

From (8.52) let

$$F_1(p,r) = e(p,r) = \begin{cases} \dfrac{1-p+r}{2}, p > r, \\ 1, p = r, \\ \dfrac{1-r+p}{2}, p < r \end{cases} \tag{8.53}$$

and $\quad e(q,r) = \begin{cases} \dfrac{1-q+r}{2}, q > r, \\ 1, q = r, \\ \dfrac{1-r+q}{2}, q < r \end{cases} \quad$ then

$$F_2(p,r) = e(p,q) \wedge e(q,r)$$
$$= \begin{cases} \dfrac{e(p,q) + e(q,r)}{2}, e(p,q) + e(q,r) > 1 \\ 0, e(p,q) + e(q,r) \leq 1 \end{cases} \tag{8.54}$$

But

$$F_2(p,r) = \dfrac{e(p,q) + e(q,r)}{2} \begin{cases} \left(\dfrac{1-p+q}{2} + \dfrac{1-q+r}{2} \right) / 2, p > q > r, \\ 1, p = q = r, \\ \left(\dfrac{1-q+p}{2} + \dfrac{1-r+q}{2} \right) / 2, p < q < r \end{cases} \tag{8.55}$$

$$= \begin{cases} \dfrac{2-p+r}{4}, p > q > r, \\ 1, p = q = r, \\ \dfrac{2-r+p}{4}, p < r < r \end{cases}$$

Now compare (8.55) and (8.53). It is apparent that $\forall r > p \Rightarrow \dfrac{2-p+r}{4} < \dfrac{1-p+r}{2} \Leftrightarrow r-p < 2(r-p)$. The same is true for $\forall p > r \Rightarrow \dfrac{2-r+p}{4} < \dfrac{1-r+p}{2} \Leftrightarrow p-r < 2(p-r)$.

And lastly $\dfrac{e(p,q)+e(q,r)}{2} \equiv e(p,r) \equiv 1$, when $p=r$. Given that $F_2(p,r) = e(p,q) \wedge e(q,r) \equiv 0$, $e(p,q)+e(q,r) \leq 1$, we are getting the proof of the fact that $F_2(p,r) \leq F_1(p,r) \Leftrightarrow e(p,q) \wedge e(q,r) \leq e(p,r) \mid \forall p,q,r \in L[0,1]$ (Q.E.D.).

Note that relation $e(p,q)$ is called a fuzzy equality relation, if additionally separability holds: $e(p,q)=1 \Leftrightarrow p=q$. Let us define a pseudo metric distance $d(p,q)$ for domain M, normalized to 1, as

$$e(p,q) = 1 - d(p,q). \tag{8.56}$$

From (8.52) we are getting

$$d(p,q) = \begin{cases} \dfrac{1+p-q}{2}, & p>q, \\ 0, & p=q, \\ \dfrac{1+q-p}{2}, & p<q \end{cases} = \begin{cases} \dfrac{1+|p-q|}{2}, & p \neq q \\ 0, & p=q \end{cases} \tag{8.57}$$

8.4.4 *Approximate fuzzy equivalence relations*

In [140] it was mentioned, that graduated equality of extended lines compels graduated equality of extended points. Figure 8.3(a) sketches a situation where two extended lines L and M intersect in an extended point P. If a third extended line L' is very similar to L, its intersection with M yields an extended point P' which is very similar to P. It is desirable to model this fact. To do so, it is necessary to allow graduated equality of extended points.

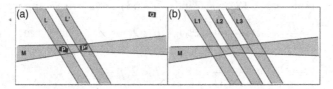

Fig. 8.3. (a) Graduated equality of extended lines compels graduated equality of extended points. (b) Equality of extended lines is not transitive

Figure 8.3(b) illustrates that an equality relation between extended objects need not be transitive. This phenomenon is commonly referred to as the Poincare paradox. The Poincare paradox is named after the famous French mathematician and theoretical physicist Henri Poincare, who repeatedly pointed this fact out, e.g. in [619], referring to indiscernibility in sensations and measurements. Note that this phenomenon is usually insignificant, if positional uncertainty is caused by stochastic variability. In measurements, the stochastic variability caused by measurement inaccuracy is usually much greater than the indiscernibility caused by limited resolution. For extended objects, this relation is reversed. The extension of an object can be interpreted as indiscernibility of its contributing points. In the present section we assume that the extension of an object is being compared with the indeterminacy of its boundary. In [307] it is shown that for modelling the Poincare paradox in a graduated context transitivity may be replaced by a weaker form [619]:

$$e(p,q) \wedge e(q,r) \wedge dis(q) \leq e(p,r). \qquad (8.58)$$

Here $dis: M \rightarrow [0,1]$ is a lower-bound measure (discernibility measure) for the degree of transitivity that is permitted by q. A pair (e, dis) that is reflexive, symmetric and weakly transitive (8.58) is called an approximate fuzzy $\wedge$ -equivalence relation. Let us rewrite (8.58) as follows

$$F_2(p,r) \wedge dis(q) \leq F_1(p,r). \qquad (8.59)$$

Where $F_2(p,r), F_1(p,r)$ are defined in (8.55) and (8.53) correspondingly. But

$$\forall p,q,r \mid p < q < r \Rightarrow F_2(p,r) \wedge dis(q)$$

$$= \begin{cases} \left(\left(\dfrac{2-r+p}{4} + dis(q)\right) / 2, \dfrac{2-r+p}{4} + dis(q) > 1 \\[4mm] 0, \dfrac{2-r+p}{4} + dis(q) \le 1 \end{cases} \qquad (8.60)$$

and

$$\forall p,q,r \mid p > q > r \Rightarrow F_2(p,r) \wedge dis(q) =$$

$$= \begin{cases} \left(\left(\dfrac{2-p+r}{4} + dis(q)\right) / 2, \dfrac{2-p+r}{4} + dis(q) > 1 \\[4mm] 0, \dfrac{2-p+r}{4} + dis(q) \le 1 \end{cases} \qquad (8.61)$$

From (8.60) and (8.61) in order to satisfy a condition (8.59) we have

$$\forall p,q,r \mid p < q < r \Rightarrow dis(q) > 1 - \frac{2-r+p}{4}$$

and $\forall p,q,r \mid p > q > r \Rightarrow dis(q) > 1 - \dfrac{2-p+r}{4}$

i.e. we have

$$dis(q) \cong \begin{cases} \dfrac{2 + |p - r|}{4}, r \ne p \\[4mm] 0, r = p \end{cases} \qquad (8.62)$$

By using (8.62) in both (8.60) and (8.61) we are getting that $\forall p,q,r \in [0,1] \Rightarrow F_2(p,r) \wedge dis(q) \equiv 0.5$. Since from (8.53) we are getting $\forall p,r \in [0,1] \Rightarrow F_1(p,r) \in [0.5,1]$ and subsequently inequality (8.59) holds. In [140] it was also mentioned that an approximate fuzzy $\wedge$ -equivalence relation is the upside-down version of a so-called pointless pseudo metric space (δ, s):

$$\delta(p,p) = 0$$
$$\delta(p,q) = \delta(q,p) \tag{8.63}$$
$$\delta(p,q) \vee \delta(q,r) \vee s(q) \geq \delta(p,r).$$

Here, $\delta : M \to \mathfrak{R}^+$ is a (not necessarily metric) distance between extended regions, and $s : M \to \mathfrak{R}^+$ is a size measure and we are using an operation disjunction (8.11) also shown in Table 8.1. Inequality $\delta(q,r) \vee s(q) \geq \delta(p,r)$ is a weak form of the triangle inequality. It corresponds to the weak transitivity (8.58) of the approximate fuzzy $\wedge$ -equivalence relation e. In case the size of the domain M is normalized to 1, e and dis can be represented by [307]

$$e(p,q) = 1 - \delta(p,q), \ dis(q) = 1 - s(q). \tag{8.64}$$

Proposition 8.10.
If a distance between extended regions $\delta(p,q)$ from (8.63) and pseudo metric distance $d(p,q)$ for domain M, normalized to 1 be the same, i.e. $\delta(p,q) = d(p,q)$, then inequality $\delta(p,q) \vee \delta(q,r) \vee s(q) \geq \delta(p,r)$ holds.
Proof:
From (8.57) we have:

$$\delta(p,q) = \begin{cases} \dfrac{1+p-q}{2}, p > q, \\ 0, p = q, \\ \dfrac{1+q-p}{2}, p < q \end{cases} \qquad \delta(q,r) = \begin{cases} \dfrac{1+q-r}{2}, q > r, \\ 0, q = r, \\ \dfrac{1+r-q}{2}, q < r \end{cases} \tag{8.65}$$

Given (8.65)

$$\delta(p,q) \vee \delta(q,r)$$

$$= \begin{cases} \left(\dfrac{1+p-q}{2} + \dfrac{1+q-r}{2} \right) / 2, \delta(p,q) + \delta(q,r) < 1, p > q > r, \\ 1, \delta(p,q) + \delta(q,r) \geq 1, \\ 0, p = q = r, \\ \left(\dfrac{1+q-p}{2} + \dfrac{1+r-q}{2} \right) / 2, \delta(p,q) + \delta(q,r) < 1, p < q < r \end{cases}$$

$$= \begin{cases} \dfrac{2+p-r}{4}, \delta(p,q) + \delta(q,r) < 1, p > q > r, \\ 1, \delta(p,q) + \delta(q,r) \geq 1, \\ 0, p = q = r, \\ \dfrac{2+r-p}{4}, \delta(p,q) + \delta(q,r) < 1, p < q < r \end{cases} \tag{8.66}$$

$$= \begin{cases} \dfrac{2+|p-r|}{4}, \delta(p,q) + \delta(q,r) < 1, p \neq q \neq r, \\ 1, \delta(p,q) + \delta(q,r) \geq 1, \\ 0, p = q = r, \end{cases}$$

But

$$\delta(p,r) = \begin{cases} \dfrac{1+p-r}{2}, p > r, \\ 0, p = r, \\ \dfrac{1+r-p}{2}, p < r \end{cases} \tag{8.67}$$

From (8.66) and (8.67) the following is apparent:

$$\delta(p,q) \vee \delta(q,r) \leq \delta(p,r). \tag{8.68}$$

Now we have to show that size measure $s(q) > 0$. From (8.62) we have

$$s(q) = 1 - dis(q) = \begin{cases} \dfrac{2 - |p - r|}{4}, r \neq p \\ 1, r = p \end{cases} \tag{8.69}$$

It is apparent that $s(q) \in (0.25,1] \mid \forall r, p, q \in [0,1]$, therefore from (8.67), (8.68) and (8.69) $\delta(p,q) \vee \delta(q,r) \vee s(q) \geq \delta(p,r)$ holds (Q.E.D.).

Note, that $\delta(p,r)$ from (8.67) we have $\forall r, p \in [0,1] \Rightarrow \delta(p,r) = \dfrac{1 + |p - r|}{2} \in [0,1]$. But as it was mentioned in [778], given a pointless pseudo metric space (δ, s) for extended regions on a normalized domain, equations (8.64) define an approximate fuzzy $\wedge$-equivalence relation (e, dis) by simple logical negation. The so-defined equivalence relation on the one hand complies with the Poincare paradox, and on the other hand retains enough information to link two extended points (or lines) via a third. For used fuzzy logic an example of a pointless pseudo metric space is the set of extended points with the following measures:

$$\delta(P,Q) := \inf \{ d(p,q) \mid p \in P, q \in Q \}, \tag{8.70}$$

$$s(P) := \sup \{ d(p,q) \mid p, q \in P \}. \tag{8.71}$$

It is easy to show that (8.69) and (8.70) are satisfied, because from $(3.57) d(p,q) \in [0,1] \mid \forall r, p, q \in [0,1]$. A pointless metric distance of extended lines can be defined in the dual space [778]:

$$\delta(L,M) := \inf \{ d(l',m') \mid l \in L, m \in M \}, \tag{8.72}$$

$$s(L) := \sup \{ d(l',m') \mid l, m \in L \}. \tag{8.73}$$

8.4.5 *Boundary conditions for granularity*

As it was mentioned in [778], in exact coordinate geometry, points and lines do not have size. As a consequence, distance of points does not matter in the formulation of Euclid's first postulate. If points and lines are allowed to have extension, both, size and distance matter. Figure 8.4 depicts the location constraint on an extended line L that is incident with the extended points P and Q.

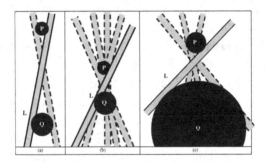

Fig. 8.4. Size and distance matter

The location constraint can be interpreted as tolerance in the position of L. In Figure 8.4(a) the distance of P and Q is large with respect to the sizes of P and Q, and with respect to the width of L. The resulting positional tolerance for L is small. In Figure 8.4(b), the distance of P and Q is smaller than it is in Figure 8.4(a). As a consequence the positional tolerance for L becomes larger. In Figure 8.4(c), P and Q have the same distance than in Figure 8.4(a), but their sizes are increased. Again, positional tolerance of L increases. As a consequence, a formalization of Euclid's first postulate for extended primitives must take all three parameters into account: the distance of the extended points, their size, and the size of the incident line.

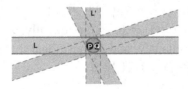

Fig. 8.5. P and Q are indiscernible for L

Figure 8.5 illustrates this case: Despite the fact that P and Q are distinct extended points that are both incident with L, they do not specify any directional constraint for L. Consequently, the directional parameter of the extended lines L and L' in Figure 8.5 may assume its maximum (at 90°). If we measure similarity (i.e. graduated equality) as inverse to distance, and if we establish a distance measure between extended lines that depends on all parameters of the lines parameter space, then L and L' in Figure 8.5 must have maximum distance. In other words, their degree of equality is zero, even though they are distinct and incident with P and Q.

The above observation can be interpreted as granularity: If we interpret the extended line L in Figure 8.5 as a sensor, then the extended points P and Q are indiscernible for L. Note that in this context grain size is not constant, but depends on the line that serves as a sensor.

Based on above mentioned a granularity enters Euclid's first postulate, if points and lines have extension: If two extended points P and Q are too close and the extended line L is too broad, then P and Q are indiscernible for L. Since this relation of indiscernibility (equality) depends not only on P and Q, but also on the extended line L, which acts as a sensor, we denote it by e(P,Q)[L], where L serves as an additional parameter for the equality of P and Q.

In [778] the following three boundary conditions to specify a reasonable behavior of e(P,Q)[L] were proposed:

1. If $s(L) \geq \delta(P,Q) + s(P) + s(Q)$, then P and Q impose no direction constraint on L (Figure 8.5), i.e. P and Q are indiscernible for L to degree 1: e (P, Q) [L] =1.

2. If $s(L) < \delta(P,Q) + s(P) + s(Q)$, then P and Q impose some direction constraint on L, but in general do not fix its location unambiguously. Accordingly, the degree of indiscernibility of P and Q lies between zero and one: 0<e (P, Q) [L] <1.

3. If $s(L) < \delta(P,Q) + s(P) + s(Q)$ and P = p, Q = q and L = l are crisp, then s (L) = s (P) = s (Q) = 0. Consequently, p and q determine the direction of l unambiguously, and all positional tolerance disappears. For this case we demand e (P, Q) [L] = 0.

In this section we are proposing an alternative approach to one from [778] to model granulated equality.

Proposition 8.11.

If Fuzzy Equivalence Relation e (P, Q) is defined in (8.52) and the width $s(L)$ of extended line L is defined in (8.73), then e (P, Q) [L] — the degree of indiscernibility of P and Q could be calculated as follows:

$$e\ (P,\ Q)\ [L] \equiv e(P,Q) \wedge s(L), \qquad (8.74)$$

and would satisfy a reasonable behavior, defined in 1-3. Here $\wedge$ - is conjunction operator from Table 8.1.

Proof:
From (8.9), (8.74) and (8.52) we have:

$$e(P,Q)[L] \equiv e(P,Q) \wedge s(L) = \begin{cases} \dfrac{e(P,Q)+s(L)}{2}, e(P,Q)+s(L) > 1, \\ 0, e(P,Q)+s(L) \leq 1 \end{cases} \qquad (8.75)$$

but from (8.52)

$$e(P,Q) = \begin{cases} \dfrac{1-p+q}{2}, p > q, \\ 1, p = q, \\ \dfrac{1-q+p}{2}, p < q \end{cases} \qquad (8.76)$$

therefore we have the following:
1. If P and Q impose no direction constraint on L which means that $s(L) = 1$ and
$\delta(P,Q) = 0 \Rightarrow e(P,Q) = 1$, then e (P, Q) [L] = 1 (proof of point 1).
2. If P and Q impose some direction constraint on L, but in general do not fix its location unambiguously, then from (8.75) and (8.76) we are get

$$e(P,Q)[[L] = \begin{cases} \dfrac{1-p+q+2\times s(L)}{4}, & \dfrac{1-p+q}{2}+s(L)>1, \\[2mm] 0, & \dfrac{1-|p-q|}{2}+s(L)\le 1, \\[2mm] \dfrac{1+s(L)}{2}, & p=q, \\[2mm] \dfrac{1-q+p+2\times s(L)}{4}, & \dfrac{1-q+p}{2}+s(L)>1 \end{cases} \in (0,1)$$

(proof of point 2).

3. If P = p, Q = q and L = l are crisp, which means that values of p and q are either 0 or 1 and since s (L) = 0, then e (P, Q) [L] = 0 (proof of point 3).

8.5 Fuzzification of the Euclid's first postulate

8.5.1 *The Euclid's first postulate formalization*

In previous section we identified and formalized a number of new qualities that enter into Euclid's first postulate, if extended geometric primitives are assumed. We are now in the position of formulating a fuzzified version of Euclid's first postulate. To do this, we first split the postulate

"Two distinct points determine a line uniquely." (8.77)

into two sub sentences:

"Given two distinct points, there exists at least one line that passes through them." (8.78)

"If more than one line passes through them, then they are equal." (8.79)

These sub sentences can be formalized in Boolean predicate logic as follows:

$$\forall p,q,\exists l,[R_{inc}(p,l)\wedge R_{inc}(q,l)] \tag{8.80}$$

$$\forall p,q,l,m[\neg(p=q)]\wedge[R_{inc}(p,l)\wedge R_{inc}(q,l)]\wedge \tag{8.81}$$
$$\wedge[R_{inc}(p,m)\wedge R_{inc}(q,m)]\to(l=m).$$

A verbatim translation of (8.80) and (8.81) into the syntax of a fuzzy logic we use yields

$$\inf_{P,Q}\sup_L[R_{inc}(P,L)\wedge R_{inc}(Q,L)] \tag{8.82}$$

$$\inf_{P,Q,L,M}\{[\neg e(P,Q)]\wedge[R_{inc}(P,L)\wedge R_{inc}(Q,L)]$$
$$\wedge[R_{inc}(P,M)\wedge R_{inc}(Q,M)]\to e(L,M)\} \tag{8.83}$$

where P, Q denote extended points, L, M denote extended lines. The translated existence property (8.82) can be adopted as it is, but the translated uniqueness property (8.83) must be adapted to include *granulated equality* of extended points.

In contrast to the Boolean case, the degree of equality of two given extended points is not constant, but depends on the extended line that acts as a *sensor*. Consequently, the term $\neg e(P,Q)$ on the left hand side of (8.83) must be replaced by two terms, $\neg e(P,Q)[L]$ and $\neg e(P,Q)[M\}$, one for each line, L and M, respectively:

$$\inf_{P,Q,L,M}\{[\neg e(P,Q)[L]\wedge\neg e(P,Q)[M]]$$
$$\wedge[R_{inc}(P,L)\wedge R_{inc}(Q,L)] \tag{8.84}$$
$$\wedge[R_{inc}(P,M)\wedge R_{inc}(Q,M)]\to e(L,M)\}.$$

We have to use weak transitivity of graduated equality. For this reason the *discernibility measure* of extended connection $\overline{PQ}$ between extended points P and Q must be added into (8.84)

$$\inf_{P,Q,L,M} \{[\neg e(P,Q)[L] \wedge \neg e(P,Q)[M] \wedge dis(\overline{P}\overline{Q})]$$

$$\wedge [R_{inc}(P,L) \wedge R_{inc}(Q,L)] \tag{8.85}$$

$$\wedge [R_{inc}(P,M) \wedge R_{inc}(Q,M)] \to e(L,M)\}$$

But from (8.75) we get

$$\neg e(P,Q)[L] = \begin{cases} \dfrac{2 - e(P,Q) - s(L)}{2}, e(P,Q) + s(L) > 1, \\ 1, e(P,Q) + s(L) \leq 1 \end{cases} \tag{8.86}$$

and

$$\neg e(P,Q)[M] = \begin{cases} \dfrac{2 - e(P,Q) - s(M)}{2}, e(P,Q) + s(M) > 1, \\ 1, e(P,Q) + s(M) \leq 1 \end{cases} \tag{8.87}$$

By using (8.86) and (8.87) in (8.85) we get

$$\neg e(P,Q)[L] \wedge \neg e(P,Q)[M]$$

$$= \begin{cases} \dfrac{4 - 2 \times e(P,Q) - s(L) - s(M)}{4}, \dfrac{4 - 2 \times e(P,Q) - s(L) - s(M)}{2} \\ > 1, e(P,Q) + s(L) > 1, e(P,Q) + s(M) > 1, \\ 0, \dfrac{4 - 2 \times e(P,Q) - s(L) - s(M)}{2} \leq 1, e(P,Q) + s(L) \\ > 1, e(P,Q) + s(M) > 1, \\ 1, e(P,Q) + s(L) \leq 1, e(P,Q) + s(M) \leq 1 \end{cases} \tag{8.88}$$

Since from (8.75) we have $[R_{inc}(P,L) \wedge R_{inc}(Q,L)] \wedge [R_{inc}(P,M) \wedge R_{inc}(Q,M)] \equiv 1$, then (8.85) could be rewritten as follows

$$\inf_{P,Q,L,M} \{[\neg e(P,Q)[L] \wedge \neg e(P,Q)[M] \wedge dis(\overline{P}\overline{Q})] \wedge 1 \to e(L,M)\} \tag{8.89}$$

It means that the "sameness" of extended lines $e(L,M)$ depends on

$$[\neg e(P,Q)[L] \wedge \neg e(P,Q)[M] \wedge dis(\overline{PQ})]$$

only and could be calculated by (8.88) and (8.89) respectively.

8.5.2 *Fuzzy logical inference for the Euclid's first postulate*

In a contrary to the approach, proposed in [778], which required a lot of calculations, we suggest to use the same fuzzy logic and correspondent logical inference to determine the value of e (L, M). For this purpose let us represent a values of following $E(p,q,l,m) = \neg e(P,Q)[L] \wedge \neg e(P,Q)[M]$ from (8.88) and $D(p,q) = dis(\overline{PQ})]$ from (8.62) functions. Note, that values from both $E(p,q,l,m) \in [E_{\min}, E_{\max}]$ and $D(p,q) \in [D_{\min}, D_{\max}]$. In our case $E(p,q,l,m) \in [0,1]$, $D(p,q) \in [0,0.75]$. We represent E as *fuzzy set* forming linguistic variables described by triplets of the form $E = \{< E_{i,}U, E >\}, E_i \in T(u), \forall i \in [0, CardU]$, where $T_i(u)$ is extended set term set of the linguistic variable *"degree of indiscernibility "* from Table 8.3, E is normal fuzzy set represented by membership function $\mu_E : U \rightarrow [0,1]$, where $U = \{0,1,2,...,10\}$ - universe set and $CardU$ is power set of the set U. We will use the following mapping $\alpha : E \rightarrow U | u_i = Ent[(CardU - 1) \times E_i] | \forall i \in [0, CardU]$, where

$$E = \int_U \mu_E(u) / u. \qquad (8.90)$$

To determine the estimates of the membership function in terms of singletons from (8.90) in the form $\mu_E(u_i) / u_i | \forall i \in [0, CardU]$ we propose the following procedure.

$$\forall i \in [0, CardU], \forall E_i \in [0,1], \mu(u_i) \qquad (8.91)$$

$$= 1 - \frac{1}{CardU - 1} \times | u_i - Ent[(CardU - 1) \times E_i] |.$$

We also represent D as *fuzzy set* forming linguistic variables described by triplets of the form $D = \{< D_j, U, D >\}$, $D_j \in T(u), \forall j \in [0, CardU]$, where $T_j(u)$ is extended set term set of the linguistic variable "*discernibility measure*" from Table 8.3, D is normal fuzzy set represented by membership function $\mu_D : U \to [0,1]$.

We will use the following mapping

$\beta : D \to U \mid v_j = Ent[(CardU - 1) \times D_j] \mid \forall j \in [0, CardU]$, where

$$D = \int_U \mu_D(u) / u. \tag{8.92}$$

On the other hand to determine the estimates of the membership function in terms of singletons from (8.92) in the form $\mu_D(u_j) / u_j \mid \forall j \in [0, CardU]$ we propose the following procedure.

$\forall j \in [0, CardU], \forall D_j \in [0, 0.75], \mu(u_j)$

$$= 1 - \frac{1}{CardU - 1} \times \mid u_j - Ent[(CardU - 1) \times D_j / 0.75] \mid. \tag{8.93}$$

Let us represent $e(L, M)$ as *fuzzy set* forming linguistic variables described by triplets of the form, where $T_k(w)$ is extended set term set of the linguistic variable "*extended lines sameness*" from Table 8.3.

$$S = \{< S_k, V, S >\}, S_k \in T(v), \forall k \in [0, CardV]$$

is normal fuzzy set represented by membership function $\mu_S : V \to [0,1]$, where $V = \{0, 1, 2, ..., 10\}$ - universe set and $CardV$ is power set of the set V.

We will use the following mapping

$\gamma : S \to V \mid v_k = Ent[(CardV - 1) \times S_k] \mid \forall k \in [0, CardV]$, where

$$S = \int_V \mu_s(v) / v. \tag{8.94}$$

Again to determine the estimates of the membership function in terms of singletons from (8.94) in the form $\mu_S(w_k) / v_k \mid \forall k \in [0, CardW]$ we propose the following procedure.

$$\forall k \in [0, CardV], \forall S_k \in [0,1], \mu(v_k)$$

$$= 1 - \frac{1}{CardV - 1} \times \mid v_k - Ent[(CardV - 1) \times S_k] \mid, \tag{8.95}$$

Table 8.3. Lindvistic variable

Value of variable			$u_i, v_j \in U, v_k \in V$
"degree of indiscernibility"	*"discernibility measure"*	*"extended lines sameness"*	$\forall i, j, k \in [0,10]$
lowest	Highest	nothing in common	0
very low	almost highest	very far	1
low	High	Far	2
bit higher than low	pretty high	bit closer than far	3
almost average	bit higher than average	almost average distance	4
average	Average	Average	5
bit higher than average	almost average	bit closer than average	6
pretty high	bit higher than low	pretty close	7
high	Low	Close	8
almost highest	very low	almost the same	9
highest	Lowest	the same	10

To get an estimates of values of $e(L,M)$ or *"extended lines sameness"*, represented by fuzzy set S from (8.94) given the values of $E(p,q,l,m)$ or *"degree of indiscernibility"* and $D(p,q)$ - *"discernibility measure"*, represented by fuzzy sets E from (8.90) and D from (8.92) respectively, we will use a *Fuzzy Conditional Inference Rule*, formulated by means of *"common sense"* as a following conditional clause:

$$P = \text{"IF (S is P1) AND (D is P2), THEN (E is Q)"} \qquad (8.96)$$

In other words we use fuzzy conditional inference of the following type:

Ant 1: If s is *P1* and d is *P2* then e is Q

Ant 2: s is *P1'* and d is *P2'*

----------------------------------, $\qquad (8.97)$

Cons: e is Q'.

Where $P1, P1, P2, P2'' \subseteq U$ and $Q, Q' \subseteq V$.

Now for fuzzy sets (8.90), (8.92) and (8.94) a *binary relationship* for the fuzzy conditional proposition of the type (8.96) and (8.97) for fuzzy logic we use so far is defined as

$$R(A_1(s,d), A_2(e)) = [P1 \cap P2 \times U] \to V \times Q$$

$$= \int_{U \times V} \mu_{P1}(u)/(u,v) \wedge \mu_{P2}(u)/(u,v) \to \int_{U \times V} \mu_Q(v)/(u,v)$$

$$= \int_{U \times V} ([\mu_{P1}(u) \wedge \mu_{P2}(u)] \to \mu_Q(v))/(u,v) \qquad (8.98)$$

Given (8.10) expression (8.98) looks like

$$[\mu_{P1}(u) \wedge \mu_{P2}(u)] \to \mu_Q(v)$$

$$= \begin{cases} \dfrac{1 - [\mu_{P1}(u) \wedge \mu_{P2}(u)] + \mu_Q(v)}{2}, [\mu_{P1}(u) \wedge \mu_{P2}(u)] > \mu_Q(v), \\ 1, [\mu_{P1}(u) \wedge \mu_{P2}(u)] \le \mu_Q(v), \end{cases} \qquad (8.99)$$

where $[\mu_{P1}(u) \wedge \mu_{P2}(u)]$ is $\min[\mu_{P1}(u), \mu_{P2}(u)]$. It is well known that given a *unary relationship* $R(A_1(s,d)) = P1' \cap P2'$ one can obtain the consequence $R(A_2(e))$ by applying compositional rule of inference (CRI) to $R(A_1(s,d))$ and $R(A_1(s,d), A_2(e))$ of type (8.98):

$$R(A_2(e)) = P1' \cap P2' \circ R(A_1(s,d), A_2(e)) \qquad (8.100)$$

$$= \int_U [\mu_{P1'}(u) \wedge \mu_{P2'}(u)]/u \circ \int_{U \times V} [\mu_{P1}(u) \wedge \mu_{P2}(u)] \rightarrow \mu_Q(v)/(u,v)$$

$$= \int_V \bigcup_{u \in U} \{[\mu_{P1'}(u) \wedge \mu_{P2'}(u)] \wedge ([\mu_{P1}(u) \wedge \mu_{P2}(u)] \rightarrow \mu_Q(v))\}/v \quad .$$

But for practical purposes we will use another *Fuzzy Conditional Rule* *(FCR)*

$$R(A_1(s,d), A_2(e)) = (P \times V \rightarrow U \times Q) \cap (\neg P \times V \rightarrow U \times \neg Q) \qquad (8.101)$$

$$= \int_{U \times V} (\mu_P(u) \rightarrow \mu_Q(v)) \wedge ((1 - \mu_P(u)) \rightarrow (1 - \mu_Q(v)))/(u,v)$$

where $P = P1 \cap P2$ and

$$R(A_1(s,d), A_2(e)) = (\mu_P(u) \rightarrow \mu_Q(v)) \wedge ((1 - \mu_P(u)) \rightarrow (1 - \mu_Q(v)))$$

$$= \begin{cases} \dfrac{1 - \mu_P(u) + \mu_Q(v)}{2}, \mu_P(u) > \mu_Q(v), \\ 1, \mu_P(u) = \mu_Q(v), \\ \dfrac{1 - \mu_Q(v) + \mu_P(u)}{2}, \mu_P(u) < \mu_Q(v). \end{cases} \qquad (8.102)$$

The *FCR* from (8.102) gives more reliable results.

8.6 *Example*

To build a binary relationship matrix of type (8.101) we use a conditional clause of type (8.96):

P = "IF (S is *"lowest"*) AND (D is *"highest"*), THEN (E is *"nothing in common"*)"   (8.103)

To build membership functions for fuzzy sets S, D and E we use (8.91), (8.93) and (8.95) respectively.

In (8.103) the membership functions for fuzzy set S (for instance) would look like:

$$\mu_s("lowest") = 1/0 + .9/1 + .8/2 + .7/3 + .6/4 + \qquad (8.104)$$
$$+ .5/5 + .4/6 + .3/7 + .2/8 + .1/9 + 0/10$$

Same membership functions we use for fuzzy sets D and E.

From (8.102) we have $R(A_1(s,d), A_2(e))$ given in Table 8.4.

Table 8.4. Fuzzy relation

	1	.9	.8	.7	.6	.5	.4	.3	.2	.1	0
1	1	.45	.4	.35	.3	.25	.2	.15	.1	.05	0
.9	.45	1	.45	.4	.35	.3	.25	.2	.15	.1	.05
.8	.4	.45	1	.45	.4	.35	.3	.25	.2	.15	.1
.7	.35	.4	.45	1	.45	.4	.35	.3	.25	.2	.15
.6	.3	.35	.4	.45	1	.45	.4	.35	.3	.25	.2
.5	.25	.3	.35	.4	.45	1	.45	.4	.35	.3	.25
.4	.2	.25	.3	.35	.4	.45	1	.45	.4	.35	.3
.3	.15	.2	.25	.3	.35	.4	.45	1	.45	.4	.35
.2	.1	.15	.2	.25	.3	.35	.4	.45	1	.45	.4
.1	.05	.1	.15	.2	.25	.3	.35	.4	.45	1	.45
0	0	.05	.1	.15	.2	.25	.3	.35	.4	.45	.1

Suppose from (8.88) a current estimate of $E(p,q,l,m) = 0.6$ and from (8.62) $D(p,q) = 0.25$. By using (8.91) and (8.93) respectively we got (see Table 8.3.)

$$\mu_E("bit\ higher\ than\ average") = .4/0 + .5/1 + .6/2 + .7/3 +.$$
$$+ 8/4 + .9/5 + 1/6 + .9/7 + .8/8 + .7/9 + .6/10$$

$$\mu_D(\text{"pretty high"}) = .7/0 + .8/1 + .9/2 + 1/3 + .9/4 +$$
$$+ .8/5 + .7/6 + .6/7 + .5/8 + .4/9 + .3/10$$

It is apparent that:

$$R(A_1(s',d')) = \mu_E(u) \wedge \mu_D(u) = .4/0 + .5/1 + .6/2 + .7/3 +$$
$$+ .8/4 + .8/5 + .7/6 + .6/7 + .5/8 + .4/9 + .3/10$$

By applying compositional rule of inference (CRI) to $R(A_1(s',d'))$ and $R(A_1(s,d), A_2(e))$ from Table 8.4.

$R(A_2(e')) = R(A_1(s',d')) \circ R(A_1(s,d), A_2(e))$ we got the following:

$$R(A_2(e')) = \mu_E(u) \wedge \mu_D(u) = .4/0 + .5/1 + .6/2 + .7/3 + .8/4 +$$
$$+ .8/5 + .7/6 + .6/7 + .5/8 + .4/9 + .3/10)$$

It is obvious that the value of fuzzy set S is laying between terms *"almost average distance"* and *"average distance"* (see Table 8.3) which means that approximate values for $e(L.M)$ are $e(L, M) \in [0.5, 0.6]$.

8.7 Decision making in visual information environment

In visual information environment a decision making problem is started as a 4-tuple $\left(\hat{S}, \hat{P}, \hat{X}, \hat{A} \succsim \right)$ where a set of states of nature $\hat{S}$, a corresponding imprecise probability distribution $\hat{P}$, a set of outcomes $\hat{X}$ are generally considered as spaces of F-lines. Set of actions $\hat{A}$ is considered then as a set of mappings from $\hat{S}$ to $\hat{X}$. Preferences $\succsim$ in its turn is to be implicit in some knowledge base described as "if-then" rules which include $\hat{S}, \hat{P}, \hat{X}, \hat{A}$-based description of decision situations faced before and a DM's or an experts' opinion-based evaluations of corresponding intrinsic values $V(f)$ of alternatives $f \in \hat{A}$.

The problem of decision making consists in determination of the best alternative as an alternative $f^* \in \hat{A}$ for which $V(f^*) = \max_{f \in \hat{A}} V(f)$.

Let us describe preferences of a decision making are expressed by fuzzy geometric "if-then" rules of the following form:

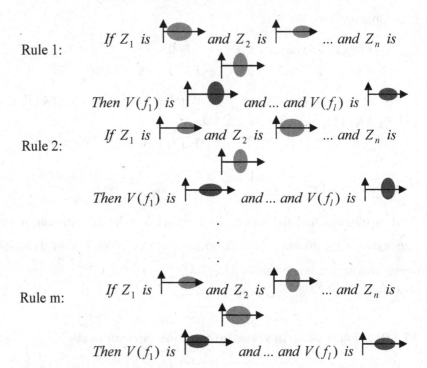

Rule 1:   *If Z_1 is* ... *and Z_2 is* ... *and Z_n is*

Then $V(f_1)$ is ... *and ... and $V(f_l)$ is*

Rule 2:   *If Z_1 is* ... *and Z_2 is* ... *and Z_n is*

Then $V(f_1)$ is ... *and ... and $V(f_l)$ is*

Rule m: *If Z_1 is* ... *and Z_2 is* ... *and Z_n is*

Then $V(f_1)$ is ... *and ... and $V(f_l)$ is*

Here $Z_i, i = 1,...,n$ is a variable to describe a decision problem under consideration. In general case, $Z_i, i = 1,...,n$ stores information about states of nature $\hat{S}$, a corresponding imprecise probability distribution $\hat{P}$ and outcomes $\hat{X}$ considered as F-lines. A current perception-based input information on values of a variables of interest is introduced by a user in form of F-lines. An entered F-line is situated in a 2D space one dimension of which supports a basic (numerical) value of a variable (e.g. probability) and the other dimension supports a truth degree associated with this basic value. Every F-line is approximated by its convex hull which represents a set of basic values of a variable of interest with the associated truth degrees. For example, consider an F-line P which describes visual perception-based information about a value of probability of a state of nature $S \in \hat{S}$. The truth degree $\varphi(p) \in [0,1]$ of a basic value p of probability is defined as a thickness of the F-line at a point representing a basic value (see Figure 8.6).

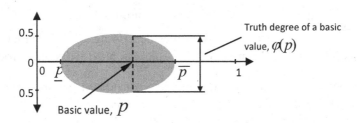

Fig. 8.6. An F-line P as a description of a value of a probability

A truth degree represents a DM's or an expert's confidence-based evaluation of the truthness of a considered basic value given an available perception-based information.

Let us describe the proposed fuzzy geometrical "if-then" rules based solution methodology for the problem of decision making with unprecisiated visual information. The methodology consists of two distinct phases of behavior. The first phase is construction of a knowledge base with fuzzy geometrical "if-then" rules. The second phase is the execution phase at which computational inference within the fuzzy geometrical "if-then" rules is performed. The step by stp explanation of the methodology is given below:

At first step construct fuzzy geometrical "if-then" rules and assign a confidence degree $Cf^{j}, j=1,...,m$. To verify the axioms (I_1-I_4) for the primitives in the "if-then" rules knowledge base(KB), set threshold r'^{KB} (say, $r'^{KB} = 0.5$) for a truth value $\underline{r}^{KB}$ as the minimal required degree of satisfaction of the axioms. For each fuzzy geometrical primitive of the fuzzy geometrical "if-then" rules determine satisfaction of the axioms (I_1-I_4) by calculating $r_i^{j}(Z_k)$, $i=1,...,4$, $k=1,...,n$, $j=1,...,m$ and $\underline{r}_k^{j} = \min_{i=1,...,4} r_{k\,i}^{j}$ as the minimal degree of satisfaction of the axioms. Verify whether the threshold condition is satisfied for all primitives in each "if-then" rule:

$$r_k^j \geq r'^{KB}.$$

For each rule $j = 1,...,m$ calculate a minimal partial truth $\underline{r}^j$ of satisfaction of the axioms for primtives describing all the n inputs and l outputs (values of alternatives) $\underline{r}^j = \min_{k=1,...,n+l} r_k^j$. Next we should proceed to the process of reasoning within the considered geometrical rules. Aggregate inputs of every rule by using t-norm:

$$Z = Z_1 \times ... \times Z_n.$$

Compute the relation matrix R between the aggregated inputs Z and each output (value of alternative) $V_j(f_k), k = 1,...,l$ on the base of implication. The computed matrices are then aggregated by using t-conorm into one aggregated relation matrix for a value of each alternative. Next we compute a partial truth of satisfaction of axioms (I_1-I_4) for the aggregated relation matrix R_k:

$$r_k = \min_{j=1,...,m} r_k^j.$$

Calculate a confidence degree Cf of the aggregated relation matrix R_k:

$$Cf = \min_{j=1,...,m} Cf^j.$$

Determine a partial truth $s_k = r_k \otimes Cf$ of the outputs of the rules which will be computed further. This step completes the first phase.

In second step DM enters fuzzy geometrical information describing perception-based evaluation of inputs Z_i^{DM} and the corresponding convex hulls $ch(Z_i^{DM})$ are constructed. A threshold r'^{DM} is set for satisfaction of axioms (I_1-I_4). If the threshold condition is satisfied then the reasoning within the fuzzy geometrical "if-then" rules is performed. If a threshold condition is not satisfied then a DM should reenter corresponding visual information until threshold is satisfied.

Aggregate fuzzy geometrical inputs provided by a DM into one input by using t-norm. Compute a composition of this input information Z with the aggregated relation matrices $R_k, k = 1,...,l$ by using t-norm and t-conorm and obtain resulting fuzzy geometrical values of alternatives $V'(f_k)$:

$$V'(f_k) = Z^{DM} \circ R_k.$$

Calculate a partial truth describing a degree of belief s_{new} to the fuzzy geometrical outputs computed at the previous step: $s_{k,new} = \min(r, \underline{r_k}) \otimes Cf, k = 1, ..., l$, where r is the truth degree for satisfaction of the axioms for the entered information. Next we arrive at geometric values of alternatives weighted by the associated partial truth $s_{k,new}$:

$$V_s(f_k) = s_{k,new} V(f_k).$$

This completes the reasoning. Compare $V_s(f_k)$, $k = 1, ..., l$, to find the best alternative as an alternative $f^* \in \hat{A}$ for which $V_s(f^*) = \max_{f \in \hat{A}} V_s(f)$.

We suggest comparing the weighted overall values of alternatives $V_s(f_k)$ on the base of their distances to the upper bound of the universe of discourse. A distance-based comparison is an adequate approach for comparison of quantities described by geometrical figures. The choice of a distance measure depends on a decision problem under consideration and behavioral features of a DM. As it is known, for decision problems under uncertainty and imprecision, the general way is to use pessimistic approach. The idea of this approach is to compare the worst realizations of alternatives within uncertainty. The pessimistic approach models behavior of an uncertainty averse DM, that is a DM who behaves in a most cautious way under uncertainty and imprecision.

Under decision relevant information described by visual perceptions the use of a pessimistic approach for comparing may be even more reasonable. In order to implement pessimistic approach in comparison of weighted overall values of alternatives, we will adopt the idea of the distance suggested in [178]. For geometrical primitives this distance is described as

$$d_w(V_s(f_k), \bar{v}) = \frac{\sum_{i=1}^{n} \alpha_i d([V_s(f_k)]^{\alpha_k}, \bar{v})}{\sum_{i=1}^{n} \alpha_i}, \qquad (8.105)$$

where $V_s(f_k) = s_{new} \cdot V'(f_k)$, $[V_s(f_k)]^{\alpha_i} = \{v \in V | \varphi(v) \geq \alpha_i, \alpha_i = \frac{i}{n}, i = 1, ..., n|\}$,

V is the universe of discourse, $\bar{v}$ is the upper bound of V, $d()$ is the Hausdorff distance [233]. Thus, formula (8.105) is a way to measure the longest distance within a fuzzy geometrical object $V_s(f_k)$ to the upper bound of V. Surely, one can adopt other ideas for constructing a distance measure, including those suggested in [233, 528, 697, 816].

The best alternative f^* is that with the minimal distance to the upper bound of V as an ideal point: $d_w(V_s(f^*), \bar{v}) = \min_{f_i \in \mathcal{A}} d_w(V_s(f_i), \bar{v})$.

One disadvantage of the considered approach to reasoning is that it is needed to store relation matrices number and sizes of which for real decision processes can be rather high. The other disadvantage is complex and a time-consuming computation of implications(with many parameters) which is not always acceptable for real decision processes.

We can use different approach to reasoning which is based on the use of similarity measures which take values from [0,1]. In this case the measure of equality of F-marks described by (8.7) is used as a similarity measure. First, a degree of similarity of the current decision situation described by f-lines $Z_k^{current}$ and the f-lines Z_{jk} of the rules in the knowledge base is computed: $eq(Z_{jk}, Z_k^{current}), k = 1, ..., n$. Next for each rule t-norm $eq_j = \bigotimes_{k=1}^{n} eq(Z_{jk}, Z_k^{current})$ is computed. The result of reasoning is a Lukasiewicz t-conorm based union of the corresponding outputs of all the rules weighted by values of the measure of equality:

$$V'(f_k) = \bigoplus_{j=1}^{m} [eq_j \otimes V_j(f_k)], \; k = 1, ..., l,$$

where $V_j(f_k)$ is the f-line for the k-th output of the j-th rule, m is the number of rules, eq_j is a measure of equality of antecedent parts of the j-th rule and the current situation, $V_j(f_k)$ is k-th output of the j-th rule.

The computations within the second approach to reasoning are significantly less time-consuming. However, the disadvantage of this approach is that results of reasoning don't depend on the form of truth distribution of f-lines which describe inputs. As a result, the outputs for relatively similar situations may not differ to each other. This may be counterintuitive.

Let us now calculate the considered distances (8.105): $d_w(V_s(f_1),\bar{v}) = 0.75$, $d_w(V_s(f_2),\bar{v}) = 0.73$.

Therefore, $d_w(V_s(f_2),\bar{v}) < d_w(V_s(f_1),\bar{v})$ and the best alternative is f_2. However, the important issue is that the computed $V(f_1)$ and $V(f_2)$ are subject to the truth degree r of satisfaction of axioms (I_1-I_4) for fuzzy geometrical objects in the KB, the truth degree r_k of satisfaction of axioms (I_1-I_4) for fuzzy geometrical objects entered by a DM (Figure 8.6) and the confidence degree Cf related to the rules in KB. Therefore, the obtained $V(f_1)$ and $V(f_2)$ are true with the degree $\min(s_{1,new}, s_{2,new}) = 0.27$. As a result, the reliability of the obtained preference $f_2 \succ f_1$ is 0.27.

Let us conduct a comparison of the suggested approach with the normal fuzzy inference system in the considered problem. Assuming that it is possible to represent the given fuzzy geometrical objects by using fuzzy sets, we applied Mamdani reasoning approach for determination of preferences. The obtained results are $V(f_1) = 0.583$ and $V(f_2) = 0.602$ which imply the same preference: $f_2 \succ f_1$. However, in this case, the related reliability is 100% as the computation does not involve necessity of verification of axioms, and confidence degrees for the rules are not used. The complete (100%) reliability is counterintuitive as visual information cannot be completely expressed by linguistic description and, therefore, by membership functions-based representation. At the same time, the completely reliable preference is not adequate under imprecise perception based decision relevant information.

Chapter 9

Interval Granular-Based Decision Making

9.1 Decision making with interval probabilities

9.1.1 *Consistency of interval probabilities*

Interval probability P is denoted as $P = \left[p^-, p^+ \right] \subseteq [0,1]$.

Definition 9.1 [554, 808]. A finite sequence $P_1, ..., P_n$ is consistent if the $p_1 + ... + p_n = 1$ condition is satisfied for at least one sequence of numeric probabilities $p_1 \in P_1, ..., P_n \in p_n$.

Definition 9.2. Interval probability of a subset of $S = \{S_1, ..., S_n\}$. Let $S = \{S_1, ..., S_n\}$ be the states of nature and let the interval probabilities $P(S_i) = [\underline{p_i}, \overline{p_i}]$ $i = 1, ..., n$ of the elements of S be given. The interval probability of a subset $\mathcal{H}$ of S is $P(\mathcal{H}) = [\underline{p}, \overline{p}]$ where the lower and upper bounds are defined as follows:

$$\underline{p} = \sum_{j, S_j \in \mathcal{H}} p_j \to \min,$$

subject to

$$\underline{p_j} \le p_j \le \overline{p}_j,$$
$$p_1 + ... + p_n = 1,$$

and

$$\bar{p} = \sum_{j, S_j \in \mathcal{H}} p_j \to \max,$$

subject to

$$\underline{p}_j \le p_j \le \bar{p}_j,$$
$$p_1 + \ldots + p_n = 1,$$

where $p_j \in P(S_j)$, $P(S_j) = [\underline{p}_j, \bar{p}_j]$.

Averaging operator for interval probabilities transforms sequence of pairs

$$\left((P_1, c_1), \ldots, (P_n, c_n) \right)$$

into a real number

$$C\left((P_1, c_1), \ldots, (P_n, c_n) \right).$$

In [808] authors proved that averaging operation has the form

$$C\left(\left(\left[p_1^-, p_1^+ \right], c_1 \right), \ldots, \left(\left[p_n^-, p_n^+ \right], c_n \right) \right) = \tilde{p}_1 \cdot c_1 + \ldots + \tilde{p}_n c_n \qquad (9.1)$$

where

$$\tilde{p}_j = \frac{\sum^+ - 1}{\sum^+ - \sum^-} \cdot p_j^- + \frac{1 - \sum^-}{\sum^+ - \sum^-} \cdot p_j^+, \qquad (9.2)$$

$$\sum{}^- = p_1^- + \ldots + p_n^-, \qquad (9.3)$$

and

$$\sum{}^+ = p_1^+ + \ldots + p_n^+. \qquad (9.4)$$

9.1.2 *Statement of the problem and its solution*

Decision making problem with interval probabilities is stated as following:

There are several alternatives f_i, the outcome of each alternative x_{ij} under situation S_j, and the interval probability $p_j = \left[p_j^-, p_j^+ \right]$ of each state of nature are given.

The problem is to select a decision f_i for which

$$U(f_i) = \tilde{p}_1 \cdot x_{i1} + ... + \tilde{p}x_{in} \rightarrow \max,$$

Here p_j are determined from (9.1)–(9.4).

Formula (9.2) can transformed to next equivalent form:

$$\tilde{p}_j = p_j^- + \frac{\Delta p_j}{\Delta p} \cdot \left(1 - p_1^- - ... - p_n^- \right) \tag{9.2a}$$

where $\Delta p_j = p_j^+ - p_j^-$, and $\Delta p = \Delta p_1 + ... + \Delta p_n$.

Formula (9.2) can be represented as

$$\tilde{p}_j = p_j^+ + \frac{\Delta p_j}{\Delta p} \cdot \left(p_1^+ - ... + p_n^+ - 1 \right) \tag{9.2b}$$

When interval probabilities coincide, i.e., $\tilde{p}_j = 1/n$ for all j, we choose an alternative f_i for which

$$U(f_i) = \frac{x_{i1} + ... + x_{in}}{n} \rightarrow \max_i$$

If only the upper bounds p_i^+ is known, i.e., if $p_i^- = 0$ for all i, then

$$\tilde{p}_j = \frac{p_j^+}{p_1^+ + ... + p_n^+}$$

And we have to choose f_i, for which

$$C = \frac{p_1^+ \cdot c_1 + \ldots + p_n^+ \cdot c_n}{p_1^+ + \ldots + p_n^+} \to \max.$$

The formula (9.2) also can be expressed as follows:

$$\tilde{p}_j = \alpha \cdot p_j^- + (1-\alpha) \cdot p_j^+, \qquad (9.2c)$$

where $\alpha = \left(\sum^+ -1\right)/\left(\sum^+ - \sum^-\right)$. α belongs to the interval [0,1]. (9.2c) is similar to decision making approach suggested by Hurwitz.

Example. *Investment multicriteria decision making with interval probabilities.* Assume that a company is planning to make an investment in three spheres: f_1 - development of small businesses, f_2 - tourism sector, f_3 - transportation. These alternatives are characterized by following criteria: C_1 - quality of product, C_2 - degree of risk, C_3 - quality of service and C_4 - volume of income.

Criteria evaluations of each alternative is performed by experts. For 3 experts (E_1, E_2, E_3) criteria evaluations are shown in Table 9.1.

Table 9.1. Criteria evaluations of the alternatives

Attribute	Experts / Alternatives	E_1	E_2	E_3
C_1 (quality of product)	f_1	(0,4-0,6)(0,6-0,7)	(0,6-0,8)(0,1-0,2)	(0,4-0,6)(0,1-0,3)
	f_2	(0,6-0,8)(0,6-0,7)	(0,4-0,6)(0,1-0,2)	(0,6-0,8)(0,1-0,3)
	f_3	(0,8-1,0)(0,6-0,7)	(0,6-0,8)(0,1-0,2)	(0,4-0,6)(0,1-0,3)
C_2 (degree of risk)	f_1	(0,6-0,8)(0,6-0,7)	(0,6-0,8)(0,1-0,2)	(0,8-1,0)(0,1-0,3)
	f_2	(0,4-0,6)(0,6-0,7)	(0,8-1,0)(0,8-1,0)	(0,6-0,8)(0,1-0,3)
	f_3	(0,8-1,0)(0,6-0,7)	(0,6-0,8)(0,1-0,2)	(0,6-0,8)(0,1-0,3)
C_3 (quality of service)	f_1	(0,8-1,0)(0,6-0,7)	(0,6-0,8)(0,1-0,2)	(0,6-0,8)(0,1-0,3)
	f_2	(0,6-0,8)(0,6-0,7)	(0,8-1,0)(0,1-0,2)	(0,8-1,0)(0,1-0,3)
	f_3	(0,4-0,6)(0,6-0,7)	(0,6-0,8)(0,1-0,2)	(0,6-0,8)(0,1-0,3)

The Results of aggregation of experts' opinions are given in Table 9.2.

Table 9.2. Aggregation of experts' opinions

	Alternatives	Experts' quantities
C_1	f_1	0,42-0,64
(quality of product)	f_2	0,56-0,78
	f_3	0,66-0,92
C_2	f_1	0,62-0,86
(degree of risk)	f_2	0,48-0,72
	f_3	0,72-0,94
C_3	f_1	0,72-0,94
(quality of service)	f_2	0,66-0,88
	f_3	0,46-0,68
C_4	f_1	0,72-0,94
(volume of income)	f_2	0,62-0,84
	f_3	0,66-0,88

Interval probabilities of criteria are given in Table 9.3.

Table 9.3. Interval probabilities of criteria

C_1	C_2	C_3	C_4
$P_1 = (0,1-0,15)$	$P_2 = (0,25-0,35)$	$P_3 = (0,05-0,3)$	$P_4 = (0,15-0,25)$

Interval expected utilities are given in Table 9.4.

Table 9.4. Interval expected utilities

Alternatives	Overall evaluation
f_1	(0,625-0,867)
f_2	(0,547-0,801)
f_3	(0,621-0,905)

Ranking of alternatives is performed on the basis of comparison of their interval expected utilities $U_1 = [\underline{U}_1, \overline{U}_1]$, $U_2 = [\underline{U}_2, \overline{U}_2]$ by using the following formula:

$$d(U_1, U_2)$$

$$= \begin{cases} \dfrac{\overline{U}_1 - \overline{U}_2}{\left|(\overline{U}_1 - \overline{U}_2) + (\underline{U}_1 - \underline{U}_2)\right|}, & \overline{U}_1 > \overline{U}_2, \ \underline{U}_1 > \underline{U}_2 \\[2mm] 1, & \overline{U}_1 = \overline{U}_2, \underline{U}_1 > \underline{U}_2 \ \text{ or } \ \overline{U}_1 > \overline{U}_2, \underline{U}_1 \geq \underline{U}_2 \ \text{ or } \ \overline{U}_1 = \overline{U}_2, \underline{U}_1 = \underline{U}_2 \\[2mm] 1 - d(U_2, U_1), & \text{otherwise} \end{cases}$$

$d(U, U)$ measures a degree to which U_1 is superior to U_2.

The results are as follows:

$d(U_1, U_2) = 1$ in the result of comparison of 1st and 2nd alternatives;

$d(U_2, U_3) = 0,416$ in the result of comparison of 2nd and 3rd alternatives;

$d(U_1, U_3) = 0,095$ in the result of comparison of 1st and 3rd alternatives.

Thus, the best option is the first alternative, f_1.

9.2 Interval-based multi-attribute decision making

Decision making with interval uncertainties includes the following steps:

1. for evaluating alternatives interval numbers are used;
2. consistency analysis of interval probabilities (weights) is performed;
3. for ranking alternatives, nearness to the ideal alternative is used.

Assume that interval multiattribute decision making problem has m alternatives $f_1, f_2, ..., f_m$ and n attributes. The weight value w_j of an attribute is an interval number $w_j \in [c_j, d_j]$, where $\sum_{j=1}^{n} w_j = 1$. An attribute score of alternative f_i is an interval number $[a_{ij}^-, a_{ij}^+]$,

$i = 1, 2, ..., m, \; j = 1, 2, ..., n$. The main steps of the solution method is as follows [873].

Step 1. Decision matrix A is expressed as follows,

$$A = \begin{bmatrix} [a_{11}^-, a_{11}^+] & [a_{12}^-, a_{12}^+] & ... & [a_{1n}^-, a_{1n}^+] \\ [a_{21}^-, a_{21}^+] & [a_{22}^-, a_{22}^+] & ... & [a_{2n}^-, a_{2n}^+] \\ ... & ... & ... & ... \\ [a_{m1}^-, a_{m1}^+] & [a_{m2}^-, a_{m2}^+] & ... & [a_{mn}^-, a_{mn}^+] \end{bmatrix}. \tag{9.5}$$

Without loss of generality, here we suppose that all elements of A are positive.

Step 2. Standardizing decision matrix $R = [r_{ij}^-, r_{ij}^+]$ is defined as follows.

$$[r_{ij}^-, r_{ij}^+] = \left[\frac{a_{ij}^-}{\|A_j\|}, \frac{a_{ij}^+}{\|A_j\|} \right], \; i = 1, 2, ..., m, \; j = 1, 2, ..., n.$$

Here A_j is the column vectors of A.

Step 3. Interval number weighted matrix $C = ([c_{ij}^-, c_{ij}^+])_{m \times n}$ is defined as

$$[c_{ij}^-, c_{ij}^+] = [c_j, d_j] \cdot [r_{ij}^-, r_{ij}^+], \; i = 1, 2, ..., m, \; j = 1, 2, ..., n.$$

Step 4. Reference number sequence is determined as the set of optimal weighted interval values.

Step 5. Calculation of connection coefficient between i[th] alternative and reference number sequence is performed as

$$r_i = \frac{1}{n} \sum_{k=1}^{n} q_i(k), \; i = 1, 2, ..., m.$$

Here

$$q_i(k) = \frac{\min\limits_{i} \min\limits_{k} \left\| [u_0^-(k), u_0^+(k)] - [c_{ij}^-, c_{ij}^+] \right\| + \rho \max\limits_{i} \max\limits_{k} \left\| [u_0^-(k), u_0^+(k)] - [c_{ij}^-, c_{ij}^+] \right\|}{\left\| [u_0^-(k), u_0^+(k)] - [c_{ij}^-, c_{ij}^+] \right\| + \rho \max\limits_{i} \max\limits_{k} \left\| [u_0^-(k), u_0^+(k)] - [c_{ij}^-, c_{ij}^+] \right\|}$$

$\rho \in (0, +\infty)$ is resolving coefficient.

Step 6. Optimal alternative is determined as follows:

$$r_{opt} = \max_{1 \leq i \leq m} r_i.$$

9.3 Interval linear programming based decision making

Decision making on the basis of linear programming with interval coefficients may be expressed as follows.

$$\text{Minimize} \quad Z = \sum_{j=1}^{n} [\underline{c}_j, \overline{c}_j] x_j,$$

$$\text{subject to} \quad \sum_{j=1}^{n} [\underline{a}_{ij}, \overline{a}_{ij}] x_j \geq [\underline{b}_i, \overline{b}_i] \quad \forall i = 1, \ldots, m, \tag{9.6}$$

$$x_j \geq 0, \quad \forall j = 1, \ldots, n.$$

Here Z is objective function, $[\underline{c}_j, \overline{c}_j]$, $[\underline{a}_{ij}, \overline{a}_{ij}]$ and $[\underline{b}_i, \overline{b}_i]$ are interval coefficients.

Let $A = [\underline{a}, \overline{a}]$, $B = [\underline{b}, \overline{b}]$, and x be a numerical (crisp) variable. In accordance with Section 3 $Ax \leq B$ may be expressed as $S(Ax \leq B) > 0$.

An equivalent description of the interval inequality is[2] :

$$Ax \leq B \Rightarrow \begin{cases} S(Ax \leq B) > 0, \\ S_U(B < Ax) \leq \alpha \in [0,1] \end{cases}, \tag{9.7}$$

Here α is optimistic threshold of decision maker. An equivalent form of (9.7) is

$$Ax \leq B \Rightarrow \begin{cases} \underline{a}x < \overline{b} \quad (\text{or equivalently } \overline{b} - \underline{a}x \geq \varepsilon), \\ \overline{a}x - \overline{b} \leq \alpha(\overline{b} - \underline{b}) + \alpha(\overline{a} - \underline{a})x, \end{cases}$$

where $\varepsilon > 0$ is a small positive value.

Similarly, for $Ax \geq B$ we have

$$Ax \geq B \Rightarrow \begin{cases} S(Ax \geq B) > 0, \\ S_U(B > Ax) \leq \alpha \in [0,1] \end{cases}$$

and

$$Ax \leq B \Rightarrow \begin{cases} \overline{a}x > \underline{b} \quad (or\ equivalently\ \overline{a}x - \underline{b} \geq \varepsilon), \\ \underline{b} - \underline{a}x \leq \alpha(\overline{b} - \underline{b}) + \alpha(\overline{a} - \underline{a})x. \end{cases}$$

The objective function in (9.6) can be transformed into the following LP [2]

$$Minimize \quad Z_{\text{left limit}}$$

$$Minimize \quad Z_{\text{right limit}} \tag{9.8}$$

Subject to the set of constraints

We have to define the non-dominated solutions of the decision making problem (9.8). This problem can be considered as simultaneous minimization the left and right limits of Z expressed as

$\lambda_1 \left(\sum_{j=1}^{n} \underline{c}_j x_j \right) + \lambda_2 \left(\sum_{j=1}^{n} \overline{c}_j x_j \right)$, where $\lambda_1, \lambda_2 \geq 0$ and $\lambda_1 + \lambda_2 = 1$. $\lambda_1 = 1$

expresses an optimistic opinion of minimizing Z, $\lambda_2 = 1$ expresses a pessimistic opinion. The linear bi-objective programming problem (9.8) can be reduced into an ordinary linear programming problem. For example, for optimistic DM we have

$$Minimize \quad \sum_{j=1}^{n} \underline{c}_j x_j,$$

$$\tag{9.9}$$

$subject\ to \quad \sum_{j=1}^{n} \overline{a}_{ij} x_j \geq \underline{b}_i \quad \left(or\ equivalently\ \sum_{j=1}^{n} \overline{a}_{ij} x_j - \underline{b}_i \geq \varepsilon \right) \quad \forall i = 1,...,m,$

$$\underline{b_i} - \sum_{j=1}^{n} \overline{a}_{ij} x_j \leq \alpha(\overline{b}_i - \underline{b_i}) + \alpha \sum_{j=1}^{n} (\overline{a}_{ij} - \underline{a}_{ij}) x_j \quad \forall i = 1,...,m$$

$$x_j \geq 0 \quad \forall j = 1,...,n.$$

Example [2, 724]. Consider the following problem:

$$Minimize \quad Z = [0.38, 0.42] x_1 + 0.2 x_2,$$

$$subject \ to \quad x_1 + x_2 = [1, 1.13] \times 1000,$$

$$[0.48, 0.52] x_1 + [0.085, 0.115] x_2 \geq [0.21, 0.23] \times 1000, \tag{9.10}$$

$$[0.005, 0.008] x_1 + 0.003 x_2 \geq [0.004, 0.006] \times 1000,$$

$$x_1, x_2 \geq 0.$$

In accordance with the approach considered above (9.10) is transformed into

$$Minimize \quad \underline{Z} = 0.38 x_1 + 0.2 x_2,$$

$$subject \ to \quad 1000 \leq x_1 + x_2 \leq 1300,$$

$$0.52 x_1 + 0.115 x_2 \geq 210 + \varepsilon,$$

$$(0.48 + 0.04\alpha) x_1 + (0.085 + 0.03\alpha) x_2 \geq 210 - 20\alpha,$$

$$0.008 x_1 + 0.003 x_2 \geq 4 + \varepsilon,$$

$$(0.005 + 0.003\alpha) x_1 + 0.003 x_2 \geq 4 - 2\alpha,$$

$$x_1, x_2 \geq 0.$$

Solution of (9.10) is presented in Table 9.5.

Table 9.5. The results of solution (for optimistic case)

α	x_1	x_2	$Z_\alpha = [\underline{z}^*, \overline{z}^*]$
0	305	825	[289.9, 293.1]
0,1	293.83	747.56	[261.17, 272.92]
0,2	289.67	710.33	[252.14, 263.73]
0,3	276.38	723.62	[249.75, 260.8]
0,4	263.16	736.84	[247.37, 257.89]
0,5	250	750	[245, 255]
0,6	236.91	763.09	[242.64, 252.12]
0,7	234.81	765.19	[242.27, 251.66]
0,8	234.81	765.19	[242.27, 251.66]
0,9	234.81	765.19	[242.27, 251.66]
1	234.81	765.19	[242.27, 251.66]

Chapter 10

Decision Making in Fuzzy Environment

10.1 Fuzzy decision theory with imperfect information

10.1.1 *State-of-the-art*

The existing decision models have been successfully applied to solving many decision problems in management, business, economics and other fields, but nowadays arises a need to develop more realistic decision models. The main drawback of the existing utility theories starting from von Neumann-Moregnstern expected utility to the advanced non-expected models is that they are designed for laboratory examples with simple, well-defined gambles which do not adequately enough reflect real decision situations. In real-life decision making problems preferences are vague and decision-relevant information is imperfect as described in natural language (NL). Vagueness of preferences and imperfect decision relevant information require using suitable utility model which would be fundamentally different to the existing precise utility models. Precise utility models cannot reflect vagueness of preferences, vagueness of objective conditions and outcomes, imprecise beliefs, etc. The time has come for a new generation of decision theories. In this study, we propose a decision theory, which is capable to deal with vague preferences and imperfect information. The theory discussed here is based on a fuzzy-valued non-expected utility model representing linguistic preference relations and imprecise beliefs.

273

Decision making theory is a holy grail of numerous studies in management science, economics and other areas. It comprises a broad diversity of approaches to modeling behavior of a decision maker realized under various information frameworks. In essence, the solution to the decision making problem is defined by a preferences framework and a type of decision-relevant information. In its turn preference and decision-relevant information frameworks are closely related. One of the approaches to formally describe preferences on the base of decision-relevant information is the use of a utility function. Utility function is a quantitative representation of prederences of a decision-maker (DM) and any scientifically grounded utility model comes with the underlying preference assumptions.

The existing utility models are developed within the two main directions of decision making theory: decision making under ignorance, decision making under risk and decision making under ambiguity.

Decision making under ignorance [308, 361] is characterized by an absence of any information about probabilities of events. Unfortunately, this is an ideal view on decision-relevant information, because in real-life a DM almost always has some limited information about probabilities. The decision making methods developed for situations of ignorance include Laplace insufficient reason criterion, Savage minimax regret criterion, Hurwitz criterion, Wald maximin solution rule, etc. Maximin solution rule models extreme pessimism in decision making, whereas its generalization, Hurwitz criterion uses linear combination of pessimistic and optimistic solutions.

In decision making under risk [177, 404, 622, 664, 733, 734, 749] it is supposed that precise objective or subjective probabilities of states of nature and precise outcomes are available. Subjective probabilities [664] are used when objective probabilities are unknown. The main methods of decision making under risk are von Neumann and Morgenstern expected utility (EU) [749], subjective expected utility (SEU) [664] and Kahneman and Tversky Prospect theory (PT) [277, 733]. As it was shown by many experiments, the the use of precise objective or subjective probabilities appeared non-realistic [70, 146, 263, 316]. On the other hand, even if objective probabilities were known, beliefs of a DM do not coincide with them but are affected by some kind of distortion — they are transformed into so-called decision weights [277, 548, 734].

A large number of studies is devoted to decision making under ambiguity [97, 146, 192, 260, 267, 269, 287, 309, 310, 312, 316, 337, 370, 410, 411]. Ambiguity is commonly referred to as uncertainty with respect to probabilities — the cases when probabilities are not known or are supposed to vary within some range. The terms 'uncertainty' and 'ambiguity' are not always clearly distinguished and defined but, in general, are related to non-probabilistic uncertainty. In turn, decision making under uncertainty often is considered as an extreme non-probabilistic case — when no information on probabilities is available. From the other side, this case is also termed as decision making under complete ignorance. At the same time, sometimes, this is considered as ambiguity represented by simultaneous consideration of all the probability distributions. The studies on decision making under ambiguity are conducted in two directions — a development of models based on multiple probability distributions, called multiple priors models [318, 755], and a formation of approaches based on non-additive measures [754, 755, 756, 768]. Mainly, these models consider so-called ambiguity aversion as a property of human behavior to generally prefer outcomes related to non-ambiguous events to those related to ambiguous ones.

The well-known approach developed for multiple priors is Maximin EU (MMEU) and its development [146, 150, 192, 266, 267, 268, 269, 309, 310, 311, 312, 317, 435, 622]. In this criterion, an alternative is evaluated by minimal or maximal expected utility with respect to all possible probability distributions. In [312] they suggest to use convex combination of minimal and maximal expected utilities.

In general, multiple priors are much more adequate but still a poor formulation of probability-relevant information available for a DM — in real-world problems a DM usually has some information that allows determining which priors are more and which are less relevant. For addressing this issue, models with second-order probabilities were suggested [97, 195, 436, 675]. In [436] they suggest so-called 'smooth ambiguity' model which generalizes the existing MMEU models. In this model a subjective probability measure reflects DM's belief on whether a considered subset of multiple priors contains a 'true' prior. The use of these models is a step toward forming a more adequate information structure. However, a construction of a second-order probability distribution over first-order probabilities become doubtful as the latter cannot be known precisely [146]. Second-order precise probability model is a non-realistic description of human beliefs characterized by imprecision and associated with some psychological aspects that need to be considered as well. The other disadvantage of the belief representation suggested in [436] is that the problem of investigation of consistency of subjective probability-relevant information is not discussed – consistent multiple priors are supposed to be given in advance. However, a verification of consistency of beliefs becomes a very important problem. An extensive investigation of this issue is covered in [756].

The alternative approach to model imperfect information about probabilities is the use of imprecise probabilities, [78, 261, 295, 338, 380, 381, 480, 590, 739, 741, 756]. Some intuitively acceptable and useful interpretations of imprecise probabilities are interval probabilities [261, 338], fuzzy (linguistic) probabilities [279, 806], to name a few viable alternatives. The first fundamental study in this framework was the Walley's theory of imprecise probabilities [756]. The key concept of the theory is the lower prevision, which can be used to model evaluations like lower and upper probabilities, belief functions, additive probability measures etc and does not impose any assumptions on the type of probability distributions. However, this theory often requires solving very complicated optimization problems.

In [338] they suggest an approach for decisions based on interval probabilities where the latter are obtained on the base of pairwise comparison of likelihood of events.

The important class of approaches to problems when a DM is uncertain about probabilities deals with imprecise hierarchical models [218, 279, 326, 545, 694, 740, 864]. In these models imprecise probabilities of states of nature are assigned at the first (lower) level. The second level is used to represent imprecise probability describing a DM's or experts' confidence about imprecise probability being assigned at the first level. However, most of the works devoted to hierarchical models deals with a large number of optimization problems.

One of the main models in this realm of application of non-additive measures (fuzzy measures) is Choquet Expected Utility (CEU) based on the Choquet integral [196]. As mentioned in [805], fuzzy measure is a unified description of various types of characterizations of uncertainty such as randomness, lack of specifity, and imprecision [115, 231, 232, 379, 710, 751]. CEU is a one of the most successful utility models, it is used as a criterion of decision making under ambiguity and decision making under risk.

Concerning real-world information about probabilities, Savage wrote [664]:

"...there seem to be some probability relations about which we feel relatively 'sure' as compared with others.... The notion of 'sure' and 'unsure' introduced here is vague, and my complaint is precisely that neither the theory of personal probability as it is developed in this book, nor any other device known to me renders the notion less vague".

In our opinion, the issue is that real relevant information perceived by DMs involves possibilistic uncertainty. Fuzzy probabilities [134, 218, 265, 447, 590, 600, 711, 806] are tools for addressing this issue to a significant extent.

Fuzzy probabilities are successful interpretation for linguistic estimates of probabilities such as "this is likely", "probability is low" etc. [846]. In comparison to multiple priors consideration, for majority of cases, a DM has some additional linguistic information coming from his experience or even naturally present which reflects unequal levels of belief or possibility for different probability distributions. This means, that it is more adequate to consider sets of probability distributions as fuzzy sets which allow for taking into account various degrees of belief or possibility for different probability distributions. This involves second-order uncertainty, namely, probability-possibility modeling of information.

Different types of decision relevant information require an application of different theories for solving a decision-making problem. In order to view the situations of decision-relevant information that one can be faced with and the utility models that can be applied, let us look at Table 10.1.

Table 10.1. Classification of decision-relevant information

		Probabilities			
Outcomes	**Utilities**	Precise	Complete Ignorance	Ambiguous	Imperfect
Precise	Precise	Situation 1	Situation 2	Situation 3	Situation 4
	Fuzzy	Situation 5	Situation 6	Situation 7	Situation 8
Complete Ignorance	Precise	Situation 9	Situation 10	Situation 11	Situation 12
	Fuzzy	Situation 13	Situation 14	Situation 15	Situation 16
Ambiguous	Precise	Situation 17	Situation 18	Situation 19	Situation 20
	Fuzzy	Situation 21	Situation 22	Situation 23	Situation 24
Imperfect	Precise	Situation 25	Situation 26	Situation 27	Situation 28
	Fuzzy	Situation 29	Situation 30	Situation 31	Situation 32

In this table, we identify three important coordinates (dimemsions) essential to our investigations. The first one concerns information available for probabilities, the second captures information about outcomes, while the third looks at the nature of utilities and their description. The first two dimensions include precise information (risk), ignorance (absence of information), ambiguous information, and imperfect information. Two main types of utilities are considered, namely precise and fuzzy. Decision-relevant information setups are represented at the crossing of these coordinates; those are cells containing Situations from 1 to 32. They capture combinations of various types of probabilities, outcomes, and utilities. The most developed scenarios are those positioned in entries numbered from 1 to 4 (precise utility models). A limited attention has paid to situations 5-8 with fuzzy utilities, which are considered in works [71, 125, 313, 501]. For the situations 9-12 with complete ignorance with respect to outcomes and with precise utilities a few works related to interactive obtaining of information were suggested. For situations 13-16, in our opinion, no works were suggested. Few studies are devoted to the situations with ambiguous outcomes (situations 17-20) [359, 365, 370] and precise utilities and no works to ambiguous outcomes with fuzzy utilities are available (situations 21-24). For situations 25-32 a very few studies were reported including the existing fuzzy utility models [71, 125, 313, 501]. In this study, we consider the case with imperfect probabilities, imperfect outcomes, and fuzzy utilities (situation 32) for which all other situations excluding those with complete ignorance (as there is no information) are subsumed by it. Unfortunately, for this situation no adequate utility model has been established so far.

Fuzzy logic [15, 36, 520, 521, 735, 848, 852] has emerged as a tool to handle vague estimates. There is a significant number of studies devoted to fuzzy and linguistic preference relations (FPR and LPR, for short) [304, 566, 568, 569]. They are motivated by the fact that vagueness is more adequately articulated in terms of fuzzy concepts. As a result, fuzzy degree-based preference axiomatization arises as a more adequate representation as it is closer to the essentials of human thinking [600, 849]. In view of this, LPR form a natural generalization of classical preference relations to underline the human-like utility model.

Along the direction of imperfect information and vague preference-based models, a series of works was devoted to the fuzzy utility models and decisions under fuzzy uncertainty [14, 71, 114, 125, 223, 313, 336, 337, 501]. In [125] they presented axioms for LPR in terms of linguistic probability distributions over fuzzy outcomes and defined fuzzy expected utility on this basis. But, unfortunately, an existence of a fuzzy utility function has not been proved. [114] is an extensive work devoted to the representation of FPR. In this paper, an existence of a utility function representing a fuzzy preorder is proved. However, in this work a utility function itself is considered as a non-fuzzy real-valued function. In [501] it is formulated conditions for existence and continuity of a numerical and fuzzy-valued expected utility under some standard conditions of a FPR (viz. reflexivity, transitivity, continuity, etc.). The author proves theorems on existence of a fuzzy expected utility for the cases of probabilistic and possibilistic information on states of nature. The possibilistic case, as it is correctly identified by the author, appears to be more adequate to deal with real-world problems. However, in this model, probabilities and outcomes are considered as numerical entities. This notably limits the use of the suggested model for real-life decision problems where almost all the information is described in NL. A new approach for decision making under possibilistic information on states of nature when probabilistic information is absent is considered in [337]. In [313] they suggest representation of a fuzzy preference relation by fuzzy number-valued expected utility on the basis of fuzzy random variables. However, an existence of a fuzzy utility function has not been shown. In [71] they consider a fuzzy utility as a fuzzy-valued Choquet integral with a real-valued fuzzy measure obtained based on a set of possible probability distributions and with a fuzzy integrand. Unfortunately, the existence of the suggested fuzzy utility is not proved.

The existing decision theories yield good results, but nowadays there is a need in generation of more realistic theories. The problem is that the existing theories are good for laboratory examples with simple, well-defined gambles. The existing approaches to model impreciseness of beliefs are based on non-realistic and complicated techniques which are far from adequate modeling vagueness of perceptions. At the same time, the use of Savage's formulation of states of nature as "a space of mutually exclusive and exhaustive states" is inadequate to real decision problems, when DM often cannot exhaustively determine all possible objective conditions and cannot precisely differentiate between them. From the other side, in the existing theories they use numerical description of outcomes as results of actions under various events. However, a DM almost always cannot precisely determine future outcomes and have to use imprecise quantities like high profit, medium cost etc.

Despite that development of preference frameworks has passed a long way the modern preferences frameworks lack an important feature of human-like preferences: human-like preferences are vague [600] and are described in NL. Humans compare alternatives using linguistic techniques like "much better", "much worse", "a little better", "almost equivalent" etc [849]. Such vague estimates cannot be handled and described in terms of classical logic.

In real-life decision problems, the relevant information on states of nature, probabilities, outcomes and utilities is imperfect as perception-based and described in NL [19, 20, 40, 52, 55-58,]. As Prof. Zadeh states, imperfect information is information which in one or more regards is imprecise, uncertain, incomplete, unreliable, vague or partially true [855]. Moreover, real-life problems are characterized by a second-order uncertainty, or uncertainty^2, for short. The cases of uncertainty^2 are fuzzy probabilities, second-order probabilities, type-2 fuzzy sets etc [829].

In this section, we construct fundamentals of the theory of decision making with imperfect information for solving problems when all the relevant in formation is NL-described. The suggested theory utilizes fuzzy logic and fuzzy mathematics [100, 541] and is capable of dealing with the second-order uncertainty represented by fuzzy probabilities. The theory is based on the representation theorems on a fuzzy number-valued utility represented as a fuzzy-valued Choquet integral with a fuzzy integrand and a fuzzy-valued fuzzy measure for the framework of linguistic preferences, fuzzy states of nature, fuzzy probabilities, and fuzzy outcomes.

As opposed to the existing approaches with imprecise beliefs like multiple priors models (e.g. MMEU), second-order precise and imprecise beliefs models (smooth ambiguity and hierarchical models), models with non-additive beliefs (e.g. CEU, Prospect theory) etc, the suggested theory uses fuzzy probabilities and fuzzy-valued fuzzy measures [40, 334, 335, 447, 545, 869] which are closer to DMs' beliefs described in NL. In the suggested theory, in contrast to the existing theories, a state of nature is considered as a fuzzy set taking into account that in real problems not only beliefs but also underlying events are often described in NL. This helps to model vagueness and proximity of real objective conditions. For evaluation of outcomes, in the developed theory we use fuzzy numbers as more reliable for NL-based descriptions than numerical values used in the existing decision models like MMEU, CEU etc, especially when one deals with non-monetary outcomes like health, time, reputation, quality etc [694].

In the suggested theory we use linguistic preference relation which, as opposed to classical logic-based preference relations used the existing theories, are able to adequately describe human preferences under imperfect information described in NL. Fuzzy-valued utility function used in the suggested theory, as opposed to its numerical counterpart used in the famous theories like MMEU, CEU, PT etc is a natural interpretation quantifying vague preferences and imprecise beliefs.

10.1.2 *Definitions*

Let E^n [233, 453] be a space of all fuzzy subsets of R^n. These subsets satisfy the conditions of normality, convexity, and are upper semicontinuous with compact support. It is obvious that E^1 is the set of fuzzy numbers defined over R. Then let us denote by $E^1_{[0,1]}$ the corresponding space of fuzzy numbers defined over the unit interval $[0,1]$.

Definition 10.1 [20, 21, 49]. *Fuzzy Hausdorff distance.* Let $V, W \in E^n$. The fuzzy Hausdorff distance d_{fH} between V and W is defined as

$$d_{fH}(V,W) = \bigcup_{r \in [0,1]} r \left[d_H(V^1, W^1), \sup_{r \leq \bar{r} \leq 1} d_H(V^{\bar{r}}, W^{\bar{r}}) \right],$$

where d_H is the Hausdorff distance [233, 454] and V^1, W^1 denote the cores of fuzzy sets V, W respectively.

Example. Let V and W be triangular fuzzy sets $V = (2,3,4)$ and $W = (6,8,12)$. Then the fuzzy Hausdorff distance d_{fH} between V and W is defined as a triangular fuzzy set $d_{fH}(V,W) = (5,5,8)$.

Definition 10.1 is a generalization of the definition 2.6 given by Zhang G-Q in [869].

Let Ω be a nonempty set and $F(\Omega) = \{V | \mu_V : \Omega \to [0,1]\}$ be the class of all fuzzy subsets of Ω.

Hukuhara difference [233, 254]. Let $X, Y \in E^n$. If there exists $Z \in E^n$ such that $X = Y + Z$, then Z is called a Hukuhara difference of X and Y and is denoted as $X -_h Y$.

Note that with the standard fuzzy difference for Z produced of X and Y, $X \neq Y + Z$. We use Hukuhara difference when we need $X = Y + Z$.

Example. Let X and Y be triangular fuzzy sets $X = (3,7,11)$ and $Y = (1,2,3)$. Then Hukuhara difference of X and Y is $X -_h Y = (3,7,11) -_h (1,2,3) = (3-1,7-2,11-3) = (2,5,8)$. Indeed, $Y + (X -_h Y) = (1,2,3) + (2,5,8) = (3,7,11) = X$.

Definition 10.2 [869, 876]. A subclass F of $F(\Omega)$ is called a fuzzy σ-algebra if it has the following properties:

(1) $\varnothing, \Omega \in F$

(2) if $V \in F$, then $V^c \in F$

(3) if $\{V_n\} \subset F$, then $\bigcup_{n=1}^{\infty} V_n \in F$

Definition 10.3 [869]. Let A be a fuzzy number. For every positive real number M, there exists a $r_0 \in (0,1]$ such that $M < A_2^{r_0}$ or $A_1^{r_0} < -M$. Then A is called fuzzy infinity, denoted by ∞.

Definition 10.4 [869]. For $A, B \in E^1$, we say that $A \leq B$, if for every $r \in (0,1]$,

$A_1^r \leq B_1^r$ and $A_2^r \leq B_2^r$.

We consider that $A < B$, if $A \leq B$, and there exists an $r_0 \in (0,1]$ such that

$A_1^{r_0} < B_1^{r_0}$, or $A_2^{r_0} < B_2^{r_0}$.

We consider that $A = B$ if $A \leq B$, and $B \leq A$

Denote $E_+^1 = \{A \in E | A \geq 0\}$.

Definition 10.5 [869]. A fuzzy number-valued fuzzy measure $((z)$ fuzzy measure) on F is a fuzzy number-valued fuzzy set function $\eta : F \rightarrow E_+^1$ with the properties:

(1) $\eta(\varnothing) = 0$;

(2) if $V \subset W$ then $\eta(V) \leq \eta(W)$;

(3) if $V_1 \subset V_2 \subset ..., V_n \subset ... \in F$, then $\eta(\bigcup_{n=1}^{\infty} V_n) = \lim_{n \to \infty} \eta(V_n)$;

(4) if $V_1 \supset V_2 \supset ..., V_n \in F$, and there exists n_0 such that $\eta(V_{n_0}) \neq \infty$,

then $\eta(\bigcap_{n=1}^{\infty} V_n) = \lim_{n \to \infty} \eta(V_n)$.

Here limits are taken in terms of the d_{fH} distance.

$(\Omega, F(\Omega))$ is called a fuzzy measurable space and $(\Omega, F(\Omega), \eta)$ is called a (z) fuzzy measure space.

Definition 10.6 [869]. Let $(\Omega, F(\Omega), \eta)$ be a (z) fuzzy measure space. A mapping $f : \Omega \to (-\infty, +\infty)$ is called a fuzzy measurable function if $\chi_{F_\beta} \in F(\Omega)$, where $F_\beta = \{\omega \in \Omega | f(\omega) \geq \beta\}$ and

$$\chi_{F_\beta}(\omega) = \begin{cases} 1 & \textit{iff} \quad \omega \in F_\beta, \\ 0 & \textit{iff} \quad \omega \notin F_\beta, \end{cases} \text{ with } \beta \in (-\infty, +\infty).$$

Let N_R be the set of all closed intervals of the real line.

Definition 10.7 [814]. $\overline{f} : \Omega \to N_R$ is fuzzy measurable if both $f_1(\omega)$, the left end point of interval $\overline{f}(\omega)$, and $f_2(\omega)$, the right end point of interval $\overline{f}(\omega)$, are fuzzy measurable functions of ω.

Definition 10.8 [814]. Let $\overline{f} : \Omega \to N_R$ be a fuzzy measurable interval-valued function on Ω and $\tilde{\eta}$ be a fuzzy number-valued fuzzy measure on F. The Choquet integral of $\overline{f}$ with respect to η is defined by:

$$\int \overline{f} d\eta = \left\{ \int f d\eta \mid f(\omega) \in \overline{f}(\omega) \ \forall \omega \in \Omega, \ f : \Omega \to R \quad \text{is} \quad \text{fuzzy} \right.$$

measurable}.

Definition 10.9 [814]. A fuzzy-valued function $f : \Omega \to E^1$ is fuzzy measurable if its r-cut $\overline{f}^r(\omega) = \{y | \mu_{f(\omega)}(y) \geq r\}$ is a fuzzy measurable set function for every $r \in (0,1]$, where $\mu_{f(\omega)}$ is the membership function of the value of f at ω.

Definition 10.10 [814]. Let $f : \Omega \to E^1$ be a fuzzy measurable fuzzy-valued function on Ω and η be a fuzzy-number-valued fuzzy measure on F. The Choquet integral of f with respect to η is defined by:

$$\int_\Omega f d\eta = \bigcup_{r \in [0,1]} r \int_\Omega \overline{f}^r d\eta.$$

Definition 10.11 [125]. The set of linguistic probabilities $P^l = \{P_1, ..., P_i, ..., P_n\}$ and corresponding values $\{X_1, ..., X_i, ..., X_n\}$ of a random variable X are called a distribution of linguistic probabilities of this random variable.

Definition 10.12 [125]. *Fuzzy set-valued random variable.* Let a discrete variable X takes a value from the set $\{X_1, ..., X_n\}$ of possible linguistic values, each of which is a fuzzy variable $\langle x_i, U_x, X_i \rangle$ described by a fuzzy set $X_i = \int_{U_x} \mu_{x_i}(x)/x$. Let the probability that X take a linguistic value X_i to be characterized by a linguistic probability $P_i \in P^l$, $P^l = \left\{ P \middle| P \in E^1_{[0,1]} \right\}$. The variable X is then called a fuzzy set-valued random variable.

Definition 10.13 [125]. *Linguistic lottery.* Linguistic lottery is a fuzzy set-valued random variable with known linguistic probability distribution. Linguistic lottery is represented by a vector:

$$L = \left(P_1, X_1; ...; P_i, X_i; ...; P_n, X_n \right).$$

10.1.3 *Statement of the problem*

In our study, we generalize the axiomatizations of decision making problem used by Anscombe and Aumann [77] and Schmeidler [668, 669], which are constructed for perfect information framework. For real-world problems, probabilities, outcomes and utilities are not exactly known and are described in natural language. Taking into account that such problems are essentially characterized by imperfect information relevant to decision making, our generalization involves the following aspects: 1) Spaces of fuzzy sets [233, 454] instead of a classical framework are used for modelling states of nature and outcomes 2) Fuzzy probabilities are considered instead of numerical probability distributions 3) Linguistic preference relation [125, 849] (LPR) is used instead of binary logic-based preference relations 4) Fuzzy number-valued utility functions [20, 24, 454] are used instead of real-valued utility functions 5) Fuzzy number-valued fuzzy measure [869] is used instead of a real-valued nonadditive probability.

These aspects form fundamentally a new statement of the problem - the problem of decision making with imperfect information. This problem is characterized by second-order uncertainty, namely by fuzzy probabilities. In this framework, we prove representation theorems for a fuzzy-valued utility function. Fuzzy-valued utility function will be described as a fuzzy-valued Choquet integral [20, 814] with fuzzy number-valued integrand and fuzzy number-valued fuzzy measure. Fuzzy number-valued integrand will be used to model imprecise linguistic utility evaluations. It is contemplated that fuzzy number-valued fuzzy measure that can be generated by fuzzy probabilities will better reflect the features of impreciseness and non-additivity related to human behavior. The Fuzzy utility model we consider here is a generalization of Schmeidler's CEU and is more suitable for human evaluations and vision of decision problem and related information.

Let $S = \{S_1,...,S_n\} \subset E^n$ be a set of fuzzy states of the nature, $X = \{X_1,...,X_n\} \subset E^n$ be a set of fuzzy outcomes, Y be a set of *distributions of linguistic probabilities* over X, i.e. Y is a set of *fuzzy number-valued functions* [100, 233, 454]: $Y = \left\{y \middle| y : X \to E^1_{[0,1]}\right\}$. For notational simplicity we identify X with the subset $\{y \in Y | y(X) = 1 \, for \, some \, X \in X\}$ of Y. Denote by F_S a σ-algebra of subsets of S. Denote by A_0 the set of all F_S-measurable [541, 814] fuzzy finite valued step functions [762] from S to Y and denote by A_c the constant fuzzy functions in A_0. We call a function $f : S \to Y$ a fuzzy finite valued step function if there is a finite partition of S to $H_i \subset S, i = 1,2,...,n$, $H_j \cap H_k = \varnothing$, for $j \neq k$, such that $f(S) = y_i$ for all $S \in H_i$. In this case $g : S \to Y$ is called a constant fuzzy function if for some $g(S) = y$ for all $S \in S$, $y \in Y$. Thus the constant fuzzy function is a special case of a fuzzy finite valued step function.

Let A be a convex subset [547] of Y^S which includes A_c. Y can be considered as a subset of some linear space, and Y^S can then be considered as a subspace of the linear space of all fuzzy functions from

S to the first linear space. Let us now define convex combinations in Y pointwise [547]: for y and z in Y, and $\lambda \in (0,1)$, $\lambda y + (1-\lambda)z = r$, where $r(X) = \lambda y(X) + (1-\lambda)z(X)$, $y(X), z(X) \in E^1_{[0,1]}$. The latter expression is defined based in the Zadeh's extension principle. Let $\mu_{r(X)}, \mu_{y(X)}, \mu_{z(X)} : [0,1] \to [0,1]$ denote the membership functions of fuzzy numbers $r(X), y(X), z(X)$, respectively. Then for $\mu_{r(X)} : [0,1] \to [0,1]$ we have:

$$\mu_{r(X)}(r(X)) = \sup_{\substack{r(X)=\lambda y(X)+(1-\lambda)z()X \\ y(X)+z(X)\leq 1}} \min (\mu_{y(X)}, (y(X)), \mu_{z(X)}, (z(X))),$$

$$r(X), y(X), z(X) \in [0,1].$$

Convex combinations in A are also defined pointwise, i.e., for f and g in A $\lambda f + (1-\lambda)g = h$, where $\lambda f(S) + (1-\lambda)g(S) = h(S)$ on S.

To model LPR, let's introduce a linguistic variable "degree of preference" with term-set $T = (T_1,...,T_n)$. Terms can be labeled, for example, as "equivalence", "little preference", "high preference", and can each be described by a fuzzy number defined over some scale, for example, $[0,1]$. The fact that preference of f against g is described by some $T_i \in T$ is expressed as $f T_i g$. We denote LPR as $\succsim_l$ and below we sometimes, for simplicity, write $f \succsim^i_l g$ or $f \succ^i_l g$ instead of $f T_i g$.

Definition 10.14. Two acts f and g in Y^S are said to be co-monotonic if there are no S_i and S_j in S, $f(S_i) \succ_l f(S_j)$ and $g(S_j) \succ_l g(S_i)$ hold.

Two real-valued functions a and b are co-monotonic iff $(a(S_i) - a(S_j))(b(S_i) - b(S_j)) \geq 0$ for all S_i and S_j in S.

For a fuzzy number-valued function a: S $\to$ E^1 denote by a^r, $r \in (0,1]$ its r-cut and note that $a^r = \left[a^r_1, a^r_2 \right]$, where $a^r_1, a^r_2 : S \to R$.

Two fuzzy functions $a,b: S \to E^1$ are said to be co-monotonic iff the real-valued functions $a_1^r, b_1^r : S \to R$, $a_2^r, b_2^r : S \to R$, $r \in (0,1]$ are co-monotonic.

A constant act $f = y^S$ for some y in Y, and any act g are co-monotonic. An act f whose statewise lotteries $\{f(S)\}$ are mutually indifferent, i.e., $f(S) \sim_l y$ for all S in S, and any act g are co-monotonic.

In the suggested framework, we extend a classical neo-Bayesian nomenclature as follows: elements of X are fuzzy outcomes; elements of Y are linguistic lotteries; elements of A are fuzzy acts; elements of S are fuzzy states of nature; and elements of F_S are fuzzy events.

It is common knowledge that under degrees of uncertainity humans evaluate alternatives or choices linguistically using certain evaluation techniques such as "much worse", "a little better", "much better", "almost equivalent" etc. In contrast to the classical preference relation, imposed on choices made by humans, LPR consistently expresses "degree of preference" allowing the analysis of preferences under uncertainity.

Below we give a series of axioms of the LPR $\succsim_l$ over A [20].

(i) Weak-order:

(a) Completeness of LPR. Any two alternatives are comparable with respect to LPR: for all f and g in A: $f \succsim_l g$ or $g \succsim_l f$. This means that for all f and g there exists such $T_i \in T$ that $f \succsim_l^i g$ or $g \succsim_l^i f$

(b) Transitivity. For all f, g and h in A: If $f \succsim_l g$ and $g \succsim_l h$ then $f \succsim_l h$. This means that if there exist such $T_i \in T$ and $T_j \in T$ that $f \succsim_l^i g$ and $g \succsim_l^j h$, then there exists such $T_k \in T$ that $f \succsim_l^k h$. Transitivity of LPR is defined on the base of the extension principle and fuzzy preference relation [849]. This axiom states that any two alternatives are comparable and assumes one of the fundamental properties of preferences (transitivity) for the case of fuzzy information.

(ii) Co-monotonic Independence: For all pairwise co-monotonic acts f, g and h in A if $f \succsim_l g$, then $\alpha f + (1-\alpha)h \succsim_l \alpha g + (1-\alpha)h$ for all $\alpha \in (0,1)$. This means that if there exist such $T_i \in T$ that $f \succsim_l^i g$ then there exists such $T_k \in T$ that $\alpha f + (1-\alpha)h \succsim_l^k \alpha g + (1-\alpha)h$, with f, g and h pairwise co-monotonic. The axiom extends the independency property for co-monotonic actions as opposed to independence axiom for the case of fuzzy information.

(iii) Continuity: For all f, g and h in A: if $f \succ_l g$ and $g \succ_l h$ then there are α and β in $(0,1)$ such that $\alpha f + (1-\alpha)h \succ_l g \succ_l \beta f + (1-\beta)h$. This means that if there exist such $T_i \in T$ and $T_j \in T$ that $f \succsim_l^i g$ and $g \succsim_l^j h$ then there exist such $T_k \in T$ and $T_m \in T$ that define preference of $\alpha f + (1-\alpha)h \succsim_l^k g \succsim_l^m \beta g + (1-\beta)h$. The axiom is an extension of classical continuity axiom for the case of fuzzy information.

(iv) Monotonicity. For all f and $\tilde{g}$ in A: If $f(S) \succsim_l g(S)$ on S then $f \succsim_l g$. This means that if for any $S \in S$ there exists such $T \in T$ that $f(S) \succsim_l g(S)$, then there exists $T_i \in T$ such that $f \succsim_l^i g$. The axiom is an extension of the classical monotonicity axiom for the case of fuzzy information.

(v) Nondegeneracy: Not for all $f, g \in A$, $f \succsim_l g$.

LPR $\succsim_l$ on A induces LPR denoted also by $\succsim_l$ on Y: $y \succsim_l z$ iff $y^S \succsim_l z^S$, where y^S and z^S denotes the constant functions y and z on S.

The presented axioms are formulated to reflect human preferences under a mixture of fuzzy and probabilistic information. Such formulation requires the use of a fuzzy-valued utility function. Formally, it is required to use a fuzzy-valued utility function U such that

$$\forall f, g \in A, f \succsim_l g \Leftrightarrow U(f) \geq U(g).$$

The problem of decision making with imperfect information consists in determination of an optimal $f^* \in A$, that is, $f^* \in A$ for which $U(f^*) = \max_{f \in A} U(f)$.

Fuzzy utility function U we adopt will be described as a fuzzy number-valued Choquet integral with respect to a fuzzy number-valued fuzzy measure. In its turn fuzzy number-valued fuzzy measure can be obtained from NL-described knowledge about probability distribution over S. NL-described knowledge about probability distribution over S is expressed as $P^l = P_1 / S_1 + P_2 / S_2 + P_3 / S_3 =$ small/small + high/medium + small/large, with the understanding that a term such as high/medium means that the probability, that $S_2 \in S$ is medium, is high. So, P^l is a linguistic (fuzzy) probability distribution.

In the discussions above, we have mentioned the necessity of the use of a fuzzy utility function as a suitable quantifying representation of vague preferences. Below we present a definition of a fuzzy number-valued utility function representing LPR (i)-(v) over an arbitrary set Z of alternatives.

Definition 10.15 [20, 40]. Fuzzy number-valued function $U(\cdot) : Z \to E^1$ is a utility function if it represents linguistic preferences $\succsim_l$ such that for any pair of alternatives $Z_1, Z_2 \in Z$, $Z_1 \succsim_l^i Z_2$ holds if and only if $U(Z_1) \geq U(Z_2)$, where T_i is determined on the base of $d_{fH}(U(Z_1), U(Z_2))$.

Here we consider a set Z of alternatives as if they are a set A of actions $f : S \to Y$.

Below we present representation theorems showing the existence of a fuzzy number-valued Choquet-integral-based fuzzy utility function [20, 517] that represents LPR defined over the set A of alternatives under conditions of linguistic probability distribution P^l over a set S.

Theorem 10.1. Assume that LPR $\succsim_l$ on $A = A_0$ satisfies (i) weak order, (ii) continuity, (iii) co-monotonic independence, (iv) monotonicity, and (v) nondegeneracy. Then there exists a unique fuzzy number-valued fuzzy measure η on F_S and an affine fuzzy number-valued function u on Y such that for all f and g in A:

$$f \succsim_l g \quad \text{iff} \quad \int_S u(f(S))d\eta \geq \int_S u(g(S))d\eta,$$

where u is unique up to positive linear transformations.

Theorem 10.2. For a nonconstant affine fuzzy number-valued function u on Y and a fuzzy number-valued fuzzy measure η on F_S a fuzzy number-valued Choquet integral induces such LPR on A that satisfies conditions (i)–(v). Additionally, u is unique up to positive linear transformations.

The proofs of the theorems are given in [20].

If S is a finite set $S = \{S_1,...,S_n\}$, $U(f)$ is determined as follows:

$$U(f) = \sum_{i=1}^{n} \left(u(f(S_{(i)})) -_h u(f(S_{(i+1)})) \right) \eta(H_{(i)}). \tag{10.1}$$

Subscript $(\cdot)$ shows that the indices are permuted in order to have $u(f(S_{(1)})) \geq ... \geq u(f(S_{(n)}))$, using some fuzzy ranking method, $u(f(S_{(n+1)})) = 0$, and $H_{(i)} = \{S_{(1)},...,S_{(i)}\}$. Here η is a fuzzy-number-valued fuzzy measure that can be obtained from linguistic probability distribution P^l on the base of the methodology presented in [850]. For this case we denote a fuzzy-number-valued fuzzy measure η_{P^l}. The optimal action f^* is found as an action with a fuzzy utility value $U(f^*) = \max_{f \in A} \left\{ \int_S u(f(S)) d\eta_{P^l} \right\}$. If A is a finite set $A = \{f_1,...,f_m\}$, then after determining fuzzy utility values for all alternatives, the best alternative can be found using some fuzzy ranking method.

In brief, a value of fuzzy utility function for action is determined as a fuzzy number-valued Choquet integral [20, 24, 40]:

$$\begin{aligned} U(f) &= \int_S u(f(S)) d\eta_{P^l} \\ &= \sum_{i=1}^{n} \left(u(f(S_{(i)})) -_h u(f(S_{(i+1)})) \right) \cdot \eta_{P^l}(H_{(i)}) \end{aligned} \tag{10.2}$$

Here $\eta_{P^l}()$ is a fuzzy number-valued fuzzy measure obtained from linguistic probability distribution over S [20, 24, 40] and $u(f(S))$ is a fuzzy number-valued utility function used to describe NL-based evaluations of utilities, (i) means that utilities are ranked such that

$u(f(S_{(1)})) \geq ... \geq u(f(S_{(n)}))$, $\mathrm{H}_{(i)} = \left\{ S_{(1)},...,S_{(i)} \right\}$, $u(f_j(S_{(n+1)})) = 0$, and for each (i) there exists $u(f(S_{(i)})) -_h u(f(S_{(i+1)}))$. Mutliplication $\cdot$ is realized in the sense of the Zadeh's extension principle. An optimal $f^* \in A$, that is $f^* \in A$ for which $U(f^*) = \max_{f \in A} \left\{ \int_S u(f(S)) d\eta_{p^l} \right\}$, can be determined by using a suitable fuzzy ranking method.

The crucial problem in the determination of an overall fuzzy utility of an alternative is a construction of a fuzzy number-valued fuzzy measure η_{p^l}. We will consider η_{p^l} as a fuzzy number-valued lower probability constructed from linguistic probability distribution P^l. Linguistic probability distribution P^l implies that a state $S_i \in S$ is assigned a linguistic probability P_i that can be described by a fuzzy number defined over [0,1]. However, fuzzy probabilities P_i cannot initially be assigned for all $S_i \in S$ [829]. Initial data are represented by fuzzy probabilities for $n-1$ fuzzy states of nature whereas for one of the given fuzzy states the probability is unknown. Subsequently, it becomes necessary to determine unknown fuzzy probability $P(S_j) = P_j$ [273]. In the framework of Computing with Words [36, 515, 845, 847], the problem of obtaining the unknown fuzzy probability for state S_j given fuzzy probabilities of all other states is a problem of propagation of generalized constraints [823, 829, 848]. Formally this problem is formulated as [125, 829]:

$$\text{Given } P(S_i) = P_i; \ S_i \in \mathrm{E}^n, \ P_i \in \mathrm{E}^1_{[0,1]}, \ i = \left\{ 1,...,j-1, j+1,...,n \right\} \quad (10.3)$$

$$\text{find unknown } P(S_j) = P_j, \ P_j \in \mathrm{E}^1_{[0,1]} \quad (10.4)$$

It reduces to a variational problem of constructing the membership function $\mu_{P_j}(\cdot)$ of an unknown fuzzy probability P_j:

$$\mu_{P_j}(p_j) = \sup_\rho \min_{i = \{1,...,j-1,j+1,...,n\}} (\mu_{P_i}(\int_S \mu_{S_i}(s)\rho(s)ds)) \quad (10.5)$$

subject to $\qquad \int_S \mu_{S_j}(s)\rho(s)ds = p_j, \int_S \rho(s)ds = 1$ (10.6)

Here $\mu_{S_j}(s)$ is the membership function of a fuzzy state S_j.

When P_j has been determined, linguistic probability distribution P^l for all states S_i is determined: $P^l = P_1/S_1 + P_2/S_2 + ... + P_n/S_n$.

If we have linguistic probability distribution over fuzzy values of some fuzzy set-valued random variable S, the important problem that arises is the verification of its consistency, completeness, and redundancy [14, 125]. Given consistent, complete and not redundant linguistic probability distribution P^l we can obtain from it a fuzzy set P^ρ of possible probability distributions $\rho(s)$. We can construct a fuzzy measure from P^ρ as its lower probability function (lower prevision) [553] by taking into account a degree of correspondence of $\rho(s)$ to P^l. Lower prevision is a unifying measure as opposed to the other existing additive and non-additive measures [754, 755]. We denote the fuzzy-number-valued fuzzy measure by η_{p^l} [20, 22, 24, 40, 44, 52] because it is derived from the given linguistic probability distribution P^l. A degree of membership of an arbitrary probability distribution $\rho(s)$ to P (a degree of correspondence of $\rho(s)$ to P^l) can be obtained by the formula

$$\pi_P(\rho(s)) = \min_{i=1,n}(\pi_{P_i}(p_i)),$$

where $p_i = \int_S \rho(s)\mu_{S_i}(s)ds$ is numeric probability of S_i defined by $\rho(s)$.

$\pi_{P_i}(p_i) = \mu_{P_i}\left(\int_S \rho(s)\mu_{S_i}(s)ds\right)$ is the membership degree of p_i to P_i.

To derive a fuzzy-number-valued fuzzy measure η_{p^l} we use the following formulas [20, 40]:

$$\eta_{p^l}(H) = \bigcup_{r \in (0,1]} r\left[\eta_{p^l_1}^r(H), \eta_{p^l_2}^r(H)\right]$$ (10.7)

where

$$\eta_{p^l 1}^r(H) = \inf\left\{\int_S \rho(s)\mu_H(s)ds \middle| \rho(s) \in P^{\rho^r}\right\}, \eta_{p^l 2}^r(H)$$

$$= \inf\left\{\int_S \rho(s)\mu_H(s)ds \middle| \rho(s) \in core(P^\rho)\right\}, \tag{10.8}$$

$$P^{\rho^r} = \left\{\rho(s) \middle| \min_{i=1,n}(\pi_{P_i}(p_i)) \geq r\right\}, core(P^\rho) = P^{\rho^{r=1}}, H \subset S$$

The support of η_{p^l} is defined as $\operatorname{supp} \eta_{p^l} = cl\left(\bigcup_{r\in(0,1]}\eta_{p^l}^r\right)$.

For special case, when states of nature are just some elements, fuzzy number-valued fuzzy measure η_{p^l} is defined as

$$\eta_{p^l}(H) = \bigcup_{r\in(0,1]} r\left[\eta_{p^l 1}^r(H), \eta_{p^l 2}^r(H)\right], H \subset S = \{S_1,...,S_n\}$$

where

$$\eta_{p^l}^r(H) = \inf\left\{\sum_{s_i \in H} p(s_i) \middle| (p(s_1),...,p(s_n)) \in P^{\rho^r}\right\},$$

$$P^{\rho r} = \left\{(p(s_1),...,p(s_n)) \in P_1^r \times ... \times P_n^r \middle| \sum_{i=1}^n p(s_i) = 1\right\},$$

here $P_1^r,...,P_n^r$ are r-cuts of fuzzy probabilities $P_1,...,P_n$ repectively, $p(s_1),...,p(s_n)$ are basic probabilities for $P_1,...,P_n$ respectively, $\times$ denotes the Cartesian product.

10.2 Fuzzy optimality based decision making

In the realm of decision making under uncertainty, the general approach is the use of the utility theories. The main disadvantage of this approach is that it is based on an evaluation of a vector-valued alternative by means of a scalar-valued quantity. This transformation is counterintuitive and leads to loss of information. The latter is related to restrictive assumptions on preferences underlying utility models like independence, completeness, transitivity etc. Relaxation of these assumptions results into more adequate but less tractable models.

In contrast, humans conduct direct comparison of alternatives as vectors of attributes' values and don't use artificial scalar values. Although vector-valued utility function-based methods exist, a fundamental axiomatic theory is absent and the problem of a direct comparison of vectors remains a challenge with a wide scope of research and applications.

In the realm of multicriteria decision making there exist approaches like TOPSIS and AHP to various extent utilizing components-wise comparison of vectors. Basic principle of such comparison is the Pareto optimality which is based on a counterintuitive assumption that all alternatives within a Pareto optimal set are considered equally optimal.

The above mentioned mandates necessity to develop new decision approaches based on direct comparison of vector-valued alternatives. In this section we suggest a Fuzzy Pareto optimality (FPO) based approach to decision making with fuzzy probabilities representing linguistic decision-relevant information. We use FPO concept to differentiate "more optimal" solutions from "less optimal" solutions. This is intuitive, especially when dealing with imperfect information.

10.2.1 *State-of the-art*

In the realm of formal methods of decision making, the general approach is the use of the utility theories which are based on an evaluation of a vector-valued alternative by means of an appropriate scalar-valued quantity. In real-life, human being does not proceed from vectors of attributes' values to scalar values for comparison in reasoning or decision making. Also, preferences as human judgments are often described in natural language (NL) and cannot be described by exact numerical values. For such cases, when application of utility function meets significant difficulties, scoring of alternatives may be conducted by direct ranking of alternatives. Then, as a rule, instead of a utility function it is used binary relations that provide finding an optimal or near to optimal alternative(s). There exists a spectrum of works in this area.

For performing outranking of alternatives, some methods had been developed for the traditional multiattribute decision making (MADM) problem [482, 863]. One of the first among these methods was ELECTRE method [369, 642, 643]. The general scheme of this method can be described as follows. A DM assigns a weight for each criterion and concordance and discordance indices are constructed. After this, a decision rule is constructed including construction of a binary relation on the base of information received from a DM. Once a binary relation is constructed, a DM is provided with a set of non-dominated alternatives and chooses one alternative from among them as a final decision.

Similar methods like TOPSIS [209, 563, 817], VIKOR [563-565] are based on the idea that optimal vector-valued alternative(s) should have the shortest distance from the positive ideal solution and farthest distance from the negative ideal solution. An optimal alternative in the VIKOR is based on the measure of "closeness" to the positive ideal solution. TOPSIS and VIKOR methods use different aggregation functions and different normalization methods. There exists a series of works based on applying interval and fuzzy techniques to extend AHP [264, 482], TOPSIS [467, 482, 578] and VIKOR [473, 581] methods to fuzzy environment.

In [744] a fuzzy balancing and ranking method for MADM is suggested. They appraise the performance of alternatives against criteria via linguistic variables based on triangular fuzzy numbers (TFNs).

The above mentioned approaches including the classical MADM methods and their fuzzy extensions suffer from serious disadvantages. Classical MADM methods require to provide perfect decision relevant information (e.g. to assign precise weights to criteria). This difficult problem sometimes is resolved by intensive involving of a DM. The fuzzy extensions of the existing methods are more tolerant. However, the fuzzy set theory does not play in these methods a main role, the main role is again belongs to the framework of the classical methods although equipped with ability to process linguistic information. Another important issue is that all these approaches are not developed to solve problems of decision making under uncertainty.

The above mentioned circumstances mandate necessity to develop new decision approaches which, from one side, may be based on a direct pairwise comparison of vector-valued alternatives. From the other side, there is a need to model the way humans actually think and reason with information described in NL in making decisions, for which it is adequate to use original capabilities of the fuzzy set theory.

In order to address the above mentioned problems, it is adequate to use computing with words (CW) approaches [354, 355, 459, 495, 496, 511] to provide an intuitive, human friendly way to decision making. In [273] they suggest a fuzzy Pareto optimality (FPO) concept for MADM problems. This concept is an implementation of the ideas of CW-based redefinitions of the existing scientific concepts [829]. In this approach, by directly comparing alternatives, they arrive at total degrees to which one alternative is better than, is equivalent to and is worse than another one. These degrees are determined as graded sums of differences between criteria values for considered alternatives. Such comparison is closer to the way humans compare alternatives by confronting their criteria values.

In the present section we suggest FPO concept-based approach to decision making under uncertainty in which relevant information on states of nature, probabilities and outcomes is imperfect as described in NL. As compared to the existing approaches, the suggested approach has fundamental capability of a direct comparison of NL-described alternatives by using linguistic preference degrees. Linguistic degrees are obtained by soft constraining of a Pareto optimal set of alternatives on the base of their degrees of optimality. The decision analysis in this approach is free from complex operations like construction of utility function or intensive involving of a DM. Computations with linguistic information is mainly based on simple operations.

10.2.2 *Some preliminary information*

Let $\mathcal{E}^n$ be a space of all fuzzy subsets of $\mathcal{R}^n$, which satisfies the conditions of normality, convexity, and are upper semicontinuous with compact support. It is obvious that $\mathcal{E}^1$ is the set of fuzzy numbers defined over $\mathcal{R}$. Then, let's denote by $\mathcal{E}^1_{[0,1]}$ the corresponding space of fuzzy numbers defined over $[0,1]$.

For a TFN $a = (a_1, a_2, a_3)$, the generalized mean value $gmv(A)$ may be defined as [460]:

$$gmv(A) = \frac{a_1 + a_2 + a_3}{3}. \tag{10.9}$$

Denote $\mathcal{A} = \{f_1, f_2, ..., f_N\}$ the set of alternatives and $\mathcal{S} = \{s_1, s_2, ..., s_M\}$ the set of states of nature. Let $\mathcal{X}$ be a set of outcomes, $\mathcal{X} = \{x_{ij}\}$, where x_{ij} is an outcome of an action f_i taken at a state s_j and is denoted $f_i(s_j)$.

Definition 10.16 (Pareto Dominance). For any two points (candidate solutions) $f_i, f_k \in \mathcal{A}$, f_i is said to dominate f_k in the Pareto sense (P-dominate) if and only if the following conditions hold:

$$f_i(s_j) \geq f_k(s_j) \quad \text{for all } j \in \{1, 2, ..., M\}, \tag{10.10}$$

$$f_i(s_{j'}) > f_k(s_{j'}) \quad \text{for at least one } j' \in \{1, 2, ..., M\}. \tag{10.11}$$

Definition 10.17 (Pareto Optimality). $f^* \in \mathcal{A}$ is Pareto optimal if there is no $f_i \in \mathcal{A}$ such that f_i P-dominates f^*.

Definition 10.18 (Pareto Set and Front). We call Pareto optimal set $\mathcal{S}_P$ and Pareto optimal front $\mathcal{F}_P$ the set of Pareto otpimal solutions in design domain and objective domain respectively.

***Consistency, completeness and redundancy of linguistic probability distribution* [125].** Let the set of linguistic probabilities $P^l = \{P_1, ..., P_j, ..., P_M\}$ correspond to the set of linguistic values $\{s_1, ..., s_j, ..., s_M\}$ of a random variable s. If one formalizes linguistic probabilities and linguistic values by fuzzy sets, then, for special case, a linguistic probability distribution P^l is inconsistent when the condition

$$p_j = \int_S \mu_{s_j}(s)\rho(s)ds \qquad (10.12)$$

or

$$\mu_{P_j}\left(\int_S \mu_{s_j}(s)\rho(s)ds\right) = 1 \qquad (10.13)$$

is not satisfied for any density ρ from the set of evaluations of densities. Here $s \in S$, where S is a universe of discourse.

The degree of inconsistency (denoted **contr**) of a linguistic probability distribution P^l could be determined as

$$\text{contr } P^l = \min_\rho \left| 1 - \int_S \rho(s)ds \right| \qquad (10.14)$$

where ρ satisfies conditions (10.4) and (10.5). Obviously, $\text{contr } P^l = 0$ when the required density ρ exists.

Let a linguistic probability distribution P^l be consistent, that is $\text{contr } P^l = 0$. If this distribution is given as a set of crisp probabilities p_j, then its incompleteness (denoted **in**) and redundancy (denoted **red**) can be expressed as

$$\text{in } P^l = \max\left\{0, 1 - \sum_j p_j\right\} \qquad (10.15)$$

$$\text{red } P^l = \max\left\{0, \sum_j p_j - 1\right\} \qquad (10.16)$$

If P^l is given by using linguistic probabilities P_j then its incompleteness and redundancy can be expressed as

$$\text{in } P^l = \max\left\{0, 1 - \sup_{\gamma \in \Gamma} \gamma\right\} \tag{10.17}$$

$$\text{red } P^l = \max\left\{0, \inf_{\gamma \in \Gamma} \gamma - 1\right\} \tag{10.18}$$

where $\Gamma = \{\gamma | \mu_\Lambda(\gamma) = 1\}$. Here Λ is a sum of linguistic probabilities $P_j \in P^l$.

10.2.3 *Statement of the problem*

Let $S = \{s_1, s_2, ..., s_M\} \subset E^n$ be a set of fuzzy states of the nature and $\mathcal{X} \subset \mathcal{E}^n$ be a set of fuzzy outcomes. Fuzziness of states of nature is used for a fuzzy granulation of objective conditions when pure partitioning of the latter is impossible due to vagueness of the relevant information described in NL. A set of alternatives is considered as a set $\mathcal{A}$ of fuzzy functions f from S to $\mathcal{X}$ [20, 24, 850]. Linguistic information on likelihood P^l of the states of nature is formalized by fuzzy probabilities P_j of the states s_j.

Due to vagueness of real-world objective conditions and uncertainty of future, relevant information on states of nature and the related probabilities is often described in NL. These are the cases when objective probabilities are not known due to absence of good statistical data and precise subjective probabilities are not reliable. Assuming three states of nature, NL-described information about corresponding probability distribution *Prob*() can be expressed as follows:

Prob(State1)/State1 + Prob(State2)/State2 + Prob(State3)/State3 =
small/small + high/medium + very small/large,

with the understanding that a term *high/medium* means that the probability that the state of nature is *medium* is *high*. The considered linguistic description can be precisiated by using fuzzy sets with typical membership functions, say triangular-shaped one. Then the precisiation will be formally written as:

$$P^l = P_1 / s_1 + P_2 / s_2 + P_3 / s_3$$

Here, for instance, s_2 and P_2 are TFNs used as precisiation for the terms *medium* and *high* respectively. Thus, P^l is a distribution of the fuzzy probabilities over the fuzzy states of nature. Let us mention that construction of this distribution does not consist in just assessing appropriate fuzzy numbers but requires solving a complex optimization problem which is described in the next section.

Vague preferences over a set of imprecise alternatives is modeled by a linguistic preference relation over $\mathcal{A}$. For this purpose it is adequate to introduce a linguistic variable "degree of preference" [125, 474] with a term-set $T = (T_1, ..., T_K)$. Terms can be labeled as, for example, "equivalence", "little preference", "high preference", and each can be described by a fuzzy number defined over some scale like [0,1] or [0,10] etc. The fact that $\tilde{f}_i$ is linguistically preferred to f_k is written as $f_i \succsim_l f_k$. The latter means that there exist some $T_i \in T$ as a linguistic degree $Deg(f_i \succsim_l f_k)$ to which f_i is preferred to f_k: $Deg(f_i \succsim_l f_k) \approx T_i$.

A decision making problem with linguistic information can be formalized as a 4-tuple $\left(\mathcal{S}, P^l, \mathcal{A}, \succsim_l\right)$ and consists in determination of $\succsim_l$. The latter are described on the base of degrees of optimality of alternatives. A degree of optimality of an alternative $\tilde{f}_i$ denoted $do(f_i)$ is an overall degree to which f_i dominates all the other alternatives. The linguistic preference $f_i \succsim_l f_k$ of f_i with respect to f_k is described by a degree $Deg(f_i \succsim_l f_k) = do(f_i) - do(f_k)$ iff $do(f_i) > do(f_k)$ and $Deg(f_i \succsim_l f_k) = 0$ otherwise.

10.2.4 *Method of solution*

The FPO formalism suggested in [273] is developed for a perfect information structure, i.e. when all the decision relevant information is represented by precise numerical evaluations. From the other side, this approach is developed for multiattribute decision making. We will extend the FPO formalism for the considered framework of decision making with imperfect information. The method of solution is described below.

The solution of the considered problem consists in determination of a linguistic degree of preference of f_i to f_k for all $f_i, f_k \in A$ by direct comparison of f_i and f_k as vector-valued alternatives.

At the first stage it is needed for fuzzy probabilities P_j to be known for each fuzzy state of nature s_j. However, it can be given only partial information represented by fuzzy probabilities for all fuzzy states except one. The unknown fuzzy probability cannot be assigned but must be computed based on the known fuzzy probabilities. Computation of an unknown fuzzy probability is an optimization problem as it requires construction of a membership function. The problem of obtaining the unknown fuzzy probability $P(s_j) = P_j$ is formulated.

The important problem that arises for the obtained P^l, is the verification of its consistency, completeness and redundancy (see formulas (10.12)-(10.18)).

At the second stage, given consistent, complete and not-redundant distribution of the fuzzy probabilities over all the states of nature it is needed to determine the total degrees of statewise superiority, equivalence and inferiority of f_i with respect to f_k taking into account fuzzy probability P_j of each fuzzy state of nature s_j. The total degree nbF of statewise superiority, the total degree neF of statewise equivalence, and the total degree nwF of statewise inferiority of f_i with respect to f_k are determined on the base of differences between fuzzy outcomes of f_i and f_k at each fuzzy state of nature as follows:

$$nbF(f_i, f_k) = \sum_{j=1}^{M} \mu_b^j (gmv((f_i(s_j) - f_k(s_j)) \cdot P_j)), \qquad (10.19)$$

$$neF(f_i, f_k) = \sum_{j=1}^{M} \mu_e^j (gmv((f_i(s_j) - f_k(s_j)) \cdot P_j)), \qquad (10.20)$$

$$nwF(f_i, f_k) = \sum_{j=1}^{M} \mu_w^j (gmv((f_i(s_j) - f_k(s_j)) \cdot P_j)), \qquad (10.21)$$

where $\mu_b^j, \mu_e^j, \mu_w^j$ are membership functions for linguistic evaluations "better", "equivalent" and "worse" respectively, determined as in [273]. For any j-th state $\mu_b^j, \mu_e^j, \mu_w^j$ are constructed such that Ruspini condition holds, which, in turn, results in the following condition:

$$nbF(f_i, f_k) + neF(f_i, f_k) + nwF(f_i, f_k) = \sum_{j=1}^{M} (\mu_b^j + \mu_e^j + \mu_w^j) = M. \qquad (10.22)$$

On the base of $nbF(f_i, f_k)$, $neF(f_i, f_k)$, and $nwF(f_i, f_k)$, $(1-kF)$-dominance is determined as dominance in the terms of its degree. This concepts suggests that f_i $(1-kF)$-dominates f_k iff

$$neF(f_i, f_k) < M, \quad nbF(f_i, f_k) \geq \frac{M - neF(f_i, f_k)}{kF + 1}, \qquad (10.23)$$

with $kF \in [0,1]$.

In order to determine the greatest kF such that f_i $(1-kF)$-dominates f_k, a function d is introduced:

$$d(f_i, f_k) = \begin{cases} 0, & \text{if } nbF(f_i, f_k) \leq \dfrac{M - neF(f_i, f_k)}{2} \\ \dfrac{2 \cdot nbF(f_i, f_k) + neF(f_i, f_k) - M}{nbF(f_i, f_k)}, & \text{otherwise} \end{cases} \qquad (10.24)$$

Given d, the desired greatest kF is found as $1 - d(f_i, f_k)$.

$d(f_i, f_k) = 1$ implies Pareto dominance of f_i over f_k whereas $d(f_i, f_k) = 0$ implies no Pareto dominance of f_i over f_k.

In contrast to determine whether f^* is Pareto optimal, in FPO they determine whether f^* is a Pareto optimal with the considered degree kF. f^* is kF optimal if and only if there is no $f_i \in A$ such that f_i $(1-kF)$-dominates f^*.

The main idea of FPO concept suggests to consider f^* in terms of its degree of optimality $do(f^*)$ determined as follows:

$$do(f^*) = 1 - \max_{f_i \in \mathbb{A}} d(f_i, f^*) \, . \tag{10.25}$$

A function *do* can be considered as the membership function of a fuzzy set describing the notion of *kF* -optimality.

At the fourth stage, the degree $Deg(f_i \succsim_l f_k)$ of preference of f_i to f_k for any $f_i, f_k \in \mathbb{A}$ should be determined based on $do()$. For simplicity, one can calculate $Deg(f_i \succsim_l f_k)$ as follows:

$$Deg(f_i \succsim_l f_k) = do(f_i) - do(f_k) \, .$$

The supplier selection problem solution by using the proposed method is given in [61]. Comparative analysis of this method and method given in [744] also is considered in [61].

10.3 Decision making with combined states

Behavioral decision making is an area of multidisciplinary research attracting growing interest of scientists and practitioners, economists, and business people. A wide spectrum of successful theories is present now, including multiple priors models, studies on altruism, trust and fairness. However, these theories are developed for precise and complete information, whereas real information concerning behavior and environment is imperfect, qualitative, and, as a result, often described in NL. We suggest an approach based on modeling a DM's behavior by a set of states. Each state represents a certain principal behavior. In our approach, states of nature and DM's states constitute a single space of combined states. For formalizing relevant information described in NL, we use fuzzy set theory. The utility model is based on Choquet-like integration over combined states. The investigations show that Expected Utility, Choquet Expected Utility and Cumulative Prospect Theory (CPT) are special cases of the suggested approach.

10.3.1 *State-of-the-art*

There is a large number of works on decision analysis including multicriteria decision making [312, 318, 436, 644]. The existing decision models yielded good results. Nowadays it is needed new generation of decision theories due to necessity to deeply account for behavioral features of decision makers. During the development of decision theories scientists try to take into account features of human choices in formal models to make the latter closer to real decision activity. Risk issues were the first basic behavioral factors taken into account in the construction of decision methods. Three main categories of risk-related behaviors: risk aversion, risk seeking and risk neutrality were introduced. Gain-loss attitudes [749] and ambiguity attitudes [318] were revealed as other important behavioral features. A large group of investigations is devoted to modeling such important psychological, moral and social aspects of decisions as reciprocity [205, 208, 271], altruism [76, 205], trust [108, 208] etc.

A large area of research concerns mental-level models [127, 201, 262, 502, 552, 688] in which a DM's behavior is modeled by a set of states. Each state describes a DM's possible decision-relevant condition and is referred to as "mental state", "state of mind" etc. In these models, they consider relations between mental state and state of environment [204, 347, 785] (nature). In [127, 688] a mental state and a state of nature form a state of the whole system called a "global state". Within the scope of mental-level models there are two main research areas: internal modeling [127, 808] and implementation-independent modeling [127]. The first one is based on modeling a mental state by a set of characteristics (variables) and the second one is based on modeling a mental state on the base of beliefs, preferences and decision criterion [127, 299, 627].

We observe a significant progress in the development of a series of successful decision theories based on behavioral factors. Real-life choices are based on interaction among numerous factors as risk, ambiguity, altruism and others. Humans conduct an intelligent, substantive comparison of alternatives in a whole, as some mixes of factors. However, one of the disadvantages of the existing decision theories is an absence of a due attention to interaction among the factors. Variables describing the factors are introduced into a decision model without consideration of how these factors really interact. From the other side, the fact that information on a DM's behavior is imperfect is not taken into account. For example, in the CPT they imperatively consider that a DM is risk averse in domain of gains and risk seeking in domain of losses. This is too simplified view and in reality we don't have such complete information concerning a considered DM in a considered situation. In α-MMEU DM's ambiguity aversion is modeled by a precise value α, whereas real information about the ambiguity attitude is imprecise. Moreover, behavioral factors are included by using complex expressions – nonlinearities, second-order probabilities etc. As a result, the existing models are not transparent and cannot adequately describe human decision activity.

Humans are not fully rational DMs and their decisions are based on perceptions about imperfect environment. The necessity to consider that humans are not fully rational was first addressed by Herbert Simon [691]. He proposed the concept of bounded rationality to reflect limitations of humans' knowledge and computational abilities. Despite its significant importance, the idea of bounded rationality did not find its mathematical formalism adequate to realize real decisions. The theory which offers an adequate formalism for bounded rationality is the fuzzy set theory introduced by L.A. Zadeh [490, 558, 828]. The reason is that this theory deals with the formalization of linguistically (qualitatively) described imprecise or vague information and partial truth. Due to limitation of knowledge and computational abilities, humans use linguistic description of information as more tolerant for imprecision and vagueness than precise numbers. Fuzzy set theory and its successive technologies [190, 703] as tools for processing linguistic information may help to arrive at perception-friendly and mathematically consistent decisions.

The necessity of considering interaction of behavioral factors under imperfect information is the main insight for development of new decision approaches. Following this, we suggest to use fuzzy granulation of a space of variables describing behavioral factors (for example, risk and ambiguity attitudes) into main fuzzy subspaces. Each fuzzy subspace represents one principal behavior as a DM's state in which he/she may be when making choices [41]. The use of fuzzy sets reflects the facts that a DM's state cannot be sharply bounded. Form the other side this will help to describe qualitative nature of such concepts as altruism, trust etc. Occurrence of a state of a DM is to be described by a linguistic (fuzzy) probability due to imprecision and complexity of interaction of the behavioral factors underlying a DM's behavior.

Concerning states of nature, it is also not often possible to construct an ideal description. For example, in many real problems they should not be considered as exclusive: the evaluations like "moderate growth of economy" and "strong growth of economy" don't have sharp boundaries and may overlap.

In order to address the above mentioned issues of real-world behavioral decision making it is needed to model at a fundamental level dependence of human behavior on objective conditions (environment) under imperfect relevant information. In view of this we suggest to consider the space of states of nature and space of DM's states as a single space of combined states [41, 50], i.e. to consider Cartesian product of these two important spaces as a fundamental basis for comparison of alternatives. Likelihood of each combined space as a pair of a state of nature and a DM's state is to be described by fuzzy probability of their joint occurrence. This fuzzy joint probability (FJP) will model imperfect information on dependence of a DM's behavior on objective conditions. For example, FJP may represent our belief on whether a considered DM will exhibit risk aversion in a considered situation characterized by losses. Utilities of outcomes are also to be distributed over combined states reflecting naturally various evaluation of the outcomes by a DM in his/her various states. For instance, a DM's mental evaluation of an outcome obtained at a state of nature characterized by ambiguity depends on whether a state of DM represents ambiguity aversion or ambiguity seeking. Consideration of DM's behavior by space of states and its Cartesian product with space of states of nature will allow for transparent analysis of decisions. The reason is that in this approach relations between objective conditions and a DM behavior are not 'hidden' in complex mathematical expressions but are made transparent. For a utility representation in the suggested model we adopt the generalized fuzzy Choquet-like aggregation with respect to a fuzzy-valued bi-capacity.

We suggest to model a DM's behavior by a set of his/her states reflecting principal behaviors hi/she may exhibit (analogously to the idea of states of nature). Within the existing works, our theory belongs to the so-called mental-level models [347, 502, 552, 640]. States of nature (or states of environment) and DM's states in these models constitute a global space as their Cartesian product, an element of which is a pair composed of a state of nature and a DM's state". In [127] they suggest to model a DM's mental state in terms of beliefs, preferences and a decision criterion. This description is called implementation-independent description of the agent. They explain the reasons of describing a DM's state not by using the values of various registers, or those of state variables, but by using notions of beliefs, preferences, and a decision criterion. The mentioned reasons are intuitiveness and generality of the description (because beliefs, preferences and decision criteria is widely used notions in decision models) and easiness from computational and analytical point of view.

However, such a model is developed for idealized information structure: information on states of nature is represented by ignorance – no probability information is available (belief is represented by a subset of states of nature space); outcomes are deterministic (sometimes as precise numbers, clear consequences etc); utilities are precise; states of nature are mutually exclusive, mental states are mutually exclusive; no probability information is available for mental states. As a result, the criteria for decisions under uncertainty are used in this model. This ignores intrinsic imperfect nature of DM's related information represented by imprecise beliefs and outcomes and vague preferences. As a result, this formalism-based model is more suitable for inanimate agents like robots, controllers etc functioning in an ideal or primitive environment and not for human DMs. In [127] they consider such agents or human DMs in simple thought experiments.

In [201] they consider mental-level model for decisions under risk: precise probabilities, deterministic outcomes, mutually exclusive states of nature and mutually exclusive states of mind of DM. In this model, as opposed to the model in [127], they consider determination of the precise joint probabilities over pairs of states of nature and DM's states. The joint distribution is to be constructed from precise probabilities of states of mind and conditional probabilities of states of nature for states of mind.

In contrast to works in [127, 201], we try to describe imperfect information related to nature and DM, represented by impreciseness of beliefs, vagueness and ambiguity of states of nature and DM's states and their joint occurrence and impreciseness of outcomes which lead to vagueness of preferences. Internal modeling of a DM by means of fuzzy states and the associated fuzzy probabilities allows to realistically model behavior-related information in real-life problems, which is, as a rule, linguistically described. The proposed imperfect-information based internal modeling, of course, complicates decision analysis, but this complexity is the price we need to pay for using assumptions on the relevant information which are closer to real decision situations. From the other side, internal modeling as opposed to external modeling (implementation-independent) itself is a more relevant in behavioral aspect because is based on a unite and direct description of a DM and not on indirect description on the base of external elements (beliefs, outcomes, preferences). We also, in general, disagree with the authors in [127] that implementation-independent modeling is easy from analytical point of view. It is known that incorporating various attitudes and features of a DM into preferences sufficiently complicates the latter (for example, consider complicated preferences of CPT [175] which cover gain-loss, risk and non-additivity issues).

The other main theory to be compared with our approach is CPT – a successful theory reflecting important behavioral aspects. However, in CPT only gain-loss, risk and ambiguity attitudes are considered. Our approach is able to take into account also other aspects such as trust, reciprocity, altruism etc. Moreover, in CPT a DM is considered as risk averse when dealing with gains and risk seeking when dealing with losses. However, this is not always the case in real life and we suggest to simultaneously consider all possible DM's behaviors both for gains and losses.

As opposed to CPT, we model risk attitudes by assigning imprecise (fuzzy) probabilities to the risk aversion, risk neutrality and risk seeking DM's states. This reflects natural mix of possibilistic and probabilistic uncertainties present in information related to a DM and nature. This is not taken into account in the other approaches. On the basis of fuzzy probabilities of states of nature and DM's states and information on dependence between them we construct a FJP distribution over space "nature-DM". FJP models natural impreciseness of information on a likelihood of joint occurrence of DM-related and nature-related events. For this information, the use of a single distribution is not justifiable and use of multiple priors is not sufficiently adequate. At the same time we suggest to assess various fuzzy utilities to outcomes for various DM's states. This reflects various evaluations of outcomes under various behaviors and also reflects natural uncertainty related to an evaluation of outcomes by a DM. The overall utility for an action in our approach is to be determined as a fuzzy-valued Choquet integral with respect to fuzzy-valued bi-capacity. The fuzziness of an overall utility naturally follows from fuzziness of joint distribution and fuzziness of utilities.

Both parametric and non-parametric approaches to introducing such social aspects as trust, reciprocity, altruism, fairness etc to utility function were proposed by James C. Cox and his colleagues [205-209] and other authors [3, 76, 108, 271]. They developed a non-parametric theory of reciprocal altruism for games behavior. In their theory they formalize a player's preferences as depending on both his/her and others' monetary payoffs. They formalize how choices of a single player influence preferences of the other. However, the proposed approach is designed for perfect information framework. We propose to take into account by using fuzzy set theory natural impreciseness, vagueness and partial truth of decision-relevant information for which the use of precise techniques is not suitable.

The suggested approach as compared to the existing approaches has the following advantages. The first is a consideration of a Cartesian product of a set of states of nature and a set of DM's states with a joint probability distribution [50, 52]. This allows to model dependence of a DM's state on a state of nature, that is, to clearly model dependence of human behavior on objective conditions. The second is that the suggested approach allows to model natural vagueness, imprecision, partial truth and other imperfectness of the information related to behavioral decision activity. This issue is not in general addressed in the existing theories, including the famous works of Cox and colleagues, Kahnemann and Tversky and others. Humans make decisions based on perceptions, which are intrinsically imprecise, and not on precise estimates.

In the suggested approach, complexity is one of the main issues that should be analyzed and compared with that of the other approaches. It is well-known that decision theories based on simple computational schemes like EU are often inconsistent with human decisions. In order to make a decision criterion closer to human choices it is required to use more complex representations, in particular, multiple priors, which leads to optimization problems. In our approach we use possibilistic constraint on a set of priors and fuzzy-valued utilities. The first is conditioned by the fact, that probabilistic information on states of nature and DM's states is usually represented by linguistic estimations. The latter are, in turn, soft (smooth) constraints on values of probabilities implying that relevance of a prior to a set of priors is matter of a degree. The second is also conditioned by imprecise evaluations of outcomes and utilities by humans in real decision problems. However, one can mention the model in [436] where smooth constraint on multiple priors is used in form of probability distribution. However, as compared to our approach of modeling probability-relevant information, this approach has two main disadvantages. In general, the belief representation by second-order probability is counterintuitive. Human behavior and thinking can hardly be based on so strict and specific model as probabilistic beliefs over priors. From the other side, construction of a subjective probability over multiple priors is a rather problematic task. The other disadvantage is that investigation of consistency of subjective probability-relevant information is not considered – consistent multiple priors are supposed to be given. However, verification of consistency is very important problem. For instance, an investigation of this issue is conducted in [756].

The sources of computational complexity in our approach are time-consuming processing of membership functions including determination of a membership of unknown fuzzy marginal probability and fuzzy number-valued bi-capacity construction. Here we need to solve optimization problems and even variational problems. At the same time, construction of a FJP distribution is also a difficult problem conditioned by partially known dependence and other problems. However, these problems can be rather fast solved by the existing mathematical software like Maple and Matlab [133]. To a smaller extent, complexity is conditioned by mathematical operations over fuzzy numbers. Yes, anyway, our model is more general than the others as accumulating fuzzy and probabilistic uncertainty which leads to loss of preciseness and affects power of prediction. However, our approach is based on formalization of linguistic estimations which are more in line with human-originated information. In developing the suggested theory we try to obey the J. Keynes rule: *"it is better to be roughly right than precisely wrong"* to create less precise but more realistic approach. The higher complexity is a price one needs to pay to arrive at linguistic solutions as more acceptable for human intuition.

10.3.2 *Statement of the problem*

Let $S = \{s_1, s_2, ..., s_M\} \subset E^n$ be a space of fuzzy states of nature and X be a space of fuzzy outcomes as a bounded subset of E^n. Denote by $H = \{h_1, h_2, ..., h_N\} \subset E^n$ a set of fuzzy states of a DM [50, 52]. Then we call $\Omega = S \times H$ a space "nature-DM", elements of which are combined states $w = (s, h)$ where $s \in S, h \in H$.

Denote by $\mathcal{F}_\Omega$ a σ-algebra of subsets of Ω. Then consider $A = \{f \in A | f : \Omega \to X\}$ the set of fuzzy actions as the set of all F_Ω-measurable fuzzy functions from Ω to X [50, 52].

Then a problem of behavioral decision making with combined states under imperfect information (BDMCSII) can be denoted as $D_{BDMCSII} = (\Omega, X, A, \succsim_l)$ where $\succsim_l$ are linguistic preferences of a DM.

In general, it is not known which state of nature will take place and what state of a DM will present at the moment of decision making. Only some partial knowledge on probability distributions on S and H is available. An information relevant to a DM can be formalized as a linguistic probability distribution over his/her states: $p_1 / h_1 + p_2 / h_2 + ... + p_N / h_N$, where p_i is a linguistic belief degree or a linguistic probability. So, p_i / h_i can be formulated as, for example, "a probability that a DM's state is h_i is p_i".

For a detailed description of human behavior and imperfect information on Ω we use a fuzzy number-valued bi-capacity $\eta = \eta(V, W), V, W \subset \Omega$. Value or utility of an outcome $y = f(s, h)$ in various DM's states will also be various, and then can be formalized as a function $u(y) = u(f(s, h))$. We can claim that the value function of Kahneman and Tversky $v = v(f(s))$ [732] appears then as a special case. So, an overall utility $U(f)$ of an action f is to be determined as a fuzzy number-valued bi-capacity-based aggregation of $u(f(s, h))$ over space Ω. Then the BDMCSII problem consists in determination of an optimal action $f^* \in A$ with $U(f^*) = \max_{f \in A} \int_{\Omega} U(f(w)) d\eta$.

10.3.3 *Utility model axiomatization*

As the basis for our model we use the framework of bi-capacity [451] formulated by Labreuche and Grabisch. The bi-capacity is a natural generalization of capacities where we are able to describe interaction between attractive and repulsive values (outcomes, criteria values), particularly, gains and losses. We extend this framework to the case of imperfect information by using linguistic preference relation [14, 849]. The linguistic preference means that the preference among actions f and g is modeled by a degree $Deg(f \succsim_l g)$ to which f is at least as good as g and a degree $Deg(g \succsim_l f)$ to which g is at least as good as f. The degrees are from [0,1]. The closer $Deg(f \succsim_l g)$ to 1 the more f is preferred to g. These degrees are used to represent vagueness of preferences, that is, situations when decision relevant information is too vague to definitely determine preference of one alternative against another. For special case, when $Deg(g \succsim_l f) = 0$ and $Deg(f \succsim_l g) \neq 0$ we have the classical preference, i.e. we say that f is preferred to g.

We use bi-capacity-adopted integration [451] at the space "nature-DM" for determination of an overall utility of an alternative. The base for our model is composed by intra-combined state information and inter-combined states information. Intra-combined state information is used to form utilities representing preference over outcomes $f(w_i) = x_i$, where $w_i = (s_{i_1}, h_{i_2})$ of an act $f \in A$ with understanding that these are preferences at state of nature s_{i_1} conditioned by a state h_{i_2} of a DM.

Inter-combined states information will be used to form fuzzy-valued bi-capacity representing dependence between combined states as human behaviors under incomplete information.

Proceeding from these assumptions, for an overall utility U of action f we use an aggregation operator based on the use of a bi-capacity. Bi-capacity is a more powerful tool to be used in a space "nature-DM". More specifically, we use a fuzzy-valued generalized Choquet-like aggregation with respect to fuzzy-valued bi-capacity over Ω:

$$U(f) = \sum_{l=1}^{n} (u(f(w_{(l)})) -_h u(f(w_{(l+1)})))\eta((1),...,(l)), \qquad (10.26)$$

provided $u(f(w_{(l)})) \geq u(f(w_{(l+1)}))$; $N^+ = \{w \in \Omega : u(f(w)) \geq 0\}$,

$N^- = \Omega \setminus N^+$,

$\eta((1),...,(l)) = \eta(\{w_{(1)},...,w_{(l)}\} \cap N^+, \{w_{(1)},...,w_{(l)}\} \cap N^-)$ is a fuzzy number-valued bi-capacity $\eta(\cdot,\cdot)$.

In (10.26) under level r we have an interval $U^r(f) = [U_1^r(f), U_2^r(f)]$ of possible precise overall utilities, where $U_1^r(f), U_2^r(f)$ are described as follows:

$$U_1^r(f) = \left(\left| u_1^r(f(w_{(1)})) \right| - \left| u_1^r(f(w_{(2)})) \right| \right) \eta_{p^l_1}^r(\{w_{(1)}\} \cap N^+, \{w_{(1)}\} \cap N^-) +$$

$$+ \left(\left| u_1^r(f(w_{(2)})) \right| - \left| u_1^r(f(w_{(3)})) \right| \right) \eta_{p^l_1}^r(\{w_{(1)}, w_{(2)}\} \cap N^+, \{w_{(1)}, w_{(2)}\} \cap N^-) +$$

$$+ ... + \left| u_1^r(f(w_{(n)})) \right| \eta_{p^l_1}^r(\{w_{(1)}, w_{(2)}, ..., w_{(n)}\} \cap N^+, \{w_{(1)}, w_{(2)}, ..., w_{(n)}\} \cap N^-),$$

$$U_2^r(f) = \left(\left| u_2^r(f(w_{(1)})) \right| - \left| u_2^r(f(w_{(2)})) \right| \right) \eta_{p^l_2}^r(\{w_{(1)}\} \cap N^+, \{w_{(1)}\} \cap N^-) +$$

$$+ \left(\left| u_2^r(f(w_{(2)})) \right| - \left| u_2^r(f(w_{(3)})) \right| \right) \eta_{p^l_2}^r(\{w_{(1)}, w_{(2)}\} \cap N^+, \{w_{(1)}, w_{(2)}\} \cap N^-) +$$

$$+ ... + \left| u_2^r(f(w_{(n)})) \right| \eta_{p^l_2}^r(\{w_{(1)}, w_{(2)}, ..., w_{(n)}\} \cap N^+, \{w_{(1)}, w_{(2)}, ..., w_{(n)}\} \cap N^-),$$

provided that

$$\left| u_1^r(f(w_{(1)})) \right| \geq ... \geq \left| u_1^r(f(w_{(n)})) \right|, \quad \left| u_2^r(f(w_{(1)})) \right| \geq ... \geq \left| u_2^r(f(w_{(n)})) \right| \quad \text{and}$$

$$\left| u_1^r(f(w_{(n)})) \right| = \left| u_2^r(f(w_{(n)})) \right| = 0.$$

So, $U_i^r(\tilde{f})$, $i = 1, 2$ is a common Choquet-like precise bi-capacity based functional [451], with u_i^r and $\eta_{p^l_i}^r$ $i = 1, 2$ being a precise utility function and a precise bi-capacity respectively. This representation captures imprecision of utility and bi-capacity arising from imprecision of outcomes and probabilities encountered in real-life decision problems.

An optimal action $f^* \in A$, that is $f^* \in A$ for which $U(f^*) = \max_{f \in A} \left\{ \int_\Omega u(f(s, h) d\eta_{p^l} \right\}$ is found by a determination of $Deg(f \succsim_l g)$, $f, g \in A$: optimal action $f^* \in A$ is an action for which $Deg(f^* \succsim_l f) \geq Deg(f \succsim_l f^*)$ is satisfied for all $f \in A, f \neq f^*$. The determination of $Deg(f \succsim_l g)$ is based on comparison of $U(f)$ and $U(g)$ as the basic values of $U(f)$ and $U(g)$ respectively as follows. The membership functions of $U(f)$ and $U(g)$ describe possibilities of their various basic values $U(f)$ and $U(g)$ respectively, that is, possibilities for various precise values of overall utilities of f and g. In accordance with these membership functions, there is possibility $r \in (0, 1]$ that precise overall utilities of f and g are equal to

$U_1^r(f), U_2^r(f)$ and $U_1^r(g), U_2^r(g)$ respectively. Therefore, we can state that there is possibility $r \in (0,1]$ that the difference between precise overall utilities of f and g is $U_i^r(f) - U_j^r(g), i, j = 1, 2$. As f is preferred to g when overall utility of f is larger than that of g, we will consider only positive $U_i^r(f) - U_i^r(g)$. Consider now the following functions:

$$\sigma(r) = \sum_{i=1}^{2} \sum_{j=1}^{2} \max(U_i^r(f) - U_j^r(g), 0);$$

$$\delta_{ij}(r) = \begin{cases} \dfrac{\max(U_i^r(f) - U_j^r(g), 0)}{|U_i^r(f) - U_j^r(g)|}, & \text{if } U_i^r(f) - U_j^r(g) \neq 0 \\ 0, & else \end{cases} \quad i, j = 1, 2.$$

$$\delta(r) = \sum_{i}^{2} \sum_{j}^{2} \delta_{ij}(r)$$

$\sigma(r)$ shows the sum of all positive differences between $U_1^r(f), U_2^r(f)$ and $U_1^r(g), U_2^r(g)$ and $\delta(r)$ shows the number of these differences. Consider now the quantity $\dfrac{\int_0^1 r\sigma(r)dr}{\int_0^1 r\delta(r)dr}$ as a weighted average of differences $U_i^r(f) - U_j^r(g), i, j = 1, 2$ where weights are their possibilities $r \in (0,1]$. Then the degree $Deg(f \succ_l g)$ is determined as follows:

$$Deg(f \succsim_l g) = \frac{\int_0^1 r\sigma(r)dr}{(u_{\max} - u_{\min})\int_0^1 r\delta(r)dr} \tag{10.27}$$

In other words, $Deg(f \succsim_l g)$ is computed as a percentage of a weighted average of differences $U_i^r(f) - U_j^r(g)$, $i, j = 1, 2$ with respect to $u_{max} - u_{min}$ being maximally possible difference (as for all $f, g \in A$ the inequality $U_i^r(f) - U_j^r(g) \leq u_{max} - u_{min}; i, j = 1, 2$ is satisfied). By other words, the closer the difference $U_i^r(f) - U_j^r(g)$ of the equally possible values of precise overall utilities of f and g to $u_{max} - u_{min}$ the higher the extent to which f is better than g is.

As it is shown in [60] the famous existing utility models are special cases of the proposed combined states-based fuzzy utility model.

10.3.4 *Solution of the problem*

The solution of the problem consists in determination of an optimal action $f^* \in A$ with $U(f^*) = \max\limits_{f \in A} \left\{ \int_\Omega u(f(s,h))d\eta \right\}$. The problem is solved as follows. At the first stage it becomes necessary to assign linguistic utility values $u(f(s_i, h_j))$ to every action $f \in A$ taken at a state of nature $s_i \in S$ when a DM's state is h_j. The second stage consists in construction of a FJP distribution P^l on Ω proceeding from partial information on marginal distributions over S and H which is represented by given fuzzy probabilities for all states except one. This requires constructing unknown fuzzy probability for each space [20, 24]. Given marginal distribution of fuzzy probabilities for all the states, it is needed to verify consistency, completeness and redundancy of this distribution [50]. Finally, on the base of fuzzy marginal distributions (for S and H) and information on dependence between states of nature $s \in S$ and a DM's states $h \in H$ it is needed to construct FJP distribution P^l on Ω.

At the third stage it is necessary to construct a fuzzy-valued bi-capacity $\eta(\cdot, \cdot)$ based on FJP P^l on Ω. For simplicity one can determine a fuzzy-valued bi-capacity as the difference of two fuzzy-valued capacities.

Next the problem of calculation of an overall utility $U(f)$ for every action $f \in A$ is solved by using formula (10.26). In (10.26) differences between fuzzy utilities $u(f(s,h))$ assigned at the first stage are multiplied on the base of the Zadeh's extension principle by the values of the fuzzy valued bi-capacity $\eta(\cdot,\cdot)$ constructed at the third stage.

Finally, an optimal action $f^* \in A$ as the action with the maximal fuzzy valued utility $U(f^*) = \max_{f \in A} \left\{ \int_\Omega u(f(s,h))d\eta \right\}$ is determined by comparing fuzzy overall utilities $U(f)$ for all $f \in A$ (see formula (10.27)).

10.4 Fuzzy economics and decision making

Tracing the development of economics since 19th century up to present days makes it evident that at its core there is a sequence of rather precise and mathematically sophisticated axiomatic theories. At the same time, there is always a noticeable and persistent gap between the economic reality and economic predictions derived from these theories.

The main reason for why economic theories have not been successful so far in modelling economic reality is the fact that these theories are formulated in terms of hard sciences characterized by their nature of preciseness.

As a complex multi-agent humanistic system, in Economics, motivations, intuition, human knowledge and human behaviour, such as perception, emotions and norms, play dominant roles. Consequently, real economical and socio-economical world problems are too complex to be translated into classical mathematical and bivalent logic languages, solved and interpreted in the language of the real world. The traditional modelling methodology (economics deals with models of economic reality) is perhaps not relevant or at least not powerful enough to satisfy the requirements of human reasoning and decision making activities. A new much more effective modelling language is needed to capture the economic reality. According to Prof. L. Zadeh, in general, Fuzzy logic-based modelling languages have higher power of cointension than their bivalent logic based counterparts and present the potential for playing an essential role in modelling economic, social and political systems.

The sheer complexity of causation in the economic arena mandates a fuzzy approach. We argue that many economic dynamical systems naturally become fuzzy due to the uncertain initial conditions and parameters.

We consider economic system as human centric and imperfect information based realistic multi-agent system with fuzzy-logic-based representation of the economic agents' behavior and with imprecise constraints. We use fuzzy "if-then" language and fuzzy differential equations for modeling the economic agents.

This study looks beyond the standard assumptions of economics that all people are similarly rational and self-interested. To be able to include motivation input variables of economic agents into their models, we created behavioral model of agents by using fuzzy If-Then rules.

Nowadays, adding norms and motivations to utility function has become an issue to economists and business people. They also recognized that something is missing in standard utility function and even in standard economic theory. Everything is not as simple as just profit or utility maximization under budget constraint. They recognized that during all these years they have ignored the most important thing: norms and motivations which actually directed the human nature.

It is obvious that these norms and motivations cannot be captured by statistical analysis, there are deeper and more subtle uncertain relationships between well-being and its determinants. We suggest fuzzy graph based approach to utility function construction. The proposed approach is consistent with the behavioral and the uncertainty paradigms of decision makers. Here we put emphasis on mathematical background rather than real case analysis.

Neoclassical assumptions regarding the opportunity and efficiency of economic agents are not realistic [9, 243, 638]. As George Akerlof argues, in New Classical macroeconomics the important element: motivation is missing– it fails to incorporate the norms of decision makers [9].

The more advanced macroeconomics interprets behavior of economical agents through preferences that include norms, which are people's views regarding how they, and others, should or should not behave. Although these preferences are a central feature of sociological theory, they have been ignored by majority of economists. Sociologists consider norms to be central to motivation; because people tend to live up to the views and principles they accept and are happy only when they can manage them. Daniel Kahneman and Amos Tversky [404] have studied people unwillingness to take favorable odds in small bets due to loss aversion. They explain that people have a mental frame, that makes them reluctant to take losses.

Unlike traditional neoclassical theory, assumptions are not fundamental to the construction of economic models in behavioural economics. The Herbert Simon tradition in behavioural economics maintains that intelligent behaviour need not produce the type of optimal or efficient behaviours predicted by traditional neoclassical theory. The behavioural model makes it possible to have multiple equilibria or a fuzzy set solution to the choice set afforded to economic agents in the fundamentally important domain of production. For this reason, the behavioural model can interpret important economic facts that contradict the analytical predictions of neoclassical economic theory (variety of complex outcomes in competitive equilibrium, is indicative of the substance of economic life.)

In a complex environment with a large number of heterogeneous interacting agents there is a high degree of uncertainty about their interaction and relevant information. Also agents will constantly try to find better representations of the perceived reality and will therefore experience and learn. We need a way of modelling the "mental models" of economic agents that operate within such an economic environment.

Main reasons why economic theories have not been successful in modelling economic reality is directly related with the subject of this study, i.e. these theories are formulated in terms of classical mathematics, bivalent logic and classical theory of additive measures. Human reasoning and decision making is based on high degrees of uncertainty (usually nonstatistical) and classical mathematics is not capable of expressing this kind of uncertainty. Human preferences for complex choices are not determined, in general, by the rules of additives measures.

As stated above, well known economists such as Akerlof, Kahneman, and Altman have advocated reformulation of economic models to include factors such as motivations and norms of agents that influence economic behaviour. However, to date, no comprehensive mathematical framework has been suggested for this economic paradigm.

This research attempts to model economic system as human centric and imperfect information based realistic multi-agent system with fuzzy-logic [824, 828, 842] based representation of economic agents behaviour.

British economist Shackle has argued since the late 1940s that probability theory, is not useful for capturing the nature of uncertainty in economics. He has suggested that uncertainty associated with actions with unknown outcomes should be expressed in terms of degrees of possibility rather than by probabilities [684].

C. Ponsard presented that fuzzy optimization makes it possible to consider that the objective or the constraint are fuzzy [620]. Fuzzy optimization accounts for either the imprecision of the utility function or the imprecision of budget constraint.

C. R. Barret *et al.* explored the problem of aggregation of ordinary fuzzy individual preferences into ordinary fuzzy social preferences [94]. S. Ovchinnikov *et al.* established existence of fuzzy models for strict preference, indifference and incomparability satisfying all classical properties [567]. Fuzzy individual and social preference relations based new solution concepts in group decision making, and presentation of new «soft» degrees of consensus are given by J. Kacprzyk *et al.* [401]. B. R. Munier put into question the expected utility hypothesis as a pattern of rational decision under risk or uncertainty [542].

A comparative review of the application of fuzzy sets theory in economics was conducted by A. Billot [115, 116]. There are also various papers (for example by J.G. Aluja, A. Kaufmann) where fuzzy microeconomics models were considered [73, 74, 422, 882].

Various simulations of different real world problems, including macro-economical problems described by fuzzy differential equations, among which there are supply and demand economic problem, national economy model etc were considered by J. J. Buckley, L.J. Jowers [132].

Optimal control of complex dynamic economical system was considered in a series of works (for example, by Silberberg and Suen, by Zhukovsky and Salukvadze etc) [332, 353, 680, 689, 879].

Fuzzy control for stabilizing economic processes to implement stabilization strategies in a user-friendly way, by means of a linguistically expressed algorithm is suggested in paper by V. Georgescu [305].

In recent years, a great number of papers and several books have explored the use of fuzzy logic as a tool for designing intelligent systems in business, finance, management and economics [36, 124, 181, 646, 672]. These books present recent progress in the application of constituents of Soft Computing (SC) methodologies, in particular neural networks, fuzzy logic, chaos etc. The book [36] highlights some of the recent developments in practical applications of SC in business and economics.

Economy as complex systems is composed of a number of agents interacting in distributed mode. Advances in distributed artificial intelligence, intelligent agent theory and soft computing technology make it possible for these agents as components of complex system to interact, cooperate, contend and coordinate in order to form global behavior of economic system. Recently, there has been great interest in development of Intelligent Agents (IA) and Multi-agent systems in economics, in particular in decision analysis and control of economic systems [477, 482, 717, 775].

It should be noted that economic agents often deal with incomplete, contradictory, missing and inaccurate data and knowledge [35, 48, 243, 403]. Furthermore, the agents have to make decision in uncertain situations, i.e. in the real world multi-agent economical systems function within an environment of uncertainty and imprecision.

Two main approaches to multi-agent economic system exist: conventional concept and alternative concept. In conventional concept of multi-agent distributed intelligent systems the main idea is granulation of functions and powers from a central authority to local authorities. In these terms, economy is composed of several agents, such as firms, plants and enterprises that can perform their own functions independently, and, therefore, have information, authority and power necessary to perform only their own function. These intelligent agents can communicate together to work, cooperate and be coordinated in order to reach a common goal of the economy [35, 302, 403].

An alternative concept of a multi-agent distributed intelligent system with cooperation and competition among agents, distinguished from the conventional approach by the following: each intelligent agent acts fully autonomously; each intelligent agent proposes full solution of the problem (not only for own partial problem); each agent has access to full available input information; total solution of the problem is determined as proposal of one of the parallel functioning agents on the basis of a competition procedure (not by coordinating and integrating partial solutions of agents, often performed iteratively); agents' cooperation produces desired behavior of the system; cooperation and competition acts in the systems are performed simultaneously (not sequentially) [42, 275, 342].

A similar idea of decomposition of the overall system into agents with cooperation and competition among them is implemented in several papers [395, 728, 867].

Zhang proposed a way to synthesize final solutions in systems where different agents use different inexact reasoning models to solve a problem. In this approach a number of expert systems propose solutions to a given problem. These solutions are then synthesized using ego-altruistic approach [430].

Let us consider conventional approach [46, 48]. We will mainly consider systems with so-called "fan" structure in which the economic system consists of N agents in the lower level and one element in the higher level (called center).

The state of *i-th* agent ($i \in [1:N]$) is characterized by vector x_i. The vector x_i should meet the local constraints

$$x_i \in X_i \subset E^{n_i} \tag{10.28}$$

where X_i - is a set in n_i dimensional Euclidean space. A specificity of these hierarchical systems is information aggregation at the higher level.

This means that the only agent of the higher level, the center, is not concerned with individual values of variables x_i, but some indexes evaluating elements' activities (states) produced from those values. Let's denote the vector of such indexes as:

$$F_i(x_i) = (f_{i1}(x_i), ..., f_{im_i}(x_i)), i \in [1 : N].$$ (10.29)

The state of the center is characterized by vector F_0, the components of which are the indexes of the agents of the lower level:

$$F_0 = (F_1, ..., F_N), \text{ where } F_i = F_i(x_i)$$ (10.30)

Commonly, the decision making process implies the existence of a person making the final decision at the higher level.

$$H_0(F_1, ..., F_N) \to \max;$$ (10.31)

$$H(F_1, ..., F_N) \geq b;$$ (10.32)

$$F_i \in S_i^F = \left\{ F_i / F_i = F_i(x_i), x_i \in P_i^X \left(\text{or } x_i \in R_i^X \right) \right\},$$ (10.33)

where $P_i^x(R_i^x)$ is the set of effective (semi-effective) solutions of the problem

$$\Phi_i(x_i) = (\varphi_{i1}(x_i), ..., \varphi_{ik_i}(x_i)) \to {}'\max';$$ (10.34)

$$x_i \in X_i$$ (10.35)

We suggest two methods to solution to (10.31)-(10.33)

a) Non-iterative method

Non-iterative optimization method includes three main phases. At the first stage, the local problems of vector optimization are dealt. The solutions of these problems are sets P_i^X and sets $S_i^F(Q_i^F)$ or any approximations of these sets. The second stage implies the implementation of the center's task (10.31)-(10.33) as result of which we get the optimal values of the agents' criteria $F^* = (F_1^* ... , F_N^*)$. Vector F_i^*

is then passed to i-th agent which implements the third stage by solving the problem:

$$F_i(x_i) = F_i^*; x_i \in X_i \qquad (10.36)$$

Solution of (10.36) represents local variables x_i^*. In case of existing several solutions, one is selected based on preferences of the i-th agent.

Note that the center receives the information only about the indexes F_i, not about the vector x_i. Because the dimension of F_i is usually significantly less than the dimension of vector x_i, it considerably reduce amount of data circulating between the levels.

b) Iterative method

Let $\Omega_i \subset E^{k_i}$ - is a subset in the space of criteria. Let's call the elements $\omega_i \in \Omega_i$ from this subset as coordinating signals.

Definition 10.19 [48]. The function $\overline{F}_i(\omega_i) = (\overline{f}_{i1}(\omega_i), ..., \overline{f}_{im_i}(\omega_i))$ is named a coordinating function if the following conditions are satisfied:

a) For $\forall \omega_i \in \Omega_i$ there exists such element $\overline{x}_i(\omega_i) \in R_i^x$, for which $\overline{F}_i(\omega_i) = F_i(\overline{x}_i(\omega_i))$;

b) Inversely, for any element x_i^0 - of subset P_i^X, there exists such coordinating signal $\omega_i^0 \in \Omega_i$, for which $\overline{F}_i(\omega_i^0) = F_i(x_i^0)$.

From the definition above, it follows that the problem (10.31)-(10.33) is equivalent to the problem given below:

$$\left. \begin{aligned} &H_0(\overline{F}_1(\omega_1), ..., \overline{F}_N(\omega_N)) \to \max; \\ &H(\overline{F}_i(\omega_i), ..., \overline{F}_N(\omega_N)) \geq b; \\ &\omega_i \in \Omega_i, i \in [1:N]. \end{aligned} \right\} \qquad (10.37)$$

Thus, the variables of problem (10.37) are coordinating signals ω_i, defined on the set of acceptable coordinating signals Ω_i. The rationale for such transformation is simpler structure of set Ω_i compared to the set of effective elements (points). Choosing among different coordinating functions $\overline{F}_i(\omega_i)$ and different solution algorithms of problem (10.37) it is possible to construct a large number of iterative coordinating algorithms [46, 47]. It can be shown that the known decomposition algorithms such as Dantzig-Wolf algorithm [215], Kornai-Liptak algorithm [445], or the algorithm based on the interaction prediction principle [526] are special cases of the proposed algorithm [48].

The alternative approach is considered in [15, 36, 42, 275].

10.5 Type-2 fuzzy clustering

In many real-world problems involving pattern recognition, system identification and modeling, control, decision making, and forecasting of time-series, available data are quite often of uncertain nature. An interesting alternative is to employ type-2 fuzzy sets, which augment fuzzy models with expressive power to develop models, which efficiently capture the factor of uncertainty. The three-dimensional membership functions of type-2 fuzzy sets offer additional degrees of freedom that make it possible to directly and more effectively account for model's uncertainties. Type-2 fuzzy logic systems developed with the aid of evolutionary optimization forms a useful modeling tool subsequently resulting in a collection of efficient "If-Then" rules.

10.5.1. *State-of-the-art*

During the past decades, intelligent technologies have been emerged as an interesting and relevant alternative to solve many real-world problems in forecasting, decision making, control, and decision analysis. Among these approaches, Soft Computing encompassing fuzzy logic, neural networks, and evolutionary optimization methods, has been viewed as an interesting and useful alternative. Fuzzy logic systems (i.e., type-1 fuzzy logic systems) have been successfully used in various applications.

To design of "ordinary" fuzzy logic systems, knowledge of human experts along with available data are utilized for the construction of fuzzy rules and membership functions based on available linguistic or numeric information [582]. However, in many cases available information or data are associated with various forms of uncertainty which should be taken into account. The uncertainty can be captured by using higher order and/or higher type fuzzy sets. In this regard, type-2 fuzzy sets have been considered as a viable conceptual and algorithmic vehicle to design intelligent systems. In many cases reported in the literature, it was demonstrated that type-2 fuzzy sets contribute to the robustness and stability of the resulting constructs (namely, models, inference schemes, classifiers, etc.) [169, 374, 394, 413, 414, 415, 417].

The concept and properties of type-2 fuzzy sets were originally introduced by Zadeh [851] and were further pursued by others [413, 414, 417, 470, 513]. Recently type-2 fuzzy sets have been applied to several areas including control of mobile robots [497, 787], decision making [169, 801], forecasting of time-series [415], identification of nonlinear plants [759], diagnosis [374], scheduling [394], and others.

In this applied context, one should make a remark that the use of type-2 fuzzy logic systems usually increases the computational complexity in comparison with the level of computational overhead encountered in type-1 systems due to the use and optimization of three-dimensional membership functions describing type-2 fuzzy sets [521]. Given that the use of type-2 fuzzy logic system could provide a significant level of improvement of performance, it is worth accepting the increased computational complexity associated with their usage [373].

In [373] authors focused on interval type-2 fuzzy clustering problems by studying an extension of the commonly known Fuzzy C-Means (FCM algorithm). In this research, the uncertainty becomes associated with various values of the fuzzifier parameter m that controls the amount of fuzziness present in the final partition, see also [730]. In [142] the author suggests a method for accelerating fuzzy clustering by using gradient-based neural network training algorithms. Authors of [284, 658] apply evolutionary algorithms for generation of clusters. In [571] discussed was an important question of determination of effective upper and lower bounds of the fuzzifier parameter m.

Some studies appeared recently on type-2 fuzzy inference systems [356] or, being more general, on type-2 fuzzy neural networks and their efficient training algorithms [164, 523]. Very limited research has been realized on applications of type-2 fuzzy sets in the area of fuzzy rule extraction. In [759] type-2 fuzzy logic system cascaded with neural network is presented to handle uncertainty with dynamical optimal learning. The considered type-2 fuzzy neural system consists of type-2 fuzzy sets forming the antecedent part while a two-layer interval neural network is used to form the consequent part. One could agree with the authors of [341] that from the conceptual standpoint, one can view the publication [759], in spite of some of its mathematical flaws, as the first study on type-2 fuzzy neural network aimed at uncertainty handling.

In spite of intensive developments of the theory and design methods for type-2 fuzzy logic systems [164, 356, 368, 413, 414, 513, 523], there has been a fairly limited progress in the area of type-2 fuzzy rule extraction, tuning of parameters of membership functions used in the rules, merging type-2 fuzzy logic system with other components of Soft Computing, namely, with neural networks, evolutionary computing, and type-2 inference schemes. These are visible shortcomings which have suppressed pursuits in the realm of type-2 fuzzy modeling.

10.5.2. *Type-2 fuzzy clustering and rule extraction*

Our aim is to develop a design methodology and discuss ensuring algorithmic aspects arising within the realm of designing of type-2 DE fuzzy neural networks. More specifically, we

(1) generate type-2 fuzzy "If-Then" rule base from data by making use of clustering augmented by the mechanisms of evolutionary optimization (in this study, we confine ourselves to the optimization framework of Differential Evolution (DE)), and

(2) adjust (optimize) the parameters of the initial rule-base on the basis of a type-2 fuzzy neural inference system using the DE optimization (DEO, for short).

Given n input-output pairs of data $\{\mathbf{X}_1 / Y_1, \mathbf{X}_2 / Y_2, ..., \mathbf{X}_n / Y_n\}$ and the required accuracy of the model ($\varepsilon \geq 0$), we form the minimal number of the rules and parameters of the type-2 membership functions (for instance, 6 parameters describing each interval valued triangular membership function described here as $T(LL, LR, ML, MR, RL, RR)$ for input and output terms) so that the error function $Err = \sum_{i=1,n} \|y(\mathbf{X}_i) - Y_i\|$

(where $y(\mathbf{X})$ is the inference system's numeric output for any given input data vector $\mathbf{X}$ of dimension s: $\mathbf{X} = [x_1 \, x_2 \ldots x_s]^{\mathrm{T}}$) satisfies the inequality $Err < \varepsilon$. The model output will be obtained on the basis of the inferencing from the following "If-Then" rules:

$$R^i : \text{If } x_1 \text{ is } \tilde{A}_1^i \text{ and } x_2 \text{ is } \tilde{A}_2^i \text{ and} \ldots x_s \text{ is } \tilde{A}_s^i \text{ Then } y \text{ is } \tilde{B}^i, \quad (10.38)$$

where x_j $(j = \overline{1,s})$ and y are input and output variables, respectively; $\tilde{A}_j^i$, $\tilde{B}^i$ are antecedent and consequent type-2 fuzzy sets, respectively.

Fuzzy clustering is a well-established paradigm used to generate the initial type-2 fuzzy "If-Then" model. When dealing with fuzzy clustering [373], there are several essential parameters whose values need to be decided upon in advance. We can think of uncertainty, which is inherently associated with the selection of the specific numeric values of these parameters. In the FCM-like family of fuzzy clustering, the fuzzification coefficient (fuzzifier) plays a visible role as it directly translates into the shape (geometry) of resulting fuzzy clusters. Let us recall that for the values of "m" close to 1, the membership functions become very close to the characteristic functions of sets whereas higher values of "m" (say, over 3 or 4) result in "spiky" membership functions.

The type-2 fuzzy clustering may be formulated as follows (for simplicity, we consider here interval fuzzy clustering). n data vectors $P = \{\mathbf{p}_1, \mathbf{p}_2, \ldots, \mathbf{p}_n\}$ are given. We partition the data P into c fuzzy clusters so that the following objective function is minimized:

$$J_{\tilde{m}} = \sum_{i=1}^{n} \sum_{j=1}^{c} \tilde{u}_{ij}^{\tilde{m}} \left\| \mathbf{p}_i - \tilde{\mathbf{v}}_j \right\|, \quad (10.39)$$

where $\left\| * \right\|$ is Euclidean distance.

The minimization of (10.39) is carried out under the two "standard" requirements commonly imposed on the partition matrix: (1) the clusters are non-empty and there are more than a single cluster; (2) the sum of membership degrees of any data point is equal to 1. Here the fuzzifier $\widetilde{m}$ represents interval (type-1 fuzzy) value ($[m_1, m_2]$); $\widetilde{\mathbf{v}}_j$ is the prototype of the j-th cluster generated by fuzzy clustering; $\widetilde{u}_{ij}$ is the membership degree of the i-th data belonging to the j-th cluster represented by the prototype $\widetilde{\mathbf{v}}_j$.

The choice of the number of clusters can be realized on a basis of some cluster validity criterion, like the one suggested in [178]. Here, we adopt the following validity measure [178] for type-2 fuzzy clustering:

$$V(u,c) = \frac{1}{n}\sum_{k=1}^{n}\max(u_{ij}) - \frac{1}{K}\sum_{i=1}^{c-1}\sum_{j=i+1}^{c}\left[\underbrace{\frac{1}{n}\sum_{k=1}^{n}\min(u_{ik}, u_{jk})}_{i}\right] \qquad (10.40)$$

where $K = \sum_{i=1}^{c-1} i$.

The number of clusters can be defined on the basis of the maximal value of V, which is picked up for different values of $\widetilde{m}$. The minimum number of clusters and, therefore, the number of the fuzzy rules themselves is very important for interpretability reasons. However, this number may need to be increased based on the required accuracy (expressed via the MSE performance index).

Clustering is completed through the minimization of the values of the objective function $J_{\widetilde{m}}$ with the fuzzifier being considered as a fuzzy (interval) number $\widetilde{m} = [m_1, m_2]$. The most widely used clustering is that of the Fuzzy C-Means (FCM) [169, 373] due to its efficiency and simplicity. Standard FCM is an iterative procedure that leads to a local minimum of the objective function (10.39).

Based on the experimental work reported in [571] we reformulate the problem (10.38) as:

$$J_{m1} = \sum_{i=1}^{n}\sum_{j=1}^{c}u_{ij}^{m_1}\left\|\mathbf{p}_i - \mathbf{v}_j^{(1)}\right\| \to \min,$$

$$J_{m2} = \sum_{i=1}^{n} \sum_{j=1}^{c} u_{ij}^{m_2} \left\| \mathbf{p}_i - \mathbf{v}_j^{(2)} \right\| \to \min, \qquad (10.41)$$

subject to constraints:

$$0 < \sum_{i=1}^{n} u_{ij} < n \ \ (j = 1, 2, ..., c) \text{ and } \sum_{j=1}^{c} u_{ij} = 1 \ (i = 1, 2, ..., n).$$

The vector $\tilde{\mathbf{v}}_i$ is formed as:

$$\tilde{\mathbf{v}}_i = [\min(\mathbf{v}_i^{(1)}, \mathbf{v}_{Ind_i}^{(2)}), \max(\mathbf{v}_i^{(1)}, \mathbf{v}_{Ind_i}^{(2)})], \qquad (10.42)$$

where $Ind_i = \arg\min_j \left\| \mathbf{v}_i^{(1)}, \mathbf{v}_j^{(2)} \right\|$. The conclusion is based on the result that the change in the location of the prototypes associated with a change of the values of m is of monotonic character. The above assumption allows to replace (10.39) by (10.41) and significantly reduce computational burden when searching for cluster centers using different optimization methods. As shown in [571] the meaningful range for m is [1.4, 2.6].

In [373], the authors presented a interval type-2 fuzzy version of the FCM. However, gradient-based optimization methods (such as the FCM itself) exhibit here some disadvantages. One of significant drawbacks is that they may not produce a global minimum but instead could get stuck in some local minimum. On the other hand, the standard iterative scheme may not be applicable directly to the considered problem, especially when various distance functions other than the Euclidean one are being used. As pointed out in [588], a better approach could be to consider a population-based algorithm such as genetic algorithm, DE, or PSO. In this work we use DEO – a simple, yet powerful global optimizer. An illustrative example of the clustering problem is shown in Fig. 10.1. There is a collection of two-dimensional data with clearly visible four clusters. The data points are separated into 4 clusters. Fig.10.1 (a) shows the clusters found by the standard FCM with m=2. Fig.10.1 (b) shows type-2 fuzzy clustering result for the same problem. In Fig. 10.1(b) the squares around the cluster centers, shown by cross-signs (×), incorporate the cluster centers found for a variety of m within the range [1.05, 9.0]; the clusters found with $m=2$ are connected with the thin dotted line. It should be noted that, following our experiments, DE converges more successfully than the standard FCM within the considered range of m. It can be seen from Fig.10.1 (a) and (b) that in the case when $m_1 = m_2$, i.e. for type-1 FCM the cluster centers are located within the bounds of the cluster squares obtained by type-2 FCM. At the same time, the cluster squares allows capturing more uncertainty in data than one-point cluster centers. Even for narrower ranges of m, say $m = [1.4, 2.6]$ DE as a global search algorithm is expected to be more advantageous that standard FCM for the case of large number of highly-dimensional data vectors. To show this, we run the following experiment. We generate 1,000 data vectors of dimension 10 on the basis of 7 original vectors C1, C2, C3, C4, C5, C6, C7 as follows (Table 10.2).

$$p_{ik} = C_{((i-1)\%7+1),k} + 1.5 \cdot (\text{Rand}() - 0.5); i = 1, 2, ..., 1000;$$

$k = 1, 2, ..., 10$, where Rand() is a random number drawn from the uniform distribution [0,1] and % is the operation of determining a remainder of integer division.

Table 10.2. Data vectors

j	1	2	3	4	5	6	7	8	9	10
$C_1=$	1.0	2.0	3.0	4.0	5.0	4.0	3.0	2.0	1.0	2.0
$C_2=$	2.0	7.0	8.0	3.0	7.0	8.0	4.0	7.0	8.0	5.0
$C_3=$	1.0	1.0	1.5	1.0	1.0	1.5	1.0	1.0	1.0	1.0
$C_4=$	4.0	6.0	7.0	5.0	8.0	3.0	5.0	4.0	9.0	9.0
$C_5=$	2.0	7.5	8.0	3.0	7.5	8.0	4.0	7.0	8.0	4.5
$C_6=$	1.0	1.0	1.0	1.0	1.0	2.0	1.0	1.0	1.0	1.0
$C_7=$	1.0	6.0	3.0	3.0	5.0	5.0	2.0	6.0	6.0	8.0

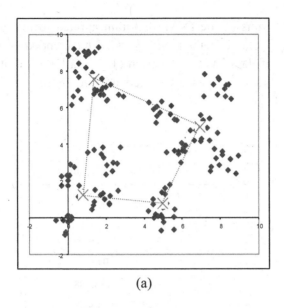

(a)

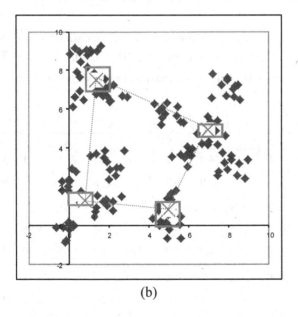

(b)

Fig. 10.1. Clustering results produced by the FCM (a) and the DE-based type-2 fuzzy clustering (b)

Consecutive 5 runs of the FCM algorithm applied to the generated 1,000 for finding 7 cluster centers with $m = 2.5$ have ended up with the following values of the objective function (10.39) after 1,000 iterations (at which point the FCM has converged and no more iterations are required, Table 10.3):

Table 10.3. Objective function values

Experiment	Objective function ($J_{m=2.5}$)
1	88.148
2	96.902
3	84.988
4	94.693
5	118.788
6	84.988

The application of the global search DE algorithm (ps=200) allowed us to minimize the objective function (10.40) down to $J_{m=2.5} = 79.076$. The clusters found by the DE based clustering are shown below:

Table 10.4. Fuzzy clusters

J	1	2	3	4	5	6	7	8	9	10
$\mathbf{v}_1$	1	1.95	2.98	4.01	4.97	3.98	3	2.01	1	1.98
$\mathbf{v}_2$	1.98	7.05	7.98	2.99	6.99	7.97	4	6.96	7.94	5.01
$\mathbf{v}_3$	1.99	7.46	8.02	2.99	7.48	7.96	4	6.96	8.06	4.5
$\mathbf{v}_4$	3.99	5.97	6.99	4.95	8.01	3	4.95	3.99	8.98	8.98
$\mathbf{v}_5$	0.99	5.99	3.01	2.99	4.99	4.99	2.01	5.99	6	8
$\mathbf{v}_6$	0.99	0.99	1.49	0.99	0.99	1.5	1	0.99	1.01	1
$\mathbf{v}_7$	1	0.99	1.01	0.99	0.99	1.98	0.99	0.98	0.99	0.99

Note that the actual minimum value of the objective function for this example (found by the optimization with initial cluster centers set to the original 7 data vectors instead of random numbers) is approximately 77.7.

The parameters to be optimized by the DEO when minimizing the objective function are the centers of the clusters, $\mathbf{v}_i^{(1)}, \mathbf{v}_i^{(2)}$, $i = 1, 2, ..., c$. The DE-based clustering algorithm can be formally described as follows:

1. Set the number of clusters $c = 2$ (start with the minimal number of clusters, that is $c = 2$).

2. Compute cluster centers for m_1: $\mathbf{v}_i^{(1)}$ ($i = 1, 2, ..., c$).

2.1. Create a population of random solutions (population size is ps), i.e., cluster centers $\mathbf{v}_i^{(1)}$: $P = \{\mathbf{S}_1, \mathbf{S}_2, ..., \mathbf{S}_{ps}\}$ (Each $\mathbf{S}_j (j = 1, 2, ..., ps)$ represent a combination of cluster centers for given data).

2.2. Randomly select 4 different trial vectors from P: $\mathbf{S}_{r1}, \mathbf{S}_{r2}$, $\mathbf{S}_{r3}, \mathbf{S}_{r4}$, $1 \leq r_1 \neq r_2 \neq r_3 \neq r_4 \leq ps$.

2.3. Compute the new trial solution as $\mathbf{S}_n = (\mathbf{S}_{r1} - \mathbf{S}_{r2})f + \mathbf{S}_{r3}$.

2.4. Set the cost function to J_{m1}. Compute the cost value of $\mathbf{S}_n$. If Cost($\mathbf{S}_n$)<Cost($\mathbf{S}_{r4}$), replace $\mathbf{S}_{r4}$ by $\mathbf{S}_n$.

2.5. If the maximal number of generations has not been reached, go to Step 2.2, else go to Step 3.

2.6. Find the solution with the minimum cost value, $\mathbf{S} = \mathbf{S}_{best}$, where Cost($\mathbf{S}_{best}$)$\leq$Cost($\mathbf{S}_r$), $r = 1, 2, ..., ps$. Retrieve optimal cluster centers $\mathbf{v}_i^{(1)}$ from $\mathbf{S}_{best}$.

3. Compute cluster centers for m_2: $\mathbf{v}_i^{(2)}$ ($i = 1, 2, ..., c$).

3.1. Create the population of random solutions (cluster centers $\mathbf{v}_i^{(2)}$): $P = \{\mathbf{S}_1, \mathbf{S}_2, ..., \mathbf{S}_{ps}\}$.

3.2. Randomly select 4 different trial vectors from P: $\mathbf{S}_{r1}, \mathbf{S}_{r2}, \mathbf{S}_{r3}, \mathbf{S}_{r4}$, $1 \leq r_1 \neq r_2 \neq r_3 \neq r_4 \leq ps$.

3.3. Compute the new trial solution as $\mathbf{S}_n = (\mathbf{S}_{r1} - \mathbf{S}_{r2})f + \mathbf{S}_{r3}$.

3.4. Set the cost function to J_{m2}. Compute the cost value of $\mathbf{S}_n$. If $\text{Cost}(\mathbf{S}_n)<\text{Cost}(\mathbf{S}_{r4})$, replace $\mathbf{S}_{r4}$ by $\mathbf{S}_n$.

3.5. If the number of generations has not reached go to Step 3.2, else go to Step 4.

3.6. Find the solution with minimum cost value $\mathbf{S} = \mathbf{S}_{best}$, where Cost $(\mathbf{S}_{best})\leq\text{Cost}(\mathbf{S}_r)$, $r = 1, 2, ..., ps$. Retrieve optimal cluster centers $\mathbf{v}_i^{(2)}$ from $\mathbf{S}_{best}$.

4. Check if the validity criterion $V = \min(V_{m1},V_{m2})$ attains higher value than a predefined threshold (e.g., 0.6). If yes, then go to Step 5, otherwise increase c by one ($c = c+1$) and repeat from Step 2.

5. On the basis of optimal cluster centers $\mathbf{v}_i^{(1)}$ and $\mathbf{v}_i^{(2)}$ form the interval cluster centers: $\tilde{\mathbf{v}}_i = [\min(\mathbf{v}_i^{(1)},\mathbf{v}_{Ind_i}^{(2)}), \quad \max(\mathbf{v}_i^{(1)},\mathbf{v}_{Ind_i}^{(2)})]$, where $Ind_i = \arg\min_j\left\|\mathbf{v}_i^{(1)},\mathbf{v}_j^{(2)}\right\|$.

6. Stop

Examples

Estimation of a non-linear model. As a simple, yet highly illustrative example, let us consider a certain numeric mapping as shown in Figure 10.2 (dashed curve). Assume that no explicit model is available – just only a few rules are known that are provided by an expert. Other numerical input-output data that describe the relationship are uncertain or contain noise. We consider that any numeric data is affected by noise and comes with a level of error of up to 10%. In this case, an available datum v can be adequately expressed as a certain interval being reflective of the associated error, that is [0.95v, 1.05v].

Let us assume that the linguistic rules coming from the expert are of the form:

    IF X **IS** "VERY LOW" **THEN** Y **IS** "LOW"
    IF X **IS** "LOW" **THEN** Y **IS** "HIGH"
    IF X **IS** "HIGH" **THEN** Y **IS** "VERY LOW"
    IF X **IS** "VERY HIGH" **THEN** Y **IS** "VERY HIGH"

Here X and Y represent input and output variables, respectively. X takes values from type-2 fuzzy termset: A={"VERY LOW"(X), "LOW"(X), "HIGH"(X), "VERY HIGH"(X)} and Y takes value from type-1 fuzzy termset B={"VERY LOW"(Y), "LOW"(Y), "HIGH"(Y), "VERY HIGH"(Y)}.

The initial input type-2 fuzzy terms in the form $\tilde{A}_i = [[LL_i, LR_i], [ML_i, MR_i], [RL_i, RR_i]]$ and output type-1 fuzzy terms in form $B_i = [L_i, ML_i, MR_i, R_i]$ are generated manually by help of the expert. The initial terms can be drawn by precisiation of the available linguistic information using the considered type-1 (ordinary trapezoid) and type-2 (type-2 trapezoid) fuzzy number representation. The construction of type-2 fuzzy terms is done on the basis of some hints about the width of FOU of type-2 membership function generated by the expert.

The initial defuzzified input/output relationship of the system produced on the basis of expert given rules and initial termsets is shown in Fig. 10.2.

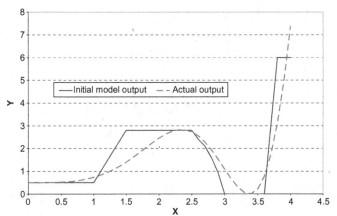

Fig. 10.2. Input/output relationship produced by T2FINN with the use of initial rules (termset) vis-à-vis the actual curve

The final membership functions of A and B obtained after the network has been trained with the use of the DE optimization come in the form:

For X:

VERY LOW = [[0.00, 0.30], [2.09, 2.12], [3.16, 4.00]],

LOW = [[3.57, 3.82], [4.35, 4.54], [4.84, 5.00]],

HIGH = [[1.02, 2.60], [2.60, 2.69], [2.70, 2.95]],
VERY HIGH = [[1.42, 1.77], [2.03, 2.33], [2.72, 3.12]].

For Y:
VERY LOW = [[2.03, 2.03], [4.65, 5.30], [7.81, 7.81]],
LOW = [[0.00, 0.00], [0.01, 0.56], [1.84, 1.84]],
HIGH = [[3.57, 3.57], [4.07, 8.08], [10.00, 10.00]],
VERY HIGH = [[1.85, 1.85], [3.58, 5.06], [7.80, 7.80]].

Fig.10.3 includes the comparison of the actual output of the system being identified and the output generated by the proposed T2FINN. The MSE obtained by the DE learning is $4.71 \cdot 10^{-4}$ (for comparison, the MSE obtained by experiments with similar system (the same number of rules and dimensions of term-sets) based on type-1 logic is $1.03 \cdot 10^{-3}$).

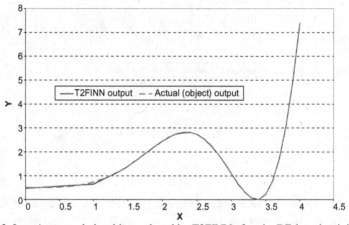

Fig.10.3. Input/output relationship produced by T2FINN after the DE-based training

Nonlinear System Identification. This benchmark problem for nonlinear system identification was taken from [178]. The dynamic system is governed by the following equation:

$$x(k) = g(x(k-1), x(k-2)) + u(k) \qquad (10.43)$$

where

$$g(x(k-1), x(k-2)) = \frac{x(k-1)x(k-2)(x(k-1)-0.5)}{1 + x^2(k-1) + x^2(k-2)}. \qquad (10.44)$$

The goal is to construct the T2FINN for the non-linear system (10.43)-(10.44). 200 input-output data pairs were used for training and 200 others for testing.

Applying the DE-based clustering, we obtain the following 5 rules

IF $x(k-2)$ **IS** A1 **AND** $x(k-1)$ **IS** B1 **THEN** $x(k)$ **IS** C1
IF $x(k-2)$ **IS** A2 **AND** $x(k-1)$ **IS** B2 **THEN** $x(k)$ **IS** C2
IF $x(k-2)$ **IS** A3 **AND** $x(k-1)$ **IS** B3 **THEN** $x(k)$ **IS** C3
IF $x(k-2)$ **IS** A4 **AND** $x(k-1)$ **IS** B4 **THEN** $x(k)$ **IS** C4
IF $x(k-2)$ **IS** A5 **AND** $x(k-1)$ **IS** B5 **THEN** $x(k)$ **IS** C5

The progression of the DE optimization is quantified in terms of the values of the MSE reported in successive iterations, see Fig. 10.4. It becomes noticeable that the reduction of the error is quite fast and the optimization proceeds smoothly without any significant oscillations.

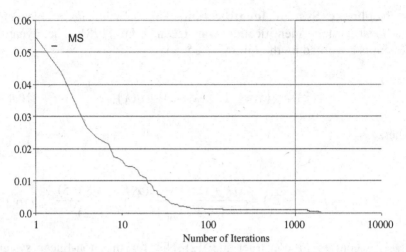

Fig. 10.4. Minimized performance index in successive iterations of the DE optimization

The type-2 fuzzy terms obtained after the training are the following:
Type-2 fuzzy terms for x(k-2):
A1 = [[-29.46, -14.39], [-3.38, -3.38], [4.50, 40.91]]
A2 = [[-13.40, -9.95], [-9.89, 9.39], [9.39, 16.29]]
A3 = [[-6.12, -0.58], [1.84, 3.04], [8.37, 10.12]]
A4 = [[-12.70, -1.69], [2.93, 3.50], [6.60, 7.09]]
A5 = [[-17.17, -15.70], [-2.12, -2.03], [-2.03, 5.40]]

Type-2 fuzzy terms for x(k-1):
B1 = [[-20.98, -20.72], [3.18, 4.91], [35.59, 38.01]]
B2 = [[-16.90, -1.38], [-0.83, 2.19], [2.43, 6.73]]
B3 = [[-17.95, -8.29], [-2.78, -1.58], [0.10, 1.59]]
B4 = [[-2.03, -1.37], [-0.95, 1.40], [1.41, 1.52]]
B5 = [[-8.96, -3.84], [-3.57, -0.30], [10.84, 15.49]]

Type-2 fuzzy terms for x(k):
C1 = [[-6.77, -6.77], [-6.74, -1.86], [15.46, 15.46]]

C2 = [[-5.92, -5.92], [-2.01, 9.87], [13.53, 13.53]]
C3 = [[-10.28, -10.28], [-0.81, 2.08], [22.32, 22.32]]
C4 = [[-15.85, -15.85], [-4.91, 2.10], [9.80, 9.80]]
C5 = [[-19.73, -19.73], [-14.11, -1.69], [8.39, 8.39]]

For further visualization, the obtained FOUs for the type-2 fuzzy terms A1, A2, A3, A4, and A5 after training are illustrated in Fig. 10.5.

The values of the MSE obtained on the training data and on the testing data were equal to $2.11 \cdot 10^{-4}$ and $2.84 \cdot 10^{-4}$, respectively. For comparison, as reported in [178], the MSE for the same problem was $1.90 \cdot 10^{-4}$ (training data) and $3.80 \cdot 10^{-4}$ (testing data). For the type-1 fuzzy based system, the best result obtained for the same problem was $9.50 \cdot 10^{-4}$ on the testing data. All the results are concisely summarized in Table 10.5.

The comparison of the actual response of the system and the output of the model is included in Fig. 10.6 (the results are shown for testing data).

Table 10.5. MSE values produced by different versions of the network

	MSE (train data)	MSE (test data)
Fuzzy Model [178] (type-1)	$1.90 \cdot 10^{-4}$	$3.80 \cdot 10^{-4}$
Type-1 FINN	$5.40 \cdot 10^{-4}$	$9.50 \cdot 10^{-4}$
Type-2 FINN	$2.11 \cdot 10^{-4}$	$2.84 \cdot 10^{-4}$

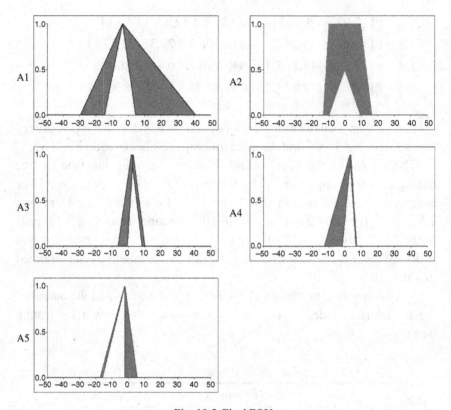

Fig. 10.5. Final FOUs

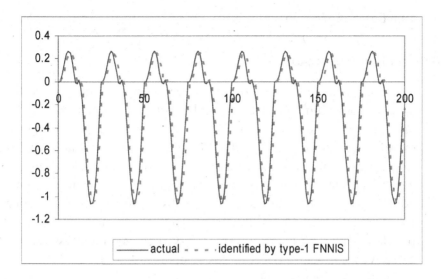

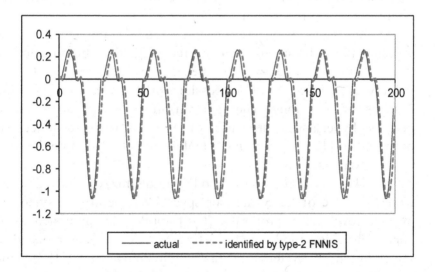

Fig. 10.6. The actual system response and the output of the model

10.6 Fuzzy regression analysis

10.6.1 *State-of-the-art*

Complex systems, such as industry, economy, finance, marketing, and ecology function in the real world in an environment of uncertainty and imprecision. Such systems require decisions based on human thinking and judgment and involve human–machine interactions. In such environments we often cannot obtain exact numerical data about a system. The nature of information about complex systems with vagueness is frequently fuzzy. In general fuzzy regression seems intuitively more adequate for real life problems [587, 714]. Therefore, fuzzy regression analysis is more effective for modeling of complex systems [399, 587, 714].

In the pioneering work [715] in this field the authors use Zadeh's extension principle [828], a-level procedure, interval arithmetic, and linear programming techniques to develop a fuzzy linear regression analysis. A modification of this approach for nonlinear case is reported in [93].

A simple fuzzy regression model introducing the corresponding distances is considered in [234]. Minimization of these distances in fuzzy number space with respect to the unknown parameters of regression models leads to solving systems of equations. The generalization of this approach to general hyperplanes and use of Hausdorff-like distances is proposed in [12, 93]. The methodology for global approximation of fuzzy data is given in [84].

In [647] linear regression model fitting fuzzy-valued data by using a metric of fuzzy number space by integral of distance of every a-level set is proposed. [648] applies this approach to S-curve regression model and creating of this model is reduced to the solution of systems of linear equations. In [764] genetic algorithm is used to classify the input data for increasing the effectiveness of fuzzy regression analysis based on [714, 715]. However, genetic algorithm was not applied directly for the determination of unknown fuzzy coefficients of fuzzy regression model.

In [665] the method proposed in [715] is enhanced through a two-step procedure where first the peak values of fuzzy regression coefficients are determined, and then the linear program is solved. In [432] parameters of the triangular fuzzy regression coefficients are determined using ordinary linear regression procedures. Both of the above methods are restricted to the crisp inputs/fuzzy outputs data.

The above approaches to fuzzy regression analysis are based on a-level sets and interval arithmetic, and require specifying and solving a set of linear programming problems or system of equations. Also, in these approaches fuzzy data and unknown fuzzy coefficients are frequently represented as fuzzy symmetrical triangular membership functions, whereas in reality they may be of a variety of shapes. This simplification significantly reduces the accuracy of solutions. The above approaches result in not- soeasy calculating problems. Therefore, there is a need to consider relatively more general regression equations and more effective approaches to estimate their parameters.

Another significant drawback of the above approaches is that the comparison of the calculated and the desired output is not considered in the process of determining fuzzy regression coefficients. [136] advocated the use of fuzzy chaos for fuzzy regression. In this approach the direct comparison of the desired and actual outputs is used. Other advantages of the approach proposed in [136] include the idea of extension of the method to the polynomial regression, and avoidance of using a-level procedures, the disadvantages of which has been mentioned above. The disadvantage of the proposed method is that the search for fuzzy regression coefficients is undirected.

In this study we propose fuzzy regression analysis using genetic algorithms for defining of unknown fuzzy coeffi- cients of fuzzy regression models. The overall complexity of the proposed method is less than above mentioned approaches. The idea of using genetic algorithms for fuzzy regression analysis had been mentioned in [589, 797]. Here we present a methodology for constructing fuzzy regression models on the basis of fuzzy arithmetic and genetic algorithms.

10.6.2 *Statement of problem*

Assume, K fuzzy data expressed as fuzzy numbers are given for multiple input – single output system. The problem is to define regression model for fitting this type of data. The following fuzzy regression model is considered:

$$y^M(x_1, x_2, ..., x_N) = a_0 + \sum_{i=1}^{N} a_i \cdot x_i + \sum_{i=1}^{N} b_i \cdot x_i^2 + \sum_{\substack{i=1 \\ i<j}}^{N} \sum_{j=1}^{N} c_{ij} \cdot x_i \cdot x_j \qquad (10.45)$$

It is required to determine fuzzy coefficients (numbers) $a_i, b_i,$ and $c_{ij}, i = \overline{0, N}, j = \overline{1, N},$ given fuzzy input date $x_{ik}, i = \overline{1, N}, k = \overline{1, K},$ and output date $y_{ik}, k = \overline{1, K},$ so that

$$d(y^M, y) = \sum_{i=1}^{K} \left| y_i - y_i^M \right| \to \min \qquad (10.46)$$

Here d is Hamming fuzzy distance in general fuzzy number space between each fuzzy datum y_i and the corresponding fuzzy number y_i^M calculated by (10.45).

In order to define unknown parameters (shapes and centers of membership functions) $a_i, b_i,$ and $c_{ij}, i = \overline{0, N}, j = \overline{1, N},$ the aggregated distance d (10.46) is minimized. Use of least squares and gradient based methods for solving the problem (10.45-10.46) is not feasible, because d in (10.46) is non differentiable, fuzzy numbers are from general fuzzy number space, and the regression model is general. In this section we use genetic algorithms for solving this problem.

10.6.3 *Genetic algorithm for defining parameters of fuzzy regression model*

Genetic algorithms (GA) are optimization techniques based on the principle of evolution and survival of the fittest [325, 362, 527]. GA operates on the population of potential solutions, also called chromosomes. Traditionally binary representation is used for chromosome encoding. The objective function of the problem needs to be transformed into the fitness function, which associates each chromosome with the corresponding fitness value.

Maximizing the value of fitness function is equivalent to solving the original optimization problem.

During the simulated evolution the fitter chromosomes have larger chance of surviving and producing offspring for the next generation. Mutation and crossover operators are used during evolution. Mutation changes a value of randomly chosen bit in a chromosome (gene), thus, implementing random search. Crossover chooses a pair of chromosomes, and exchanges their parts at random, providing information exchange between different directions of search. This iterative process leads to finding closeto-optimal solutions.

The only requirement for the fitness function is that it should adequately represent the objective function of the original problem. The fitness function does not have to be differentiable. This feature is particularly useful when the objective function of the problem at hand is not differentiable which is the case with fuzzy regression analysis.

The fitness function is defined by the following formula:

$$F = \left[1 + d\right]^{-1}, \qquad (10.47)$$

where d is the aggregate distance between the desired and actual outputs of a regression model.

Inputs and output data and regression coefficients are represented as arbitrary fuzzy numbers in this work. The calculations are performed based on the fuzzy arithmetic operations [59, 249]. Each fuzzy regression coefficient is represented by q strings of bits, where q is the number of parameters of a fuzzy number. Using pointwise representation may result in generating non-valid fuzzy numbers, i.e. one cannot guarantee that all the points for the parameters of fuzzy numbers would be in the correct order. Therefore, the parametric representation of fuzzy numbers is used to represent fuzzy coefficients. Combination of all strings for all regression coefficients is a chromosome, i.e. a potential specification for the parameters of a regression model.

Initially, a pool of binary chromosomes is randomly generated. Each chromosome is then translated into the set of fuzzy coefficients using prespecified ranges for the parameters for those coefficients. Every coefficient can be an arbitrary fuzzy number represented in the following general form [293]:

$$a(x) = \begin{cases} 1 & for\ x \in [a_L, a_U] \\ l(x) & for\ x \in [-\infty, a_L] \\ r(x) & for\ x \in [a_U, +\infty] \end{cases}, \qquad (10.48)$$

where a_L and a_U are the lower and upper bounds of the core of $\tilde{a}$ respectively; l is a monotonic, increasing, continuous from the right function from $(-\infty, a_L)$ to $[0, 1]$, and such that $l(x) = 0$ for $x \in (-\infty, a_{SL})$; r is a monotonic, decreasing, continuous from the left function from (a_U, ∞) to $[0,1]$, and such that $r(x) = 0$ for $x \in (a_{SU}, \infty)$. Functions l and r are determined m and n parameters respectively. Then, every fuzzy coefficient will be deter-mined by $m+n+1$ (one extra parameter for the peak of fuzzy number) parameters if $a = b$ in (10.48), and by $m+n+2$ parameters if a < b. In this case every fuzzy regression coefficient can be expressed as:

$$\left(\underbrace{\underbrace{0111}_{a_{ip}} \underbrace{00110}_{a_{il1}} \underbrace{101101}_{a_{il2}}...\underbrace{111010}_{a_{ilm}} \underbrace{101}_{a_{ir1}} \underbrace{111000}_{a_{ir2}}...\underbrace{00001}_{a_{im}}}_{\tilde{a}_i} \right)$$

Here, a_{ip} is the peak value of fuzzy coefficient a_i; $a_{ilj}, j = \overline{1, m}$ and $a_{irk}, k = \overline{1, n}$ are the jth and kth parameters of functions l and r respectively. In particular, assume that fuzzy regression coefficients have triangular form and are represented in L-R format:

$$a = (a_p, a_L, a_R)_{LR} \tag{10.49}$$

Then, the following chromosome encodes fuzzy coefficients of (10.46) represented in form (10.49):

$$\left(...\underbrace{\underbrace{01100}_{a_{ip}} \underbrace{11101}_{a_{iL}} \underbrace{01000}_{a_{iR}}}_{\tilde{a}_i'}... \underbrace{\underbrace{11100}_{b_{ip}} \underbrace{10111}_{b_{iL}} \underbrace{11100}_{b_{iR}}}_{\tilde{b}_i}... \underbrace{\underbrace{10010}_{c_{ijp}} \underbrace{11101}_{c_{ijL}} \underbrace{01100}_{c_{ijR}}}_{\tilde{c}_{ij}}... \right)$$

Here, a_i are fuzzy regression coefficients, and a_{ip}, a_{iL}, a_{iR} are the values for the peak and left and right deviations of a fuzzy triangular coefficient. In this example each parameter is encoded as a five-bit string.

$$\left(...\underbrace{01100\,11101\,01000}_{\tilde{a}_i}... \underbrace{11100\,101 \,\overset{SP}{\mid}\, 11\,11100}_{\tilde{b}_i}... \underbrace{10010\,11101\,01100}_{\tilde{c}_{ij}}... \right)$$

$$\left(...\underbrace{10100001\,11\,11010}_{\tilde{a}_i'}... \underbrace{01110\,001 \,\overset{SP}{\mid}\, 01\,00000}_{\tilde{b}_i'}... \underbrace{01111\,0000110101}_{\tilde{c}_{ij}'}... \right)$$

The coefficients are plugged into the fuzzy model and the fuzzy outputs (y_i^M) are calculated for the set of given fuzzy inputs. These outputs are compared to the desired outputs (y_i) and the distance is calculated. Then, the value of fitness is determined using (10.47) for that chromosome.

$$\left(\underbrace{\dots 01100\,11101\,01000}_{\tilde{a}_i'} \dots \underbrace{11100\,101 \overset{SP}{\mid} 01\,00000}_{\tilde{b}_i''} \dots \underbrace{01111\,00001\,10101 \dots}_{\tilde{c}_{ij}'} \right)$$

$$\left(\underbrace{\dots 10100\,00111\,11010}_{\tilde{a}_i'} \dots \underbrace{01110\,001 \overset{SP}{\mid} 11\,11100}_{\tilde{b}_i'''} \dots \underbrace{10010\,11101\,01100 \dots}_{c_{ij}} \right)$$

After all the chromosomes in the population have been evaluated in terms of their fitness values, the selection process takes place. During selection the new generation is created by randomly choosing chromosomes from old population with the probabilities proportional to the fitness values of the chromosomes. We used elitist approach, where the best chromosome is preserved in the new population, i.e. the best solution always survives.

After selection the newly generated population undergoes crossover and mutation operations. The probabilities of mutation and crossover control the level of exploration exploitation in solution search process. The crossover operation randomly chooses two chromosomes with the specified probability and exchanges their parts. First, the split point is randomly selected. Then, two child chromosomes are generated each of them having a substring up to the split point from one parent, and another substring from the other parent chromosome. The following example demonstrates the crossover operator for two chromosomes representing two different sets of potential fuzzy regression coefficients.

Before crossover:

Here SP stands for "split point". After crossover the child chromosomes become:

As the result of crossover the child chromosome inherits part of uzzy coefficients from one parent, and part from the other parent. Most probably one of the coefficients will not belong to either parents, because the split point may fall inside the substring for that coefficient as it is shown in the example above.

Mutation chooses a bit in a chromosome with the specified probability of mutation and flips it to the opposite value. For example:

Before mutation:

$$
\left(\ldots \underbrace{01100\ 11101\ 01000}_{a_i} \ldots \underbrace{11100\ 1\ \overset{Mt}{0}\ 111\ 11100}_{b_i} \ldots \underbrace{10010\ 11101\ 01100}_{c_{ij}} \ldots \right)
$$

After mutation:

$$
\left(\ldots \underbrace{01100\ 11101\ 01000}_{a_i} \ldots \underbrace{11100\ 1\ \overset{Mt}{1}\ 111\,11100}_{b_i'} \ldots \underbrace{10010\ 11101\ 01100}_{c_{ij}} \ldots \right)
$$

Here Mt marks the gene that undergoes mutation. In effect, a single mutation operation randomly changes one of the parameters of some fuzzy coefficient. The algorithm for performing fuzzy regression can be summarized as follows:

Step 1. Mapping solution space $\left(a_i, b_i, c_{ij}\right)$ into genetic search space X (binary strings). Constructing fuzzy fitness function F using fuzzy measure of Ω distance d (10.46) (objective function).

Step 2. Creating initial population (set of chromosomes) randomly, i.e. a population of fuzzy regression coefficients which are randomly specified.

Step 3. Evaluating each chromosome in the population in terms of fitness value using (10.47).

Step 4. If termination conditions are met go to Step 8.

Step 5. Generating new population using selection operator. This operator randomly selects chromosomes from the current population with the probabilities proportional to the values of fitness of the chromosomes.

Step 6. Creating new chromosomes by mating randomly selected (with some specified probability called probability of crossover, Pc) chromosomes. The resulting offspring replaces the original parent chromosomes in the population.

Step 7. Mutating some randomly selected (with some specified probability called probability of mutation, Pm) chromosomes. Return to Step 3.

Step 8. Stop, return the best chromosome and translate it into the fuzzy regression coefficients.

The stop criterion may be, for example, maximum number of generations. This iterative process leads to the improved performance of candidate set of fuzzy coefficients.

10.6.4 *Simulations*

We used GA-based fuzzy regression fuzzy regression example given in [713]. For measuring the performance of fuzzy regression fuzzy error (10.46) was used. The fuzzy error is compared with the case of perfect match of the regression outputs with the desired outputs. Because of fuzzy subtraction operation used, the right and left deviation of fuzzy error is not expected to be crisp zero [135]. Therefore, to assure learning is acceptable, it is necessary to define a set that would reflect the required accuracy [135]. Let the interval $\left[y_{iL}^d, y_{iR}^d \right]$ be the support of y_i^d represented as a triangle LR – fuzzy number $y_i^d = \left(y_{ip}^d, y_{iL}^d, y_{iR}^d \right)$ then left and right end points of support of y_i^d can be easily calculated as:

$$y_{iSL}^d = y_{ip}^d - y_{iL}^d; \quad y_{iSU}^d = y_{ip}^d + y_{iR}^d. \tag{10.50}$$

If $y_i = y_i^d$, then the support of $\tilde{d}$ is $[0, \lambda]$, where

$$\lambda = \sum_{i=1}^K \left| y_{iSU}^d - y_{iLU}^d \right|. \tag{10.51}$$

If the fuzzy error derived from (10.45) is within the boundaries specified by (10.51) plus some user-specified acceptance level ε, then we accept the model. $\varepsilon > 0$ is a small acceptable positive number. It is chosen, like in classical case, with the consideration of the required accuracy for the problem at hand. If we want the error to be zero $(0, 0.5, 0.5)$, ε is defined considering how close to zero the error should be, e.g. it should be in the interval $[-0.5 - \varepsilon; 0.5 + \varepsilon]$.

Tanaka *et al.* [713] used data with crisp input and fuzzy output numbers to fit a fuzzy linear regression model. This data was also used in [432, 665]. Fuzzy regression model is represented in the following linear form:

$$y^M = a_0 + a_1 x \tag{10.52}$$

a_0 and a_1 are represented as fuzzy numbers with triangular membership functions. In [432] the following difference measure is used:

$$E = \frac{\int_{S_Y \cap S_{Y^M}} \left| \mu_Y(x) - \mu_{Y^M}(x) \right| dx}{\int_{S_Y} \mu_Y(x) dx}, \tag{10.53}$$

where $\mu_Y(x)$ and $\mu_{Y^M}(x)$ are membership functions for observed and estimated fuzzy numbers, and S_Y and S_{YM} are the corresponding supports. We have used the same data for the GA-based fuzzy regression. The parameters of GA used for this problem are listed in Table 10.6. The following estimates of fuzzy coefficients were obtained:

$$a_0 = (4.893; 1.827; 2.01); a_1 = (1.621; 0.184; 0.095).$$

More refined estimates can be obtained by further tuning the GA parameters. The pre-specified acceptance interval was set to [0; 30] $(\text{with } \lambda = 23.2)$. The calculated fuzzy distance expressed pointwise was $(0; 5.6; 29.19)$, which falls within the acceptable region. We also calculated the fuzzy difference (10.53) as suggested in [432] for our model. Table 10.7 gives the comparison of errors using the methods described in [432,665,713] and GA-based fuzzy regression (GAFR). As one can see from the table the method proposed here outperforms the above methods in terms of total error as measured by fuzzy difference. Note, that our approach is not restricted to the case of crisp inputs as, for example, the one proposed in [432].

Table 10.6. GA parameters

Population size	50
Chromo some length	50
Number of generations	500
Probability of crossover	0.7
Probability of mutation	0.01
Selection method	Elitist

Table 10.7. Comparison of errors

Method/Obs.	1	2	3	4	5	Total error
FLR [23]	1.86	1.3	0.58	0.86	1.0	5.6
FLSLR [13]	1.54	1.52	0.7	1.16	0.86	5.78
FMLS [14]	1.22	1.38	0.4	1.12	0.36	4.48
GAFR	1.31	1.27	0.18	1.32	0.09	4.17

Chapter 11

The Z-Restriction Centered Decision Theory

11.1 The Z-restriction based general decisions theory

11.1.1 *Motivation*

The majority of the existing decision theories, starting from von Neumann and Morgenstern Expected Utility theory, are based on sound mathematical background and yielded good results. However, they are developed for solving particular decision situations. Consequently, nowadays there is no theory to unite main directions of decision analysis. Let us try to outline main shortcomings of the present state-of-the art of decision theories. First, numerical, precise modeling techniques are still used whereas real-world information is imprecise and constraints are soft as represented by humans in NL. Indeed, it should be taken into account that a human being reasons with linguistic description of information. In particular, even the advanced models are based on the use of precise probability measures, whereas a long time ago J. Keynes mentioned that real-world probabilities are imprecise. Second, whereas our knowledge about future is not perfect, they use mutually exclusive and exhaustive states of nature. Third, the use of binary logic-based preference relations does not fit well the fact that vagueness of real preferences resulting from the fact that humans find difficulty to make choices in imperfect decision environment. Forth, parametrical modeling of behavioral determinants does not allow taking into account qualitative nature of information related to their interaction. Fifth, a small attention is paid to account for the fact that reliability of decision-relevant information is often partially but not completely reliable. Thus, it is needed to develop a general theory of decisions that would be free of the limitations outlined above. In this section, we consider the fundamentals of the new general theory of decisions which is based on complex consideration of imperfect decision-relevant information issues and behavioral aspects. We illustrate that the existing theories including Expected Utility of von Neumann and Morgenstern, Prospect Theory, Choquet Expected Utility, Cumulative Prospect Theory and other theories are special cases of the suggested general theory of decisions. We provide axioms and principles, the corresponding mathematical methodologies of decision analysis and auxiliary formal techniques.

Prior to describe the proposed general decision theory, let us discuss the following properties that any general theory of decisions should have [289, 700]: 1) Generality; 2) Congruence with reality; 3)Tractability.

Let us discuss what these properties imply. *Generality* of a theory implies that every existing decision making theory would be its particular case. This requires using a unified decision model at its nutshell which could unite the existing models into a single whole. As a result, the existing decision theories would be particular cases of a new general theory of decisions, because they are developed for modeling particular evidences. A unified decision model will help us understand more about how various interacting factors of decision making including behavioral determinants compose an ensemble inspiring real-world decisions.

In order to achieve *congruence with reality* it is needed to understand what is the basis of real-world decision making. Due to imprecision, vagueness, partial truth and partial reliability of real-world decision-relevant information and complexity of considered phenomena, this information is supported by perceptions. Often, perception-based information has linguistic, i.e., natural language-based representation. Initially, any problem is described verbally, and then they try to construct a formal model reflecting observed regularities. However, formalisms of the majority of the existing theories account for imperfect nature of only probability-relevant information. Indeed, the imperfect information related to states of nature, outcomes, behavioral determinants and other elements of a decision problem, is missed. The problem is that when we proceed from imperfect information to a precise numerical model we deal with inevitable coarsening, loss and distortion of information. Concerning behavioral determinants like risk, ambiguity and losses attitudes, fairness, reciprocity and others, the most important issue in development of a new general theory is modeling of their interaction. Indeed, a mental state of a DM is a complex system of these factors. The main disadvantage of the existing theories is that this issue has not been fundamentally addressed.

It should be mentioned that the properties of generality and congruence with reality are closely related. Without taking into account interaction of behavioral determinants and imperfect nature of decision relevant information, a general theory of decisions cannot be created. It is reasonable to recall that taking into account real-world ambiguity of probabilities resulted in construction of the theories more general than the expected utility theories. Subsequent introduction of ambiguity attitudes and human expertise led to the further generalization [312].

The main difficulty related to the use of general theories is related to computational complexities. However, modern computational resources allow achieving *tractability* [771] of a general theory by overcoming the problems of decision analysis under second-order uncertainty and linguistic information.

We suggest that behavioral determinants, i.e. subjective conditions, should be considered at the same fundamental level of decision analysis as states of nature, i.e. objective conditions. Moreover, objectives and subjective conditions should be linked together as a human behavior naturally depends on·objective conditions. However, in the existing approaches the basis of decision analysis is the space of states of nature only, whereas behavioral determinants are just introduced parametrically.

Behavioral decision analysis in the general theory of decisions will be based on a concept of a combined state. The space of combined states is both more fundamental and a more transparent basis of behavioral decision analysis. A state of a DM should in general be considered as a vector whose components are behavioral factors, which are important for the problem at hand. For example, a state of an investor may be characterized by risk attitude [404], ambiguity attitude, reciprocity and social responsibility. The same applies to a state of nature (e.g. economy), for which such indexes as inflation rate, GDP, unemployment level may be considered. Consideration of a combined state, therefore, becomes a promising task.

The principle of a combined state is very close to the idea underlying discrete choice models. However, let us contrast these two approaches. At first we should mention, that discrete choice is considered for the cases of qualitative decision-relevant information. In real-world, qualitative information about alternatives is described by people using NL, as it is indeed imprecise, partially true and, sometimes, is vague. As a result, in contrast to assumptions of the existing discrete choice models, it is not possible to perfectly differentiate among values of attributes of alternatives. It is known, that there exist three important issues that complicates construction of a discrete choice model. First, a DM often has incomplete and partially true information on alternatives. Second, a researcher often has incomplete and partially true information on alternatives. Third, a researcher often has imperfect information about behavioral determinants of a DM. In the existing discrete choice model these problems are treated by applying probabilistic models. However, as it was shown by simple laboratory experiments, a probability measure often fails to model decision phenomena [70, 263]. The use of only a probabilistic approach is not sufficient to treat imprecision, ambiguity, partial truth. The approach suggested in the present section is more adequate for dealing with qualitative information about a decision environment and a DM because it is based on synergy of probability theory and fuzzy set theory. This allows to deal with imprecise probabilities as important constituent of real choices.

The proposed principles of the new general theory of decisions open a door to improvement and progress of such important directions as multicriteria decisions and group decision making [763]. For multicriterial decisions, the use of states of a DM would help to overcome incorrect, improper choices of a human being which can be conditioned by the fact that emotions, biases etc may hinder constructive consideration of criteria and their importance. For group decision making, the use of a formalism of states of a DM may help to discover at a more fundamental level an expertise and professionalism of members of a group. This, in turn would lead to more adequate and clear ranking of them and, therefore, a better determination of an optimal group decision.

The suggested general theory of decisions may help to better understand the phenomena of motivation, bounded rationality [691, 813] and imperfect information as leading factors of economic agents behavior.

Let us now proceed to formalization of the suggested general theory of decisions. The suggested theory is based on a framework of discrete information processing.

11.1.2 A unified decision model

11.1.2.1 Formal framework

In the majority of the existing theories, a formal decision framework includes the following elements: a set of states of nature $\mathcal{S}$ that describes external environment conditions, a set of outcomes $\mathcal{X}$, a set of alternatives $\mathcal{A}$ as a set of actions $\mathcal{A} = \{f \mid f : \mathcal{S} \to \mathcal{X}\}$ generating outcomes $\mathcal{X}$ subject to external environment conditions $\mathcal{S}$, and preferences of a DM $\succsim$ representing choice over a set $\mathcal{A}$. In the suggested formal framework, we introduce a set of states of a DM $\mathcal{H}$ in order to model subjective conditions of a choice in line with the objective conditions in an evident manner.

The suggested framework is a framework of processing of discrete information. Taking into account the fact that real problems are characterized by linguistic information which is, as a rule, described by a discrete set of meaningful linguistic terms, in our study we consider discrete Z-numbers.

Let $\mathcal{S} = \{S \mid S \in \mathcal{S}\}$ be a discrete space of vector-valued states of nature and $\mathcal{H} = \{\hat{h} \mid \hat{h} \in \mathcal{H}\}$ a discrete space of vector-valued states of a DM, such that

$$S = (S_1, ..., S_m), \quad \hat{h} = (\hat{h}_1, ..., \hat{h}_n),$$

where components $S_i, i = 1, ..., m$ are important factors of decision environment (for economic problems the factors like *GDP*, *interest rates* etc) and components $\hat{h}_j = (\tilde{A}_{h_j}, \tilde{B}_{h_j})$ $j = 1, ..., n,$ are behavioral determinants (for example, *risk attitude, ambiguity attitude, reciprocity, trust* etc). Denote $S^{(i)} = \{S_1^{(i)}, ..., S_{m_i}^{(i)}\}$ a discrete set of values of S_i and denote $H^{(j)} = \{\hat{h}_1^{(j)},...,\hat{h}_{n_j}^{(j)}\}$ a discrete set of values of $\hat{h}_j$.

Let us denote $\mathcal{X} = \{\hat{X}_1,...,\hat{X}_l\}$, $\hat{X}_k \in \mathcal{Z}, k=1,...,l$, a space of Z-valued vector outcomes. We call $\Omega = \mathcal{S} \times \mathcal{H}$ a space "nature-DM", elements of which are combined states $\hat{\omega} = (S, \hat{h})$ where $S \in \mathcal{S}, \hat{h} \in \mathcal{H}$. Consider $\mathcal{A} = \{\hat{f} | \hat{f} : \Omega \to \mathcal{X}\}$ the set of Z-valued actions as the set of Z-valued functions from Ω to $\mathcal{X}$. Let us denote $\hat{X}_i = \{\hat{f}(\hat{\omega}_i) \mid \hat{f} \in \mathcal{A}, \hat{\omega}_i \in \Omega\}$. It is obvious that $\mathcal{X} = \bigcup_{i=1}^{nm} \hat{X}_i$.

In the suggested framework, linguistic preference relation (LPR) [179] is used to account for vagueness of real-world preferences. The LPR used in our general model is composed by intra-combined state information and inter-combined states information. Intra-combined state information is used to form utilities representing preferences over outcomes $\hat{f}(\hat{\omega}_i) = \hat{X}_i$, where $\hat{\omega}_i = (S_{i_1}, \hat{h}_{i_2})$, of an act $\hat{f} \in \mathcal{A}$ with understanding that these are preferences at state of nature S_{i_1} conditioned by a state $\hat{h}_{i_2}$ of a DM.

Inter-combined states information is used to represent preferences inspired by dependence between combined states as human behaviors under imperfect information.

To model LPR, let's introduce a linguistic variable "*degree of preference*" with term-set $T = (T_1,...,T_n)$. The fact that preference of $\hat{f}$ against $\hat{g}$ is described by some $T_i \in T$ is expressed as $\hat{f} T_i \hat{g}$. We denote LPR as $\succsim_l$ and below we sometimes, for simplicity, write $\hat{f} \succsim_i^j \hat{g}$ or $\hat{f} \succ_i^j \hat{g}$ instead of $\hat{f} T_i \hat{g}$. Denote $0_i \in \mathcal{X}_i$ neutral, $-1_i \in \mathcal{X}_i$ the worst and $1_i \in \mathcal{X}_i$ the best outcomes from $\mathcal{X}_i$.

Intra-combined state information.

Z-valued utilities of outcomes $\hat{u}_i^\varsigma : \mathcal{X}_i \to \mathcal{Z}_\varsigma, \varsigma \in \{+,-\}$, satisfy

Monotonicity $\forall \hat{X}_i, \hat{Y}_i, (\hat{X}_i, 0_i) \succsim_l (\hat{Y}_i, 0_i) \Leftrightarrow \hat{u}_i(\hat{X}_i) \geq \hat{u}_i(\hat{Y}_i)$

Interval scale condition

$\forall \hat{X}_i, \hat{Y}_i, \hat{Z}_i, \hat{W}_i$ such that $\hat{u}_i(\hat{X}_i) > \hat{u}_i(\hat{Y}_i)$ and $\hat{u}_i(\hat{W}_i) > \hat{u}_i(\hat{Z}_i)$ one has

$$\frac{\hat{u}_i(\hat{X}_i) - \hat{u}_i(\hat{Y}_i)}{\hat{u}_i(\hat{Z}_i) - \hat{u}_i(\hat{W}_i)} = \hat{k}(\hat{X}_i, \hat{Y}_i, \hat{Z}_i, \hat{W}_i) \in \mathcal{D}^1_{[0,\infty)} \times \{1\}$$

iff the difference of satisfaction degree that the DM feels between $(\hat{X}_i, 0_i)$ and $(\hat{Y}_i, 0_i)$ is $\hat{k}(\hat{X}_i, \hat{Y}_i, \hat{Z}_i, \hat{W}_i)$ as large as the difference of satisfaction between $(\hat{W}_i, 0_i)$ and $(\hat{Z}_i, 0_i)$.

Normalization

$\hat{u}_i^+(0_i) = (0,1), \hat{u}_i^+(1_i) = (1,1), \hat{u}_i^-(0_i) = (0,1)$ and $\hat{u}_i^-(-1_i) = (-1,0)$.

Multiplicative transitivity

$\forall \hat{X}_i, \hat{Y}_i, \hat{Z}_i, \hat{W}_i, \hat{R}_i, \hat{V}_i$ such that $\hat{u}_i(\hat{X}_i) > \hat{u}_i(\hat{Y}_i)$, $\hat{u}_i(\hat{W}_i) > \hat{u}_i(\hat{Z}_i)$ and $\hat{u}_i(\hat{R}_i) > \hat{u}_i(\hat{V}_i)$ we have

$$\hat{k}(\hat{X}_i, \hat{Y}_i, \hat{Z}_i, \hat{W}_i) \times \hat{k}(\hat{Z}_i, \hat{W}_i, \hat{R}_i, \hat{V}_{ii}) = \hat{k}(\hat{X}_i, \hat{Y}_i, \hat{R}_i, \hat{V}_i)$$

$\hat{u}_i^s$ is stable under positive linear transformation.

The ratio $\dfrac{\hat{u}_i(\hat{X}_i) - \hat{u}_i(\hat{Y}_i)}{\hat{u}_i(\hat{Z}_i) - \hat{u}_i(\hat{W}_i)}$ does not change if $\hat{u}_i$ is changed to $\alpha \hat{u}_i + \beta$, $\alpha > 0, \beta \geq 0$.

Inter-combined states information.

Z-valued bi-capacity $\hat{\eta}$ satisfies:

Monotonicity

$$\hat{\eta}(\mathcal{V}, \mathcal{V}) \geq \hat{\eta}(\mathcal{W}, \mathcal{W}) \Leftrightarrow (1_\mathcal{V}, -1_\mathcal{V}, 0_{-(\mathcal{V} \cup \mathcal{V})}) \succsim (1_\mathcal{W}, -1_\mathcal{W}, 0_{-(\mathcal{W} \cup \mathcal{W})})$$

Interval scale condition

$$\frac{\hat{\eta}(\mathcal{V}, \mathcal{V}') - \hat{\eta}(\mathcal{W}, \mathcal{W}')}{\hat{\eta}(\bar{\mathcal{V}}, \bar{\mathcal{V}}') - \hat{\eta}(\bar{\mathcal{W}}, \bar{\mathcal{W}}')} - \hat{k}(\mathcal{V}, \mathcal{V}', \mathcal{W}, \mathcal{W}', \bar{\mathcal{V}}, \bar{\mathcal{V}}', \bar{\mathcal{W}}, \bar{\mathcal{W}}')$$

iff the difference of satisfaction degrees that the DM feels between $(1_\mathcal{V}, -1_\mathcal{V}, 0_{-(\mathcal{V} \cup \mathcal{V})})$ and $(1_\mathcal{W}, -1_\mathcal{W}, 0_{-(\mathcal{W} \cup \mathcal{W})})$ is as large as the difference of satisfaction between $(1_{\bar{\mathcal{V}}}, -1_{\bar{\mathcal{V}}}, 0_{-(\bar{\mathcal{V}} \cup \bar{\mathcal{V}})})$ and $(1_{\bar{\mathcal{W}}}, -1_{\bar{\mathcal{W}}}, 0_{-(\bar{\mathcal{W}} \cup \bar{\mathcal{W}})})$.

Normalization

$$\hat{\eta}(\varnothing, \varnothing) = (0,1), \hat{\eta}(N, \varnothing) = (1,1) \text{ and } \forall (\mathcal{V}, \mathcal{V}') \in \mathfrak{A}(N), \ \hat{\eta}(\mathcal{V}, \mathcal{V}') \in \mathcal{Z}^1_{[-1,1]}$$

Multiplicative transitivity

$\forall \mathcal{V}, \mathcal{V}', \mathcal{W}, \mathcal{W}', \bar{\mathcal{V}}, \bar{\mathcal{V}}', \bar{\mathcal{W}}, \bar{\mathcal{W}}', \mathcal{K}, \mathcal{K}', \mathcal{L}, \mathcal{L}' \subset N$ such that
$\hat{\eta}(\mathcal{V}, \mathcal{V}') > \hat{\eta}(\mathcal{W}, \mathcal{W}')$, $\hat{\eta}(\bar{\mathcal{V}}, \bar{\mathcal{V}}') > \hat{\eta}(\bar{\mathcal{W}}, \bar{\mathcal{W}}')$ and $\hat{\eta}(\mathcal{K}, \mathcal{K}') > \hat{\eta}(\mathcal{L}, \mathcal{L}')$ one
has

$$\hat{k}(\mathcal{V}, \mathcal{V}', \mathcal{W}, \mathcal{W}', \bar{\mathcal{V}}, \bar{\mathcal{V}}', \bar{\mathcal{W}}, \bar{\mathcal{W}}', \mathcal{K}, \mathcal{K}', \mathcal{L}, \mathcal{L}') \times \hat{k}(\bar{\mathcal{V}}, \bar{\mathcal{V}}', \bar{\mathcal{W}}, \bar{\mathcal{W}}', \mathcal{K}, \mathcal{K}', \mathcal{L}, \mathcal{L}')$$
$$= \hat{k}(\mathcal{V}, \mathcal{V}', \mathcal{W}, \mathcal{W}', \mathcal{K}, \mathcal{K}', \mathcal{L}, \mathcal{L}')$$

Homogeneity

The ratio $\dfrac{\hat{u}_i(\hat{X}_i) - \hat{u}_i(\hat{Y}_i)}{\hat{u}_i(\hat{Z}_i) - \hat{u}_i(\hat{W}_i)}$ does not change if $\hat{\eta}$ changes to $\gamma\hat{\eta}$, $\gamma \in R$.

If the preferences $\succsim_l$ of a DM over $\mathcal{A}$ satisfies the above mentioned assumptions then they can be described by a Z-valued overall utility $\hat{U}(\hat{f})$ of $\hat{f} \in \mathcal{A}$ expressed as a Z-valued Choquet-like aggregation of $\hat{u}(\hat{f}(S,\hat{h}))$ w.r.t. Z-number-valued bi-capacity:

$$\hat{U}(\hat{f}) = \sum_{l=1}^{L} (\hat{u}(\hat{f}(\hat{\boldsymbol{\omega}}_{(l)})) -_h \hat{u}(\hat{f}(\hat{\boldsymbol{\omega}}_{(l+1)}))) \hat{\eta}(\mathcal{V}, \mathcal{W})$$

$$= \sum_{l=1}^{n} ((A_{u(f(\hat{\boldsymbol{\omega}}_{(l)}))}, B_{u(f(\hat{\boldsymbol{\omega}}_{(l)}))}) -_h (A_{u(f(\hat{\boldsymbol{\omega}}_{(l+1)}))}, B_{u(f(\hat{\boldsymbol{\omega}}_{(l+1)}))}))(A_{\eta(\mathcal{V},\mathcal{W})}, B_{\eta(\mathcal{V},\mathcal{W})}). \tag{11.1}$$

where indices (l) implies $\hat{u}(\hat{f}(\hat{\boldsymbol{\omega}}_{(l)})) \geq \hat{u}(\hat{f}(\hat{\boldsymbol{\omega}}_{(l+1)}))$; $\hat{u}(\hat{f}(\hat{\boldsymbol{\omega}}_{(L+1)})) = (0,1)$ by convention; $\mathcal{V} = \{\hat{\boldsymbol{\omega}}_{(1)},...,\hat{\boldsymbol{\omega}}_{(l)}\} \cap N^+$, $\mathcal{W} = \{\hat{\boldsymbol{\omega}}_{(1)},...,\hat{\boldsymbol{\omega}}_{(l)}\} \cap N^-$, $N^+ = \{\hat{\boldsymbol{\omega}} \in \Omega : \hat{u}(\hat{f}(\hat{\boldsymbol{\omega}})) \geq (0,1)\}$, $N^- = \Omega \setminus N^+$. $\hat{\eta} : \Omega \times \Omega \to \mathcal{Z}_{[-1,1]}$ is a Z-number-valued bi-capacity.

An optimal $\hat{f}^* \in \mathcal{A}$, that is, such $\hat{f}^* \in \mathcal{A}$ that $\hat{U}(\hat{f}^*) = \max\limits_{\hat{f} \in \mathcal{A}}$ $\left\{ \int_{\Omega} \hat{u}(\hat{f}(S,\hat{h})) d\hat{\eta} \right\}$, is determined by using the method of ranking of Z-numbers (Section 6.6).

11.1.3 *Discussion of some special cases*

We would like to briefly discuss here application of the suggested theory to special cases in the existing literature. Let us show that the existing decision theories like EU, CEU, PT and CPT which are the basic existing utility models applied on space S are special cases of the suggested general theory of decisions. A general representation of combined states space Ω is given in Table 11.1:

Table 11.1. General representations of a CSs space

	S_1	$\cdots$	S_i	$\cdots$	S_n
$\hat{h}_1$	$(S_1,\hat{h}_1)$	$\cdots$	$(S_i,\hat{h}_1)$	$\cdots$	$(S_n,\hat{h}_1)$
$\vdots$					
$\hat{h}_j$	$(S_1,\hat{h}_j)$	$\cdots$	$(S_i,\hat{h}_j)$	$\cdots$	$(S_n,\hat{h}_j)$
$\vdots$					
$\hat{h}_m$	$(S_1,\hat{h}_m)$	$\cdots$	$(S_i,\hat{h}_m)$	$\cdots$	$(S_n,\hat{h}_m)$

First, let us suppose that all the decision relevant information is completely reliable, that is, for any Z-number $Z = (A, B)$, the part B is taken as a singleton $B = 1$. In this case the framework of decision making under Z-valued information (partially reliable information) will reduce to decision making under fuzzy information and the utility model will reduce to fuzzy-valued aggregation with respect to fuzzy-valued bi-capacity. Thus, $\hat{U}(\hat{f})$ in (11.1) is reduced to:

$$\hat{U}(\hat{f}) = \sum_{l=1}^{L} (\hat{u}(\hat{f}(\hat{\boldsymbol{\omega}}_{(l)})) -_h \hat{u}(\hat{f}(\hat{\boldsymbol{\omega}}_{(l+1)})))\hat{\eta}(\mathcal{V}, \mathcal{W})$$

$$= \sum_{l=1}^{L} ((A_{u(f(\boldsymbol{\omega}_{(l)}))}, B_{u(f(\boldsymbol{\omega}_{(l)}))}) -_h (A_{u(f(\boldsymbol{\omega}_{(l+1)}))}, B_{u(f(\boldsymbol{\omega}_{(l+1)}))}))(A_{\eta(\mathcal{V},\mathcal{W})}, B_{\eta(\mathcal{V},\mathcal{W})})$$

$$= \sum_{l=1}^{L} ((A_{u(f(\boldsymbol{\omega}_{(l)}))}, 1) -_h (A_{u(f(\boldsymbol{\omega}_{(l+1)}))}, 1))(A_{\eta(\mathcal{V},\mathcal{W})}, 1)$$

$$= \sum_{l=1}^{L} (A_{u(f(\boldsymbol{\omega}_{(l)}))} -_h A_{u(f(\boldsymbol{\omega}_{(l+1)}))})A_{\eta(\mathcal{V},\mathcal{W})}$$

$$= \sum_{l=1}^{L} (u(f(\boldsymbol{\omega}_{(l)})) -_h u(f(\boldsymbol{\omega}_{(l+1)})))\eta(\mathcal{V}, \mathcal{W})$$

Thus, a fuzzy-valued utility functional is obtained:

$$U(f) = \sum_{l=1}^{L} (u(f(\omega_{(l)})) -_h u(f(\omega_{(l+1)}))) \eta(\mathcal{V}, \mathcal{W}).$$

Let us note that Z-valued utility (11.1) can be considered as fuzzy type-2 Choquet-like aggregation on the basis of relationships between type-2 fuzzy sets and Z-numbers shown in [38, 802, 803].

Let us now simplify this fuzzy model to its non-fuzzy variant. This results in the following expression:

$$U(f) = \sum_{l=1}^{n} (u(f(w_{(l)})) - u(f(w_{(l+1)}))) \eta(\mathcal{C}, \mathcal{D}) \qquad (11.2)$$

This is a real-valued utility with real-valued integrand and bi-capacity.

Let us at first consider EU model. Let r_j in (11.2) be a probability measure on Ω. Then we have (11.2) as:

$$U(f) = \sum_{k=1}^{mn} u(f(w_k)) p(w_k) = \sum_{j=1}^{m} \sum_{i=1}^{n} u(f(s_i, h_j)) p(s_i, h_j) \qquad (11.3)$$

In traditional EU they consider a DM exhibiting the same behavior in any state of nature. This means that only one state of a DM exists. Then, we exclude all h_j except one h_k in (11.3). This means $p(s_i, h_j) = 0, \forall j \neq k$ and we have

$$U(f) = \sum_{i=1}^{n} u(f(s_i, h_k)) p(s_i, h_k)$$

As a DM is always at h_k whatever s_i takes place, we have $p(s_i, h_k) = p(s_i)$. In EU a DM is *risk averse*, *risk seeking* or *risk neutral*. Therefore, h_k can represent one of these behaviors. Denote $u'(f(\cdot)) = u(f(\cdot, h_k))$ and then we have

$$U(f) = \sum_{i=1}^{n} u'(f(s_i)) p(s_i)$$

which is nothing but a traditional EU.

The suggested theory as opposed to EU allows to take into account DM's various risk attitudes at various states of nature.

Let us now consider CEU model. Let η_j in (11.2) be a capacity. Then we have (11.2) as:

$$U(f) = \sum_{l=1}^{n} (u(f(w_{(l)})) - u(f(w_{(l+1)}))) \eta(\{w_{(1)},...,w_{(l)}\}) \qquad (11.4)$$

$w_{(l)} = (s_j, h_k), u(f(w_{(l)})) \geq u(f(w_{(l+1)}))$. Assuming that only some h_k exists, we have $\forall w \in \Omega, w = (s_i, h_k)$, that is $\Omega = S \times \{h_k\}$. Then $u(f(w_{(l)})) - u(f(w_{(l+1)})) = 0$ for $w_{(l)} = w_{(l+1)} = (s_i, h_k)$. Only $u(f(w_{(l)})) - u(f(w_{(l+1)}))$ for which $w_{(l)} = (s_i, h_k), w_{(l+1)} = (s_j, h_k), i \neq j$ may not be equal to zero.

As a result, we have:

$$U(f) = \sum_{i=1}^{n} (u(f(s_{(i)}, h_k)) - u(f((s_{(i+1)}, h_k)))) \eta(\{(s_{(1)}, h_k),...,(s_{(i)}, h_k)\})$$

Now, using notations $u'(f(\cdot)) = u(f(\cdot, h_k))$ and $\eta'(\{s_{(1)},...,s_{(i)}\}) = \eta(\{(s_{(1)}, h_k),...,(s_{(i)}, h_k)\})$ we can write

$$U(f) = \sum_{i=1}^{n} (u'(f(s_{(i)})) - u'(f(s_{(i+1)}))) \eta'(\{s_{(1)},...,s_{(i)}\})$$

This is CEU representation. CEU is often used to represent uncertainty attitude. So, if h_k represents ambiguity aversion (ambiguity seeking) then $\eta(\{(s_{(1)}, h_k),...,(s_{(i)}, h_k)\})$ can be chosen as lower prevision (upper prevision).

Let us now compare the suggested unified model with the PT utility model. Let probabilities $p(s_{(1)}),...,p(s_{(i)})$ be known. Then PT utility model will be as follows:

$$U(f) = \sum_{i=1}^{n} (v(f(s_i)) - v(f(s_{i+1})))w\left(\sum_{j=1}^{i} p(f(s_j)) \right)$$

where w is a weighting function and v is a value function.

As w is non-additive, then considering $w\left(\sum_{j=1}^{i} p(f(s_j)) \right)$ as a value of

a non-additive measure $\eta(\{s_1,...,s_i\}) = w\left(\sum_{j=1}^{i} p(f(s_j)) \right)$, one arrives at

CEU representation [669]:

$$U(f) = \sum_{i=1}^{n} (v(f(s_{(i)})) - v(f(s_{(i+1)})))\eta(\{s_{(1)},...,s_{(i)}\}),$$

which is a special case of the suggested unified decision model. Therefore, PT utility model is a special case of the suggested unified decision model.

It can also be shown that the CPT representation is also a special case of the suggested theory as this representation is a sum of two Choquet integrals.

11.1.4 *Methodology for the general theory of decisions*

An application of the suggested general theory requires solving several related problems. As the basis of decision analysis in the suggested theory is the space of combined states, the adequate determination of the structure of a state of nature and a state of a DM is important. This begins with determination of influential factors $S_1,...,S_m$ of objective conditions which are influential for the considered alternatives. On the base of analysis of the considered alternatives and factors $S_1,...,S_m$, a vector of behavioral determinants $\hat{h}=(\hat{h}_1,...,\hat{h}_n)$ which are important for a considered choice, should be determined. In turn, for each component $S_i, i = 1,...,m$ and $\hat{h}_j, j = 1,...,n$ it is needed to determine discrete sets $S^{(i)}$ and $H^{(j)}$ of their possible values. For example, if $\hat{h}_j$ is *risk attitude* then the set $H^{(j)}$ may be [44]

$$H^{(j)} = \{\hat{h}_1^{(j)} = (risk\,averse, high), \hat{h}_2^{(j)} = (risk\,neutral, medium),$$
$$\hat{h}_3^{(j)} = (risk\,seeking, low)\}$$

If S_i is *GDP* then the set $S^{(i)}$ may be

$$S^{(i)} = \{S_1^{(i)} = low, S_2^{(i)} = medium, S_3^{(i)} = high\}.$$

A space of combined states as a space of multidimensional vectors $(\boldsymbol{S}, \hat{\boldsymbol{h}}) = (S_{i_1}^{(1)}, ..., S_{i_m}^{(m)}, \hat{h}_{j_1}^{(1)}, ..., \hat{h}_{j_n}^{(n)}) = (S_{k_1}^{(1)}, ..., S_{k_m}^{(m)}, \hat{h}_{k_{m+1}}^{(m+1)}, ..., \hat{h}_{k_{m+n}}^{(m+n)})$ can then be used for comparison of alternatives. For this purpose, for each alternative it is necessary to determine Z-valued utilities $\hat{u}(\hat{f}(\boldsymbol{S}, \hat{\boldsymbol{h}}))$ of its Z-valued outcomes at all the combined states. These utilities measure attractiveness or repulsiveness of each outcome from a DM's condition point of view. This can be done by using experience based-evaluation or by applying well-known techniques. The other necessary information for comparison of alternatives is measuring degrees of dependence of a DM's condition on objective conditions. These degrees will be represented by means of Z-valued joint probabilities. For determination of Z-valued joint probabilities, it is needed to estimate Z-valued marginal probabilities of $(S_1, ..., S_m), (\hat{h}_1, ..., \hat{h}_n)$. Inturn, this requires the use of information on Z-valued probability distributions over $S^{(i)}$ and $H^{(j)}$:

$$\hat{P}(S_i) = \hat{P}_1^{(i)} / S_1^{(i)} + ... + \hat{P}_{m_i}^{(i)} / S_{m_i}^{(i)}, \ i = 1, ..., m,$$

$$\hat{P}(\hat{h}_j) = \hat{P}_1^{(j)} / \hat{h}_1^{(j)} + ... + \hat{P}_{n_j}^{(j)} / \hat{h}_{n_j}^{(j)}, \ j = 1, ..., n,$$

where $\hat{P}_1^{(i)} = (A_{P_1^{(i)}}, B_{P_1^{(i)}})$, ... , $\hat{P}_{m_i}^{(i)} = (A_{P_{m_i}^{(i)}}, B_{P_{m_i}^{(i)}})$, $\hat{P}_1^{(j)} = (A_{P_1^{(j)}}, B_{P_1^{(j)}})$, ... , $\hat{P}_{n_j}^{(j)} = (A_{P_{n_j}^{(j)}}, B_{P_{n_j}^{(j)}})$. Note that the condition $B_{P_1^{(i)}} = ... = B_{P_{m_i}^{(i)}} = B_{P^{(i)}}$, $B_{P_1^{(j)}} = ... = B_{P_{n_j}^{(j)}} = B_{P^{(j)}}$ should be satisfied for the purpose of consistency of Z-valued probability distributions. Given $\hat{P}(S_i)$ and $\hat{P}(\hat{h}_j)$, the Z-valued marginal probability distributions $\hat{P}(\boldsymbol{S})$ and $\hat{P}(\hat{\boldsymbol{h}})$ will be represented as follows:

$$\hat{P}(S) = \hat{P}(S_1)/S_1 + ... + \hat{P}(S_m)/S_m,$$

$$\hat{P}(\hat{h}) = \hat{P}(\hat{h}_1)/\hat{h}_1 + ... + \hat{P}(\hat{h}_n)/\hat{h}_n.$$

Given marginal $\hat{P}(S)$ and $\hat{P}(\hat{h})$, and information about signs of dependences between components of S and $\hat{h}$, it is needed to determine the Z-valued joint probabilities over combined states

$$\hat{P}(S,\hat{h}) = \hat{P}(S_{i_1}^{(1)},...,S_{i_m}^{(m)},\hat{h}_{j_1}^{(1)},...,\hat{h}_{j_n}^{(n)}) = \hat{P}(S_{k_1}^{(1)},...,S_{k_m}^{(m)},\hat{h}_{k_{m+1}}^{(m+1)},...,\hat{h}_{k_{m+n}}^{(m+n)}):$$

$$\hat{P}(S_{k_1}^{(1)},...,S_{k_m}^{(m)},\hat{h}_{k_{m+1}}^{(m+1)},...,\hat{h}_{k_{m+n}}^{(m+n)}) = \phi(\hat{P}(S_{k_1}^{(1)}),...,\hat{P}(S_{k_m}^{(m)}),\hat{P}(\hat{h}_{k_{m+1}}^{(m+1)}),...,\hat{P}(\hat{h}_{k_{m+n}}^{(m+n)}))$$

The main problem in determination of $\hat{P}(S,\hat{h})$ is to obtain information about interdependencies of $S_{k_1}^{(1)},...,S_{k_m}^{(m)},\hat{h}_{k_{m+1}}^{(m+1)},...,\hat{h}_{k_{m+n}}^{(m+n)}$. Taking into account the complexity of relations between $S_{k_1}^{(1)},...,S_{k_m}^{(m)},\hat{h}_{k_{m+1}}^{(m+1)},...,\hat{h}_{k_{m+n}}^{(m+n)}$, an adequate approach to obtain such information is the use of some intelligent procedure based on expert evaluations [96, 113, 292, 455, 561, 636].

On the base of the Z-valued joint probabilities $\hat{P}(\hat{\omega}) = \hat{P}(S,\hat{h}) = (A_{P(\omega)}, B_P)$ a Z-valued bi-capacity $\hat{\eta}$ is then constructed to model relation between combined states under imprecise and partially reliable information, especially taking into account interaction between attractive and repulsive outcomes. A Z-valued bi-capacity $\hat{\eta}$ is to be constructed as the difference between two Z-valued capacities:

$$\hat{\eta}(\mathcal{V},\mathcal{W}) = \hat{\upsilon}_1(\mathcal{V}) - \hat{\upsilon}_2(\mathcal{W})$$

Z-valued fuzzy capacities $\hat{\upsilon}_1(\mathcal{V}), \hat{\upsilon}_2(\mathcal{W})$ can be constructed as lower or upper probabilities or their convex combinations. As lower and upper probabilities, one can use lower and upper envelops of the set of priors which is defined by Z-valued restrictions $\hat{P}(\hat{\omega}) = \hat{P}(S,\hat{h}) = (A_{P(\omega)}, B_P)$. The lower envelope $\hat{\upsilon}(\mathcal{V})$ can be found as [44]

$$\hat{v}(\mathcal{V}) = (A_v(\mathcal{V}), B_v), \quad B_v = B_P$$

$$A_v(\mathcal{V}) = \bigcup_{\alpha \in (0,1]} \alpha \left[A_{v1}^{\alpha}(\mathcal{V}), A_{v2}^{\alpha}(\mathcal{V}) \right], \quad \mathcal{V} \subset \Omega = \{\hat{\omega}_1, ..., \hat{\omega}_L\} \tag{11.5}$$

where

$$A_{v1}^{\alpha}(\mathcal{V}) = \inf \left\{ \sum_{\hat{\omega}_l \in V} p(\hat{\omega}_l) \Big| (p(\hat{\omega}_1), ..., p(\hat{\omega}_L)) \in A_P^{\alpha} \right\},$$

$$A_P^{\alpha} = \left\{ (p(\hat{\omega}_1), ..., p(\hat{\omega}_L)) \in A_{P(\omega_1)}^{\alpha} \times ... \times A_{P(\omega_L)}^{\alpha} \Big| \sum_{l=1}^{L} p(\hat{\omega}_l) = 1 \right\}. \tag{11.6}$$

Here $A_{P(\omega_1)}^{\alpha}, ..., A_{P(\omega_L)}^{\alpha}$ are α-cuts of fuzzy probabilities $A_{P(\omega_1)}, ..., A_{P(\omega_L)}$ respectively, $p(\hat{\omega}_1), ..., p(\hat{\omega}_L)$ are basic probabilities for $A_{P(\omega_1)}, ..., A_{P(\omega_L)}$ respectively, $\times$ denotes the Cartesian product. The upper prevision can be obtained by substituting inf by sup in (11.6).

For each alternative $\hat{f}$, given its utilities for all the combined states and the Z-valued bi-capacity modeling dependence between combined states, the overall utility $\hat{U}(\hat{f})$ can be determined according to (11.1). The best alternative is further found by determining the highest value of the Z-valued utility $\hat{U} : A \rightarrow Z$. The determination of the highest value of $\hat{U}$ can be done by applying fuzzy Pareto optimality principle-based comparison of Z-numbers suggested in Section 6.6.

11.2. Z-number based linear programming

Linear Programming (LP) is the operations research technique frequently used in the fields of Science, Economics, Business, Management Science and Engineering. Although it is investigated and applied for more than six decades, and LP models with different level of generalization of information about parameters including models with interval, fuzzy, generalized fuzzy, and random numbers are considered, till now there is no approach to account for reliability of information within the framework of LP. The use of Z-information is more adequate and intuitively meaningful for formalizing information structure of a decision problem. In this section we consider a study of fully Z-number based LP (Z-LP) model in order to better fit real-world problems within the framework of LP. We consider the method to solve Z-LP problems which utilizes differential evolution optimization and Z-number arithmetic developed in [17].

11.2.1 *State-of-the art*

Linear Programming (LP) is the well-known operations research technique frequently in various fields theory and practice. LP models representing real-world situations usually include a lot of parameters which are assigned by experts. In classical LP models values of these parameters required to be fixed, precisely known. But in real-world in many cases it becomes impossible to determine the precise values of parameters due to uncertainty and imprecision of relevant information. Interval analysis, Type-1 and Type-2 fuzzy set theories have been applied in formulation of LP models, and the corresponding methods to better capture uncertainty of an investigated real-world problem were developed [230, 237, 238, 300, 389].

An interval arithmetic-based LP approach is considered in [68, 280]. The first research on taking into account real-world soft constraints in LP problem by using fuzzy sets was suggested in the famous work by Zadeh and Bellman [105]. The concept of fuzzy LP was first given in [881]. Nowadays there is a wide spectrum of works within application of the fuzzy set theory to modeling of imperfect information within LP problems. A lot of works are devoted to LP with parameters considered as fuzzy numbers [147, 225, 400, 486, 491, 712]. In [626] a new concept of duality in fuzzy LP, weak and strong duality theorems are suggested. A series of works is devoted to comparison of fuzzy and stochastic LP problems [376, 639]. Some works are devoted to LP problems with fuzzy parameters described by typical forms of membership functions [296, 375].

In [131] an evolutionary algorithm-based solution to the fully fuzzified linear programming problem is proposed. In [26] they propose fuzzy chaos-based approach to solution of fuzzy linear programming problem and provide its application to product mix problem. In [238] solving of the Type-2 fuzzy linear programming problems by using two phases method is proposed. In [448] the authors propose generalized simplex algorithm to solve fuzzy LP problems with parameters described by generalized fuzzy numbers (GFNs). To our knowledge, this work is the first research on fuzzy LP with GFNs, which is close to an implementation of an idea to account for reliability of decision-relevant information. In this paper, on the base of the proposed new approach to ranking of GFNs, the authors develop generalized fuzzy simplex algorithm to solve real-world LP problems.

We can conclude that there is a large progress in taking into account uncertainty, imprecision, partial truth and soft constraints in real LP problems. However, the main drawback of the works mentioned above is that in these works the reliability of the decision relevant information is not taken into consideration to a considerable extent. Moreover, in the majority of works they only take into account imperfect information on parameters of LP models, whereas decision variables are considered accurate.

In this section we describe a new LP model, namely Z-number based LP (Z-LP) model which is based on Z-numbers arithmetic [33]. This approach utilizes LP model with both the parameters and decision variables are described by Z-numbers in order to better fit the real-world problems to LP with imprecise and partially reliable information.

11.2.2 *Statement of a Z-number based linear programming problem*

We consider solving a fully Z-number based linear programming problem, i.e. with Z-valued decision variables and Z-valued parameters.

The general formulation of a Z-LP problem may be described as follows:

$$Z_f(Z_{x_1}, Z_{x_2}, ..., Z_{x_n}) = Z_{c_1} Z_{x_1} + Z_{c_2} Z_{x_2} + ... + Z_{c_n} Z_{x_n} \rightarrow \max \qquad (11.7)$$

subject to

$$Z_{a_{11}} Z_{x_1} + Z_{a_{12}} Z_{x_2} + ... + Z_{a_{1n}} Z_{x_n} \preceq Z_{b_1},$$
$$Z_{a_{21}} Z_{x_1} + Z_{a_{22}} Z_{x_2} + ... + Z_{a_{2n}} Z_{x_n} \preceq Z_{b_2},$$

$$...$$

$$Z_{a_{m1}} Z_{x_1} + Z_{a_{m2}} Z_{x_2} + ... + Z_{a_{mn}} Z_{x_n} \preceq Z_{b_m},$$

(11.8)

$$Z_{x_1}, Z_{x_2}, ..., Z_{x_n} \succeq Z_0$$

(11.9)

Here decision variables and parameters are described by Z-numbers $Z_{x_i} = (A_{x_i}, B_{x_i})$, $Z_{c_i} = (A_{c_i}, B_{c_i})$, $Z_{a_{ij}} = (A_{a_{ij}}, B_{a_{ij}})$, $Z_{b_j} = (A_{b_j}, B_{b_j})$, $i = 1, ..., n, j = 1, ..., m$, $Z_0 = (0,1)$.

To properly define the Z-LP problem we have to clarify what is $\max Z_f$ and what is Z-inequality. In this work $\max Z_f$ and Z-inequality are defined in terms ranking of Z-numbers described in Section 6.6 and, the problem (11.7)-(11.9) may be transformed into the problem described below:

$$Z_f(Z_{x_1}, Z_{x_2}, ..., Z_{x_n}) = Z_{c_1} Z_{x_1} + Z_{c_2} Z_{x_2} + ... + Z_{c_n} Z_{x_n} \rightarrow \max \quad (11.10)$$

subject to

$$Z_{a_{11}} Z_{x_1} + Z_{a_{12}} Z_{x_2} + ... + Z_{a_{1n}} Z_{x_n} \leq^Z Z_{b_1},$$
$$Z_{a_{21}} Z_{x_1} + Z_{a_{22}} Z_{x_2} + ... + Z_{a_{2n}} Z_{x_n} \leq^Z Z_{b_2},$$

$$...$$

$$Z_{a_{m1}} Z_{x_1} + Z_{a_{m2}} Z_{x_2} + ... + Z_{a_{mn}} Z_{x_n} \leq^Z Z_{b_m},$$

(11.11)

$$Z_{x_1}, Z_{x_2}, ..., Z_{x_n} \geq^Z Z_0.$$

(11.12)

Let us consider solving of this problem. To our knowledge, there is no a method for solving the Z-LP problem (11.10)-(11.12), that is to obtain optimal (max or min) value of Z_f. We will use a directed search method, namely DE optimization method described in Section 11.2.3, to find an optimal solution to the considered problem.

Definition 11.1. *A Z-valued slack variable.* Suppose that an *i*-th constraint of a Z-LP problem is

$$\sum_{j=1}^{n} Z_{a_{ij}} Z_{x_j} \leq^Z Z_{b_i} \ .$$

A Z-valued variable $Z_{x_{n+i}}$ such that

$$\sum_{j=1}^{n} Z_{a_{ij}} Z_{x_j} + Z_{x_{n+i}} = Z_{b_i}, \quad Z_{x_{n+i}} \geq^Z Z_0$$

is called a Z-valued slack variable.

Definition 11.2. *A Z-valued surplus variable.* Suppose that an *i*-th constraint of a Z-LP problem is

$$\sum_{j=1}^{n} Z_{a_{ij}} Z_{x_j} \geq^Z Z_{b_i}$$

A Z-valued variable $Z_{x_{n+i}}$ such that

$$\sum_{j=1}^{n} Z_{a_{ij}} Z_{x_j} - Z_{x_{n+i}} = Z_{b_i}, \quad Z_{x_{n+i}} \geq^Z Z_0$$

is called a Z-valued surplus variable.

Definition 11.3. *A Z-valued feasible solution.* Any Z_x in (11.10) which satisfies constraints (11.11)-(11.12) is called a Z-valued feasible solution of (11.10)-(11.12).

Denote $\mathbf{Z}_s$ a set of all Z-valued feasible solutions of (11.10)-(11.12).

Definition 11.4. *A Z-valued optimal solution.* A Z-valued feasible solution $Z_{x_{opt}} \in \mathbf{Z}_s$ is called a Z-valued optimal solution of (11.10)-(11.12) if

$Z_f(Z_{x_{opt}}) \leq^Z Z_f(Z_x)$. Let us proceed to solving of the problem (11.10)-(11.12).

At first we add the Z-valued slack variables:

$$Z_f(Z_{x_1}, Z_{x_2}, ..., Z_{x_n}) = Z_{c_1} Z_{x_1} + Z_{c_2} Z_{x_2} + ... + Z_{c_n} Z_{x_n} \to \max$$

subject to

$$Z_{a_{11}} Z_{x_1} + Z_{a_{12}} Z_{x_2} + ... + Z_{a_{1n}} Z_{x_n} + Z_{x_{n+1}} = Z_{b_1},$$
$$Z_{a_{21}} Z_{x_1} + Z_{a_{22}} Z_{x_2} + ... + Z_{a_{2n}} Z_{x_n} + Z_{x_{n+2}} = Z_{b_2},$$
$$...$$
$$Z_{a_{m1}} Z_{x_1} + Z_{a_{m2}} Z_{x_2} + ... + Z_{a_{mn}} Z_{x_n} + Z_{x_{n+m}} = Z_{b_m}, \qquad (11.13)$$
$$Z_{x_1}, Z_{x_2}, ..., Z_{x_n}, Z_{x_{n+1}}, Z_{x_{n+2}}, ..., Z_{x_{n+m}} \geq^Z Z_0.$$

Next we rewrite the considered problem in the following equivalent form:

$$Z_g(Z_{x_1}, Z_{x_2}, ..., Z_{x_n}, Z_{x_{n+1}}, Z_{x_{n+2}}, ..., Z_{x_{n+m}}) = -(Z_{c_1} Z_{x_1} + Z_{c_2} Z_{x_2}$$
$$+ ... + Z_{c_n} Z_{x_n}) + + (Z_{b_1} - (Z_{a_{11}} Z_{x_1} + Z_{a_{12}} Z_{x_2} + ... + Z_{a_{1n}} Z_{x_n} + Z_{x_{n+1}}))$$
$$+ (Z_{b_2} - (Z_{a_{21}} Z_{x_1} + Z_{a_{22}} Z_{x_2} + ... + Z_{a_{2n}} Z_{x_n} + Z_{x_{n+2}})) + ... +$$
$$+ (Z_{b_m} - (Z_{a_{m1}} Z_{x_1} + Z_{a_{m2}} Z_{x_2} + ... + Z_{a_{mn}} Z_{x_n} + Z_{x_{n+m}})) \to \max$$

$$(11.14)$$

subject to

$$Z_{x_1}, Z_{x_2}, ..., Z_{x_n}, Z_{x_{n+1}}, Z_{x_{n+2}}, ..., Z_{x_{n+m}} \geq^Z Z_0 \qquad (11.15)$$

The solution method for solving of optimization problem (11.14)-(11.15) is described in Section 11.2.3.

11.2.3 *Solution method*

Recently many heuristic algorithms have been proposed for global optimization of nonlinear, non-convex, and non-differential functions [11, 170, 210, 594, 767]. These methods are more flexible than classical as they do not require differentiability, continuity, or other properties to hold for optimizing functions. Some of such methods are genetic algorithm [15, 321, 661], evolutionary strategy, particle swarm optimization, and differential evolution (DE) optimization. In this study we consider the use of the DE algorithm.

As a stochastic method, DE algorithm uses initial population randomly generated by uniform distribution, differential mutation, probability crossover, and selection operators [621]. The population with N individuals (each individual is one candidate solution) is maintained with each generation. A new vector is generated by mutation which in DE means randomly selecting from the population 3 individuals– vectors $r_1 \neq r_2 \neq r_3$ and adding a weighted difference vector between two individuals to a third individual (population member).

The mutated vector is then undergone the crossover operation with another vector generating new offspring vector.

The selection process is done as follows. If the resulting vector yields a lower value of the objective function (assuming a lower value is a better one as is usually done in DE cost objective function) than a predetermined population member does, then in the following generation the newly generated vector will replace the vector with which it was compared.

Extracting distance and direction information from the population to generate random deviations results in an adaptive scheme with excellent convergence properties. DE has been successfully applied to solve a wide range of problems such as image classification, clustering, optimization etc.

Figure 11.1 shows the process of generation of a new trial solution, X_{new} vector, from randomly selected population members X_{r1}, X_{r2}, X_{r3} (vector X_{r4} is then the candidate for replacement by the new vector, if the new vector is better (i.e. its value of objective function is lower). Here we assume that the solution vectors are of dimension 2 (i.e. 2 optimization parameters).

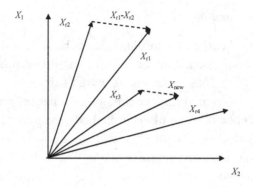

Fig. 11.1. Realization of DE optimization: a two-dimensional case

In this section we describe the solution method for Z-LP (11.14)-(11.15). At the first stage we set the parameters of the DE algorithm, define the DE cost function as the objective function Z_f (11.14), and choose the population size PN. As a rule of thumb, the population size is set at least ten times the number of optimization variables. Thus, as a Z-number has two components, the population size is $PN = 2 \cdot 10 N_{var}$, where N_{var} is the number of optimization variables. Then the DE optimization is started.

First we construct template parameter vector u of dimension $2N_{var}$ for holding data of all decision variables Z_x. Then we set algorithm parameters: F (mutation rate)=0.8, CR (crossover rate)=0.7.

Next PN parameter vectors are randomly generated and a population $P = \{u_1, u_2, \ldots, u_{PN}\}$ is formed.

While the termination condition (a number of predefined generations is reached or a required error level is obtained) is not met, new parameter sets are generated. For a next vector u_i ($i=1, \ldots, PN$) 3 different vectors u_{r1}, u_{r2}, u_{r3} are chosen randomly from P each of which is different from the current u_i. A new trial vector $u_{new} = u_{r1} + F \cdot (u_{r2} - u_{r3})$ is used to generate a new vector in the population. Individual vector parameters of u_i are inherited with probability CR into the new vector u_{new}. If the cost function for u_{new} is better (lower) than the cost function for u_i then the current u_i is replaced in population P by u_{new}. Next the parameter vector

u_{best} is selected with the best value of cost function (objective function) from population P.

The above process is continued until the termination condition is met. When the condition is met, we select the parameter vector u_{best} (best decision variables) with the lower cost function Z_f from population P. Finally, we extract from u_{best} all the decision variables.

11.3 Fair price based decision making under interval, set-valued, fuzzy, and Z-number uncertainty

In this section, we explain how to define a fair price for a participation in a decision, and then select an alternative for which the corresponding fair price is the largest. This idea is explained on the examples of interval uncertainty, set-valued, fuzzy, and Z-number uncertainty.

In many practical situations, we have several alternatives, and we need to select one of these alternatives. For example:

– a person saving for retirement needs to find the best way to invest money;

– a company needs to select a location for its new plant;

– a designer must select one of several possible designs for a new airplane;
– a medical doctor needs to select a treatment for a patient.

Decision making is easier if we know the exact consequences of each alternative selection.

Often, however, we only have an incomplete information about consequences of different alternative, and we need to select an alternative under this uncertainty.

Traditional decision making theory mostly concentrates on the case of probabilistic uncertainty, when for each alternative a, we know the probability $p_i(a)$ of different outcomes i; [283, 483, 625]. In this case, it can be proven that preferences of a rational decision maker can be described by assigning, to each possible outcome, a value u$_i$ called its *utility.* Then, the attractiveness of each alternative to this particular decision maker can be characterized by the corresponding expected value of its utility $\bar{u}(a) \stackrel{def}{=} \sum_i p_i(a) \cdot u_i$; the larger the expected utility, the better the alternative.

Often, however, we do not know these probabilities. For example, sometimes, we only know the range $[\underline{u}, \bar{u}]$ of possible utility values, but we do not know the probability of different values within this range. It has been shown that in this case, it makes sense to select an alternative for which the expression $\alpha_H \cdot \bar{u} + (1 - \alpha_H) \cdot \underline{u}$ is the largest possible, where a number $\alpha_H \in [0,1]$ described the optimism level of a decision maker.

• When $\alpha_H = 1$, the decision maker completely ignores the worst-case possibility $\underline{u}$ and bases his/her decision exclusively on the best-case scenario, with outcome $\bar{u}$. This case corresponds to the maximum *optimism*.

• When $\alpha_H = 0$, the decision maker completely ignores the best-case possibility $\bar{u}$ and bases his/her decision exclusively on the worst-case scenario, with outcome $\underline{u}$. This case corresponds to the maximum *pessimism*.

Most actual decision makers take both worst-case and best case outcomes into account, so their decisions correspond to the values $\alpha_H \in (0,1)$. This idea was first proposed by the Nobelist L. Hurwicz; it is known as the *Hurwicz optimism-pessimism criterion* [371, 483].

What if we have fuzzy uncertainty? There are many semiheuristic methods of decision making under fuzzy uncertainty, methods which have led to many practical applications; [371, 483]. In [38], a consistent approach to decision making under fuzzy (and more general) uncertainty is described – which is based on the extension of the notion of utility to interval, fuzzy, and Z-number uncertainty.

In spite of all these successes, there are still many practical problems in which it is not completely clear how to make an appropriate decision, so there is still a need for a consistent general methodology for decision making under uncertainty.

Here, we provide foundations for the new methodology of decision making under uncertainty, a methodology which is based on a natural idea of a *fair price*.

When we have a full information about an object, we can express our desirability of each possible situation, e.g., by declaring a price that we

are willing to pay to get involved in this situation. Once these prices are set, selecting the most preferable alternative is easy: we just select the alternative for which the participation price is the highest — since this is clearly the most desirable alternative.

In decision making under uncertainty, the situation is not so clear, since it is not easy to come up with a fair price. A natural idea is to develop techniques for producing such fair prices – these prices can then be used in decision making, to select an appropriate alternative.

11.3.1 *Case of interval uncertainty*

Let us start with a simple case of uncertainty, in which, instead of knowing the exact gain u of selecting an alternative, we only know the lower bound $\underline{u}$ and the upper bound $\overline{u}$ on this gain – and we have no information on which values from the corresponding interval $[\underline{u}, \overline{u}]$ are more probable or less probable. This situation, in which the only information that we have about the gain u is that this gain belongs to the interval $[\underline{u}, \overline{u}]$, is called *interval uncertainty*.

We want to assign, to each interval $[\underline{u}, \overline{u}]$, a number $P(\underline{u}, \overline{u}|)$ describing the fair price of this interval. In other words, we need a function $P(\underline{u}, \overline{u}|)$ that takes an interval as an input and returns a real number. There are several reasonable requirements that this function must satisfy.

First, since in all cases, the gain is larger than or equal to $\underline{u}$ and is smaller than or equal to $\overline{u}$, it is reasonable to require that the price should also be larger than or equal to $\underline{u}$ and smaller than or equal to $\overline{u}$:
$\underline{u} \leq P([\underline{u}, \overline{u}]) \leq \overline{u}$.

Second, if we keep the lower endpoint $\underline{u}$ intact but increase the upper bound, this means that we are keeping all the previous possibilities, but we are allowing new possibilities with a higher gain. In this case, it is reasonable to require that the corresponding price increases (or at least that it does not decrease). In other words, if $\underline{u} = \underline{v}$ and $\overline{u} = \overline{v}$, then $P([\underline{u}, \overline{u}]) \leq P([\underline{v}, \overline{v}])$.

Similar, if we dismiss some low-gain alternatives, this should increase (or at least not decrease) the fair price. So, in general, if $\underline{u} = \underline{v}$ and $\overline{u} = \overline{v}$, then we should have $P([\underline{u}, \overline{u}]) \leq P([\underline{v}, \overline{v}])$.

To describe the third requirement, let us consider the situation when we have two consequent decisions. Let us assume that these decisions are *independent* from each other, in the sense that the second decision does not depend on the first one. We can view this situation in two different ways:

• we can consider two decision processes separately, or

• we can consider a single decision process in which we select a pair of alternatives:

• the first alternative corresponding to the first decision process, and

• the second alternative corresponding to the second decision process.

If we know the exact gains u and v in each of the decision processes, this means that we are willing to pay:

• the amount u to participate in the first process,

• the amount v to participate in the second decision process, and

• the total of $u + v$ to participate in both decision processes.

In general, it is reasonable to require that even under uncertainty, the fair price $u + v$ of selecting two alternatives in the two decision processes is equal to the sum of the fair prices u and v of selecting each of these alternatives in the corresponding decision process.

Let us describe this requirement for the case when the consequences of each alternative are only known with interval uncertainty. About the gain u from the first alternative, we only know that this (unknown) gain value belongs to the interval $[\underline{u}, \overline{u}]$. About the gain v from the second alternative, we only know that this gain belongs to the interval $[\underline{v}, \overline{v}]$. The overall gain $u + v$ can thus take any value from the interval $[\underline{u}, \overline{u}] + [\underline{v}, \overline{v}] = [\underline{u} + \underline{v}, \overline{u} + \overline{v}]$. Thus, the above requirement about the fair prices takes the form

$$P([\underline{u} + \underline{v}, \overline{u} + \overline{v}]) = P([\underline{u}, \overline{u}]) + P([\underline{v}, \overline{v}])$$ (11.16)

Thus, we arrive at the following definition.

Definition 11.5. By a fair price under interval uncertainty, we mean a function $P[\underline{u}, \overline{u}]$ that assigns, to every interval, a real number, and which satisfies the following properties:

- $\underline{u} \leq P([\underline{u}, \overline{u}]) \leq \overline{u}$ for all u (conservativeness);

- if $\underline{u} = \underline{v}$ and $\overline{u} = \overline{v}$, then $P([\underline{u}, \overline{u}]) \leq P([\underline{v}, \overline{v}])$ (monotonicity);

- for all $\underline{u}, \overline{u}, \underline{v}$ and $\overline{v}$, we have

$$P([\underline{u} + \underline{v}, \overline{u} + \overline{v}]) = P([\underline{u}, \overline{u}]) + P([\underline{v}, \overline{v}])$$ (11.17)

(additivity).

Proposition 11.1 [506]. Each fair price under interval uncertainty has the form

$$P([\underline{u}, \overline{u}]) = \alpha_H \cdot \overline{u} + (1 - \alpha_H) \cdot \underline{u}$$ (11.18)

for some real number $\alpha_H \in [0,1]$

We thus get a new justification of the Hurwicz optimism-pessimism criterion that we described above. We reproduce the proof from [506] since other proofs from this section use its ideas and techniques.

Proof

1. Let us first consider the value $\alpha_H \stackrel{def}{=} P([0,1])$ corresponding

to the simplest possible interval [0, 1]. Due to conservativeness, we have $0 \le \alpha_H \le 1$.

2. Let us now compute the value $P([0,m])$ for positive integer values m.

The interval $[0,m]$ can be represented as the sum of m intervals equal to [0, 1]:

$[0,m] = [0, 1] + \ldots + [0, 1]$ (m times).

Thus, due to additivity, we have

$P([0,m]) = P([0, 1]) + \ldots + P([0, 1])$ (m times) $=$

$\alpha_H + \ldots + \alpha_H$ (m times) $= \alpha_H \cdot m$.

3. Now, let us compute the value $z \stackrel{def}{=} P\left(\left[0,\dfrac{1}{n}\right]\right)$ for a positive integer n.

In this case, the interval [0, 1] can be represented as the sum of n intervals equal to $\left[0,\dfrac{1}{n}\right]$:

$$[0,1] = \left[0,\dfrac{1}{n}\right] + \ldots + \left[0,\dfrac{1}{n}\right] \quad (n \text{ times})$$

Thus, due to additivity, we have

$\alpha_H = z + \ldots + z$ (n times)

i.e., $\alpha_H = z \cdot n$ and hence $z = \alpha_H \cdot \dfrac{1}{n}$,

4. For every two positive integers $m > 0$ and $n > 0$, the interval $\left[0, \dfrac{m}{n}\right]$ can be represented as the sum of m intervals equal to $\left[0, \dfrac{1}{n}\right]$. Thus

$$P\left(\left[0, \frac{m}{n}\right]\right) = m \cdot P\left(\left[0, \frac{1}{n}\right]\right) = m \cdot \left(\alpha_H \cdot \frac{1}{n}\right) = \alpha_H \cdot \frac{m}{n} .$$

5. We have proved that for rational values $r = \dfrac{m}{n}$, we have $P([0, r]) = \alpha_H \cdot r$. Let us prove that the same property $P([0, r]) = \alpha_H \cdot x$ holds for every positive real value x.

To prove this property, we use monotonicity. Each real number x can be approximated, with arbitrary accuracy, by two rational numbers $r < x < r'$. Due to monotonicity, we have $P([0, r]) \leq P([0, x]) \leq P([0, r'])$. Due to Part 4 of this proof, we thus conclude that $\alpha_H \cdot r \leq P([0, x]) \leq \alpha_H \cdot r'$. When $r \to x$ and $r' \to x$, we get $\alpha_H \cdot r \to \alpha_H \cdot x$ and $\alpha_H \cdot r' \to \alpha_H \cdot x$ and thus, $P([0, x]) = \alpha_H \cdot x$.

6. Now, we are ready to prove the proposition. For each $\underline{u}$ and $\overline{u}$, we have $[\underline{u}, \overline{u}] = [\underline{u}, \underline{u}] + [0, \overline{u} - \underline{u}]$. Thus, due to additivity,

$$P([\underline{u}, \overline{u}]) = P([\underline{u}, \underline{u}]) + P([0, \overline{u} - \underline{u}]) \tag{11.19}$$

For the first term, due to conservativeness, we have $\underline{u} \leq P([\underline{u}, \underline{u}]) \leq \underline{u}$, and thus, $P([\underline{u}, \underline{u}]) = \underline{u}$. For the second term, due to Part 5 of this proof, we get $P([0, \overline{u} - \underline{u}]) = \alpha_H \cdot (\overline{u} - \underline{u})$ Thus, the above additivity formula leads to

$$P([\overline{u}, \underline{u}]) = \overline{u} + \alpha_H \cdot (\overline{u} - \underline{u}), \qquad (11.20)$$

which is exactly $\alpha_H \cdot \overline{u} + (1 - \alpha_H) \cdot \underline{u}$. The proposition is proven.

11.3.2 *Case of set-valued uncertainty*

Let's give description of the case. In some cases, in addition to knowing that the actual gain belongs to the interval $[\underline{u}, \overline{u}]$, we also know that some values from this interval cannot be possible values of this gain. For example, if we buy an obscure lottery ticket for a simple prize-or-no-prize lottery from a remote country, we either get the prize or lose the money. In this case, the set of possible values of the gain consists of two values.

In a closer-to-home lottery, we usually have an additional information about the outcomes that we can take into account when making a decision: e.g., we usually know the probability of a prize (or prizes, if there are different prizes). However, for an obscure lottery, it is reasonable to imagine that we have no additional information. In this case, the only information that we have is the (2-element) set of possible outcomes.

In general, instead of a (bounded) *interval* of possible values, we can consider a more general bounded *set* of possible values. It makes sense to consider bounded sets S that contain all their limits points. Indeed, if $x_n \in S$ for all n and $x_n \to x$, then, for any given accuracy, x is undistinguishable from some possible value x_n — thus, in effect, the value x itself is possible. Such sets are known as *closed* sets. So, in this section, we will consider bounded closed sets.

We want to assign, to each bounded closed set S, a number $P(S)$ describing the fair price of this set. In other words, we need a function $P(S)$ that takes a set as an input and returns a real number. There are several reasonable requirements that this function must satisfy.

First, for the case when the set S is an interval, we must get the fair price as described by Proposition 11.1.

Second, if we have two independent alternatives described by sets S and S', then we should have $P(S + S') = P(S) + P(S')$, where

$$S + S' \overset{def}{=} \{x + x' : x \in S \text{ and } x' \in S'\} \tag{11.21}$$

is the set of all possible sums $x + x'$.

Thus, we arrive at the following definition.

Definition 11.6. By a fair price under set-valued uncertainty, we mean a function P(S) that assigns, to every bounded closed set S, a real number, and which satisfies the following properties:

• a restriction of this function to intervals $S + [\underline{u}, \overline{u}]$ is a fair price under interval uncertainty – in the sense of Definition 11.5 (conservativeness);

• for every two sets S and S', we have P(S + S') = P(S) + P(S') (additivity).

Proposition 11.2. Each fair price under interval uncertainty has the form $P([\underline{u}, \overline{u}]) = \alpha_H \cdot \sup S + (1 - \alpha_H) \cdot \inf S$ for some real number $\alpha_H \in [0, 1]$.

Proof is given in [479].

11.3.3 *Case of Z-valued uncertainty*

In the previous sections, we assumed that we are 100% certain that the actual gain is contained in the given interval (or set). In reality, mistakes are possible, so usually, we are only certain that u belongs to the corresponding interval or set with some probability $0 < p < 1$. In such situations, to fully describe our knowledge, we need to describe both the interval (or set) *and* this probability p.

In the general context, after supplementing the information about a quantity with the information of how certain we are about this piece of information, we get what L. Zadeh calls a *Z-number* [821]. Because of this:

• we will call a pair consisting of a (crisp) number and a (crisp) probability a crisp Z-number;

• we will call a pair consisting of an interval and a probability a Z-interval; and

• we will call a pair consisting of a set and a probability a Z-set.

In this section, we will describe fair prices for crisp Z-numbers, Z-intervals, and Z-sets for situations when the probability p is known exactly.

When we have two independent sequential decisions, and we are 100% sure that the first decision leads to gain u and the second decision leads to gain v, then, as we have mentioned earlier, the user's total gain is equal to the sum $u + v$. In this section, we consider the situation in which:

• for the first decision, our degree of confidence in the gain estimate u is described by some probability p;

• for the second decision, our degree of confidence in the gain estimate v is described by some probability q.

The estimate u + v is valid only if both gain estimates are correct. Since these estimates are independent, the probability that they are both correct is equal to the product p · q of the corresponding probabilities. Thus:

• for crisp Z-numbers (u, p) and (v, q), the sum is equal to (u + v, p · q);

• for Z-intervals $([\underline{u},\overline{u}],p)$ and $([\underline{v},\overline{v}],q)$, the sum is equal to $([\underline{u}+\underline{v},\overline{u}+\overline{v}],p\cdot q)$;

• finally, for Z-sets (S, p) and (S', q), the sum is equal to (S + S', p · q).

Let us analyze these cases one by one.

Case of crisp Z-numbers. Since the probability p is usually known with some uncertainty, it makes sense to require that the fair price of a crisp Z-number (u, p) continuously depend on p, so that small changes in p lead to small changes in the fair price – and the closer our estimate to the actual value of the probability, the closer the estimated fair price should be to the actual fair price.

Thus, we arrive at the following definitions.

Definition 11.7. By a crisp Z-number, we mean a pair (u, p) of two real numbers such that $0 < p \le 1$.

Definition 11.8. By a fair price under crisp Z-number uncertainty, we mean a function P(u, p) that assigns, to every crisp Z-number, a real number, and which satisfies the following properties:

- P(u, 1) = u for all u (conservativeness);

- for all u, v, p, and q, we have P(u + v, p $\cdot$ q) =P(u, p) + P(v, q) (additivity);

- the function P(u, p) is continuous in p (continuity).

Proposition 11.3. Each fair price under crisp Z-number uncertainty has the form P(u, p) = u − k $\cdot$ ln(p) for some real number k.

Proof is given in [479].

Cases of Z-intervals and Z-sets. Similar results hold for Z-intervals and Z-sets; in both results, we will use the fact that we already know how to set a fair price for the case when $p = 1$.

Definition 11.9. By a Z-interval, we mean a pair $([\underline{u}, \overline{u}], p)$ consisting of an interval $[\underline{u}, \overline{u}]$ and a real numbers p such that $0 < p \leq 1$.

Definition 11.10. By a fair price under Z-interval uncertainty, we mean a function $P([\underline{u}, \overline{u}], p)$ that assigns, to every Z-interval, a real number, and which satisfies the following properties:

- for some $\alpha_H \in [0,1]$ and for all $\underline{u} \leq \overline{u}$, we have $P([\underline{u}, \overline{u}], 1)$ = $\alpha_H \cdot \overline{u} + (1 - \alpha_H) \cdot \underline{u}$ (conservativeness);

- for all $\underline{u}, \overline{u}, \underline{v}, \overline{v}$, p, and q, we have

$$P([\underline{u} + \underline{v}, \overline{u} + \overline{v}], p \cdot q = P([\underline{u}, \overline{u}], p) + P([\underline{v}, \overline{v}], q) \tag{11.22}$$

(additivity).

Proposition 11.4. Each fair price under Z-interval uncertainty has the form $P([\underline{u}, \overline{u}], p) = \alpha_H \cdot \overline{u} + (1 - \alpha_H) \cdot \underline{u} - k \cdot \ln(p)$ for some real numbers $\alpha_H \in [0,1]$ and k.

Proof is given in [479].

Definition 11.11. By a Z-set, we mean a pair (S, p) consisting of a closed bounded set S and a real numbers p such that $0 < p \leq 1$.

Definition 11.12 By a fair price under Z-set-valued uncertainty, we mean a function P(S, p) that assigns, to every Z-interval, a real number, and which satisfies the following properties:

• for some $\alpha_H \in [0,1]$ and for all sets S, we have

$$P(S,1) = \alpha_H \cdot \sup S + (1 - \alpha_H) \cdot \inf S \qquad (11.23)$$

(conservativeness);

• for all S, S', p, and q, we have P(S + S', p $\cdot$ q) =P(S, p) + P(S', q) (additivity).

Proposition 11.5. Each fair price under Z-set-valued uncertainty has the form

$$P(S,p) = \alpha_H \cdot \sup S + (1 - \alpha_H) \cdot \inf S - k \cdot \ln(p)$$

for some real numbers $\alpha_H \in [0,1]$ and k.

Proof is given in [479].

When we know the exact probabilities p and q that the corresponding estimates are correct, then the probability that both estimates are correct is equal to the product $p \cdot q$.

Similarly to the fact that we often do not know the exact gain, we often do not know the exact probability p. Instead, we may only know the interval $[\underline{p}, \overline{p}]$ of possible values of p, or, more generally, a set P of possible values of p. If we know p and q with such uncertainty, what can we then conclude about the product $p \cdot q$?

For positive values p and q, the function $p \cdot q$ is increasing as a function of both variables: if we increase p and/or increase q, the product increases. Thus, if the only information that we have the probability p is that this probability belongs to the interval $[\underline{p}, \overline{p}]$, and the only information that we have the probability q is that this probability belongs to the interval $[\underline{q},\overline{q}]$, then:

- the smallest possible value of $p \cdot q$ is equal to the product $\underline{p} \cdot \underline{q}$ of the smallest values;

- the largest possible value of $p \cdot q$ is equal to the product $\overline{p} \cdot \overline{q}$ of the largest values; and

- the set of all possible values $p \cdot q$ is the interval

$$[\underline{p} \cdot \underline{q}, \overline{p} \cdot \overline{q}] .$$

For sets P and Q, the set of possible values $p \cdot q$ is the set

$$P \cdot Q \stackrel{def}{=} \{p \cdot q : p \in P \text{ and } q \in Q\} \qquad (11.24)$$

Let us find the fair price under such uncertainty.

Let us start with the case of crisp Z-numbers under such uncertainty.

Definition 11.13. By a crisp Z-number under interval p-uncertainty, we mean a pair $(u,[\underline{p},\overline{p}])$ consisting of a real number u and an interval $[\underline{p},\overline{p}] \subseteq (0,1]$.

Definition 11.14. By a fair price under crisp Z-number p-interval uncertainty, we mean a function $P(u,[\underline{p},\overline{p}])$ that assigns, to every crisp Z-number under interval p-uncertainty, a real number, and which satisfies the following properties:

- for some real number k, we have

$$P(u, [p, p]) = u - k \cdot \ln(p) \qquad (11.25)$$

for all u and p (conservativeness);

- for all $u, v, \underline{p}, \overline{p}, \underline{q}$ and $\overline{q}$, we have

$$P(u + v,[\underline{p} \cdot \underline{q}, \overline{p}, \overline{q}] = P(u,[\underline{p}, \overline{p}]) + P(v,[\underline{q},\overline{q}]) \qquad (11.26)$$

(additivity);

• the function $P(u,[\underline{p},\overline{p}])$ is continuous in $\underline{p}$ and $\overline{p}$ (continuity).

Proposition 11.6. Each fair price under crisp Z-number p-interval uncertainty has the form

$$P(u,[\underline{p},\overline{p}]) = u - (k - \beta) \cdot \ln(\overline{p}) - \beta \cdot \ln(\underline{p}) \qquad (11.27)$$

for some real numbers k and $\beta \in [0, 1]$.
Proof is given in [479].

Definition 11.15. By a crisp Z-number under set-valued puncertainty, we mean a pair (u,P) consisting of a real number u and a bounded closed set $P \subseteq (0, 1]$.

One can easily show that for each closed set $P \subseteq (0, 1]$, we have inf $P > 0$.

Definition 11.16. By a fair price under crisp Z-number p-setvalued uncertainty, we mean a function P(u,P) that assigns, to every crisp Z-number under set-valued p-uncertainty, a real number, and which satisfies the following properties:

• for some real numbers k and β, we have

$$P(u,[\underline{p},\overline{p}]) = u - (k - \beta) \cdot \ln(\overline{p}) - \beta \cdot \ln(\underline{p}) \qquad (11.28)$$

for all u, $\underline{p}$, and $\overline{p}$ (conservativeness);

• for all u, v, P, and Q, we have

$$P(u + v,P \cdot Q) = P(u,P) + P(v,Q) \qquad (11.29)$$

(additivity).

Proposition 11.7. Each fair price under crisp Z-number p-setvalued uncertainty has the form

$$P(u,P) = u - (k - \beta) \cdot \ln(\sup P) - \beta \cdot \ln(\inf P) \qquad (11.30)$$

for some real number $\beta \in [0, 1]$.

Proof is given in [479].

Let us extend the above results to Z-sets (and to their particular case: Z-intervals).

Definition 11.17. By a Z-set under set-valued p-uncertainty, we mean a pair (S,P) consisting of a bounded closed set S and a bounded closed set $P \subseteq (0,1]$.

Definition 11.18. By a fair price under Z-set p-set-valued uncertainty, we mean a function P(S,P) that assigns, to every Z-set under set-valued p-uncertainty, a real number, and which satisfies the following properties:

• for some real number $\alpha_H \in [0,1]$, we have

$$P(S,1) = \alpha_H \cdot \sup S + (1 - \alpha_H) \cdot \inf S \qquad (11.31)$$

for all S (conservativeness);

• for some real numbers k and β, we have

$$P(u,P) = u - (k - \beta) \cdot \ln(\sup P) - \beta \cdot \ln(\inf P) \qquad (11.32)$$

for all u and P (conservativeness);

• for all S, S′, P, and Q, we have

$$P(S + S', P \cdot Q) = P(S,P) + P(Q,Q) \qquad (11.33)$$

(additivity).

Proposition 11.8. Each fair price under Z-set p-set-valued uncertainty has the form

$$P(S,P) = \alpha_H \cdot \sup S + (1 - \alpha_H) \cdot \inf S - (k - \beta) \cdot \ln(\overline{p}) - \beta \cdot \ln(\underline{p}). \quad (11.34)$$

11.3.4 *Case of fuzzy uncertainty*

In the above text, we first considered situations when about each value of gain u, the expert is either absolutely sure that this value is possible or absolutely sure that this value is not possible. Then, we took into account the possibility that the expert is not 100% certain about that — but we assumed that the expert either knows the exact probability p describing his/her degree of certainty, or that the expert is absolutely sure which probabilities can describe his/her uncertainty and which cannot.

In reality, an expert is often uncertain about the possible values, and uncertain about possible degrees of uncertainty. To take this uncertainty into account, L. Zadeh introduced the notion of a *fuzzy set* [438, 555, 828] where, to each possible value of u, we assign a degree $\mu(u) \in [0, 1]$ to which this value u is possible. Similarly, a fuzzy set $\mu_p : [0,1] \rightarrow [0,1]$ can describe the degrees to which different probability values are possible.

In this section, we restrict ourselves to *fuzzy numbers s*, i.e., fuzzy sets for which the membership function is different from 0 only on a bounded set, where it first monotonically increases until it reaches a point $\overline{s}$ at which $\mu(\overline{s}) = 1$, and then monotonically decreases from 1 to 0.

Operations on fuzzy numbers are usually described in terms of Zadeh's extension principle: if two quantities u and v are described by membership functions $\mu_1(u)$ and $\mu_2(v)$, then their sum w = u + v is described by the membership function $\mu(w) = \max_{u,v:u+v=w} \min(\mu_1(u),(\mu_2(v))$, and their product $w = u \cdot v$ is described by the membership function $\mu(w) = \max_{u,v:u \cdot v=w}$ $\min(\mu_1(u),(\mu_2(v))$.

It is known that these operations can be equivalently described in terms of the *α-cuts*. An α-cut of a fuzzy number $\mu(u)$ is defined as an interval $u(\alpha) = [u^-(\alpha), u^+(\alpha)]$, where

$$u^-(\alpha) \stackrel{def}{=} \inf\{u : \mu(u) \geq \alpha\} \text{ and}$$

$$(11.35)$$

$$u^+(\alpha) \stackrel{def}{=} \sup\{u : \mu(u) \geq \alpha\}.$$

The α-cuts corresponding to the sum $w = u + v$ can be described, for every α, as

$$[w^-(\alpha), w^+(\alpha)] = [u^-(\alpha), u^+(\alpha)] + [v^-(\alpha), v^+(\alpha)], \qquad (11.36)$$

or, equivalently, as

$$[w^-(\alpha), w^+(\alpha)] = [u^-(\alpha) + v^-(\alpha), u^+(\alpha) + v^+(\alpha)], \qquad (11.37)$$

Similarly, the α-cuts corresponding to the product $w = u \cdot v$ can be described as

$$[w^-(\alpha), w^+(\alpha)] = [u^-(\alpha), u^+(\alpha)] \cdot [v^-(\alpha), v^+(\alpha)]. \qquad (11.38)$$

If both fuzzy numbers u and v are non-negative (e.g., if they are limited described as to the interval [0, 1]), then the α-cuts corresponding to the product can be

$$[w^-(\alpha), w^+(\alpha)] = [u^-(\alpha) \cdot v^-(\alpha), u^+(\alpha) \cdot v^+(\alpha)]. \qquad (11.39)$$

Let us start with describing the fair price of fuzzy numbers. Similarly to the interval case, a natural requirement is monotonicity: if for all α, we have $s^-(\alpha) \leq t^-(\alpha)$ and $s^+(\alpha) \leq t^+(\alpha)$, then the fair price of t should be larger than or equal to the fair price of s. It is also reasonable to require continuity: that small changes in $\mu(u)$ should lead to small changes in the fair price.

Definition 11.19. By a fair price under fuzzy uncertainty, we mean a function P(s) that assigns, to every fuzzy number s, a real number, and which satisfies the following properties:

• if a fuzzy number s is located between $\underline{u}$ and $\bar{u}$, then $\underline{u} \leq P(s) \leq \bar{u}$ (conservativeness);

• if a fuzzy number w is the sum of fuzzy numbers u and v, then we have P(w) = P(u) + P(v) (additivity);

• if for all α, we have

$$s^-(\alpha) \leq t^-(\alpha) \text{ and } s^+(\alpha) \leq t^+(\alpha). \tag{11.40}$$

then we have P(s) $\leq$ P(t) (monotonicity);

• if a sequence of membership functions μn uniformly converges to μ, then we should have $P(\mu_n) \to P(\mu)$ (continuity).

We will see, the fair price of a fuzzy number is described in terms of a Riemann- Stieltjes integral.

Proposition 11.9. For a fuzzy number s with a continuous membership function $\mu(x)$, α-cuts $[s^-(\alpha), s^+(\alpha)]$ and a point s0 at which $\mu(s_0) = 1$, the fair price is equal to

$$P(S) = s_0 \int_0^1 k^-(\alpha) ds^-(\alpha) - \int_0^1 k^+(\alpha) ds^+(\alpha), \tag{11.41}$$

for appropriate functions $k^-(\alpha)$ and $k^+(\alpha)$.

When the function g(x) is differentiable, the Riemann-Stieltjes integral $\int_a^b f(x) dg(x)$ is equal to the usual integral

$$\int_a^b f(x) \cdot g'(x) dx$$

where g'(x) denotes the derivative. When the function f(x) is also differentiable, we can use integration by part and get yet another equivalent form

$$f(b) \cdot g(b) - f(\alpha) \cdot g(\alpha) + \int_a^b F(x)g(x)dx, \qquad (11.42)$$

with $F(x) = -f'(x)$. In general, a Stieltjes integral can be represented in a similar form for some *generalized function* F(x) [303]; generalized function are also known as *distributions*; we do not use this term to avoid confusion with probability distributions). Thus, the above general formula can be described as

$$P(s) = s_0 \int_0^1 K^-(\alpha) \cdot s^-(\alpha)d\alpha + \int_0^1 K^+(\alpha) \cdot s^+(\alpha)d\alpha \qquad (11.43)$$

for appropriate generalized functions $K^-(\alpha)$ and $K^+(\alpha)$.
Conservativeness means that for a crisp number located at s_0, we should have $P(s) = s_0$. For the above formula, this means that

$$\int_0^1 K^-(\alpha)d\alpha + \int_0^1 K^+(\alpha)d\alpha = 1 \qquad (11.44)$$

For a fuzzy number which is equal to the interval $[\underline{u}, \overline{u}]$, the above formula leads to

$$P(s) = (\int_0^1 K^-(\alpha)d\alpha) \cdot \underline{u} + (\int_0^1 K^+(\alpha)d\alpha) \cdot \overline{u} \qquad (11.45)$$

Thus, Hurwicz optimism-pessimism coefficient α_H is equal to $\int_0^1 K^+(\alpha)d\alpha$. In this sense, the above formula is a generalization of Hurwicz's formula to the fuzzy case.

Proof is given in [479].

Case of Z-number uncertainty. In this case we have two fuzzy numbers: the fuzzy number s which describes the values and the fuzzy number p which describes our degree of confidence in the piece of information described by s.

Definition 11.20. By a fair price under Z-number uncertainty, we mean a function P(s, p) that assigns, to every pair of two fuzzy numbers s and p such that p is located on an interval $[p_0, 1]$ for some $p_0 > 0$, a real number, and which satisfies the following properties:

• if a fuzzy number s is located between $\underline{u}$ and $\overline{u}$, then $\underline{u} \leq P(s,1) \leq \overline{u}$ (conservativeness);

• if w = u + v and r = p · q, then

$$P(w, r) = P(u, p) + P(v, q) \qquad (11.46)$$

(additivity);

• if for all α, we have

$$s^-(\alpha) \leq t^-(\alpha) \text{ and } s^+(\alpha) \leq t^+(\alpha) \qquad (11.47)$$

then we have P(s, 1) ≤ P(t, 1) (monotonicity);

• if $s_n \to s$ and $p_n \to p$, then $P(s_n, p_n) \to P(p, s)$ (continuity).

Proposition 11.10. For a fuzzy number s with α-cuts $[s^-(\alpha), s^+(\alpha)]$, and a fuzzy number p with α-cuts $[p^-(\alpha), p^+(\alpha)]$, we have

$$P(s,p) = \int_0^1 K^-(\alpha) \cdot s^-(\alpha)d\alpha + \int_0^1 K^+(\alpha) \cdot s^+(\alpha)d\alpha$$

$$+ \int_0^1 L^-(\alpha) \cdot \ln(p^-(\alpha))d\alpha + \int_0^1 L^+(\alpha) \cdot \ln(p^+(\alpha))d\alpha$$

for appropriate generalized functions $K^\pm(\alpha)$ and $L^\pm(\alpha)$.

Proof is given in [479].

11.4 Z-regression analysis

In order to simplify operations over Z-numbers for problems where approximated solutions are acceptable bandwidth method is very effective.

A bandwidth method [821]. This method is based on an approximation of a fuzzy number A of a Z-number by an interval as its bandwidth $A_1^{Bandwidth}$. As a bandwidth, an α-cut can be used $A_1^{Bandwidth} = A^{\alpha=0.5}$ (Fig. 11.2).

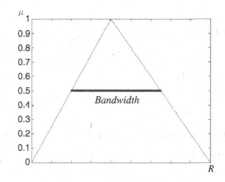

Fig. 11.2. Interval-valued approximation to triangular fuzzy number

Let $Z_1 = (A_1, B_1)$ and $Z_2 = (A_2, B_2)$ be two Z-numbers and $* \in \{+, -, /, \times\}$ be a basic arithmetic operation. In this case we can write for any operation over Z-numbers:

$$(A_1^{Bandwidth}, B_1) * (A_2^{Bandwidth}, B_2) = (A_1^{Bandwidth} * A_2^{Bandwidth}, B_1 \times B_2) \quad (11.48)$$

where $*$ is a binary operation and $B_1 \times B_2$ is the product of the fuzzy numbers B_1 and B_2. The bandwidth method allows to approximate operations of probabilistic arithmetic within computation of Z-numbers to multiplication of fuzzy values of probability measures B_1 and B_2. This allows to significantly reduce complexity operations over Z-numbers.

11.4.1 Z-regression model

Let us consider a multi input-single output process characterized by Z-number valued information. Let $Z_{X_1}, Z_{X_2}, ..., Z_{X_N}$ denote Z-numbers describing values of $X_1, X_2, ..., X_N$ and Z_Y denote the Z-number describing the corresponding value of the output Y.

Assume a series of Z-valued observation data $Z_{X_{i,j}}, i = 1, ..., N$ and $Z_{Y,k}, k = 1, ..., K$ are given (K is a number of observations). For simplicity we consider a Z-valued linear regression model of a process under study:

$$Z_{Y^M}(Z_{X_1}, Z_{X_2}, ..., Z_{X_N}) = Z_{C_0} + \sum_{i=1}^{N} Z_{C_i} Z_{X_i} \quad (11.49)$$

By using the bandwidth method (11.48), we will have for operation of multiplication in (11.49):

$$Z_{C_i} \times Z_{X_i} = ((A_{C_i}^{Bandwith} \times A_{X_i}^{Bandwith}), (B_{C_i} \times B_{X_i})).$$

The operation of addition is treated analogously and the model (11.49) will be expressed as follows:

$$Z_{Y^M} = Z_{C_0} + Z_{C_1} \times Z_{X_1} + ... + Z_{C_N} \times Z_{X_N} =$$
$$(A_{C_0}^{Bandwith} + (A_{C_1}^{Bandwith} \times A_{X_1}^{Bandwith}) + ... + (A_{C_N}^{Bandwith} \times A_{X_N}^{Bandwith}),$$
$$B_{C_0} \times (B_{C_1} \times B_{X_1}) \times ... \times (B_{C_N} \times B_{X_N}))$$

Construction of regression model (11.49) is related to computation with a large number of Z-numbers. In this case, the issue of computational complexity becomes very important. In order to achieve a trade-off between adequacy and computational complexity, we propose to use the bandwidth method for the arithmetic operations in (11.49). The problem of construction of Z_{y^M} requires to determine Z-valued coefficients (Z-numbers) Z_{C_0}, Z_{C_i} given Z-valued input $Z_{X_i,k}, i = 1, ..., N$ and output data Z_{Y_k} so that the following error is minimized:

$$\sum_{k=1}^{K} \left| Z_{Y,k}^M - Z_{Y,k} \right| \to \min , \qquad (11.50)$$

" – " denotes the standard subtraction of Z-numbers, $| \; |$ denotes the absolute value of a Z-number and Σ denotes addition of Z-numbers. These operations are handled by using the bandwidth method.

Model (11.49) describes a general case, when all the variables and coefficients of a regression model are Z-numbers. In such case, the use of classical techniques, e.g. gradient based methods, for construction of the regression model is not suitable due to complexity of representation of derivative of a Z-valued function. Problem (11.49)-(11.50) can be solved by DE optimization method shown in Section 11.2.

Chapter 12

Simulation and Applications

12.1 Decision making for well interventions under interval probability

Optimization of oil field development performances and producing well operational conditions are one of the key issues in the oil extraction processes. For this purpose, various measures are taken at all stages of field development, particularly at the final stage. All additional measures taken at this stage are focused on the increase in overall oil production and therefore improvement of engineering and economic performances. For this purpose, carrying out of geological and engineering operations in parallel with routine work is of special importance.

One of the most advanced methods of regulation of producing well technological process parameters and optimization of their flow rate is the injection of polymeric solutions into the space behind the well bore [331]. Injection of polymeric solutions into the well reduces hydraulic losses in the well bore, facilitates flowing of mixtures (oil, gas, water) entering from strata through the bore, creates favorable conditions for normal operation of the lift and as a result promotes increase in the well productivity.

However implementation of any operation and obtaining positive results in the oil extraction practice depend on the right choice of a well. Thus, first of all, well's condition should be normal and meet appropriate requirements for implementation of any operations, otherwise, effectiveness of such operations will be inadequate. Thus, the problem consists in determination of the number of producing wells in the oil production enterprise's stock for which well intervention will be carried out, i.e. the total number of wells. As experience shows, it is impossible to obtain high efficiency for all wells in the result of intervention. In certain cases a decrease in capacity of 10-15% of wells under intervention is observed. In this context, it is important to make the right decision on carrying out of intervention and to determine an optimal number of wells.

One of the main factors that complicates decision making on a choice of an optimal number of wells is imprecision of relevant information. Indeed, information on amount of oil production and related probabilities is naturally imprecise. In such cases, the use of the classical probability theory based approaches of decision making [77, 664, 749] is inadequate. The issue is that in decision making with imprecise probabilities, human beliefs exhibit non-additivity property. Decision making with imprecise probabilities and non-additive beliefs constitute nowadays a wide area of research aimed at dealing with real-world problems [71, 115, 338, 739]. In this example we consider a problem of decision making on a choice of an optimal number of oil wells when decision relevant information is described by interval-valued outcomes and probabilities. For solving the considered decision making problem, an interval-valued Choquet integral based utility function is used.

12.1.1 *Statement of the problem*

The primary objective of carrying out of well interventions in oil extraction processes is to obtain high revenue by increasing oil production. The basis of this process management consists in oil production increase maximization (and accordingly increase in revenue) and investment risk minimization [345].

Effectiveness of the methods applicable for improving well operation conditions to a large extent depends on accurate determination of the total number of wells where research will be conducted. In addition, although long-term operation of wells is impossible due to carrying out of various operations, no general procedure was developed for current operations effectiveness estimation. In such conditions, determination of appropriate volume of intervention in the producing well stock has come to the fore as the major practical issue. In addition, currently there are practically no criteria for determination of an optimal number of wells which would take into account engineering and economic parameters for taking various well productivity optimization measures.

Thus, a need arises in decision making on determination of an optimal number of wells to improve wells productivity. The considered problem is a problem of decision making under uncertainty characterized by imprecise decision relevant information. More concretely, for each available option (alternative number of wells) possible outcomes (oil production) and their probabilities are naturally imprecise.

Thus, we will consider determination of an optimal number of well in case of the highest increase in well flow rate [441] as a problem of decision making with interval-valued information.

The considered problem of decision making can be formalized as 4-tuple $(S, \mathcal{P}, \mathcal{A}, X, \succeq)$ [20, 669]:

$S = \{S_1, ..., S_n\}$ is a space of mutually exclusive and exhaustive states of nature that describe possible objective conditions which determine oil production;

$\mathcal{P}$ is a distribution of interval probabilities of states of nature, $P(S_i), i = 1, ..., n$, $S_i \in S$;

X is a set of interval-valued outcomes (oil production);

$\mathcal{A}$ is a set of alternatives (alternative number of wells) that are $\mathcal{F}_S$-measurable functions $f : S \rightarrow X$, where $\mathcal{F}_S$ is a σ-algebra of subsets of S, $B \subset S$.

$\succeq$ is a non-additive preference relation over $\mathcal{A}$ which satisfy the properties of weak order, transitivity, continuity, comonotonic independence, monotonicity and non-degeneracy [20, 669].

The problem is to determine preferences $\succeq$ among alternatives $\mathcal{A}$.

12.1.2 *Solution of the problem*

The utility models based on the Choquet integral [393] is more adequate for modeling decision-maker (DM) behavior because it is based on the use of non-additive measures and not on probability measures [175, 256, 281, 348, 584, 634, 670, 752]. The model can reflect a number of typical properties associated with risk and uncertainty attitude of a DM.

Alternatively, most available utility models assume that the utility function and probability distribution are precisely known. Studies [18, 20, 54, 60] suggest new decision models which allow to solve decision making problems characterized by imprecise decision relevant information. These models are based on a fuzzy valued Choquet integral. We will apply this model to the considered decision making problem characterized by interval-valued information. The interval-valued Choquet integral based utility of an alternative $f_i \in \mathcal{A}$ is described as follows:

$$U(f_i) = \sum_{j=1}^{m} (X_{i(j)} - X_{i(j+1)}) \eta_{\{(1),...,(j)\}},$$

where $\eta_{\{(1),...,(j)\}}$ is a non-additive measure, $X_{i(j)} = f_i(S_{(j)})$ is an interval-valued outcome of alternative f_i at a state $S_{(j)}$, () index means that $X_{i(j)}$ values are enumerated such that, $X_{i(j)} \geq X_{i(j+1)}$ and $X_{i(m+1)} = 0$ by convention. By means of this measure non-additivity of DM's preferences under ambiguity (e.g. a safe to a certain extent decision or a risky to a certain extent decision made under uncertainty) can be modeled.

Let us assume that a DM wants to make a safe choice under interval valued information on probabilities $P(S_i) = [\underline{p}_i, \overline{p}_i]$. Then, a lower probability can be used as a non-additive measure to describe a DM's beliefs [768]. In other words, we assume that a DM thinks about the worst possible case of oil production events within the probability ranges. The lower probability η is defined as follows.

$$\eta\{S_{(1)},...,S_{(j)}\} = p_{(1)} + ... + p_{(j)} \to \min$$

$$\underline{p}_{(1)} \le p_{(1)} \le \overline{p}_{(1)},$$

.

.

.

$$\underline{p}_{(j)} \le p_{(j)} \le \overline{p}_{(j)},$$
$$p_{(1)} + \ldots + p_{(n)} = 1$$

Here p_0 denotes possible numeric probability of S_0. As we can see, this problem is the problem of linear programming.

Thus, the problem under consideration (choosing an optimal number of wells) is to determine an alternative with maximal value of the interval-valued utility function U:

$$U(f^*) = \max_{f_i \in \mathcal{A}} U(f_i)$$

Determination of the maximal value of an interval-valued utility function is based on an appropriate method of comparison of intervals.

12.1.3 *A numerical solution*

Practical solution of the problem is as follows: let us determine the set of alternatives (the number of wells) $\mathcal{A} = \{f_1, f_2, f_3, f_4\}$: f_1 is an intervention in 10 wells, f_2 is an intervention in 20 wells, f_3 is an intervention in 30 wells, f_4 is intervention in 40 wells. States of nature are considered as possible geological conditions $S = \{S_1, S_2, S_3, S_4\}$ which influence outcomes of the alternatives (oil production). Due to significant uncertainty and imprecision of decision-relevant information in the considered problem, we consider interval-valued probabilities of states of nature and interval-valued outcomes of the alternatives. The decision relevant information is represented in Table 12.1.

Now, we need to determine utilities of alternatives. For simplicity of notation, denote $\eta_{\{(1),...,(j)\}} = \eta\{S_{(1)},...,S_{(j)}\}$. Then, the utility of alternative f_1 will be determined as:

$$U(f_1) = \sum_{j=1}^{m} (X_{1(j)} - X_{1(j+1)})\eta_{\{(1),...,(j)\}} = (X_{1(1)} - X_{1(2)})\eta_{\{(1)\}} +$$
$$(X_{1(2)} - X_{1(3)})\eta_{\{(1),(2)\}} + (X_{1(3)} - X_{1(4)})\eta_{\{(1),(2),(3)\}} + X_{1(4)}\eta_{\{(1),(2),(3),(4)\}}.$$

Permutation of indices is based on the method of comparison of intervals proposed in [338]. According to this method, for two intervals $A_1 = [a_{11}, a_{12}]$ and $A_2 = [a_{21}, a_{22}]$, one has $A_1 \geq A_2$ iff $a_{11} \geq a_{21}$ and $a_{12} \geq a_{22}$. Thus, given the information in Table 12.1, we will obtain:

$$U(f_1) = (X_{14} - X_{13})\eta_{\{4\}} + (X_{13} - X_{12})\eta_{\{3,4\}} + (X_{12} - X_{11})\eta_{\{2,3,4\}} + X_{11}\eta_{\{1,2,3,4\}}$$

Table 12.1. Decision problem with interval-valued information

	S_1	S_2	S_3	S_4
f_1	$X_{11} = [50,60]$,	$X_{12} = [120,150]$,	$X_{13} = [190,200]$	$X_{14} = [240,260]$,
	$P_{11} = [0.2,0.25]$	$P_{12} = [0.3,0.35]$	$P_{13} = [0.25,0.3]$	$P_{14} = [0.1,0.25]$
f_2	$X_{21} = [80,100]$,	$X_{22} = [130,155]$,	$X_{23} = [210,230]$,	$X_{24} = [270,290]$,
	$P_{21} = [0.23,0.27]$	$P_{22} = [0.24,0.27]$	$P_{23} = [0.29,0.32]$	$P_{24} = [0.14,0.24]$
f_3	$X_{31} = [110,120]$,	$X_{32} = [160,180]$,	$X_{33} = [240,260]$,	$X_{34} = [285,310]$,
	$P_{31} = [0.22,0.26]$	$P_{32} = [0.27,0.3]$	$P_{33} = [0.29,0.32]$	$P_{34} = [0.12,0.22]$
f_4	$X_{41} = [135,150]$,	$X_{42} = [190,220]$,	$X_{43} = [270,300]$,	$X_{44} = [305,330]$,
	$P_{41} = [0.21,0.24]$	$P_{42} = [0.29,0.32]$	$P_{43} = [0.3,0.33]$	$P_{44} = [0.11,0.2]$

Utilities of the other alternatives are determined in a similar way. For calculation of utility values U we will construct measure η as the lower probability [553]. For example, calculation of $\eta_{\{2,3,4\}}$ is as follows:

$$\eta_{\{2,3,4\}} = p_2 + p_3 + p_4 \to \min$$

$$0.3 \leq p_2 \leq 0.35,$$
$$0.25 \leq p_3 \leq 0.3,$$
$$0.1 \leq p_4 \leq 0.25,$$
$$p_1 + \ldots + p_4 = 1$$

By solving this problem, we obtain $\eta_{\{2,3,4\}} = 0.75$. Similarly, we get: $\eta_{\{3,4\}} = 0.4$, $\eta_{\{4\}} = 0.1$ and it is clear that $\eta_{\{1,2,3,4\}} = 1$. Then we have for $U(f_1)$:

$$U(f_1) = ([240,260] - [190,200])0.1 + ([190,200] - [120,150])0.65 +$$
$$([120,150] - [50,60])0.75 + [50,60] = [115,174].$$

Similarly, we obtain:

$$U(f_2) = [133,212],$$

$$U(f_3) = [169,224],$$

$$U(f_4) = [187,268].$$

Having compared the obtained interval utilities by using the method proposed in [338] we get: $U(f^*) = \max_{f_i \in A} U(f_i) = U(f_4)$. The optimal alternative is f_4. Therefore, interventions carried out in 40 wells is an optimal action.

Let us compare the obtained results of decision analysis under interval information with the use of a classical approach. As a classical approach we consider Subjective Expected Utility model [664]. However, this model is developed for a precise information framework. In this model it is assumed that a DM subjectively assigns precise probabilities when dealing with decision problems under ambiguity. Therefore, to apply this model, we need to use precise values of outcomes and probabilities in the considered problem. So, we consider the following information:

Table 12.2. Decision problem with precise information

	S_1	S_2	S_3	S_4
f_1	$X_{11} = 55,$	$X_{12} = 130,$	$X_{13} = 195,$	$X_{14} = 250,$
	$P_{11} = 0.23$	$P_{12} = 0.33$	$P_{13} = 0.27,$	$P_{14} = 0.17$
f_2	$X_{21} = 90,$	$X_{22} = 140,$	$X_{23} = 220,$	$X_{24} = 280,$
	$P_{21} = 0.25$	$P_{22} = 0.25$	$P_{23} = 0.3$	$P_{24} = 0.2$
f_3	$X_{31} = 120,$	$X_{32} = 180,$	$X_{33} = 260$	$X_{34} = 310$
	$P_{31} = 0.22$	$P_{32} = 0.27$	$P_{33} = 0.29$	$P_{34} = 0.22$
f_4	$X_{41} = 135,$	$X_{42} = 190,$	$X_{43} = 270,$	$X_{44} = 305,$
	$P_{41} = 0.24$	$P_{42} = 0.32$	$P_{43} = 0.3$	$P_{44} = 0.14$

The values of Expected utility for these alternatives are as follows.

$$U(f_1) = 150.7,$$

$$U(f_2) = 179.5,$$

$$U(f_3) = 218.6,$$

$$U(f_4) = 216.9.$$

As one can see, the best alternative is f_3, though it is slightly better than f_4. This result differs with what we obtained when dealing with interval-valued information. Thus, disregarding of imprecision of the original information (which is always characterized by loss of information) leads to improper results.

12.2 Fuzzy production–distribution planning in supply chain management

Aggregate production–distribution planning (APDP) is one of the most important activities in supply chain management (SCM). When solving the problem of APDP, we are usually faced with uncertain market demands and capacities in production environment, imprecise process times, and other factors introducing inherent uncertainty to the solution.

Using deterministic and stochastic models in such conditions may not lead to fully satisfactory results. Using fuzzy models allows us to remove this drawback. It also facilitates the inclusion of expert knowledge. However, the majority of existing fuzzy models deal only with separate aggregate production planning without taking into account the interrelated nature of production and distribution systems. This limited approach often leads to inadequate results. An integration of the two interconnected processes within a single production–distribution model would allow better planning and management. Due to the need for a joint general strategic plan for production and distribution and vague planning data, in this section we develop a fuzzy integrated multi-period and multi-product production and distribution model in supply chain. The model is formulated in terms of fuzzy programming and the solution is provided by genetic optimization (genetic algorithm). The use of the interactive aggregate production–distribution planning procedure developed on the basis of the proposed fuzzy integrated model with fuzzy objective function and soft constraints allows sound trade-off between the maximization of profit and fillrate.

12.2.1 *State-of-the-art*

A significant number of research studies have addressed the development of aggregate production and distribution planning in Supply Chain (SC). A review of the works on strategic production–distribution models is given in [748]. The authors consider a global supply chain models with an emphasis on integer programming models. Deterministic models for production–distribution and inventory-distribution problems are investigated in [720]. In [110] separate stochastic production model and distribution model are used to establish a material requirement policy in a supply chain system.

The model suggested in [363] is one of the best known classical models for tackling aggregated production and inventory planning problems. In [352] this approach was extended into a stochastic programming model considering the randomness of product demand. Stochastic programming based model is used in [120] for determining multi-period production plans under stochastic demand. While the stochastic approach is useful, it is not always possible to use it due to existence of uncertainty in data or even a lack of sufficient historical data. There is a close linkage between production and distribution that necessitates coordination of production and distribution operations in supply chain systems. The SCM systems studies pointed out above do not consider the necessity to coordinate the models and solve the problems of production and distribution, respectively.

To avoid the drawback of the above-mentioned works, in [462] an optimal joint production–distribution planning hybrid method in supply chain management combining mathematical programming and simulation model is suggested. The production and distribution capacity constrains in the analytic model are considered as stochastic variables that are adjusted in accordance with general production–distribution characteristics, obtained from the simulation model. The review of integrated production–distribution systems is given in [663, 692]. The problem to find an integrated schedule of production and distribution that provides trade-of between the distribution cost and the customer service level is considered in [191]. The heuristic algorithm is developed which is capable of generating near-optimal solution of joint production–distribution schedule. It should be noted that the authors have completed an interesting research and showed the possible benefits of using the integrated production–distribution model when compared to sequential model where production and distribution operations are scheduled sequentially and separately.

Another set of models related to joint production, inventory, and distribution problems in the supply chain management can be found in [168, 200]. These models of production or integrated production–distribution in SCM are categorized into deterministic [110, 363] and stochastic [110, 363] programming models. It is not simple to apply these models to most realistic problems of SCM. In paper [242] the authors consider the optimization of integrated supply chain including raw materials supply, intermediate supply, manufacturing, distribution, retail and customers. The integer linear programming is applied for solution of strategic planning problem. The optimization strategy is applied for planning of networks of desktop computer production. In papers [239, 298] the authors consider e-supply chain optimization between different stages of the chain, i.e. between suppliers and consumers, manufacturers and retailers.

Many companies have been trying to optimize their production and distribution systems separately, but using this approach limits any possible increase in profit [583]. The papers [396, 583] propose a solution for integrated production and distribution planning in complicated environments where the objective is to maximize the total profit. These papers state that the supply chain environment requires a production–distribution planning system to enable collaboration between production and distribution units and confirm the substantial advantage of the integrated planning approach over the decoupled one.

The main disadvantage of the discussed deterministic production–distribution models is that they ignore the existing SC network uncertainty. Stochastic models are usually based on representation of existing uncertainty approximately by probability concepts and are, consequently, limited to tackling the uncertainties captured by some probability distributions.

The plans obtained on the basis of stochastic models can only take the form of a distribution function, which can do little to help decision making in practical situations. As it is shown in [274] SC is a dynamic network of several business entities that involve a high degree of imprecision. This is mainly due to its real-world character, where uncertainties in activities extending from the suppliers to the customers make SC imprecise. Authors of [274] further point out that ''... fuzzy set theory is a suitable tool to come up with such a complicated system''.

Therefore, there is a strong need for research on production–distribution planning to take into account of uncertainties sourced from market demand and manufacturing [274].

Some researchers investigated fuzzy production planning problems in SC in [463, 624, 633, 760]. Aggregate production planning model and algorithm using fuzzy logic is developed in [633]. Fuzzy aggregate production planning for single product types with fuzzy objective function, fuzzy demand in different time periods is considered in [463]. Planning model is based on a linear programming model with fuzzy objective and soft constraints. In [760] the authors developed fuzzy-genetic approach for solving fuzzy linear production planning problem in SC. Decision analysis in e-supply chain using fuzzy set approach mainly on the basis of fuzzy reasoning Petry nets is considered in [297]. The method proposed in [471] aims at simultaneous minimization of total distribution costs and the total delivery time on the basis of fuzzy available supply, total budget, fuzzy forecast demand, and warehouse space. Paper [185] suggests an approach to deriving the membership function of the fuzzy minimum total cost of the multi-period SC model with fuzzy parameters.

The considered fuzzy production planning models and methods are mainly a single product type and separate production planning model without integration with distribution problems.

Computational intelligence is widely used in economics and finance [36, 180, 686, 859]. Application of fuzzy logic can provide two significant advantages for SCM. First, it allows construction of compromises between conflicting objectives usually present in SCM by considering an overall satisfaction degree as trade-off between several objectives and constraints. Second, intersection of fuzzy constraints and overall objectives can be smoother (less cutting) increasing the chance to get a better solution within the overlapping areas of constraints and objectives [1, 105, 327].

The overall objective of the SC aggregate plan is to satisfy demand and maximize profit in SC. The input data on production capacities and demand forecasts are available, but are always approximate. The actual data is often different from the forecasted (projected) one, because of unforeseen changes in the environment. Given the profit maximization as a criterion, the purpose is to determine near-optimal solution, consisting of a choice of production volumes and logistic decisions that would remain stable or tolerant.

The objective of this section is to develop an integrated multi-period, multi-product fuzzy production and distribution aggregate planning model in supply chain by providing a sound trade-off between fillrate of fuzzy market demand and the profit. The suggested integrated production–distribution planning model is based on fuzzy mathematical programming with fuzzy objective functions, soft constraints, and fuzzy decision variables. The optimization problem is solved by genetic algorithm that provides a general near-optimal plan with more realistic results.

12.2.2 *Statement of the problem*

Let us consider the following production–distribution planning SC model. There are nPU plants (denoted as PU, production units), nDC distribution centers (DC), and nCZ customer zones (CZ). Several PUs produce product items. Cost of production of a certain item at different PUs can be different. Each PU is characterized by its own fixed cost per period and production capacity. Several Distribution Centers are used to store the production produced at DC. No difference is made as in storage or maintenance cost to the same kind of production from different PUs. DCs are differentiated on the storage capacities, fixed costs, and storage costs. Storage cost may not be a linear function of the number of items. Production capacities of PUs and storage capacities of DCs are represented by triangular or trapezoidal fuzzy numbers as these parameters are sensitive to many unforeseen factors, and thus are often described in ranges rather than standalone numbers and have fuzzy boundaries. This allows solutions, falling near the boundaries of corresponding constrains, be more realistic. Selling price for the same kind of item can be different at different CZs. Only customer-ordered items are transported to CZs (CZs do not have storage; CZs can store items only within a current period, after which the items are considered to be lost). At any given time period t, fuzzy demand forecasts for future time periods for all CZs are available. All items (produced at this or previous periods as well as ordered but not yet delivered) are stored in DCs. A PU can supply to any DC and A DC can supply to any CZ, however different transportation costs are related to different routes. Some DCs can supply to others some semi-products, but not end- products. The transportation costs depend on the locations of relevant PUs, DCS, and CZs. The cost function may not be a linear function of the number of transported items (e.g. items can be transported in bunches).

The notations used for the considered problem are listed below:

* $V_{t,ij}^{proj}$ is the number (fuzzy) of items projected to be transported from PU i to DC j at period t;

* $W_{t,jk}^{proj}$ is the number of items (fuzzy) projected to be transported from DC j to CZ k at time t;

* $M_{t,ip}^{proj}$ is the number of items of product p projected to produce by PU i at time t;
* $W_{t,j0}^{proj}$ is the number of items in DC j to be supplied to various CZ at time t;
* F is total (projected) profit;
* R is total (projected) return after sales;
* E is total (projected) expenses;
* E_{DC} is total (projected) DC expenses;
* E_{PU} is total (projected) PU expenses,
* E_T is total (projected) transportation expenses;
* $N_{t,kp}^{proj}$ is the number of items of product p projected to be supplied and sold at CZ k at period t (i.e. the evaluated supply);
* $N_{t,kp}$ is the number of items of product p actually supplied to CZ k at period t (i.e. actual supply);
* $W_{t,jk}$ is the number of items actually transported from DC j to CZ k at period t;
* W_{j0}^i is the actual number of items remaining at DC j at period t (items remaining at DC from the previous time period $t - 1$, e.g. due to a lower value of actual sales);
* $W_{j\,max}$ is the fuzzy value representing the maximum number of items that can be stored in DC j;
* T_{ij} is the cost of transportation of (a bunch of) items from PU i to DC j;
* U_{jk} is the cost of transportation of (a bunch of) items from DC j to CZ k;
* $D_{t,kp}^{proj}$ is the forecasted fuzzy demand for item of product p in CZ k at period t;
* P_{kp} is the selling price of item of product p in CZ k;
* S_{i0} is the fixed cost for exploitation of PU i during a period;
* Q_{j0} is the fixed cost for exploitation of DC j during a period;
* Q_j is the cost for storing one item in DC j during a period;
* C_{ip} is the cost for production of one item of product p at PUi;
* $V_{i\,max}$ is the fuzzy value representing the maximum production capacity (i.e. the maximum number of items that can be produced at PU i during a period t);
* $D_{t,kp}$ is the actual demand for product p (the product actually sold);

$W_{t,j0p}^{proj}$ is the number of items of product p in DC j projected for supply to various CZs at period t;

*n is the considered number of periods: $t = 1, 2, \ldots n$.

The mathematical formulation of the considered production distribution problem is presented in the following way. The primary objective function, describing the maximization of the overall profit, comes in the form:

$$\text{Maximize } F = (R - E) \text{ (maximize the profit)}, \qquad (12.1)$$

where

$$R = \sum_{t=1}^{n} \sum_{k} \sum_{p} N_{t,kp}^{proj} P_{kp} \text{ (the projected total revenue from sales); } \quad (12.2)$$

$$E = E_{DC} + E_{PU} + E_T \text{ (the projected overall expenses)}. \qquad (12.3)$$

In the sequel, the components of E are described in the form

$$E_{DC} = \sum_{t=1}^{n} \left(\sum_{j} Q_{j0} + \sum_{j} Q_j W_{t,j0}^{proj} \right)$$

$$= n \sum_{j} Q_{j0} + \sum_{t=1}^{n} \sum_{j} Q_j W_{t,j0}^{proj}$$

(the projected total expenses for DCs (fixed expenses Q_{j0} may be considered only if $W_{t,j0}^{proj} > 0$));

$$E_{PU} = \sum_{t=1}^{n} \left(\sum_{i} S_{i0} + \sum_{i} \sum_{p} C_{ip} M_{t,ip}^{proj} \right)$$

$$= n \sum_{i} S_{i0} + \sum_{t=1}^{n} \sum_{i} \sum_{p} C_{ip} M_{t,ip}^{proj} \qquad (12.4)$$

(the projected total expenses for PUs (fixed expenses S_{i0} may be considered only if $M_{t,ip}^{proj} > 0$));

$$E_T = \sum_{t=1}^{n} \sum_i \sum_j T_{ij} V_{t,ij}^{proj} + \sum_{t=1}^{n} \sum_j \sum_k U_{jk} W_{t,jk}^{proj}$$ (the projected total

transportation cost)   (12.5)

The maximization of F is subject to the following constraints:

$$V_{t,ij}^{proj} \geq 0 \text{ for all } i \text{ and } j \tag{12.6}$$

$$W_{t,jk}^{proj} \geq 0 \text{ for all } i \text{ and } k \tag{12.7}$$

$$W_{t,j0}^{proj} \geq 0 \text{ for all } j \tag{12.8}$$

$$\sum_j V_{t,ij}^{proj} \leq V_{i\max} \text{ for all } i \tag{12.9}$$

$$W_{t,j0}^{proj} \leq W_{j\max} \text{ for all } j \tag{12.10}$$

$$N_{t,kp}^{proj} \geq D_{t,kp}^{proj} \text{ for all } k \tag{12.11}$$

$$\sum_p M_{t,ip}^{proj} = \sum_j V_{t,ij}^{proj} \text{ for all } i \text{ and } p \tag{12.12}$$

$$\sum_p N_{t,kp}^{proj} = \sum_j W_{t,jk}^{proj} \text{ for all } k \tag{12.13}$$

$$W_{t,j0}^{proj} = W_{t-1,j0}^{proj} + \sum_i V_{t,ij}^{proj} - \sum_k W_{t,jk}^{proj} \text{ for all } j \tag{12.14}$$

where the decision variables are:

$V_{t,ij}^{proj}$ (the number of items projected to be transported from PU i to DC j at period t);

$W_{t,jk}^{proj}$ (the number of items projected to be transported from DC j to CZ k at time t);

$M_{t,ip}^{proj}$ (the number of items of product p projected to produce by PU i at time t);

$W_{t,j0}^{proj}$ (the number of items in DC j to be supplied to various CZ at time t).

Constraint (12.6)–(12.8) reflect the fact that the number of items produced and sent to a DC, the number of items in a DC sent to a CZ, and the number of items stored in a DC cannot be negative. Constraint (12.9) says that no more items can be taken from a plant than can be produced in it. Constraint (12.10) is to provide that items currently in the store cannot exceed the maximum storage capacity. Constraint (12.11) means that the demand must be met at a required fillrate. Constraint (12.12) ensures that all produced items are sent to DCs. Constraint (12.13) means that all items supplied from DCs is equal to all items supplied to CZs. Constraint (12.15) means that what there are currently in the store equals to what there were in the store plus what are received minus what are sent. The way fuzzy constraints (12.9)–(12.14) are treated will be described below.

Note that the production–distribution model introduced above is of general form and some additional constraints may be necessary to consider when dealing with some particular cases of practical relevance (e.g. we might be interested in capturing relationships among production units regarding exchange of semi-products or components, some specific agreements and conditions etc.).

As was indicated above, the primary objective of optimization is to maximize the overall profit that is the return from sales less production, transportation, and storage and maintenance expenses. Transportation expenses and storage expenses can be of non-linear nature when looking at the number of items transported or stored. The optimization should be done for several periods ahead provided that the demand forecasts for those periods are known. The fuzzy demand forecasts, obtained from a forecasting agent, for several succeeding periods in the future are considered. The optimization should be performed anew as a better forecast becomes available and in this case all the plans and schedules on the affected periods need to be recalculated.

However, there is another objective in the optimization to be considered that is to keep the fillrate (expressing customer demand satisfaction or service level, considered as a fuzzy constraint in the optimization problem, $0 \leq$ fillrate ≤ 0) from falling below a specified level (a lower bound fillrate). The actual fillrate level is based on the degree to which the fuzzy comparison $N \geq D$ (the degree to which fuzzy supply is possibly greater or equal than fuzzy demand) is satisfied for a considered case. Experiments with different minimum allowable fillrate values were performed and a more desirable value for lower bound fillrate level (in the trade-off between cost and required demand satisfaction) was identified to be between 0.90 and 0.95. The next section describes a generalized production–distribution planning procedure.

12.2.3 *A solution of the production–distribution problem*

Finding an optimal solution is not an easy task and the use of traditional methods based on linear and non- linear programming models is accompanied with heavy computing overhead. Having this in mind, we have decided to pursue evolutionary optimization, and genetic algorithms (GAs), in particular. The principle of GA optimization differs substantially from most traditional search and optimization methods. GA conducts a search through the space of solutions by exploiting a population of points in parallel rather than a single point; GA requires neither information expressed in terms of gradient of the optimized objective function nor other auxiliary knowledge: only the objective function and the corresponding fitness levels influence the directions of search; GA uses probabilistic transition rules instead of deterministic ones; GA is generally more straightforward to apply; GA can provide a number of potential solutions to a given problem, leaving the user to make the final decision. Moreover, our experience and many examples found in the literature have proven genetic algorithm to be better choice for tackling optimization problems containing fuzzy parameters [36, 589, 760]. Taking into account the above, we use a genetic algorithm to optimize the considered production–distribution process.

To apply the genetic algorithm technique all considered decision variables, i.e. $V_{t,ij}^{proj}$, $W_{t,jk}^{proj}$, $M_{t,ip}^{proj}$ and $W_{t,j0}^{proj}$ need to be coded to a data structure named a chromosome or a genome. Since, in this research we use binary coding, our genomes represent bitstrings each storing a coded potential solution. Fuzzy parameters are converted to binary form and linked-up in a single bitstring (genome) S. The parameters are linearly transformed into integers of l bits accuracy (in our experiments $l = 32$ bits) with constant limits for every variable. Depending on the type of fuzzy number, different quantity of such integer numbers p may be required for each fuzzy number, e.g. 3 – for triangle, 4 – for trapezoid etc.

The population elements (genomes) are completely defined by their strings: Population $= \{S_1, S_2, ..., S_{PopSize}\}$. A population of bitstring (initially generated randomly) is repeatedly undergone a series of genetic operators (crossover, mutation, selection, elitism, etc.) until new "better" genomes are produced. The quality of a genome is evaluated by the fitness function. The fitness value of a genome reflects the quality of the coded solution and is produced by the fitness function given the actual values of decision variables coded in the genome. The number of iterations (or generations) necessary to produce an acceptable solution varies depending on the complexity of problem. Genetic operators have probability based parameters (e.g. probability of cross-over, probability of mutation, probability of selection, probability of parent genomes to pass to the next generation unchangeably, etc.). The abovesaid genetic operators depend on the type of coding used in GA and can be implemented in different ways. In this research we use the multipoint binary mutation operator, to switch bits in a genome according to predefined mutation probability, and the multipoint binary crossover operator, exchanging bits of two parent genomes according to a predefined crossover probability. Figure 12.1 illustrates a general flowchart of the single-population genetic algorithm.

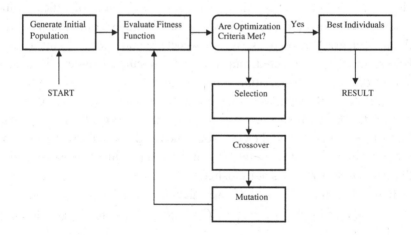

Fig. 12.1. Single-population genetic algorithm

Each of constraints (12.6)–(12.9), (12.10), (12.13), (12.14) is considered to be satisfied if the degree of accomplishment of the related fuzzy condition is higher than the degree of accomplishment of the inverse condition, e.g.: for a fuzzy condition $W_{t,j0}^{proj} \leq W_{j\max}$ to be hold, the satisfaction of the crisp condition Degree $(W_{t,j0}^{proj} \leq W_{j\max}) \geq$ Degree $(W_{j\max} \leq W_{t,j0}^{proj})$ is necessary. Condition 11 ($N_{t,kp}^{proj} \geq D_{t,kp}^{proj}$ is considered in a different way; its degree of accomplishment is directly used in calculation of the fitness function.

The fitness function (to be minimized, i.e. lower values represent better solutions) is calculated on the basis of forecast values of demand as follows:

$$\text{Fitness} = \begin{cases} F_{\max}, \text{ if } \text{ constraints } (13.6) - (13.9), (13.10), \\ \quad (13.13), (13.14) \text{ are } \text{ not satisfied}; \\ \\ F_{\max} \cdot \left(1 - \begin{cases} 1, \text{ if } \bigwedge_{k}\left[\text{Degree}(N_{t,kp}^{proj} \geq D_{t,k}^{proj})\right] \geq \\ \text{MinFillRate}; \\ \bigwedge_{k}\left[\text{Degree}(N_{t,k}^{proj} \geq D_{t,k}^{proj})\right], \\ \text{otherwise} \end{cases} \right) - \text{ETP}, \text{ otherwise} \end{cases} \quad (12.15)$$

where $F_{\max}$ is chosen possible maximum (worst) value of fitness value which is necessary for balancing the effects in fitness function from the fillrate and profit objectives; ETP (expected total profit) is the (crisp) defuzzified fuzzy projected total profit F calculated under given data and production/transportation and demand forecast assumptions; MinFillRate is chosen minimum admissible level for fillrate (e.g. 0.9).

Note that in the considered case, the better genomes are those with lower fitness function value and the GA is designed to do search to minimize the fitness function. The fitness function takes the maximum (the worst) value if any of the constraints is not satisfied.

If all constraints are satisfied, we calculate
$\bigwedge_{k}\left[\text{Degree}(N_{t,k}^{proj} \geq D_{t,k}^{proj})\right] \geq \text{MinFillRate}$, which is the minimum value of the fuzzy satisfaction degree of fuzzy condition $N_{t,k}^{proj} \geq D_{t,k}^{proj}$ over all CZs.

As can be seen, the effect of fillrate is put on the fitness function only if the fullrate is below the required level and it would have no effect on the fitness function if the fillrate is within the interval [MinFillRate, 1]. If the fillrate requirement is met then the optimization is performed to maximize the projected total profit (by minimizing the negative value: -ETP).

Overall, the generalized optimal production–distribution planning procedure can be outlined in the following way:

1. Obtain the demand forecasts for the current (t) quarter and $n - 1$ succeeding quarters (t+1, t+2, t+n-1, etc.). Update the values of other data (e.g. DC/PU costs, product selling prices, etc.). Enter input production–distribution data and GA characteristics.

2. Perform GA based optimization:

(a) Prepare a genome structure to hold coded representation of the values of parameters to be optimized (i.e. $V_{t,ij}^{proj}$, $W_{t,jk}^{proj}$, $M_{t,ip}^{proj}$ and $W_{t,j0}^{proj}$).

(b) Randomly generate a population of genomes (coded representations of potential solutions):

Population $= \{S_1, S_2, ..., S_{\text{PopSize}}\}$. Real solutions from the previous periods transformed to genomes can be added to the population (as well as selected parent genomes from previous generations).

(c) Evaluate the fitness value for every genome. The fitness values of genomes leading to solutions with higher profit will have lower (better in our choice) values. The fitness values for such genomes, representing solutions of which do not satisfy the realistic (fuzzy or crisp) constraints will be set to the highest possible (the worst in our choice) value.

(d) Apply genetic operators of crossover, and mutation to generate new genomes.

(e) Apply selection and elitism operators. Choose better genomes to form the new generation.

(f) Restore the best current solution from the chosen population of genomes. If a predefined number of iterations (generations) have already been done, a decision maker evaluates if further optimization is necessary. If an acceptable solution has already found go to Step 3. Otherwise, continue from Step 2c.

3. Prepare production and transportation plans for the current (next) period and the following $n - 1$ periods. If any better evaluations for demand are known during the current period (this is especially important if the forecasted demand exceed actual demand i.e. actual sales), the optimization for current period can be run anew to reroute transportation from DCs to CZs, searching for schedules leading to less E_{DC} expenses (thereby increasing the profit).

12.2.4 *Experimental investigation*

The considered example of SC is a simplified model based on the case of the General Appliance Company described in [241]. The considered SC network contains two PUs ($n_{PU} = 2$), two DCs ($nDC = 2$), and two CZs ($n_{CZ} = 2$) (Fig. 12.2). The number of periods $n = 2$. The PU1 produces end-products (washers) for DC_1 and DC_2 and two kinds of components (cabinets and motors) for PU_2. PU_2 assembles end-products (washers) from components (cabinets and motors) supplied by PU_1 and deliver end-products to DC_1 and DC_2. The production and transportation volumes are evaluated on the basis of demand for end-products (washers) at customer zones CZ_1 and CZ_2 (evaluated as fuzzy values).

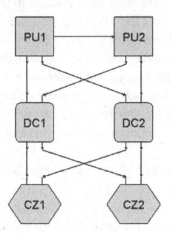

Fig. 12.2. An example SCM network considered for simulation

The production unit (PU) and distribution center (DC) cases, production volumes, transportation routes, and storage volumes are found on the basis of an optimization procedure based on genetic algorithm with the main objective of maximizing the overall profit from product sales subject to the material constraints (e.g. limited production and storage capacities), natural con straints (e.g. positive volumes to produce, store and transport), and a soft constraint (demand satisfaction) providing the fillrate at a level 90% or above.

Input data are given in Tables 12.3 and 12.4. Table 12.3 contains capacity and cost data for the considered PUs and DCs and product selling price at considered CZs. Table 12.4 contains transportation cost data for different routes. The table contains cost for transportations between different PUs and DCs and between DCs and CZs. The following input variables are fuzzy: projected (forecasted) demand volumes at customer zones, maximum production capacities, and maximum storage capacities. Note also that here we consider 1 end-product supplied to customers by PU_1 and PU_2 and two semi-products (necessary to assemble a unit of end-product) produced by PU1 and supplied to PU2.

Table 12.3. PUs, DCs, and CZs data

Maximum fuzzy production capacity ($V_{i\max}$), items

PU_1	PU_2
(195,000; 200,000; 205,000)	(95,000; 100,000; 105,000)

Maximum fuzzy storage capacity ($W_{i\max}$), items

DC_1	DC_2
(125,000; 130,000; 135,000)	(165,000; 170,000; 175,000)

Fixed cost (S_{i0}), USD

PU_1	PU_2
250,000	200,000

Production cost (C_i), USD

PU_1	PU_2
65	75

Fixed cost (Q_{j0}), USD

DC_1	DC_2
45,000	54,000

Storage cost (Q_j), USD

DC_1	DC_2
3	2

(*Continued*)

Table 12.3. (*Continued*)

Maximum fuzzy production capacity ($V_{i\,max}$), items	
Selling price (Pk), USD	
CZ$_1$	CZ$_2$
95	110

Table 12.4. Transportation costs (for 1 item in bunches of 1000 items)

Transportation cost (T_{ij}), USD	Received by:
	DC$_1$
Sent from:	PU$_1$ 10
	PU$_2$ 12
Transportation cost (U_{jk}), USD	Received by:
	CZ$_1$
Sent from:	DC$_1$ 16
	DC$_2$ 11

The objective of computer experiments is to investigate the effectiveness of the suggested fuzzy integrated production–distribution planning model.

To this end, the experiments were made to compare production–distribution planning (PDP) models built on the basis of crisp and fuzzy approaches; to compare integrated and disintegrated PDP models; and to analyze the effect of the fillrate/profit trade-off on the effectiveness of fuzzy integrated PDP models.

For a forecasted demand shown in Table 12.5, Tables 12.6–12.8 show the known ideal crisp solution to this problem with the objective (maximize the profit (12.1)) and constraints (12.6)–(12.14) formulated for the numeric case.

Table 12.5. Forecasted demand for items in CZs

Forecasted quantity of items for sales ($D_{t,k}^{proj}$) in 1000 items

t	CZ$_1$	CZ$_2$	Total
1	(168,170,172)	(94,96,98)	(262,266,270)
2	(170,173,176)	(98,101,1	(268,274,280

Table 12.6. Production plan for PUs

t	Quantity of items to produce (defuzzified), items		
	PU$_1$	PU2	Total
1	200,000 (end-product) 66,000 (component1) 66,000 (component2)	66,000(end product)	266,000
2	200,000 (end-product) 74,000 (component1) 74,000 (component2)	74,000 (end-product)	274,000

Table 12.7. Transportation plan (defuzzified values are shown)

Transported quantities $V^{proj}_{PU,t=1,ij}$ items		Received by: PU$_2$		
Sent from:	PU$_1$	Semiproduct 1 66,000		Semiproduct 2 66,000
Transported quantities $V^{proj}_{t=1,ij}$ items		Received by:		All DCs
		DC$_1$	DC$_2$	
Sent from:	PU$_1$	96,000	104,000	200,000
	PU$_2$	0	66,000	66,000
	All PUs	96,000	170,000	266,000
Transported quantities $W^{proj}_{t=1,ij}$ items		Received by:		
		CZ$_1$	CZ$_2$	All CZs
Sent from:	DC$_1$	0	96,000	96,000
	DC$_2$	170,000	0	170,000
	All DCs	170,000	96,000	266,000
Transported quantities $V^{proj}_{PU,t=2,ij}$ items		Received by: PU$_2$		
Sent from:	PU$_1$	Semiproduct 1 0		Semiproduct 2 0
Transported quantities $V^{proj}_{t=2,ij}$ items		Received by:		All DCs
		DC$_1$	DC$_2$	
Sent from:	PU$_1$	105,000	95,000	200,000
	PU$_2$	0	74,000	74,000
	All PUs	105,000	169,000	274,000
Transported quantities $W^{proj}_{t=2,ij}$ items		Received by:		
		CZ$_1$	CZ$_2$	All CZs
Sent from:	DC$_1$	4000	101,000	91,000
	DC$_2$	169,000	0	109,000
	All DCs	173,000	101,000	274,000

Table 12.8. Projected performance charac-teristics for the all (2) periods

Characteristics	Projected value
Total revenue from sales, USD	54,255,000
PU expenses, USD	37,400,000
DC expenses, USD	1,479,000
Transportation expenses, USD	13,200,000
Total profit, USD	2,176,000

However, the proposed solution is not realistic because the capacity constraints and demand forecasts for the next two periods are taken to be accurate crisp values, and the performance value is based completely on the exact accomplishment of the predefined assumptions. However, the capacity may change for next periods and the demand can significantly decline which is different from the initially known forecasts (especially for further and longer periods).

As an illustration, let us consider the following numeric example. In the above case, the numeric solution implies that the demand would be exactly 170,000 (CZ_1) and 96,000 (CZ_2) for period 1 and 173,000 (CZ_1) and 101,000 (CZ_2) for period 2. However, if the actual demand is lower than the forecasted by only 1–2% in both customer zones in period 2 (e.g. down to 170,000 and 96,000), the actual profit would be less by USD 835,000. If, in addition, the plant capacities go down by 1%, the constraints (12.9), (12.10), (12.14) will not be satisfied and there will be no crisp solution (e.g. 96,000 + 104,000 ≤ 200,000 − 2000: constraint (12.9) is wrong). As can be seen, in actual cases when the demand and capacity change, there is a significant risk of large profit losses. Experiments showed that profit would go down even to negative values in some situations.

Tables 12.9–12.11 show a solution provided by the proposed method, found by GA based optimization, that considers fuzzy production and capacity constraints as well as fuzzy demand forecasts. The "Projected" in Table 12.9 means the projected values of variables while the "Actual" shows the values after completion of current time period and recalculation. This solution is more stable to changes of the environment parameters. The proposed above demand change will not decrease the profit. The decrease in capacity considered above will not cause the constraint

(12.9) to fail $(86{,}913 + 110{,}931 = 197{,}844 \leq \{190{,}000;\ 200{,}000;\ 210{,}000\} - 2000 = \{188{,}000;\ 198{,}000;\ 208{,}000\})$ is true [36] ("possibly true" because $1 > 0.9844$ and "necessarily true" because $0.0156 > 0$, where $\{190{,}000;\ 200{,}000;\ 210{,}000\}$ is the fuzzy capacity described as a triangle fuzzy number [36, 39].

A number of experiments have been performed to investigate the sensitivity of overall profit on lower bound fillrate level. These experiments have shown that decreasing the lower bound level of fillrate can lead in some cases to an increase in overall profit. These are cases when the actual demand appears to be lower than the projected demand (sales levels), and we can save on transportation, production,

Table 12.9. Production plan for PUs (defuzzified values shown)

Quantity of items to produce $M_{t,ip}^{proj}$ items

t	PU1	PU2	Total
1	197,844 (end-product) 51,705 (component1) 51,705 (component2)	51,705 (end product)	249,549
2	199,997 (end-product) 62,695 (component1) 62,695 (component2)	62,695 (end-product)	262,692

Table 12.10. Transportation plan (defuzzifed values are shown)

Transported quantities $V_{PU,t=1,ij}^{proj}$ items		Received by: PU2		
Sent from:	PU1	Semiproduct 1 51,705		Semiproduct 2 51,705
Transported quantities $V_{t=1,ij}^{proj}$ items		Received by:		All DCs
		DC_1	DC_2	
Sent from:	PU1	86,913	110,931	197,844
	PU2	13,887	37,818	51,705
	All PUs	100,800	148,749	249,549
Transported quantities $W_{t=1,ij}^{proj}$ items		Received by:		
		DC_1	DC_2	All DCs
Sent from:	DC_1	56,875	43,925	100,800
	DC_2	106,250	42,499	148,749
	All DCs	163,125	86,424	249,549

(*Continued*)

Table 12.10. (*Continued*)

Transported quantities $V^{proj}_{t=2,ij}$ items		Received by:		
		DC$_1$	DC$_2$	All DCs
Sent from:	PU$_1$	99,999	99,998	199,997
	PU$_2$	0	62,695	62,695
	All PUs	99,999	162,693	262,692
Transported quantities $V^{proj}_{PU,t=2,ij}$ items		Received by:		
		PU$_2$	DC$_2$	All DCs
Sent from:	PU$_1$	Semiproduct1		Semiproduct2
		62,695		62,695
Transported quantities $W^{proj}_{t=2,jk}$ items		Received by:		
		CZ$_1$	CZ$_2$	All CZs
Sent from:	DC$_1$	8,999	91,000	99,999
	DC$_2$	158,982	3,711	162,693
	All DCs	167,981	94,711	262,692

Table 12.11. Performance summary for the all (2) periods after using GA

Characteristics	Projected	Actual
Total revenue from sales, USD	51,379,920	51,096,725
PU expenses, USD	35,339,665	35,209,860
DC expenses, USD	1,423,281	1,423,281
Transportation expenses, USD	13,251,272	13,226,312
Total profit, USD	1,365,702	1,237,272
Fillrate	0.94	0.94

and storage costs. In cases, however, when the actual demand exceeds the forecasted one, we sometimes lose on the profit as result of deficit of the end-product in great demand (we do not consider here the possibility for customers to switch to another producer, though this may be a concern as well).A higher fillrate give us higher overall profit only if the forecasted demand is very close to the actual demand (actual sales level). In cases when the actual demand (actual sales level) is low, we experience losses because of inability to sell end-product in excess. When, however, the actual demand is high, we experience losses in overall profit as result of more expenses needed for production, storage, and transportation: experiments show that a comparative or even higher profit in this case can be got with some less production volumes.

Along with allowance for soft constraint bounds providing reasonable stability, the risk level can be controlled by manipulations of the lower bound fillrate (MinFillRate) parameter (keeping the current fillrate, evaluated as degree of accomplishment of fuzzy inequality (12.11), at a value higher than or equal to MinFillRate). MinFillRate can be set lower to minimize the risk of demand decrease. The experiments have shown that an effective value of lower bound fillrate is a value between 0.90 and 0.95. The considered above solution is found for MinFillRate = 90%.

A number of experiments have been performed to demonstrate the effect of integration of planning and distribution tasks. Table 12.12 quantifies the performance when using separate planning and distribution processes. As can be seen, the projected profit is lower than the one obtained in the case when we considered the integrated case. Experiments in which we considered production and transportation as two separate activities have resulted in the total profit being 9–11% less than in the integrated case. Experiments considering optimization of each time period t separately in the average showed lower performance resulting in up to 7% loss of profit.

Table 12.12. Performance summary for disintegrated case

Characteristics	Projected	Actual
Total revenue from sales, USD	54,145,000	54,052,435
PU expenses, USD	37,740,000	37,737,375
DC expenses, USD	1,496,000	1,423,281
Transportation expenses, USD	14,206,000	14,655,154
Total profit, USD	703,000	236,625
Fillrate	0.98	0.94

In the majority of our GA optimization experiments we used the following parameters: Size of population: 100 (or 50), Number of parent genomes to pass to next generation: 10 (or 5), Number of randomly chosen genomes added to next generation: 0 (or 5), Number of generations: 500–2000, Probability of binary multi- point mutation: 0.05, Probability of binary multipoint crossover: 0.25. A fuzzy number is coded as 64 (or 128) bits length subbitstring. With these parameters, the time one experiment took was 20–40 min on a Pentium 4 class PC. The software was written in C#(C sharp) programming language. An increase in dimensionality has a noticeable impact in computing times because the genome size (the bitstring length) increases. However, the impact can be set down by decreasing size of population and precision of solution and fuzzy number coding method.

Figure 12.3 shows an example of the values of the fitness obtained in successive generations. It shows very clearly that the GA provides a continuous improvement of the solutions produced during the course of progression of the genetic optimization. The application of the capacities of PUs and DCs expressed as fuzzy numbers made it possible to correctly tackle solution vectors falling near constraints boundaries, which afterwards allowed to produce more realistic results. The use of fuzzy demand brings also an effective evaluation of the fillrate on the basis of degree of holding of the fuzzy inequality $\overline{N}_k \geq \overline{D}_k$.

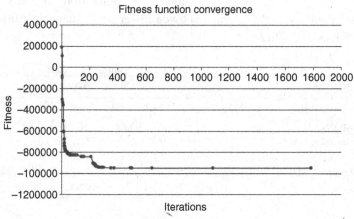

Fig. 12.3. The evolutionary process. GA optimizes production–distribution solution

Constraints (12.5)-(12.14) are treated as follows. Given two fuzzy numbers N and D with membership functions $\mu_N(x)$ and $\mu_D(x)$ defined on the universe of discourse $U(x \in U \subset R)$, the possibility measure and necessity measure that N is greater than or equal to D is defined as follows:

$$\text{Possibility}(N \geq D) = \sup_x \min(\mu_N(x), \mu_{[D,+\infty)}(x))$$

$$\text{Necessity}(N \geq D) = \inf_x \max(1 - \mu_N(x), \mu_{[D,+\infty)}(x)),$$

where $\mu_{[D,+\infty)}(y) = \sup_{x \leq y} \mu_D(x)$.

The possibility measure and necessity measure that D is less than or equal to N is defined as follows:

$$\text{Possibility}(D \leq N) = \text{Possibility}(N \geq D)$$

$$\text{Necessity}(D \leq N) = \text{Necessity}(N \geq D).$$

Given two fuzzy numbers N and D with membership functions $\mu_N(x)$ and $\mu_D(x)$ defined on the universe of discourse $U(x \in U \subset R)$, the degree that N is greater than of equal to D is defined as follows:

$$\text{Degree}(N \geq D) = \beta \cdot \text{Possibility}(N \geq D) + (1 - \beta) \cdot \text{Necessity}(N \geq D),$$

where β is the decision maker's attitude parameter, $0 \leq \beta \leq 1$. If β is greater than 0.5 then this attitude is optimistic, otherwise it is pessimistic.

For checking satisfaction of conditions in fuzzy constraints, the following rule is used:

If $\text{Degree}(N \geq D) > \text{Degree}(D \geq N)$, then $N \geq D$ ($N \geq D$ is satisfied), else if

$\text{Degree}(N \geq D) < \text{Degree}(D \geq N)$, then $N \leq D(N \geq D$ is not satisfied),

else $N = D$.

All presented solutions have been found for the decision maker's attitude parameter equal to 1 (optimistic), however the risk-averse decision maker may apply the pessimistic decision strategy based on his own assumptions. As can be seen, the application of fuzzy technology permits account for the imprecision and ranges of input constraints, leading to more reliable and feasible solutions.

12.3 Application of fuzzy logic in economics

In this study the Fuzzy Economics is defined as human-centric and closer to the reality Economics with fuzzy-logic based representation of the economic agent's behavior. Using fuzzy agents this section investigates different problems of fuzzy economics and methods of their solutions, namely, time path and stability of the fuzzy dynamic economic systems.

12.3.1 *Fuzzy language in modeling of an economic agent*

Rule-based models occupy a central position in a broad spectrum of linguistic models [15, 596]. Fuzzy-rule-bases can be used for representations of an economic agent's knowledge and usually consist of a set of fuzzy rules such as:

"If the inflation differential between Europe and the USA is low, then the rate of appreciation of the Euro will be high".

A complete and consistent fuzzy rule-base can be automatically generated on the basis of a numerical database. Nevertheless, the user may influence the results in many ways and therefore always keeps control over the output.

These criteria, and possible trade-offs have been a subject of many investigations.

The quest for models that are accurate, transparent and user-friendly has characterized intelligent system for decades.

The theory of differential equations has become an essential tool of economic analysis particularly since computer has become commonly available. It would be difficult to comprehend the contemporary literature of economics if one does not understand basic concepts (such as bifurcations and chaos) and results of modern theory of differential equations.

Fuzzy differential equations serve many functions in economics. They are used to determine the conditions for dynamic stability in microeconomic models of market general equilibria and to trace the time path of growth under various conditions and uncertainty in microeconomics. Given the growth rate of a function, differential equations enable the economist to find the function whose growth is described; from point elasticity, they enable the economist to estimate the demand function.

12.3.2 *Fuzzy stability*

Stability is one of the most essential properties of complex dynamical systems, no matter whether technical or human-oriented (social, economical, etc.) In classical terms, the stability property of a dynamical system usually is quantified in a binary form and this quantification states whether the system under consideration reaches equilibrium state after being affected by disturbances. Even if we define a region of stability, in every point of operation of the system we can only conclude that "*the system is stable*" or "*the system is unstable*". No particular quantification as to a degree of stability could be offered. In many cases when such a standard bivalent two-valued definition of stability is being used, we may end up with counterintuitive conclusions.

In contrast, human generated statements would involve degrees of stability which are expressed linguistically and expressed by some fuzzy number which links with some quantification of stability located somewhere in-between absolutely stable and absolutely unstable states, i.e., a stability degree could be expressed by a fuzzy number defined over the unit interval in which 0 is treated as absolutely unstable and 1 corresponds to that state that is absolutely stable. It is then advantageous to introduce linguistic interpretation of degrees of stability, i.e., a degree of stability becomes a linguistic variable assuming terms such as "unstable", "*weakly* stable", "*more or less* stable", "*strongly* stable", "*completely* stable" each of them being described by the corresponding fuzzy numbers defined over [0,1] [63].

We can conclude that the concept of stability is a fuzzy concept in the sense that it is a matter of degree.

Accuracy has been a dominant feature in mathematics. However, as the systems under study become more and more complex, nonlinear or uncertain, the use of well-positioned tools of fully deterministic analysis tends to exhibit some limitations and show a lack of rapport with the real world problem under consideration. As a matter of the fact, this form of limitation has been emphasized by the principle of incompatibility [825].

In many cases, information about a behavior of a dynamical system becomes uncertain. In order to obtain a more realistic model, we have to take into account a existing components of uncertainty. Furthermore, uncertainties might not be of probabilistic type. The generalized theory of uncertainty (GTU), outlined by Prof. L.A. Zadeh in [826], breaks with the tradition in real-world problems to view uncertainty as a province of probability and puts it in a much broader perspective. In this setting, the language and formalism of the dynamic fuzzy "if-then" rules and fuzzy differential equations (FDE) become a natural ways to model dynamical systems.

Let us consider a fuzzy differential system

$$x' = f(t,x),$$
(12.16)

where f in (12.16) is continuous and has continuous partial derivatives $\dfrac{\partial f}{\partial x}$ on $R_+ \times E^n$ i.e. $f \in C^1 \left| R_+ \times E^n, E^n \right|$, and $x(t_0) = y(t_0) \in E^n, t \geq t_0$, $t_0 \in R_+$.

Definition (Zadeh-Aliev) 12.1. The solution $x(t,t_0,y_0)$ of the system (12.16) is said to be fuzzy Lipschitz stable with respect to the solution $x(t,t_0,x_0)$ of the system (12.16) for $t \geq t_0$, where $x(t,t_0,x_0)$ is any solution of the system (12.16), if there exists a fuzzy number $M = M(t_0) > 0$, such that

(12.17)

$$\left\| x(t,t_0,y_0) -_h x(t,t_0,x_0) \right\|_{fH} \leq M(t_0) \left\| y_0 -_h x_0 \right\|_{fH}$$

If M is independent on t_0, then the solution $x(t,t_0,y_0)$ of the system (12.16) is said to be uniformly fuzzy Lipschitz stable with respect to the solution $x(t,t_0,x_0)$.

Let $x(t,t_0,x_0)$ be the solution to (12.16) for $t \geq t_0$. Then $\Phi(t,t_0,x_0) = \dfrac{\partial x(t,t_0,x_0)}{\partial x_0}$ exists and is the fundamental matrix solution of the variational equation

$$z' = \frac{\partial f(t,x(t,t_0,x_0))}{\partial x} z,$$
(12.18)

and $\dfrac{\partial x(t,t_0,x_0)}{\partial t_0}$ exists, is a solution of (12.18), and satisfies the relation:

$$\frac{\partial x(t,t_0,x_0)}{\partial t_0} + \Phi(t,t_0,x_0)f(t_0,x_0) = 0, \text{ for } t \geq t_0.$$

Definition (Zadeh-Aliev) 12.2. The solution $x(t,t_0,y_0)$ of the system (12.16) through (t_0,y_0) for $t \geq t_0$ is said to be *fuzzy Lipschitz stable* with respect to the solution $x(t,t_0,x_0)$ of (12.16) for $t \geq t_0$, where $x(t,t_0,x_0)$ is any solution of the system (12.16) if and only if there exist $M = M(t_0) > 0$ and $\delta > 0$ such that $\left\| x(t,t_0,y_0) -_h x(t,t_0,x_0) \right\|_f \leq$ $\leq M(t_0)\left\| y_0 -_h x_0 \right\|_f$ for $t \geq t_0$, provided $\left\| y_0 - x_0 \right\|_f \leq \delta$. If M is independent of t_0, then the solution $x(t,t_0,y_0)$ of the system (12.16) is *uniformly fuzzy Lipschitz stable* with respect to the solution $x(t,t_0,x_0)$.

The theory of FDE which utilizes the Hukuhara derivative has a certain disadvantage that the *diam* $((x(t))^\alpha)$ of the solution $x(t)$ of FDE is a nondecreasing function of time. As it was mentioned in [465], this formulation of FDE cannot reflect any reach behavior of solutions of ODE, such as stability, periodicity, bifurcation and others, is not well suited for modeling purposes. In view of this it is useful to utilize b)-type of strongly generalized differentiability [21, 98–100]. For example, let us consider the following FDE:

$$x' = -x.$$

The solution of the numeric analog $y' = -y$ of this equation is $y = y_0 e^{-t}$ which is stable. If we use (a)-type of strongly generalized differentiability [98–100], then α-cut of its solution is [21]

$$x_l^\alpha = \frac{1}{2}(x_{l0}^\alpha - x_{r0}^\alpha)e^t + \frac{1}{2}(x_{l0}^\alpha + x_{r0}^\alpha)e^{-t},$$

$$x_r^\alpha = \frac{1}{2}(x_{r0}^\alpha - x_{l0}^\alpha)e^t + \frac{1}{2}(x_{l0}^\alpha + x_{r0}^\alpha)e^{-t}.$$

In general it is not stable, and so, we lose the stability property. But if we use b)-type of strongly generalized differentiability, then α-cut of its solution is $x_l^\alpha = x_{l0}^\alpha e^{-t}, x_r^\alpha = x_{r0}^\alpha e^{-t}$. It is stable and coincides with the solution obtained before for the numeric case.

Stability Criteria

Theorem 12.1. Let us consider the solutions $x(t,t_0,y_0)$, $t \geq t_0$, and $x(t,t_0,x_0)$, $t \geq t_0$ of the system (12.16). Let us assume the following

1) There exists a fuzzy number $L(t_0)$, such that $\int_{t_0}^{\infty} \lambda(s)ds = L(t_0)$, where

$$\lambda(s) \in C\big[[0,\infty), E_+ \subset E\big], E_+ = \{\lambda \in E, \mathrm{supp}(\lambda) \geq 0\}.$$

2) f satisfies the following fuzzy Lipschitz condition with respect to x:

$$\big\| f(t,v(t,t_0,v_0)+x(t,t_0,x_0)) -_h f(t,x(t,t_0,x_0)) \big\|_{fH} \leq \lambda(t) \big\| v(t) \big\|_{fH},$$

where $v(t,t_0,v_0) = x(t,t_0,y_0) -_h x(t,t_0,x_0)$.

Then the solution $x(t,t_0,y_0)$ of the system (12.16) is fuzzy Lipschitz stable with respect to $x(t,t_0,x_0)$.

Theorem 12.2. Let $\Phi(t,t_0)$ be the fundamental matrix of (12.16). If there exist positive continuous functions $k(t)$ and $h(t) \in E^1$, $t \geq t_0$, such that

$$\int_{t_0}^{t} h(s) \| \Phi(t,s) \|_f \, ds \leq k(t) \quad \text{for } t \geq t_0 \geq 0, \tag{12.19}$$

and

$$k(t) \exp\left(-\int_{t_1}^{t} \frac{h(s)}{k(s)} ds \right) \leq K \quad \text{for } t \geq t_1 \geq t_0, \tag{12.20}$$

where $K \in E^1$ is a fixed positive constant, then the solution $x(t,t_0,y_0)$ of (12.16) is uniformly fuzzy Lipschitz stable.

12.3.3 *Stability and time path planning of national economy*

A simple model for the national economy of some country may be described by system of fuzzy differential equations

$$I' = I - \alpha C, \alpha > 1 \tag{12.21}$$

$$C = b(I - C - G), b \geq 1 \tag{12.22}$$

$$G = G_0 + kI$$

where I - the national income, C - the rate of consumer spending, G - the rate of government expenditures and $I'(C')$ is the time derivative of $I(C)$.

All the parameters are a, b, G_0, k and the two initial conditions. Let us assume that the government effect is fuzzy and the other parameters are all unknown and fuzzy.

The solutions $I(t)$ and $C(t)$ are also fuzzy. The system now becomes a continuous fuzzy system whose trajectories are fuzzy so that any slice through a trajectory at some time t is a fuzzy number. We wish to estimate the stability and time path growth of given economical system.

Let $k = 0$, and the other parameters are described by triangular fuzzy numbers: $G_0 = (20000, 30000, 40000)$, $a = (1.4, 1.5, 1.6)$, $b = (1.1, 1.2, 1.3)$. Let the initial conditions be also described by triangular fuzzy numbers:

In this case the system is fuzzy Lipschitz stable because $\left\| \Phi \right\|_f \leq M,$ where Φ is the fundamental matrix solution of the system (12.21)-(12.22). It means that the inequality

$$\left\| x(t, t_0, y_0) - x(t, t_0, x_0) \right\|_f \leq M(t_0) \left\| y_0 - x_0 \right\|,$$

is satisfied with M being a triangular fuzzy number:

$$M = (2.668, 2.9526, 3.4165).$$

The fuzzy degree of stability is

$$Deg = (0.9274, 0.99, 1).$$

The degree was calculated by the following formula:

$$Deg = \frac{\int_0^\delta \left(M \parallel \Delta x_0 \parallel \ - \parallel \Delta x \parallel \ \right) d \parallel \Delta x_0 \parallel}{\int_0^\delta \left(M \parallel \Delta x_0 \parallel \ \right) d \parallel \Delta x_0 \parallel}. \tag{12.23}$$

The graphs of the National Income and Consumer Spending which illustrate the behavior of the stable system are shown below in the Figs. 12.4 and 12.5.

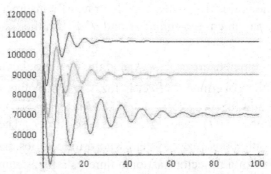

Fig. 12.4. Fuzzy trajectory for national income (core and support behavior)

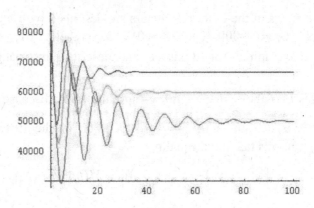

Fig. 12.5. Fuzzy trajectory for consumer spending (core and support behavior)

Let us now change only the parameter b:

$$k = 0, G_0 = (20000, 30000, 40000), \alpha = (1.4, 1.5, 1.6), b = (0.7, 0.8, 0.9),$$
$$I_0 = (90000, 100000, 110000), C_0 = (75000, 80000, 85000).$$

In this case the economic system is unstable and one can see it looking at Figs. 12.6 and 12.7.

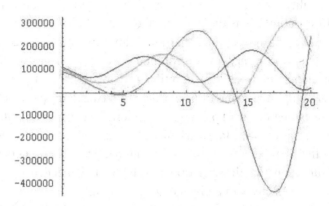

Fig. 12.6. Fuzzy trajectory for national income (core and support behavior)

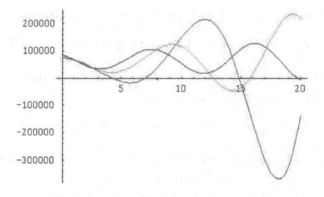

Fig.12.7. Fuzzy trajectory for consumer spending (core and support behavior)

12.3.4 *Economic growth control problem*

Let us consider the problem of control of macroeconomic system's behavior in long-term period. We assume that the system is competitive and macroeconomic trajectories are comes out from behavior of a large amount o interacting producers and consumers (agents). The model of the economical growth is described by a fuzzy differential equation:

$$k' = sk^{0.5} - vk - c \qquad (12.24)$$

Here $k = K / L$, k -a capital ratio; K - capital; L - labor; s - proportionality constant between rate of change of capital and production output of economy, v is the per capita growth rate, c is the consumption per labor. We do not assume that gross investment is a fixed part of a product. On the contrary, in control model we look for in some sense the best correlation between consumption and investment. It is needed the choice of an optimal value of non-productive consumption which defines size of investment, size of a capital and, therefore, size of an output.

In our problem the state variable is the capital ratio, and the control variable that defines a trajectory of economic growth in a perspective is the consumption function per effective labor. It is needed to synthesize an economic system with a given degree of stability.

Choosing c in the form $c = bk$ we obtain different degrees of stability for different values of b. Let the parameters of the system (12.24) and initial conditions are described by triangular fuzzy numbers:

$$s = (0.297, 0.33, 0.363), v = (0.036, 0.04, 0.044), k_0 = (34, 35, 36).$$

For the case when $b = 0.01$ the system is stable and the fuzzy degree of stability is a triangular fuzzy number

$$Deg = (0.568, 0.635, 0.635).$$

Thus we can say that the system is "*more or less*" stable. The degree was calculated by the formula (12.23).

The graph of the capital ratio dynamics which illustrates the behavior of the stable system is shown below in the Fig. 12.8.

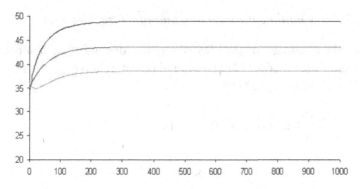

Fig. 12.8. Fuzzy trajectory of a capital ratio (core and support behavior)

For the case when $b = 0.02$ the system is stable and the fuzzy degree of stability is a triangular fuzzy number

$$Deg = (0.76, 0.85, 0.85)$$

So, we can conclude that the system is "*strongly*" stable. The graph of the capital ratio dynamics which illustrates the behavior of the stable system is shown belowin the Fig. 12.9.

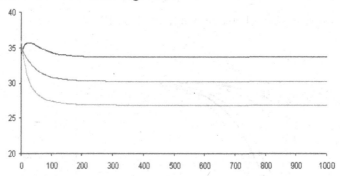

Fig. 12.9. Fuzzy trajectory of a capital ratio (core and support behavior)

12.3.5 *Fuzzy nonlinear model of a manufacture dynamics*

A simple nonlinear model describing the dynamics of a manufacture represents the relation between the level of relative production output and its rate of change [731]:

$$\frac{dq(t)}{dt} = q(t) -_h q^2(t), \quad q(0) = q_0, \quad q(t), \quad q_0 \in E^1, \tag{12.25}$$

where $q(t)$ is a relative production output. $q(t) = Q/Q^*$, where Q is production output and Q^* is its equilibrium value [731]. Production output is one of the main indices of macroeconomics.

For $\alpha = 1$, the fundamental matrix solution is

$$\Phi^{\alpha=1} = \frac{e^{t+t_0}}{\left(e^{t_0}\left(q_0^{\alpha=1}-1\right) - e^t q_0^{\alpha=1}\right)^2}.$$

The graphs of the two fuzzy solutions of (12.25) with the initial conditions $q_{l0}^{\alpha=0} = 0.3$, $q_0^{\alpha=1} = 0.4$, $q_{r0}^{\alpha=0} = 0.5$, $qq_{l0}^{\alpha=0} = 0.8$, $qq_0^{\alpha=1} = 0.9$, $qq_{r0}^{\alpha=0} = 1$ are shown in the Fig. 12.10.

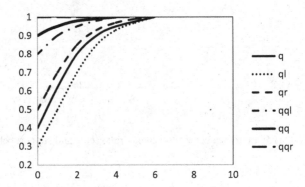

Fig. 12.10. Plot of the fuzzy solutions to (12.25)

If $q_{i0}^{\alpha=0} \geq 0.1$ and $t_0 = 0$ then $\| \Phi(t,t_0,q_0) \|_f \leq M$, where $M = (1,1,2.8)$, and thus

$$\left\| q(t,t_0,\overline{q_0}) -_h q(t,t_0,q_0) \right\|_f \leq M \left\| \overline{q_0} -_h q_0 \right\|_f.$$

M is independent of t_0, and thus solution of (12.25) is uniformly fuzzy Lipschitz stable in variation. The degree of stability is $Deg = (0.396562, 0.5404, 0.679825)$. The possibility measures computed for this fuzzy number and the terms "*weakly* stable", "*more or less* stable" and "*strongly* stable" are about 0.26, 0.918, 0.37 respectively. In essence, the system is *more or less* stable.

12.3.6 *Fuzzy approach to portfolio construction*

In this section, a fuzzy portfolio selection model based on fully fuzzified linear programming with fuzzy goal (fuzzy risk), fuzzy constraints (fuzzy expected return), and fuzzy variables (fuzzy invested proportions) is suggested. To solve a portfolio selection problem on the basis of this model, we use genetic algorithm which provides a global near-optimal solution without conversion of the initial natural fuzzy linear programming (LP) method to crisp linear programming models. The model provides higher accuracy of solution with less computational complexity in near-optimal portfolio construction.

The use of fully fuzzified LP model with soft constraints and genetic algorithm for solving the portfolio selection problem allows management of the conflict between expected rate of return rate and risk by providing a trade-off between them. The fuzzy portfolio optimization model can be formulated as [376]:

$$z = \frac{1}{T} \sum_{t=1}^{T} \left| \min\{0, \sum_{j=1}^{n} (r_{jt} - R_j)x_j\} \right| \to \min \tag{12.26}$$

$$\sum_{j=1}^{n} R_j x_j \geq p - q(1 - \mu_B(y)), \tag{12.27}$$

$$x_1, x_2, \dots, x_n \geq 0$$

Here R_j is the fuzzy value of expected return, p is the minimum rate of return, x_j are fuzzy values of portfolio allocation in security j over the entire period T, and r_{jt} is return of security j over period t. The problem is to determine such values of x_j under fuzzy inequalities and equality conditions (12.27), that would minimize the fuzzy value of objective function (12.26).

The input data for fuzzy portfolio selection model are historical returns data and fuzzy values of expected returns in future. The expected values of returns are determined by expert perception by using fuzzy numbers. A fuzzy portfolio selection model based on fuzzy linear programming (12.26)-(12.27) was solved by genetic algorithm that provides for finding a global near-optimal solution with a reduction in computational complexity compared to the existing methods.

Using portfolio model (12.26) and (12.27) and statistical data, an efficient frontier for portfolio model is constructed. The effcient frontier is obtained for different values of portfolio return. In the simulation fifty chromosomes are generated for each asset. In Fig. 12.11 the portfolio efficient frontier for twelve stocks, after defuzzification of the fuzzy return and fuzzy risk, is shown.

For comparison, deterministic portfolio selection modeling was carried out using the same historical data. For each stock the expected returns were determined through arithmetic means of historical return rates. Then, applying deterministic semiabsolute deviation model and genetic algorithm the optimal values of invested proportions were determined. In Fig. 12.12 the efficient frontier which is constructed by deterministic model is shown. Note that the values of objective risk function in fuzzy portfolio are less than in deterministic models. Thus, it can be said that deterministic model is more risky than the fuzzy model.

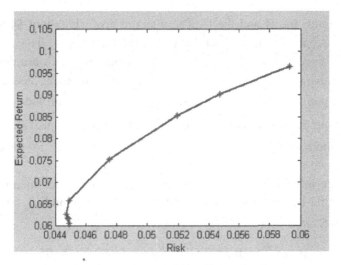

Fig. 12.11. Fuzzy portfolio efficient frontier

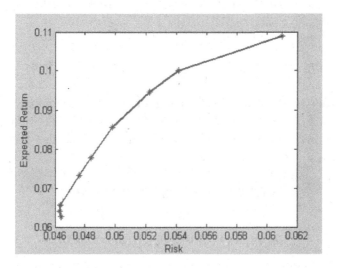

Fig. 12.12. Efficient frontier obtained from deterministic model

12.4 Decision making in a products mix problem

Consider a decision problem on a choice of production planning. A manufacturing company must determine the mix of its commercial products B and C to be produced next year. The company produces two product lines, the B and the C. The average profit is (about $400, very likely) for each B and (about $800, likely) for each C. The resources limitations are fabrication and assembly capacities which are described by Z-numbers to account for possible faults of equipment. Assume that the solution of the considered problem (x_1^1, x_2^1) provides overall profit(about $100 *mln*, likely), and the solution (x_1^2, x_2^2) provides overall profit (about $90 *mln*, very likely). The problem is to rank these solutions.

Let the information about imprecise random quantities mentioned in the example be described by Z-numbers $Z_1 = (A_1, B_1)$ and $Z_2 = (A_2, B_2)$ given (in $ *mln*):

$$A_1 = 0/95 + 0.5/97.5 + 1/100 + 0.5/102.5 + 0/105,$$

$$B_1 = 0/0.75 + 0.5/0.775 + 1/0.8 + 0.5/0.825 + 0/0.85;$$

$$A_2 = 0/85 + 0.5/87.5 + 1/90 + 0.5/92.5 + 0/95,$$

$$B_2 = 0/0.85 + 0.5/0.875 + 1/0.9 + 0.5/0.925 + 0/0.95.$$

In order to solve the considered problem, let us compare these Z-numbers on the basis of the proposed approach. In accordance with approach Section 6.6 first we calculated values of the functions n_b, n_e, n_w:

$$n_b(Z_1, Z_2) = 0.095,\ n_b(Z_2, Z_1) = 0.105,$$
$$n_e(Z_1, Z_2) = 1.8,\ n_e(Z_2, Z_1) = 1.8,$$
$$n_w(Z_1, Z_2) = 0.105,\ n_w(Z_2, Z_1) = 0.095.$$

At the second step, a function d is calculated according approach Section 6.6:

$$d(Z_1, Z_2) = 0;\ d(Z_2, Z_1) = 0.095.$$

Next, $do(Z_1) = 0.905$ and $do(Z_2) = 1$ are obtained on the basis of approach Section 6.6. Therefore, Z_2 is formally more optimal than $Z_1 : Z_2 > Z_1$. However, the considered Z-numbers are almost of the same optimality and the use of a human being's opinion may help to rank solutions (x_1^1, x_2^1) and (x_1^2, x_2^2). Let us consider a human-oriented ranking of these Z-numbers with degree of pessimism $\beta = 0.6$. For this case we will have:

$$r(Z_1, Z_2) = 0.943 < \frac{1}{2}(0.905 + 1) = 0.953.$$

Therefore, $Z_1 > Z_2$. Indeed, as two options have sufficiently high reliabilities, a human being may prefer an option with the higher profit.

12.5 Multi-attribute decision making for web services selection

12.5.1 *State-of-the-art*

The process of multi-attribute criteria decision making (MADM) is to find the best all of the existing alternatives. The use of one or another multi-attribute decision theory depends mainly on decision making situations.

One of the widely used theories to model human decisions is of fuzzy set theory. Some of the most popular theories that emerged for uncertainty modeling were fuzzy sets [18, 27, 828] and possibility theory [246, 857], the rough set theory [586], Dempster [229] and Shafer's [685] evidence theories. It is needed to find the relevant methodology suitable for a particular problem. Some of these methods are the Analytical Hierarchy Process (AHP) [656], Analytic Network Process (ANP) [655], Technique for Order Preference by Similarity to Ideal Solution (TOPSIS) [372], Multi-criteria Optimization and Compromise Solution (VIKOR) [563-565], Simple Additive Weighting Method (SAW) [197], Elimination Et Choice Translating EReality (ELECTRE) [644], Preference Ranking Organization METHODS for Enrichment Evaluations (PROMETHEE) [129], Fuzzy expert systems [31] etc. Unfortunately, up to day there are scarce research on multi-attribute decision making under Z-environment [66]. In this section, we suggest a new approach to study of multi-attribute decision analysis using Z-number concept.

12.5.2 *Statement of the problem and its solution*

Assume that $A = \{A_1, A_2, ..., A_n\}$ is a set of alternatives and $C = \{C_1, C_2, ..., C_m\}$ is a set o attributes. Every attribute C_j, $j = \overline{1, m}$ is characterised by weight W_j assigned by expert or decision maker. As we deal with Z-information valued decision environment, the characteristic of the alternative A_i, $i = \overline{1, n}$ on attribute $C_j \left(j = \overline{1, m} \right)$ is described by the form

$$A_i = \left\{ (Z(A_{i1}, B_{i1}), Z(A_{i2}, B_{i2}), ..., Z(A_{ij}, B_{ij}), Z(A_{im}, B_{im}) \right\} \qquad (12.28)$$

where $Z(A_{ij}, B_{ij})$ is evaluation of an alternative A_i with respect to a attribute C_j. Value of attributes and weights of attributes are usually derived from decision maker or experts and are vague and characterized with partial reliability. In this case, the weights W_j, $i = \overline{1, m}$ are represented as

$$W_j = \left\{ Z(A_j^w, B_j^w) \right\}, \ j = \overline{1, m} \qquad (12.29)$$

where A_j^w is value of weight of j-th is attribute, B_j^w is reliability of this value.

Hence, we can represent decision matrix D_{nmx} as Table 12.13.

Table 12.13. Decision matrix

	C_1	C_2	...	C_m
A_1	$\left[Z(A_{11}, B_{11}) \right]$	$\left[Z(A_{12}, B_{12}) \right]$	...	$\left[Z(A_{1m}, B_{1m}) \right]$
A_2	$\left[Z(A_{21}, B_{21}) \right]$	$\left[Z(A_{22}, B_{22}) \right]$	...	$\left[Z(A_{2m}, B_{2m}) \right]$
$\vdots$	$\vdots$	$\vdots$	$\vdots$	$\vdots$
A_n	$\left[Z(A_{n1}, B_{n1}) \right]$	$\left[Z(A_{n2}, B_{n2}) \right]$	...	$\left[Z(A_{nm}, B_{nm}) \right]$

The common approach in the MADM is the use of the utility theories. This approach leads to transformation of a vector-valued alternative to a scalar-valued quantity. This transformation leads to loss of information. It is related to restrictive assumptions on preferences underlying utility models. In human decision it is not needed to use artificial transformation.

In this case we will use the concept of positive and negative ideal point in multi-attribute decision making [188]. We present an ideal Z-point for attributes as

$$A_p^{id} = \left(Z\left(A_{p1}^{id}, B_{p1}^{id} \right), Z\left(A_{p2}^{id}, B_{p2}^{id} \right), ..., Z\left(A_{pm}^{id}, B_{pm}^{id} \right) \right) \tag{12.30}$$

A negative attributes ideal point will be discribed as

$$A_p^{id} = \left(Z\left(A_{N_1}^{id}, B_{N_1}^{id} \right), Z\left(A_{N_2}^{id}, B_{N_2}^{id} \right), ..., Z\left(A_{N_m}^{id}, B_{N_m}^{id} \right) \right) \tag{12.31}$$

Solution at the stated decision making problem, i.e. choice best alternative among $A = \{ A_1, A_2, ..., A_n \}$ consist of the following steps:

1. Weighted distances d_{ip} i-th alternative and positive ideal solutions (12.30) is defined.

2. Weighted distances d_{iN} between i-th alternative and negative ideal solutions (12.30) is defined.

3. Degree of membership $r_i, i = \overline{1, n}$,of each alternatives belonging to the positive ideal solution is calculated. For this (12.32) is used [722]:

$$r_i = \frac{1}{1 + \left(\dfrac{d_{ip}}{d_{iN}} \right)} \tag{12.32}$$

4. Final decision alternative is selected as $\max(r_i), i = 1, n$

12.5.3 *Practical example*

We consider multi-attribute decision making for Web services selection problem [66]. Today a wide variety of services are offered that can satisfy quality of services for agents. The number of options, i.e. Web services is 8 A_1, A_2, A_3 ... A_8. An agent has to make a decision taking into account 5 attributes C_1 (cost), C_2 (time), C_3 (reliability), C_1 (availability), C_5 (repetition). In this case all 8 alternatives are evaluated under 5 attributes by Z-numbers. Components of these Z-numbers are presented by triangle fuzzy number and scaled decision matrix shown in Tables 12.14a and 12.14b.

Table 12.14a. Decision matrix

	C_1	C_2	C_3
A₁	((0.45 0.5 0.55),	(0.441 0.49 0.539)	(0.621 0.69 0.759))
	(0.5 0.6 0.7))	(0.5 0.6 0.7)	(0.5 0.6 0.7)
A₂	(0.126 0.14 0.154)	(0.531 0.59 0.649)	(0.423 0.47 0.517))
	(0.5 0.6 0.7)	(0.5 0.6 0.7)	(0.5 0.6 0.7)
A₃	(0.225 0.25 0.275)	(0.711 0.79 0.869)	(0.27 0.3 0.33))
	(0.5 0.6 0.7)	(0.7 0.8 0.9)	(0.5 0.6 0.7)
A₄	(0.612 0.68 0.748)	(0.603 0.67 0.737)	(0.378 0.42 0.462))
	(0.5 0.6 0.7)	(0.5 0.6 0.7)	(0.5 0.6 0.7)
A₅	(0.333 0.37 0.407)	(0.225 0.25 0.275)	(0.522 0.58 0.638))
	(0.5 0.6 0.7)	(0.5 0.6 0.7)	(0.5 0.6 0.7)
A₆	(0.432 0.48 0.528)	(0.549 0.61 0.671))	(0.621 0.69 0.759))
	(0.5 0.6 0.7)	(0.5 0.6 0.7)	(0.5 0.6 0.7)
A₇	(0.738 0.82 0.902)	(0.324 0.36 0.396))	(0.522 0.58 0.638))
	(0.7 0.8 0.9)	(0.5 0.6 0.7)	(0.5 0.6 0.7)
A₈	(0.531 0.59 0.649)	(0.378 0.42 0.462)	(0.648 0.72 0.792)
	(0.5 0.6 0.7)	(0.5 0.6 0.7)	(0.7 0.8 0.9)

Table 12.14b. Decision matrix

	C_4	C_5
A₁	(0.702 0.78 0.858) (0.5 0.6 0.7)	(0.126 0.14 0.154) (0.5 0.6 0.7)
A₂	(0.585 0.65 0.715) (0.5 0.6 0.7)	(0.828 0.92 1.012) (0.7 0.8 0.9)
A₃	(0.747 0.83 0.913) (0.7 0.8 0.9)	(0.576 0.64 0.704) (0.5 0.6 0.7)
A₄	(0.405 0.45 0.495) (0.5 0.6 0.7)	(0.342 0.38 0.418) (0.5 0.6 0.7)
A₅	(0.351 0.39 0.429) (0.5 0.6 0.7)	(0.243 0.27 0.297) (0.5 0.6 0.7)
A₆	(0.621 0.69 0.759) (0.5 0.6 0.7)	(0.702 0.78 0.858) (0.5 0.6 0.7)
A₇	(0.216 0.24 0.264) (0.7 0.8 0.9)	(0.324 0.36 0.396)) (0.5 0.6 0.7)
A₈	(0.522 0.58 0.638) (0.5 0.6 0.7)	(0.252 0.28 0.308) (0.5 0.6 0.7)

For the simplicity the weights vector of the 5 attributes is given as follows: for C_1 is $W_1 = 0.3$, for C_2 is $W_2 = 0.2$, for C_3 is $W_3 = 0.12$, for C_4 is $W_4 = 0.18$ and for C_5 is $W_2 = 0.2$.

The positive ideal alternative is presented as

$A_p^{id} = ((0.738 \quad 0.82 \quad 0.902)(0.7 \quad 0.8 \quad 0.9),(0.711 \quad 0.79 \quad 0.869)(0.7 \quad 0.8 \quad 0.9),(0.648 \quad 0.72 \quad 0.792)(0.7 \quad 0.8 \quad 0.9),(0.747 \quad 0.83 \quad 0.913)(0.7 \quad 0.8 \quad 0.9),(0.828 \quad 0.92 \quad 1.012)(0.7 \quad 0.8 \quad 0.9))$

The negative ideal alternative is presented as

$A_N^{id} = ((0.126 \quad 0.14 \quad 0.154)(0.5 \quad 0.6 \quad 0.7), (0.225 \quad 0.25 \quad 0.275)(0.5 \quad 0.6 \quad 0.7), (0.27 \quad 0.3 \quad 0.33)(0.5 \quad 0.6 \quad 0.7), (0.216 \quad 0.24 \quad 0.264)(0.5 \quad 0.6 \quad 0.7), (0.126 \quad 0.14 \quad 0.154)(0.5 \quad 0.6 \quad 0.7))$

The weighted distances between Z-vectors of alternatives and positive ideal solution Z-vector are obtained as.

$d_{p1} = 0.32 \qquad d_{p2} = 0.42 \qquad d_{p3} = 0.375 \qquad d_{p4} = 0.24$

$d_{p5} = 0.315 \qquad d_{p6} = 0.261 \qquad d_{p7} = 0.246 \qquad d_{p8} = 0.274$

Analogously we have obtained weighted distances between Z-vectors of alternatives and negative ideal solution Z- vector:

$$d_{N1} = 0.18 \qquad d_{N2} = 0.32 \qquad d_{N3} = 0.24 \qquad d_{N4} = 0.27$$
$$d_{N5} = 0.114 \qquad d_{N6} = 0.22 \qquad d_{N7} = 0.429 \qquad d_{N8} = 0.225$$

The membership degree $r_i, i = \overline{1,8}$ are calculated according to (12.32) and have obtained

$$r_1 = 0.27 \; r_2 = 0.37 \; r_3 = 0.29 \; r_4 = 0.56 \; r_5 = 0.12 \; r_6 = 0.42 \; r_7 = 0.75 \; r_8 = 0.4$$

The final decision is determined as

$$\max(r_1, r_2, r_3, r_4, r_5, r_6, r_7, r_8) = 0.75$$

The best alternative is A_7.

12.6 Z-number modeling in psychological research

12.6.1 *Set of problem*

The investigation of the effect of physical activities on motivation, attention, anxiety, and educational performances of students is one of the important research areas in psychology. Hannaford in [349] noticed that "Thinking and learning are not all in our head. Our movements that not only express knowledge and facilitate greater cognitive function, they actually grow the brain as they increase in complexity. Our entire brain structure is intimately connected to and grown by the movement mechanism within our body." Recently some research works, demonstrating the achievement of the academic performances through physical activities, have been published in different sources. In [285] is given a review showing the effectiveness of aerobic, resistance, and multi modal exercise interventions on a wide range of outcome measures, including cognition, general physical function, mobility, strength, balance, flexibility, quality of life. It was shown [199] that the students with the highest fitness level performed better on standardized tests and students with the lowest fitness level performed lower in class grades. In [255, 425, 721] it was found that the physical activity improves a cognitive function, learning, and academic achievement. Salmon in [660] presented cross-sectional and longitudinal studies analyzing the effect of physical exercises on anxiety, depression, and sensitivity to stress.

Increased physical activity therefore reduces premature mortality [278] and the establishment and maintenance of exercises' habits has become target for clinical psychologists [572].

The above research studies consider impact of psychological activities on performances of students using different psychological parameters. Considering and modeling the effect of physical activities on basic psychological parameters of humans acquire great importance. In this section, we suggest the model that takes the parameters — motivation, attention, and anxiety — into account and improves educational achievement of students through Pilates exercises. There is broad agreement in the literature that the physical exercises and particularly Pilates exercises are associated with the motivation, attention, anxiety, and educational achievement [10, 143, 358, 618, 635, 738]. The classical statistical approach is used today for finding the relationship between Pilates and above mentioned psychological parameters. Application of statistical techniques allows estimating the relationship between input (effect of Pilates) and output (achievement) from probabilistic point of view. This approach embraces only statistical uncertainty, but not fuzzy uncertainty inherent in psychological phenomena.

- The mind-body approach is a basic of Pilates principles: centering, concentration, control, precision, flow, and breath [143, 163, 618, 738].

Pilates has physical, psychological, and social impacts [10, 143, 358, 635, 738].

12.6.2 *Z-modeling of educational achievement*

The relationships between educational achievement and the above mentioned psychological variables are presented as *Z-if. . .then* rules (Table 12.15) by the following linguistic variables: H - high; L - low; M - medium; G - good; E - excellence; U - usually; P - plausible; R - rare.

Z-rule base concept plays pivotal role in economics, decision making, forecasting, and other human centric systems functioning in Z-information environment. The Z-rule base is complete when for all the possible observations there exists at least one rule whose Z-antecedent part overlaps the current antecedent Z-valuation, at least partially.

Otherwise, the Z- rule base is incomplete. In case that there is incomplete (sparse) Z-rule base, the classical reasoning methods based on compositional rule of inference (Zadeh [822], Mamdani [492], and R. A. Aliev and R. R. Aliev [15]) or Takagi and Sugeno [709] reasoning approach are not so effective to adapt generating an output for the observation covered by none of the rules. Consequently, we will use inference techniques which in the lack of matching rules can perform an approximate reasoning, namely, Z-interpolated methods.

Table 12.15 Z-if. . .then rules

Number of rules	Motivation	Attention	Anxiety	Achievement
1	(L, U)	(L, U)	(H, U)	(L, U)
2	(L, U)	(M, U)	(M, U)	(M, U)
3	(L, U)	(M, U)	(L, U)	(G, U)
4	(L, U)	(H, U)	(L, U)	(G, U)
5	(L, U)	(H, U)	(L, U)	(E, U)
6	(L, U)	(L, U)	(M, U)	(L, U)
7	(L, U)	(H, U)	(M, U)	(G, U)
8	(M, U)	(H, U)	(L, U)	(E, P)
9	(M, U)	(M, U)	(M, U)	(G, U)
10	(M, U)	(M, U)	(M, U)	(M, U)
11	(M, U)	(M, U)	z(H, U)	(L, U)
12	(M, U)	(H, U)	(L, U)	(G, U)
13	(M, U)	(H, U)	(L, U)	(E, U)
14	(M, U)	(H, U)	(H, U)	(M, U)
15	(M, U)	(M, U)	(M, U)	(M, U)
16	(M, U)	(H, U)	(M, U)	(G, U)
17	(M, U)	(H, U)	(M, U)	(E, U)
18	(H, U)	(H, U)	(L, U)	(E, R)
19	(H, U)	(H, U)	(L, U)	(G, U)
20	(H, U)	(H, U)	(M, U)	(E, U)
21	(H, U)	(H, U)	(M, U)	(G, U)
22	(H, U)	(M, U)	(M, U)	(G, U)
23	(H, U)	(M, U)	(L, U)	(G, U)
24	(H, U)	(M, U)	(L, U)	(M, U)
25	(H, U)	(L, U)	(H, U)	(L, U)
26	(H, U)	(L, U)	(M, U)	(M, U)
27	(H, U)	(L, U)	(L, U)	(L, U)
28	(H, U)	(L, U)	(L, U)	(M, U)

A problem of Z-interpolation is an interpolation of fuzzy is given below [33, 397].
Given the following Z-rules:

If X is $(A_{X,1}, B_{X,1})$ then Y is $(A_{Y,1}, B_{Y,1})$

If X is $(A_{X,2}, B_{X,2})$ then Y is $(A_{Y,2}, B_{Y,2})$

...

If X is $(A_{X,n}, B_{X,n})$ then Y is $(A_{Y,n}, B_{Y,n})$

and the fact that

$$X \text{ is } (A_X, B_X),$$

find the Z-value of Y on the basis of the approach given in section 6.5.

The idea underlying the suggested interpolation approach is that the ratio of distances between the conclusion and the consequent parts is identical to ones between the observation and the antecedent parts. For Z-rules interpolation we have:

$$Z_Y = \frac{\sum_{i=1}^{n} \frac{1}{dist(Z_X, Z_{X,i})} Z_{Y,i}}{\sum_{k=1}^{n} \frac{1}{dist(Z_X, Z_{X,i})}},$$

where *dist* is the distance between Z-numbers. As *dist*, method suggested in [397] can be used.

Let us consider the special case of the considered problem of Z-rules interpolation.

Given the Z-rules

If X is $A_{X,1}$ then Y is $(A_{Y,1}, B)$

If X is $A_{X,2}$ then Y is $(A_{Y,2}, B)$

...

If X is $A_{X,n}$ then Y is $(A_{Y,n}, B)$

and the fact that X $is\,(A_X, B_X)$, find the value of Y.

For this case, we have

$$Z_Y = \frac{\displaystyle\sum_{i=1}^{n} \frac{1}{dist(Z_X, Z_{X,i})} Z_{Y,i}}{\displaystyle\sum_{k=1}^{n} \frac{1}{dist(Z_X, Z_{X,i})}} = \frac{\displaystyle\sum_{i=1}^{n} \frac{1}{dist(A_X, A_{X,i})}(A_{Y,i}, B)}{\displaystyle\sum_{k=1}^{n} \frac{1}{dist(A_X, A_{X,i})}}.$$

For example, using supremum metric d of fuzzy numbers will be

$$Z_Y = \frac{\displaystyle\sum_{i=1}^{n} \frac{1}{dist(A_X, A_{X,i})}(A_{Y,i}, B)}{\displaystyle\sum_{k=1}^{n} \frac{1}{dist(A_X, A_{X,i})}} = \frac{\displaystyle\sum_{i=1}^{n} \frac{1}{d(A_X, A_{X,i})}(A_{Y,i}, B)}{\displaystyle\sum_{k=1}^{n} \frac{1}{d(A_X, A_{X,i})}}.$$

Taking into account that $\dfrac{1}{d(A_X, A_{X,i})}$ is a scalar and applying the

approach to multiplication of a Z-number by a scalar described in [33] we will have:

$$Z_Y = (A_Y, B), \text{ with } A_Y = \frac{\displaystyle\sum_{i=1}^{n} \frac{1}{d(A_X, A_{X,i})} A_{Y,i}}{\displaystyle\sum_{k=1}^{n} \frac{1}{d(A_X, A_{X,i})}}.$$

Let the knowledge base of 26 Z-rules of the following form is used:

$$\text{If } X_1 \text{ is } \hat{Z}_{i1} = (A_{i1}, B_{i1})$$

$$X_2 \text{ is } \hat{Z}_{i2} = (A_{i2}, B_{i2})$$

$$X_3 \text{ is } \hat{Z}_{i3} = (A_{i3}, B_{i3})$$

$$\text{then } Y \text{ is } \hat{Z}_{Y,i} = (A_{Y_i}, B_{Y_i}),$$

$$i = 1,...,26.$$

The considered Z-rules base described in terms of linguistic labels of A_{ij}, B_{ij}, is shown in Table 12.15.

Consider a problem of reasoning within the given Z-rules base by using Z-interpolation approach. Let the current input information is described by the following Z-numbers $\hat{Z}_1 = (Z_{A_1}, Z_{B_1})$, $\hat{Z}_2 = (Z_{A_2}, Z_{B_2})$, $\hat{Z}_3 = (Z_{A_3}, Z_{B_3})$:

$$Z_{A_1} = {}^{0.1}\!/\!_{0.3} + {}^{0.5}\!/\!_{0.35} + {}^{1}\!/\!_{0.4} + {}^{0.5}\!/\!_{0.45} + {}^{0.1}\!/\!_{0.5},$$

$$Z_{B_1} = {}^{0.1}\!/\!_{0.6} + {}^{0.5}\!/\!_{0.65} + {}^{1}\!/\!_{0.7} + {}^{0.5}\!/\!_{0.75} + {}^{0.1}\!/\!_{0.8};$$

$$Z_{A_2} = {}^{0.1}\!/\!_{0.2} + {}^{0.5}\!/\!_{0.25} + {}^{1}\!/\!_{0.3} + {}^{0.5}\!/\!_{0.35} + {}^{0.1}\!/\!_{0.4},$$

$$Z_{B_2} = {}^{0.1}\!/\!_{0.6} + {}^{0.5}\!/\!_{0.65} + {}^{1}\!/\!_{0.7} + {}^{0.5}\!/\!_{0.75} + {}^{0.1}\!/\!_{0.8};$$

$$Z_{A_3} = {}^{0.1}\!/\!_{0.62} + {}^{0.5}\!/\!_{0.67} + {}^{1}\!/\!_{0.7} + {}^{0.5}\!/\!_{0.73} + {}^{0.1}\!/\!_{0.8},$$

$$Z_{B_3} = {}^{0.1}\!/\!_{0.6} + {}^{0.5}\!/\!_{0.65} + {}^{1}\!/\!_{0.7} + {}^{0.5}\!/\!_{0.75} + {}^{0.1}\!/\!_{0.8}.$$

Z-interpolation approach based reasoning consists of two main stages.

1) For each rule compute distance D_i between the current input Z-information $\hat{Z}_1 = (Z_{A_1}, Z_{B_1})$, $\hat{Z}_2 = (Z_{A_2}, Z_{B_2})$, $\hat{Z}_3 = (Z_{A_3}, Z_{B_3})$ and Z-antecedents of Z-rules base $\hat{Z}_{i1} = (A_{i1}, B_{i1})$, $\hat{Z}_{i2} = (A_{i2}, B_{i2})$, $\hat{Z}_{i3} = (A_{i3}, B_{i3})$ as follows:

$$D_i = \sum_{j=1}^{3} D(\hat{Z}_j, \hat{Z}_{ij}),$$

where $D(\hat{Z}_j, \hat{Z}_{ij})$ is the supremum metric:

$$D\left(\hat{Z}_j, \hat{Z}_{ij}\right) = d_H\left(\tilde{A}_j, \tilde{A}_{ij}\right) + d_H\left(\tilde{B}_j, \tilde{B}_{ij}\right), \tag{12.33}$$

with

$$d_H\left(A_j, A_{ij}\right) = \sup\left\{d_H(A_j{}^\alpha, A_{ij}{}^\alpha)\big|0 < \alpha \le 1\right\},$$

$$d_H\left(B_j, B_{ij}\right) = \sup\left\{d_H(B_j{}^\alpha, B_{ij}{}^\alpha)\big|0 < \alpha \le 1\right\}. \tag{12.34}$$

Consider computation of D_i for 1st and 15th rules. Z-antecedents of the 1st rule are Z-numbers $\hat{Z}_{11} = (Z_{A_{11}}, Z_{B_{11}})$, $\hat{Z}_{12} = (Z_{A_{12}}, Z_{B_{12}})$, $\hat{Z}_{13} = (Z_{A_{13}}, Z_{B_{13}})$:

$$Z_{A_{11}} = \frac{1}{0.1} + \frac{0.75}{0.2} + \frac{0.5}{0.3} + \frac{0.25}{0.4} + \frac{0.1}{0.5},$$

$$Z_{B_{11}} = \frac{0.1}{0.7} + \frac{0.5}{0.75} + \frac{1}{0.8} + \frac{0.5}{0.85} + \frac{0.1}{0.9};$$

$$Z_{A_{12}} = \frac{1}{0.1} + \frac{0.75}{0.2} + \frac{0.5}{0.3} + \frac{0.25}{0.4} + \frac{0.1}{0.5},$$

$$Z_{B_{12}} = \frac{0.1}{0.7} + \frac{0.5}{0.75} + \frac{1}{0.8} + \frac{0.5}{0.85} + \frac{0.1}{0.9};$$

$$Z_{A_{13}} = \frac{0.1}{0.5} + \frac{0.25}{0.57} + \frac{0.5}{0.65} + \frac{0.75}{0.72} + \frac{1}{0.8},$$

$$Z_{B_{13}} = \frac{0.1}{0.7} + \frac{0.5}{0.75} + \frac{1}{0.8} + \frac{0.5}{0.85} + \frac{0.1}{0.9}.$$

Thus, we need to compute $D_1 = \sum_{j=1}^{3} D\left(\hat{Z}_j, \hat{Z}_{1j}\right)$ where $D\left(\hat{Z}_1, \hat{Z}_{11}\right)$, $D\left(\hat{Z}_2, \hat{Z}_{12}\right)$, $D\left(\hat{Z}_3, \hat{Z}_{13}\right)$ are computed on the base of (12.33). We have obtained the results:

$$D\left(\hat{Z}_1, \hat{Z}_{11}\right) = d_H\left(A_1, A_{11}\right) + d_H\left(B_1, B_{11}\right) = 0.5 + 0.5 = 1,$$

$$D\left(\hat{Z}_2, \hat{Z}_{12}\right) = 1,$$

$$D\left(\hat{Z}_3, \hat{Z}_{13}\right) = 0.62.$$

Thus, the distance for 1st rule is

$$D_1 = 2.62$$

The inputs of the 15th rule $\hat{Z}_{15,1} = (Z_{A_{15,1}}, Z_{B_{15,1}})$, $\hat{Z}_{15,2} = (Z_{A_{15,2}}, Z_{B_{15,2}})$, $\hat{Z}_{15,3} = (Z_{A_{15,3}}, Z_{B_{15,3}})$ are

$$Z_{A_{15,1}} = \frac{1}{0.1} + \frac{0.75}{0.2} + \frac{0.5}{0.3} + \frac{0.25}{0.4} + \frac{0.1}{0.5},$$

$$Z_{B_{15,1}} = \frac{0.1}{0.7} + \frac{0.5}{0.75} + \frac{1}{0.8} + \frac{0.5}{0.85} + \frac{0.1}{0.9};$$

$$Z_{A_{15,2}} = \frac{1}{0.1} + \frac{0.75}{0.2} + \frac{0.5}{0.3} + \frac{0.25}{0.4} + \frac{0.1}{0.5},$$

$$Z_{B_{15,2}} = \frac{0.1}{0.7} + \frac{0.5}{0.75} + \frac{1}{0.8} + \frac{0.5}{0.85} + \frac{0.1}{0.9};$$

$$Z_{A_{15,3}} = \frac{0.1}{0.5} + \frac{0.25}{0.57} + \frac{0.5}{0.65} + \frac{0.75}{0.72} + \frac{1}{0.8},$$

$$Z_{B_{15,3}} = \frac{0.1}{0.7} + \frac{0.5}{0.75} + \frac{1}{0.8} + \frac{0.5}{0.85} + \frac{0.1}{0.9}.$$

Analogously, we computed the distance for 15th rule as

$$D\left(\hat{Z}_1, \hat{Z}_{15,1}\right) = 0.8,$$

$$D\left(\hat{Z}_2, \hat{Z}_{15,2}\right) = 1,$$

$$D\left(\hat{Z}_3, \hat{Z}_{15,3}\right) = 1.02;$$

$$D_{15} = 2.82.$$

The distances computed for the rest of the rules are

$$D_1 = 2.62;\; D_7 = 3.02;\; D_{13} = 2.9;\; D_{19} = 3;\; D_{25} = 2.52;$$

$$D_2 = 2.92;\; D_8 = 2.9;\; D_{14} = 2.42;\; D_{20} = 2.92;\; D_{26} = 2.52;$$

$$D_3 = 3;\; D_9 = 2.72;\; D_{15} = 2.82;\; D_{21} = 2.92;$$

$$D_4 = 3.1;\; D_{10} = 2.72;\; D_{16} = 2.82;\; D_{22} = 2.82;$$

$$D_5 = 3.1;\; D_{11} = 2.32;\; D_{17} = 2.82;\; D_{23} = 2.9;$$

$$D_6 = 3.02;\; D_{12} = 2.9;\; D_{18} = 3;\; D_{24} = 2.9.$$

(2) Computation of the aggregated output Z_Y for Z-rules base by using linear Z-interpolation:

$$Z_Y = \sum_{i=1}^{n} w_i Z_{Y,i},\; w_i = \frac{1}{D_i \sum_{k=1}^{n} \frac{1}{D_k}}.$$

Thus, we need to compute convex combination of outputs of the rules base. The outputs of the Z-rules base are as follows:

$$Z_{A_{Y_1}} = \frac{1}{0.1} + \frac{0.75}{0.2} + \frac{0.5}{0.3} + \frac{0.25}{0.4} + \frac{0.1}{0.5},$$

$$Z_{B_{Y_1}} = \frac{0.1}{0.6} + \frac{0.5}{0.65} + \frac{1}{0.7} + \frac{0.5}{0.75} + \frac{0.1}{0.8};$$

$$\cdots$$

$$Z_{A_{Y_{15}}} = \frac{0.1}{0.1} + \frac{0.5}{0.3} + \frac{1}{0.5} + \frac{0.5}{0.62} + \frac{0.1}{0.75},$$

$$Z_{B_{Y_{15}}} = \frac{0.1}{0.1} + \frac{0.5}{0.15} + \frac{1}{0.2} + \frac{0.5}{0.25} + \frac{0.1}{0.3}.$$

Therefore, the aggregated output Z_Y is defined as

$$Z_Y = 0.042 Z_{Y_1} + 0.037 Z_{Y_2} + ... + 0.038 Z_{Y_{26}} = (A_Y, B_Y).$$

We have obtained the following result:

$$A_Y = 0.1/0.395 + 0.5/0.518 + 1/0.627 + 0.5/0.644 + 0.25/0.656,$$

$$B_Y = 0.1/0.7 + 0.5/0.75 + 1/0.8 + 0.5/0.85 + 0.1/0.9.$$

In accordance with codebook we have: Achievement is "medium" and the reliability is "usually".

The analysis shows that there are no significant differences between the mean of results obtained by conventional statistical method and Z-number based modeling. The standard deviations of the outputs estimated by statistical method and Z-number based modeling show significant differences of results. The less variance in the Z-number based modeling method is related with the ability of this method to control uncertainty in data.

12.7 Optimal port choice under Z-information

One of the most crucial factors to influence the operational and business performance of the organizations. The existing decision theories are not sufficiently adequate to account for imprecision and partial reliability of decision-relevant information in real-world problems. In this section, we consider a hierarchical multiattribute decision problem of an optimal port choice under Z-number-based information. The solution of the problem is based on the use of Z-valued weighted average aggregation operator.

12.7.1 *State-of-the-art*

Port selection decisions of shippers are crucial for policy formulation in ports and shipping lines [719]. Researches use a discrete choice model where each shipper faces a choice of 14 alternatives based on shipping line and port combinations, and makes his decision on the basis of various shipper and port characteristics. The results show that the distance of the shipper from port, distance to destination, port congestion and shipping line's the play an important role.

Providers of port infrastructure and services are interested in finding out critical port choice factors as rational basis for formulating sustainable port reform policy. In [562], questionnaires were distributed to collect data on observed port choice made by shippers under study. A discrete choice model was applied to estimate the shipper's port utility function. Policy implications of the estimated utility function are discussed.

In [228] fuzzy analytic network process and extended fuzzy VIKOR methodologies are used for solving the problem of cruise port place selection in Istanbul. Comparison of the obtained results is provided.

Analysis proposed in [725] is based on a survey conducted among major shipping lines operating in Singapore and Malaysia. The results show that port charges and wide range of port services are the only significant factors in port choice. However, the results show no consistency between the stated and revealed preferences of shipping lines. In [746] appraisal of the container terminals or ports is implemented by using a fuzzy multicriteria decision making method. This model is illustrated with a numerical example.

In [388] five port intangible resources were identified. A survey questionnaire (prepared by using standard techniques [5, 213, 214, 641]) was sent to 21 experts. It was found that customer and relational resource contributes most to the delivery of port service quality. The port of Hong Kong appeared to be the port where intangible resources were most highly evaluated.

This research helps to enrich the literature on port service quality and port choice evaluation.

In [172] they identify the factors affecting shipping companies' port choice based on a survey to a sample of shipping companies. Six factors were considered: local cargo volume; terminal handling charge; berth availability; port location; transshipment volume and feeder network. Exploratory factor and confirmatory factor analyses identified five port choice categories, i.e. advancement/convenience of port; physical/operational ability of port; operational condition of shipping lines; marketability; and port charge. Moreover, the main haul shipping lines are more sensitive to port cost factors.

The studies investigating the port selection process had one thing in common: they analyze the declared preferences of the port agents. In [301] it is suggested to study the port choice through revealed port selection instead of asking port stakeholders about the main factors in port selection.

In [549] they identified factors that affect port selection. They consider three ports: Antwerp, Rotterdam and Hamburg and three types of decision makers: shippers, carriers and freight forwarders. Also, it is discussed how port policymakers must continuously make an effort to understand what factors influence port users' port choice. The Analytical Hierarchy Process method was applied. The results show the following ranking of port selection criteria in decreasing order of importance: port costs, geographical location, quality of hinterland connections, productivity and capacity. Of the three ports studied, Antwerp was found to be the most attractive, followed by Rotterdam and then Hamburg.

Several authors have been invested decision making by use of fuzzy approach [5, 20, 24, 114, 125, 313]. We have to mention that a port selection problem, as a real-world problem, is characterized by imprecise and partially reliable information. Unfortunately, this is not taken into account in the existing studies. In this section we consider multiattribute decision making on port selection under Z-number-valued information. All the criteria evaluations and criteria importance weights are described by Z-numbers.

12.7.2 *Decision making on port selection under Z-number-valued information*

The literature review reveals a considerable range of factors that have an influence on the decision of port choice studies. The key influencing factors for port selection are identified in [117, 212, 220, 544]. After carefully examining the relevant literature, selected experts have determined the all possible evaluation criteria prior to port choice selection (Table 12.16, see page 467). Each criterion and sub-criterion has its importance weight.

Thus, we have seven criteria $C_j, j = 1,...,7$: hinterland condition, C_1, port services, C_2, logistics cost, C_3, connectivity, C_4, convenience, C_5, availability, C_6, regional center, C_7. Suppose that a decision maker should choose the best port by using the criteria and sub-criteria given in Table 12.16. The considered alternatives are: port of Busan, port of Tokyo, port of Hong Kong, port of Qingdao, port of Shanghai, port of Kaohsiung, port of Shenzhen. Decision relevant information in the considered problems is characterized by imprecision and partial reliability. In view of this, criteria evaluations and importance weights are expressed by Z-numbers (Tables 12.17 a, b, c). Codebooks of fuzzy numbers as A and B components of Z-numbers are shown in Tables 12.18 and 12.19. Let us solve the considered problem of choosing the best alternative. At first we should compute overall evaluation of each port. Below we provide computation for the port of Hong Kong, computation for the other ports is analogous.

Step 1. Compute the Z-valued criteria evaluations $Z_{y_{ij}}$ for i-th alternative, $i = 1,...,7$, with respect to j-th criterion, $j = 1,...,7$, by using weighted average-based aggregation of the corresponding sub-criteria evaluations. The weighted average is based on operations over Z-numbers which are given in Section 6.3 and is expressed in Table 12.18.

$$Z_{y_{ij}} = \frac{\sum_{k}^{K_j} Z_{x_{ijk}} \cdot Z_{w_{jk}}}{\sum_{k}^{K_j} Z_{w_{jk}}},$$

where $Z_{x_{ijk}}$ is a Z-number-valued evaluation of i-th alternative with respect to k-th sub-criterion of j-th criterion, $Z_{w_{jk}}$ is a Z-number-valued importance weight of k-th sub-criterion of j-th criterion. The obtained results for the port of Hong Kong are as follows.

$$Z_{y_{11}} = \frac{\sum_{k=1}^{3} Z_{x_{11k}} \cdot Z_{w_{1k}}}{\sum_{k=1}^{3} Z_{w_{1k}}} = \frac{(M,EL)\cdot(H,EL)+(H,L)\cdot(H,VL)+(VH,EL)\cdot(H,EL)}{(H,EL)+(H,VL)+(H,EL)}$$

$$= \big((1.7 \quad 4 \quad 8)(0.52 \quad 0.57 \quad 0.93)\big);$$

$$Z_{y_{12}} = \frac{\sum_{k=1}^{3} Z_{x_{12k}} \cdot Z_{w_{2k}}}{\sum_{k=1}^{3} Z_{w_{2k}}} = \frac{(VH,VL)\cdot(M,L)+(VH,EL)\cdot(VH,L)+(VH,VL)\cdot(H,VL)}{(M,L)+(VH,L)+(H,VL)}$$

$$= \big((2.2 \quad 5 \quad 8.5)(0.96 \quad 0.99 \quad 1)\big);$$

$$Z_{y_{13}} = \frac{\sum\limits_{k=1}^{3} Z_{x_{13k}} \cdot Z_{w_{3k}}}{\sum\limits_{k=1}^{3} Z_{w_{2k}}} = \frac{(L,L) \cdot (M,L) + (M,NVL) \cdot (H,VL) + (L,L) \cdot (H,L)}{(M,L) + (H,VL) + (H,L)}$$

$$= \big((0.7 \quad 2.4 \quad 6)(0.5 \quad 0.7 \quad 0.8)\big);$$

$$Z_{y_{14}} = \frac{\sum\limits_{k=1}^{2} Z_{x_{14k}} \cdot Z_{w_{4k}}}{\sum\limits_{k=1}^{2} Z_{w_{4k}}} = \frac{(M,NVL) \cdot (M,L) + (L,L) \cdot (M,L)}{(M,L) + (M,L)}$$

$$= \big((0.5 \quad 2.5 \quad 7.6)(0.4 \quad 0.6 \quad 0.7)\big);$$

$$Z_{y_5} = \frac{\sum\limits_{k=1}^{3} Z_{x_{15k}} \cdot Z_{w_{5k}}}{\sum\limits_{k=1}^{3} Z_{w_{5k}}} = \frac{(VH,VL) \cdot (H,EL) + (H,L) \cdot (M,VL) + (M,VL) \cdot (H,VL)}{(H,EL) + (M,VL) + (H,VL)}$$

$$= \big((1.44 \quad 4 \quad 8.48)(0.65 \quad 0.71 \quad 0.72)\big);$$

$$Z_{y_6} = \frac{\sum\limits_{k=1}^{2} Z_{x_{16k}} \cdot Z_{w_{6k}}}{\sum\limits_{k=1}^{2} Z_{w_{6k}}} = \frac{(H,EL) \cdot (VH,EL) + (VH,EL) \cdot (VH,VL)}{(VH,EL) + (VH,VL)}$$

$$= \big((2.36 \quad 4.5 \quad 6.23)(0.94 \quad 0.98 \quad 0.99)\big);$$

$$Z_{y_7} = \frac{\sum\limits_{k=1}^{2} Z_{x_{17k}} \cdot Z_{w_{7k}}}{\sum\limits_{k=1}^{2} Z_{w_{7k}}} = \frac{(M,L) \cdot (M,L) + (L,L) \cdot (L,L)}{(M,L) + (L,L)}$$

$$= \big((0.45 \quad 2.6 \quad 11.6)(0.44 \quad 0.77 \quad 0.8)\big).$$

Step 2. Compute the overall port evaluation Z_y as the weighted average-based aggregation of the criteria evaluations $Z_{y_j}, j = 1, ..., 7$ obtained at Step 1:

$$Z_y = \frac{\sum\limits_{j=1}^{7} Z_{y_j} \cdot Z_{w_j}}{\sum\limits_{j=1}^{7} Z_{w_j}} = \big((0.89 \quad 3.9 \quad 9.5)(0.85 \quad 0.98 \quad 0.99)\big).$$

Analogously we computed the overall port evaluations Z_y for all the other ports:

$$Z_y^{Busan} = ((0.8 \quad 3.5 \quad 10.7)(0.5 \quad 0.7 \quad 0.8));$$

$$Z_y^{Shanghai} = ((0.5 \quad 3.32 \quad 12.9)(0.48 \quad 0.81 \quad 0.82));$$
$$Z_y^{Kaohsiung} = ((0.62 \quad 2.98 \quad 10.3)(0.48 \quad 0.7 \quad 0.72));$$

$$Z_y^{Qingdao} = ((0.7 \quad 3.5 \quad 13.4)(0.66 \quad 0.96 \quad 0.97));$$

$$Z_y^{Shenzhen} = ((0.71 \quad 3.54 \quad 13.6)(0.4 \quad 0.6 \quad 0.7));$$

$$Z_y^{Tokyo} = ((0.48,3,10)(0.48 \quad 0.7 \quad 0.8)).$$

Step 3. Rank the obtained overall evaluations of the all seven ports. For this purpose we use the approach given in Section 6.6. The obtained results are given below:

Port Hong-Kong vs. Port of Busan:

$$do(Z_y^{HK}) = 1, \; do(Z_y^{Busan}) = 0.08;$$

Port Hong-Kong vs. Port of Qingdao:

$$do(Z_y^{HK}) = 1, \; do(Z_y^{Qingdao}) = 0.91;$$

Port Hong-Kong vs. Port of Tokyo:

$$do(Z_y^{HK}) = 1, \; do(Z_y^{Tokyo}) = 0;$$

Port Hong-Kong vs. Port of Shanghai:

$$do(Z_y^{HK}) = 1, \; do(Z_y^{shanghai}) = 0.26;$$

Port Hong-Kong vs. Port of Kaohsiung:

$$do(Z_y^{HK}) = 1, \; do(Z_y^{Kaohsiung}) = 0;$$

Port Hong-Kong vs. Port of Shenzhen:

$$do(Z_y^{HK}) = 1, \; do(Z_y^{Shenzhen}) = 0.23.$$

Thus, the port of Hong-Kong is the best port.

Table 12.16 : Evaluation criteria

Criteria & Sub-criteria			
C1: HINTERLAND CONDITION	C2: PORT SERVICES	C3:LOGISTICS COST	C4:CONNECTIVITY
1. Professionals and skilled labors in port operation 2. Size and activity of FTZ in port hinterland 3. Volume of total container cargo	1. Prompt response 2. 24hours/7 a week service 3. Zero waiting time	1. Inland transportation cost 2. Cost related vessel and cargo entering 3. Free dwell time on the terminal	1. Land distance and connectivity to major supplier 2.Efficient inland transport network
C5:CONVENIENCE	C6: AVAILABILITY	C7:REGIONAL CENTER	
1.Wather depth in approach channel and at berth 2. Sophistication level of port information & its application scope 3. Stability of Port's labour	1.Availability of vessel berth on arrival in port 2. Port Congestion	1.Port Accessibility 2.Deviation from main trunk routes	

Table 12.17a. Aggregation group decision of criteria evaluation of alternatives

Item	Port of Busan	Weighting	Port of Hong Kong	Weighting	Port of Kaohsiung
Criteria & Sub-criteria					
C1:HINTERLAND CONDITION	(M, EL)	(H,L)	(M,VL)	(VH, VL)	(L, L)
1.Professionals and skilled labors in port operation	(VH, EL)	(H,VL)	(M,EL)	(H, EL)	(M, EL)
2.Size and activity of FIZ in port interland	(M, L)	(H, L)	(H, L)	(H, VL)	(H, L)
3.Volume of total container cargo	(H, L)	(M, L)	(VH, EL)	(H, EL)	(H, L)
C2:PORT SERVICES	(H, EL)	(VH,VL)	(H, VL)	(VH, VL)	(H, VL)
1.Prompt response	(H, VL)	(M, L)	(VH, VL)	(M, L)	(L, VL)
2.24 hours/7 a week service	(H, L)	(M, L)	(VH, EL)	(VH, L)	(L, VL)
3.Zero waiting time	(VH, VL)	(H, VL)	(VH, VL)	(H, VL)	(M, VL)
C3: LOGISTICS COST	(L, EL)	(L, L)	(M, EL)	(L, L)	(H, EL)
1.Inland transportation cost	(L, L)	(M, L)	(L, L)	(M, L)	(M, L)
2.Cost related vessel and cargo entering	(M,NVL)	(H,VL)	(M, NVL)	(H, VL)	(M, L)
3.Free dwell time on the terminal	(L, L)	(H, L)	(L, L)	(H, L)	(M, VL)
C4: CONNECTIVITY	(M, L)	(M, NVL)	(H, L)	(M,NVL)	(H, L)
1.Land distance and connectivity to major supplier	(M, NVL)	(M, L)	(M, NVL)	(M, L)	(H, NVL)
2.Efficient inland transport network	(M, L)	(M, L)	(L, L)	(M, L)	(M, L)
C5:CONVENIENCE	(H, EL)	(VH,VL)	(H, EL)	(VH, VL)	(M, EL)
1.Wather depth in approach channel an berth	(VH, VL)	(H, VL)	(VH,VL)	(H, EL)	(M, VL)
2.Sophisication level of port in information & its application scope	(L, L)	(M, VL)	(H, L)	(M, VL)	(H, VL)
3.Stability of Port's labour	(M, VL)	(M, VL)	(M, VL)	(H, VL)	(M, VL)
C6:AVAILABILITY	(H, L)	(M, L)	(M, L)	(M, L)	(L, L)
1.Availability of vessel berth on arrival in port	(H, L)	(M, L)	(H, EL)	(VH, EL)	(L, L)
2.Port Congestion	(VH, VL)	(M, L)	(VH, EL)	(VH, VL)	(VH, VL)
C7:REGIONAL CENTER	(M, L)	(H, NVL)	(M, VL)	(M, VL)	(H, L)
1.Port Accessibility	(M, L)	(M, L)	(M, L)	(M, L)	(M, L)
2.Deviation from main trunk routes	(L,VL)	(M, L)	(L, L)	(L, L)	(M, VL)

Table 12.17b. Aggregation group decision of criteria evaluation of alternatives

Item	Weighting	Port of Qingdao	Weighting	Port of Shanghai	Weighting
Criteria & Sub-criteria					
C1:HINTERLAND CONDITION	(VH,L)	(VH, EL)	(VH, VL)	(H, EL)	(M, L)
1.Professionals and skilled labors in port operation	(H, VL)	(H, EL)	(H, EL)	(M, EL)	(M, VL)
2.Size and activity of FIZ in port interland	(VH, L)	(H, L)	(H, VL)	(M, L)	(H, L)
3.Volume of total container cargo	(M, L)	(VH, EL)	(H, EL)	(M, VL)	(M, VL)
C2:PORT SERVICES	(VH, VL)	(M, EL)	(VH, VL)	(H, L)	(H, L)
1.Prompt response	(M, L)	(M, VL)	(M, L)	(H, L)	(M, L)
2.24 hours/7 a week service	(H, VL)	(H, VL)	(VH, L)	(M, L)	(M, VL)
3.Zero waiting time	(H, VL)	(M, VL)	(H, VL)	(H, VL)	(H, VL)
C3: LOGISTICS COST	(L, L)	(L, EL)	(L, L)	(H, EL)	(L, L)
1.Inland transportation cost	(M, L)	(L, NVL)	(M, L)	(M, L)	(VH, L)
2.Cost related vessel and cargo entering	(H, VL)	(M, NVL)	(H, VL)	(VH, VL)	(VH, VL)
3.Free dwell time on the terminal	(H, L)	(M, L)	(H, L)	(M, L)	(H, L)
C4: CONNECTIVITY	(M, NVL)	(H, L)	(M, NVL)	(M, L)	(M, NVL)
1.Land distance and connectivity to major supplier	(M, L)	(M, VL)	(M, L)	(H, L)	(VH, U)
2.Efficient inland transport network	(M, L)	(M, L)	(M, L)	(M, L)	(M, L)
C5:CONVENIENCE	(VH, VL)	(M, EL)	(VH, VL)	(H, EL)	(VH, L)
1.Wather depth in approach channel an berth	(H, VL)	(VH, VL)	(H, EL)	(VH, VL)	(H, EL)
2.Sophisication level of port in information & its application scope	(M, VL)	(L, L)	(M, VL)	(H, L)	(M, L)
3.Stability of Port's labour	(H, VL)	(M, VL)	(H, VL)	(M, VL)	(H, VL)
C6:AVAILABILITY	(M, L)	(M, L)	(M, L)	(M, L)	(M, L)
1.Availability of vessel berth on arrival in port	(M, L)	(M, EL)	(VH, EL)	(H, L)	(M, L)
2.Port Congestion	(M, L)	(M, VL)	(VH, VL)	(L, L)	(M, L)
C7:REGIONAL CENTER	(H, NVL)	(H, VL)	(M, VL)	(M, L)	(H, L)
1.Port Accessibility	(M, L)	(H, L)	(M, L)	(M, L)	(M, EL)
2.Deviation from main trunk routes	(M, L)	(H, L)	(L, L)·	(H, VL)	(H, EL)

Table 12.17c. Aggregation group decision of criteria evaluation of alternatives

Item	Port of Shenzhen	Weighting	Port of Tokyo	Weighting
Criteria & Sub-criteria				
C1:HINTERLAND CONDITION	(H, L)	(VH, L)	(M, L)	(VH, L) ▪
1.Professionals and skilled labors in port operation	(H, EL)	(H, VL)	(M, EL)	(H, VL)
2.Size and activity of FIZ in port interland	(VH, L)	(VH, L)	(M, L)	(VH, L)
3.Volume of total container cargo	(H, L)	(M, L)	(H, L)	(M, L)
C2:PORT SERVICES	(H, EL)	(VH, VL)	(H, VL)	(VH, VL)
1.Prompt response	(L, VL)	(M, L)	(M, L)	(M, L)
2.24 hours/7 a week service	(M, VL)	(H, VL)	(L, VL)	(H, VL)
3.Zero waiting time	(M, VL)	(H, VL)	(M, VL)	(H, VL)
C3: LOGISTICS COST	(M, EL)	(L, L)	(L, EL)	(L, L)
1.Inland transportation cost	(M, EL)	(M, L)	(M, L)	(M, L)
2.Cost related vessel and cargo entering	(H, EL)	(H, VL)	(L, L)	(H, VL)
3.Free dwell time on the terminal	(M, VL)	(H, L)	(H, VL)	(H, L)
C4: CONNECTIVITY	(H, L)	(M, NVL)	(M, L)	(M, NVL)
1.Land distance and connectivity to major supplier	(H, NVL)	(M, L)	(M,NVL)	(M, L)
2.Efficient inland transport network	(M, L)	(M, L)	(M, L)	(M, L)
C5:CONVENIENCE	(L, EL)	(VH, VL)	(M, EL)	(VH, VL)
1.Wather depth in approach channel an berth	(VH, EL)	(H, L)	(L, EL)	(H, VL)
2.Sophisication level of port in information & its application scope	(H, VL)	(L, L)	(L, EL)	(M, VL)
3.Stability of Port's labour	(M, EL)	(M, VL)	(M, VL)	(H, VL)
C6:AVAILABILITY	(M, L)	(M, NVL)	(H, VL)	(M, L)
1.Availability of vessel berth on arrival in port	(H, VL)	(L, L)	(H, VL)	(M, L)
2.Port Congestion	(L, EL)	(H, EL)	(VH,VL)	(M, L)
C7:REGIONAL CENTER	(H, L)	(H, NVL)	(H, L)	(H, NVL)
1.Port Accessibility	(M, L)	(M, L)	(M, L)	(M, VL)
2.Deviation from main trunk routes	(M, VL)	(M, L)	(M, VL)	(M, L)

Table 12.18. The encoded linguistic terms for A components of Z-numbers

Scale	Level	Linguistic value
1.	Very Low	$\left\{ \frac{1}{1}, \frac{1}{1}, \frac{0}{0} \right\}$
2.	Low	$\left\{ \frac{0}{1}, \frac{1}{2}, \frac{0}{3} \right\}$
3.	Medium	$\left\{ \frac{0}{2}, \frac{1}{3}, \frac{0}{4} \right\}$
4.	High	$\left\{ \frac{0}{3}, \frac{1}{4}, \frac{0}{5} \right\}$
5.	Very High	$\left\{ \frac{0}{4}, \frac{1}{5}, \frac{1}{5} \right\}$

Table 12.19. The encoded linguistic terms for B components of Z-numbers

Scale	Level	Linguistic value
1.	Unlikely	$\left\{ \frac{1}{0.05}, \frac{1}{0.05}, \frac{0}{0.25} \right\}$
2.	Not very likely	$\left\{ \frac{0}{0.05}, \frac{1}{0.25}, \frac{0}{0.5} \right\}$
3.	Likely	$\left\{ \frac{0}{0.25}, \frac{1}{0.5}, \frac{0}{0.75} \right\}$
4.	Very likely	$\left\{ \frac{0}{0.5}, \frac{1}{0.75}, \frac{0}{1} \right\}$
5.	Extremely likely	$\left\{ \frac{0}{0.75}, \frac{1}{1}, \frac{1}{1} \right\}$

Bibliography

1. Abbasbandy, S. and Asady, B. (2006). Ranking of fuzzy numbers by sign distance, *Inform. Sci.*, 176(16), pp. 2405–2416.
2. Abbasi, M. A. and Khorram, E. (2007). Linear programming problem with interval coefficients and an interpretation for its constraints. *IRAN J Sci. Technol A*, 31(A4), pp. 369–390.
3. Abbink, K., Irlenbusch, B. and Renner, E. (2000). The moonlighting game: An empirical study on reciprocity and retribution, *J. Econ. Behav. Organ.*, 42, pp. 265–277.
4. Abu Aarqob, O. A., Shawagfeh, N. T. and AbuGhneim, O. A. (2008). Functions defined on fuzzy real numbers according to Zadeh's extension. *Int. Math. Forum*, 3(16), pp.763–776.
5. Adler, M. and Ziglio, E. (1996). *Gazing into the Oracle*. (Jessica Kingsley Publishers, Bristol, PA).
6. Aerts, D. and Sozzo, S. (2016). From ambiguity aversion to a generalized expected utility. Modeling preferences in a quantum probabilistic framework, *J. Math. Psychol.*, 74, pp. 117–127.
7. Agüero, J. R. and Vargas, A. (2007). Calculating functions of interval type-2 fuzzy numbers for fault current analysis, *IEEE T. Fuzzy Syst.*, 15(1), pp. 31–40.
8. Aguilo, I., Suner, J. and Torrens, J. (2010). A characterization of residual implications derived from left-continuous uninorms, *Inform. Sciences*, 180, pp. 3992–4005.
9. Akerlof, G. A. (2007). The missing motivation in macroeconomics. *Am. Econ. Rev*, 97(1), pp. 5–36.
10. Aladro-Gonzalvo, A. R., Machado-D´ıaz, M., Moncada- Jim´enez, J., Hern´andez-Elizondo, J. and Araya-Vargas, G. (2012). The effect of Pilates exercises on body composition: A systematic review, *J. Bodyw. and Mov. Ther.*, 16(1), pp. 109–114.
11. Al-Anzi, F. S. and Allahverdi, A. (2007). A self-adaptive differential evolution heuristic for two-stage assembly scheduling problem to minimize maximum lateness with setup times, *Eur. J. Oper. Res.*, 182, pp. 80–94.
12. Albrecht, M. (1992). Approximation of functional relationships to fuzzy observations, *Fuzzy Sets Syst.*, 49, pp. 301–305.
13. Alefelda, G. and Mayerb, G. (2000). Interval analysis: Theory and applications, *J. Comput. Appl. Math.*, 121, pp. 421–464.
14. Alexeyev, A. V., Borisov, A. N., Glushkov, V. I., Krumberg, O. A., Merkuryeva, G. V., Popov, V. A. and Slyadz, N. N. (1987). A linguistic approach to decision-making problems, *Fuzzy Set. Syst.*, 22, pp. 25–41.
15. Aliev, R. A. and Aliev, R. R. (2001). *Soft Computing and Its Application*. (World Scientific, New Jersey, London, Singapore, Hong Kong).
16. Aliev, R. A., Alizadeh A. V., Huseynov O. H. (2015). The arithmetic of discrete Z-numbers, *Inform. Sciences*, 290(1), pp.134–155.

17. Aliev, R. A., Alizadeh, A. V., Huseynov, O. H. and Jabbarova, K.I. (2015). Z-number based Linear Programming. *Int. J. Intell. Syst.*, 30, pp. 563–589.

18. Aliev, R. A. (2013) *Fundamentals of the Fuzzy Logic-Based Generalized Theory of Decisions.* (Springer, NewYork, Berlin).

19. Aliev, R. A. and Huseynov, O. H. (2014). Fuzzy geometry-based decision making with unprecisiated visual information, *Int. J. Inf. Tech. Decis.*, 13(05), pp. 1051–1073.

20. Aliev, R. A., Pedrycz, W., Fazlollahi B., Huseynov O. H., Alizadeh A. V. and Guirimov, B. G. (2012). Fuzzy logic-based generalized decision theory with imperfect information, *Inform. Sciences,* 189, pp.18–42.

21. Aliev, R. A. and Pedrycz, W. (2009). Fundamentals of a fuzzy-logic-based generalized theory of stability, *IEEE T. Syst. Man CY. B.,* 39(4), pp. 971–988.

22. Aliev, R. A., Pedrycz, W., Huseynov, O. H. and Zeinalova, L. M. (2011). Decision making with second order information granules. In: *Granular Computing and Intelligent Systems,* (Springer-Verlag), pp. 327–374.

23. Aliev, R. and Memmedova, K., (2015). Application of Z-number based modeling in psychological research, *Comput. Intel. Neurosc.*, Article ID 760403, Vol. 2015, 7 pages, https://www.hindawi.com/journals/cin/2015/760403/.

24. Aliev, R. A., Pedrycz, W. and Huseynov, O. H. (2012). Decision theory with imprecise probabilities, *Int. J. Inf. Tech. Decis.*, 11(2), pp. 271–306.

25. Aliev, R. A. and Mamedova, G. A. (1990). Analysis of fuzzy models of industrial processes, *Fuzzy Set Syst.,* 37, pp. 13–21.

26. Aliev, R. A, Akif V. A. and Shirinova U. K. (2003). Fuzzy Chaos Approach to fuzzy linear programming problem, *Proc. 6th Int. Conf. on Soft Comp. and Comp. with Words in Syst. Anal., Decis. and Control,* ICSCCW, pp. 287–294.

27. Aliev, R. A., Mamedova, G. A. and Aliev, R. R. (1993). *Fuzzy Sets Theory and its Application.* (Tabriz University Press, Iran).

28. Aliev, R. A. and Tserkovny, A. E. (2011). Systemic approach to fuzzy logic formalization for approximate reasoning, *Inform. Sciences,*181, pp. 1045–1059.

29. Aliev, R. A. and Zeinalova, L. M. (2014). Decision making under Z-information, (eds). Guo, P., Pedrycz, W., *Human-Centric Decision-Making Models for Social Sciences (Studies in Computational Intelligence),* (Springer), pp. 233–252.

30. Aliev, R. A. and Guirimov, B. (1997). Handwritten image recognition by using neural and fuzzy approaches: Intelligent control and decision making systems, *Thematic Collected Articles, Baku, Publishing House of Azerb. State Oil Academy,* 1, pp. 3–7.

31. Aliev, R. A. (1994) Fuzzy expert systems. In Aminzadeh, F. and Jamshidi, M. (eds.) *Soft Computing: Fuzzy Logic, Neural Networks and Distributed Artificial Intelligence* (PTR Prentice Hal, New Jersey) pp. 99–108.

32. Aliev, R. A. and Tserkovny, A. E. (1988). The knowledge representation in intelligent robots based on fuzzy sets, *Soviet Math. Doklady*, 37, pp. 541–544.

33. Aliev, R. A, Huseynov, O. H., Aliyev, R. R. and Alizadeh, A. V. (2015). *The Arithmetic of Z-numbers. Theory and Applications,* World Scientific (Singapore).

34. Aliev, R. A., Aliev, F. and Babaev M. (1991). *Fuzzy Process Control and Knowledge Engineering in Petrochemical and Robotic Manufacturing,* Verlag TUV Rheinland.

35. Aliev, R. A. and Aliwev R. R. (1997) Fuzzy Distributed Intelligent Systems for Continuous Production. In: Jamshidi, M., Titli, M., Zadeh, L., and Boverie, S.

(eds.) *Application of Fuzzy Logic Towards High Machine Intelligence Quotient Systems*, pp. 301–320. (Prentice Hall PTR, Upper Saddle River, New Jersey, USA)

36. Aliev, R. A., Fazlollahi, B. and Aliev, R. R. (2004) *Soft Computing and its Application in Business and Economics*. (Springer-Verlag, Berlin, Heidelberg).

37. Aliev, R.A., Guirimov, B., Bonfig, K., and Steinmann (2000). *A neuro-fuzzy algorithm for recognition of nonstylized images*, In proceedings of Fourth International Conference on Application of Fuzzy Systems and Soft Computing, ICAFS'2000, Siegen, Germany, pp. 238–241.

38. Aliev, R.A. and Kreinovich V. (2017) Z-Numbers and Type-2 Fuzzy Sets: A Representation Result, *Intell Autom Soft Co*, accepted.

39. Aliev, R.A., Fazlollahi, B. and Guirimov, B. G. (2007). Fuzzy-genetic approach to aggregate production-distribution planning in supply chain management. *Inform. Sciences*, 177, pp. 4241–4255.

40. Aliev, R.A. (2009). Decision Making Theory with Imprecise Probabilities. *Proc. of the Fifth International Conference on Soft Computing and Computing with Words in System Analysis, Decision and Control,* ICSCCW-2009, pp. 1.

41. Aliev, R. A. (2011). Decision making with combined states under imperfect information. *Proc. of the Sixth International Conference on Soft Computing and Computing with Words in System Analysis, Decision and Control,* ICSCCW, pp. 3–4.

42. Aliev, R. A., Fazlollahi, B. and Vahidov, R. M. (2000). Soft computing based multi-agent marketing decision support systems, *J. Intell. Fuzzy Syst.*, 9, pp. 1–9.

43. Aliev, R. A., Mamedova, G. A. and Tserkovny, A. E. (1991) *Fuzzy Control Systems*. (Energoatomizdat, Moscow).

44. Aliev, R. A. and Huseynov O.H. (2014). *Decision theory with imperfect information*. New Jersey, London, Singapure: World Scientific, 444 p.

45. Aliev, R. A. and Kreinovich, V. (2011). Estimating mean and variance under interval uncertainty: dynamic case. *Proc. of the Sixth International Conference on Soft Computing, Computing with Words and Perceptions in System Analysis, Decision and Control,* ICSCCW, pp. 85–94.

46. Aliev, R. A., Krivosheev, V. P. and Liberzon, M. I. (1982). Optimal decision coordination in hierarchical systems, *News of Academy of Sciences of USSR, Tech. Cybernetics*, 2, pp. 72–79 (in English and Russian).

47. Aliev, R. A. and Liberzon, M. I. (1986). Non-iterative algorithms of coordination in two-level systems. *News of Academy of Sciences of USSR, Tech. Cybernetics*, 3, pp.163–166 (in Russian).

48. Aliev, R. A. and Liberzon, M. I. (1987) Coordination methods and algorithms for integrated manufacturing systems. (Radio I svyaz, Moscow) (in Russian).

49. Aliev, R. A. (2008). Modelling and stability analysis in fuzzy economics. Appl. Comput. Math., 7(1), pp. 31–53.

50. Aliev, R. A. and Huseynov, O. H. (2011). A new approach to behavioral decision making with imperfect information. *Proc. of the Sixth International Conference on Soft Computing and Computing with Words in System Analysis, Decision and Control, ICSCCW*, pp. 227–237.

51. Aliev, R. A. and Huseynov, O. H. (2013). Fuzzy behavioural decision model with imperfect information. *International Journal of Economics and Management Engineering*, Vol. 3 Iss. 6, pp. 221–235.

52.   Aliev, R. A. and Huseynov, O. H. (2010). Decision making under imperfect information with combined states. Proc. of the Ninth International Conference on Application of Fuzzy Systems and Soft Computing, ICAFS, pp. 400–406.

53.   Aliev, R. A. (2013). Toward a general theory of decisions. *Proc. 7th Int. Conf. On Soft Comp. and Comp. With Words in Syst. Anal., Decis. and Control*, ICSCCW, pp. 13–16.

54.   Aliev, R. A., Pedrycz, W., Kreinovich, V. and Huseynov, O.H. (2016). The General Theory of Decisions. *Inform. Sciences,* 327(10), pp. 125–148.

55.   Aliev, R. A. (2009). Decision and Stability Analysis in Fuzzy Economics. *Annual Meeting of the North American Fuzzy Information Processing Society*, NAFIPS, pp. 1–2.

56.   Aliev, R. A. (2010). Theory of decision making under second-order uncertainty and combined states, *Proc. 9th Int. Conf. on Appl. of Fuzzy Syst. and Soft Comp.*, ICAFS, pp. 5–6.

57.   Aliev, R. A. (2010). Theory of Decision Making with Imperfect Information. *Annual Meeting of the North American Fuzzy Information Processing Society*, NAFIPS, pp. 1–5.

58.   Aliev, R. A. and Huseynov, O. H. (2013). Fuzzy geometry-based decision making with unprecisiated visual information, *Int. J. Inf. Tech. Decis.*, vol. 13(5), pp. 1051–1074.

59.   Aliev, R. A., Aliev, F. T. and Babaev, M. D. (1991) *Fuzzy Process Control and Knowledge Engineering.* (Verlag TUV Rheinland, Koln).

60.   Aliev, R. A., Pedrycz, W. and Huseynov, O. H. (2013). Behavioral decision making with combined states under imperfect information, *Int. J. Inf. Tech. Decis.*, 12(3), pp. 619–645.

61.   Aliev, R. A., Pedrycz, W., Alizadeh, A. V. and Huseynov, O. H. (2013). Fuzzy optimality based decision making under imperfect information without utility, *Fuzzy Optim. Decis. Ma.*, 12(4), pp. 357–372.

62.   Aliev, R. A., Alizadeh, A. V. and Huseynov, O. H. (2016). The arithmetic of continuous Z-numbers. *Inform. Sciences*, 373, pp. 441–460.

63.   Aliev, R.A. and Pedrycz, W. (2007). Toward a Generalized Theory of Stability. *Proc.4th Int. Conf.on Soft Computing and Computing with Words in System Analysis, Decision and Control*, pp.1–2.

64.   Aliyev R. A., Fazlollahi B., Vahidov R. (2002) Genetic algorithms based fuzzy regression analysis. *Soft computing* 6, Springer Verlag, pp.470–475.

65.   Aliyev R. A. and Aliyev R. R. (2004). *Soft computing (theory, technology and practice),* Baku, Chashioghlu, 624 p.

66.   Aliyev R. R. (2015). Similarity based multi-attribute decision making under Z-information. Proc. 8th Int. Conf. on Soft Computing with Words and Perceptions in System Analysis, Decision and Control, pp.33–39.

67.   Alizadeh, A., Saberi, M., Atashbar, N. Z, Chang, E. and Pazhoheshfar, P. (2013). Z-AHP: A Z-number extension of fuzzy analytical hierarchy process. *Proc. of the 7th IEEE International Conference on Digital Ecosystems and Technologies,* DEST, pp. 141–147.

68.   Allahdadi, M. and Mishmast Nehi, H. (2013). The optimal solution set of the interval linear programming problems, *OptimLett.,* 7, pp.1893–1911.

69.   Allahviranloo, T. and Salahshour, S. (2011). Fuzzy symmetric solutions of fuzzy linear systems. *J.Comput. Appl. Math.,* 235(16), pp. 4545–4553.

70. Allais, M. and Hagen, O. (1979). *Expected Utility Hypotheses and the Allais Paradox: Contemporary Discussions of the Decisions under Uncertainty with Allais' Rejoinder.* (D. Reidel Publishing Co., Dordrecht).

71. Alo, R., de Korvin, A. and Modave, F. (2002). Using fuzzy functions to select an optimal action in decision theory, *Proc. of the North American Fuzzy Information Processing Society,* NAFIPS, pp. 348–353.

72. Altman, M. (2005). Behavioral Economics, Power, rational Inefficiencies, Fuzzy Sets, and Public Policy. *J.Econ Issues,* XXXIX(3), pp. 683–706.

73. Aluja, J. G. and Kaufmann, A. (2002). Introducción de la teoría de la incertidumbre en la gestión de empresas [Introduction to the uncertainty theory in enterprises management]. Ed. Milladoiro-Academy of Doctors. Vigo-Barcelona (Spain), Reial Academia De Doctors (English version Ed. Springer 2003).

74. Aluja, J.G. and Kaufmann, A. (1986). Introducción de la teoría de los subconjuntos borrosos a la gestión de las empresas. [Introduction of fuzzy subsets theory to business management]. Santiago de Compostela: Milladoiro.

75. Kumar, A., Singh, P., Kaur, P. and Kaur, A. (2011). A new approach for ranking of L–R type generalized fuzzy numbers, *Expert Sys Applications,* 38(9), 10906–10910.

76. Andreoni, J. and Miller, J. (2002). Giving according to garp: an experimental test of the consistency of preferences for altruism. *Econometrica,* 70, pp. 737–753.

77. Anscombe, F.J. and Aumann, R.J. (1963). A definition of subjective probability. *The Annals of Mathematical Statistics,* 34, pp. 199–205.

78. Augustin, T., Miranda, E., Vejnarova, J. (2009). Imprecise probability models and their applications. *Int J Approx Reason,* 50(4), pp.581–582.

79. Azadeh A., Saberi, M., Atashbar, N. Z., Chang, N. Z. and Pazhoheshfar, P. (2013). Z-AHP: A Z-number extension of fuzzy analytical hierarchy process, International Conference on Digital Ecosystems and Technologies (DEST): 141–147.

80. Azadeh, A., Kokabi, R., Saberi, M., Hussain, F.K. and Hussain, O.K. (2014). Trust Prediction Using Z-numbers and Artificial Neural Networks. *In Proc. of IEEE Int. Conf. on Fuzzy Systems,* FUZZ-IEEE, pp. 522– 528.

81. Azadeh, I., Fam, I.M., Khoshnoud, M. and Nikafrouz, M. (2008). Design and implementation of a fuzzy expert system for performance assessment of an integrated health, safety, environment (HSE) and ergonomics system: The case of a gas refinery. *Inform. Sciences.* 178(22), pp. 4280–4300.

82. Bakar, A. S.A. and Gegov, A. (2015). MultiLayer Decision Methodology for Ranking Z-Numbers. *Int. J. Comput. Int. Sys.,* 8(2), 395–406.

83. Baltussen, G., Thierry, P. and van Vliet, P. (2006). Violations of cumulative prospect theory in mixed gambles with moderate probabilities, *Manage. Sci.,* 52(8), pp. 1288–1290.

84. Bandemer, H. and Nather, W. (1992). *Fuzzy Data Analysis.* (Kluwer Academic Publishers, Boston).

85. Bandemer H. and W. Näther, (1992). *Fuzzy data analysis, Theory and Decision Library, Series B: Mathematical and Statistical Methods, Vol. 20,* (Springer Netherlands).

86. Bandler, W. and Kohout, L.J. (1980), Fuzzy power sets and fuzzy implication operators. *Fuzzy Set Syst.,* 4, pp.13–30.

87. Bandler, W. and Kohout, L.J. 1980). *Fuzzy relational products as a tool for analysis of complex artificial and natural systems,* Wang P.P., Chang S.K. (eds.)

Fuzzy Sets; Theory and Applications to Policy Analysis and Information Systems, (Plenum Press, New York), pp. 311–367.

88.   Bandler, W. and Kohout, L.J. (1985). Probabilistic vs. fuzzy production rules in expert systems. *Int. J. Man-Machine Studies,* 22, pp. 347–353.

89.   Bandler, W. and Kohout, L.J. (1980). Semantics of fuzzy implication operators and relational products. *Int. J. Man-Machine Studies,* 12, pp. 89–116.

90.   Bandler, W. and Kohout, L.J. (1984). The four modes of inference in fuzzy expert systems, *Proc. of the 7th European Meeting on Cybernetics and Systems Research,* EMCSR, pp. 581–586.

91.   Bandler, W. and Kohout, L. J. (1980). The identification of hierarchies in symptoms and patients through computation of fuzzy relational products, *Proc. of the Conf. of British Computer Society: Information Technology for the Eighties,* BCS, pp. 191–194.

92.   Banerjee, R. and Pal, S. K. (2013). The Z-Number Enigma: A study through an experiment, Yager R. R., Abbasov A. M., Reformat M. Z., Shahbazova S. N. (Eds.), Soft Computing: State of the Art Theory and Novel Applications (Studies in Fuzziness and Soft Computing), 291, pp. 71–88.

93.   Bardossy, A. (1990). Note on fuzzy regression. *Fuzzy Sets Syst.,* 37, pp. 65–75.

94.   Barret, C. R., Pattanaik, P. K. and Salles, M. (1992). Rationality and aggregation of preferences in an ordinary fuzzy framework. *Fuzzy Sets Syst.,* 49, pp.9–13.

95.   Bashar, M. A. and Shirin, S. (2005). Squares and square roots of continuous fuzzy numbers. *Dhaka Univ. J. Sci.,* 53(2), pp.131–140.

96.   Baumfield V. M., Conroy, J. C., Davis R. A. and Lundie, D. C. (2012). The Delphi method: gathering expert opinion in religious education, *British Journal of Religious Education,* 34(1), pp. 5–19.

97.   Becker, J. and Sarin, R. (1990). *Economics of ambiguity in probability,* Working paper, (UCLA Graduate School of Management).

98.   Bede, B. and Stefanini, L. (2013). Generalized differentiability of fuzzy-valued functions, *Fuzzy Set. Syst.,* 230, pp. 119–141.

99.   Bede, B. (2013). *Mathematics of Fuzzy Sets and Fuzzy Logic.* Springer-Verlag Berlin Heidelberg.

100.   Bede, B. and Gal, S.G. (2005). Generalizations of the differentiability of fuzzy-number-valued functions with applications to fuzzy differential equations, *Fuzzy. Set. Syst.,* 151, 581–599.

101.   Bedregal, B. C., Dimuro, G. P., Santiago, R. H. N. and Reiser, R. H. S. (2010). On interval fuzzy S-implications, *Inform. Sciences,* 180, pp. 1373–1389.

102.   Bell, D.E., Raiffa, H. and Tversky A. (1988*). Decision Making: Descriptive, Normative, and Prescriptive Interactions.* Cambridge: University Press.

103.   Belles-Sampera, J., Merigó, J. M., Guillén, M. and Santolino, M. (2014). Indicators for the characterization of discrete Choquet integrals. *Inform. Sciences,* 267, 201–216.

104.   Belles-Sampera, J., Merigó, J.M., Guillén, M. and Santolino, M. (2013). The connection between distortion risk measures and ordered weighted averaging operators. *Insurance: Mathematics and Economics,* 52(2), pp. 411–420.

105.   Bellman, R. E, Zadeh, L. A. (1970). Decision making in a fuzzy environment. *Manage Sci,*17, pp. 141–164.

106. Belohlavek, R., Sigmund, E. and Zacpal, J. (2011). Evaluation of IPAQ questionnaires supported by formal concept analysis, *Inform. Sciences,*181(10), pp. 1774–1786.

107. Ben-Akiva, M. and Lerman, S. R. (1985) *Discrete Choice Analysis: Theory and Application to Travel Demand.* (MIT Press, MA, Cambridge).

108. Berg, J., Dickhaut J. and McCabe, K. (1995). Trust, reciprocity, and social history, *Game Econ. Behav.,* 10, pp. 122–142.

109. Berger, J. O. (1985) *Statistical Decision Theory and Bayesian Analysis,* (Springer-Verlag, New York).

110. Bergstrom, G.L. and Smith, B.E. (1970). Multi-item production planning–an extension of the HMMS rules. *Manage. Sci.,*16, pp. 614–629.

111. Berger, J. O. (1985) *Statistical Decision Theory and Bayesian Analysis,* (Springer-Verlag, New York).

112. Bezdek, J. and Pal, S. (ed.). (1992). *Fuzzy Models for Pattern Recognition.* New York: IEEE Press.

113. Bilal, M. A. (2001). *Elicitation of Expert Opinions for Uncertainty and Risks.* (CRC Press LLC, Boca Raton, Florida).

114. Billot, A. (1995). An existence theorem for fuzzy utility functions: a new elementary proof, *Fuzzy Set. Syst.,* 74, pp. 271–276.

115. Billot, A. (1992). From fuzzy set theory to non-additive probabilities: how have economists reacted? *Fuzzy Set Syst.,* 49, pp. 75–90.

116. Billot, A. (1992). *Economic Theory of Fuzzy Equilibria. An Axiomatic Analysis.* Springer-Verlag, New York, p. 164.

117. Bird, J. and Bland, G. (1988). Freight forwarders speak: the Perception of Route Competition via Seaports in the European Communities Research Project. *Marit. Policy Manag.,* 15(11.15), pp. 35–55.

118. Birnbaum, M. H. (2008). New tests of cumulative prospect theory and the priority heuristic: probability-outcome tradeoff with branch splitting, *Judgm. Decis. Mak.,* 3(4), pp. 304–316.

119. Birnbaum, M. H., Johnson, K. and Longbottom, J.L. (2008). Tests of cumulative prospect theory with graphical displays of probability, *Judgm. Decis. Mak.,* 3(7), pp. 528–546.

120. Bitran, G. R. and Yanassee, H.H. (1984). Deterministic approximations to stochastic production problems. *Oper. Res.,* 32, pp. 999–1018.

121. Bloch, I. (2011). Lattices of fuzzy sets and bipolar fuzzy sets, and mathematical morphology, *Inform. Sciences,*181(10), pp. 2002–2015.

122. Boading, L., (2007). *Uncertainty theory.* 2nd ed., Springer-Verlag, Berlin.

123. Bobillo, F. and Straccia, U. (2010). Reasoning with the finitely many-valued Lukasiewicz fuzzy Description Logic. *Inform. Sciences.* In Press, Uncorrected Proof, Available online 23.

124. Bojadziev, G., Bojadziev, M. (1997). *Fuzzy Logic for Business, Finance, and Management.* World Scientific.

125. Borisov, A. N., Alekseyev, A. V., Merkuryeva, G. V., Slyadz, N. N., and Gluschkov, V. I. (1989) *Fuzzy Information Processing in Decision Making Systems,* (Radio i Svyaz, Moscow) (in Russian).

126. Borisov, A. N., Krumberg, O. A. and Fyodorov, I. P. (1990). *Decision Making Based on Fuzzy Models: Application Examples.* Riga: Zinatne Press, (in Russian), p.184.

127. Brafman, R. I. and Tennenholz, M. (1997). Modeling agents as qualitative decision makers, *Artif. Intell.*, 94(1–2), pp. 217–268.
128. Braithwaite, R. B. (1931) The Foundations of Mathematics and other Logical Essays, eds. Ramsey, F.P. (1926) "Truth and Probability", in Ramsey, 1931, Chapter 7, (Kegan, Paul, Trench, Trubner & Co., London; Harcourt, Brace and Company, New York) pp. 156–198.
129. Brans, J. P., Vincke, P. and Mareschal, B. (1986). How to select and how to rank projects: The PROMETHEE method. *Eur J Oper Res*; 24, pp. 228–238.
130. Brunelli, M., Mezei, J. (2013). How different are ranking methods for fuzzy numbers? A numerical study. *Int. J. Approx. Reason.*, 54(5), 627–639.
131. Buckley, J. and Feuring, T. (2000). Evolutionary algorithm solution to fuzzy problems: fuzzy linear programming. *Fuzzy Set Syst.*, 109, pp. 35–53.
132. Buckley, J. J. and Jowers, L. J. (2006). *Simulating Continuous Fuzzy Systems*, 188, Springer.
133. Buckley, J. J. (2005). *Fuzzy probabilities*. Heidelberg: Springer-Verlag, Berlin.
134. Buckley, J. J. (2003). *Fuzzy Probability and Statistics*. (Springer-Verlag, Heidelberg, Berlin).
135. Buckley, J. J., Hayashi, Y. (1994). Fuzzy neural networks. In: Yager R, Zadeh L (eds), Fuzzy Sets, Neural Networks, and Soft Computing, Van Nostrand Reinhold, New York, NY.
136. Buckley, J. J., Hayashi, Y. (1998). Applications of fuzzy chaos to fuzzy simulation. *Fuzzy Sets Syst.*, 99, 151–157.
137. Buckley, J. J. and Leonard, J. J. (2008). *Monte Carlo Methods in Fuzzy Optimization,* Chapter 4 "Random fuzzy numbers and vectors in:, Studies in Fuzziness and SoftComputing 222, Springer-Verlag, Heidelberg, Germany.
138. Burgin, M. (1995). Neoclassical analysis: Fuzzy continuity and convergence, *Fuzzy Set. Syst.*, 75(3), pp. 291–299.
139. Burgin, M. (2000). Theory of fuzzy limits, *Fuzzy Set. Syst.*, 115, pp. 433–443.
140. Busemann, H., Kelly, P.J. (1953). *Projective Geometry and Prospective Metrics*. Academic Press Inc., Publishers.
141. Bustince, H., Barrenechea, E., Fernandez, J., Pagola, M., Montero, J. and Guerra, C. (2010). Contrast of a fuzzy relation, *Inform. Sciences*, 180, pp. 1326–1344.
142. Borgelt C. (2009). Accelerating fuzzy clustering. *Inform. Sciences*, 179(23), pp. 3985–3997.
143. Caldwell, K., Harrison M., Adams M. and Travis Triplett N. (2009). Effect of Pilates and taiji quan training on self-efficacy, sleep quality, mood, and physical performance of college students. *Journal of Bodywork and Movement Therapies*, 13(2), pp. 155–163.
144. Camerer, C., Loewenstein, G., Prelec, D. (2005). Neuroeconomics: How Neuroscience Can Inform Economics, J. Econ. Lit., XLIII, pp. 9–64.
145. Camerer, C., Loewenstein, G., Prelec, D.. Neuroeconomics: How Neuroscience Can Inform Economics, Journal of Economic Literature XLIII (2005) 9–64.
146. Camerer, C. and Weber, M. (1992). Recent developments in modeling preferences, *J. Risk Uncertainty*, 5, pp. 325–370.
147. Campos, L. and Verdegay, J. L. (1989). Linear programming problems and ranking of fuzzy numbers,*Fuzzy Set. Syst.*, 32, pp.1–11.

148. Cantarell, G. E. and Fedele V. (2003). Fuzzy Utility Theory for Analysing Discrete Choice Behaviour. *Proc. of the 4rth Int. Symposium on Uncertainly Modeling and Analysis*, ISUMA, IEEE.

149. Carotenuto, G. and Gerla, G. (2013). Bilattices for deductions in multi-valued logic, *Int. J. Approx. Reason*, 54(8), pp. 1066–1086.

150. Casadesus-Masanell, R., Klibanoff, P. and Ozdenoren, E. (2000). Maxmin expected utility through statewise combinations, *Econ. Lett.*, 66, pp. 49–54.

151. Casasnovas, J. and Torrens, J. (2003). Scalar cardinalities of finite fuzzy sets for t-norms and t-conorms. Int *J. Uncertain. Fuzz.*, 11, pp. 599–615.

152. Casasnovas, J. and Riera, J. V. (2007). Discrete fuzzy numbers defined on a subset of natural numbers, *Adv. Soft Comp.*, 42, pp:573–582.

153. Casasnovas, J. and Riera, J. V. (2006). On the addition of discrete fuzzy numbers. *WSEAS Transactions on Mathematics*, 5(5), pp.549–554.

154. Seizing, R. and Gonzalez, V. S. (2012) *Soft Computing and Humanities in Social Sciences* 273, eds. Casasnovas, J. and Riera, J.V., Chapter 18 "Weighted means of subjective evaluations," STUDFUZZ, (Springer, Berlin, Heidelberg), pp. 323–345.

155. Casasnovas, J. and Riera, J.V. (2009).Lattice Properties of Discrete Fuzzy Numbers under Extended Min and Max. *IFSA/EUSFLAT Conf.*, pp. 647–652.

156. Casasnovas, J. and Riera, J. V. (2010). Triangular norms and conorms on the set of discrete fuzzy numbers. Information Processing and Management of Uncertainty in Knowledge-Based Systems. Theory and Methods. *Comm Com Inf Sc*, 80, pp. 683–692.

157. Casillas, J., Cordón, O., Herrera Triguero, T., Magdalena, L. (2003). Interpretability Improvements to Find the Balance Interpretability-Accuracy in Fuzzy Modeling: An Overview, *Interpretability Issues in Fuzzy Modeling*, eds. Casillas, J., Cordón, O., Herrera Triguero, T., Magdalena L. Berlin, Heidelberg: Springer, pp. 3–22.

158. Castillo, O. and Melin, P. (2012). A review on the design and optimization of interval type-2 fuzzy controllers, Appl .Soft Comput., 12(4), pp. 1267–1278.

159. Castillo, O. and Melin, P. (2008). *Type-2 Fuzzy Logic: Theory and Applications.* (Springer, Berlin).

160. Castillo, O., Melin, P. and Pedrycz W. (2011). Design of interval type-2 fuzzy models through optimal granularity allocation, Appl. Soft Comput, 11(8), 5590–5601.

161. Castillo O. (2008) *Type-2 Fuzzy Logic: Theory and Applications* (Springer, Berlin).

162. Castillo O. (2011) *Type-2 Fuzzy Logic in Intelligent Control Applications,* (Springer, USA).

163. Castle P. and S. Buckler, "What Was I Saying? Concentration and Attention," https://uk.sagepub.com/sites/default/files/upm-binaries/28824_02_Castle_%26_Buckler_Ch_02.pdf

164. Castro J.R., O.Castillo, P.Melin, A.Rodríguez-Díaz, A hybrid learning algorithm for a class of interval type-2 fuzzy neural networks, *Information Sciences*, Volume 179, Issue 13, 2009, pp. 2175–2193.

165. Castle P., Buckler S. (2009). *How to be a Successful Teacher: Strategies for Personal and Professional Development.* (SAGE Publications Ltd).

166. Castro, J. R., Castillo, O., Melin P. (2009). A.Rodríguez-Díaz, A hybrid learning algorithm for a class of interval type-2 fuzzy neural networks. *Inform. Sciences*, 179(13), pp. 2175–2193.

167. Chajda, I. and Halas, R., Rosenberg, I. G. (2010). On the role of logical connectives for primality and functional completeness of algebras of logics. *Inform. Sciences*, 180, pp. 1345–1353.

168. Chandra P. M. and Fisher L. (1994). Coordination of production and distribution planning. *Euro. J. Oper. Res.*, 72, pp. 503–517.

169. Chaneau, J. L., Gunaratne, M. and Altschaeffl, A. G. (1987). An application of type-2 sets to decision making in engineering," in Analysis of Fuzzy Information, vol. II: Artificial Intelligence and Decision Systems, J. Bezdek, Ed. Boca Raton, FL: CRC Press.

170. Chang, W. D. (2007). Nonlinear system identification and control using a real-coded genetic algorithm. *Appl Math Model,*; 31, pp. 541–550.

171. Chang, Y-C. and Chen, S-M. (2008). A new method for multiple fuzzy rules interpolation with weighted antecedent variables, *The 10th IEEE Int Conf SMC*, pp.76–81.

172. Chang, Y-T, Lee S-Y, Tongzon J L. (2008). Port selection factors by shipping lines: Different perspectives between trunk liners and feeder service providers. Mar. Policy, 32, pp. 877–885.

173. Chapell, M. S., Blanding, Z. B., Takahashi, M. and *et al.*, (2005). Test anxiety and academic performance in undergraduate and graduate students, *J. Educ. Psychol.*, 97(2), pp. 268–274.

174. Charles, M., Grinstead, J. and Snell, L. (1997) *Introduction to Probability.* (American Mathematical Society, USA).

175. Chateauneuf, A. P., and Wakker, P. (1993). An Axiomatization of Cumulative Prospect Theory. *J. Risk Uncertainty,* 7(7), pp. 147–176.

176. Chateauneuf, A. and Faro, J. (2009). Ambiguity through confidence functions, *J. Math. Econ.,* 45(9–10), pp. 535–558.

177. Chateauneuf, A. and Wakker, P. (1999). An axiomatization of cumulative prospect theory for decision under risk, *J. Risk Uncertainty*, 18(2), pp. 137–145.

178. Chaudhuri, B. B. and Rosenfeld, A. (1999). A modified Hausdorff distance between fuzzy sets, *Inform. Sciences*, 118, pp. 159–171.

179. Chen, S., Liu, J., Wang, H., Xub, Y., Augusto, J. C. (2014). A linguistic multi-criteria decision making approach based on logical reasoning, *Inform. Sciences,* 258, pp. 266–276.

180. Chen, S. H. (2005). Computational intelligence in economics and finance: carrying on the legacy of Herbert Simon. *Inform. Sciences,* 170(1), 121–131.

181. Chen, S. H. (2002). *Genetic Algorithms. Evolutionary Computation in Economics and Finance.* Physica-Verlag.

182. Chen, S. M., Munif, A., Chen, G. S., Liu H. C, Kuo, B. C. (2012). Fuzzy risk analysis based on ranking generalized fuzzy numbers with different left heights and right heights. *Expert Syst Appl*, 39(7), pp. 6320–6334.

183. Chen, S. M., Chang, Y. C., Chen, Z. J., Chen, C. L. (2013). Multiple Fuzzy Rules Interpolation with Weighted Antecedent Variables in Sparse Fuzzy Rule-Based Systems. *Int. J. Patt. Recogn. Artif. Intell,.* 27, DOI: https://doi.org/10.1142/S0218001413590027.

184. Chen, S. M., Chen, Z. J. (2016). A new weighted fuzzy rule interpolation method based on GA-based weights-learning techniques, *Inform. Sciences*, 329, pp. 503–523.

185. Chen, S. P., Chang, P. C. (2006). A mathematical programming approach to supply chain models with fuzzy parameters. *Eng. Optimiz.*, 38 (6), pp. 647–669.

186. Chen, T.-Y. (2011). A Multimeasure Approach to Optimism and Pessimism in Multiple Criteria Decision Analysis Based on Atanassov Fuzzy Sets, Expert. Syst. Appl., 38(10), pp. 12569–12584.

187. Chen, T.-Y. (2010). An Outcome-Oriented Approach to Multicriteria Decision Analysis with Intuitionistic Fuzzy Optimistic/Pessimistic Operators, *Expert Syst. Appl.*, 37(12), pp. 7762–7774.

188. Chen, T.-Y. (2011). Bivariate Models of Optimism and Pessimism in Multi-Criteria Decision-Making Based on Intuitionistic Fuzzy Sets, *Inform. Sciences*, 181(11), pp. 2139–2165.

189. Chen, T. (2010). Optimistic and pessimistic decision making with dissonance reduction using interval-valued fuzzy sets, *Inform. Sciences*, 181(3), pp. 479–502.

190. Chen, T.-Y. (2011). Signed distanced-based TOPSIS method for multiple criteria decision analysis based on generalized interval-valued fuzzy numbers, *Int. J. Inf. Tech. Decis.*, 10(6), pp. 1131–1159.

191. Chen, Z-L. (2005). Integrated scheduling of production and distribution operations. *Manage. Sci.*, 51(4), pp. 614–628.

192. Chen, Z. and Epstein, L. G. (2002). Ambiguity, risk, and asset returns in continuous time, *Econometrica*, 70, pp. 1403–1443.

193. Cheng, S.-H., Chen, S.-M., Chen, C.-L. (2016). Adaptive fuzzy interpolation based on ranking values of polygonal fuzzy sets and similarity measures between polygonal fuzzy sets. *Inform. Sciences*, 342, pp. 176–190.

194. Chew S. H., Epstein l., and Zilcha I. (1988) A correspondence theorem between expected utility and smooth utility, *J. Econ. Theory* 46, pp. 186–193.

195. Chew, S. H., Karni, E. and Safra, Z. (1987). Risk aversion in the theory of expected utility with rank-dependent probabilities, *J. Econ. Theory*, 42, pp. 370–381.

196. Choquet, G. (1953). Theory of capacities, *Ann. I. Fourier*, 5, pp. 131–295.

197. Chou, S. Y., Chang, Y. H. and Shen, C. Y. (2008). A fuzzy simple additive weighting system under group decision-making for facility location selection with objective/subjective attributes. *.Eur. J. Oper. Res.*, pp. 189: 132–145.

198. Cleary, J. C. (1987). Logical arithmetica. *Future Computing Systems*, 2, pp. 125–149.

199. Coe, D. P., Pivarnik, J. M., Womack, C. J., Reeves, M. J., and Malina, R. M. (2012). Health-related fitness and academic achievement in middle school students. *J. Sports Med. Phys. Fitness.*, 52(6), pp. 654–660.

200. Cohen, M. A. and Lee, H. L. (1988). Strategic analysis of integrated production-distribution systems: Models and methods, *Oper. Res.*, 36 (2), pp. 216–228.

201. Compte, O. and Postlewaite, A. (2009). *Mental processes and decision making*, Working paper, (Yale University, New Haven, USA). https://economics.wustl.edu/files/economics/imce/refs4658520000000000025.pdf

202. Couso, I., and Dubois, D. (2015). A perspective on the extension of stochastic orderings to fuzzy random variables, *16th World Congress of the Int. Fuzzy Systems Association*, IFSA, pp. 1486–1492.

203. Couso I. and Dubois, D. (2014). Statistical reasoning with set-valued information: Ontic vs. epistemic views. *Int. J. Approx. Reason*, 55(7), pp. 1502–1518.

204. Cover, T. and Hellman, M. (1970). Learning with finite memory, *Ann. Math. Stat.,* 41, pp.765–782.
205. Cox, J. C., Friedman D. and Sadiraj, V. (2008). Revealed altruism, *Econometrica,* 76(1), pp. 31–69.
206. Cox, J.C., Friedman, D., Gjerstad, S. (2007). A tractable model of reciprocity and fairness. *Game Econ. Behav.,* 59, 17–45.
207. Cox J.C., Ostrom, E., Walker, J.M., Castillo, A.J., Coleman, E., Holahan, R., Schoon, M.and Steed, B. (2009). Trust in private and common property experiments. *Southern Econ. J.,*75(4), pp. 957–975.
208. Cox, J. C. (2004). How to identify trust and reciprocity, *Game Econ. Behav.,* 46, pp. 260–281.
209. Cox J.C., Sadiraj, K. and Sadiraj, V. (2008). Implications of trust, fear, and reciprocity for modeling economic behavior, *Exp. Econ.,* 11, pp. 1–24.
210. Crina, G. and Ajith, A. (2009). A novel global optimization technique for high dimensional functions. *Int. J. Intell. Syst.,* 24, pp. 421–440.
211. Sheskin, D. J. (2007). *Handbook of Parametric and Nonparametric Statistical Procedures,* Boca Raton Chapman & Hall/CRC.
212. D'Este, G. and Meyrick, S. (1992). Carrier selection in a RO/RO ferry trade. *Marit. Policy Manag.,* 19(2), pp. 115–126.
213. Dalkey, N and Helmer, O. (1963). An experimental application of the Delphi method to the use of experts. *Manage. Sci.,* 9, pp. 458–467.
214. Dalkey, N. (1969). *The Delphi method: An experimental study of group opinion.* Santa Monica; CA: Rand Corporation.
215. Dantzig, G. B. (1998). *Linear Programming and Extensions.* Princeton University Press's, pp. 648.
216. Davvaz, B., Zhan, J. and Shum, K. P. (2008). Generalized fuzzy Hv-submodules endowed with interval valued membership functions, *Inform. Sciences,* 178, pp. 3147–3159.
217. Dawood H. (2011). *Theories of Interval Arithmetic: Mathematical Foundations and Applications.* LAP Lambert Academic Publishing, Germany.
218. De Cooman, G. (2005). A behavioral model for vague probability assessments. *Fuzzy Set Syst.,*154, pp. 305–308.
219. De Finetti, B. (1974) *Theory of Probability,* 1. (Wiley, New York).
220. De Langen, P. (2007). Port competition and selection in contestable hinterlands; the case of Austria. *Eur J Transp Infrast,* 7(1), 1–14.
221. De Meyer, H., De Baets, B. and De Schuymer, B. (2007). On the transitivity of the comonotonic and countermonotonic comparison of random variables, *J. Multivariate Anal.,* 98(1), pp. 177–193.
222. De Schuymer, B., De Meyer, H. and De Baets, B. (2005). Transitive comparison of random variables, *J. Multivariate Anal.,* 96(2), pp. 352–373.
223. De Wilde, P. (2004). Fuzzy utility and equilibria, *IEEE T. Syst. Man CY. B.,* 34(4), 1774–1785.
224. Deci, E. L. and Ryan, R. M. (2008). Self-determination theory: a macrotheory of human motivation, development, and health. *Can. Psychol.,* 49(3), pp. 182–185.
225. Delgado, M., Verdegay, J. L. and Vila, M. A. (1989). A general model for fuzzy linear programming. *Fuzzy Set Syst.,* 29, pp. 21–29.
226. Demirci, M. (2002). Fundamentals of m-vague algebra and m-vague arithmetic operations. *Int. J. Uncertain. Fuzz.,* 10, pp. 25–75.

227. Demirci, M. (1999). Fuzzy functions and their fundamental properties. *Fuzzy Set. Syst.*, 106, pp. 239–246.
228. Demirel, N. Ç.,Yücenur, G. N. (2011). The Cruise Port Place Selection Problem with Extended VIKOR and ANP Methodologies under Fuzzy Environment. *Proc.of the World Congress on Engineering, II.*
229. Dempster, A. P. (1967). Upper and lower probabilities induced by a multivalued mapping, *Ann. Math. Stat.*, 38, pp. 325–339
230. D-F., Li, Chen, G-H. and Huang, Z-G. (2010). Linear programming method for multiattribute group decision making using IF sets, *Inform. Sciences,* 180, pp. 1591–1609.
231. Denneberg, D. (2000). *Non-additive measure and integral, basic concepts and their role for applications,* in: Grabisch, M., Murofushi, T. and Sugeno M., eds. Fuzzy Measures and Integrals: Theory and Applications, Physica-Verlag, pp. 42–69.
232. Denneberg, D. (1994). *Non-additive Measure and Integral.* Kluwer Academic Publisher, Boston, p. 196.
233. Diamond, P. and Kloeden, P. (1994) *Metric Spaces of Fuzzy Sets, Theory and Applications.* (World Scientific, Singapore).
234. Diamond, P. (1988). Fuzzy least squares. Inform.Sciences, 46, pp. 141–157.
235. Dian, J. (2010). A meaning based information theory–inform logical space: Basic concepts and convergence of information sequences, *Inform. Sciences, 180,* Special Issue on Modeling Uncertainty, 15, pp. 984–994.
236. Landowski, M. (2014). Differences between Moore's and RDM interval arithmetic, *Proceedings of the 13th International Workshop on Intuitionistic Fuzzy Sets and Generalized Nets, Warsaw, Poland,* pp. 331–340.
237. Dinagar, S. D. and Anbalagan, A. (2011). Two-phase approach for solving Type-2 fuzzy linear programming problem. *Int. J. Pure Appl. Math.,*70, pp. 873–888.
238. Dinagar, S. D. and Anbalagan, A. (2011). Fuzzy programming based on type-2 generalized fuzzy numbers, *International J. of Math. Sci. and Engg. Appls.,* 5(4), pp. 317–329.
239. Disney, S. M., Naim, M.M., Potter, A. (2004). Assessing the impact of e-business on supply chain dynamics. *Int. J. Prod. Econ.,* 89(2), pp. 109–118.
240. Dompere, K. K.(2009). *Fuzziness and Approximate Reasoning. Epistemics on Uncertainty, Expectation and Risk in Rational Behavior.* Stud. Fuzz. Soft Comp., Springer-Verlag, Berlin.
241. Dornier, P.-P., Ernst, R., Fender, M., Konvelis, P. (1998). *Global operations and logistics. Text and cases.* John Wiley and Sons Inc.
242. Dotoli, M., Fanti, M.P., Meloni, C., Zhou, M. (2006) .Design and optimization of integrated e-supply chain for agile and environmentally conscious manufacturing, *IEEE Trans. Syst. Man Cyb. Part A: Syst. Hum.,* 36(1), pp. 62–75.
243. Dowling, J. M. and Chin-Fang, Y. (2007). *Modern Developments in Behavioral Economics. Social Science Perspectives on Choice and Decision making.* (World Scientific, Singapore).
244. Dubois, D. and Prade, H. (1999). Fuzzy sets in approximate reasoning, Part 1: Inference with possibility distributions, *Fuzzy Set Syst.,* 100(1), pp. 73–132.

245. Dubois, D., Durrieu, C., Prade, H., Rico, A., Ferro, Y. (2015). *Extracting Decision Rules from Qualitative Data Using Sugeno Integral: A Case-Study, In Symbolic and Quantitative Approaches to Reasoning with Uncertainty,* Destercke, S., Denoeux T., eds. Switzerland: Springer, pp. 14–24.

246. Dubois, D. and Prade, H. (2015). *Possibility Theory and Its Applications: Where Do We Stand?"* in Springer Handbook of Computational Intelligence, Kacprzyk J. and Pedrycz, W. eds. Berlin, Heidelberg: Springer, pp. 31–60.

247. Dubois, D., Prade, H. and Schockaert, S. (2014). *Reasoning about Uncertainty and Explicit Ignorance in Generalized Possibilistic Logic,* in *Frontiers in Artificial Intelligence and Applications,* Schaub, T., Friedrich, G., O'Sullivan B., eds., IOS Press, 263, pp. 261–266.

248. Dubois, D., Liu, W., Ma, J., Prade, H. (2016). The basic principles of uncertain information fusion. An organized review of merging rules in different representation frameworks. *Inform. Fusion,* 32, pp. 12–39.

249. Dubois, D. and Prade, H. (1980) *Fuzzy Set. Syst.: Theory and Applications.* (Academic Press, New York).

250. Dymova, L. and Sevastjanov P. (2009). A new method for solving interval and fuzzy equations: linear case, *Inform. Sciences,* 17, pp. 925–937.

251. Dymova, L. and Sevastjanov P. (2008). Fuzzy solution of interval linear equations, *Lecture Notes in Comput. Sciences,* pp. 1392–1399.

252. Dymova, L. (2011). Soft computing in economics and finance, (Springer–Verlag, Berlin, Heidelberg).

253. Evgeny, D., Kreinovich, V., Wolpert, A. and Xiang, G. (2006). Population Variance under Interval Uncertainty: A New Algorithm, Reliable Computing, 12(4), pp. 273–280.

254. Eduardo, M.V. (2010). Permutation-based finite implicative fuzzy associative memories, *Inform. Sciences,,* 180, pp. 4136–4152.

255. Edwards, J.U., Mauch, L. and Winkelman, M. R. (2011). Relationship of nutrition and physical activity behaviors and fitness measures to academic performance for sixth graders in a Midwest city school district, *J School Health,* 81(2), pp. 65–73.

256. Edwards, W. (1954a). Probability Preferences Among Bets with Differing Expected Values, *American J. Psychol.,* 67, pp. 55–67.

257. Efstathuio, J. and Rajrovich, V. (1980). Multi-attribute decision-making using a fuzzy heuristic approach, *Int. J. Man-Machine Studies,* 12(2), pp.141–156.

258. Eichberger, J. and Guerdjikova, A. (2013). Ambiguity, data and preferences for information–A case-based approach, *J. Econ. Theory,* 148, pp. 1433–1462.

259. Eichberger, J. and Kelsey, D. (1999). E-Capacities and the Ellsberg paradox, *Theor. Decis.,* 46, pp. 107–138.

260. Einhorn, H. and Hogarth, R. (1985). Ambiguity and uncertainty in probabilistic inference, *Psychol. Rev.,* 92, pp. 433–461.

261. Ekenberg, L. and Thorbiornson, J. (2001). Second–order decision analysis, International Journal of Uncertainty, *Fuzziness and Knowledge-Based Systems,* 9(1), pp. 13–37.

262. El-Ghamrawy, S.M. and Eldesouky, Ali I. (2012). An agent decision support model based on granular rough model. *Int. J. Inf. Technol. and Decision Making,* 11(4), pp. 793–820.

263. Ellsberg, D. (1961). Risk, ambiguity and the Savage axioms, *Q. J. Econ.*, 75, pp. 643–669.

264. Enea, M. & Piazza, T. (2004). Project Selection by Constrained Fuzzy AHP. *Fuzzy Optim Decision Ma*, 3(1), pp. 39–62.

265. En-lin, L. and You-ming, Z. (2003). Random variable with fuzzy probability, *Applied Mathematics and Mechanics*, 24(4), pp. 491–498.

266. Epstein, L.G. and Zhang, J. (2001). Subjective Probabilities on Subjectively Unambiguous Events, *Econometrica*, 69, pp. 265–306.

267. Epstein, L.G. and Schneider, M. (2008). Ambiguity, information quality and asset pricing, *J.Financ*, 63(1), pp. 197–228.

268. Epstein L.G. and Wanf, T. (1994). Intertemporal Asset Pricing under Knightian Uncertainty, *Econometrica*, 62, pp. 283–322.

269. Epstein, L.G. (1999). A definition of uncertainty aversion, *Rev. Econ. Stud.*, 66, pp. 579–608.

270. Epstein, L.G. and Schneider M. (2008). Ambiguity, information quality and asset pricing, *J. Financ.*, 63(1), pp. 197–228.

271. Falk, A. and Fischbacher, U. (2006). A theory of reciprocity, *Game Econ. Behav.*, 54, pp. 293–315.

272. Fan, Z-P. and Feng, B. (2009). A multiple attributes decision making method using individual and collaborative attribute data in a fuzzy environment, *Inform. Sciences*, 179, pp. 3603–3618.

273. Farina, M. and Amato, P. (2004). A fuzzy definition of "optimality" for many-criteria optimization problems. *IEEE T. Sys., Man. Cyb., Part A: Systems and Humans*, 34(3), pp. 315–326.

274. Fazel Zarandi, M.H., Turksen, I.B. and Saghiri, S. (2002). Supply chain: crisp and fuzzy aspects, *Int. J. Appl. Math. Comput. Sciences*, 12(3), pp. 423–435.

275. Fazlollahi, B., Vahidov R.M. and Aliev R.A. (2000). Multi-Agent Distributed Intelligent Systems Based on Fuzzy Decision-Making, *Int. Journal of Intell. Sys.*, 15, pp. 849–858.

276. Fedrizzi, M. and Fuller, R. (1992). Stability in Possibilistic Linear Programming Problems with Continuous Fuzzy Number Parameters, *Fuzzy Set Syst.*, 47, pp. 187–191.

277. Fenema, H. and Wakker, P. (1997). Original and Cumulative Prospect Theory: a discussion of empirical differences, *J Behav. Decis. Making.*, 10, pp. 53–64.

278. Fentem, P.H. (1994). Benefits of exercise in health and disease, *Bmj Brit. Med. J.*, 308(6939), pp. 1291–1295.

279. Ferson, S., Ginsburg, L. and Kreinovich, V. Uncertainty in risk analysis: Towards a general second-order approach combining interval, probabilistic, and fuzzy techniques, In *Proceedings of FUZZ-IEEE*, pp. 1342–1347.

280. Fiedler, M., Nedoma, J., Ramik, J. and Zimmermann, K. (2006). Linear optimization problems with inexact data, (Springer, New York) pp. 214.

281. Finetti, B. (1974). Theory of Probability: A Critical Introductory Treatment, 1, Translated by A.Machi and A.Smith. (New York: Wiley).

282. Fischer, G.W. (1989). Prescriptive decision science: Problems and opportunities, Annals of Operations Research, 19 (1), pp. 489–497.

283. Fishburn, P. C. (1988). Nonlinear Preference and Utility Theory, John Hopkins Press, Baltimore, Maryland.

284. Folino, G., Forestiero, A. and Spezzano, G. (2009). An adaptive flocking algorithm for performing approximate clustering, *Inform. Sciences*, 179(18), pp. 3059–3078.

285. Fox, B. B., Hodgkinson, B. and Parker, D. (2014). The effects of physical exercise on functional performance, quality of life, cognitive impairment and physical activity levels for older adults aged 65 years and older with a diagnosis of dementia: a systematic review, *The JBI Database of Systematic Reviews and Implementation Reports*.

286. Francisco, J. Valverde-Albacete and Pelaez-Moreno, C. (2010). Extending conceptualization modes for generalized Formal Concept Analysis, *Inform. Sciences*, pp. 27.

287. Franke, G. (1978). Expected utility with ambiguous probabilities and "Irrational Parameters", *Theor. Decis.*, 9, pp. 267–283.

288. Franksen, O.I. (1978). Group representation of finite polyvalent logic, In: A. Niemi (ed.) *Proceedings 7th Triennial International federation of automatic control World Congress*, (Pergamon, IFAC, Helsinki).

289. Fudenberg, D. (2006). Advancing Beyond "Advances in Behavioral Economics", *J.Econ. Lit.*, 44, pp. 694–711.

290. Fukami, S., Mizumoto, M. and Tanaka, K. (1980). Some considerations of fuzzy conditional inference, *Fuzzy Set Syst.*, 4, pp. 243–273.

291. Fuller, R. and Zimmermann, H.-J. (1993). On Zadeh's compositional rule of inference, in: R. Lowen, M. Roubens (Eds.), Fuzzy Logic: State of the Art, Theory and Decision Library, Series D, (Kluwer Academic Publisher, Dordrecht), pp. 193–200.

292. Fumika, O., (2004). A literature review on the use of expert opinion in probabilistic risk analysis, *World Bank Policy Research Working Paper*, 3201, http://documents.worldbank.org/curated/en/346091468765322039/A-literature-review-on-the-use-of-expert-opinion-in-probabilistic-risk-analysis

293. George, K. and Yuan, B. (1995). *Fuzzy Sets and Fuzzy Logic*, (Prentice Hall, Upper Saddle River, New Jersey).

294. Guolei, X., Ceberio, M. and Kreinovich, V. (2007). Computing population variance and entropy under interval uncertainty: linear-time algorithms, *Reliable Computing*, 13(6), pp. 467–488.

295. Gajdosa, T., Hayashib, T., Tallona, J.-M. and Vergnauda, J.-C. (2008). Attitude toward imprecise information, *J.Econ. Theory*, 140(1), pp. 27–65.

296. Ganesan, K, and Veeramani, P. (2006). Fuzzy linear programs with trapezoidal fuzzy numbers. *Ann Oper Res*, 143, pp. 305–315.

297. Gaok, M., Zhou, M.C. and Tang, Y. (2004). Intelligent decision making in disassembly process based on fuzzy reasoning Petri nets, *IEEE Trans. Syst. Man. Cyb. B: Cyb.* 34 (5), pp. 2029–2084.

298. Gaonkar, R. and Viswanadham, N. (2005). Strategic sourcing and collaborative planning in internet-enabled supply chain networks producing multigeneration products, *IEEE Trans. Autom. Sci. Eng.*, 2(1), pp. 54–66.

299. Garcia, J., Borrajo, F. and Fernandez, F. (2012). Reinforcement learning for decision-making in a business simulator, *Int. J. Inform. Technol. and Decis. Making*, 11(05), pp. 935–960.

300. Garcia, J.C.F. (2011). Interval type-2 fuzzy linear programming: Uncertain constraints. IEEE Symposium on Advances in Type-2 Fuzzy Logic Systems (T2FUZZ), pp. 94–101.

301. Garcia-Alonso, L, and Sanchez-Soriano, J. (2009). Port selection from a hinterland perspective. *Marit. Econ. Logist.*, 11, pp. 60–269.
302. Gasser, L. and Huhns, M. (1989). Distributed Artificial Intelligence,2, (Morgan Koufmann, San Mateo, California), pp. 259–290.
303. Gelfand, I.M., Shilov, G. E. and Vilenkin, N. Ya. (1964). Generalized Functions, *Academic Press, New York.*
304. Genç, S., Emre Boran, F., Akay, D. and Xu, Z. (2010). Interval multiplicative transitivity for consistency, missing values and priority weights of interval fuzzy preference relations, *Inform. Sciences*, 180(24), pp. 4877–4891.
305. Georgescu, V., (2001). Fuzzy Control Applied to Economic Stabilization Policies, *Studies in Informatics and Control*, 10(1), pp. 37–60.
306. Gerhke, M., Walker, C. L. and Walker, E. A. (2003). Normal forms and truth tables for fuzzy logics, *Fuzzy Set Syst*, 138, pp. 25–51.
307. Gerla, G. (2008). Approximate Similarities and Poincare Paradox, *Notre Dame J. Formal Logic*, 49(2), pp. 203–226.
308. Ghirardato, P. (2001). Coping with ignorance: unforeseen contingencies and non-additive uncertainty, *Econ. Theory* 17, pp. 247–276.
309. Ghirardato, P. and Marinacci, M. (2001). Range convexity and ambiguity averse preferences, *Econ. Theory*, 17, pp. 599–617.
310. Ghirardato, P. and Marinacci, M. (2002). Ambiguity made precise: a comparative foundation, *J. Econ. Theory*, 102, pp. 251–289.
311. Ghirardato, P., Klibanoff, P. and Marinacci, M. (1998). Additivity with multiple priors, *J. Math. Econ.*, 30, pp. 405–420.
312. Ghirardato, P., Maccheroni F., and Marinacci M. (2004). Differentiating ambiguity and ambiguity attitude, *J. Econ. Theory*, 118, pp. 133–173.
313. Gil M.A. and Jain, P. (1992). Comparison of Experiments in Statistical Decision Problems with Fuzzy Utilities, *IEEE Tran.Syst., Man, Cyb.*, 22(4), pp. 662–670.
314. Gilboa, I. (2009) Questions in DecisionTheory, Annual Review of Economics, Annual Reviews, 2(1), pp. 1–19.
315. Gilboa, I. and Schmeidler, D. (2001). A Theory of Case-Based Decisions. *Camb. University Press.*
316. Gilboa I. (2009). Theory of Decision under Uncertainty (Cambridge University Press, Cambridge).
317. Gilboa, I., Andrew, W. P. and Schmeidler, D. (2008). Probability and Uncertainty in Economic Modeling, *J.Econ. Perspect.*, 22(3), pp. 173–188.
318. Gilboa, I. and Schmeidler, D (1989). Maximin expected utility with a non-unique prior, *J. Math. Econ.*, 18, pp. 141–153.
319. Gilboa, I., Maccheroni, F., Marinacci, M. and Schmeidler, D. (2010). Objective and subjective rationality in a multiple prior model, *Econometrica*, 78(2), pp. 755–770.
320. Gilboa, I. and Schmeidler, D. (1995). Case-Based Decision Theory, *Q. J. Econ.*,110, pp. 605–639.
321. Giovanni, A., Vincenzo, L., Saverio, S. and Autilia A. (2012). Hybrid evolutionary approach for solving the ontology alignment problem. *Int J Intell Sys*, 27, pp. 189–216.
322. Glen, A. G., Leemis, L. M. and Drew, J. H. (2004). Computing the distribution of the product of two continuous random variables, *Comput. Stat. Data An.*,,44, pp. 451–464.

323. Glen, A. G., Leemis, L. M. and Drew, J. H. (2004). Computing the distribution of the product of two continuous random variables. *Comput. Stat. Data An.*,44, pp. 451–464.
324. Goetschell, R. and Voxman, W.(1986). Elementary calculs, *Fuzzy Set. Syst.*, 18, pp. 31–43.
325. Goldberg D.E., (1989). Genetic Algorithms in Search, Optimization, and Machine Learning, Addison-Wesley, Reading, MA.
326. Good, I. J. (1962). Subjective probability at the measure of non-measurable set, *Proc. 1st Congress of Logic, Methodology and Philosophy of Science*, CLMPS, pp. 319–329.
327. Gottwald, S. (2005). Mathematical fuzzy logic as a tool for the treatment of vague information, *Inform. Sciences.*, 172(1–2), pp. 41–71.
328. Grabisch, M., Marichal, J., Pap, E. and Mesiar, R. (2011). Aggregation functions: Construction methods, conjunctive, disjunctive and mixed classes, *Inform. Sciences,* 181, pp. 23–43.
329. Grabisch, M., Murofushi, T., Sugeno, M., Kacprzyk, J. (2000). Fuzzy Measures and Integrals. Theory and Application. (Berlin, Heidelberg: Physica Verlag).
330. Grabisch, M., Orlovski, Sergei A., Yager, R.R. and Ronald R. (1998). Fuzzy Aggregation of Numerical Preferences. In R. Slowinski (Ed.), Fuzzy Sets in Decision Analysis, Operations Research and Statistics. *The Handbooks of Fuzzy Sets Series* (Boston–Dordrecht–London: Springer), pp. 131–168.
331. Grigorashenko, G.I., Zaitsev, Y.V., Mirzadjanzadeh, A.Kh. and Nedra, M. (1978). Application of polymers in an oil production, pp. 216.
332. Grigorenko, I., "Optimal Control and Forecasting of Complex Dynamical Systems". World Scientific Publishing Co. Pte. Ltd. Singapore 2006, p.198.
333. Grzegorzewski, P., (2011). On possible and necessary inclusion of intuitionistic fuzzy sets, *Inform. Sciences,* 181, pp. 342–350.
334. Guo, C. and Zhang, D. (2004). On set-valued fuzzy measures, *Inform. Sciences,* 160(1–4), pp. 13–25.
335. Guo, C. and Zhang, D. (2007). On Choquet integrals of fuzzy-valued functions with respect to fuzzy-valued fuzzy measures, *Int. Conf. Mach. Learn.*, pp. 3653–3656.
336. Guo P. and Tanaka, H. (2003). Decision Analysis based on Fused Double Exponential Possibility Distributions, *Eur. J.Oper. Res.,* 148, pp. 467–479.
337. Guo, P. (2011). One-Shot decision theory, *IEEE T. Syst. Man Cy. A,* 41(5), pp. 917–926.
338. Guo, P. and Tanaka, H. (2010). Decision making with interval probabilities. *Eur. J. Oper. Res.*, 203, pp. 444–454.
339. Gupta, S., & Chakraborty, M. (1998). Job Evaluation in Fuzzy Environment. *Fuzzy Set. Syst.*, 100, pp. 71–76.
340. Habib, E.A.E. (2012). Geometric Mean For Negative And Zero Values. *International Journal of Research and Reviews in Applied Sciences*, 11(3), pp. 419–432.
341. Hagras H. (2006) Comments on Dynamical Optimal Training for Interval Type-2 Fuzzy Neural Network (T2FNN), *IEEE T. Syst. Man. CY. B.: Cybernetics*, vol. 36(5), pp.1206–1209.

342. Hagras H., Faiyaz D., Callaghan V., and Lopez A. (2007). An Incremental Adaptive Life Long Learning Approach for Type-2 Fuzzy Embedded Agents in Ambient Intelligent Environments. *IEEE T. Fuzzy Syst.*, 15(1), pp. 41–55.

343. Hahn, G. J. and Shapiro, S. S. (1967) *Statistical Models in Engineering.* (John Wiley and Sons, New York).

344. Hájek P. (1998) *Metamathematics of Fuzzy Logic* (Kluwer, Dordrecht).

345. Hajiyev H.K., Akhundov M.S. (1983). Criteria for selection of the optimum number of wells to carry out measures to improve their working conditions. *Azerbaijan Oil Industry*, 11, pp. 21–24.

346. Halgamuge S. and Glesner, M. (1992). A fuzzy neural approach for pattern classification with generation of rules based on supervised learning. *Proceedings of Nuro Nimes* 92, pp. 165–173.

347. Halpern J. Y., and Moses Y. (1990). Knowledge and common knowledge in a distributed environment, *Journal of the Association of Computing Machinery*, 37(3), pp. 549–587.

348. Handa J. (1977) Risk, Probabilities and a New Theory of Cardinal Utility. *J Polit Econ*, 85(1), pp. 97–122.

349. Hannaford C. (2005) *Smart Moves: Why Learning Is Not All in Your Head, 2nd edition.* (Creat River Books, Salt Lake City, Utah).

350. Hansen, L. and Sargent, T. (2001). Robust control and model uncertainty, *Am. Econ. Rev.*, 91, pp. 60–66.

351. Hanss M. (2005). *Applied Fuzzy Arithmetic. An Introduction with Engineering Applications* (Springer-Verlag Berlin Heidelberg).

352. Hausman W.H., McClain J.D. (1971) A note on the Bergstrom-Smith multi-item production planning model, *Manage. Sci.*, 17, pp. 783–785.

353. Heal G., Kristrom B. (2008) A note on national income in a dynamic economy. *Econ Lett*, 98(1), pp. 2–8.

354. Herrera, F. Alonso, S., Chiclana, F., and Herrera-Viedma, E. (2009). Computing With Words in Decision Making: Foundations, Trends and Prospects. *Fuzzy Optim. Decis. Ma.*, 8(4), 337–364.

355. Herrera, F., and Herrera-Viedma, E. (2000). Linguistic Decision Analysis: Steps for Solving Decision Problems under Linguistic Information. *Fuzzy Set Syst.*, 115, 67–82.

356. Hidalgo, D., Castillo, O. and Melin, P. Type-1 and type-2 fuzzy inference systems as integration methods in modular neural networks for multimodal biometry and its optimization with genetic algorithms. *Inform. Sciences*, 179(13), 2009, pp. 2123–2145.

357. Hilbert, D. (1962). *Grundlagen der Geometrie.* Teubner Studienbuecher Mathematik.

358. Hillman, C. H., Erickson, K. I. and Kramer, A. F. (2008). Be smart, exercise your heart: exercise effects on brain and cognition. *Nat Rev Neurosci*, 9,(1), pp. 58–65.

359. Ho Joanna L.Y., Keller, L.R., and Keltyka, P. (2002). Effects of Outcome and Probabilistic Ambiguity on Managerial Choices, *J. Risk Uncertainty*, 24(1), pp. 47–74.

360. Hodges, J. L., and Lehmann, E. (1952). The use of previous experience in reaching statistical decisions. *The Ann. Math. Stat.*, 23, pp 396–407.

361. Hogarth, R. M. and Kunreuther, H. (1995). Decision making under ignorance: Arguing with yourself. *J Risk Uncertainty*, 10(1), pp. 15–36.

362. Holland, J. H. (1975). *Adaptation in Natural and Artificial Systems*. Ann Arbor: University of Michigan Press.

363. Holt C.C. *et al.* (1960). *Planning Production Inventories and Workforce*. Englewood Cliffs, NJ: Prentice Hall.

364. Horton, A. (2011). A general theory of decisions:psychological economics, A unified model of decision-making under uncertainty. *Foundations & Individual Choice*. http://fliphtml5.com/jujt/ejgo/basic/.

365. Hsu, M., Bhatt, M., Adolphs, R., Tranel, D. and Camerer, C. F. (2005) Neural systems responding to degrees of uncertainty in human decision-making, *Science*, 310(5754), 1680–1683.

366. https://www.statlect.com/probability-distributions/normal-distribution-linear-co mbinations.

367. Hu, Q., Yu, D. and Guo, M. (2010). Fuzzy preference based rough sets, *Inform. Sciences*, 180, pp. 2003–2022.

368. Huang, H. and Wu, C. (2009). Approximation capabilities of multilayer fuzzy neural networks on the set of fuzzy-valued functions. *Inform. Sciences*, 179(16), pp. 2762–2773.

369. Huangm, W.-C. and Chen, C.-H. (2005). Using the ELECTRE II method to apply and analyze the differentiation theory, *Proc. of the Eastern Asia Society for Transportation Studies, Vol. 5*, EASTS, pp. 2237–2249.

370. Huettel, S. A., Stowe, C. J., Gordon, E. M., Warner, B. T., and Platt, M. L. (2006). Neural signatures of economic preferences for risk and ambiguity, *Neuron*, 49, pp. 765–775.

371. Hurwicz, L. (1951). Optimality Criteria for Decision Making Under Ignorance, Cowles Commission Discussion Paper, *Statistics*, 370.

372. Hwang, C. and Yoon, K. (1981).*Multiple attribute decision making methods and application*. New York: Springer.

373. Hwang, C. and Rhee, F.C.-H. (2007). Uncertain fuzzy clustering: Interval Type-2 Fuzzy Approach to C-Means. *IEEE T. Fuzzy Syst.*, pp.107–120.

374. Innocent, P. R., Belton, I. P., Finlay, D. B. L., and John, R. I. (2001). Type-2 Fuzzy Representations of Lung Scans to Predict Pulmonary Emboli. *Proc. of Joint 9th IFSA World Congress and 20th NAFIPS Int. Conf.*, pp. 1902–1907.

375. Inuiguichi, M., Ichihashi, H. and Kume, Y. (1990). A solution algorithm for fuzzy linear programming with piecewise linear membership function, *Fuzzy Set. Syst.*, 34, pp. 15–31.

376. Inuiguichi, M. and Ramik, J. (2000). Possibilistic linear programming: a brief review of fuzzy mathematical programming and a comparison with stochastic programming in portfolio selection problem, *Fuzzy Set. Syst.*, 111, pp. 3–28.

377. Ishibuchi, H. and Nojima, Y. (2007). Analysis of interpretability-accuracy tradeoff of fuzzy systems by multiobjective fuzzy genetics-based machine learning. *Int. J. Approx. Reason*, 44(1), pp. 4–31.

378. Jaffal, H. and Tao, C. (2011). *Multiple Attributes Group Decision Making by Type-2 Fuzzy Sets and Systems*. Blekinge Institute of Technology, Master Degree Thesis no: 2011:1.

379. Jaffray, J. Y. (1991). *Belief functions, convex capacities and decision making*. Doignon, J.-P. and Falmagne, J.-C., eds. Mathematical Psychology: Current Developments. Springer Verlag, New York, pp.127–134.

380. Jaffray, J.-Y. and Philippe, F. (1997). On the existence of subjective upper and lower probabilities. *Math. Oper. Res.*, 22, pp. 165–185.

381. Jaffray, J.-Y. (1999). *Rational decision making with imprecise probabilities*, eds. de Cooman G., Cozman, F.G., Moral, S., Walley, P. ISIPTA 99, Proceedings of the First International Symposium on Imprecise Probabilities and their Applications, Ghent, Belgium, Imprecise Probability Project, pp. 324–332.

382. Jalal-Kamali, A., Kreinovich, V. and Longpre, L. (2011). *Estimating covariance for privacy case under interval (and fuzzy) uncertainty*, eds. Yager, R. R., Reformat, M. Z., Shahbazova, S. N. and Ovchinnikov, S. Proceedings of the World Conference on Soft Computing, San Francisco, CA, May 23–26.

383. Jamshidi, Y. and Nezamabadi-pour, H. (2014). Rule inducing by fuzzy lattice reasoning classifier based on metric distances(FLRC-MD). *Appl. Soft. Comput.*, 24, pp. 603–611.

384. Jantzen, J. (1995). Array approach to fuzzy logic, *Fuzzy Set. Syst.*, 70, pp. 359–370.

385. Jaroszewicz, S. and Korzen, A. (2012). Arithmetic Operations On Independent Random Variables: A Numerical Approach. *SIAM J. SCI. Comput.* 34(3), pp. 1241–1265.

386. Jayaram, B. and Mesiar, R. (2009). I-Fuzzy equivalence relations and I-fuzzy partitions, *Inform. Sciences,* 179, pp. 1278–1297.

387. Jenei, S. (1999). Continuity in Zadeh's compositional rule of inference, *Fuzzy Set. Syst.*, 104, pp. 333–339.

388. Ji Y.P., Vinh V.T., Gi T.Y. (2015) Fuzzy MCDM Approach for Evaluating Intangible Resources Affecting Port Service Quality. *The Asian Journal of Shipping and Logistics*, 31, pp. 459–468.

389. Jiafu, T., Dingwei, W., Fung, R.Y.K., Yung K.L. (2004) Understanding Of Fuzzy Optimization: Theories And Methods. *J Syst Sci Complex*, 17, pp. 117–136.

390. Jiao, L., Pana, Q., Denœux, T., Liang, Y., Feng, X. (2015) Belief rule-based classification system: Extension of FRBCS in belief functions framework. *Inform. Sciences*, 309, pp. 26–49.

391. Jin S., R. Diao, C. Quek, and Q. Shen, "Backward Fuzzy Rule Interpolation," *IEEE T Fuzzy Syst*, 22(6), pp. 1682–1698.

392. Jin S., Diao R., Shen Q. (2014). α-cut-based backward fuzzy interpolation. *The 13th IEEE INT Cognitive Informatics & Cognitive Computing*, pp. 211–218.

393. John D. H., Lotito G. and Maffioletti A. (2007). Choquet OK? Discussion Papers from Department of Economics, University of York, York, UK http://eprints.luiss.it/771/1/0712_HEY_2007.pdf

394. John R. (1996). Type-2 inferencing and community transport scheduling. *Proc.4th Euro. Congress on Intelligent Techniques Soft Computing*, Aachen, Germany, pp. 1369–1372.

395. Jong, Y., Liang, W. and Reza, L. (1997). Multiple fuzzy systems for function approximation, *Proc. of Annual Meeting of the North American Fuzzy Information Processing Society*, NAFIPS, pp. 154–159.

396. Jung, H., Jeong, B. (2005) Decentralized production-distribution planning system using collaborative agents in supply chain network. *Int. J. Adv. Manuf. Technol.* 25(1–2), pp. 167–173.

397. Koczy, L.T. and Hirota, K. (1993) Approximate reasoning by linear rule interpolation and general approximation. *Int. J. Approx. Reason.*, vol. 9, no. 3, pp. 197–225.

398. Kaburlasos V. G., Athanasiadis I.N., and Mitkas P.A. (2007) Fuzzy lattice reasoning (FLR) classifier and its application for ambient ozone estimation. *Int. J. Approx. Reason.*, vol. 45, iss. 1, pp. 152–188.

399. Kacprzyk J, Fedrizzi M. (1992). *Fuzzy Regression Analysis* (Omnitech Press, Warsaw, and Physica, Heidelberg).

400. Kacprzyk J. (1983). A generalization of fuzzy multistage decision making and control via linguistic quantifiers. *Int J Control* 38, pp. 1249–1270.

401. Kacprzyk J., M. Fedrizzi, H. Nurmi. (1992). Group decision making and consensus under fuzzy preferences and fuzzy majority. *Fuzzy Set. Syst.* 49, pp. 21–31.

402. Kacprzyk, J. (2008) Neuroeconomics: Yet Another Field Where Rough Sets Can Be Useful? In: Chan CC., Grzymala-Busse J.W., Ziarko W.P. (eds) Rough Sets and Current Trends in Computing. RSCTC 2008. Lecture Notes in Computer Science, vol 5306. Springer, Berlin, Heidelberg.

403. Kahneman D., Slovic P., Tversky A. (1982) *Judgment Under Uncertainty: Heuristics and Biases.* (Cambridge University Press).

404. Kahneman, D. and Tversky, A. (1979). Prospect theory: an analysis of decision under uncertainty, *Econometrica,* 47, pp.263–291.

405. Kallala, M. and Kohout, L. J. (1986). A 2-stage method for automatic handwriting classification by means of norms and fuzzy relational inference, *Annual Meeting of the North American Fuzzy Information Processing Society,* NAFIPS.

406. Kallala, M. and Kohout, L. J. (1984). The use of fuzzy implication operators in clinical evaluation of neurological movement disorders, *International Symposium on Fuzzy Information Processing in Artificial Intelligence and Operational Research* (Christchurch College, Cambridge University).

407. Kandel, A. and Last, M. (2007). Special issue on advances in fuzzy logic, *Inform. Sciences,* 177, pp. 329–331.

408. Kang, B., Wei, D., Li, Y., Deng, Y. (2012). Decision making using Z-numbers under uncertain environment, *Journal of Information and Computational Science,* 8(7), pp. 2807–2814.

409. Kang, B., Wei, D., Li, Y., Deng, Y. (2012) Decision making using Z-numbers under uncertain environment. *Journal of Computational Information Systems,* 8(7), pp. 2807–2814

410. Kang B., Wei D., Li Y., Deng Y. (2012) A method of converting Z-number to classical fuzzy number. *Journal of Information & Computational Science* 9(3), pp. 703–709.

411. Karni, E., Schmeidler, D. and Vind, K. (1983). On state-dependent preferences and subjective probabilities. *Econometrica* 51(4), pp. 1021–31.

412. Karni, E. (1985) *Decision Making under Uncertainty: The Case of State Dependent Preferences.* (Harvard University Press, Cambridge).

413. Karnik N.N. and J. M. Mendel (1998). Introduction to type-2 fuzzy logic systems, *in Proc. 1998 IEEE FUZZ Conf.,* pp. 915–920.

414. Karnik N.N. and Mendel J. M. (2001). Operations on type-2 fuzzy sets. *Fuzzy Set. Syst.,* 122, pp. 327–348.

415. Karnik N.N. and Mendel J. (1999). Application of type-2 fuzzy logic systems to forecasting of time series. *Inform. Sciences* Vol. 120, pp. 89–111.

416. Karnik, N. N. and Mendel, J. M. (2001). Operations on Type-2 Fuzzy Sets. *Fuzzy Set. Syst.,* 122, pp. 327–348.

417. Karnik, N. N., Mendel, J. M. and Liang, Q. (1999). Type-2 Fuzzy Logic Systems, *IEEE T. Fuzzy Syst.*, No. 6, vol. 7, pp. 643–658.

418. Kartik P., Mondal S.K. (2015) Fuzzy risk analysis using area and height based similarity measure on generalized trapezoidal fuzzy numbers and it sapplication. *Appl Soft Comput*, pp. 276–284.

419. Kaufman, A. (1973). *Introduction to Theory of Fuzzy Sets.* (Academic Press, Orlando).

420. Kaufman, A. and Gupta, M.M. (1985). *Introduction to Fuzzy Arithmetic: Theory and Applications* (Van Nostrand Reinhold Company, New York).

421. Kaufman, A. (1975). *Introduction to the theory of fuzzy sets* (Academic Press, Orlando).

422. Kaufmann A., Aluja J. G. (1990). Las Matemáticas Del Azar Y De La Incertidumbre. Elementos Básicos Para Su Aplicación En Economía. Editorial Centro De Estudios Ramon Areces, Madrid 1990, p.298.

423. Kearfott B. (1996). *Rigorous Global Search: Continuous Problems* (Kluwer Academic Publishers, The Netherlands).

424. Kearfott R.B., Kreinovich V. (1996). Applications of Interval Computations: An Introduction. In: R.B. Kearfott, V. Kreinovich (Eds.), *Applications of Interval Computations*, pp. 1–22, Kluwer, Dordrecht, 1996.

425. Keeley T.J.H. and Fox K.R. (2009). The impact of physical activity and fitness on academic achievement and cognitive performance in children. *Int Rev Sport Exer P*, vol. 2, no. 2, pp. 198–214.

426. Kehagias A. (2010). Some remarks on the lattice of fuzzy intervals. *Inform. Sciences*, 181(10), pp. 1863–1873.

427. Keller L.R. (1989). Decision Research with Descriptive, Normative, and Pre-scriptive Purposes-Some Comments. *Ann Oper Res* 19 (volume on Choice Under Uncertainty edited by Peter Fishburn and Irving H. LaValle), pp. 485–487.

428. Keller L.R. (1989). The Role of Generalized Utility Theories in Descriptive, Prescriptive, and Normative Decision Analysis. *Inform Decis Technol*, 15, pp. 259–271.

429. Kenneth, E. T. (2007). *Discrete Choice Models with Simulation.* (Cambridge University Press, New York).

430. Khan, N. A. and Jain, R. (1985). Uncertainty management in a distributed knowledge base system, *Proc. 9th International Joint Conference on Artificial Intelligence*, IJCAI, pp. 318–320.

431. Khorasani, E. S., Patel, P., Rahimi, S., Houle, D. (2012). An inference engine toolkit for computing with words. *J Amb Intel Hum Comp*, 4(4), pp. 451–470.

432. Kim B., Bishu R.R. (1998). Evaluation of fuzzy linear regression models by comparing membership functions. *Fuzzy Set. Syst* 100, pp. 343–352.

433. Kiszka, J. B., Kochanska, M. E. and Sliwinska, D. S. (1985). The influence of some fuzzy implication operators on the accuracy of a fuzzy model, *Fuzzy. Set. Syst.*, 15, (Part1) pp. 111–128; (Part2) pp. 223–240.

434. Klawonn F. (2000). Fuzzy points, fuzzy relations and fuzzy functions. In: V. Novák, I. Perfilieva (Eds.), *Discovering the World with Fuzzy Logic*, Springer, Berlin, pp. 431–453.

435. Klibanoff, P. (2001). Characterizing uncertainty aversion through preference for mixtures, *Soc. Choice Welfare*, 18, pp. 289–301.

436.   Klibanoff, P., Marinacci, M. and Mukerji, S. (2005). A smooth model of decision making under ambiguity, *Econometrica,* 73(6), pp. 1849–1892.

437.   Klir, G. J., Clair, U. S. and Yuan, B. (1997). *Fuzzy Set Theory, Foundations and Applications,* (PTR Prentice Hall, New Jersey).

438.   Klir, G., Yuan, B. (1996). *Fuzzy Sets, Fuzzy Logic, and Fuzzy Systems: Selected Papers by Lotfi Asker Zadeh.* (World Scientific, Singapore).

439.   Kóczy, L. T., Hirota, K.: (1991). Rule Interpolation by α-Level Sets in Fuzzy Approximate Reasoning, *J. BUSEFAL,* 46, pp. 115–123.

440.   Kóczy L.T. (1993). Approximate reasoning by linear rule interpolation and general approximation. *Int. J. Approx. Reason.,* vol. 9, no. 3, pp. 197–225.

441.   Koffman A., For R. (1966). *Let us study the operations.* (Mir, Moscow).

442.   Kohout, L. J. (1986). *A Perspective on Intelligent Systems: A Framework for Analysis and Design.* (Chapman & Hall, UK).

443.   Kohout, L. J. and Bandler, W. (1985). Relational-product architecture for information processing, *Inform. Science,* 37, pp. 25–37.

444.   Kolesarova, A. and Mesiar, R. (2010). Lipschitzian De Morgan triplets of fuzzy connectives, *Inform. Sciences,* 180, pp.3488–3496.

445.   Kornai I., Liptak T. (1965). *Planning at two levels. Application of Mathematics in Economic Research.* (Mysl, Moscow).

446.   Kreinovich, V. (2015). *Decision Making Under Interval Uncertainty.* (Walter De Gruyter Inc.)

447.   Krzysztof P. (1986) On the Bayes formula for fuzzy probability measures. *Fuzzy Set. Syst.* 18(2) pp. 183–185.

448.   Kumar, A., Singh P. and Kaur, J. (2010). Generalized Simplex Algorithm to Solve Fuzzy Linear Programming Problems with Ranking of Generalized Fuzzy Numbers. *TJFS,* 1, pp. 80–103.

449.   Kumar M. (2014). Applying weakest t-norm based approximate intuitionistic fuzzy arithmetic operations on different types of intuitionistic fuzzy numbers to evaluate reliability of PCBA fault. *Appl. Soft. Comput.,* 23, pp. 387–406.

450.   Luc J., Kieffer M., Didrit O., and Walter E. (2001). *Applied Interval Analysis, with Examples in Parameter and State Estimation, Robust Control and Robotics* (Springer-Verlag, London).

451.   Labreuche, C. and Grabisch, M. (2006). Generalized Choquet-like aggregation functions for handling bipolar scales, *Eur. J. of Oper. Res.,* 172, pp. 931–955.

452.   Lai, J. and Xu, Y. (2010). Linguistic truth-valued lattice-valued propositional logic system *lP(X)* based on linguistic truth-valued lattice implication algebra, *Inform. Sciences, 180, Special Issue on Intelligent Distributed Information Systems,* pp. 1990–2002.

453.   Lakshmikantham V., Vatsala, A.S. (2000). Existence of fixed points of fuzzy mappings via theory of fuzzy differential equations. *J. Comput. Appl. Math.,* 113(1–2), pp. 195–200.

454.   Lakshmikantham, V. and Mohapatra, R. (2003). *Theory of Fuzzy Differential Equations and Inclusions.* (Taylor and Francis, London, New York).

455.   Landeta, J. (2006). Current validity of the Delphi method in social sciences, *Technological Forecasting and Social Change,* Vol. 73, No. 5, pp. 467–82.

456.   Landowski M. (2015). Differences between Moore and RDM Interval Arithmetic. In: Angelov P. *et al.* (eds) *IEEE conf. on Intelligent Systems'2014.*

Advances in Intelligent Systems and Computing, vol 322, pp. 331–340, Springer, Cham.

457. Landowski, M. (2017). RDM interval method for solving quadratic interval equation. *Przeglad Elektrotechniczny*, 1, pp. 65–68.

458. László T. K. (1993). Approximate reasoning by linear rule interpolation and general approximation, *Int. J. Approx. Reason.* 9(3) pp. 197–225.

459. Lawry, J. (2001). An alternative to computing with words. *Int. J. Uncertain Fuzz*, 9, pp. 3–16.

460. Lee, E. S. & Li, R.-J. (1998). Comparison of fuzzy numbers based on the probability measure of fuzzy events. *Computers and Mathematics with Applications*, 15(10), 887–896.

461. Lee C. (1990). Fuzzy logic in control systems: Fuzzy logic controller, *IEEE T. Syst. Man. CY*, 20(2), pp. 404–435.

462. Lee, Y.H., S.H. Kim. (2000). Optimal production-distribution planning in supply chain management using a hybrid simulation-analytic approach, *Proc. of the 2000 Winter Simulation Conference*, pp. 1252–1259.

463. Lee Y.Y. (1990). Fuzzy set theory approach to aggregate production planning and inventory control. Ph.D. Dissertation, Department of Industrial Engineer, Kansas State University, Manhattan.

464. Leung F.H.F., Lam H.K., Ling S.H., and Tam P.K.S. (2001). Tuning of the Structure and Parameters of Neural Network using an Improved Genetic Algorithm. *Proceedings of the 27th Annual Conference of the IEEE Industrial Electronics Society, IECON'2001*, Denver, 2001, pp. 25–30.

465. Leung, F.H.F., Lam, H.K., Ling, S.H., Tam, P.K.S. (2003). Tuning of the Structure and Parameters of a Neural Network Using an Improved Genetic Algorithm. *IEEE T Neural Networ*, Vol. 14, No. 1, pp. 79–88.

466. Levy, P. (2010). From social computing to reflexive collective intelligence: The IEML research program, *Inform. Sciences, 180, Special Issue on Collective Intelligence*, pp. 71–94.

467. Li, D.-F. (2007). A fuzzy closeness approach to fuzzy multi-attribute decision making, *Fuzzy Optim. Decis. Ma.*, 6(3), pp. 237–254.

468. Li Y., Qin, K., He X., Meng D. (2016). Properties of Raha's similarity-based approximate reasoning method. *Fuzzy Set Syst.*, vol. 294, pp. 48–62.

469. Liang D., Liu D. (2014). Systematic studies on three-way decisions with interval-valued decision-theoretic rough sets. *Inform. Sciences* 27, pp. 186–203.

470. Liang Q.and Mendel, J.M. (2000). Interval type-2 fuzzy logic systems: theory and design. *IEEE T. Fuzzy Syst.*, vol. 8, pp. 535–550.

471. Liang T.-F. (2006). Distribution planning decisions using interactive fuzzy multi-objective linear programming, *Fuzzy Sets Syst.* 157 (10), pp. 1303–1316.

472. Lisboa P., Vellido, A. Edinbury B. (2000). Neural Networks. Business Applications of Neural Networks. (World Scientific).

473. Liu, P. and Wang, M. (2011). An extended VIKOR method for multiple attribute group decision making based on generalized interval-valued trapezoidal fuzzy numbers, *Sci. Res. Essays*, 6(4), pp. 766–776.

474. Liu, W. J., and Zeng, L. (2008). A new TOPSIS method for fuzzy multiple attribute group decision making problem, *J. Guilin Univ. Electron. Technol.*, 28(1), pp. 59–62.

475. Liu, S., Lin Forest, J.Y. (2010) *Grey systems, theory and applications.* (Springer, Berlin, Heidelberg).

476. Lizasoain, I. & Moreno, C. (2013). OWA operators defined on complete lattices. Fuzzy Set. Syst., 224, 36–52.

477. Loia, V. (2002). *Soft Computing Agents: A New Perspective for Dynamic Information Systems*, eds. (IOS Press, Netherlands).

478. Long, Z., Liang, X. and Yang, L. (2010). Some approximation properties of adaptive fuzzy systems with variable universe of discourse, *Inform. Sciences,*180, pp. 2991–3005.

479. Lorkowski, J., Aliev, R. and Kreinovich, V. (2014). Towards Decision Making under Interval, Set-Valued, Fuzzy, and Z-Number Uncertainty: A Fair Price Approach., FUZZ-IEEE, pp. 2244–2253.

480. Lossin S.-H. (2005). Decision making with imprecise and fuzzy probabilities–a Comparison. *Procs. of the Fourth International Symposium on Imprecise Probabilities Their Applications*, pp. 222–229.

481. Lu J., Zhang G., *Ruan D.* (2008). Intelligent multi-criteria fuzzy *group decision*-making for situation assessments. *Soft Computing*, 12(3), pp. 289–299.

482. Lu J., G. Zhang, D. Ruan, F. Wu. (2007). *Multi-Objective Group Decision Making. Methods, Software and Applications with Fuzzy set techniques.* (Imperial College Press, London).

483. Luce R. D. and Raiffa R. (1989). *Games and Decisions: Introduction and Critical Survey*. (Dover, New York).

484. Luce, R. D., Bush, R. R. and Galanter, E. H. (1965). *Handbook of Mathematical Psychology*, eds. Luce, R. D. and Suppes, P. "Preferences, Utility and Subjective Probability," vol. III (Wiley, New York) pp. 249–410.

485. Luce, R.D., Winterfeldt, D. (1994). What Common Ground Exists for Descriptive, Prescriptive, and Normative Utility Theories. *Manage Sci*, 40(2) pp. 263–279.

486. Luhandjula M.K. (1987). Linear programming with a possibilistic objective function. *Eur J Oper* Res, 31, pp. 110–117.

487. Luo M., N. Yao. (2013). Triple I algorithms based on Schweizer–Sklar operators in fuzzy reasoning, *Int. J. Approx. Reason.*, 54(5) pp. 640–652.

488. Ma, H. (2010). An analysis of the equilibrium of migration models for biogeography-based optimization, *Inform. Sciences*, 180, pp. 3444–3464.

489. Maccheroni, F., Marinacci, M. and Rustichini, A. (2005). Ambiguity aversion, robustness, and the variational representation of preferences, *Econometrica*, 74, pp. 1447–1498.

490. Magni C.A., S. Malagoli, and Mastroleo G. (2012). Approaches to leniency reduction in multi-criteria decision making with interval-valued fuzzy sets and an experimental analysis, *Int. J. Inf. Tech. Decis.*, 11(03), pp. 579–608.

491. Małeki H.R., Tata M., Mashinchi M. (2000). Linear programming with fuzzy variables. *Fuzzy Set. Syst.*, 109, pp. 21–33.

492. Mamdani E.H. (1977). Applications of fuzzy logic to approximate reasoning using linguistic systems. *IEEE T Comp*, vol. 26, no. 12, pp. 1182–1191.

493. Mammadova K. (2014). Modeling of impact of Pilates on students performance under Z-information. *Proc. of the Eighth World Conference on Intelligent Systems for Industrial Automation, WCIS-2014*, Tashkent, Uzbekistan, pp. 171–178.

494. Manski, C. F. (2001). Daniel McFadden and the econometric analysis of discrete choice, *Scand. J. Econ.*, vol. 103, No.2, pp. 217–229.

495. Martin, O. and Klir, G.J. (2006). On the problem of retranslation in computing with perceptions. *Int. J. Gen. Syst.*, 35(6), pp. 655–674.

496. Martinez, L., Ruan, D., & Herrera, F. (2010). Computing with words in decision support systems: an overview on models and applications. *International Journal of Computational Intelligence Systems*, 3(4), 382–395.

497. Martínez R., Castillo O., Aguilar L.T. (2009). Optimization of interval type-2 fuzzy logic controllers for a perturbed autonomous wheeled mobile robot using genetic algorithms, *Inform. Sciences*, 179(13), pp. 2158–2174.

498. Mas, M., Monserrat, M., Torrens, J. and Trillas, E. (2007). A survey on fuzzy implication functions, *IEEE T. Fuzzy Syst.*, 15(6), pp. 1107–1121.

499. Mas, M., Monserrat, M. and Torrens, J. (2009). The law of importation for discrete implications, *Inform. Sciences,* 179, pp. 4208–4218.

500. Mathai, A. M. (1973). A Review of the Different Techniques used for Deriving the Exact Distributions of Multivariate Test Criteria., *The Indian Journal of Statistics*, vol. 35, series A, pp. 39–60.

501. Mathieu-Nicot, B. (1986). Fuzzy expected utility, *Fuzzy Set. Syst.*, 20(2), pp. 163–173.

502. McCarthy J. (1979). Ascribing mental qualities to machines, In M. Ringle (Ed.), *Philosophical Perspectives in Artificial Intelligence.* (Atlantic Highlands, NJ: Humanities Press, pp. 161–195.

503. McFadden D.L., Economic Choices. Nobel Prize Lecture, 2000. http://www.nob elprize.org/nobel_prizes/economic-sciences/laureates/2000/mcfadden-lecture.pdf

504. McFadden, D. and Train, K. (2000). Mixed MNL models of discrete response, *J. Appl. Econometr.*, 15, pp. 447–470.

505. McFadden D. (1989). A method of simulated moments for estimation of discrete choice models without numerical integration. *Econometrica* 57, pp. 995–1026.

506. McKee J., J. Lorkowski, and T. Ngamsantivong (2014) Note on Fair Price under Interval Uncertainty. *Journal of Uncertain Systems*, 8(3), pp.186–189.

507. Medina J, Ojeda-Aciego M. (2010) Multi-adjoint t-concept lattices, *Inform. Sciences*, 180, pp. 712–725.

508. Meghdadi A. H., Akbarzadeh-T M.-R. (2001). Probabilistic fuzzy logic and probabilistic fuzzy systems. *The 10th IEEE INT CONF FUZZY*, Melbourne, pp. 1127–1130.

509. Melin P., Castillo O. (2013). A review on the applications of type-2 fuzzy logic in classification and pattern recognition, *Expert Syst. Appl.,* 40(13), pp. 5413–5423.

510. Melin, P. (2012). *Modular Neural Networks and Type-2 Fuzzy Systems for Pattern Recognition.* (Springer, Berlin).

511. Mendel, J.M., Zadeh, L.A., Yager, R.R., Lawry, J., Hagras, H. & Guadarrama, S. (2010). What computing with words means to me. *IEEE Comput Intell M*, 5(1), pp. 20–26.

512. Mendel J. M. and D. Wu (2010). *Perceptual Computing: Aiding People in Making Subjective Judgments*, (IEEE Press and Wiley, New York).

513. Mendel J. M. (2001). *Uncertain Rule-Based Fuzzy Logic Systems: Introduction and New Directions*, (Prentice-Hall, Upper Saddle River).

514. Mendel J. (2014). *Type-2 Fuzzy Logic Control: Introduction to Theory and Application.* (New-Jersey: Wiley-IEEE Press).

515. Mendel J.M. (2007). Computing with words and its relationships with fuzzistics. *Inform. Sciences*, 179(8), pp. 988–1006.

516. Mendel J.M. (2009). On answering the question 'Where do I start in order to solve a new problem involving interval type-2 fuzzy sets?'. *Inform. Sciences*, 179, pp. 3418–3431.

517. Mendel J. M. (2007). Type-2 fuzzy sets and systems: an overview. *IEEE Comput Intell M*, vol. 2, pp. 20–29.

518. Mendel, J. M. (2003). Fuzzy Sets for Words: a New Beginning, *Proc. 12th IEEE International Conference on Fuzzy Systems, FUZZ*, pp. 37–42.

519. Mendel, J. M. (2007). Advances in type-2 Fuzzy Sets and Systems. *Inform. Sciences*, 177, pp. 84–110.

520. Mendel, J. M. (2002). An Architecture for Making Judgments Using Computing With Words. *Int. J. Appl. Math. Comput. Sci.*, vol. 12, No. 3, pp. 325–335.

521. Mendel, J. M. and John, R. I. (2002). Type–2 fuzzy sets made simple, *IEEE T. Fuzzy Syst.*, no.2, vol. 10, pp. 117–127.

522. Mendel, J. M., Jhon, R. I. and Liu, F. (2006). Interval type–2 fuzzy logic systems made simple, *IEEE T. Fuzzy Syst.*, no. 6, vol. 14, pp. 808–821.

523. Méndez G.M., Hernandez M. (2009). Hybrid learning for interval type-2 fuzzy logic systems based on orthogonal least-squares and back-propagation methods. *Inform. Sciences*, Volume 179, Issue 13, pp. 2146–2157.

524. Merigó, J.M., Casanovas, M., Liu, P. (2014). Decision making with fuzzy induced heavy ordered weighted averaging operators. *Int. J. Fuz Syst*, 16(3), pp. 277–289.

525. Merigó, J.M., Guillén, M., Sarabia, J.M. (2015). The Ordered Weighted Average in the Variance and the Covariance. *Int. J. Intell. Syst.*, 30(9), pp. 985–1005.

526. Mesarovic M. D., D. Macko, Y. (1973). Takahara Theory of Hierarchical Multilevel Systems. (Moscow, Mir).

527. Michalewicz Z. (1996) *Genetic algorithms + data structures =evolution programs*. (Springer-Verlag, Berlin).

528. Mitrovi Z., Rusov, S. Z .(2006). Similarity Measure Among Fuzzy Sets *FME Transactions* 34, pp. 115–119.

529. Mizumoto M., Zimmermann H.-J. (1982). Comparison of fuzzy reasoning methods. *Fuzzy Set Syst.*, 8, pp. 253–283.

530. Mizumoto M., S. Fukami, K. Tanaka (1979). Some methods of fuzzy reasoning, In: R. Gupta, R. Yager (eds.), *Advances in Fuzzy Set Theory Applications*, (North-Holland, New York).

531. Mizumoto, M. and Tanaka, K. (1979). Some properties of fuzzy numbers, eds. Gupta, M. M., Ragade, R. K., Yager, R. R., *Advances in Fuzzy set theory and applications* (North-Holland Publishing company).

532. Mohamad D., S.A. Ahaharani and N.H. Kamis (2014). A Z-Number-Based Decision Making Procedure with Ranking Fuzzy Numbers Method. *Proceedings of the International Conference on Quantitative Sciences and Its Applications*, pp. 160–166.

533. Mohammad H. A., and Abbasi S. (2008). Ordering comparison of negative binomial random variables with their mixtures, *Stat. Probabil Letters* 78(14) pp. 2234–2239.

534. Molai A. A., Khorram E. (2008). Linear Programming Problem With Interval Coefficients And An Interpretation For Its Constraints. *Iranian Journal Of Science & Technology*, Transaction A, Vol. 31, No. A4, pp. 369–390.

535. Molai A.A., Khorram E. (2008). An algorithm for solving fuzzy relation equations with max-T composition operator. *Inform. Sciences*, 178, pp. 1293–1308.

536. Mondal B., Raha, S. (2011). Similarity-Based Inverse Approximate Reasoning. *IEEE Trans. Fuzzy Syst.*, vol. 19, issue 6, pp. 1058–1071.

537. Montgomery-Smith S. J., Alexander R. Pruss, (2001). A Comparison Inequality for Sums of Independent Random Variables, *Journal of Mathematical Analysis and Applications*, 254(1) 35–42.

538. Moore R.E. (1962). Interval Arithmetic and Automatic Error Analysis in Digital Computing. PhD thesis, Stanford University, USA.

539. Moore, R.E., Kearfott, R.B., Cloud, J.M. (2009). *Introduction to interval analysis*. (SIAM, Philadelphia).

540. Moore, R.E. (1966). Interval analysis. (Prentice Hall, Englewood Cliffs, New Jersey).

541. Mordeson, J. N. and Nair, P. S. (2001). *Fuzzy Mathematics: an Introduction for Engineers and Scientists* (Springer Physica-Verlag, Heidelberg).

542. Munier B. R. (1992). Expected utility versus anticipated utility: Where do we stand? *Fuzzy Set Syst.*, 49, pp. 55–64.

543. Munoz-Hernandez, S., Pablos-Ceruelo, V. and Strass, H. (2011). RFuzzy: Syntax, semantics and implementation details of a simple and expressive fuzzy tool over Prolog, *Inform. Sciences*, 181(10), pp. 1951–1970.

544. Murphy P, Daley J, Dalenberg D. (1988). A contemporary perspective on international port operations. *Transportation Journal*, 28:23–32.

545. Musayev, A. F., Alizadeh, A. V., Guirimov, B. G. and Huseynov, O. H. (2009). Computational framework for the method of decision making with imprecise probabilities, *Proc. 5th Int. Conf. on Soft Comp. and Comp. with Words in Syst. Anal., Decis. and Control*, ICSCCW, pp. 287–290.

546. Nachtegael, M., Sussner, P., Melange, T. and Kerre, E. E. (2011). On the role of complete lattices in mathematical morphology: From tool to uncertainty model, *Inform. Sciences*, 181(10), pp. 1971–1988.

547. Nanda, S. (1991). Fuzzy linear spaces over valued fields, *Fuzzy Set. Syst.*, 42(3), pp. 351–354.

548. Narukawa Y., Murofushi T. (2004). Decision Modeling Using the Choquet Integral, *Lecture Notes in Computer Science*, 3131, pp. 183–193.

549. Nazemzadeh M., Vanelslander T. (2015). The Container Transport System: Selection Criteria and Business Attractiveness for North-European Ports. *Marit Econ Logist*; 17 pp. 221–245.

550. Negoita C. V. and Ralescu D. A. (1975). *Applications of Fuzzy Sets to Systems Analysis*, Wiley (John Wiley & Sons, New York).

551. Neilson, W. and Stowe, J. (2002). A further examination of cumulative prospect theory parameterizations, *The J. Risk Uncertainty*, 24(1), pp. 31–46.

552. Newell A. (1981). The knowledge level, *AI Magazine* 2(2), pp. 1–20.

553. Nguyen H.T. and Walker E.A. (2006). *A First Course in Fuzzy Logic* (Chapman and Hall/CRC, Boca Raton, Florida).

554. Nguyen H. T., Kreinovich V., and Zuo Q. (1997). Interval-valued degrees of belief: applications of interval computations to expert systems and intelligent control. *International Journal of Uncertainty, Fuzziness, and Knowledge Based Systems*, Vol. 5, No. 3, pp. 317–358.

555. Nguyen, H. T. and Walker, E. A. (1996). *A First Course in Fuzzy Logic*, (CRC Press, Boca Raton).

556. Nguyen H.T., Kreinovich V. (1996). Nested intervals and sets: concepts, relations to fuzzy sets, and applications. *Appl Optimizat*, pp. 245–290.

557. Nieto-Morote A., Ruz-Vila, F. (2012). A fuzzy AHP multi-criteria decision-making approach applied to combined cooling, heating, and power production systems. *International Journal of Information Technology & Decision Making* 10(03), pp. 497–517.

558. Nobre F.S., Tobias A.M., and Walker D.S. (2009) The impact of cognitive machines on complex decisions and organizational change. *Artificial Intelligence and Society* 24, pp. 365–381.

559. Noguera C., Esteva F., Godo L. (2010). Generalized continuous and left-continuous t-norms arising from algebraic semantics for fuzzy logics. *Inform. Sciences*, 180, pp. 1354–1372.

560. Oh, K.-W. and Bandler, W. (1987). Properties of fuzzy implication operators, *Int. J. Approx. Reason.*, 1(3), pp. 273–285.

561. O'Hagan A., Caitlin E.B., Daneshkhah A., Eiser, J.R., Garthwaite, P.H., Jenkinson D.J., Oakley J.E., Rakow T. (2006). *Uncertain Judgments: Eliciting Experts' Probabilities* (Wiley).

562. Onwuegbuchunam D.E. (2013). Port selection criteria by shippers in Nigeria: a discrete choice analysis. *Int J Ship Trans Log* 5, pp. 532–550.

563. Opricovic, S. and Tzeng, G. H. (2004). Compromise solution by MCDM methods: a comparative analysis of VIKOR and TOPSIS, *Eur. J. Operat. Res.*, 156(2), pp. 445–455.

564. Opricovic, S. (1998). Multicriteria optimization of civil engineering systems. P.hD Thesis, Faculty of Civil Engineering, Belgrade.

565. Opricovic, S. and Tzeng, G. H. (2007). Extended VIKOR method in comparison with outranking methods, *Eur. J. Operat. Res.*, 178(2), pp. 514–529.

566. Orlovsky S.A. (1978). Decision-making with a fuzzy preference relation. *Fuzzy Set. Syst.* 1, pp. 155–167.

567. Ovchinnikov S., Roubens, M. Salles M. (1992). On fuzzy strict preference, indifference and incomparability relations. *Fuzzy Set. Syst.* 49, pp.15–20.

568. Ovchinnikov, S. (1991). On fuzzy preference relations, *Int. J. Intell. Syst.*, 6, pp. 225–234.

569. Ovchinnikov S. (1991). On modeling fuzzy preference relations. In: *Uncertainty in Knowledge Bases*, B. Bouchon-Meunier, R. Yager, and L. Zadeh (eds.), Lecture Notes in Computer Science Springer-Verlag, 521, pp. 154–164.

570. Ozdamar L., Bozyel M.A., Birbil S.I. (1988). A hierarchical decision support system for production planning (with Case Study). *Euro. J. Oper. Res.* 104, pp. 403–422.

571. Ozkan I., Turksen I.B. (2007). Upper and Lower Values for the Level of Fuzziness in FCM, *Inform. Sciences*, Volume 177, Issue 23, pp. 5143–5152.

572. Paffenbarger Jr. R. S. and Hyde R.T. (1988). Exercise adherence, coronary heart disease and longevity. In *Exercise Adherence: Its Impact on Public Health*, R. K. Dishman, Ed., pp. 41–73, Human Kinetics Books, Champaign, USA.

573. Pal S. K. and D. P. Mandal (1991). Fuzzy Logic and Approximate Reasoning: An Overview. *Journal of the Institution of Electronics and Telecommun. Engineers*, vol. 37, no. 5&6, pp. 548–560.

574. Pal S. K., Banerjee R. (2013). Context granulation and subjective-information quantification. *Theoretical Computer Science* 488, pp. 2–14.

575. Pal S. K., Banerjee R., Dutta S., Sarma S. S. (2013). An Insight into the Z-number Approach to CWW, *Fundamenta Informaticae* 124, pp. 197–229.

576. Pana H., Lia Y., and Cao Y. (2015). Lattice-valued simulations for quantitative transition systems. *Int. J. Approx. Reason*, vol. 56, pp. 28–42.

577. Pancho D.P., Alonso J.M., Cordon O., Quirin A., Magdalena L. (2013). FINGRAMS: Visual Representations of Fuzzy Rule-Based Inference for Expert Analysis of Comprehensibility. *IEEE Trans. Fuzzy Syst.*, vol. 21, issue 6, pp. 1133–1149.

578. Paolo, P. *Cumulative prospect theory and second order stochastic dominance criteria: an application to mutual funds performance*, Working paper. https:// ideas.repec.org/p/vnm/wpaper/157.html.

579. Papoulis, A. and Pillai, S.U. (2002). *Probability, Random Variables and Stochastic Processes, 4th edition*. (McGraw Hill).

580. Papoulis, A. (1965). *Probability, Random Variables, and Stochastic Processes* (McGraw-Hill, New York).

581. Park, J.H., Cho, H.J. & Kwun, Y.C. (2011). Extension of the VIKOR method for group decision making with interval-valued intuitionistic fuzzy information. *Fuzzy Optim. Decis. Ma.*, 10(3), pp. 233–253.

582. Park S., Lee-Kwang H. (2001). A Designing Method for Type-2 Fuzzy Logic Systems Using Genetic Algorithms. *Joint 9th IFSA World Congress and 20th NAFIPS International Conference*, pp. 2567–2572.

583. Park Y.B. (2005). An integrated approach for production and distribution planning in supply chain management. *Int. J. Prod. Res.* 43(6), pp. 1205–1224.

584. Paul J.H.S. (1982). The Expected Utility Model: Its Variants, Purposes, Evidence and Limitations. *Journal of Economic Literature*, Vol. 20, no. 2, pp. 529–563.

585. Pavel S. (2007). Numerical methods for interval and fuzzy number comparison based on the probabilistic approach and Dempster–Shafer theory, *Inform. Sciences*, 177(21) pp. 1645–4661.

586. Pawlak Z. (1982). Rough sets. *Int J Comput Inf Sci*; 11, pp. 341–356.

587. Pedrycz W. (1996). *Fuzzy Modeling: Paradigms and Practice*, Kluwer Academic Publishers, Boston, MA.

588. Pedrycz W, Hirota K. (2007). Fuzzy vector quantization with particle swarm optimization: A study in fuzzy granulation-degranulation information processing. *J Signal Process*, 87 pp. 2061–2074.

589. Pedrycz W. (1997). *Fuzzy Evolutionary Computation*. (Kluwer Academic Publishers).

590. Pedrycz W. and Gomide F. (2007). *Fuzzy Systems Engineering. Toward Human-Centric Computing*. (John Wiley & Sons, Hoboken, New Jersey).

591. Pedrycz W. and Peters J.F. (1998). *Computational Intelligence in Software Engineering. Advances in Fuzzy Systems, Applications and Theory*. (World Scientific, Singapore).

592. Pedrycz W. (1993). *Fuzzy Control and Fuzzy Systems. Second Revised Edition.* (John Willey and Sons, NY).
593. Pedrycz W., Peters J.F. (1998). *Computational Intelligence in Software Engineering. Advances in Fuzzy Systems, Applications and Theory, vol. 16* (World Scientific, Singapore).
594. Pedrycz W. (2015) Concepts and Design Aspects of Granular Models of Type-1 and Type-2. *Int. J. Fuzzy Logic and Intelligent Systems* 15(2), pp. 87–95.
595. Pedrycz, W. and Chen S.-M. (2011). *Granular Computing and Intelligent Systems*, eds. Aliev, R. A., Pedrycz, W., Huseynov, O. H. and Zeinalova, L. M., Chapter 7 "Decision Making with Second Order Information Granules," (Springer-Verlag, Berlin, Heidelberg) pp. 117–153.
596. Pedrycz, W. (2005). *Knowledge based clustering. From Data to Information Granules* (John Wiley & Sons, Hoboken, New Jersey).
597. Pedrycz, W., Skowron, A. and Kreinovich, V. (2008). *Handbook of Granular Computing*, eds. Mendel, J. M., Chapter 25 "On Type–2 Fuzzy Sets as Granular Models for Words," (Wiley, England) pp. 553–574.
598. Pei D. (2014). A survey of fuzzy implication algebras and their axiomatization. *Int. J. Approx. Reason.*, vol. 55, iss. 8, pp. 1643–1658.
599. Pei D. (2008). Unified full implication algorithms of fuzzy reasoning. *Inform. Sciences* 178 pp. 520–530.
600. Pena, J. P-P. and Piggins, A. (2007). Strategy-proof fuzzy aggregation rules, *J. Math. Econ.*, 43, pp. 564–580.
601. Perfilieva I. (2016). Closeness in similarity-based reasoning with an interpolation condition. *Fuzzy Set Syst.*, vol. 292, pp. 333–346.
602. Perfilieva I. (2013). Finitary solvability conditions for systems of fuzzy relation equations. *Inform. Sciences*, 234, pp. 29–43.
603. Perfilieva I. (2004). Fuzzy function as an approximate solution to a system of fuzzy relation equations, *Fuzzy Set. Syst.* 147, pp. 363–383.
604. Perfilieva I. (2011). Fuzzy Function: Theoretical and Practical Point of View. *In Proc. 7th Conf. of the European Society for Fuzzy Logic and Technology (EUSFLAT 2011) and «les rencontres francophones sur la Logique Floue et ses Applications» (LFA 2011)*, Aix-les-Bains, France, 2011, pp. 480–486.
605. Perfilieva I. (2013). Solvability of a system of fuzzy relation equations: Easy to check conditions. *Neural Netw. World* 13, pp. 571–580.
606. Piegat A., Plucinski M. (2015). Computing with words with the use of Inverse RDM Models of Membership Functions. *Applied Mathematics and Computer Science* 25(3), pp. 675–688.
607. Piegat A., Plucinski M. (2015). Fuzzy number addition with the application of horizontal membership functions. The Scientific World Journal, Article ID 367214, vol. 2015, p. 16.
608. Piegat A. (2005). Cardinality approach to fuzzy number arithmetic. *IEEE T. Fuzzy Syst.*, vol. 13, no. 2, pp. 204–215.
609. Piegat A., Tomaszewska K. (2013). Decision-making under uncertainty using Info-Gap Theory and a new multi-dimensional RDM interval arithmetic. *Electr Rev-London*, vol. 89, no. 8, pp. 71–76.
610. Piegat A., Landowski, M. (2014). Correctness-checking of uncertain-equation solutions on example of the interval-modal method. In: *Modern Approaches in Fuzzy Sets, Intuitionistic Fuzzy Sets, Generalized Nets and Related Topics,*

Volume I: Foundations, T. Atanassov, Ed., pp. 159–170, IBS PAN, Warsaw, Poland.

611. Piegat A. (2001). *Fuzzy Modeling and Control* (Physica, New York).
612. Piegat, A., Plucinski M. (2015). Some Advantages of the RDM-arithmetic of Intervally-Precisiated Values. *Int J Comput Int Sys*, 8(6), pp. 1192–1209.
613. Piegat, A., Landowski, M. (2012). Is the conventional interval-arithmetic correct? *Journal of Theoretical and Applied Computer Science*, vol. 6, no. 2, pp. 27–44.
614. Piegat, A., Landowski, M. (2013). Multidimensional approach to interval uncertainty calculations. In: *New Trends in Fuzzy Sets, Intuitionistic: Fuzzy Sets, Generalized Nets and Related Topics, Volume II: Applications*, ed. K.T. Atanassov et al., IBS PAN -SRI PAS, Warsaw, Poland, pp. 137–151.
615. Piegat, A., Landowski, M. (2013). Two Interpretations of Multidimensional RDM Interval Arithmetic-Multiplication and Division. *Int J Fuzzy Syst*, vol. 15 no. 4, pp. 488–496.
616. Piegat, A. (2005). On practical problems with the explanation of the difference between possibility and probability. *Control and Cybern*, 34(2), pp. 505–524.
617. Pilarek M. (2010). Solving systems of linear interval equations using the "interval extended zero" method and multimedia extensions. *Scientific Research of the Institute of Mathematics and Computer Science*, vol. 9, iss. 2, pp. 203–212.
618. Pilates J. and Robbins J. (2012). *Pilates' Return to Life Through Contrology.Revised Edition for the 21st Century*, (Originally published by Joseph Pilates in 1945) (Presentation Dynamics).
619. Poincare H. (1905). *Science and Hypothesis* (Walter Scott Publishing, London).
620. Ponsard C. (1982). Producers spatial equilibria with fuzzy constraints. *Eur J Oper Res* 10, pp. 302–313.
621. Price K.V., Storm R.M., Lampinen J.A. (2005). *Differential evolution – a practical approach to global optimization*. (Springer Science+Business Media, New York)
622. Quiggin, J. (1982). A theory of anticipated utility, *J. Econ. Behav. Organ.*, 3, pp. 323–343.
623. Ralescu A., Ralescu D. (1984). Probability and Fuzziness. *Inform. Sciences* 34, pp. 85–92.
624. R.Y.K. Fung, Tang J., Wang D. (2003). Multiproduct aggregate production planning with fuzzy demand and fuzzy capacities, *IEEE Trans.Syst. Man Cyb. Part A: Syst. Hum.* 33 (3), pp. 663–663.
625. Raiffa H., *Decision Analysis*, McGraw-Hill, Columbus, Ohio, 1997.
626. Ramik, J. (2005). Duality in fuzzy linear programming: some new concepts and results, *Fuzzy Optim.Decis.Ma.*, 4, pp. 25–39.
627. Rao, A. S. and Georgeff, M. P. (2010). Trader species with different decision strategies and price dynamics in financial markets: an agent-based modeling perspective, *Int. J. Inf. Tech. Decis.*, 9(2), pp. 327–344.
628. Rao C., Peng, J. (2009). Fuzzy group decision making model based on credibility theory and gray relative degree. *Int. J. Inf. Tech. Decis* 8(3) pp. 515–527.
629. Rasmani, K.A. & Shahari, N.A. (2007). Job Satisfaction Evaluation Using Fuzzy Approach. *In Proc. of Third International Conference on Natural Computation*, Hainan, China, pp. 544–548.
630. Rescher, N. (1969). *Many-Valued Logic*. (McGraw-Hill, New York).
631. Riera, J. V. and Torrens, J. (2013). Residual implications on the set of discrete fuzzy numbers, *Inform. Sciences*, 247, pp. 131–143.

632. Riera, J.V., & Torrens, J. (2011). Fuzzy implications defined on the set of discrete fuzzy numbers. *Proc. EUSFLAT-LFA*, pp. 259–266.

633. Rinks D.B. (1982). The performance of fuzzy algorithm models for aggregate planning and differing cost structures. In: M.M. Gupta, E. Sanchez (Eds.), *Approximate Reasoning in Decision Analysis*, North Holland, The Netherlands, pp. 267–278.

634. Roberts H. (1963). Risk, Ambiguity and the Savage Axioms: Comment. *Q J Econ*, v. 77, pp. 327–336.

635. Rodenroth K. (2010). *A study of the relationship between physical fitness and academic performance [Partial fulfillment of the requirements for the degree doctor of education*, Liberty University.

636. Roger, M. (1991). *Cooke Experts in Uncertainty: Opinion and Subjective Probability in Science* (Oxford University Press, New York).

637. Rohatgi V.K. (1976). An Introduction to Probability Theory Mathematical Statistics. (*John Wiley & Sons, New York*).

638. Romer D. (2006). *Advanced Macroeconomics. Third Edition* (McGraw-Hill/Irvin, New York).

639. Rommelfanger H. (2007). A general concept for solving linear multicriteria programming problems with crisp, fuzzy or stochastic values. *Fuzzy Set Syst*, 158, pp. 1892–1904.

640. Rosenschein S.J. (1985). Formal theories of knowledge in AI and robotics, *New Generation Computing* 3(4) pp. 345–357.

641. Rowe G., Wright G. (1999). The Delphi technique as a forecasting tool: Issues and analysis, *Int J Forecasting*, 15, pp. 353–375.

642. Roy, B. (1996). *Multicriteria Methodology for Decision Aiding.* (Kluwer Academic Publishers, Dordrecht).

643. Roy, B. and Berlier, B. (1972). La Metode ELECTRE II. Sixieme Conf. Internationale de rechearche operationelle.

644. Roy B. (1978). ELECTRE III: Unalgorithme de classements fon désurune représentationfloue des préférences en présence de criteres multiples. *Cahiers du CERO*, 20, pp. 3–24.

645. Ruan, Da. (2010). *Computational Intelligence in Complex Decision Systems*, (Atlantis Press, World Scientific, Amsterdam-Paris).

646. Ruan D., M. Fedrizzi, J. Kacprzyk (eds.) (2001). *Soft Computing for Risk Evaluation and Management: Applications in Technology, Environment and Finance,* (Springer-Verlag), (31).

647. Ruoning X. (1991). A linear regression model in fuzzy environment, *Adv Modeling Simul* 27, pp. 31–40.

648. Ruoning X. (1997). S-curve regression model in fuzzy environment, *Fuzzy Sets Syst*, 90, pp. 317–326.

649. Rutkowski, L. and Cpalka, K. (2003). Flexible neuro-fuzzy systems, *IEEE T. Neural Networ.*, 14(3), pp. 554–573.

650. Scott F., Ginzburg L., Kreinovich V., Longpre L. and Aviles M. (2002). Computing Variance for Interval Data is NP-Hard, *ACM SIGACT News*, 33(2) pp. 108–118.

651. Scott F., Ginzburg L., Kreinovich V., Longpre L. and Aviles M. (2005). Exact Bounds on Finite Populations of Interval Data, *Reliable Computing*, 11(3) pp. 207–233.

652. Scott F., Kreinovich V., Hajagos J., Oberkampf W. and Ginzburg L. (2007). Experimental Uncertainty Estimation and Statistics for Data Having Interval Uncertainty, *Sandia National Laboratories, Report SAND* 2007–0939.

653. Semyon R. (2005). *Measurement Errors and Uncertainties: Theory and Practice*, (Springer Verlag, USA).

654. Saastamoinen K., Könönen V. and Luukka P. (2002). A classifier based on the fuzzy similarity in the Lukasiewicz structure with different metrics, *Proc. of IEEE International Conference on Fuzzy Systems*, FUZZ-IEEE'02: 363–367.

655. Saaty T.L. (2001). Analytic network process. In Encyclopedia of Operations Research and Management Science Springer US 117: pp. 28–35.

656. Saaty T.L. (1990). How to make a decision: the analytic hierarchy process. *Eur J Oper Res*, 48: pp. 9–26.

657. Sadeghian, A., Mendel, J. M. and Tahayori, H. (2013). *Advances in Type–2 Fuzzy Sets and Systems. Theory and Applications*. (Springer, New York).

658. Saha S., Bandyopadhyay S. (2009). A new point symmetry based fuzzy genetic clustering technique for automatic evolution of clusters, *Information Sciences*, Vol. 179, Issue 19, pp. 3230–3246.

659. Salari M., Bagherpour M. and Wang J. (2014). A novel earned value management model using Z-number, *International Journal of Applied Decision Sciences* 7(1) 97–119.

660. Salmon P. (2001). "Effects of physical exercise on anxiety, depression, and sensitivity to stress: a unifying theory," *Clinical Psychology Review*, 21(1), pp. 33–61.

661. Sánchez A.M, Lozano M, Villar P, Herrera F. (2009). Hybrid crossover operators with multiple descendents for real-coded genetic algorithms: Combining neighborhood-based crossover operators. *Int J Intell Syst*, 24, pp.540–567.

662. Sanna L.J., Chang E.C. (2003). The Past Is Not What It Used To Be: Optimists' Use of Retroactive Pessimism to Diminish the Setting of Failure, *Journal of Research in Personality*, 37(5) pp. 388–404.

663. Sarmiento A.M., Nagi R. (1999). A review of integrated analysis of production-distributed systems, *IIE Trans.*, 31, pp. 1061–1074.

664. Savage, L. J. (1954). *The Foundations of Statistics*, (Wiley, New York).

665. Savic D.A., Pedrycz W. (1991). Evaluation of fuzzy linear regression models, Fuzzy Sets Syst 39, pp. 51–63.

666. Scheier M.F., Carver C.S. (1985). Optimism, Coping and Health: Assessment and Implications of Generalized Outcome Expectancies, *Health Psychology*, 4(3) pp. 219–247.

667. Scheier M.F., Matthews K.A., Owens J.F., Magovern G.J., Lefebvre R.C., Abbott R.A., Carver C.S. (1989). Dispositional Optimism and Recovery from Coronary Artery Bypass Surgery: The Beneficial Effects on Physical and Psychological Well-Being, *Journal of Personality and Social Psychology*, 57(6) pp.1024–1040.

668. Schmeidler, D. (1986). Integral representation without additivity, *P. Am. Math. Soc.*, 97(2), pp. 255–261.

669. Schmeidler, D. (1989). Subjective probability and expected utility without additivity, *Econometrita*, 57(3), pp. 571–587.

670. Schneeweiss H. (1974). Probability and Utility – Dual Concepts in Decision Theory. In: G.Menges (ed.). *Information, Inference and Decision*. Dordrecht: *D.Reidel*, pp. 113–144.

671. Schoemaker P.J.H. (1980). Experiments on Decisions Under Risk: The Expected Utility Theorem, Boston: Martinus Nijhoff Publishing.
672. Schott B, Whalen T. (1994). "Fuzzy Uncertainty in Imperfect Competition". *Information Sci,* 76, pp. 339–654.
673. Schwartz D.G. (2009). A Logic for Qualified Syllogisms. *Advanced Techniques in Computing Sciences and Software Engineering,* pp.45–50.
674. Schweizer B. (1985). Distribution functions: Numbers of the future, In: A. Di Nola, A.G.S. Ventre (eds.), La Matematica dei Sistemi Fuzzy Inst: di Matematica del la Facoltà di Architettura (Universitàdegli Studi di Napoli, Italy,) pp.137–149.
675. Segal, U. (1987). The Ellsberg paradox and risk aversion: An anticipated utility approach, *Int. Econ. Rev.*, 28, pp. 175–202.
676. Seising, R. and González, V.S. (2012) *Soft Computing in Humanities and Social Sciences.* Stud.Fuzz. Soft Comp. (Springer-Verlag, Berlin, Heidelberg), 273, p. 519.
677. Seki H., Mizumoto M. (2011). "On the Equivalence Conditions of Fuzzy Inference Methods—Part 1: Basic Concept and Definition," *IEEE Trans. Fuzzy Syst.*, 19(6), pp. 1097–1106.
678. Seo, K. (2009) Ambiguity and second-order belief, Econometrica, 77(5), pp. 1575–1605.
679. Serruier M., Dubois D., Prade H., Sudkamp T. (2007). Learning fuzzy rules with their implication operator, *Data & Knowledge Engineering,* 60, pp. 71–89.
680. Sethi S. P., Thompson G. L. (2000). *Optimal Control Theory. Applications to Management Science and Economics,* Second Edition, Springer (New York), p. 504.
681. Setnes M. (1997). Compatibility-Based Ranking of Fuzzy numbers, *Annual Meeting of the North American Fuzzy Information Proc. Society,* (NAFIPS '97), pp. 305–310.
682. Sevastianov P. (2007). Numerical methods for interval and fuzzy number comparison based on the probabilistic approach and Dempster–Shafer theory, *Information Sciences*, 177(21), pp. 4645–4661.
683. Sevastjanov P., Dymova L., Bartosiewicz P. (2012). A framework for rule-base evidential reasoning in the interval settings applied to diagnosing type 2 diabets, *Expert Systems with Applications,* 39, 4190.
684. Shackle G.L. (1961). *Decision, order and Time in Human Affairs.* Cambridge University Press (New York and Cambridge, U.K.).
685. Shafer, G. A. (1976). *Mathematical Theory of Evidence.* (Princeton University Press, New Jersey).
686. Sheen J.N. (2005). Fuzzy financial profitability analyses of demand side management alternatives from participant perspective, *Inform. Sci.*, 169(3–4), pp.329–364.
687. Shieh, B.-S. (2008). Infinite fuzzy relation equations with continuous t-norms, *Inform. Sciences,* 178, pp. 1961–1967.
688. Shoham Y., and S. B. Cousins, (1994). Logics of mental attitudes in AI: a very preliminary survey, In G. Lakemeyer & B. Nebel (Eds.), *Foundations of knowledge representation and reasoning* (Springer Verlag,), pp. 296–309.
689. Silberberg E., Suen W. (2001). *"The Structure of Economics. A Mathematical Analysis".* Third Edition, Irwin McGraw-Hill, (New York), p. 668.

690. Silva C.W. (1995). *Intelligent Control*. Florida: CRC Press.
691. Simon, H. (1997). *Models of Bounded Rationality: Empirically Grounded Economic Reason* (MIT Press, MA, Cambridge).
692. Simpson N.C., Vakharia A.J. (1999). Integrated production/distribution planning in supply chains: an invited review, *Euro. J. Oper. Res.,* 115, pp. 219–236.
693. Small, K. A. and Rosen, H. S. (1981). Applied welfare economics with discrete choice models, *Econometrica*, vol. 49, no. 1, pp. 105–130.
694. Smith V. (1969). Measuring Nonmonetary Utilities in Uncertain choices: the Ellsberg Urn, *Quarterly Journal of Economics,* 83, pp. 324–329.
695. Spector P.E. *Job satisfaction: Application, assessment, causes, and consequences*. (London: Sage, 1997).
696. Springer M. D. (1979). *The Algebra of Random Variables*. (John Wiley and Sons Inc, New York).
697. Sridevi B., R. Nadarajan, Fuzzy Similarity Measure for Generalized Fuzzy Numbers, *International Journal of Open Problems in Computer Science and Mathematics* 2 (2009) 240–253.
698. Starmer C. (2000). Developments in non-expected utility theory: The hunt for a descriptive theory of choice under risk, *Journal of Economic Literature* 38 pp. 332–382.
699. Stefanini L. (2010). A generalization of Hukuhara difference and division for interval and fuzzy arithmetic, *Fuzzy Set. Syst.,* 161(11), pp. 1564–1584.
700. Stigler G. (1965). *Essays in the History of Economics*. (University of Chicago Press).
701. Stojaković M. (2011). Imprecise set and fuzzy valued probability, *J. Comput. Appl. Math.*, 235(16), pp. 4524–4531.
702. Stoll R. R. (1979). *Set Theory and Logic*. (Dover Publications, New York, Dover edition).
703. Su Z.-X. (2011). A hybrid fuzzy approach to fuzzy multi-attribute group decision-making. *International Journal of Information Technology and Decision Making,* 10(4), 695–712.
704. Sugeno M. (1988). *Fuzzy Control,* (North-Holland).
705. Sugeno, M. (1974). *Theory of fuzzy integrals and its application,* Doctoral thesis, (Tokyo Institute of Technology).
706. Szmidt E. (2014). Distances and similarities in intuitionistic fuzzy sets, Springer.
707. T. H. Cormen, C. E. Leiserson R. L. (2009). Rivest, and C. *Stein, Introduction to Algorithms*, (MIT Press, Cambridge, Massachusetts).
708. Tadayon, S. and Tadayon, B. (2012). Approximate Z-number evaluation based on categorical sets of probability distributions, *Proc. 2nd World Conf. on Soft Computing*, WConSC.
709. Takagi T. and Sugeno M. (1985). "Fuzzy identification of systems and its applications to modeling and control," *IEEE Transactions on Systems, Man and Cybernetics*, 15(1), pp. 116–132.
710. Takahagi E. (2008). A fuzzy measure identification method by diamond pairwise comparisons and φ_s transformation, *Journal of Fuzzy Optimization and Decision Making*, 7(3), pp. 219–232.
711. Talasova, J. and Pavlacka, O. (2006), Fuzzy probability spaces and their applications in decision making, *Aujstat*, 35(2 and 3), pp. 347–356.
712. Tanaka, H. and Asai, K. (1984). Fuzzy linear programming with fuzzy numbers, *Fuzzy Set. Syst.*; 13, pp.1–10.

713. Tanaka H, Hayashi I, Watada J. (1989). Possibilistic linear regression analysis for fuzzy data, *European J Operations Res* 40: pp. 389–396.

714. Tanaka H., Ishibuchi H. (1992). Possibilistic regression analysisbased on linear programming, In: Kacprzyk J, Fedrizzi M (eds), Fuzzy Regression Analysis, (Omnitech Press, Warsaw, and Physica, Heidelberg), pp. 47–60.

715. Tanaka H., Uejima S, Asai K. (1982). Linear regression analysis with fuzzy modeling, *IEEE Transactions on Systems, Man, and Cybernetics* 12: pp. 903–907.

716. Tang Y., X. Yang, (2013) Symmetric implicational method of fuzzy reasoning, International Journal of Approximate Reasoning, 54(8), pp. 1034–1048.

717. Teraji Sh. (2008). Culture, effort variability, and hierarchy, *Journal of Socio-Economics*, 37(1), pp. 157–166.

718. Thimme J., Völkert C. (2015). High order smooth ambiguity preferences and asset prices, *Review of Financial Economics*, 27, pp. 1–15.

719. Tiwari P, Itoh H, Shippers' DM. (2003). Port and Carrier Selection Behaviour in China: A Discrete Choice Analysis. *Marit Econ Logist*, 5, pp. 23–39.

720. Tomas D.J., Griffn P.N. (1996). Coordinated supply chain management, *Euro. J. Oper. Res.*, 94, pp. 1–15.

721. Tomporowski P. D., Davis C. L., Miller P. H., and Naglieri J. A (2008). "Exercise and children's intelligence, cognition, and academic achievement," *Educational Psychology Review*, 20(2), pp. 111–131.

722. Tong H., Zhang S. A. (2006). Fuzzy Multi-attribute Decision Making Algorithm for Web Services Selection Based on QoS. *IEEE Asia-Pacific Conference on Services Computing*, pp. 51–57.

723. Tong R.M. (1976). Analysis of fuzzy control algorithms using the relation matrix, *Internat J. Man–Machine Stud.* 8, pp. 679–686.

724. Tong, S. (1994). Interval number and fuzzy number linear programming, *Fuzzy Sets Syst.*, 66, 301.

725. Tongzon J. (2007). Port choice in a competitive environment: from the shipping lines' perspective. *Appl Econ*; 39, pp. 477–492.

726. Touazi F., Cayrol C. and Dubois D. (2015). "Possibilistic reasoning with partially ordered beliefs," *Journal of Applied Logic*, 13(4), pp. 770–798.

727. Trillas E., Moraga, C., Guadarrama S., Cubillo S., and Casticeira E. (2007). Computing with Antonyms, eds. Nikravesh M., Kacprzyk J., Zadeh, L. A., *"Forging New Frontiers: Fuzzy Pioneers I, Studies in Fuzziness and Soft Computing,"*(Springer-Verlag, Berlin Heidelberg), pp. 133–153.

728. Tsuji, T., Jazidie, A. and Kaneko, M. (1997). Distributed trajectory generation for cooperative multi-arm robots via virtual force interactions, *IEEE T. Syst. Man. CY. B.: Cybernetics*, 27(5), pp. 862–867.

729. Turban E., *Decision support and expert systems: management support systems.* (Prentice Hall PTR, 1990).

730. Türkşen I.B. (1994). Non-specificity and interval valued fuzzy sets, *Fuzzy Set. Syst.* (Invited Special Issue).

731. Turnovsky, S. (1995). Methods of Macroeconomiç Dynamics, Cambridge, The MIT Press.

732. Tversky, A. and Kahneman, D. (1992). Advances in Prospect theory: Cumulative Representation of Uncertainty, *J. Risk Uncertainty,* 5(4), pp. 297–323.

733. Tversky, A., Kahneman, D. (1986). Rational Choice and the Framing of Decisions. *The Journal of Business*, 59(4), pp. S251-S278.

734. Tversky, A., Kahneman, D. (1991). Loss Aversion in Riskless Choice: A Reference-Dependent Model, *The Q J Econ*, 106(4), pp. 1039–1061.

735. Tzafestas S.G., Chen C.S., Fokuda T., Harashima F., Schmidt G., Sinha N.K., Tabak D., Valavanis K. (Eds.) (2006). Fuzzy logic applications in engineering science, *in: Microprocessor based and Intelligent Systems Engineering*, (Springer, Netherlands), 29, pp. 11–30.

736. Uebele V., Abe S., and Lan M. (1995). *A neural-network based fuzzy classifier*, IEEE Transactions on Systems, Man, and Cybernetics, 23(3), pp. 353–361.

737. Ufuk Cebeci, Da Ruan. (2007). A multi-attribute comparison of Turkish quality consultants by fuzzy AHP, *International Journal of Information Technology & Decision Making*, 06(01), pp. 191–207.

738. Ungaro A. (2002). *Pilates: Body inMotion*, Dorling Kindersley Publishing, (London, UK).

739. Utkin L.E. (2005). Imprecise second-order hierarchical uncertainty model. *International Journal of Uncertainty, Fuzziness and Knowledge-Based Systems*, 13(2), pp. 177–193.

740. Utkin, L. V. (2007). Risk Analysis and Decision Making under Incomplete Information (Nauka, St. Petersburg, (in Russian).

741. Utkin, L.V. and Augustin, T. (2003). Decision making with imprecise second-order probabilities, in: Bernard, J.M., Seidenfeld, T., Zaffalon, M. (Eds.), *ISIPTA'03, Proc. 3rd Int. Symposium on Imprecise Probabilities and Their Applications, Lugano, Switzerland, Carleton Scien.*, Waterloo, pp. 545–559.

742. Vladik, K., Xiang, G., Starks, S. A., Longpre, L., Ceberio, M., Araiza, R., Beck, J., Kandathi, R., Nayak, A.,Torres, R. and Hajagos, J. (2006). Towards combining probabilistic and interval uncertainty in engineering calculations: algorithms for computing statistics under interval uncertainty, and their computational complexity, *Reliable Computing*, 12(6), pp. 471–501.

743. Vladik, K., Longpr'e, L., Starks, S. A., Xiang, G., Beck, J., Kandathi, R., Nayak, A., Ferson, S. and Hajagos, J. (2007). Interval versions of statistical techniques, with applications to environmental analysis, bioinformatics, and privacy in statistical databases, *J. Comput. Applied Math.*, 199(2), pp. 418--423.

744. Vahdani, B. and Zandieh, M. (2010). Selecting suppliers using a new fuzzy multiple criteria decision model: the fuzzy balancing and ranking method, *Int. J. Prod. Res.*, 48(18), pp. 5307–5326.

745. Van-Nam H., Nakamori, Y., Lawry, J. A. (2008). Probability-Based Approach to Comparison of Fuzzy Numbers and Applications to Target-Oriented Decision Making, *IEEE Transactions on Fuzzy Systems*, 16(2), pp. 371–387.

746. Venkatasubbaiah, K., Narayana Rao K. and Malleswara Rao M. (2014). Evaluation of performance of container terminals through DEMATEL-AHP. *Intern. J.Quality Res.*, 8, pp. 533–542.

747. Vetterlein T., Zamansky, A. (2016). Reasoning with graded information: The case of diagnostic rating scales in healthcare, *Fuzzy Set Syst.*, 298, pp. 207–221.

748. Vidal C.J. and Goetschalckx, M. (1998). Strategic production-distribution models: a critical review with emphasis on global supply chain models, *Euro. J. Oper. Res.* 98, pp. 1–18.

749. von Neumann, J. and Morgenstern, O. (1944). Theory of Games and Economic Behaviour (Princeton University Press, USA).

750. Voxman, W. (2001). Canonical representations of discrete fuzzy numbers, *Fuzzy Set. Syst.* 54, pp. 457–466.

751. Wakker P. (1989). Continuous subjective expected utility with non-additive probabilities, Journal of Mathematical Economics, 18, pp. 1–27.

752. Wakker, P. P., and Zank, H. (1999). State dependent expected utility for Savage's state space, *Math. Oper. Res.*, 24(1), pp. 8–34.

753. Wald, A. (1950). Basic ideas of a general theory of statistical decision rules. Proceedings of the *Int.Cong. Math.*, vol. 1.

754. Walley, P. and De Cooman, G. (2001). A behavioral model for linguistic uncertainty, *Inform. Sciences*, 134(1–4), pp. 1–37.

755. Walley, P. (1996). Measures of uncertainty in expert systems, *Artif. Intell.*, 83(1) pp. 1–58.

756. Walley, P. (1991). Statistical Reasoning with Imprecise Probabilities (Chapman and Hall, London).

757. Wan, S.-P. and Dong, J.-Y. (2015). Power geometric operators of trapezoidal intuitionistic fuzzy numbers and application to multi-attribute group decision making, *Appl. Soft. Comput.*, 29, pp.153–168.

758. Wang, Y. M. and Elhag, T. M. S. (2006). Fuzzy TOPSIS method based on alpha level sets with an application to bridge risk assessment, *Expert Syst. Appl.*, 31(2), pp. 309–319.

759. Wang, C.H., Cheng, C.S. and Lee, T.T. (2004). Dynamical Optimal Training for Interval Type-2 Fuzzy Neural Network (T2FNN), *IEEE Trans. Syst. Man.Cyb.* B,34(3), pp.1462–1477.

760. Wang,D. and Fang, S.-C. (1997). A genetics-based approach or aggregate production planning in fuzzy environment, *IEEE Trans. Syst. Man.Cyb.* A, 27, pp. 636–645.

761. Wang, G., Wu, C. and Zhao, C. (2005). Representation and Operations of discrete fuzzy numbers, *Southeast Asian Bulletin of Math.*, 28, pp. 1003–1010.

762. Wang, G. and Li, X. (1999) On the convergence of the fuzzy valued functional defined by μ-integrable fuzzy valued functions, *Fuzzy Set. Syst.*, 107(2), pp. 219–226.

763. Wang, J., Peng, L., Zhang, H. and Chen, X. (2014). Method of multi-criteria group decision-making based on cloud aggregation operators with linguistic information, *Inform. Scien.*, 274, pp. 177–191.

764. Wang, L., Zhang, L., Itoh, H. and Seki, H. (1994). A fuzzy regression method based on genetic algorithm, In: Proc 3rd Int Conf on Fuzzy Logic, Neural Nets and Soft Computing, Iizuka, pp. 471–472.

765. Wang,M.-L., Wang, H.-F. and Lin, C.-L. (2005). Ranking fuzzy number based on lexicographic screening procedure. *Int. J.Inf. Technol. Decision Making*, 04(04), pp. 663–678 .

766. Wang, Q., Su, Z.-G., Rezaee, B. and Wang, P.-H. (2015). Constructing T–S fuzzy model from imprecise and uncertain knowledge represented as fuzzy belief functions, *Neurocomputing*, 166, pp. 319–336.

767. Wang, Y.J., Zhang, J.S. and Zhang, G.Y. (2007). A dynamic clustering based differential evolution algorithm for global optimization. *Eur J Oper Res*, pp. 56–73.

768. Wang, Z. and Wang, W. (1995). Extension of lower probabilities and coherence of belief measures, *Lect. Notes Comput. Sc.,* 945, pp. 62–69.
769. Wang, J.H. and Hao, J. (2009). An approach to aggregation of ordinal information in multi-criteria multi-person decision making using Choquet integral of Fubini type, *Fuzzy Optimization and Decision Making,* 8, pp. 365–380.
770. Wang, T. (2003). A class of multi-prior preferences, Discussion paper, Mimeo, University British Columbia. http://citeseerx.ist.psu.edu/viewdoc/summary?doi=10.1.1.201.6745.
771. Weirich, P. (2004) Realistic Decision Theory: Rules for Nonideal Agents in Nonideal Circumstances, (Oxford University Press, New York).
772. Weiss, D.J., Dawis, R. V., England, G.W. and Lofquist L. H. (1967). Manual for the Minnesota Satisfaction Questionnaire. 22.
773. Wenstøp, F. (1980). Quantitative analysis with linguistic values, Fuzzy Set. Syst., 4(2), pp. 99–115.
774. Whalen, T. and Usuality, S.B. (1992). Regularity, and fuzzy set logic. *Int.J. Approx. Reason.,* 64, pp.81–504.
775. Whinston, A. (1997). Intelligent agents as a basis for decision support systems, *Decis. Support. Syst.,* 20(1), pp. 1–2.
776. Wilde, P. D. (2004). Fuzzy Utility and Equilibria. *IEEE Trans. Syst. Man.Cyb. B Cyb,*34(4), pp.1774–1785.
777. Wilke, G. (2009). Approximate geometric reasoning with extended geographic objects, Proc. of the Workshop on Quality, *Scale and Analysis Aspects of City Models* (Lund, Sweden).
778. Wilke, G. and Frank, A.U. (2010). Tolerance Geometry – Euclid's First Postulate for Points and Lines with Extension. *18th ACM SIGSPATIAL International Symposium on Advances in Geographic Inform. Systems,* (San Jose, CA, USA, Proceedings).
779. Wilke, G. (2015). Equality in approximate tolerance geometry. In Intelligent Systems' 2014. (Springer International Publishing). pp. 365–376.
780. Wilke, G. (2015). Granular Geometry. In Towards the Future of Fuzzy Logic. (Springer International Publishing). pp. 79–115.
781. Wilke, G. (2012). Towards approximate tolerance geometry for gis – a framework for formalizing sound geometric reasoning under positional tolerance. Ph.D. dissertation, (Vienna University of Technology).
782. Williamson, R. C. and Downs, T. (1990). Probabilistic arithmetic. I. Numerical methods for calculating convolutions and dependency bounds, *Int. J. Approx. Reason,* 4(2), pp. 89–158.
783. Williamson R. C. (1989). Probabilistic Arithmetic. Ph.D. dissertation, University of Queensland, Australia, https://www.ime.usp.br/~jstern/miscellanea/General/Williamson87.pdf.
784. Willmott, R. (1978). Two fuzzier implication operators in the theory of fuzzy power sets, *In: Fuzzy Research Project.*
785. Wilson, A.(2004). Bounded memory and biases in information processing, *NAJ Economics,* 5.
786. Wise, B.P. and Henrion, M. (1985). A framework for comparing uncertain inference systems to probability, *Proc. 1st Annual Conf. on Uncertainty in Artificial Intelligence,* UAI, pp. 69–83.
787. Wu, K. (1996). Fuzzy interval control of mobile robots, *Comput. Elect. Eng.,* 22, pp.211–229.

788. Wu, Z.Q., Masaharu, M. and Shi, Y. (1996). An improvement to Kóczy and Hirota's interpolative reasoning in sparse fuzzy rule bases, *Int. J.Approx. Reason.*, 15(3), pp. 185–201.

789. Wu, Z.Q., Masaharu, M., Shi, Y., Kóczy, L.T. and Hirota, K. (1993). Approximate reasoning by linear rule interpolation and general approximation, *Int. J.Approx. Reason.*, 9(3), pp.197–225.

790. Wu, G. and Markle, A. B. (2008). An empirical test of gain-loss separability in prospect theory, *Manage. Sci.*, vol. 54, no. 7, pp. 1322–1335.

791. Xie, A. and Qin, F. (2010). Solutions to the functional equation $I(x, y) = I(x, I(x, y))$ for a continuous D-operation, *Inform. Sciences*, 180, 2487–2497.

792. Xu, Y., Liu, J., Ruan, D. and Li, X. (2010). Determination of [alpha]-resolution in lattice-valued first-order logic LF(X), *Inform. Sciences,*181(10), pp. 1836–1862.

793. Xu, Z. and Cai, X. (2010). Recent advances in intuitionistic fuzzy information aggregation. *Fuzzy Optimization and Decision Making*, 9(4), pp. 359–381.

794. Xu, Z. (2006). Induced uncertain linguistic OWA operators applied to group decision making, *Inform. Fusion*, 7(2), pp. 231–238.

795. Xue W. and X. Zhi, (2014). Optimistic and pessimistic decision making based on interval-valued intuitionistic fuzzy soft sets, *Computer Modelling & New Technologies*, 18(12C), pp. 1284–1290.

796. Yanfeng, O., Y., Wang, Z. and Zhang, H. (2010). On fuzzy rough sets based on tolerance relations, *Inform. Sciences*, 180, pp. 532.

797. Yabuchi, Y. Watada J. and Tatsumi K. (1994). Fuzzy regression analysis of data with error, *Jpn J Fuzzy Theory and Systems 6*: pp. 673–685.

798. Yager, R. R. (1991). Deductive approximate reasoning systems, *IEEE Trans. Knowl. Data Eng.*, 3(4), pp. 399–414.

799. Yager, R. R. (2010). A framework for reasoning with soft information, *Inform. Sciences*, vol. 180, Issue 8, pp. 1390–1406.

800. Yager, R. R. (1999). On global requirements for implication operators in fuzzy modus ponens, *Fuzzy Set. Syst.*, 106, pp. 3–10.

801. Yager, R. (1980). Fuzzy subsets of type II in decisions, *J.Cybern*, 10, pp. 137–159.

802. Yager, R. R. (2012). On Z-valuations using Zadeh's Z-numbers, *Int. J. Intell. Syst.*, 27, pp. 259–278.

803. Yager, R. R. (2012). On a view of Zadeh's Z-numbers, *J. Adv. Comput. Intell. Informat.*, 299, pp. 90–101.

804. Yager, R.R. (1994). On theory of approximate reasoning, Controle Automacao, 4, pp. 116–125.

805. Yager, R.R., (2001). A general approach to uncertainty representation using fuzzy measures. *In Proceedings of the 40th Int. Florida Artificial Intelligence Research Society Conference (FLAIRS-01):* pp. 619–623.

806. Yager, R. R. (1999). Decision making with fuzzy probability assessments, *IEEE T. Fuzzy Syst.*, vol.7, no.4, pp. 462–467.

807. Yager, R.R. (1992). Fuzzy sets and approximate reasoning in decision and control, *IEEE Int Conf Fuzzy*, pp. 415–428.

808. Yager, R.R. and Kreinovich, V. (1999). Decision Making Under Interval Probabilities. *Int J Approx Reason*, 22, pp. 195–215.

809. Yager, R.R. (1986). On Implementing Usual Values. UAI '86: *Proceedings of the Second Annual Conference on Uncertainty in Artificial Intelligence*, (Philadelphia: University of Pennsylvania).

810. Yager, R.R. (1998). On measures of specificity, *Proc. Computational Intelligence: Soft Computing and Fuzzy-Neuro Integration with Applications*, pp. 94–113.

811. Yager, R.R. and Alajlan N. (2015). On the consistency of fuzzy measures in multi-criteria aggregation, *Fuzzy Optimization and Decision Making*, 14(2), pp. 121–137.

812. Yager, R.R. (1988). On ordered weighted averaging aggregation operators in multi-criteria decision making, *IEEE T Syst Man Cyb*, 18, pp. 183–190.

813. Yana, H.B., Huynhb, V.N., Maa, T. and Nakamorib. Y. (2013). Non-additive multi-attribute fuzzy target-oriented decision analysis,. Inform. Sciences,240, pp. 21–44.

814. Yeo, G-T, Kyng, A., Lee P. T.-W. and Yang Z. (2014) Modeling port choice in an uncertain environment. *Marit Policy Manag*, 41, pp. 251–267.

815. Ye, X., Suen, C.and Cheriet, M. (2000). A generic system to extract and clean handwritten data from business forms, *In Prof. Int. Workshop on Frontiers in handwriting Recognition*, (Amsterdam), pp.63–72.

816. Yong, D., Wenkang, S., Feng, D. and Qi, L. (2004). A new similarity measure of generalized fuzzy numbers and its application to pattern recognition, Pattern Recognition Letters, 25, pp. 875–883.

817. Yoon, K. (1987). A reconciliation among discrete compromise solutions. *J.Oper. Res. Soc.*, 38(3), pp. 272–286.

818. Yu, V. F., Chi, H. T. X., Dat, L. Q., Phuc, P. N. K. and Shen, C-W. (2013). Ranking generalized fuzzy numbers in fuzzy decision making based on the left and right transfer coefficients and areas, *Applied Math.Modelling*, 37(16–17), 8106–8117.

819. Yu, V. F. and Dat, L. Q. (2014). An improved ranking method for fuzzy numbers with integral values, *Appl. Soft. Comput.*, 14, pp. 603–608.

820. Zadeh, L. A. (1975). *Calculus of fuzzy restrictions*, eds. Zadeh L. A., Fu K. S., Tanaka K. and Shimura M.,Fuzzy sets and Their Applications to Cognitive and Decision Processes, (Academic Press, New York), pp. 1–39.

821. Zadeh, L. A. (2011). A note on Z-numbers, *Inform. Sciences*, 181, pp. 2923–2932.

822. Zadeh, L. A. (1971). Fuzzy orderings. *Inform. Sciences*, 3, pp. 117–200.

823. Zadeh, L. A. (2008). Is there a need for fuzzy logic? *Inform. Sciences*, 178, pp. 2751–2779.

824. Zadeh, L. A. (1973). Outline of a new approach to the analysis of complex system and decision processes, *IEEE T. Syst. Man. Cyb.*3, pp. 28–44.

825. Zadeh, L. A. (1975). The concept of a linguistic variable and its applications in approximate reasoning, *Inform. Sciences*, 8, pp.43–80, pp. 301–357; 9, pp. 199–251.

826. Zadeh, L. A. (2005). Toward a generalized theory of uncertainty — an outline, *Inform. Sciences*, 172, pp. 1–40.

827. Zadeh, L. A. (1975). Fuzzy logic and approximate reasoning. *Synthese* 30(3–4), pp. 407–428.

828. Zadeh, L. A. (1965). Fuzzy Sets, *Inform. Control*, 8, pp. 338–353.

829. Zadeh, L. A. (2006). Generalized theory of uncertainty (GTU) – principal concepts and ideas, *Comput. Stat. Data An.,* 51, pp. 15–46.

830. Zadeh, L. A. (1992). Interpolative reasoning in fuzzy logic and neural network theory, *Proc. of the First IEEE Int. Conf. Fuzzy,* San-Diego, CA, Mar. 1992, p. 1–1.

831. Zadeh, L. A. (2012). Outline of a restriction-centered theory of reasoning and computation in an environment of uncertainty and imprecision. *Proc. of the 13th IEEE International Conference on Information Reuse and Integration (IRI),* Las Vegas, USA, pp. xxi–xxii.

832. Zadeh, L. A. (2013). Z-numbers — a new direction in the analysis of uncertain and complex systems, The 7th IEEE Int. Conf. on Digital Ecosystems and Technologies, *IEEE-DEST.* Menlo Park, California, USA, July 24–26, pp. 3–3.

833. Zadeh, L.A. (1983). A computational approach to fuzzy quantifiers in natural languages. *Comput Math App,* 9, pp. 149–184.

834. Zadeh, L.A. (1984). A computational theory of dispositions. *In: Proc. of 1984 Int. Conference on Computation Linguistics. Stanford,* pp. 312–318.

835. Zadeh, L.A. (1984). Fuzzy sets and commonsense reasoning. (Berkeley: Institute of Cognitive Studies report 21), University of California.

836. Zadeh, L.A. (1983). Fuzzy sets as a basis for the management of uncertainty in expert systems. *Fuzzy Set. Syst.,* 11, pp. 199–227.

837. Zadeh, L. A. (2012). Methods and Systems for Applications with Z-Numbers, United States Patent, Patent No.: US 8,311,973 B1, Date of Patent: Nov. 13, 2012.

838. Zadeh, L.A. (1996). Outline of a theory of usuality based on fuzzy logic, Fuzzy sets, fuzzy logic, and fuzzy systems. (USA: World Scien.Publishing Co.), Inc. River Edge; pp. 694–712.

839. Zadeh, L. A. (1968). Probability measures of fuzzy events, *J. Math. Anal. Appl.,* 23(2), pp. 421–427.

840. Zadeh, L.A. (1985). Syllogistic reasoning in fuzzy logic and its application to reasoning with dispositions. *IEEE T. Syst. Man. Cyb.,* 15: pp. 754–763.

841. Zadeh, L. A. (2013). Toward a restriction-centered theory of truth and meaning (RCT), *Inform. Sciences,* Vol. 248, 1, pp. 1–14.

842. Zadeh, L. A. (1988). Fuzzy logic, *IEEE Computer,* 21(4), pp. 83–93.

843. Zadeh L.A. (1980). Inference in fuzzy logic. *Proceedings of the 10th International Symposium on Multiple-Valued Logic, Northwestern University, Evanston, Illinois,* pp. 124–131.

844. Zadeh, L.A. (1992). Interpolative reasoning in fuzzy logic and neural network theory, *Proc. of the First IEEE Int. Conf. Fuzzy,* (San-Diego, CA, Mar.).

845. Zadeh, L. A. (2001). A new direction in AI — toward a computational theory of perceptions, *AI Mag.,* 22(1), pp. 73–84.

846. Zadeh, L. A. (2008). Computation with imprecise probabilities, *Proc. of the 8th Int. Conf. on Appl. of Fuzzy Syst. and Soft Comp.,* ICAFS, pp. 1–3.

847. Zadeh, L. A. (1999). From computing with numbers to computing with words – from manipulation of measurements to manipulation with perceptions, *IEEE T. Circuits-I,* 45(1), pp. 105–119.

848. Zadeh, L. A. (1996). Fuzzy logic computing with words, *IEEE T. Fuzzy Syst.,* 4(2), pp. 103–111.

849. Zadeh, L.A. (1996). Linguistic characterization of preference relations as a basis for choice in social systems. In L.A. Zadeh, G. Klir (Ed.), B. Yuan (Ed.) Fuzzy sets, fuzzy logic, and fuzzy systems: selected papers By Lotfi Asker Zadeh., *World Scien.* Publishing Co.

850. Zadeh, L.A., Aliev, R.A., Fazlollahi, B., Alizadeh, A.V., Guirimov, B.G. and Huseynov. O.H. (2009). Decision Theory with Imprecise Probabilities. Contract on "Application of Fuzzy Logic and Soft Computing to communications, planning and management of uncertainty".

851. Zadeh L.A., (1974). Numerical vs. linguistic variables, *Newsletter of the Circuits and Systems Society* 7, pp. 3–4.

852. Zadeh, L. A. (1997). Toward a theory of fuzzy information granulation and its centrality in human reasoning and fuzzy logic, *Fuzzy Set. Syst.*, 90(2), pp. 111–127.

853. Zadeh, L. A. (1979). Fuzzy sets and information granularity, eds. Gupta, M., Ragade R. and Yager R. "Advances in Fuzzy Set Theory and Applications,"(North- Holland Publishing Co., Amsterdam), pp. 3–18.

854. Zadeh, L. A. (1996). Fuzzy logic and the calculi of fuzzy rules and fuzzy graphs, *Multiple-Valued Logic 1*, pp. 1–38.

855. Zadeh, L. A. (2009). Computing with words and perceptions—a paradigm shift. *Proc. of the IEEE Int. Conf.Inform.Reuse and Integ.*, pp. 450–452.

856. Zadeh, L. A. (2009). Toward extended fuzzy logic. A first step, *Fuzzy Set. Syst.*, 160, pp. 3175–3181.

857. Zadeh, L. A. (1981). Possibility theory, soft data analysis, eds. In: Cobb L. and Thrall R.M. Math. Frontiers of the Social and Policy Sci.,(Westview Press, Boulder, CO), pp. 69–129.

858. Zadeh, L. A., Fu, K. S. and Shimura, M. A. (1975). *Fuzzy Sets and Their Applications to cognitive and Decision Processes*, eds. Yeh, R. T. and Bang, S. Y., "Fuzzy Relations, Fuzzy Graphs, and Their Applications to Clustering Analysis," (Academic Press, New York), pp. 125–149.

859. Zadroznya, S. and Kacprzyk, J. (2006). Computing with words for text processing: an approach to the text categorization, *Inform. Sciences,* 176 (4), pp. 415–437.

860. Zahedi, F. (1986). Group consensus function estimation when preferences are uncertain, *Oper. Res.*, 34(6), pp. 883–894.

861. Zamri, N., Abdullah, L., Hitam, M.S., Noor, M., Maizura, N. and Jusoh, A. (2013). A novel hybrid fuzzy weighted average for MCDM with interval triangular type-2 fuzzy sets, *WSEAS Transactions on Systems*, 4(12), pp.212–228.

862. Zeinalova, L.M.(2014). Choquet aggregation based decision making under Z-Information. *ICTACT Journal on Soft Computing,* 4(4), pp. 819–824.

863. Zeleny, M. (1982). Multiple Criteria Decision Making (New York, McGraw-Hill).

864. Zeynalova, L.M., (2010). Decision making under the second-order imprecise probability, *In Proceedings of the 9th Int. Conf. on Application of Fuzzy Systems and Soft Computing*, pp. 108–122.

865. Zhai, D. and Mendel, J. (2011). Uncertainty measures for general type-2 fuzzy sets, *Inform. Sciences*, 181(3), pp. 503–518.

866. Zhan, L. and Cai, K.-Y. (2004). Optimal fuzzy reasoning and its robustness analysis. *Int.J.Intelligent Syst.*, 19(11), pp. 1033–1049.

867. Zhang, C. (1992). Cooperation under uncertainty in distributed expert systems, *Artif. Intell.*, 56, pp. 21–69.
868. Zhang, G., Lu, J. and Gao, Y. (2015). Multi-Level Decision Making. Models, Methods and Applications, (Berlin, Heidelberg: Springer).
869. Zhang, G-Q. (1992). Fuzzy number-valued fuzzy measure and fuzzy number-valued fuzzy integral on the fuzzy set, *Fuzzy Set. Syst.*, 49, pp. 357–376.
870. Zhang, G. (1987). Fuzzy distance and limit of fuzzy numbers, BUSEFAL 33, pp. 19–30.
871. Zhang, J. and Yang, X. (2010). Some properties of fuzzy reasoning in propositional fuzzy logic systems, *Inform. Sciences,* 180, pp. 4661–4671.
872. Zhang, X., Yao, Y. and Yu, H. (2010). Rough implication operator based on strong topological rough algebras, *Inform. Sciences,* 180, pp. 3764–3780.
873. Zhang, J., Wu, D. and Olson, D.L. (2005). The method of grey related analysis to multiple attribute decision making problems with interval numbers, *Math Comp Model,* 42(9–10), pp. 991.
874. Zhao, S. and Tsang, E. C. C. (2008). On fuzzy approximation operators in attribute reduction with fuzzy rough sets, *Inform. Sciences,* 178, pp. 3163–3176.
875. Zhi-Ping, F., Yang L. and Feng, B. (2010) A method for stochastic multiple criteria decision making based on pairwise comparisons of alternatives with random evaluations, *EUR J Oper Res,* 207(2), pp. 906–915.
876. Zhong, Q. (1990). On fuzzy measure and fuzzy integral on fuzzy set, *Fuzzy Set. Syst.*, 37(1), pp.77–92.
877. Zhou, S., Chen, Q. and Wang, X. (2014). Fuzzy deep belief networks for semi-supervised sentiment classification, *Neurocomputing,* 131, pp. 312–322.
878. Zhou, S.-M., Chiclana, F., John, R. I., and Garibaldi, J. M. (2011). Alpha-level aggregation: a practical approach to type-1 OWA operation for aggregating uncertain information with applications to breast cancer treatments. *IEEE T Knowl Data En,* 23(10), pp. 1455–1468.
879. Zhukovskiy, V.I. and Salukvadze, M.E. (2004). Risks and Outcomes in Multi-criteria Control Systems (in Russian), *Intellect Edition, Moscow-Tbilisi,* p. 356.
880. Zimmermann, H. J. (1978). Fuzzy programming and linear programming with several objective functions,*Fuzzy Set. Syst.,*1, pp. 45–55.
881. Zimmermann, H.-J. (1993). *Fuzzy set theory and its applications* (Kluwer, Boston, second edition).
882. Zopounidis, C., Pardalos, P. M. and Baourakis G. (2001). *Fuzzy Sets in Management, Economics and Marketing* (World Scientific Singapore).

Index

Printed in the United States
By Bookmasters